Schriften zum Migrationsrecht

edited by

Volume 43

Kevin Fredy Hinterberger

Regularisations of Irregularly Staying Migrants in the EU

A Comparative Legal Analysis of Austria, Germany and Spain

HART

Nomos

Der Wissenschaftsfonds.

Translations were prepared and published with financial support of the Austrian Science Fund (FWF): PUB 828-G.

universität wien

Advanced Research School in Law and Jurisprudence

The publication was further supported by the Ars Iuris Vienna – Doctoral School of the University of Vienna.

The Deutsche Nationalbibliothek lists this publication in the Deutsche Nationalbibliografie; detailed bibliographic data are available on the Internet at http://dnb.d-nb.de

ISBN: HB (Nomos) 978-3-8487-7270-4 (Print)
ePDF (Nomos) 978-3-7489-1279-8 (ePDF)

British Library Cataloguing-in-Publication Data
A catalogue record for this book is available from the British Library.

ISBN: HB (Hart) 978-1-5099-4751-5 (Print)

Library of Congress Cataloging-in-Publication Data
Hinterberger, Kevin Fredy
Regularisations of Irregularly Staying Migrants in the EU
A Comparative Legal Analysis of Austria, Germany and Spain
Kevin Fredy Hinterberger
398 pp.
Includes bibliographic references.

ISBN 978-1-5099-4751-5 (hardcover Hart)

1st Edition 2023

Published by
Nomos Verlagsgesellschaft mbH & Co. KG
Waldseestraße 3–5 | 76530 Baden-Baden
www.nomos.de

Production of the printed version:
Nomos Verlagsgesellschaft mbH & Co. KG
Waldseestraße 3–5 | 76530 Baden-Baden

ISBN 978-3-8487-7270-4 (Print)
ISBN 978-3-7489-1279-8 (ePDF)
ISBN 978-1-5099-4751-5 (hardcover Hart)
DOI https://doi.org/10.5771/9783748912798

Onlineversion
Nomos eLibrary

Preface

The following book is the revised and updated translation of my PhD thesis which was originally written in German and which I completed with distinction at the University of Vienna in May 2019. This English translation includes the legislation, case law and literature up to 31 July 2022. The update also looks at new European Court of Justice case law and the recent reform of the 'roots' (*arraigo*) regularisations in Spain (Royal Decree 629/2022).

First and foremost, I would like to thank *Jonathon Watson* for his careful and precise translation of this study as well as for the pleasant and productive cooperation during the translation process.

I would also like to express my gratitude to all those who supported me in completing the thesis, most importantly my PhD supervisor, Prof. *Theo Öhlinger* from the Department of Constitutional and Administrative Law at the University of Vienna. He believed in this study from the outset. Prof. *Jürgen Bast* and Prof. *Konrad Lachmayer* are also to be mentioned for the constructive remarks made in their respective evaluations of my thesis.

My thanks also extend to the many who have accompanied me from the inception of the project to its completion. The inspiration to pursue this research came during my volunteer work as a legal advisor and representative for irregularly staying migrants and asylum seekers at the NGO 'Deserteurs- und Flüchtlingsberatung' in Vienna. Prof. *Anuscheh Farahat*, whom I first met in 2015 at the Network Migration's autumn conference, has continued to support me both as a colleague and friend in an incomparably great way. The same is true for *Philipp Janig* since 'day one' of my academic career (Jessup Moot Court). Associate Prof. *Félix Vacas Fernández* has served as an important academic point of contact in Madrid since my Erasmus semester in 2013.

Throughout the course of writing my thesis, I also had the privilege to undertake research at different institutions, contributing particularly to the comparative legal analysis of the Austrian, German and Spanish law. I would like to thank Prof. *Jürgen Bast* for welcoming me to his Chair for Public Law and European Law at the University of Giessen as a guest researcher from April to July 2016. From January to June 2017, I worked as a research assistant in the Department for Labour Market and Integration Policy at the Austrian Federal Chamber of Labour, where I have been employed since March 2019.

I am especially thankful to *Johannes Peyrl* for always being available for professional and personal discussions.

I was able to continue my work from July 2017 to June 2018 as a researcher at the Research Centre Human Rights at the University of Vienna, headed by Prof. *Manfred Nowak*. Through this period, I also spent time at the Instituto Universitario de Estudios sobre Migraciones at the University Pontificia Comillas in Madrid (September-December 2017) where Prof. *Cristina Gortázar Rotaeche* supported me on many levels. Finally, I completed my research at the Centre for European Integration Research (EIF) at the University of Vienna from July 2018 to March 2019.

It would not have been possible to complete this study without the financial assistance from various bodies. Between January 2016 and March 2019, I received a scholarship from the Austrian Academy of Sciences (DOC) at the Department of Constitutional and Administrative Law at the University of Vienna. Additionally, I received a scholarship from the 'Heinrich Graf Hardegg'sche Stiftung' and the thesis was awarded the Theodor-Körner-Prize (2016) as well as the Dr. Alois Mock-Science Prize (2021). The English translation and publication was financed by a FWF Stand-Alone Publication grant and the University of Vienna has contributed to the publication through the Ars Iuris Vienna – Doctoral School.

I thank the editors for accepting the thesis in the series 'Schriften zum Migrationsrecht', and the publishers, Nomos as well as Hart Publishing for the excellent cooperation. At Nomos, I am especially grateful to *Matthias Knopik* and Prof. *Johannes Rux*, who both put their trust and energy into this – at times daring – translation project, and *Kristina Stoll* for the great editing work.

This thesis would have never been completed without my wonderful friends who take me the way I am (which is not always an easy task) and who I consider family: I would like to thank *Stefan Bermadinger* for the countless hours talking about life; *Raphaela Haberler* for her sharp and honest opinions; *Philipp Heiling*, my oldest friend; *David Lun* for 'simply' always being there in the good and bad times; *Max Märzinger* for his ever valuable contributions to my life; *Hanna Palmanshofer* for her support in difficult times and *Jorge Horacio Restrepo Moreno*, mi consejero colombo-español.

Finally, the thesis is dedicated to my mother, sister and brother, who have always believed in me and my work. I thank my mother who literally raised me in the spirit of the Notorious B.I.G. quote: 'Stay far from timid, only make moves when your heart's in it'.

Vienna, 13 January 2023 *Kevin Fredy Hinterberger*

Contents

Abbreviations

AEUV	Vertrag über die Arbeitsweise der Europäischen Union (Treaty on the Functioning of the European Union)
AJIL	American Journal of International Law
AöR	Archiv des öffentlichen Rechts
Art(s)	Article(s)
ASVG	Allgemeines Sozialversicherungsgesetz in the version BGBl 108/2022 (Austria: General Social Security Act)
AsylbLG	Asylbewerberleistungsgesetz in the version of 10.12.2021 (BGBl I 5162) (Germany: Act on Benefits for Asylum Seekers)
AsylG (A)	Asylgesetz 2005 in the version BGBl I 83/2022 (Austria: Asylum Act)
AsylG (G)	Asylgesetz in the version of 9.7.2021 (BGBl I 2467) (Germany: Asylum Act)
ATC	Auto del Tribunal Constitucional (Decision of the Spanish Constitutional Court)
AufenthG	Aufenthaltsgesetz in the version of 23.5.2022 (BGBl I 760) (Germany: Residence Act)
AuslBG	Ausländerbeschäftigungsgesetz in the version BGBl I 106/2022 (Austria: Employment of Foreign Nationals Act)
AuslG 1990	Ausländergesetz in the version of 9.7.1990 (BGBl I 1354) (Germany: Foreigners Act 1990)
AVG	Allgemeines Verwaltungsverfahrensgesetz in the version BGBl I 58/2018 (Austria: General Administrative Procedure Act)
AVV-AufenthG	Allgemeine Verwaltungsvorschrift zum Aufenthaltsgesetz in the version of 26.10.2009 (Germany: General Administrative Provisions on the Residence Act)
BeckOK	Beck Onlinekommentar
BeschV	Beschäftigungsverordnung in the version of 20.7.2022 (BGBl I 1325) (Germany: Order on the Employment of Foreigners)
BFA	Bundesamt für Fremdenwesen und Asyl (Austria: Federal Office for Immigration and Asylum)

BFA-G	Bundesamt für Fremdenwesen und Asyl-Einrichtungsgesetz in the version BGBl I 56/2018 (Austria: Act establishing the Federal Office for Immigration and Asylum)
BFA-VG	Bundesamt für Fremdenwesen und Asyl-Verfahrensgesetz in the version BGBl I 83/2022 (Austria: Act on the Proceedings of the Federal Office for Immigration and Asylum)
BGBl	Bundesgesetzblatt (Austria and Germany: Federal Gazette)
BVerfGG	Bundesverfassungsgerichtsgesetz in the version of 20.11.2019 (BGBl I 1724) (Germany: Act on the Federal Constitutional Court)
B-VG	Bundes-Verfassungsgesetz in the version BGBl I 141/2022 (Austria: Federal Constitutional Law)
BlgNR	Beilage zu den Stenographischen Protokollen des Nationalrates (Austria: supplement to the stenographic records of the National Council)
BOE	Boletín Oficial del Estado (Spain: Official State Gazette)
BR-Drs	Bundesratsdrucksache (Germany: Official Document of the Federal Council)
BVerwG	Bundesverwaltungsgericht (Germany: Federal Administrative Court)
CE	Constitución Española, BOE 311 of 29.12.1978 in the version of 27.9.2011 (Spanish Constitution)
Cf.	Confer
CFR	Charter of Fundamental Rights of the European Union, OJ 2012 C 326/391
CMLRev	Common Market Law Review
CP	Ley Orgánica 10/1995, de 23 de noviembre, del Código Penal, BOE 281 of 24.11.1995 in the version of 29.7.2022 (Spanish Criminal Code)
DÖV	Die Öffentliche Verwaltung
DRdA	Das Recht der Arbeit
e.g.	for example
ECJ	European Court of Justice
ECRE	European Council on Refugees and Exiles
ECtHR	European Court of Human Rights
edn	edition
ed(s)	editor(s)
EEA	European Economic Area
EJML	European Journal of Migration and Law

ELR	European Law Review
EMN	European Migration Network
Employers Sanctions Directive	Directive 2009/52/EC of the European Parliament and of the Council of 18 June 2009 providing for minimum standards on sanctions and measures against employers of illegally staying third-country nationals, OJ 2009 L 168/24
ErläutRV	Erläuterungen zur Regierungsvorlage (Austria: Explanatory remarks to a government bill)
etc.	et cetera
EU	European Union
EuR	Zeitschrift Europarecht
EuZW	Europäische Zeitschrift für Wirtschaftsrecht
f(f)	and the following page(s)
FABL	Die fremden- und asylrechtlichen Blätter
Family Reunification Directive	Council Directive 2003/86/EC of 22 September 2003 on the right to family reunification, OJ 2003 L 251/12
FJ	fundamento jurídico (legal basis for the decision)
Fn	Footnote
FRA	European Union Agency for Fundamental Rights
FPG	Fremdenpolizeigesetz in the version BGBl I 206/2021 (Austria: Aliens' Police Act)
FrG	Fremdengesetz 1997, BGBl I 75/1997 (Austria: Aliens' Act)
FS	Festschrift (liber amicorum)
GC	Grand Chamber
GG	Grundgesetz für die Bundesrepublik Deutschland in the version of 28.6.2022 (BGBl I 968) (Basic Law of the Federal Republic of Germany)
GP	Gesetzgebungsperiode (legislative period)
GVV	Grundversorgungsvereinbarung, BGBl I 80/2004 (Austria: Basic Welfare Agreement)
HRLR	Human Rights Law Review
Human Trafficking Directive	Council Directive 2004/81/EC of 29 April 2004 on the residence permit issued to third-country nationals who are victims of trafficking in human beings or who have been the subject of an action to facilitate illegal immigration, who cooperate with the competent authorities, OJ 2004 L 261/19
ICLQ	International & Comparative Law Quarterly
ICON	International Journal of Constitutional Law

i.e.	that is
IJRL	International Journal of Refugee Law
InfAuslR	Informationsbrief Ausländerrecht
IntG	Integrationsgesetz (Austria: Integration Act)
IOM	International Organization for Migration
JRP	Journal für Rechtspolitik
JZ	Juristenzeitung
LEVD	Ley 4/2015, de 27 de abril, del Estatuto de la víctima del delito, BOE 101 of 28.4.2015 in the version of 23.2.2021 (Spain: Law 4/2015 on the standing of victims of crime)
LJCA	Ley 29/1998, de 13 de julio, reguladora de la Jurisdicción Contencioso-administrativa, BOE 167 of 14.7.1998 in the version of 5.5.2021 (Spain: Law 29/1998 governing the jurisdiction of the administrative courts)
LODYLE	Ley Orgánica 4/2000 sobre derechos y libertades de los extranjeros en España y su integración social, BOE 10 of 12.1.2000 in the version of 23.2.2021 (Organic Law 4/2000 on the rights and freedoms of foreigners in Spain and their social integration)
LOE	Ley Orgánica 7/1985, de 1 de julio, sobre derechos y libertades de los extranjeros en España, BOE 158 of 3.7.1985 (Organic Law 7/1985 on the rights and freedoms of foreigners in Spain)
LOMPIVG	Ley Orgánica 1/2004, de 28 de diciembre, de Medidas de Protección Integral contra la Violencia de Género, BOE 313 of 29.12.2004 in the version of 5.6.2021 (Spain: Organic Law 1/2004 on comprehensive measures concerning the protection against gender-based violence)
Long Term Residence Directive	Council Directive 2003/109/EC of 25 November 2003 concerning the status of third-country nationals who are long-term residents, OJ 2004 L 16/44
LOTC	Ley Orgánica 2/1979, de 3 de octubre, del Tribunal Constitucional, BOE 239 of 5.10.1979 in the version of 17.10.2015 (Spain: Organic Law 2/1979 on the Constitutional Court)
LPAC	Ley 39/2015, de 1 de octubre, de Procedimiento Administrativo Común de las Administraciones Públicas, BOE 236 of 2.10.2015 in the version of 13.7.2022 (Spain: Law 39/2015 on the Common Administrative Procedure for Public Administration)
mn(s)	marginal number(s)

NAG	Niederlassungs- und Aufenthaltsgesetz in the version of BGBl I 83/2022 (Austria: Settlement and Residence Act)
NJW	Neue Juristische Wochenschrift
NN	unknown author
No(s).	Number(s)
NS-Ausländer-polizeiverordnung	Nationalsozialistische Ausländerpolizeiverordnung of 11.5.1938, Imperial Law Gazette I 1053/1938 (Austria and Germany: National Socialist Police Order on Foreigners)
NVwZ	Neue Zeitschrift für Verwaltungsrecht
NVwZ-RR	Neue Zeitschrift für Verwaltungsrecht-Rechtsprechungs-Report
NZS	Neue Zeitschrift für Sozialrecht
OECD	Organisation for Economic Co-operation and Development
OJ	Official Journal of the European Union
ÖJT	Österreichischer Juristentag
ÖJZ	Österreichische Juristen-Zeitung
ÖZPR	Österreichische Zeitschrift für Pflegerecht
PERCO	Platform for European Red Cross Cooperation on Refugees, Asylum Seekers and Migrants
Qualification Directive	Directive 2011/95/EU of the European Parliament and of the Council of 13 December 2011 on standards for the qualification of third-country nationals or stateless persons as beneficiaries of international protection, for a uniform status for refugees or for persons eligible for subsidiary protection, and for the content of the protection granted, OJ 2011 L 337/9
Recommendation (EU) 2017/432	Commission Recommendation (EU) 2017/432 of 7 March 2017 on making returns more effective when implementing the Directive 2008/115/EC of the European Parliament and of the Council, OJ 2017 L 66/15
REDYLE	Real Decreto 557/2011, de 20 de abril, por el que se aprueba el Reglamento de la Ley Orgánica 4/2000, sobre derechos y libertades de los extranjeros en España y su integración social, tras su reforma por Ley Orgánica 2/2009, BOE 103 of 30.4.2011 in the version of 27.7.2022 (Royal Decree 557/2011 approving the Regulation implementing Organic Law 4/2000 on the rights and freedoms of foreign nationals in Spain and their social integration, as recast by Organic Law 2/2009)
Refugee Convention	United Nations Convention of 28 July 1951 relating to the status of refugees and its New York Protocol of 31 January 1967

Residence Permit Regulation	Council Regulation (EC) No. 1030/2002 of 13 June 2002 laying down a uniform format for residence permits for third-country nationals, OJ 2002 L 157/1
Return Directive	Directive 2008/115/EC of the European Parliament and of the Council of 16 December 2008 on common standards and procedures in Member States for returning illegally staying third-country nationals, OJ 2008 L 348/98
Return Handbook 2017	Commission Recommendation (EU) 2017/2338 of 16 November 2017 establishing a common 'Return Handbook' to be used by Member States' competent authorities when carrying out return-related tasks, OJ 2017 L 339/83
Royal Decree 2393/2004	Real Decreto 2393/2004, de 30 de diciembre, por el que se aprueba el Reglamento de la Ley Orgánica 4/2000, de 11 de enero, sobre derechos y libertades de los extranjeros en España y su integración social, BOE 6 of 7.1.2005 in the version of 15.3.2014 (Royal Decree 2393/2004 approving the regulations of Organic Law 4/2000 on the rights and freedoms of foreigners in Spain and their social integration)
SBC	Regulation (EU) 2016/399 of the European Parliament and of the Council of 9 March 2016 on a Union Code on the rules governing the movement of persons across borders (Schengen Borders Code), OJ 2016 L 77/1
Schengen Agreement	Convention implementing the Schengen Agreement of 14 June 1985 between the Governments of the States of the Benelux Economic Union, the Federal Republic of Germany and the French Republic on the gradual abolition of checks at their common borders, OJ 2000 L 239/19
Sent.	Sentence
SGB II	Sozialgesetzbuch Zweites Buch in the version of 19.6.2022 (BGBl I 921) (Germany: Social Insurance Code II)
SGB V	Sozialgesetzbuch Fünftes Buch in the version of 28.6.2022 (BGBl I 969) (Germany: Social Insurance Code V)
SGB XII	Sozialgesetzbuch Zwölftes Buch in the version of 23.5.2022 (BGBl I 760) (Germany: Social Insurance Code XII)
Single Permit Directive	Directive 2011/98/EU of the European Parliament and of the Council of 13 December 2011 on a single application procedure for a single permit for third-country nationals to reside and work in the territory of a Member State and on a common set of rights for third-country workers legally residing in a Member State, OJ 2011 L 343/1
SIS	Schengen Information System

STC	Sentencia del Tribunal Constitucional (Decision of the Spanish Constitutional Court)
StGB (A)	Strafgesetzbuch in the version BGBl I 242/2021 (Austria: Criminal Code)
STS	Sentencia del Tribunal Supremo (Decision of the Spanish Supreme Court)
STSJ	Sentencia del Tribunal Superior de Justicia (Spain: Decision of the High Court of an Autonomous Community)
Students and Researchers Directive	Directive (EU) 2016/801 of the European Parliament and of the Council of 11 May 2016 on the conditions of entry and residence of third-country nationals for the purposes of research, studies, training, voluntary service, pupil exchange schemes or educational projects and au pairing, OJ 2016 L 132/21
TEC	Treaty Establishing the European Community, OJ 1992 C 191/1
Temporary Protection Directive	Council Directive 2001/55/EC of 20 July 2001 on minimum standards for giving temporary protection in the event of a mass influx of displaced persons and on measures promoting a balance of efforts between Member States in receiving such persons and bearing the consequences thereof, OJ 2001 L 212/12
TEU	Treaty on European Union, OJ 2008 C 115/15
TFEU	Treaty on the Functioning of the European Union, OJ 2012 C 326/01
Travel Document Regulation	Regulation (EU) 2016/1953 of the European Parliament and of the Council of 26 October 2016 on the establishment of a European travel document for the return of illegally staying third-country nationals, and repealing the Council Recommendation of 30 November 1994, OJ 2016 L 311/13
VfGG	Verfassungsgerichtshofgesetz in the version BGBl I 125/2022 (Austria: Constitutional Court Act)
VfGH	Verfassungsgerichtshof (Austria: Constitutional Court)
VGH	Verwaltungsgerichtshof (Germany: Higher Administrative Court)
Visa Regulation	Regulation (EU) 2018/1806 of the European Parliament and of the Council of 14 November 2018 listing the third countries whose nationals must be in possession of visas when crossing the external borders and those whose nationals are exempt from that requirement, OJ 2018 L 303/39
Vol	Volume

VVDStRL	Veröffentlichungen der Vereinigung der Deutschen Staatsrechtslehrer
VwGG	Verwaltungsgerichtshofgesetz in the version BGBl I 109/2021 (Austria: Administrative Court Act)
VwGH	Verwaltungsgerichtshof (Austria: Supreme Administrative Court)
VwGO	Verwaltungsgerichtsordnung in the version of 20.7.2022 (BGBl I 1325) (Germany: Administrative Court Code of Procedure)
VwGVG	Verwaltungsgerichtsverfahrensgesetz in the version BGBl I 109/2021 (Austria: Administrative Court Procedure Act)
VwVfG	Verwaltungsverfahrensgesetz in the version of 25.6.2021 (BGBl I 2154) (Germany: Administrative Procedure Act)
WP	Working Paper
ZaöRV	Zeitschrift für ausländisches öffentliches Recht und Völkerrecht
ZAR	Zeitschrift für Ausländerrecht und Ausländerpolitik
ZEuP	Zeitschrift für Europäisches Privatrecht
ZEuS	Zeitschrift für europarechtliche Studien
ZfV	Zeitschrift für Verwaltung
ZVglRWiss	Zeitschrift für vergleichende Rechtswissenschaft

Introduction

A. The challenge at hand

'Combatting' irregular migration,[1] which covers the 'fight' against both irregular entry and irregular stays, is one of the key challenges to migration management at EU level. The EU debates on this issue have often been intense, has exemplified by 'the long summer of migration'[2] of 2015 and the closure of the 'Balkan route'.[3] However, the structural problems underlying the 'fight' against irregular migration are often not easy to grasp and as such are not addressed appropriately.[4] This study focuses on one of the most pressing problems: the low return rate of irregularly staying migrants.[5] More specifically, it examines the reasons for the present deficits in the EU's return policy and proposes a legal solution that concentrates on

---

1 Art 79(1) TFEU. See Chapter 2.C.I. and cf. *Lutz*, Non-removable Returnees under Union Law: Status Quo and Possible Developments, EJML 2018, 50; *Menezes Queiroz*, Illegally Staying in the EU: An Analysis of Illegality in EU Migration Law (2018) 1ff and *EMN*, The effectiveness of return in EU Member States 2017 (15.2.2018), http://emn.ie/files/p_201802260500242017_emn_synthesis_return_23.02.2018.pdf (31.7.2022) 13.

2 I prefer the expression 'long summer of migration' rather than 'refugee crisis' (or similar) as refugee movements were a contributing factor to a historical and structural collapse of the EU border regime; cf. *Hess/Kasparek/Kron/Rodatz/Schwertl/Sontowski* (eds), Der lange Sommer der Migration: Grenzregime III (2016). In addition *Thym*, The "refugee crisis" as a challenge of legal design and institutional legitimacy, CMLRev 2016, 1545; *den Heijer/Rijpma/Spijkerboer*, Coercion, Prohibition and Great Expectations: The Continuing Failure of the Common European Asylum System, CMLRev 2016, 607; *Depenheuer/Grabenwarter* (eds), Der Staat in der Flüchtlingskrise: Zwischen gutem Willen und geltendem Recht (2017). For an analysis of the closure of the Balkan route see *Dérens/Rico*, Auf der Balkanroute, Le Monde diplomatique (English version) April 2016, 4.

3 One may also take into consideration asylum policy, securing Europe's external borders, and legal migration; see COM(2015) 240 final.

4 Cf. *Desmond*, The Development of a Common EU Migration Policy and the Rights of Irregular Migrants: A Progress Narrative?, HRLR 2016, 247 (248) or *Carrera/Parkin*, Protecting and Delivering Fundamental Rights of Irregular Migrants at Local and Regional Levels in the European Union (14.11.2011), https://www.ceps.eu/ceps-publications/protecting-and-delivering-fundamental-rights-irregular-migrants-local-and-regional/ (31.7.2022) 1f.

5 Cf. *Menezes Queiroz*, Illegally Staying 4.

ending the irregularity of migrants. As the legal systems of the EU Member States feature various approaches, this study will analyse and compare the legislative approaches in Austria, Germany and Spain.[6] These three Member States use, inter alia, differentiated systems of regularisation (i.e. the award of residency rights) to 'combat' the problem of irregularly staying migrants. For the purposes of this study, regularisation is understood as each legal decision that awards legal residency to irregularly staying migrants when particular minimum requirements are satisfied.[7]

Chapter 1 narrows the scope of persons to be analysed in the study. It defines the residency status as irregular when a migrant does not have (or no longer has) a right to stay in a territory because the legal requirements have not been met, such as for persons who have entered irregularly and stay as such. Alternatively, a stay may be deemed irregular where the legal requirements have been breached, such as by those individuals who have entered the Member State legally, yet continue to remain even after the period for their permitted stay has expired (a so-called 'overstayer'[8]). In principle, the term 'migrant' covers all non-citizens, though immigration law distinguishes between privileged and non-privileged migrants. For the purposes of this study it will be shown that only nationals of third-countries and stateless persons are eligible as non-privileged migrants.[9]

Instances of irregular migration typically occur when a person enters a territory without a right to do so – be this as a right of entry or a right to stay – and/or remains. As national laws restrict the movement within the territory, 'irregular migration is not an independent social phenomenon but exists in relation to state policies and is a social, political and legal construction'.[10] Conceptionally speaking, irregular migration has two distinct aspects. Firstly, in accordance with international law, a state must have a defined territory, a population and an effective government,[11] thereby allowing for the control of migration within its territory. We are thus

---

6 See Introduction D.II.1. and Chapter 3 and Chapter 4.

7 See Chapter 1.A.

8 See *EMN*, Asylum and Migration Glossary 3.0 (October 2014), https://www.emn.at/wp-content/uploads/2016/11/emn-glossary-en-version.pdf (31.7.2022) 208.

9 See Chapter 1.A.II.1.

10 *Düvell*, Paths into Irregularity: The Legal and Political Construction of Irregular Migration, EJML 2011, 275 (276); cf. also *Tapinos*, Irregular Migration in *OECD* (ed), Combating the Illegal Employment of Foreign Workers (2000) 13.

11 Cf. *Jellinek*, Allgemeine Staatslehre[3] (1914) 394ff and *Shaw*, International Law[9] (2021) 179ff.

faced with a core aspect of state sovereignty.[12] Secondly, the concept of irregular migration is a political and social problem created via norms:[13] irregularity arises through the norms created by the state.[14] Accordingly, the concept underpinning irregular migration thus applies to every state that uses legal norms to regulate migration within its territory;[15] all EU Member States satisfy such criteria. Furthermore, irregular migration also features a temporal aspect, as irregularity may end through deportation, when the migrant leaves the territory or through regularisations.[16]

The EU's political and legal efforts towards 'combatting' irregular migration aim at the effective return of irregularly staying migrants;[17] the Return Directive serves as the EU's central piece of legislation in this respect.[18] This Directive obliges Member States to issue a return decision to any third-country national staying illegally on their territory.[19] However, a return decision does not automatically mean that the migrant in question is actually returned. Whereas the Member States do indeed issue return decisions, annually only approximately 40 % of all return decisions are actually enforced and, at less than 30 %, the return rate to African countries is even lower.[20] For example, of the 516,115 return decisions issued in 2015 in all EU Member States, only approximately 188,905 migrants returned

12 Chapter 1.A.II.1.

13 For an in-depth discussion see *Willen*, Toward a Critical Phenomenology of "Illegality": State Power, Criminalization, and Abjectivity among Undocumented Migrant Workers in Tel Aviv, Israel, International Migration 2007, 8; more recently *Morticelli*, Human Rights of Irregular Migrants in the European Union (2021) 26ff.

14 Cf. *Błuś*, Beyond the Walls of Paper. Undocumented Migrants, the Border and Human Rights, EJML 2013, 413 (424ff); *Koser*, International Migration (2007) 54f. See in particular *Carrera/Guild*, Addressing Irregular Migration, Facilitation and Human Trafficking: The EU's Approach in *Carrera/Guild* (eds), Irregular Migration, Trafficking and Smuggling of Human Beings (2016) 1 (3f); also *Klarmann*, Aspekte migrationsspezifischer Illegalisierung im Unionsrecht in *Thym/Klarmann* (eds), Unionsbürgerschaft und Migration im aktuellen Europarecht (2017) 127.

15 *Angenedt*, Irreguläre Migration als internationales Problem. SWP Study (December 2007), https://www.swp-berlin.org/fileadmin/contents/products/studien/2007_S33_adt_ks.pdf (31.7.2022) 11.

16 Cf. *Tapinos* in *OECD* 15.

17 See the Recommendation (EU) 2017/432.

18 See for an overview of the return-related EU legal instruments *Molnár*, The Interplay between the EU's Return Acquis and International Law (2021) 70f.

19 Art 6(1) Return Directive; see Chapter 2.B.I.

20 COM(2017) 558 final, 9 and COM(2017) 200 final, 2.

voluntarily or were deported (327,111).[21] Following *Lutz*, one can therefore cautiously estimate that annually there are approximately 300,000 migrants who are non-returnable.[22] It is therefore clear that the EU is experiencing a shortfall in the return of irregularly staying migrants.[23]

The scale of the issue is readily apparent in the 2008 CLANDESTINO-Study,[24] which concluded that irregularly staying migrants comprise around 1 % of the European population; 1.9–3.8 million irregularly staying migrants were spread across the Member States.[25] The European Commission assumes that in 2017 approximately one million migrants were illegally present in the EU.[26] However, the accuracy of such numbers is to be questioned[27] as the definition of 'third country nationals found to be illegally present' only includes those 'who are apprehended or otherwise come to the attention of national immigration authorities'.[28] As not all

21 *European Commission*, A stronger and more effective European return policy (12.9.2018), https://ec.europa.eu/info/sites/default/files/soteu2018-factsheet-returns-policy_en.pdf (31.7.2022).

22 As expressed by *Lutz*, EJML 2018, 30.

23 Cf. *Lutz*, EJML 2018, 29f and *Farcy*, Unremovability under the Return Directive: An Empty Protection? in *de Bruycker/Cornelisse/Moraru* (eds), Law and Judicial Dialogue on the Return of Irregular Migrants from the European Union (2020) 437 (437f).

24 Cf. *Kovacheva/Vogel*, The Size of the Irregular Foreign Resident Population in the European Union in 2002, 2005 and 2008: Aggregated Estimates. WP 4/2009 (2009), https://irregular-migration.net/wp-content/uploads/2021/06/WP4_Kovacheva-Vogel_2009_EuropeEstimate_Dec09.pdf (31.7.2022) 11; *European Commission*, Clandestino Project. Final Report (23.11.2009), http://www.statewatch.org/news/2015/mar/eu-com-clandestino-final-report-november-2009.pdf (31.7.2022) 106. On the factors to assess the data quality see *Vogel/Kovacheva*, Classification report: Quality assessment of estimates on stocks of irregular migrants. WP 1/2008 (2008). For criticism see *Lazaridis*, International Migration into Europe: From Subjects to Abjects (2015) 10, who describes the statistics as 'guesstimates'. See also *Singleton*, Migration and Asylum Data for Policy-making in the European Union: The problem with numbers. CEPS WP No. 89 (March 2016), https://www.ceps.eu/system/files/LSE%2089%20AS%20Migration%20and%20Asylum%20Data.pdf (31.7.2022).

25 Cf. *European Commission*, Clandestino (23.11.2009) 11f and 105f.

26 COM(2017) 558 final, 9.

27 Cf. *Wehinger*, Do amnesties pull in illegal immigrants? An analysis of European apprehension data, International Journal of Migration and Border Studies 2014, 231 (234–236) and for a critical analysis of the Eurostat statistics concerning asylum seekers see *Kleist*, Warum weit weniger Asylbewerber in Europa sind, als angenommen wird: Probleme mit Eurostats Asylzahlen, ZAR 2015, 294.

28 *Eurostat*, Enforcement of Immigration Legislation: Eurostat metadata (30.4.2015), http://ec.europa.eu/eurostat/cache/metadata/en/migr_eil_esms.htm (31.7.2021).

migrants 'illegally present' and, respectively, persons unknown to the national authorities, fall under this definition, one may presume that the numbers have remained at the same level as in 2008 (1.9–3.8 million).[29] Moreover, it is conceivable that the 'long summer of migration 2015' even contributed to an increase in the number of irregularly staying migrants. This may be explained primarily by the comparably high number of asylum applications in 2015 and 2016,[30] though indeed not all applications (will) have been successful.[31] Furthermore, the number of persons staying irregularly in Austria in 2015 has been estimated as ranging between 95,000 and 254,000.[32] As this corresponds to 1.1 and 2.9 % of Austria's total population, the importance of this subject for society as a whole is clear.[33]

Irregularly staying migrants may in fact reside in the EU, yet they are often precluded from those rights available to legal residents.[34] It is therefore

29 Cf. *Triandafyllidou/Vogel*, Irregular Migration in the European Union: Evidence, Facts and Myths in *Triandafyllidou* (ed), Irregular Migration: Myths and Realities (2010) 291 (298f).

30 *Eurostat*, Record number of over 1.2 million first time asylum seekers registered in 2015, news release 44/2016 (4.3.2016), https://ec.europa.eu/eurostat/documents/2995521/7203832/3-04032016-AP-EN.pdf/790eba01-381c-4163-bcd2-a54959b99ed6 (31.7.2022); *Eurostat*, 1.2 million first time asylum seekers registered in 2016, news release No. 46/2017 (16.3.2017), https://ec.europa.eu/eurostat/documents/2995521/7921609/3-16032017-BP-EN.pdf/e5fa98bb-5d9d-4297-9168-d07c67d1c9e1 (31.7.2022) and *Eurostat*, 650 000 first-time asylum seekers registered in 2017, news release No. 47/2018 (20.3.2018), https://ec.europa.eu/eurostat/documents/2995521/8754388/3-20032018-AP-EN.pdf/50c2b5a5-3e6a-4732-82d0-1caf244549e3 (31.7.2022). Cf. *Farcy* in *de Bruycker/Cornelisse/Moraru* 437.

31 See also *Desmond*, HRLR 2016, 272.

32 One must again doubt the reliability of the data because the basis for these numbers is not readily apparent from the report; cf. *Migrationsrat für Österreich*, Bericht des Migrationsrats (2016) 20.

33 Cf. also *Dumon*, Effects of Undocumented Migration for Individuals concerned, International Migration 1983, 218 (227f).

34 Cf. *Boswell*, The Politics of Irregular Migration in *Azoulai/De Vries* (eds), EU Migration Law: Legal Complexities and Political Rationales (2014) 41 (41); *Lazaridis*, International Migration 22, 132; *Engbersen*, The Unanticipated Consequences of Panopticon Europe: Residence Strategies of Illegal Immigrants in *Guiraudon/Joppke* (eds), Controlling a New Migration World (2001) 222; with regard to regularisations see *Wehinger*, International Journal of Migration and Border Studies 2014, 241; *Hoffmann*, Leben in der Illegalität – Exklusion durch Aufenthaltsrecht in *Falge/Fischer-Lescano/Sieveking* (eds), Gesundheit in der Illegalität: Rechte von Menschen ohne Aufenthaltspapiere (2009) 13 (15).

undisputed that irregularly staying migrants are particularly vulnerable.[35] *Tohidipur* is thereby correct in asserting that the irregular residency does not release the political community from its responsibility and thus may not lead to a loss of rights.[36] Accordingly, the requirements to be satisfied by irregularly staying migrants in order to (re-)obtain legal residency are especially pertinent to this study.[37] This issue has been neglected by the European legislator.[38]

In light of the shortfall in returns and the aforementioned numbers of irregularly staying migrants, the increase of the return rate and the decrease of the numbers of irregularly staying migrants are high on the EU's political agenda.[39] This is shown by various measures. In particular, the 2016 Regulation on the establishment of a European travel document for the return of illegally staying third-country nationals[40] aims to increase the rate of return by harmonising the format and technical specifications

---

35 Cf. *Raposo/Violante*, Access to Health Care by Migrants with Precarious Status During a Health Crisis: Some Insights from Portugal, Human Rights Review 2021; *Fox-Ruhs/Ruhs*, The Fundamental Rights of Irregular Migrant Workers in the EU: Understanding and reducing protection gaps (July 2022), https://www.europarl.europa.eu/RegData/etudes/STUD/2022/702670/IPOL_STU(2022)702670_EN.pdf (31.7.2022) 9, 55ff; *PERCO*, PERCO Position Paper on the Vulnerabilities of Migrants which are caused by the Lack of a Legal Status (8.5.2015), https://drk-wohlfahrt.de/uploads/tx_ffpublication/PERCO_Position_Paper_on_Vulnerabilities_along_the_migratory_trails_to_the_EU_and_to_the_Schengen_area_03.pdf (31.7.2022); *Cholewinski*, Control of Irregular Migration and EU Law and Policy: A Human Rights Deficit in *Peers/Rogers* (eds), EU Immigration and Asylum Law: Text and Commentary (2006) 899 (900f); *European Commission*, Clandestino (23.11.2009) 22; see already *Carlin*, Statement by the ICM Director James L. Cadin, International Migration 1983, 97 (97); *Böhning*, Regularising the Irregular, International Migration 1983, 159 (160). *Lazaridis*, International Migration 14, notes that irregularly staying migrants are often unable to make their voices heard.

36 *Tohidipur*, Grund- und Menschenrechte illegalisierter Migrantinnen und Migranten in *Fischer-Lescano/Kocher/Nassibi* (eds), Arbeit in der Illegalität: Die Rechte von Menschen ohne Aufenthaltspapiere (2012) 41 (44).

37 See Chapter 4.

38 Cf. *Thym*, EU migration policy and its constitutional rationale: A cosmopolitan outlook, CMLRev 2013, 709 (733f) and see Chapter 2 and Chapter 5.

39 Cf. *EMN*, Practical Measures to Reduce Irregular Migration. Synthesis Report (October 2012). For criticism see *Boswell* in *Azoulai/De Vries* 47f, who considers that the EU does not at all want to lower the number of irregularly staying migrants.

40 More commonly known as the Travel Document Regulation.

of travel documents for irregularly staying migrants.[41] In addition, a new Entry/Exit System (EES) shall record the (cross-border) movements of migrants within the EU and shall contribute to the swift identification of irregularly staying migrants.[42] The 2015 'EU Action Plan on return'[43] and the 2017 'Renewed Action Plan'[44] both contain further suggestions for improvements, for instance additional assistance for voluntary return which already constitutes 40 % of all returns. The recent proposal to reform the Return Directive also heads in this direction.[45] Nonetheless, on the whole the EU has made little headway with regard to the standards set out in the Return Directive.

The EU's efforts also focus on preventing illegal entry by migrants, for example through an isolationist policy in the form of strict entry requirements, such as visas.[46] These are expressed in various so-called *'non-entrée'* EU policies,[47] for example externalisation and extra-territorialisation.[48]

---

41 Recital 3 Travel Document Regulation and COM(2015) 668 final, 2.

42 Regulation (EU) 2017/2226 establishing an Entry/Exit System (EES) to register entry and exit data and refusal of entry data of third-country nationals crossing the external borders of the Member States, OJ 2017 L 327/20. Cf. *Klaus*, Überwachung von Reisen Drittstaatsangehöriger durch das Entry/Exit System (EES): Anfang vom Ende aller Overstays?, ZAR 2018, 246; *Cole/Quintel*, Data Retention under the Proposal for an EU Entry/Exit System (EES): Analysis of the impact on and limitations for the EES by Opinion 1/15 on the EU/Canada PNR Agreement of the Court of Justice of the European Union (October 2017), http://orbilu.uni.lu/bitstream/10993/35446/1/Legal%20Opinion.PDF (31.7.2022) and *Jeandesboz/Rijpma/Bigo*, Smart Borders Revisited: An assessment of the Commission's revised Smart Borders proposal (October 2016), http://www.europarl.europa.eu/RegData/etudes/STUD/2016/571381/IPOL_STU%282016%29571381_EN.pdf (31.7.2022).

43 COM(2015) 453 final, 3f.

44 COM(2017) 200 final.

45 COM(2018) 634 final; COM(2020) 609 final; SWD(2020) 207 final, 67ff and see Chapter 2.B.I. for details.

46 Cf. *Costello*, The Human Rights of Migrants and Refugees in European Law (2015) 3 and 231ff; *Gil-Bazo*, The Practice of Mediterranean States in the context of the European Union's Justice and Home Affairs External Dimension. The Safe Third Country Concept Revisited, IJRL 2006, 571 (593 and 599f).

47 Cf. *Hathaway*, The Emerging Politics of Non-Entrée, Journal of Refugee Studies 1992, 40 (40f) and *Gammeltoft-Hansen/Hathaway*, *Non-Refoulement* in a World of Cooperative Deterrence, University of Michigan Law and Economics Research Paper No. 14-016, 5ff.

48 See *Eisele*, The External Dimension of the EU's Migration Policy (2014); *Bröcker*, Die externen Dimensionen des EU-Asyl- und Flüchtlingsrechts im Lichte der Menschenrechte und des Völkerrechts (2010).

These terms describe the efforts towards shifting the border and migration controls as far as possible beyond its external borders[49].[50] The following study will not focus on irregular entry as the numbers of those migrants play a much lesser role than often portrayed.[51] For example, the image of migrants attempting to scale the border fence in Ceuta and Melilla does not accurately depict the reality that the largest group of irregularly staying migrants in the EU are in fact 'overstayers' – those who enter legally on a visa but remain irregularly after their visa has expired.

As the aforementioned EU policies regarding irregular migration are not exhaustive, the following study will focus on regularisation. Member States already make extensive use of this legal instrument in order to 'combat' irregular migration and which represents an alternative to return. Regularisation ends the irregular stay by granting a right to stay.[52] This domestic measure allows states to (again) manage this part of the population,[53] specifically in the context of immigration law.[54] Positive aspects include, for instance, population management, tackling illegal employment and increasing government revenue through taxation and social security payments.[55] Moreover, regularisations allow migrants access to welfare systems and the labour market due to their residency status.[56]

49 Cf. in this regard Arts 67(2) and 77(1)(b), (c) as well as (2)(d) TFEU.

50 On external migration control see *Ryan/Mitsilegas* (eds), Extraterritorial Immigration Control (2010); *Gammeltoft-Hansen*, Access to Asylum: International Refugee Law and the Globalization of Migration Control (2011); *den Heijer*, Europe and Extraterritorial Asylum (2012); *Moreno-Lax*, (Extraterritorial) Entry Controls and (Extraterritorial) Non-Refoulement in EU Law in *Maes/Foblets/de Bruycker* (eds), The External Dimensions of EU Asylum and Immigration Policy (2011) 415.

51 Cf. *Triandafyllidou/Vogel* in *Triandafyllidou* 294.

52 See Chapter 1.A.II.2.

53 Cf. *Hampshire*, The Politics of Immigration (2013) and *Kraler*, Regularization of Irregular Migrants and Social Policies: Comparative Perspectives, Journal of Immigrant and Refugee Studies 2019, 94 (107–109 and 97).

54 Cf. *Trinidad García*, Los inmigrantes irregulares en la Ley 4/2000 y en su reforma: una regularización que no cesa, Revista de Derecho Migratorio y Extranjería 2002/1, 99 (100, 105).

55 COM(2004) 412 final, 10–12 and Chapter 2.D.IV. and Chapter 4.

56 The following is also to be emphasised from the migrants' perspective: 'On the whole, the beneficiaries of regularization interviewed for this study perceived regularization as a positive factor that enabled them to exercise a greater degree of control over different aspects of their life'; *Kraler*, Journal of Immigrant and Refugee Studies 2019, 107.

B. Hypothesis and structure

The study proceeds from the following hypothesis: EU regularisations supplementing the present return policy are more effective at 'combatting' irregular migration at EU level.

This hypothesis gives rise to three closely linked questions that each require further examination. (1) What are the regularisations in Austrian, German and Spanish immigration law? (2) How and to what extent could regularisations be used as an effective regulatory instrument to 'combat' irregular stays? (3) Does a harmonisation of regularisations at EU level offer any advantages over domestic rules? The aforementioned hypothesis and these three questions will be explored in more depth and examined in three parts comprising a total of five chapters.

Part I examines across two chapters the concepts underpinning irregular migration and regularisations as well as the EU regulatory framework. Chapter 1 focuses on the conceptual aspects of regularisations and provides the necessary definition and categories of regularisations for the analysis in Chapter 2 of the EU's competences regarding irregular migration and regularisation. The initial analysis concerns EU secondary law, namely the Return Directive, with the subsequent analysis of primary law clearly showing that the EU indeed has the necessary competence to legislate on regularisation at EU level. Both provide my own doctrinal clarifications of the concepts and notions in need of interpretation.

The second question, namely whether regularisations could be used as an effective regulatory instrument to 'combat' irregular stays, will be assessed using the standards under EU constitutional law.[57] As will be shown in Chapter 2, each EU legal act must fulfil a particular purpose. The fact that primary law requires a measure to at least be able to achieve a particular objective indicates that primary law itself demands that legal acts obtain a certain level of effectiveness.[58] In this study, administrative law is generally viewed in relation to its 'regulatory approach',[59] whereby

57 On the question concerning the effectiveness of the law see *Schmidt-Aßmann*, Das allgemeine Verwaltungsrecht als Ordnungsidee[2] (2006) Chapter 2 mns 20ff and Chapter 2.C. and Chapter 4.

58 See Chapter 2.C.I.

59 *Schmidt-Aßmann*, Verwaltungsrecht Chapter 1 mn 33.

the law is a 'suitable means of regulation'[60] that needs to be improved.[61] As for every legal field, the fields of law analysed in this study are subject to particular (factual) limitations.[62] In this respect, the resources of national authorities and the will to enforce legal requirements have foremost influence on the effectiveness of migration management. The design and features of the law are further key aspects in achieving the legislator's political and legal goals.[63]

The two chapters in Part II examine and compare the regularisations in Austria, Germany and Spain,[64] thus answering the first question of the regularisations available in each of these legal systems. The comparison employs the critical-contextual approach.[65] Chapter 3 examines particular features of each national framework as far as is necessary for the comparison in Chapter 4, such as the development of the relevant national legislation. This approach thus avoids the risk of unnecessary repetitions in the course of the comparison. Unlike a comparison based on national reports, the integrated approach applied in Chapter 4 adopts the purposes of the regularisations themselves as the basis for the comparison.

To conclude, Part III (more precisely Chapter 5) presents a proposal for a future 'Regularisation Directive'. Hereby I collate the results of the earlier research and present the accompanying concept of 'migration from within'. The question whether harmonisation of regularisation at EU level offers any advantages over domestic rules will also be answered.

---

60 *Schmidt-Aßmann*, Verwaltungsrecht Chapter 1 mns 33f with further references; *Scharpf*, Politische Steuerung und Politische Institutionen, Politische Vierteljahresschrift 1989, 10. For criticism from a socio-scientific viewpoint see *Luhmann*, Politische Steuerung: Ein Diskussionsbeitrag, Politische Vierteljahresschrift 1989, 4.

61 On the current discussion regarding migration management see, for example, *Bast*, Aufenthaltsrecht und Migrationssteuerung (2011); *Thym*, Migrationssteuerung im Einklang mit den Menschenrechten – Anmerkungen zu den migrationspolitischen Diskursen der Gegenwart, ZAR 2018, 193; *Berlit*, Migration und ihre Folgen – Wie kann das Recht Zuwanderung und Integration in Gesellschaft, Arbeitsmarkt und Sozialordnung steuern? (Teil 1), ZAR 2018, 229; *Berlit*, Migration und ihre Folgen – Wie kann das Recht Zuwanderung und Integration in Gesellschaft, Arbeitsmarkt und Sozialordnung steuern? (Teil 2), ZAR 2018, 287.

62 In general, *Schmidt-Aßmann*, Verwaltungsrecht Chapter 1 mns 38f.

63 Cf. *Bast*, Illegale Migration und die Rechte von illegalen Migrantinnen und Migranten als Regelungsgegenstände des Europarechts in *Fischer-Lescano/Kocher/Nassibi* (eds), Arbeit in der Illegalität (2012) 71 (71ff with further references).

64 On the choice of these three Member States see Introduction D.II.1.

65 See Introduction D.I.–II.

C. Current research

This study closes several gaps in current research, most notably the absence of an up-to-date comparison of the regularisations in Austria, Germany and Spain. Closing these gaps, however, requires further explanation.

As far as could be ascertained, there has been no systematic examination of the residency status of irregularly staying migrants. Although contributions to a 2011 issue of the European Journal of Migration and Law[66] provide key insights on irregular migration from various different perspectives (primarily from the social and political sciences), these for the most part do not adopt the perspective of legal science. Part II closes the gap.

An effective comparison of the different national laws requires an in-depth discussion of the concept of 'regularisation'. Existing research does feature such discussions, yet they are limited.[67] Chapter 1 therefore contains the first conceptual discussion of regularisations as a whole.

The last comparative analysis of regularisations in Europe is now over 20 years old.[68] With the exception of the REGINE-Study, which only gives a broad overview of the issue from the perspective of political science, there are no detailed legal comparisons of regularisations.[69] *Desmond* provides a short, but concise, comparison on the most common use of regularisa-

---

66 *Düvell*, The Pathways in and out of Irregular Migration in the EU: A Comparative Analysis, EJML 2011, 245; *Triandafyllidou/Ambrosini*, Irregular Immigration Control in Italy and Greece: Strong Fencing and Weak Gate-keeping serving the Labour Market, EJML 2011, 251; *Düvell*, EJML 2011, 275; *Kraler*, Fixing, Adjusting, Regulating, Protecting Human Rights – The Shifting Uses of Regularisations in the European Union, EJML 2011, 297; *Vollmer*, Policy Discourses on Irregular Migration in the EU – 'Number Games' and 'Political Games', EJML 2011, 317; *Raffaeli*, Criminalizing Irregular Immigration and the Returns Directive: An Analysis of the El Dridi Case, EJML 2011, 467.

67 See the overview in Chapter 1.A.I.

68 *De Bruycker* (ed), Les regularisations des étrangers illégaux dans l'union européenne. Regularisations of illegal immigrants in the European Union (2000). A summary of the study was published as *Apap/de Bruycker/Schmitter*, Regularisation of Illegal Aliens in the European Union. Summary Report of a Comparative Study, EJML 2000, 263; see Chapter 1.B.I.

69 *Baldwin-Edwards/Kraler*, REGINE Regularisations in Europe: Study on the practices in the area of regularization of illegally staying third-country nationals in the Member States of the EU. Final Report (January 2009), https://ec.europa.eu/migrant-integration/sites/default/files/2009-04/docl_8193_345982803.pdf (31.7.2022) and Chapter 1.B. See also *Kraler*, Journal of Immigrant and Refugee Studies 2019.

tions, though the focus is on the EU and the United States.[70] *Schieber*, whose dissertation concerns non-returnable persons and their right to stay, must also be considered.[71] Although there are overlaps with the study undertaken here, *Schieber* focuses mainly on the international protection, i.e. refugees and subsidiary protection, and the corresponding protective mechanisms.[72] In short, *Schieber* analyses irregular migration from the perspective of asylum procedures. By contrast, Part II of this study examines all decisions in Austria, Germany and Spain which underpin a right to stay[73] and which concern irregularly staying migrants. *Schieber* does indeed compare national laws, including Germany and Austria, but her comparison also includes Belgium, Sweden and the United Kingdom, and favours national reports over the integrated approach used in this study.[74] Further research also concerns the 'different national practices concerning granting of non-EU harmonised protection statuses'[75] – this is only covered in part in this study.[76] It can therefore be stated that the comparison of regularisations in Part II (Chapter 3 and Chapter 4) closes this gap in the current research.

Reference may also be made to several studies concerning non-returnees. Applying the ECJ's definition, which will be discussed in greater detail below,[77] a person is non-returnable when 'it is not, or has not been, possible to implement a return decision'.[78] Similar to *Schieber*, *Gosme* tackles the question of the 'limbo spaces between illegal and legal stay'.[79] More recently, *Lutz* has examined 'non-removable returnees' and the corresponding shortfalls in enforcement, but only touches lightly upon regularisations.[80]

70 *Desmond*, Regularization in the European Union and the United States. The Frequent Use of an Exceptional Measure in *Wiesbrock/Acosta Arcarazo* (eds), Global Migration: Old Assumptions, New Dynamics. Vol 1 (2015) 69.

71 *Schieber*, Komplementärer Schutz: Die aufenthaltsrechtliche Stellung nicht rückführbarer Personen in der EU (2013).

72 *Schieber*, Komplementärer Schutz 44ff.

73 See the definition in Chapter 1.A.II.3.

74 See Introduction D.II.2.

75 Cf. *EMN*, The different national practices concerning granting of non-EU harmonised protection statuses (December 2010).

76 Cf. *Kraler*, EJML 2011, 297.

77 See Chapter 2.B.II.

78 ECJ 5.6.2014, C-146/14, ECLI:EU:C:2014:1320, *Mahdi*, para 87.

79 Cf. *Gosme*, Limbo spaces between illegal and legal stay: resulting from EU management of non-removable third country nationals, Dissertation 2014, Sciences Po Paris, https://spire.sciencespo.fr/hdl:/2441/30a6ffj78696ja3eov65066e05/resources/2014iepp0037-gosme-charles-these.pdf (31.7.2022).

80 *Lutz*, EJML 2018, 46–50.

The same applies vis-à-vis a 2018 study by *Menezes Queiroz* discussing, inter alia, the situation of 'non-removable migrants' and 'access to legality in the EU'.[81] *Farcy* adopts the same direction in an analysis of the guarantees prior to return and the access to rights by non-returnable migrants against the backdrop of the legal obstacles to deportation and the resulting consequences for non-returnables.[82] Finally, the empirical and legal analysis of the 'return procedures applicable to rejected asylum seekers in the EU and options for their regularisation'[83] undertaken by *Strban/Rataj/Šabič* is also to be mentioned as it covers several topics relevant to this study, albeit with some differences. Firstly, *Strban/Rataj/Šabič* focus only on rejected asylum seekers and their particular situation in the EU.[84] The category of persons covered is thus much narrower, though with much broader content as the attention is directed towards the return procedure. Secondly, *Strban/Rataj/Šabič* do not examine the different regularisations in detail, but give just a broad overview of the practices in 17 Member States.[85] Last but not least, a 2014 study on the detention of non-returnable migrants contains several examples of 'best practices'.[86]

Each of the aforementioned studies have the common feature that they do not make any specific suggestions regarding the problem of non-returnable migrants (and in this respect the low return rate). Chapter 5 addresses this gap in current research by first presenting the accompanying concept of 'migration from within', outlining the reasons why the existing EU migration policy requires a new direction with regard to irregularly staying migrants and that this can best be achieved through the introduction of a Regularisation Directive at EU level. Proceeding from this concept – and building on the comparison in Part II – I present my proposal for such a Directive.

---

81 *Menezes Queiroz*, Illegally Staying 81–116 and 153–181.

82 *Farcy* in *de Bruycker/Cornelisse/Moraru*.

83 *Strban/Rataj/Šabič*, Return Procedures Applicable to Rejected Asylum-Seekers in the European Union and Options for their Regularisation, Refugee Survey Quarterly 2018, 1.

84 *Strban/Rataj/Šabič*, Refugee Survey Quarterly 2018, 4.

85 The authors sent a questionnaire with 28 questions to national experts; cf. *Strban/Rataj/Šabič*, Refugee Survey Quarterly 2018, 4.

86 *Vanderbruggen/Phelps/Sebtaoui/Kovats/Pollet*, Point of No Return: The Futile Detention of Unreturnable Migrants (January 2014), https://detentionaction.org.uk/wp-content/uploads/2018/12/PONR_report.pdf (31.7.2022).

In summary, the following study will close several gaps in the current research, with the first ever comparative analysis of regularisations in Austria, Germany and Spain at the core.

D. Methodology

The aforementioned problem, hypothesis and the current research now serve as a foundation for the explanation of the methodology employed to answer the three questions central to this study. This section will first introduce the critical-contextual approach to the comparative legal analysis (I.)[87] before explaining the application of this approach in this study (II.) as well as particular features of this English language version (III.).

I. Critical-contextual approach

The study applies the critical-contextual method, which is a critical evolution of functionalism. A critical-contextual comparison can be best understood by picturing a three-piece Matryoshka doll. Using said picture, functionalism forms the basis and, consequently, the centre of the Matryoshka doll. Contextualism and the critical approaches to comparative law form the second and third pieces, respectively. A critical-contextual comparison draws upon all three methods/approaches and fuses them together. Following *Frankenberg*,[88] context-sensitive, critical and reflexive comparisons are 'thick' in nature.

---

87 A detailed description of the critical-contextual method has been published in *Hinterberger*, A Critical-Contextual Approach in Comparative Migration Law, International Journal of Migration and Border Studies 2023, forthcoming.

88 *Frankenberg*, Comparative Law as Critique (2019) 225ff; *Legrand*, European Legal Systems are not Converging, ICLQ 1996, 52 (56) and *Husa*, A New Introduction to Comparative Law (2015) 155 who refer in a similar vein to the work of *Geertz*, Thick Description: Toward an Interpretive Theory of Culture in *Geertz*, The Interpretation of Cultures (1973) 3.

1. The starting point: functionalism

The comparison of public law[89] applies various methods.[90] Functionalism forms the core of the three-piece Matryoshka doll and, thus, of a critical-contextual comparison. Functionalists compare norms, in their function as solutions to particular problems.[91] This allows the focus on the question of the function (role and contribution) of the norm or institution within the respective legal system and society.[92] According to the functional approach, different legal norms in different legal systems answer the question or solve the problem similarly or differently.[93] The so-called presumption of similarity is necessary to understand the functional method whereby it has to be noted that there is not one, but many functional methods.[94]

The functional method is not without its criticisms.[95] One fundamental critique is that it may be difficult or even impossible to ascertain the function the law strives to perform.[96] It is correct that a legal provision, depending on the perspective, may fulfil different functions, yet it does not mean that the provision cannot be examined with regard to a specific function. I therefore believe that the chosen function and perspective has to be clearly identified and outlined to tackle this criticism.[97] Furthermore,

---

89 For detail on the particular features of a comparison of public law see *Bernhardt*, Eigenheiten und Ziele der Rechtsvergleichung im öffentlichen Recht, ZaöRV 1964, 431; *Krüger*, Eigenart, Methode und Funktion der Rechtsvergleichung im öffentlichen Recht in FS Martin Kriele (1997) 1393; *Bell*, Comparing Public Law in *Harding/Örücü* (eds), Comparative Law in the 21st Century (2002) 235 (240ff).

90 Cf. *Trantas*, Die Anwendung der Rechtsvergleichung bei der Untersuchung des öffentlichen Rechts (1998) 43–47 with further references; for the comparative methods specifically in constitutional law see *Jackson*, Comparative Constitutional Law: Methodologies in *Rosenfeld/Sajó* (eds), The Oxford Handbook of Comparative Constitutional Law (2012) 54 and *Tushnet*, Weak Courts, Strong Rights: Judicial Review and Social Welfare Rights in Comparative Constitutional Law (2009) 5ff.

91 *Kischel*, Comparative Law (2019) § 3 mns 3f.

92 *Ebert*, Rechtsvergleichung (1978) 29; *Sommermann*, Bedeutung der Rechtsvergleichung für die Fortentwicklung des Staats- und Verwaltungsrechts in Europa, DÖV 1999, 1017 (1023).

93 *Zweigert/Kötz*, An Introduction to Comparative Law[3] (1998) 40; cf. *Kamba*, Comparative Law: A Theoretical Framework, ICLQ 1974, 485 (517).

94 *Michaels*, The Functional Method of Comparative Law in *Reimann/Zimmermann* (eds), The Oxford Handbook of Comparative Law[2] (2019) 346 (347).

95 For a useful overview see *Kischel*, Comparative Law § 3 mns 6ff and *Piek*, Die Kritik an der funktionalen Rechtsvergleichung, ZEuP 2013, 60 (62ff).

96 *Kischel*, Comparative Law § 3 mn 7.

97 See Introduction D.II.3.

if it is impossible to ascertain the function the law strives to perform, it should be explicitly pointed out and, consequently, taken into account in the course of the comparison.

2. Adding the context and…

Jackson neatly sums up a further criticism regarding the functional method in stating that '[a] number of scholars have cautioned against the misleadingly homogenizing and obscuring perils of functionalism. It is all too easy, scholars such as Günter Frankenberg suggest, for a comparativist unconsciously to assume the categories of legal thought with which she is familiar, and thus to see foreign law only as either similar or different, without being able to grasp the conceptual or sociological foundations of other legal orders. Professor Bomhoff, in a similar vein, has shown how doctrines with a similar name and seemingly similar function actually mean quite different things in a practice that is shaped by more particular contexts'.[98]

In response to such critique, a contextualist approach has emerged within the functional method comprising the following: the law as a whole and thus its individual provisions and rules are to be viewed in the context of the historical, economic and political framework to obtain a more complete picture.[99]

For example, the contextual method favoured by *Kischel* is functionalist at the core and, therefore, looks at the legal and non-legal environment in which a legal norm is situated.[100] However, he proposes that the context has to be considered in every comparison. In short, a comparatist has to recognise, in which conceptual, dogmatic/doctrinal or cultural environment a legal norm is situated.

Following *Jackson* ('contextualised functionalism'), one should never fail to consider the context and the characteristics of legal systems and institutions, otherwise there is the risk of making false assumptions.[101] Functions and concepts may appear to be the same at first glance, though

---

98 *Jackson* in *Rosenfeld/Sajó* 66.

99 Cf. *Bell* in *Harding/Örücü* 235ff; *Legrand*, How to Compare Now, Legal Studies 1996, 232 (236); *Van Hoecke/Warrington*, Legal Cultures, Legal Paradigms and Legal Doctrine: Towards a New Model for Comparative Law, ICLQ 1998, 495 (532ff).

100 *Kischel*, Comparative Law § 3 mns 199ff.

101 *Jackson* in *Rosenfeld/Sajó* 70–72.

can have very different (legal and actual) effects in different societies. An in-depth understanding of the subject is therefore only possible once the characteristics, the socio-political and historical contexts are understood. *Bell* argues in this regard that 'public law is particularly influenced by historical contingencies'[102] and, therefore, the institutional setting is important to understand what social function it really entails.[103]

Depending on the subject matter, the necessary context to be taken into account differs. One has to identify the environment the legal norms are situated. It is only after this step that a comparatist is able to grasp the relevant contextual elements – like the historical, economic and political framework – that are necessary for its understanding. As will be shown below regarding the case study, understanding the different regularisations in Austria, Germany and Spain requires insights into the historical and political development of migration law.[104] However, there is no single answer to the question concerning the contextual aspects to take into account.

To sum up, both *Kischel* from a comparative public law perspective and *Jackson* from a comparative constitutional law perspective advocate for a functionalist approach enhanced with contextual elements. Taking account of the context thus helps to avoid the risk of making incorrect assumptions based on a too 'thin' understanding of law because contexts have an influence on the functioning and the interpretation of norms.

Coming back to the picture of the Matryoshka doll, the two inner pieces are now laid out. However, to be able to speak of 'thick' comparison according to *Frankenberg*, the comparison has to further be critical and reflexive.

3. …Critical approaches to functionalism

Critical comparison has already a long tradition in the field of constitutional law. It is closely linked to critical legal studies (CLS) approaches.[105] CLS cannot claim to be one coherent approach, but rather a broad variety

102 *Bell* in *Harding/Örücü* 241 and 247.

103 Cf. *Tushnet*, Weak Courts 10ff with regard to the particularities of constitutional law.

104 See Chapter 3.

105 Cf. *Mattei*, Comparative Law and Critical Legal Studies in *Reimann/Zimmermann* (eds), The Oxford Handbook of Comparative Law^2 (2019) 805 (805ff); *Frankenberg*, Comparative Law 17ff.

of critical approaches to law. Hence, the question remains of the contribution made by the qualifier 'critical' to the contextualist approach described above. In my opinion, it has the potential to address another fundamental critique from *Frankenberg*: 'The functionalist comparatist picks a social problem, always already framed in terms of law, and then moves on to its legal solution. Overconfident that law is a self-contained and autonomous system of conflict management [...]. The hermeneutic fallacy is built upon a double reduction of the approach that focuses on the interpretation and better, that is, more authentic, understanding of the law and the cultural analysis of law. [...] The hermeneutic fallacy, therefore, follows from a theory of law that is constitutive only in one direction and which denies the dynamic, dialectical law/power and law/culture relationship'.[106]

Consequently, using a critical approach broadens the view and helps to see how different concepts yield different power structures. *Frankenberg* rightly stated that '[c]ritique may help uncover and dismantle those hierarchies and asymmetries: it may deconstruct hegemony by unsettling settled knowledge'.[107] Therefore, by adding a critical approach to contextualism, the method can be developed further. Critical-contextual comparison may be used as a hegemony-critical approach and applied to analyse how different concepts are interpreted differently in different contexts.

This is particularly relevant regarding the relationship between migrants and the state and the given power-political relations in migration law. To better understand said relationship, it is necessary to refer again to the perspective taken by the comparatist. Regarding migration law, one may take the position of the state or the migrant. In my view it is particularly useful from a critical perspective to take a migrant-centred perspective as has been done in this study.[108]

Finally yet importantly, the term 'reflexive' can be considered as another layer of a critical comparison. It is understood as employing 'distancing to capture "the other" most effectively'.[109] When comparing different legal systems, the risk of bias towards one's 'home' legal system is eminent.[110] From a critical perspective, an unbiased description and evaluation of

---

106 *Frankenberg*, Comparing constitutions: Ideas, ideals, and ideology—toward a layered narrative, ICON 2006, 439 (444–446).

107 *Frankenberg*, Comparative Law ix.

108 See Introduction D.II.3.

109 *Curran*, Critiquing Günter Frankenberg's Comparative Law As Critique, German Law Journal 2020, 304 (305); cf. *Frankenberg*, Comparative Law 70ff and 229–231.

110 Cf. *Ebert*, Rechtsvergleichung 144.

such legal systems is (almost) impossible.[111] According to *Frankenberg*, comparing reflexively therefore means to 'start a critical dialog between the familiar and the unfamiliar legal cultures'.[112]

II. Critical-contextual comparison in this study

1. Content and choice of Member States

The study compares particular real-life factual circumstances in which the associated legal problems serve as a common basis for comparison.[113] In principle the method is to be based on the problem itself.[114] This favours the use of the critical-contextual method due to the considerable role played by the context of the problems to be analysed. Accordingly, the first question concerns mechanisms in Austrian, German and Spanish law which provide a means out of irregular migration.

The factual circumstances in question relate to the presence of irregularly staying migrants in EU Member States who are seeking a right to reside. Many of these migrants cannot be deported for legal or factual reasons, in particular in long term. The irregular stay gives rise to various problems, such as the denial of rights, and often such migrants are in an especially vulnerable position.[115] As a social, political and legal phenomenon, irregular migration presents the EU and the individual Member States with significant (legal) challenges.[116] Generally, it is only with the right to reside that irregularly staying migrants are 'integrated' into the state system for the first time, which is typically followed by (limited) access to the labour market, welfare benefits and healthcare.

The legal regimes in the EU's area of freedom, security and justice are partly harmonised and, consequently, similar problems arise. For this reason the presumption of similarity applies and critical-contextual com-

---

111 Cf. *Frankenberg*, Critical Comparisons: Re-thinking Comparative Law, Harvard International Law Journal 1985, 411 (439f).

112 *Frankenberg*, Comparative Law 230.

113 Cf. *Bartels*, Methode und Gegenstand intersystemarer Rechtsvergleichung (1982) 66f; *Michaels* in *Reimann/Zimmermann* 347f.

114 *Ebert*, Rechtsvergleichung 28f.

115 See Introduction A.

116 See Introduction A.

parison seems to be a particularly fruitful approach in the EU.[117] The EU Member States enjoy legislative freedom and a margin of discretion regarding regularisations. Article 6(4) Return Directive leaves Member States the possibility to regularise irregularly staying migrants instead of issuing a return decision.[118] Consequently, Austria, Germany and Spain adopt different legal approaches with regard to regularisations; this is also one reason why the description of contextual elements is necessary to fully understand regularisations. Each of the three countries is an EU Member State and part of the same supranational legal system. Accordingly, they must each follow the same EU constitutional requirements pursuant to Article 79(1) TFEU.[119] In other words, by virtue of their EU membership they have the same programmatic objectives. For instance, the objective of tackling irregular migration – one of the core elements of EU migration policy.

Hence, the case study focuses on legal possibilities for regularisation in Austria, Germany and Spain. In other words, the analysis will focus on each of the possibilities in Austria, Germany and Spain, which are available to this group regarding the award of a residency title. The relationship between the legal and the extra-legal approaches concerning irregular migration and regularisations will subsequently be examined and compared. In a broad sense these must therefore fulfil the function of allowing irregularly staying migrants to become legal residents or be related to such outcome. Asylum procedures will not be analysed as persons subject to international protection do not fall within the scope of this study.[120] For the same reason I shall not conduct a detailed examination and comparison of the expulsion systems in place.[121]

To be able to effectively describe regularisations, contextual elements had to be taken into account. The historical and political development of migration law in each of the three Member States – and the margin of discretion according to Article 6(4) Return Directive – contributed to the

---

117 Cf. *Örücü*, The Enigma of Comparative Law: Variations on a Theme for the Twenty-first Century (2004) 24f.

118 See Chapter 2.B.I.

119 See Chapter 2.C.

120 Art 2(a) Qualification Directive. The Qualification Directive divides international protection into refugee status and subsidiary protection; cf. on the difference between the concepts see *Peers/Moreno-Lax*, Qualification: Refugee Status and Subsidiary Protection in *Peers/Moreno-Lax/Garlick/Guild* (eds), EU Immigration and Asylum Law. Vol 3: EU Asylum Law^2 (2015) 65 (156ff).

121 See recently *Molnár*, Interplay.

formation of different regularisations. Understanding these contexts is key to outlining regularisations and allowing an integrated comparison.[122]

As an examination of all 27[123] EU Member States was not feasible, the study only focused on three Member States, namely Austria, Germany and Spain. Each of these Member States have different regularisations in their legal system.[124] The differences in approach towards irregular migration are reflected in the national legislation and case law as well as in extra-legal approaches. In this respect the comparison appears to be especially fruitful.

Spain used regularisation programmes in the 1990s as an extraordinary legal measure.[125] The background to such an approach lies, inter alia, in viewing regularisations as an 'alternative to immigration policy'.[126] The high demand for workers in the service industry could be covered by migrants who were in employment, but who were residing irregularly.[127] However, as in Austria and Germany, regularisation mechanisms, which permanently form part of the legal order of Member States, as opposed to ad-hoc programmes, are now the standard.[128]

The comparison answers the question whether the different legal approaches indeed achieve the same legal function whereby contextual elements play a particularly important role in this analysis. The comparison between Austria and Germany is especially informative, though at first one may assume that because of the similar legal traditions, the laws of

122 See Introduction D.II.2.

123 Since 31 January 2020 the United Kingdom is no longer an EU Member State.

124 See *European Commission*, Clandestino (23.11.2009) 42–46, 54–59, 74–79. On Austria: *Kraler/Hollomey*, Austria: Irregular Migration – A Phenomenon in Transition in *Triandafyllidou* (eds), Irregular Migration: Myths and Realities (2010) 41. On Germany: *Cyrus/Kovacheva*, Undocumented Migration in Germany: Many Figures, Little Comprehension in *Triandafyllidou* (ed), Irregular Migration: Myths and Realities (2010) 125. On Spain: *González-Enríquez*, Spain: Irregularity as a Rule in *Triandafyllidou* (ed), Irregular Migration: Myths and Realities (2010) 247.

125 On the distinction between the concepts of regularisation programmes and mechanisms see Chapter 1.B.I. See also Chapter 3.C.I.

126 *Baldwin-Edwards/Kraler*, REGINE (January 2009) 39.

127 Cf. *Baldwin-Edwards/Kraler*, REGINE (January 2009) 39f; *Pelzer*, Regularisierung des Aufenthalts von Menschen ohne Papiere: Bausteine einer liberalen Migrationspolitik? in *Fischer-Lescano/Kocher/Nassibi* (eds), Arbeit in der Illegalität: Die Rechte von Menschen ohne Aufenthaltspapiere (2012) 143 (149) and *Kraler*, Journal of Immigrant and Refugee Studies 2019, 99 and 102.

128 See Chapter 3.A.III., Chapter 3.B.III. and Chapter 3.C.III.

both countries are also similar.[129] Regularisations in Austria and Germany are linked to different requirements. Austria and Germany are considered 'ideological opponents' of regularisations,[130] yet the comparison will show that this is no longer a valid assessment as both use regularisations to bring an irregular residency to an end. Furthermore, the consequences of the 'longer summer of migration 2015' are still present in both countries, which have both seen a high number of applications for international protection.[131]

Another example of a contextual element that is taken into account is the different legal status of irregularly staying migrants in Austria, Germany and Spain which leads to differences in their factual living situations. Failing to present the (legal) contexts in question would mean overlooking that irregularly staying migrants in Spain have access to the welfare system, whereas such migrants in Germany and Austria do not, at least in principle. This is also particularly important from a migrant-centred perspective and its implications on the social conditions of these individuals.[132]

The need to include the context is also clear with regard to a further example, specifically toleration.[133] Although it does not constitute legal residency – and is thus not a regularisation – toleration is often the first level towards gaining a right to stay and thus the first step away from irregularity;[134] including this approach therefore enrichens the comparison and has to be included due to the context to provide a full picture of the factual and legal problem. The situation is different in Spain as there is no comparable legal concept. Accordingly, those who cannot be deported are tolerated, though not as a result of the law itself.[135] It is necessary nonetheless to present this non-legal approach in order to understand the Spanish regularisations in full.

---

129 Such as in relation to civil law, see *Zweigert/Kötz*, Rechtsvergleichung 130ff and *Ebert*, Rechtsvergleichung 57ff.

130 Cf. *Baldwin-Edwards/Kraler*, REGINE (January 2009) 8, 42; *Kraler/Reichel/Hollomey*, Undocumented Migration: Country Report Austria. Clandestino Project (November 2008/updated October 2009), https://www.eliamep.gr/wp-content/uploads/2017/12/clandestino_report_austria_final_2.pdf (31.7.2022). For a more reserved opinion see *Kraler*, Journal of Immigrant and Refugee Studies 2019, 99 and 102.

131 See the references in Fn 30.

132 See Introduction D.III.3.

133 See Chapter 1.B.III.1.a., Chapter 4.A.I.2. and Chapter 4.A.I.3.

134 See Chapter 1.B.III.1.a.

135 See Chapter 4.A.I.1.

There is difficulty in achieving an unbiased description and evaluation of the three legal systems because of the risk of bias towards one's 'home' legal system; in this case: Austria.[136] In order to appropriately heed such risk, generic terms are used and the knowledge acquired during research trips is linked back, as mentioned in the preface and in the introductory remarks in Part II. The terms ('irregular stay', 'migrant', 'regularisation' and 'right to stay') were specifically chosen to – or to be able to – include the context and also to reflect precise legal concepts.[137] This allows me to adopt an (almost) objective position and to view the selected legal systems from a sufficient distance.[138] I also took into consideration that, in so far as terms particular to the national legal systems are used,[139] the different meanings require explanation.

This study analyses formal, written legislation, 'law in debate', i.e. the different legal opinions,[140] and (decisions from superior courts). *Michaels* accurately describes 'judicial decisions as responses to real life situations'.[141] Consequently, the analysis looks further at the 'law in action'.[142] This concept describes how the law is practised and implemented in everyday life. *Großfeld* refers to the latter as the study of legal effect – to paraphrase *Rehbinder*, law that is not alive in practice remains dead in the books.[143] Accordingly, non-legal approaches are also examined alongside

---

136 Cf. with regard to the particular features of a 'homeward trend' *Ebert*, Rechtsvergleichung 144.

137 Cf. *Dumon*, International Migration 1983, 218, 227 and see Chapter 1.A.

138 *Trantas*, Rechtsvergleichung 41; cf. also *Sommermann*, DÖV 1999, 1023; *Von Busse*, Rechtsvergleichung 347; *Evan/Grisoli/Treves*, Rechtssoziologie und Rechtsvergleichung in *Drobnig/Rehbinder* (eds), Rechtssoziologie und Rechtsvergleichung (1997) 35 (51); similarly *Kaiser*, ZaöRV 1964, 391 (396f). For criticism see *Frankenberg*, Harvard International Law Journal 1985, 439 and *Kischel*, Comparative Law § 3 mns 186ff with further references.

139 *Zweigert/Kötz*, Rechtsvergleichung 33, describe this as the negative aspect of the principle of functionality. See also *Starck*, JZ 1997, 1026f; *Glaser*, Die Entwicklung des Europäischen Verwaltungsrechts aus der Perspektive der Handlungsformenlehre (2013) 70f in relation to the notion of modes of action (*Handlungsform*); see also *Gutteridge*, Comparative Law (1946) 117ff; *Raschauer*, Allgemeines Verwaltungsrecht[5] (2016) mn 33 with regard to EU concepts.

140 Cf. *Kischel*, Comparative Law § 3 mns 44, 234.

141 *Michaels* in *Reimann/Zimmermann* 347f.

142 See *Pound*, Law in Books and Law in Action, American Law Review 1910, 12. Cf. also *Frankenberg*, ICON 2006, 442f.

143 *Großfeld*, Kernfragen der Rechtsvergleichung (1996) 117f; *Rehbinder*, Rechtssoziologie[8] (2014) 2 § 3; see especially *Ehrlich*, Grundlegung der Soziologie des Rechts (1913) Vorrede, 394 and 405.

the legislative provisions.[144] An approach or solution is 'non-legal' if it is not formally stipulated in law. For example, it is shown below that Austria and Germany stipulate toleration in their respective laws, whereas in Spain those persons who cannot be deported are *de facto* but not legally tolerated.[145] In comparison to other areas of law, non-legal solutions have far greater influence on public law;[146] an assessment that is especially noticeable in migration law.[147] In the case study, the variety of legislation, case law, studies, newspaper articles, statistics and implementation regulations have been examined to best paint a picture of the legal reality and non-legal practices.[148] Furthermore, the information on the law and legal reality in Austria, Germany and Spain was linked, acquired through research periods in each country.[149] Nonetheless, it has to be emphasised that a complete picture of 'law in action' can never be painted.

The results from the comparison may be especially useful and may serve as a source of inspiration in the search for new solutions.[150] Accordingly, the comparisons between legal systems can contribute to solving legal issues.[151] Ultimately, comparing in a functional manner may be about finding 'better' solutions to a legal or factual 'problem'. Following *Michaels* and also in my opinion, 'functionality can serve as an evaluative criterion. Functional comparative law then becomes a "better-law comparison"—the better of several laws is that which fulfils its function better than the others'.[152]

However, according to critical approaches, there are no 'better' solutions because who defines 'better' and according to which standard? I disagree

---

144 Cf. *Trantas*, Rechtsvergleichung 72ff with further references; *Kischel*, ZVglRWiss 2005, 17ff and in particular 24f with excellent examples.

145 See Chapter 4.A.I.

146 *Schwarze*, Europäisches Verwaltungsrecht^2 (2005) 83. Similarly *Kischel*, Comparative Law § 3 mn 201; *Kaiser*, Vergleichung im öffentlichen Recht, ZaöRV 1964, 391 (396) and *Krüger* in FS Martin Kriele 1398ff.

147 Cf. *Einwallner*, Asyl- und Fremdenrecht 2010 – Bloß noch Spielball der Politik, juridikum 2010, 68.

148 See the examples in *Schmid-Drüner*, Der Begriff der öffentlichen Sicherheit und Ordnung im Einwanderungsrecht ausgewählter EU-Mitgliedstaaten (2007) 47.

149 See the comments made in the preface.

150 Cf. *Schmidt-Aßmann/Dagron*, Deutsches und französisches Verwaltungsrecht im Vergleich ihrer Ordnungsideen, ZaöRV 2007, 395 (467); *Von Busse*, Die Methoden der Rechtsvergleichung im öffentlichen Recht als richterliches Instrument der Interpretation von nationalem Recht (2015) 40.

151 Cf. *Trantas*, Rechtsvergleichung 29.

152 *Michaels* in *Reimann/Zimmermann* 348.

that it is generally impossible to compare in order to find 'better' solutions. Nevertheless, I take this criticism seriously, which is why some comparisons may not be possible because they would otherwise be too subjective unless at least a standard is defined. Hence, one limit of critical-contextual comparison is to make clear how 'better' is defined to rebut this criticism. In the case study 'better' is considered from a normative perspective. The 'better'-law is evaluated according to a specific standard: international law, in particular human rights, and EU law.

The standards are those of international and EU law – international law will be examined in Chapter 1, EU law in Chapter 2. The inclusion of higher-ranking legal norms arises from the hierarchy underpinning the legal system. The compatibility of regularisations with the relevant requirements of international and EU law will therefore be examined. Where international law is concerned, only the ECHR is included as a more detailed analysis would exceed the scope of this study. The constitutional law of each of the three Member States ranks above the mere individual pieces of legislation, but is not examined since the core constitutional guarantees regarding fundamental rights which are central to the (comparative) analysis of regularisations, are all anchored in international and EU provisions.[153] Moreover, it would extend far beyond the scope of this study. The results of the comparison and of the analysis may be used to propose a Regularisation Directive (Part III) in order to determine the content central to such a Directive. Taking international and EU law as the standard is thus key as a Regularisation Directive would have to satisfy the requirements in international and EU law. An assessment of the compatibility between regularisations and constitutional standards would therefore be irrelevant for this reason.

To sum up, the critical-contextual comparison plays a key role as I examine whether a common EU solution can be found with regard to regularisations. The results of the comparison are used to propose a Regularisation Directive at EU level. Taking international and EU law as the standard is essential as a Regularisation Directive would have to satisfy the requirements in international and EU law.

153 See Chapter 1.B.III.

2. Integrated approach

Prior to the actual comparison in Chapter 4, Chapter 3 contains separate discussions of the context surrounding migration in each of the three Member States. More specifically, the development of immigration law, the legal status of foreigners (aliens) and of each of the relevant regularisations. Furthermore, the competences, the responsible authorities as well as the legal protections in place will also be outlined. The described contextual elements create the framework for the integrated comparison in which the individual regularisations can be linked and described in detail. The integrated comparison can then refer to general aspects that are relevant to understanding the measures in place.

The comparison in the case study thus does not have the usual descriptive element that results from individual national reports.[154] The legislative provisions and non-legal solutions in the selected Member States are linked, analysed and evaluated in an integrated approach.[155] Using the relationship between the provisions and solutions allows one to determine changes in function, which may not be readily apparent at first sight.[156] In addition, separate treatment of the regularisations can also give rise to unnecessary repetitions, which are to be avoided. As *Kischel* quite rightly notes, comparison and presentation should melt together form a whole.[157]

The point of comparison is referred to as *tertium comparationis*.[158] The categorisation follows on the basis of the purpose of the regularisation, as outlined in detail below.[159] The concept centres around the decisive legal reason for awarding a right to stay, whereby (with regard to regularisations) six purposes can be derived from the three relevant levels of legal sources. The extent of their links varies with respect to each purpose of

---

154 Cf. *Von Busse*, Rechtsvergleichung 36ff. An example for such an approach as outlined by *Von Busse* is present in *Schieber*, Komplementärer Schutz 117ff or in *Schmid-Drüner*, Einwanderungsrecht 49ff. In addition, see *Kischel*, Comparative Law § 3 mns 10, 12, 50, 53.

155 *Ebert*, Rechtsvergleichung 145ff; *Kischel*, Comparative Law § 3 mns 50 und 242ff; *Trantas*, Rechtsvergleichung 48f with further references; *Zweigert/Kötz*, Rechtsvergleichung 43f.

156 Cf. *Lachmayer*, Verfassungsvergleichung durch Verfassungsgerichte, JRP 2010, 166 (170); *Ebert*, Rechtsvergleichung 154, 158.

157 *Kischel*, Comparative Law § 3 mn 243.

158 Cf. *Örücü*, Enigma 21; *Sommermann*, DÖV 1999, 1017; *Piek*, ZEuP 2013, 67f.

159 See *Kischel*, Comparative Law § 3 mn 242 for general remarks regarding categorisation; see Chapter 1.B.II. concerning the purpose of the regularisation.

the regularisation as only 'non-returnability' and 'vulnerability' are sub-divided.

3. Analysis from the perspective of irregularly staying migrants

Finally yet importantly, this study has also a (hegemony-)critical layer. A research perspective that is migrant-centred most accurately serves the above-described hegemony-critical approach.[160] This is particularly relevant to deal with the relationship between migrants and the state and the underlying power relations in migration law. 'Migrant-centred' is defined as looking at the relevant legal and non-legal approaches through the lens of migrants, thus the perspective shifts from the state to the migrants. This allows one to look at the law and how it constitutes legality/illegality in migration law[161] and, consequently, social conditions. *Klarmann* accurately pointed out in his work on the deconstruction of migration-specific illegalities that 'illegal' migrants are not factual realities.[162]

Transnational law is one approach that takes a migrant-centred perspective and may be applied in a hegemony-critical manner. Generally speaking, provisions of (EU) migration law are to be found at three levels: international law, EU law and national law. The case study considers all three levels and shows that an isolated view of one single level is no longer appropriate. This is already clear from Chapter 1 in the discussion of the relationship between the three levels. Chapter 2 – as Chapter 5 – focuses solely on EU law. The comparison in Part II (Chapter 3 and Chapter 4) centres around Austrian, German and Spanish public law measured against the EU and international standards.[163]

In this respect, the notion 'transnational law' must be emphasised.[164] The notion refers, inter alia, to law applicable to acts and circumstances

160 See Introduction D.I.1.

161 *Menezes Queiroz*, Illegally Staying 11ff.

162 *Klarmann*, Illegalisierte Migration. Die (De-)Konstruktion migrationsspezifischer Illegalitäten im Unionsrecht (2021) 31.

163 See Introduction D.II.1.

164 For the fundamentals see *Jessup*, Transnational Law (1956); cf. *Miller/Zumbansen* (eds), Comparative Law as Transnational Law (2012); *Zumbansen*, Carving Out Typologies and Accounting for Differences Across Systems: Towards a Methodology of Transnational Constitutionalism in *Rosenfeld/Sajó* (eds), The Oxford Handbook of Comparative Constitutional Law (2012) 75 (75–84); on transnational refugee law see *Goodwin-Gill/Lambert*, The Limits of Transnational Law:

beyond national borders.[165] One purpose of transnational law is to clarify the interrelationship and links between these three levels when apparent in a particular case.[166] Attention must also be drawn to one aspect of the methodology of transnational research: selected case scenarios are examined, categorised and analysed from the perspective of the addressee of the norm.[167] *Farahat* has shifted and applied this approach to the field of transnational migration.[168] This also serves as a framework for the present study and will therefore be applied.

The residency status of migrants staying irregularly in a Member State is at the centre of the legal analysis. At the same time the study is also based on the perspective of the individual. Present research on this topic has often focused on deportation law and therefore only considered the matter from the perspective of the state.[169] This study examines the topic from the other side of the coin by viewing irregularity and regularisations from a 'migrant-centred perspective'.[170] This casts (new) light on the various national, EU and international provisions[171] and the given power-political relations. This approach is also expressed by the starting point for the comparison (purpose of the regularisation), which bases decisions justifying the right to stay on a contractual structure.[172]

The right to stay, which determines the legal or illegal residence of migrants, is therefore at the heart of this study.[173] This seems to be the more contemporary and fruitful approach in view of the changing understanding of the law surrounding immigration. Accordingly, decisions

---

Refugee Law, Policy Harmonization and Judicial Dialogue in the European Union (2010).

165 Cf. *Jessup*, Transnational 1ff; *Farahat*, Progressive Inklusion: Zugehörigkeit und Teilhabe im Migrationsrecht (2014) 11 with further references.

166 *Farahat*, Progressive Inklusion 12.

167 Cf. *Farahat*, Progressive Inklusion 12f; *Jessup*, Transnational 11f.

168 Cf. *Farahat*, Progressive Inklusion 12f; *Jessup*, Transnational 11f.

169 See especially *Thym*, Schutz des Aufenthalts zwischen polizeilicher Herkunft und menschenrechtlicher Neuausrichtung in *Arndt/Betz/Farahat/Goldmann/Huber/Keil/Láncos/Schaefer/Smrkolj/Sucker/Valta* (eds), 48. Assistententagung Öffentliches Recht (2008) 221 or *Molnár*, Interplay 5.

170 *Handmaker/Mora*, 'Experts': the mantra of irregular migration and the reproduction of hierarchies in *Ambrus/Arts/Hey/Raules* (eds), The Role of 'Experts' in International and European Decision-Making Processes: Advisors, Decision Makers or Irrelevant Actors? (2014) 263.

171 *Farahat*, Progressive Inklusion 13.

172 See Chapter 1.B.II.

173 See also *Menezes Queiroz*, Illegally Staying 8, who analyses the different forms of illegality in the EU from the perspective of the right to stay.

justifying the right to stay[174] are fundamental to the structure of the right that transcends legal systems and does not take expulsion[175] as a central pillar for its development.[176] By changing the perspective, the results from research can expand on the research undertaken by viewing the challenges from the perspective of the state.

III. Translation

This study was originally published in German in 2020 as *Regularisierungen irregular aufhältiger Migrantinnen und Migranten – Deutschland, Österreich und Spanien im Rechtsvergleich*; particular topics explored in earlier drafts of Chapter 1, Chapter 2, Chapter 4 and Chapter 5 have also been published in English and German.[177]

The English version presented here revises and updates the original German version to take account of the legislation, case law and literature to 31 July 2022. Subsequent developments in case law and literature could only be considered in select instances.

---

174 See Chapter 1.A.II.3.

175 Expulsion is generally understood as the order to leave national territory.

176 See Chapter 1.B.II.

177 Chapter 1: *Hinterberger/Klammer*, Abschiebungsverbote aus gesundheitlichen Gründen: Die aktuelle Rechtsprechung des EGMR und EuGH zu Non-Refoulement und deren Auswirkungen auf die österreichische, deutsche und spanische Rechtslage – eine Verbesserung der rechtlichen Situation schwer kranker Drittstaatsangehöriger? in *Filzwieser/Taucher* (eds), Asyl- und Fremdenrecht. Jahrbuch 2017 (2017) 111 as well as the shortened version *Hinterberger/Klammer*, Abschiebungsverbote aus gesundheitlichen Gründen: Die aktuelle EGMR- und EuGH-Rechtsprechung zu Non-Refoulement und deren Auswirkungen auf die deutsche Rechtslage – eine Verbesserung der rechtlichen Situation schwer kranker Drittstaatsangehöriger, NVwZ 2017, 1180. Both articles note from the outset that I was the author of those parts that feature in this study.
Chapter 4: *Hinterberger*, Arbeitsmarktzugang von Fremden mit „Duldung" oder „Aufenthaltstitel aus besonders berücksichtigungswürdigenden Gründen" – Eine gleichheitsrechtliche Analyse, DRdA 2018, 104.
Chapter 1, Chapter 2, Chapter 4 and Chapter 5: *Hinterberger*, An EU Regularization Directive. An effective solution to the enforcement deficit in returning irregularly staying migrants, Maastricht Journal of European and Comparative Law 2019, 736 and *Hinterberger*, Eine Regularisierungsrichtlinie der EU: Eine wirksame Lösung für das Vollzugsdefizit von Rückführungen irregulär aufhältiger Migrant*innen in *Lanser/Potocnik-Manzouri/Safron/Tillian/Wieser* (eds), Social Europe? 1. Tagung junger Europarechtler*innen 2018 (2018) 45.

Part I – Regularisations and irregular migration in the EU legal framework

Part I of this study focuses first on the concepts underpinning regularisations before outlining the key aspects of the EU legislative framework surrounding irregular migration.[178] Chapter 1 explores the notion of regularisation in more detail, providing not only a definition of regularisation but also casting light on the different categories necessary for the comparison in Chapter 4. Insights into the conceptual foundations are essential for the analysis in Chapter 2 of the EU primary and secondary law concerning the extent of Union competence in the fields of irregular stays and regularisation. The attention is first directed towards EU secondary law – namely the Return Directive – with the subsequent analysis of primary law clearly demonstrating that the EU indeed has the necessary competence to pass EU legislation on regularisations.

Chapter 1 – Conceptualising regularisations

Chapter 1 provides key insights into the concept and definition of regularisations and shines further light on these tools from the immigration law toolbox which – just as a return – end an irregular status.[179] In principle regularisations are thus acts or measures which justify the transition from the status as an irregularly staying to a lawfully residing migrant.[180]

As the term 'regularisation' is not used and applied uniformly, this study is not content with providing merely a definition (A.) but rather

---

178 See on this question *Hinterberger*, Die Mehrebenendimension aufenthaltsrechtlicher Irregularität. Konzeptionelle Überlegungen zum Auftreten irregulärer Migration in der EU in *Thym/Klarmann* (eds), Unionsbürgerschaft und Migration im aktuellen Europarecht (2017) 155 as well as *Hinterberger*, A Multi-Level Governance Approach to Residence Rights of Migrants and Irregular Residence in the EU, EJML 2018, 182.

179 Extracts from an earlier version of this Chapter have been published in German in *Hinterberger* in *Lanser/Potocnik-Manzouri/Safron/Tillian/Wieser* and in English in *Hinterberger*, Maastricht Journal of European and Comparative Law 2019. See Chapter 1.A.II.2. and Chapter 2.B.

180 Cf. *Pelzer* in *Fischer-Lescano/Kocher/Nassibi* 146.

also a full explanation of the constituent elements of the definition itself. The elucidated definition of regularisation then forms the framework for creating the categories of regularisations that form the central foundation for the comparison in Part II (B.). At the same time it serves to conclude the conceptual considerations in Part I before turning in Chapter 2 to the EU framework regarding irregular migration and regularisation.

A. Definition

This section explores various definitions of regularisation (I.) turning thereafter to describing the constituent elements of the definition proposed in this study (II.).[181]

I. Overview of current definitions

The lack of a common standard in Austria, Germany, Spain[182] or in EU law[183] creates considerable challenges in finding a particular approach to defining 'regularisation'. The term itself is not anchored in the national laws of these Member States:[184] it is therefore not a legal term.[185] In principle national legal systems only distinguish between residence titles, residence rights, residence approvals, residence permits, etc.,[186] which may constitute a regularisation in certain circumstances. Defining a separate, legal notion of regularisation is therefore complicated further by finding separate definitions and clear distinctions between regularisations characterised by the change in status from 'irregular' to 'regular'.

181 For detail regarding the German term, see *Hinterberger*, Regularisierungen 106.

182 As an example of Spanish literature cf. *Puerta Vílchez*, La regularización de extranjeros. Art. 31.3 y Disposición transitoria cuarta in *Moya Escudero* (ed), Comentario sistemático a la ley de extranjería (2001) 391 (391f).

183 Cf. *Baldwin-Edwards/Kraler*, REGINE (January 2009) 7.

184 Cf. *Bydlinski*, Das bewegliche System und juristische Methodenlehre in *Bydlinski/Krejci/Schilcher/Steininger* (eds), Das Bewegliche System im geltenden und künftigen Recht (1986) 21 (25).

185 Cf. *Raschauer*, Verwaltungsrecht mn 30.

186 See for example § 4 AufenthG or Art 1(2)(a) Residence Permit Regulation. For detail see Chapter 3.A.III., Chapter 3.B.III. and Chapter 3.C.III.

The respective literature also does not feature a uniform definition of regularisation.[187] Such lack of uniformity is explained to some extent by the fact that there is not just one single type of regularisation.[188] Nonetheless, certain common elements do exist, as can be seen in the following examples:

- The 'granting on the part of the State, of a residence permit to a person of foreign nationality residing illegally within its territory'.[189]
- 'Regularisation is defined as any state procedure by which third country nationals who are illegally residing, or who are otherwise in breach of national immigration rules, in their current country of residence are granted a legal status'.[190]

In their respective definitions *Apap/de Bruycker/Schmitter* and *Baldwin-Edwards/Kraler* refer to the grant of a legal status through a state procedure. However, the definitions differ in so far as the status in the first definition is granted to a person who is 'residing illegally', whereas the second refers also to a third-country national who breaches national immigration rules.

- 'Regularisation is defined as a state procedure by which third-country nationals who are in breach of national immigration rules in their country of residence are granted a legal status, but are not accorded full citizenship rights'.[191]

The grant of lawful residence via a state procedure is also an essential factor for *Lazaridis*, yet she adds greater precision to the status granted by noting that regularisation does not imply the grant of full citizenship rights.

- 'Regularization is the means by which a government provides lawful status to foreigners in an unlawful or irregular situation in respect to admission, stay and economic activity'.[192]

---

187 See e.g. *Pelzer* in *Fischer-Lescano/Kocher/Nassibi* 143.

188 *Kluth*, Einheitliche Europäische Zuwanderungspolitik: Vertragsrechtliche Grundlagen und Vergleich der politischen Konzeptionen. Legalisierungsmaßnahmen, ZAR 2007, 20 (22).

189 *Apap/de Bruycker/Schmitter*, EJML 2000, 263.

190 *Baldwin-Edwards/Kraler*, REGINE (January 2009) 7; see also *EMN*, Asylum and Migration Glossary 3.0 (October 2014) 234, which refers to the definition in the REGINE-Study. See also *Kraler*, Journal of Immigrant and Refugee Studies 2019, 95.

191 *Lazaridis*, International Migration 132.

192 *Intergovernmental Committee for Migration*, Undocumented Migrants and the Regularization of their Status, International Migration 1983, 109 (109). See also the *IOM* definitions in *Perruchoud/Redpath-Cross* (eds), Glossary on Migration[2] (2011): 'Any process or programme by which the authorities in a State allow

The definition given by the *Intergovernmental Committee for Migration* (the predecessor of the *IOM*) also includes details concerning the 'lawful status' that is awarded. In addition to the right to stay, the definition also covers access to the job market, as is the presumed meaning of the term 'economic activity'.[193]

The complexity surrounding these definitions arises inter alia not only from their use of different terminology but also from the different content attributed to such terminology.[194] For example, reference is made in part to persons of foreign nationality and third-country nationals, to illegal status or irregular migration, with each term having its own meaning. Furthermore, the German term *Aufenthaltsrecht* could be translated into English as 'right to stay' or 'right to reside', though the former is the preferred translation. One may therefore never assume that the notion 'regularisations' refers to the same measures and/or procedures.

The aforementioned definitions overlap in so far as they refer to persons who do not have a right to stay in a particular country but who receive a residence permit (or similar) through an official procedure. *Kluth* describes this as a national measure with a legal effect and which leads to a change in a specific legal status.[195] The grant of a residence right is of particular interest here as the focus is on such national acts that effect the legal transition from the status as a migrant staying irregularly to one staying lawfully.[196]

II. Elements

It is clear from examining the notion of regularisation that a specific, separate and clear definition is required. Regularisation is therefore to be understood as decision issued by an administrative authority (or a court)

---

non-nationals in an irregular or undocumented situation to stay lawfully in the country. Typical practices include the granting of an amnesty (also known as "legalization") to non-nationals who have resided in the country in an irregular situation for a given length of time and are not otherwise found inadmissible'.

193 Cf. *Böhning*, International Migration 1983, 171 Fn 10.

194 *Kraler*, Regularisation: A misguided option or part and parcel of a comprehensive policy response to irregular migration? IMISCOE WP No. 24 (February 2009) 8.

195 Cf. *Kluth*, ZAR 2007, 21f.

196 See the definition 'irregularly staying migrants' in Chapter 1.A.II.1.

which grants irregularly staying migrants a right to stay, provided certain minimum requirements are met.

The elements of this definition of regularisation have been derived inductively from the review of the various different definitions; they are brought together based on the objectives underpinning the comparison of the national laws.[197] The proposed definition lays down key principles and may be used for other (scholarly) studies.[198] It serves to structure and depict a legal phenomenon that has not received sufficient attention in current research. Furthermore, the definition describes the aforementioned legal change in residence status. The definition proposed here comprises four elements: (1.) irregularly staying migrants, (2.) the grant of a right to stay, (3.) a decision, and (4) satisfying the minimum requirements.

The change to a migrant's legal status is at the heart of regularisations. Generally speaking, 'regularisation' is an umbrella term for the change from an unlawful to a lawful residency status.[199] Regularisations are attached to the person and their unlawful/irregular stay,[200] whereby by removing the irregularity, the grant of a right to stay thus effects a change in legal status. From the outset, however, the national legal system must recognise that such change results from the grant of the right. The elements 'irregularly staying migrants' and 'the grant of a right to stay' thereby have a constitutive function as they are vital for the change in status: without them there is ultimately no change in status and as such they form the heart of the definition. The 'decision' and 'satisfaction of the minimum requirements' are not constitutive elements as it is conceivable that they need not be included in a definition of regularisation. I have nonetheless included these two aspects because they are generally elements of regularisations and relate to the form thereof.

1. Irregularly staying migrants

A qualification as a regularisation requires a measure to at least target persons staying irregularly in a Member State – a 'geographical criterion'

197 See Introduction D.II.

198 In general on '*wissenschaftliche Begriffe*' (scientific terms) *Raschauer*, Verwaltungsrecht mn 31.

199 Cf. *Kluth*, ZAR 2007, 21f.

200 In turn this corresponds to the view taken in this study; see Introduction D.II.3.

according to *Apap/de Bruycker/Schmitter*.[201] The personal scope of application therefore encompasses irregularly staying migrants.[202] Generally, the term 'migrants' concerns all non-citizens,[203] though in the following the term refers to third-country nationals as understood in EU law. EU primary law distinguishes in principle between Union citizens and third-country nationals.[204] In this regard, the second sentence of Article 20(1) TFEU provides that third-country nationals are all persons who do not hold the nationality of a Member State. Stateless persons are treated as third-country nationals for the purposes of the policies on 'asylum, immigration and external border control',[205] as per the second sentence of Article 67(2) TFEU. All relevant provisions of EU primary and secondary law therefore apply;[206] they are thus also subsumed in this study under the term 'third-country nationals'.

However, the personal scope of application as referred to in the following is limited even further:[207] it does not concern Union citizens,[208] citizens of an EEA State or of Switzerland. As noted above, it also does not extend to persons who enjoy international protection as beneficiaries under the Qualification Directive.[209] Moreover, the scope does not extend to relatives of a person falling into one of the aforementioned categories since such persons have privileged residence rights.[210]

In principle, the term 'irregular stay' lacks a uniform legal definition.[211] The *FRA* uses 'irregular' as a synonym for the term 'illegally staying third-

201 *Apap/de Bruycker/Schmitter*, EJML 2000, 294f.

202 For an initial approach see *Guild*, Who is an irregular migrant? in *Bogusz/Cholewinski/Cygan/Szyszczak* (eds), Irregular Migration and Human Rights (2004) 3.

203 On the terminology see *Motomura*, Americans in Waiting (2007) 3f and *Costello*, Human Rights 4.

204 For an overview see *Boeles/den Heijer/Lodder/Wouters*, Migration 30ff.

205 Cf. the heading Part V Chapter 2 TFEU.

206 Especially *Weiß/Satzger* in *Streinz* (ed) EUV/AEUV Kommentar^3 (2018) Art 67 AEUV mn 32.

207 In this sense also *Morticelli*, Irregular Migrants 74.

208 However see in this regard also *Klarmann*, Illegalisierte Migration 261–270 or *Thym*, When Union Citizens Turn into Illegal Migrants: The Dano Case, ELR 2015, 249, who both describe illegalised/illegal Union citizens.

209 See Introduction D.II.1.

210 *Hinterberger*, EJML 2018.

211 Cf. for example *Düvell* in *Falge/Fischer-Lescano/Sieveking* 23ff with further references; *Fischer-Lescano/Kocher/Nassibi*, Einleitung in *Fischer-Lescano/Kocher/Nassibi* (eds), Arbeit in der Illegalität (2012) 7 (8).

country nationals' as used in Article 3 No. 2 Return Directive:[212] '"[I]llegal stay" means the presence on the territory of a Member State, of a third-country national who does not fulfil, or no longer fulfils the conditions of entry as set out in Article 5 of the Schengen Borders Code or other conditions for entry, stay or residence in that Member State; [...]'. The EU's legislative competence concerning the Return Directive is anchored in Article 79(2)(c) TFEU.[213] The term 'unauthorised residence' used in Article 79(2)(c) TFEU is to be viewed as the counterpart to 'residing legally' under Article 79(2)(b) TFEU.[214] It is therefore notable that Commission documents use the terms 'staying illegally' as well as 'irregularly staying'.[215]

Migrants 'staying illegally' fall within the scope of the Return Directive.[216] This corresponds with the aim of this Directive 'to establish an effective removal and repatriation policy, based on common standards and common legal safeguards, for persons to be returned in a humane manner and with full respect for their fundamental rights and dignity'.[217] Despite such focus on commonality, the Return Directive affords the Member States broad discretion for the return procedure,[218] with the ECJ later determining that the Return Directive is 'not designed to harmonise in their entirety the national rules on the stay of foreign nationals'.[219]

Article 2(b) of the Employers Sanctions Directive contains a near identical definition with regard to an 'illegally staying third-country national [...] present on the territory of a Member State, who does not fulfil, or no longer fulfils, the conditions for stay or residence in that Member State'. This differs from the Return Directive in so far as there is no reference to the Schengen Borders Code regarding the conditions of entry.

---

212 Cf. *FRA*, Fundamental rights of migrants in an irregular situation in the European Union. Comparative report (November 2011), https://fra.europa.eu/sites/default/files/fra_uploads/1827-FRA_2011_Migrants_in_an_irregular_situation_EN.pdf (31.7.2022) 16.

213 Cf. *Thym* in *Grabitz/Hilf/Nettesheim* (eds), Das Recht der Europäischen Union Kommentar Band I (69th edn, February 2020) Art 79 AEUV mn 34 and *Hörich*, Abschiebungen nach europäischen Vorgaben (2015) 19 as well as Chapter 2.B.I.

214 *Bast* in *Fischer-Lescano/Kocher/Nassibi* 78.

215 Recitals 11 and 19 Recommendation (EU) 2017/432.

216 Art 2(1) Return Directive; cf. *Lutz* in *Thym/Hailbronner* (eds), EU Immigration and Asylum Law. A Commentary[3] (2022) Art 2 Return Directive mns 1ff.

217 ECJ *Mahdi*, para 38.

218 See only Arts 2(2), 6(6) and 8(6) Return Directive as well as Chapter 2.B.I. With regard to Art 3 No. 4 Return Directive see ECJ 6.12.2012, C-430/11, ECLI:EU:C:2012:777, *Sagor*, para 39.

219 ECJ 6.12.2011, C-329/11, ECLI:EU:C:2011:807, *Achughbabian*, para 28.

The EU Treaties therefore view migrants as 'legal' or 'illegal'.[220] This dichotomy has quite rightly been criticised as it fails to recognise the social process of 'illegalisation'.[221] In particular, the term 'illegal' is to be rejected due to its stigmatising effect[222] and portrayal of migrants as criminals.[223] The use is also criticised by several voices in the literature.[224] The negative connotations associated with 'staying illegally' also do not contribute to removing the stigmatism or negative connotations attached to the use of 'illegal'.[225]

The expression 'irregularly staying' is therefore preferred as it best expresses the subsequent focus on the legal status of migrants[226] and on residency laws in general. 'Irregularly staying' stands for the status of those migrants who do not have (or no longer have) a right to stay due to the violation of particular legislative provisions, be this through the breach or non-fulfilment of the provisions.[227]

---

220 *Costello*, Human Rights 64 and *Menezes Queiroz*, Illegally Staying 4, 7ff and especially 91. See further Chapter 1.A.II.1.–2.

221 Recently, *Klarmann*, Illegalisierte Migration 44ff; *Bauder*, Why We Should Use the Term 'Illegalized' Refugee or Immigrant: A Commentary, IJRL 2014, 327 as well as *Costello*, Human Rights 64f.

222 *Parliamentary Assembly of the Council of Europe*, Human Rights of Irregular Migrants, Resolution 1509 (27.6.2006) § 7.

223 Cf. *Błuś*, EJML 2013, 414; *Lazaridis*, International Migration 11f; *Tohidipur* in *Fischer-Lescano/Kocher/Nassibi* 42 with further references; *Pelzer* in *Fischer-Lescano/Kocher/Nassibi* 145; *Koser*, Migration 54.

224 Cf. for instance *Cholewinski*, The Criminalisation of Migration in EU Law and Policy in *Baldaccini/Guild/Toner* (eds), Whose Freedom, Security and Justice? EU Immigration and Asylum Law and Policy (2007) 301 (305f); *Carrera/Guild* in *Carrera/Guild* 6; *Koser*, Migration 54f; *Costello*, Human Rights 64; *Dumon*, International Migration 1983, 218.

225 *Kluth*, ZAR 2007, 21 Fn 12.

226 *Costello*, Human Rights 2, refers to 'migration status' that is created by immigration and asylum laws. The term appears to be more extensive as it includes more than just a residence right. See also *Schieber*, Komplementärer Schutz.

227 Cf. also the definitions in *Uriarte Torrealday*, Algunas reflexiones críticas a partir de la jurisprudencia sobre inmigración irregular, Revista de Derecho Político 2009, 291 (297); *Düvell* in *Falge/Fischer-Lescano/Sieveking* 24; *Böhning*, International Migration 1983, 160.

The definition creates a precise legal term,[228] which harmonises the fragmented EU[229] and national[230] terminology – irregular, illegal, staying illegally, illegalised, 'sans papiers'[231], undocumented and unauthorised migrants – for the purposes of residency laws. With regard to EU law, 'irregularly staying' is to be understood as synonymous with 'illegal stay' under Article 3 No. 2 of the Return Directive.[232] Establishing such a term also contributes to modernising the language used in immigration law (in particular German terminology)[233] as the focus is placed on the migrants' perspective.[234] 'Irregular stay' is therefore used as an autonomous, dogmatic and thus specific legal term that is suitable in general for structuring the law.[235]

'Irregularly staying' comprises two elements: 'staying' requires the physical presence in the territory of a Member State whereby 'irregularity' refers to the legal status of the stay pursuant to residency laws; it therefore does not extend to applications made from abroad.

In most cases the requirement 'irregularly staying' must be satisfied at the time of the application or decision (from the administrative authorities or administrative courts[236]), or across the entire period (i.e. from application to decision).[237] In contrast to a change of status under other aspects of residency laws, it is not only possible but indeed necessary to make the application domestically, thereby allowing for an appropriate distinction to be drawn from those residence rights that can be acquired whilst abroad. A residency right acquired whilst abroad therefore cannot constitute a regularisation as the key requirement of being physically present

---

228 *Uriarte Torrealday*, Revista de Derecho Político 2009, 299, 312; cf. *Cholewinski* in *Baldaccini/Guild/Toner* 306.

229 See just *Klarmann* in *Thym/Klarmann* or *Menezes Queiroz*, Illegally Staying 26, 28–21.

230 Cf. *Baldwin-Edwards/Kraler*, REGINE (January 2009) 1f and see with regard to Austria, Chapter 3.A.II.1., for Germany, Chapter 3.B.II.1. and for Spain, Chapter 3.C.II.1.

231 Cf. *Tohidipur* in *Fischer-Lescano/Kocher/Nassibi* 41; *Hobbe*, Undokumentierte Migration in Deutschland und den Vereinigten Staaten (2004) 1ff.

232 Cf. *Menezes Queiroz*, Illegally Staying 30.

233 Cf. *Bast*, Aufenthaltsrecht 1ff, 291ff.

234 See Introduction D.II.3.

235 Cf. *Glaser*, Handlungsformenlehre 70.

236 On the law in Austria, Chapter 3.A.IV.–V., for Germany see Chapter 3.B.IV.–V., and for Spain, Chapter 3.C.IV.–V.

237 On the law in Austria, Chapter 3.A.III.2.a., for Germany see Chapter 3.B.III.2.a., and for Spain, Chapter 3.C.III.3.a.

on the domestic territory is not satisfied. It is for this reason that family reunification is not examined as the relevant applications are typically to be made when the family members are residing outside the territory of the Member State.[238] Certain circumstances allow for an application for family reunification to be made when the family members are already in the territory, but these cases are not examined here.

2. Granting a right to stay

As the legal consequence of a particular measure, the grant of a right to stay may allude to a regularisation, yet by itself does not shed light on the actual meaning and implications of such right. In principle the right to stay entitles a person to reside in a Member State, i.e. a lawful residency. *Farahat* describes such a right as establishing a relationship determined by territory.[239] At first glance this appears to be an appropriate description, yet closer examination reveals several complications. It is clear that each objective right accompanied by lawful residency may be understood as a right to stay in the narrow sense, but it is not necessary that a claim to residency arises, i.e. a subjective right.

The treatment of toleration under Austrian and German law complicates matters further as the instrument takes on different forms to allow factual residence that is not lawful *per se*. According to *Renner*, this concerns the actual stay without regard for duration, purpose and other circumstances such as, above all, the legality.[240] The person concerned is (provisionally) tolerated, though the national authorities are aware that the return cannot be enforced. Toleration may therefore be understood as a right to stay in a broad sense, at least for the purposes of understanding its position amongst the various instruments in residency laws.[241] It thus becomes clear that the notion of a right to stay features core and peripheral elements.

---

238 Art 5(3) Family Reunification Directive.

239 *Farahat*, Progressive Inklusion 61; on 'Territorium' *Bast*, Völker- und unionsrechtliche Anstöße zur Entterritorialisierung des Rechts, VVDStRL 2016/76, 278.

240 Cf. *Renner*, Ausländerrecht in Deutschland: Einreise und Aufenthalt (1998) 156; see also *Riecken*, Die Duldung als Verfassungsproblem (2006) 35f with further references.

241 Cf. *Kluth*, ZAR 2007, 22. For detail, see Chapter 1.B.III.1.a.

In light of the above, determining whether a right to stay has been granted requires an understanding of how the right is devised. The central element for this study is for a right to stay to establish a legally-recognised, lawful residence. This change in status forms the core (a.). Three further elements are also described which determine the stability and weight of a right to stay, yet are not essential for it to be granted: whether the right is temporary (b.), whether there are any rights related to the status (c.) and whether there is the possibility to consolidate the right (d.).

a) Lawful

The first and central element concerns the status of the stay as lawful. It is a fundamental requirement for the classification as a right to stay that, by granting the right, national law establishes a lawful stay in a purely domestic manner. In this context, 'purely domestic' is used when a right to stay is granted purely on the basis of domestic rules. The lawfulness of the stay follows from the TFEU, which distinguishes between legal and illegal residence,[242] as well as the Return Directive,[243] and thus is appropriate for the comparison of the national laws. Generally, a lawful stay will take the form of a residence title, residence permit or other authorisation. From the perspective of Austrian and German law, however, toleration does not constitute a right to stay as it is not considered as granting permitted/lawful residence.

b) Temporary

The second element concerns the temporal element: the lawful residence created by a right to stay is typically subject to a time constraint. Although *Kluth* refers to a temporary right to stay in such instances, he does detail the period of time that is 'temporary' in nature.[244] By contrast, the lawful stay resulting from the grant of the corresponding right may also be permanent. For the purposes of the definition used in this study, a temporary right to stay is especially pertinent as Member States usually do not grant

---

242 Cf. *Costello*, Human Rights 63ff; critically of this conception *Klarmann*, Illegalisierte Migration 118ff and Chapter 1.A.II.1.

243 See Chapter 2.B.I.

244 *Kluth*, ZAR 2007, 22.

irregularly staying migrants a permanent right to stay in the course of the regularisation process.

c) Rights linked to the status

The weight of the right to stay is determined not only by its duration but also by its content. Accordingly, the third element concerns the rights that are linked to the status, in particular the access to employment as well as certain other social rights. In this respect, *Kraler* determines that migrants consider the access to employment as one of the main reasons to seek regularisation.[245]

d) Consolidation

The fourth element focuses on the legal possibility to consolidate the right once the allocated time period has expired. The notion of consolidation, which is linked to the improvement of an existing residence status, may take the form of an extension or the grant of a different type of residence right and has been covered in a number of different studies.[246]

3. Decision

The following begins by explaining the scope of the 'decision' to describe thereafter the nature of the decision as applying to a single individual (a.). Furthermore, it will also be discussed whether the decision follows from an administrative authority or an administrative court (b.)

The right to stay is granted in principle via a decision of the administrative authority or in a (subsequent) decision from an administrative court. The expression 'decision granting the right to stay' will be used hereinafter as the umbrella term for each type of residence title, residence permit,

245 Cf. *Kraler*, Journal of Immigrant and Refugee Studies 2019, 105–107. On the law in Austria, see Chapter 3.A.II., for Germany, Chapter 3.B.II. and for Spain, Chapter 3.C.II.

246 Cf. generally *Bast*, Aufenthaltsrecht 256f with further references, and *Farahat*, Inklusion in der superdiversen Einwanderungsgesellschaft in *Baer/Lepsius/Schönberger/Waldhoff/Walter* (eds), Jahrbuch des öffentlichen Rechts der Gegenwart 66 (2018) 337 (343).

Aufenthaltstitel, autorización de residencia, etc.[247] As the decision effects the transition from irregularity to regularity, it is more appropriate to focus on the actual effect rather than on the procedure underpinning the decision itself.[248] Here it is not the procedure itself that forms the relevant point for the change in status, but rather the time of the decision (which typically marks the end of the procedure). It is to be further noted that the Member States have different rules concerning the moment at which the decision takes effect. The effect can be *ex-tunc* (*ab initio*) or *ex nunc* (*de futuro*). Whereas *ex tunc* describes the retrospective effect, whereby the status is deemed to have changed at the moment the application was made, *ex nunc* means the change in status beginning from the time of the decision.

a) Individual

A decision granting the right to stay may concern a group as well as an individual. However, as the following adopts the standpoint that regularisations are at the basis of a decision regarding an individual, the decision is therefore directed towards a single person and not towards individuals who belong to a group by virtue of their personal characteristics. German administrative law refers in this respect to a *konkret-individueller Charakter eines Aktes*, in other words the act is individual by its very nature.[249] The term 'individual' is used in the following to describe a decision regarding a particular person and thus an assessment of whether the requirements are satisfied in each separate case. I do not analyse procedures in which a right to stay is granted without such a case-by-case assessment and corresponding decision.[250]

---

247 It would also be conceivable to refer to an '*Aufenthaltsgenehmigung*' ('residence approval'); see for example *Bast*, Zehn Jahre Aufenthaltsgesetz, DÖV 2013, 214 (216).

248 Cf. *Baldwin-Edwards/Kraler*, REGINE (January 2009) 7; *Lazaridis*, International Migration 132.

249 *Maurer/Waldhoff*, Allgemeines Verwaltungsrecht[20] (2020) § 9 mns 16–18. Cf. further *Raschauer*, Verwaltungsrecht mns 852ff on Austrian administrative law.

250 See Chapter 3.A.III.4.

b) Decision from the administrative authorities or the courts

The administrative authorities[251] act with governmental authority[252] in administrative proceedings. In principle the measures can follow on the basis of an application but also *ex officio*, namely where an authority acts on its own initiative when certain requirements are satisfied.[253]

The administrative (and individual) decision in Austrian administrative proceedings is generally in the form of a *Bescheid* (an administrative decision or ruling);[254] in Germany one refers to a *begünstigender Verwaltungsakt* (a beneficial administrative act, i.e. an administrative measure which establishes or confirms a right or legal advantage),[255] and in Spain the decision falls within the category of an *acto administrativo* (administrative act).[256]

Under certain circumstances a decision from the administrative court may follow from the actions taken by the administrative authorities. The administrative courts in Austria have jurisdiction for matters under residence law.[257] The decisions are made on the basis of a so-called *Bescheidbeschwerde mittels Erkenntnis* (i.e. a judgment on an appeal brought against an administrative decision or ruling).[258] Under German law the *Verwaltungsgerichte* (administrative courts) issue an *Urteil* (judgment) with

---

251 Cf. on Austrian law, *Kolonovits/Muzak/Stöger*, Verwaltungsverfahrensrecht (2014) mns 14 and 58, for Germany *Maurer/Waldhoff*, Verwaltungsrecht § 22 mns 13ff.

252 Cf. on the use of the term (*hoheitlich*) in Austria *Kolonovits/Muzak/Stöger*, Verwaltungsverfahrensrecht mn 381; *Hengstschläger/Leeb*, AVG (1.1.2014, rdb.at) § 7 AVG mn 3; *Hengstschläger/Leeb*, AVG (1.7.2005, rdb.at) § 56 AVG mn 13; for Germany *Maurer/Waldhoff*, Verwaltungsrecht § 1 mn 25 and § 9 mns 12–14.

253 Cf. regarding the Austrian *Aufenthaltstitel aus berücksichtigungswürdigen Gründen* ('residence permits for exceptional circumstances') § 58(1) AsylG (A) and Chapter 3.A.III.2.b.

254 Cf. *Raschauer*, Verwaltungsrecht mns 812ff.

255 Cf. *Groß*, Das Ausländerrecht zwischen obrigkeitsstaatlicher Tradition und menschenrechtlicher Herausforderung, AöR 2014, 421 (423f). In general on the administrative act see § 35 VwVfG and *Maurer/Waldhoff*, Verwaltungsrecht § 9, specifically mn 48.

256 Cf. in general the comments in *Boza Martínez/Donaire Villa/Moya Malapeira*, La normativa española de extranjería y asilo: evolución y características principales in *Boza Martínez/Donaire Villa/Moya Malapeira* (eds), La nueva regulación de la inmigración y la extranjería en España (2012) 15 (19).

257 BGBl I 51/2012.

258 §§ 7ff and 28 VwGVG, see Chapter 3.A.V.1.

regard to an appeal.[259] In Spain the *Tribunal de lo Contencioso-Administrativo* (administrative court) issues a *sentencia* (judgment) in relation to a *recurso contencioso-administrativo* (act for judicial review).[260]

4. Satisfying the minimum requirements

The grant of a right to stay is subject to the satisfaction of certain (formal and substantive) requirements.[261] However, it is not particularly expedient to list all possible requirements here as this would require an analysis of all regularisations, but examples include the minimum duration, language skills or whether there are particular humanitarian grounds. It can be noted at this early stage that one of the general criteria for a decision granting the right to stay, namely a visa, does not apply.

III. Interim conclusion

The overview of existing definitions for regularisation given at the beginning of section A above allows for the conclusion that regularisations are characterised by the change in residence status from irregular to regular. Regularisations were defined as each decision of an administrative authority or administrative court which grants a right to stay to irregularly staying migrants who satisfy the minimum requirements for such right.

By providing general principles, the dogmatic nature of the definition allows for its use in other (academic) works and at the same time serves to depict and structure this legal concept. The notion 'regularisation' is preferred to 'legalisation' (and its derivatives) as the latter otherwise casts irregularly staying migrants in a bad light. As a concept, a regularisation comprises the following elements: irregularly staying migrants, grant of a right to stay, decision and satisfying minimum requirements. However, only the first two requirements are essential.

To qualify as a regularisation, a measure must at the very least concern persons staying irregularly on the territory of a Member State either at the

259 It is also additionally possible that the German Administrative Court decides via an order. See Chapter 3.B.V.1.

260 See Chapter 3.C.V.1.

261 Cf. *Groß*, AöR 2014, 423f; *Bast*, Aufenthaltsrecht 31.

time of the application, of the decision, or throughout the period between both.

Furthermore, those staying irregularly must be granted a right to stay. The elements of such right were presented to provide a framework for determining whether such right is granted. The legally-recognised, lawful residence results in the change in status, which forms the heart of the right to stay and thus the central aspect of this study. Three further elements were also described as factors relevant for the stability and weight of the right, but without which the right may still exist. This includes whether the right is temporary, whether there are accompanying rights and whether consolidation is possible.

The expression 'decision granting the right to stay' is used broadly to describe the grant of a right to stay via a decision from an administrative authority or administrative court. The decision is key to this study as it reflects the moment at which there is a change in status. Furthermore, this study assumes that regularisations refer to a single person and thus a decision is directed towards a certain person on the basis of a case-by-case assessment of the criteria. The last element of the definition therefore refers to the formal and substantive criteria to be satisfied to grant a right to stay.

B. Classification

Whereas the creation of a dogmatic concept of regularisation was examined above, the following concerns the classification of regularisations for the purposes of an integrated comparison. This is especially complicated from a methodological perspective: many aspects must be considered as the comparison of the national laws does not follow on the basis of separate national reports, but is integrated, i.e. regularisations are classed in accordance with certain criteria and then compared.[262] The following first presents and evaluates several existing categories (I.) before proposing a new category based on the purpose of the regularisation (II. and III.). The final step draws a distinction from those topics that are not included in the analysis and thus narrows the scope of this study (IV.).

262 See Introduction D.II.2.

I. Possible starting points

In their REGINE Study for the European Commission, *Baldwin-Edwards/Kraler* present categories of regularisations by using the distinction drawn in procedural law between 'programmes' and 'mechanisms'. A programme is defined as 'a specific regularisation procedure which (1) does not form part of the regular migration policy framework, (2) runs for a limited period of time and (3) targets specific categories of non-nationals in an irregular situation', with mechanisms being a procedure that is not a programme but 'by which the state can grant legal status to illegally present third country nationals residing on its territory' often based on humanitarian grounds and 'likely to be longer-term policies'.[263]

Other authors have adopted the division into programmes and mechanisms.[264] In theory, it is feasible to use this approach for the comparison, though there are good reasons to doubt the effectiveness of these criteria. The distinction between programmes and mechanisms is interesting and certainly sensible, at least for political scientists, yet such division is not appropriate from a legal perspective as, in a multi-national context, there are too few differences and thus the scientific value added is negligible.

Additional identifiable criteria can be derived from *de Bruycker's* study published in the year 2000, which contains summaries of the laws from eight Member States and – more fundamentally – a classification of five different types of regularisations.[265] Three of the five are especially notable:[266]

263 Cf. *Baldwin-Edwards/Kraler*, REGINE (January 2009) 8f.

264 Cf. for example *Pelzer* in *Fischer-Lescano/Kocher/Nassibi* 147.

265 *De Bruycker* (ed), Les regularisations des étrangers illégaux dans l'union européenne. Regularisations of illegal immigrants in the European Union (2000). The English summary is published in *Apap/de Bruycker/Schmitter*, EJML 2000 and for the French summary *Apap/de Bruycker/Schmitter*, Rapport de synthèse sur la comparaison des régularisations d'étrangers illégaux dans l'Union européenne in *de Bruycker* (ed), Les regularisations des étrangers illégaux dans l'union européenne. Regularisations of illegal immigrants in the European Union (2000) 24. The German and Spanish national reports (drafted by *Hailbronner* and *Gortázar*, respectively) are discussed in more detail in Chapter 3.B.I. and Chapter 3.C.I.

266 An analysis of 'Regularisation through Expedience or Obligation' and 'Organised or Informal Regularisation' would exceed the scope of this study and is therefore not covered in detail.

- The study distinguishes at first between 'permanent' and 'on-off' procedures.[267] The term 'permanent' is used to describe the regularisations set by law which are not subject to any time constraints. In contrast, 'on-off' procedures centre around the fulfilment of the conditions of regularisation on a particular date, whereby the study highlights the date of entry or presence within the territory on a particular date.
- The second category divides regularisations on the basis of their individual or collective nature.[268] The criterion 'individual' refers to the discretion available to the authorities.[269] 'Collective' regularisations, however, refer to objective criteria and thus the lack of discretion for the authorities. A legally enforceable claim, i.e. a subjective right, to regularisation could nonetheless arise where the criteria are satisfied.[270]
- A third distinction draws on the differing protection implied by the regularisations.[271] 'Regularisations for protection' concern those individuals who require protection from serious harm that would result from deportation; humanitarian, family or medical reasons may be taken into account. 'Fait accompli' regularisations, however, recognise the presence on the territory for a certain period. *Apap/de Bruycker/Schmitter* view the grant of a right to residence to irregularly staying migrants by virtue of the *de facto* situation as being especially controversial.[272]

The aforementioned typology is especially notable as it was legally the first of its kind to capture and depict certain patterns that are characteristic of regularisations.[273] Nonetheless, one of the central problems is that it does not allow for a categorisation that is sufficiently general and workable for comparative purposes. In describing the categories, *Apap/de Bruycker/Schmitter* acknowledge that it is hardly possible to use the pairs of criteria to categorise regularisations in a precise manner.[274] However, such precision is needed for the purposes of the integrated comparison. The characteristic necessary for the categorisation must therefore be especially

---

267 *Apap/de Bruycker/Schmitter*, EJML 2000, 266f.

268 *Apap/de Bruycker/Schmitter*, EJML 2000, 267f.

269 With regard to the use of the term 'discretion' see *Guild*, Discretion, Competence and Migration in the European Union, EJML 1999, 61.

270 See Chapter 2.B.II.2.

271 *Apap/de Bruycker/Schmitter*, EJML 2000, 268ff.

272 *Apap/de Bruycker/Schmitter*, EJML 2000, 268.

273 References are made to these in *Sunderhaus*, Regularization Programs for Undocumented Migrants: A Global Survey on more than 60 Legalizations in all Continents (2007) 29ff.

274 See just *Apap/de Bruycker/Schmitter*, EJML 2000, 268, 269.

'watertight' to avoid overlaps and repetitions as far as possible, especially as the methodology refrains from presenting national reports.

The research undertaken by *Schieber* has already been referred to in discussing the current research in this field.[275] The author examines the complementary protective measures and uses these as the basis for her comparison.[276] However, the reference to asylum procedures constitutes a fundamental difference as it does not create an independent concept of regularisation that, unlike in this study, forms the starting point for the research.[277]

A further criterion considered in the development stages of this study concerns the division and presentation of regularisations by their criteria and their legal consequences. Such division is not without flaws as it does not allow regularisations to be presented as a whole, thereby resulting in repetitions. Where the criteria are concerned, it is conceivable to categorise according to the persons affected (e.g. workers). For the legal consequences, one approach would be to distinguish between the type or legal form of the right to stay that is granted.

The reasons outlined above ultimately convinced me to favour a categorisation based on the purpose of the regularisation. Each decision underlying a right to stay is underpinned by a legal basis – the *Aufenthaltszweck* ('purpose of the stay'), to refer to the term used in Germany.[278] As the definition is designed around such individual decisions, linking the definition to the purpose of the right is the most promising and fruitful basis for devising a precise system.

II. The basis: purpose of the regularisation

A decision granting the right to stay is in principle always linked to a particular purpose. Yet what is covered by the purpose and which perspective is taken?

The term is derived from 'purpose of the stay' which describes the relevant legal basis for granting the right,[279] such as humanitarian of familial reasons. Although 'purpose of the regularisation' and 'purpose of the stay' are in essence identical, the following favours the term 'purpose of the

---

275 See Introduction C.
276 *Schieber*, Komplementärer Schutz 117ff.
277 See Chapter 1.A.
278 Cf. on the German law in general *Groß*, AöR 2014, 423ff.
279 *Bast*, Aufenthaltsrecht 245.

regularisation' over 'purpose of the stay'. It is more precise and more appropriate as it does not cover all decisions underpinning a right to stay, just those that fall within the scope of a regularisation. *Bast* is correct in observing that the 'purpose of the stay' provides a basic and overarching framework in modern residency law in which the focus is on granting residency, not on deportation.[280] Indeed, as will be demonstrated, such observation for German residency law also applies to its Austrian and Spanish counterparts, supporting the assertion that linking the definition of regularisation to the purpose of the right appears especially promising for devising a precise system.

Where German law is concerned, the 'purpose of the stay' has already been identified as a primary, horizontal criterion for classification under the Residence Act (*Aufenthaltsgesetz*; AufenthG) and it is even explicitly anchored as such in statute law.[281]

The notion 'purpose of the stay' is also regulated in the Austrian law governing settlement and residence,[282] e.g. just once in asylum law with respect to the regularisations.[283] In principle the notion may be unfamiliar to the Aliens' Police Act (*Fremdenpolizeigesetz*; FPG),[284] though this is of little consequence as this legislation only concerns the issue of entry documents and measures terminating residency, amongst others.[285] Accordingly, 'purpose of the stay' may be applied in relation to Austrian law, at least for scholarly purposes. As in German law, Austrian law also adopts the approach whereby the decision to award a right to stay is typically linked to a particular reason.[286] This is confirmed by the case law of the Austrian Supreme Administrative Court, the *Verwaltungsgerichtshof*, which often uses the term '*Aufenthaltszweck*'.[287]

280 *Bast*, DÖV 2013, 216 refers in this context to '*Aufenthaltsgenehmigungen*' (residence approvals).

281 *Bast*, Aufenthaltsrecht 218ff; *Bast*, DÖV 2013, 216 and *Groß*, AöR 2014, 423–427.

282 See just §§ 19(2), (3) or 26 NAG.

283 § 58(6) AsylG (A) and see on the regularisations Chapter 3.A.III.

284 See however § 21(2) No. 1 FPG which regulates a reason for refusing a Visa D where the purpose and conditions of the planned stay cannot be justified.

285 § 1(1) FPG.

286 Cf. *Peyrl/Neugschwendtner/Schmaus*, Fremdenrecht[7] (2018) 37ff and *Muzak*, Fremden- und Asylrecht in *Kolonovits/Muzak/Piska/Perthold/Strejcek* (eds), Besonderes Verwaltungsrecht[2] (2017) 187 (201f).

287 See just VwGH 12.11.2015, Ra 2015/21/0101 or 7.12.2016, Ra 2016/22/0013.

The above also applies to Spain.[288] The notion 'purpose of the stay' is unfamiliar to Spanish law and, as in Austrian law, lacks a regulation of such purposes,[289] but the possibility for transferred application within the context of this study remains. For instance, *Serrano Villamanta* structures the 'residence due to exceptional circumstances' on the basis of the reasons that pertinent to granting residency.[290] The 'purpose of the stay' may be equated with the '*motivo de la residencia*' in Spanish.

Determining the purpose requires consideration from the perspective of the State as well as from the migrant. According to *Motomura* and *Bast*, decisions awarding a right to stay are based on a contractual approach.[291] 'Contractual' is not to be understood here in the literal sense as a form of agreement between the parties, but rather describes the convergence between the private and public interest in awarding a right to stay.[292] In principle migrants have to comply with and subject themselves to the conditions imposed unilaterally by the State,[293] and so in effect agree to the 'standard terms and conditions' regarding the types of residence title and the rules by which they are awarded.[294] Although the State's focus is not directed towards the migrant's own personal interest in migration,[295] such as voluntary entry or remaining in the country, ultimately the State's and migrant's interests will overlap if the right to stay is granted.[296] Since every lawfully sanctioned migration process is based on this contractual approach, consideration of both

288 Cf. *Triguero Martínez*, El arraigo y los modelos actuales jurídico-políticos de inmigración y extranjería, Migraciones 2014, 433 (438).

289 See only Art 29ff LODYLE and Art 28ff REDYLE.

290 *Serrano Villamanta*, La residencia por circunstancias excepcionales. El arraigo in *Balado Ruiz-Gallegos* (ed), Inmigración, Estado y Derecho: Perspectivas desde el siglo XXI (2008) 553 (557); see also *Triguero Martínez*, Migraciones 2014, 438f.

291 Cf. *Bast*, Aufenthaltsrecht 30f with reference to *Motomura*, Americans 9–12, 15–62. *Motomura's* understanding of immigration is founded on two further notions: 'immigration as transition' as well as 'immigration as affiliation'.

292 Cf. *Bast*, Aufenthaltsrecht 219 and *Groß*, AöR 2014, 425. *Bast*, Aufenthaltsrecht 31 Fn 103 is correct in noting that this understanding is limited when applied to refugee migration as this is characterised by the involuntarily nature of entering into the migration agreement ('*durch die Unfreiwilligkeit des Eingehens des Migrationskontrakts geprägt ist*').

293 See *Groß*, AöR 2014, 425.

294 Referring here to the analogy used by *Bast*, Aufenthaltsrecht 31; cf. also *Bast*, DÖV 2013, 216.

295 *Bast*, Aufenthaltsrecht 31.

296 *Bast*, Aufenthaltsrecht 30.

the State's and the individual's personal interest are necessary to determine the purpose of the regularisation in this study.[297]

III. Purpose-based structure

The above explanations illustrate that the purpose of the regularisation is a suitable category for comparison. Regarding the methodological perspective, three different legislative sources allow the identification of the relevant purpose of the regularisation: the reasons for granting a right to stay are derived from international law, from EU law as well as from the distinctly national law of the Member States.[298]

A synopsis of the different levels shows six purposes of the regularisation that are listed in the order according to the references to international, EU, and domestic law: non-returnability (1.), social ties (2.), family unity (3.), vulnerability (4.), employment and training (5.), other national interests (6.).

Source of law	**Purpose of the regularisation**
International and/or EU law	1. Non-returnability
	2. Social ties
	3. Family unity
	4. Vulnerability
Purely domestic law	5. Employment and training
	6. Other national interests

Table 1: Purpose of the regularisation and sources of law

The purposes of the regularisation are divided into two categories depending on whether they are linked to international or EU law (1–4) or whether they are only anchored in national law (5–6). This depiction eases the understanding, but is purely schematic as the differences between the two categories or the individual purposes are only gradual.

Purposes 1–4 are influenced by international or EU law. The analysis of the regularisations in Austria, Germany and Spain shows, however, that the extent of the influence differs. Each are derived from higher-ranking provisions of international or EU law. For the sake of completeness, na-

297 See Introduction D.II.3.
298 See also *Menezes Queiroz*, Illegally Staying 2.

tional constitutional law in part contains corresponding guarantees that were created before the EU Member State became bound by provisions of international or EU law. However, where the derivation of regularisations is concerned, this aspect is disregarded as all Member States are now bound by the provisions of international or EU law, whereas the fundamental rights anchored in national constitutional law only apply domestically.[299] As this study takes into account the perspective of irregularly staying migrants – the so-called migrant-centred perspective[300] – the protection against expulsion under human rights and EU law will be presented as it is required for the analysis, but there is no in-depth analysis of the protection offered by the individual legislative provisions. The focus is directed towards the question of the higher-ranking sources of law that provide the source for the regularisations analysed in Chapter 4. This is an essential step to find a basic framework that can be referred to in Chapter 5 in devising an EU Regularisation Directive.

The provisions of international and EU law may trigger two different consequences for the Member States. On the one hand, it is possible that provisions such as Articles 3 and 8 ECHR represent a legal obstacle to return and thus guarantee particular protection against expulsion.[301] I use the expression 'obstacle to return' when, for factual or legal reasons, an obstacle arises in relation to the return. However, the term 'obstacle' indicates that the circumstances are not permanent and as such there remains the possibility for the return to occur (again). In the interest of simplicity, the term 'prohibited' is only used when it reflects the wording of legislation. The focus is on determining whether there is an 'obligation to regularise'. Nevertheless, the provisions of international and EU law do not oblige the Member States to grant a migrant a right to stay to in a given case.[302] The Member States therefore retain the discretion whether to approve residency of such persons.[303] A claim to residency can, however, arise at national level. Conversely, the migrants in such cases do not have a legal claim to regularisation due to higher-ranking provisions, yet it

299 On the standard, see Introduction D.II.1.

300 See Introduction D.II.3.

301 Cf. *Diekmann*, Menschenrechtliche Grenzen des Rückführungsverfahrens in Europa (2016) 153–163; *Tewocht*, Drittstaatsangehörige 418 with further references; *Cholewinski*, No Right of Entry in *Groenendijk/Guild/Minderhoud* (eds), In Search of Europe's Borders (2002) 107 (107ff);

302 For detail on Art 3 ECHR, Chapter 1.B.III.1.b. and Chapter 2.B.II.2.a. and on Art 8 ECHR, Chapter 1.B.III.2.–3.

303 See Chapter 2.B.I.

can be seen in practice that Member States often respond to the legal obstacles to return by granting a right to stay, even if they would not be obliged to do so by international or EU law. The European Commission therefore acknowledged in 2004 that '[m]ost Member States recognise that for pragmatic reasons the need may arise to regularise certain individuals who do not fulfil the normal criteria for a residence permit. By carrying out regularisation operations, governments attempt to bring such migrants into society rather than leaving them on the margins, subject to exploitation'.[304] I therefore argue that in such instances Member States often go beyond the provisions of international and EU law, notwithstanding that this development does not receive sufficient acknowledgement in the current legal discussion.

Assuming they are not interpreted as mere protection against expulsion, certain high-ranking provisions may, on the other hand, trigger an obligation to regularise, i.e. to grant a right to stay. This may first appear as contradiction, but it can be explained by the fact that the existence of a legal obligation to grant a right to stay (as opposed to the existence of a legal obstacle to return) is often disputed and depends on how the legislative provisions are interpreted. This will be demonstrated in relation to the principle of non-refoulement.[305] Arguments for such an obligation would afford migrants a legal claim to regularisation and therefore remove any discretion the Member States have in this regard.[306] In order to best present the effects of the higher-ranking provisions on the Member States, I will explain these in detail both in the following and in Chapter 2.B. and Chapter 4, outlining also whether or not there is an obligation for the Member States to grant a right to stay.

The purposes 5 and 6 are at present anchored foremost in national law and, in comparison to the purposes 1–4, have not been permeated by international or EU law, at least not noticeably. I assume for now that contextual aspects have contributed to the development and establishment of these particular regularisations, but will return to this assumption in the course of the comparison in Chapter 4. For example, the Member State may require more workers to cover domestic shortfalls.[307] This does not

304 COM(2004) 412 final, 9.

305 See Chapter 1.B.III.1.b. and Chapter 2.B.II.2.a.

306 See below, Chapter 2.B.II.2.a.

307 See Chapter 4.E.IV. on the discussion regarding the shortage of skilled workers in Germany or Chapter 4.E.I.–III. on social, employment or training roots in Spain.

mean that the EU does not also have competences in this area and has become legislatively active.[308] Regularisation purposes in national law may constitute a patchwork of EU and national rules, which especially shows the gradual nature of the differences between the two identified categories or six regularisation purposes.

Three of the six regularisation purposes identified above (namely 'social ties', 'family unity' and 'employment and training') correlate with the basic types of permissible purposes of residence accounted for by *Bast* in the German Residence Act (humanitarian grounds, family unity and employment).[309] 'Training' could be included as a fourth distinct type, though is to be rejected as it falls within the broad interpretation of employment (or occupation).[310] *Bast* only refers to selected parts of the German Residence Act in his analysis,[311] whereas the three additional purposes arise from the wider framework of this study.

1. Non-returnability

The Return Directive in principle obliges the Member States to terminate the irregular stay either by return or by granting a right to stay.[312] In this context, the first purpose of the regularisation is non-returnability, which is largely derived from human rights guarantees. The principle of non-refoulment is prominently anchored in Articles 2 and 3 ECHR as well as in Article 33 of the Refugee Convention. Furthermore, it is regulated almost verbatim in Article 19(2) CFR[313] and, according to Article 5 of the Return Directive, to receive due consideration in the implementation of the Directive.[314] The ECJ has qualified the principle of non-returnability

---

308 See Art 4(2)(j) TFEU.

309 *Bast*, Aufenthaltsrecht 219 refers to §§ 16–38a AufenthG.

310 For Germany, § 2(2) AufenthG as well as BeschV and for detail Chapter 3.B.II.2. For Austria, see just § 2(1) Nos. 7 and 8 NAG and on the Austrian AuslBG *Kreuzhuber/Hudsky*, Arbeitsmigration (2011) mn 61.

311 Chapter 2 Parts 4–6 AufenthG.

312 See Chapter 2.B.I.

313 Explanations relating to the Charter of Fundamental Rights, OJ 2007 C 303/17, 18 and 24. Art 4 CFR is not listed as Art 19(2) CFR is *lex specialis*; cf. *Lukan* in *Holoubek/Lienbacher* (eds), GRC-Kommentar[2] (2019) Art 4 GRC mn 1 with further references.

314 See also Recital 24 and *Hörich*, Abschiebungen 41 with further references. See also Art 9 and Art 13 Return Directive and Chapter 2.B.II.

under the Charter as a fundamental and subjective right;[315] according to Article 52(3) CFR, the rights under the Charter are identical to those of the ECHR.[316] This study refers only to the principle of non-refoulement under the ECHR (and thus indirectly to the CFR) as a deeper analysis would simply be far too extensive. The principle of non-refoulement absolutely prohibits the return of migrants to their country of origin where there is the threat of serious violations of human rights (torture and other inhuman or degrading treatment or punishment).[317] Broadly speaking, the regularisations within this purpose are derived from the principle of non-refoulement under the ECHR and CFR as well as the relevant provisions of the Return Directive. However, before the legal and factual reasons are explored in detail, it is first necessary to briefly explore toleration in residence law due to its close relationship to the above reasons and the context that is relevant for the later comparison.[318]

a) Status of toleration in residence law

The legal notion of toleration subsequently describes the statutory provisions in Austria and Germany.[319] Non-statutory toleration applies to Spain, where a person is *de facto* tolerated, but the situation is not governed by legislation.[320]

Toleration in Austria and Germany is not equivalent to lawful residency, but is not to be viewed as a mere irregular stay because of the particular

---

315 ECJ 18.12.2014, C-562/13, ECLI:EU:C:2014:2453, *Abdida*, para 46 and ECJ 19.6.2018, C-181/16, ECLI:EU:C:2018:465, *Gnandi*, para 53. See also ECJ 24.6.2015, C-373/13, ECLI:EU:C:2015:413, *HT*, para 65.

316 See just ECJ *Abdida*, para 47 on Art 19(2) CFR and ECJ 24.4.2018, C-353/16, ECLI:EU:C:2018:276, *MP*, para 37 on Art 4 CFR. Further ECJ 26.9.2018, C-180/17, ECLI:EU:C:2018:775, *X* and *Y*, para 31 with further references on Art 47 CFR.

317 Cf. *Thurin*, Der Schutz des Fremden vor rechtswidriger Abschiebung: Das Prinzip des Non-Refoulement nach Artikel 3 EMRK² (2012) 102ff; *Dembour*, When Humans Become Migrants (2015) 197–249 and *De Weck*, Non-Refoulement under the European Convention on Human Rights and the UN Convention against Torture (2016).

318 See only *Hailbronner* in *de Bruycker* 253.

319 For an analysis of the position of toleration in the German context see *Nachtigall*, Die Ausdifferenzierung der Duldung, ZAR 2020, 271 (275ff).

320 *Menezes Queiroz*, Illegally Staying 112 refers to this as 'de facto toleration'. See also Chapter 3.B.I.

status rights that are attached to toleration.[321] The concept is Janus-like. On the one hand, it unifies aspects of a right to stay, such as

- a partially temporary, partially permanent *de facto* residency acknowledged by law,
- status rights and
- elimination of administrative[322] or judicial sanctions.[323]

Yet on the other hand also combines aspects of an irregular stay, such as

- the decision to return, and
- the unlawful stay.

Furthermore, each legally regulated instance of toleration can qualify as a preliminary step towards a right to stay where there is the prospect of regularisation,[324] i.e. the possibility for a tolerated person to acquire a right to stay (as understood here). Conversely, this does not mean that there is a legal claim to a right to stay. *Kluth/Breidenbach* refer in this context to the creation of '*Vertrauensschutztatbestände*' for tolerated persons,[325] which are perhaps best described here as aspects which invoke legitimate expectations. Tolerated status must therefore be one of the relevant conditions for granting a right to stay,[326] though as will be shown, this does not carry the same weight in Austrian and German law.[327] Nonetheless, even in these cases of toleration, the features of a right to stay do not suffice to end the irregular stay.

The phrase 'qualified irregularity' will be used to describe the circumstances in which, despite toleration, there is no prospect of regularisation. Such phrase is appropriate as it clarifies that the stay is not regular, yet

---

321 *Hailbronner* in *de Bruycker* 252 refers to tolerations as a 'quasi-residence right'.

322 For Austria, § 120(5) No. 2 FPG and Chapter 4.A.I.3.

323 See for Germany the criminal offence in § 95(1) No. 2 AufenthG and Chapter 3.A.II.1. and Chapter 4.A.I.2.

324 *Hoffmann*, Geduldet in Deutschland – Teil 1: Aufenthaltsrechtliche Auswirkungen, Asylmagazin 2010, 369 (369), also goes in the same direction.

325 *Kluth/Breidenbach* in *Kluth/Heusch* (eds), BeckOK Ausländerrecht (30th edn, 1.7.2021) § 60a AufenthG mn 1. *Kraler* refers to a two-stage regularisation procedure. Although the approach is taken from the perspective of political science (and therefore being somewhat imprecise when viewed from a legal perspective), the basic notion behind the terminology is convincing; *Kraler*, IMISCOE WP No. 24 (February 2009) 8; see also *Pelzer* in *Fischer-Lescano/Kocher/Nassibi* 158 and *Hailbronner* in *de Bruycker* 253f.

326 In Germany, toleration was a central requirement of the regularisations from the 1990s; cf. *Hailbronner* in *de Bruycker* 252f and Chapter 3.B.I. This requirement still features in current Austrian and German law; see Chapter 4.A.II.1.–2. and Chapter 4.C.II.

327 See just Chapter 4.A.I.2.–3.

is more than just a mere irregular stay.[328] This refers above all to the status rights conferred as well as the assessment that the migrant cannot be (at least temporarily) be returned. However, the lack of the prospect for regularisation excludes the additional qualification as a preliminary step towards acquiring a right to stay.

Irregular stay	Mere irregular stay
	Qualified irregular stay – legal toleration without the prospect of regularisation
	Preliminary step towards a right to stay – legal toleration with the prospect of regularisation
Right to stay	Temporary right to stay
	Permanent right to stay

Table 2: Overview of residency status possibilities – graduated model[329]

b) Principle of non-refoulement under the ECHR and CFR or factual reasons

The presence of legal or factual obstacles surrounding the removal constitutes the relevant reason for regularisations under this particular category. As already mentioned, the legal reasons refer to the principle of non-refoulement. This does not apply to international protection within the meaning of the Qualification Directive, i.e. refugees and beneficiaries of subsidiary protection.[330] Consequently, the spotlight is directed only towards the regularisations that go beyond the international protection; the principle of non-refoulement regulated in Article 33 Refugee Convention will not be examined. The Member States are in principle not obliged to grant irregularly staying migrants a right to stay for reasons of non-refoulement anchored in the ECHR (and CFR[331]) and the corresponding case law.[332] The Member States perform their duty under Article 3 ECHR by protecting such migrants from expulsion. Consequently, the practice has emerged in Austria and Germany to first tolerate such migrants.[333]

328 Cf. *Klarmann*, Illegalisierte Migration 274–278 and 286–288.

329 Cf. also *Kluth*, ZAR 2007, 22.

330 See Introduction D.II.1.

331 See already the remarks in Chapter 1.B.III.1.

332 See ECtHR 15.9.2005, *Bonger/Netherlands*, 10154/04; for criticism *Dembour*, Migrants 442–481 and in general on ECtHR case law *Menezes Queiroz*, Illegally Staying 109–111.

333 See Chapter 4.A.I.2.–3.

Although this approach is in principle compatible with both the Return Directive as well as the ECtHR case law,[334] I argue that the threat of a breach of Article 3 ECHR gives rise to an obligation to regularise under the Return Directive.[335] The legal reasons for non-returnability may refer to other breaches of human or fundamental rights, such as Article 8 ECHR, the sub-category 'non-returnability' only refers to the non-refoulement principle as understood in the ECHR and CFR.

Regularisations due to factual reasons refer to the return or in part directly to the deportation process. To give an example: the return is impossible due to the lack of travel documents,[336] whereby the country of origin refuses the readmission of the person affected. The inability to determine the migrant's origin or identity, therefore excluding return, is a further example.[337] Whereas the ECHR does not provide an obligation to regularise, it is disputed whether such obligation features in the Return Directive, though in my opinion such obligation exists where the non-returnability is permanent.[338] As above for the legal reasons, migrants in Austria and Germany will first be tolerated before a right to stay is granted.[339]

2. Social ties

The second purpose is established primarily by virtue of the right to respect for private life according to Article 8 ECHR. It describes those regularisations that are awarded on the basis of humanitarian reasons (in a broad sense). The State's interest in approving residence aims to fulfil or satisfy humanitarian obligations or considerations by granting a right to stay. This excludes those reasons that constitute non-returnability since they fall within such category (or the sub-category 'principle of non-refoulement under the ECHR and CFR or factual reasons').[340]

The reasons for the award are derived from the right to respect for private life under Article 8 ECHR (which is practically identical to Article 7

334 On the Return Directive, see Chapter 2.B.I.
335 See Chapter 2.B.II.2.
336 See the Travel Document Regulation.
337 Cf. also *Menezes Queiroz*, Illegally Staying 87.
338 See Chapter 2.B.II.2.b.
339 See Chapter 4.A.I.2.–3.
340 See Chapter 1.B.III.1.

CFR[341]). According to the ECtHR case law, the right covers 'multiple aspects of the person's physical and social identity' such as 'gender identification, name and sexual orientation'.[342] However, the Member States are not obliged to grant a residence permit or special legal status due to an existing private life per Article 8 ECHR. The corresponding ECtHR case law provides that the obligation to grant a right to stay only arises in exceptional cases.[343] If expelling a person constitutes a disproportionate intervention in their private life, this would 'just' be a legal obstacle.[344] Consequently, the decision to award a right to stay remains once again at the discretion of the Member States.

3. Family unity

The third purpose covers regularisations derived from the right to respect for family life according to Article 8 ECHR. This right is not only practically identical to Article 7 CFR[345] but, pursuant to Article 24(2) CFR, the Member States must take into account the best interests of the child 'at all stages of the procedure'.[346] The ECtHR case law provides that 'family life' covers 'marriage-based relationships, and also other *de facto* "family ties" where the parties are living together outside marriage or where other factors demonstrated that the relationship had sufficient constancy'.[347] It is

341 Explanations relating to the Charter of Fundamental Rights, OJ 2007 C 303/17, 20.

342 ECtHR 4.12.2008 (GC), *S and Marper/United Kingdom*, 30562/04 and 30566/04, para 66. For detail *Da Lomba*, Vulnerability and the Right to Respect for Private Life as an Autonomous Source of Protection against Expulsion under Article 8 ECHR, Laws 2017/6/32.

343 See in particular ECtHR (GC) 16.6.2012, 26828/06, *Kurić/Slovenia* paras 358f and in detail *Bast/von Harbou/Wessels*, Human Rights Challenges to European Migration Policy. The REMAP Study (2022) 199. See further ECtHR 15.6.2006, 58822/00, *Shevanova/Latvia*, para 69 and Fn 501.

344 *Farcy* in *de Bruycker/Cornelisse/Moraru* 442 with further references; *Schieber*, Komplementärer Schutz 82–100 and *Thym*, Respect for private and family life under Article 8 ECHR in immigration cases: a human right to regularize illegal stay?, ICLQ 2008, 87; *Menezes Queiroz*, Illegally Staying 104–109.

345 Explanations relating to the Charter of Fundamental Rights, OJ 2007 C 303/17, 20.

346 ECJ 14.1.2021, C-441/19, ECLI:EU:C:2021:9, *TQ*, para 44; see also ECJ 10.5.2017, C-133/15, ECLI:EU:C:2017:354, *Chavez-Vilchez*, para 70, ECJ 8.5.2018, C-82/16, ECLI:EU:C:2018:308, *KA*, para 71.

347 ECtHR 24.1.2017 (GC), *Paradiso* and *Campanelli/Italy*, 25358/12, para 140.

thus a question of fact that depends on whether there is a close personal relationship. The relevant reason for the purpose of this regularisation aims at preserving and maintaining family ties. Providing protection against expulsion under Article 8 ECHR does not mean in principle that Member States are obliged to award a right to stay or special legal status.[348]

4. Vulnerability

The fourth purpose is characterised by the focus on vulnerable groups of people or situations. In Germany, for example, these are referred to as 'hardship' cases, which describe humanitarian or personal emergencies.[349] 'Vulnerability' indeed consists of humanitarian reasons in the broad sense, and thus displays parallels to the regularisation purpose 'social ties', but it is defined as a separate purpose and can be divided into two sub-categories: 'victim protection' is derived from higher-ranked legislative provisions (specifically from EU law), whereas the sub-category 'other emergency situations' is not derived from either international or EU law.

a) Victim protection[350]

Victim protection is derived from EU secondary law. Article 8 of the Human Trafficking Directive and Article 13(4) of the Employers Sanctions Directive are the most relevant provisions in this regard.[351] The provisions apply to victims of specific criminal offences. Neither afford the affected migrant a right to receive a right to stay, rather the decision remains at the discretion of the Member State, which only has to determine the conditions for awarding such right under domestic law. The Member States provide residency status for the victims of human trafficking and for those undocumented migrants who were employed under particularly

348 See Fn 343 and 501.

349 § 23a AufenthG; cf. *Lüke*, Humanitäre Bleiberechte außerhalb des Flüchtlingsschutzes im Rahmen des Aufenthaltsgesetzes, ZAR 2004, 397 (402); for detail, Chapter 4.D.II.1.

350 In detail *Frei*, Menschenhandel und Asyl: Die Umsetzung der völkerrechtlichen Verpflichtungen zum Opferschutz im schweizerischen Asylverfahren (2018).

351 On the Employers Sanctions Directive *Vogelrieder*, Die Sanktionsrichtlinie: ein weiterer Schritt auf dem Weg zu einer umfassenden Migrationspolitik der EU, ZAR 2009, 168.

exploitative working conditions or were illegally employed as a minor. Awarding legal residence should protect the victims from further criminal acts against them. There is also often a public interest in criminal prosecution.

b) Other emergency situations

The sub-category 'other emergency situations' represents a 'catch-all' purpose in the broader sense as it can cover various different regularisations, yet each share the common feature that they are not derived from either international or from EU law. 'Other emergency situations' concerns vulnerable groups or individuals in a vulnerable situation who have no other possibility to regularise their residency. As mentioned, the German 'granting residence in case of hardship' is one such regularisation.[352]

The duration of previous stays is a further example of a reason for awarding a right to stay. This covers cases in which the duration of particular (factual and ir/regular) previous stays are relevant for the decision granting the right to stay.[353] Furthermore, legislation may provide that the duration of previous stays has to be satisfied on a particular date. As for those regularisations that may be subsumed under 'employment and training', the duration of previous stays is one of many factors that are considered in balancing interests under Article 8 ECHR. However, for the purpose outlined here, the duration of the previous stay is central to the underlying reason for granting the right to stay.

5. Employment and training

The fifth purpose (like the sixth purpose to be analysed in the following) has so far been anchored in purely domestic law, although in comparison to the regularisation purposes 1–4 there is no such distinct permeation of international and EU law. The EU has, for example, passed the Students and Researchers Directive to regulate certain aspects and provide legal

352 § 23a AufenthG and see Chapter 4.D.II.1.

353 In some regularisations this reason constitutes one of the conditions for the award, but is often only of a subsidiary character in relation to the other conditions.

claims for certain groups (e.g. students). As noted above, a patchwork of EU and national rules underpin regularisations within this purpose.

The purpose of such regularisation is linked to employment or training/education in a broad sense. It may concern an employed or self-employed activity[354] and may also be linked to training/education. Specifically, the conditions for the regularisation thus refer to employment or training/education already exercised over a particular period of time or to commencing prospective employment. The grant of a right to stay thus aims at the continuation of existing employment or to allow prospective employment to commence legally.

Employment is also one of several factors to be considered in relation to Article 8 ECHR.[355] Unlike other regularisations based on Article 8 ECHR,[356] here employment and training concern the relevant requirement for the regularisation.

6. Other national interests

The sixth purpose describes those regularisations whose reason for granting is solely based on the protection of other national interests. For example, it may be considered to grant a right to stay to allow participation as a witness in criminal proceedings or for the protection of the political interests of a Member State. In relation to 'vulnerability' and the sub-category 'protection of victims', the main focus is on the protection of victims, as the name indicates. The purpose of the regularisation discussed here primarily serves other national interests.

---

354 § 2(2) AufenthG and see Chapter 3.A.II.2.

355 ECtHR 10.1.2017, *Salija/Switzerland*, 55470/10, para 51; ECtHR 20.9.2011, *AA/United Kingdom*, 8000/08, paras 62 and 66; ECtHR 15.1.2007 (GC), *Sisojeva/Latvia*, 60654/00, para 95; ECtHR 31.1.2006, *Sezen/Netherlands*, 50252/99, para 48. Detailed *Oswald*, Das Bleiberecht: Das Grundrecht auf Privat- und Familienleben als Schranke für Aufenthaltsbeendigungen (2012) 231–233 and *Reyhani/Nowak*, Beschäftigung von Asylsuchenden in Mangelberufen und die Zulässigkeit von Rückkehrentscheidungen (4.7.2018), https://bim.lbg.ac.at/sites/files/bim/attachments/reyhaninowak_gutachten_art_8_abs_2_emrk_04072018.pdf (31.7.2022) 8ff.

356 See Chapter 1.B.III.2.–3.

IV. Delimitation

The scope as well as the content of this study need to be distinguished from those topics that could qualify as regularisations under the above definition, but are not taken into consideration for the purposes of the comparison in Chapter 4.

1. Temporary protection

The Directive on minimum standards for giving temporary protection in the event of a mass influx of displaced persons (Temporary Protection Directive) primarily concerns displaced persons warranting protection. The Directive has already been transposed by the Member States and provides, inter alia, the possibility to provide a residence permit once the Directive has been 'activated' at EU level by a Council Decision. Accordingly, categorisation as a regularisation would be possible. However, as the Directive has never been activated at EU level until Russia's military invasion of the Ukraine in February 2022,[357] it has not been included in the scope of this study as its relevance during the research for this study could not be seen in practice despite its transposition into national law.[358]

2. Marriage and registered partnerships

Marriages and registered partnerships are ultimately family law matters and thus belong to the civil law domain.[359] Administrative law only merely concerns the examination whether there is a marriage, partnership or adoption 'of convenience'.[360] Each act giving rise to marriage, a partnership or adoption is purely of civil law nature. This may have effects on

357 See Decision (EU) 2022/382 and regarding the non-activation *Ineli-Ciger*, Time to Activate the Temporary Protection Directive, EJML 2016, 1 (13ff). See in more detail *Ineli-Ciger*, Temporary Protection in Law and Practice (2018).

358 See Chapter 3.A.III.4. and Chapter 3.B.III.4.

359 On Austrian law *Welser/Kletečka*, Grundriss des bürgerlichen Rechts: Band I^{15} (2018) mns 30, 34f and 1392ff.

360 Cf. on Austrian law §§ 117f FPG and *Messinger*, Schein oder Nicht Schein. Konstruktion und Kriminalisierung von „Scheinehen" in Geschichte und Gegenwart (2012); on German law § 27(1a) AufenthG; cf. on Spanish law Art 53(2)(b) LODYLE and *Boza Martínez*, El régimen sancionador en la normativa de extran-

the residence status of irregularly staying migrants, especially where EU citizens are involved and in circumstances in which the marriage or registered partnerships affords others the status as a family member.

In general there are no (direct) effects under residency law where irregularly staying migrants marry or enter into a registered partnership with one another. However, this study very much covers instances of marriage or adoption. Several of the regularisations analysed herein are derived from the right to respect for family life under Article 8 ECHR.[361] This right is defined, inter alia, by familial relationships that are consequently to be considered in the comparison in Chapter 4. Be that as it may, entering into marriage or registered partnership is only a matter to be considered when granting a right to stay and thus does not by itself give rise to such right. Marriages or registered partnerships may therefore not be understood as a regularisation for the purposes of this study and are thus not examined.

V. Interim conclusion

A categorisation of regularisations has been created for the purpose of the comparison of the approaches in Austria, Germany and Spain. The integrated comparison requires consideration of many different factors and thus presents a particular methodological challenge. Consequently, several existing structural approaches have been analysed with regard to their suitability as a system for regularisations.

For example, the REGINE Study divides regularisations into regularisation programmes and regularisation mechanisms. When viewed through a legal lens, however, the division into two such aspects is not appropriate as there are too few cross-jurisdictional differences to allow for a fruitful contribution. Furthermore, there is an insufficient overlap between the characteristic relevant for categorisation and the definition of regularisation used in this study. Older research is also notable due to the typology it creates, but it does not allow for a categorisation that is sufficiently general and workable for the purposes of the intended comparison.

The favoured approach is ultimately a categorisation on the basis of the purpose of the regularisation. The expression is derived from the 'purpose of the stay', which describes the relevant legal reason for granting the

---

jería in *Boza Martínez/Donaire Villa/Moya Malapeira* (eds), La nueva regulación de la inmigración y la extranjería en España (2012) 471 (482ff).

361 See Chapter 1.B.III.3.

right. Although the terms are in essence identical, the 'purpose of the regularisation' is a more precise and better suited concept as it only covers those decisions which fall within the notion of regularisation. As the definition of regularisation is centred around such individual decisions, linking the definition to the purpose of the right appears as the most promising and fruitful basis for devising a precise system.

The next step extracted the relevant purposes of regularisations from sources of law across three levels (international, EU, and national law): 'non-returnability', 'social ties', 'family unity', 'vulnerability', 'employment and training' and 'other national interests'.

As depicted in Table 1, the purposes were divided into two categories determined by their link to international and/or EU law (purposes 1–4) or to purely domestic law (purposes 5–6). These can trigger two different consequences for the Member States: on the one hand, it is possible that international or EU laws represent a legal obstacle and thereby ensure particular protection against return. Nevertheless, the Member States are not obliged to grant a right to stay. The decision to approve the residency in such cases is thus at the discretion of the Member States. However, a claim to residency may arise at national level. Conversely, the migrants in such cases do not have a legal claim to regularisation by virtue of higher-ranking provisions. Practice shows that the Member States often grant a right to stay in response to the legal obstacles to return. As they are not obliged to do so under international or EU law, they thus go beyond these higher-ranking laws. This requires greater consideration in the current legal discussions. On the other hand, particular higher-ranking provisions can trigger an obligation to regularise (i.e. to grant a right to stay) in so far as they are not interpreted as merely protecting against return. This is explained by differing interpretations of the respective higher-ranking provisions, though it is disputed whether there is a legal obligation to grant a right to stay as opposed to the existence of a legal obstacle to return.

The purposes 5 and 6 are at present only anchored in purely domestic law and are not derived from higher-ranking provisions of international or EU law. This forms the basis for my (provisional) assumption that the context has contributed to the development and establishment of such different regularisations.[362]

---

362 See Chapter 4.G.

Finally, a distinction was drawn to those topics, namely temporary protection as well as marriage and registered partnerships, that are not analysed in the comparison in Chapter 4.

Chapter 2 – EU competence concerning irregular migration and regularisations

This Chapter[363] focuses on the European Union's legislative competence regarding irregular stays and regularisations, examining in particular both primary and secondary law. The current EU *acquis* does not feature legislation concerning regularisations, though Article 6(4) Return Directive allows the Member States to regularise irregularly staying migrants.

I will first address the EU immigration policy with regard to irregular migration in general (A.). The spotlight then pans to the Return Directive (B.) as a basis for determining whether EU primary law features a regularisation policy. Answering this question first requires an analysis of the mandates anchored in Article 79(1) TFEU (C.). This allows me to demonstrate that the EU immigration policy pursued so far is not prescribed by EU primary law. The analysis then shifts to the question whether the competences under present primary law allow the EU to pass legislation aimed at regularising irregularly staying migrants (D.).

A. Irregular migration under EU immigration policy

For the purposes of this analysis, the term immigration policy is understood as each EU policy rooted in primary law, specifically in Article 79 TFEU.[364] I therefore begin with a political concept within EU law, which I then outline in relation to irregular migration.

The use of the term 'fight' in relation to illegal immigration was first used in 1991 in a report from a meeting of the European Council.[365]

---

363 Earlier drafts of parts of this Chapter were published in *Hinterberger/Klammer* in *Filzwieser/Taucher*; *Hinterberger/Klammer*, NVwZ 2017; *Hinterberger* in *Lanser/Potocnik-Manzouri/Safron/Tillian/Wieser* as well as *Hinterberger*, Maastricht Journal of European and Comparative Law 2019. See Introduction D.III.

364 For detail on the notion see *Thym*, Europäische Einwanderungspolitik: Grundlagen, Gegenstand und Grenzen in *Hofmann/Löhr* (eds), Europäisches Flüchtlings- und Einwanderungsrecht (2008) 183 (183ff).

365 *European Council*, Report from the Ministers responsible for immigration to the European Council meeting in Maastricht on immigration and asylum

The Treaty of Maastricht, which entered into force in 1993, set 'combatting unauthorized immigration, residence and work' as a matter of 'common interest' requiring cooperation between the Member States.[366] The distinction between immigration and residence is notable as it creates two distinct concepts, whereby Article 79(2)(c) TFEU now refers to 'illegal immigration and unauthorised residence'.

The entry into force of the Schengen Agreement[367] in 1995 not only abolished internal border controls but the increased security and monitoring of external borders also became characteristic of the EU political agenda concerning migration.[368] The later Treaty of Amsterdam played a highly important role for the common immigration policy by bringing the policy areas within the Community domain.[369] By creating an 'area of freedom, security and justice'[370] immigration policy became a separate policy area independent of the internal market.[371] In 1999, 'illegal immigration' and 'illegal residence' became express competences after the Treaty of Amsterdam had entered into force.[372] However, unlike the Treaty of Maastricht, the Treaty of Amsterdam did not contain an express reference to

policy (3.12.1991), SN 4038/91 (WGI 930); cf. *European Council*, Conclusions (12.12.1992), SN/456/92, No. 18.

366 Art K1(3)(c) TEC.

367 Cf. *Ter Steeg*, Das Einwanderungskonzept der EU (2006) 73ff; *Winkelmann*, 25 Jahre Schengen: Der Schengen-Acquis als integraler Bestandteil des Europarechts – Bedeutung und Auswirkung auf die Einreise- und Aufenthaltsrechte – Teil 1, ZAR 2010, 213 and *Winkelmann*, 25 Jahre Schengen: Der Schengen-Acquis als integraler Bestandteil des Europarechts – Bedeutung und Auswirkung auf die Einreise- und Aufenthaltsrechte, ZAR 2010, 270.

368 On the essence of the Schengen Agreement in its interaction with external borders see *Michl*, Dysfunktionale Außengrenze und binnenstaatliche Reaktion – zur unionsrechtlichen Zulässigkeit einseitiger Maßnahmen in Zeiten großer Migrationsströme in *Bungenberg/Giegerich/Stein* (eds), ZEuS-Sonderband: Asyl und Migration in Europa – rechtliche Herausforderungen und Perspektiven (2016) 161 (162ff). Critical, *Bigo*, Border Regimes Police Cooperation and Security in an Enlarged European Union in *Zielonka* (ed), Europe Unbound: Enlarging and Reshaping the Boundaries of the European Union (2003) 213.

369 On the development, *Bast*, Ursprünge der Europäisierung des Migrationsrechts in FS Kay Hailbronner (2013) 3 (3) or also *Desmond*, HRLR 2016, 247f.

370 Art 67ff TFEU; see for example COM(2000) 782 final and COM(2000) 167 final, with detailed contributions in *Baldaccini/Guild/Toner* (eds), Whose Freedom, Security and Justice? EU Immigration and Asylum Law and Policy (2007) as well as *Costello*, Human Rights 17ff.

371 So *Thym* in *Hofmann/Löhr* 189f with further references.

372 Art 63(3)(b) TEC in the version OJ 1997 C 340/1; for detail *Peers*, EU Justice and Home Affairs Law. Vol 1: EU Immigration and Asylum Law^4 (2016) 445f.

'combatting' or 'fighting' irregular immigration as a common interest or purpose. The use of the term 'combat' in relation to 'illegal immigration' was reintroduced in 2009 via the Treaty of Lisbon, namely in Article 79(1) TFEU.[373]

The European Commission's 2001 Communication regarding a common policy in the 'fight' against illegal immigration and human trafficking expressly highlights that 'illegal entry or residence should not lead to the desired stable form of residence'.[374] Less than three months after this Communication, in February 2002, the European Council proposed a 'comprehensive plan to combat illegal immigration and trafficking of human beings in the European Union',[375] which proposed short and medium-term measures, ranging from visas to returns.

In this sense Article 79(1) TFEU refers, inter alia, to the 'prevention of, and enhanced measures to combat, illegal immigration' as one of the current mandates in the Treaty.[376] The 2008 Return Directive makes a key contribution to this process and broadly harmonises the return policy.[377]

The (restrictive) immigration policy is also apparent in the 2015 'Agenda on Migration', in which the reduction of incentives for irregular migration – symbolically – forms the first of four key areas.[378] Overall, the EU also presses on with the policy[379] in its 2020 New Pact on Migration and Asylum.[380] According to the Commission, the Agenda strives to set out an effective and balanced migration policy that is fair, robust and realistic.[381] Whether these goals can actually or even be achieved by the legal instruments in place indeed requires critical analysis.[382]

---

373 See Chapter 2.C.I.
374 COM(2001) 672 final, 6. See also COM(2004) 412 final, 11.
375 OJ 2002 C 142/23.
376 See Chapter 2.C.I.
377 See Chapter 2.B.
378 COM(2015)240 final, 9ff; cf. *Carrera/Guild/Aliverti/Allsopp/Manieri/Levoy*, Fit for purpose? The Facilitation Directive and the criminalisation of humanitarian assistance to irregular migrants (2016), http://www.europarl.europa.eu/RegData/etudes/STUD/2016/536490/IPOL_STU%282016%29536490_EN.pdf (31.7.2022).
379 As outlined in Introduction A.
380 COM(2020) 609 final, 2 and 7–9.
381 COM(2015) 240 final, 7f.
382 *Kraler*, Journal of Immigrant and Refugee Studies 2019, 94f.

B. Return Directive

Following the above outline of EU immigration policy concerning irregular migration, this section turns to the main instrument presently used to 'combat' an irregular stay: the Return Directive. The section first explains the general structure and content (I.) before examining whether current secondary law allows the Member States to regularise irregularly staying migrants or if they are even obliged to do so (II.).

I. General structure and content

The harmonisation and effectuation of return procedures have been in EU crosshairs since 1999,[383] with the Return Directive passed almost a decade later in 2008.[384] The Directive aims foremost at an 'effective removal and repatriation policy [...] with full respect for their fundamental rights and dignity'.[385] *Hörich* states in this respect that the Directive successfully balances the interests in the effective termination of residence and the observance of the fundamental rights of the persons affected by the procedure.[386]

Chapter II of the Return Directive concerns the 'Termination of Illegal Stay' and contains the Directive's core provision, Article 6(1), whereby the irregular stay is in principle to be terminated by a return decision and the subsequent return process.[387] For the purposes of the Directive, all migrants without a residence permit or other authorisation offering a

---

383 See just COM(2017) 200 final and *Acosta Arcarazo*, The Returns Directive in *Peers/Guild/Acosta Arcarazo/Groenendijk/Moreno-Lax* (eds), EU Immigration and Asylum Law. Vol 2: EU Immigration Law^2 (2012) 455 (484ff).

384 For a useful overview of the background see *Lutz*, The Negotiations on the Return Directive: Comments and Material (2010) and *Pollet*, The Negotiations on the Return Directive: Challenges, Outcomes and Lessons learned from an NGO Perspective in *Zwaan* (ed), The Returns Directive (2011) 25.

385 ECJ *Mahdi*, para 38 referring to Recitals 2 and 11. See further ECJ 30.5.2013, C-534/11, ECLI:EU:C:2013:343, *Arslan*, paras 42, 60: 'effective removal'; Recommendation (EU) 2017/432 and *Hörich*, Abschiebungen 31f with further references.

386 *Hörich*, Abschiebungen 307. See also *Bast*, Aufenthaltsrecht 101ff.

387 Recital 11 Recommendation (EU) 2017/432: 'In accordance with Article 6(1) of Directive 2008/115/EC, the Member States should systematically issue a return decision to third-country nationals who are staying illegally on their territory'. Cf. *Acosta Arcarazo* in *Peers/Guild/Acosta Arcarazo/Groenendijk/Moreno-Lax* 490;

right to stay are staying irregularly. The expression 'irregular' is used in this study as a synonym for 'illegal' as used in the Directive.[388]

Article 6(1) of the Return Directive obliges the Member States to issue a return decision.[389] This was confirmed by the ECJ in *El Dridi*.[390] At first glance it appears as an instruction to the Member States, though I will show in the following that this is 'merely' one of two equal options. Issuing a return decision depends on whether it can be enforced,[391] as legal or factual obstacles to return may exist. The migrant in question can or should initially comply with the return decision by departing the Member State voluntary.[392] The ECJ made it clear in its case law that the voluntary departure according to Article 7(1) has priority over the forced removal.[393] Where the person does not leave the territory of the Member State on a voluntary basis, the decision may ultimately be enforced via forced removal.[394] Member States shall therefore return irregularly staying migrants instead of granting a right to stay. This is one of the reasons why the EU has not passed regularisation legislation.

The basic approach of issuing a return decision is subject to three exceptions.[395] The first requires irregularly staying migrants who hold a valid residence permit issued by another Member State to go to that Member

Boeles/den Heijer/Lodder/Wouters, European Migration Law[2] (2014) 392; *Hörich*, Abschiebungen 73ff.

388 Art 2(1) and Art 3 No. 2 Return Directive and see also Chapter 1.A.II.1.

389 Art 3 No. 4 Return Directive; *Hörich*, Abschiebungen 73.

390 ECJ 28.4.2011, C-61/11, ECLI:EU:C:2011:268, *El Dridi*, para 35; affirmed ECJ *Achughbabian*, para 31, ECJ 23.4.2015, C-38/14, ECLI:EU:C:2015:260, *Zaizoune*, para 31, ECJ *TQ*, para 41 and ECJ 3.3.2022, C-409/20, ECLI:EU:C:2022:148, *UN*, para 42. Before issuing a return decision against an unaccompanied minor, the Member State concerned must carry out a general and in-depth assessment of the situation of that minor, taking due account of the best interests of the child, though this does not mean that the return will be enforced; ECJ *TQ*, paras 60 and 74–81.

391 Cf. *Hörich*, Abschiebungen 92.

392 Art 7 Return Directive. For criticism of the terminology, *Berger/Tanzer*, Die Rückführungsrichtlinie im Spannungsfeld von effektiver Rückführungspolitik und Grundrechtsschutz – eine Analyse unter Berücksichtigung der österreichischen Gesetzeslage in *Salomon* (ed), Der Status im europäischen Asylrecht (2020) 265 (280f).

393 ECJ *UN*, para 50 with further references.

394 Art 8 Return Directive; ECJ *TQ*, paras 79f.

395 See also ECJ *Zaizoune*, para 32.

State.[396] The second provides for the procedure if a person is taken back by another Member State under a bilateral agreement.[397] The most important exception is to be found in the first sentence of Article 6(4): 'Member States may at any moment decide to grant an autonomous residence permit or other authorisation offering a right to stay for compassionate, humanitarian or other reasons to a third-country national staying illegally on their territory'.[398] The wording suggests that an individual evaluation is necessary before a residence permit can be granted to an irregularly staying migrant.[399] Generally speaking, this exception to issue a return decision rests on the national sovereignty that the Member States continue to maintain in this matter.[400] As a consequence, the first sentence of Article 6(4) allows the Member States to terminate the irregular stay by granting a residence right, i.e. via a regularisation,[401] namely a process which terminates the irregularity per the Return Directive.[402] The residence permit or 'other

---

396 Art 6(2) Return Directive. Cf. ECJ 16.1.2018, C-240/17, ECLI:EU:C:2018:8, *E*, paras 44–48.

397 Art 6(3) Return Directive. Cf. *Acosta Arcarazo* in *Peers/Guild/Acosta Arcarazo/Groenendijk/Moreno-Lax* 494 and *Hörich*, Abschiebungen 73ff.

398 See further also ECJ 9.11.2010, C-57/09 and C-101/09, ECLI:EU:C:2010:661, *B* and *D*, paras 115–121 and ECJ 18.12.2014, C-541/13, ECLI:EU:C:2014:2451, *M'Bodj*, paras 43–47 regarding the relationship between the Qualification Directive and Return Directive and the question of the cases in which the Member States may issue residence permits for humanitarian reasons which do not represent 'international protection' under the Qualification Directive.

399 *Costello*, Human Rights 96 therefore argues that there would be a tense relationship between regularisation programmes and the Return Directive. Similarly, *Augustin*, Die Rückführungsrichtlinie der Europäischen Union. Richtliniendogmatik, Durchführungspflichten, Reformbedarf (2016) 227–230; see however *Schieber*, Komplementärer Schutz 282, 311f and 334. On the aforementioned programmes, Chapter 1.B.I. and Chapter 3.C.I.

400 Cf. *Martin*, The Authority and Responsibility of States in *Aleinikoff/Chetail* (eds), Migration and International Legal Norms (2003); *Nafziger*, The General Admission of Aliens under International Law, AJIL 1983, 804; *Dauvergne*, Making People Illegal: What Globalization Means for People and Law (2008) 2ff; *Bosniak*, Human Rights, State Sovereignty and the Protection of Undocumented Migrants under the International Migrant Workers Convention, International Migration Review 1991, 737 (754).

401 Art 6(4) Return Directive; cf. ECJ *Mahdi*, para 88: 'enables' and ECJ 22.11.2022, C-69/21, ECLI:EU:C:2022:913, *X*, para 86. In this sense, *Desmond* in *Wiesbrock/Acosta Arcarazo* 75.

402 See Chapter 1.A.II.

authorisation offering a right to stay'[403] under the respective national law must afford lawful residence in order to actually terminate the irregular stay.[404] Merely tolerating the irregular stay without initiating one of the two options would contradict the Return Directive.[405]

It seems at first blush that toleration under Austrian and German law violates the Return Directive.[406] 'Tolerating' migrants means that the Austrian or German State determines that the deportation is temporarily suspended because the return decision cannot be enforced due to 'prohibitions' or 'obstacles'. 'Toleration' under Austrian and German law cannot be considered as comparable to a residence permit as it does not establish legal residency under national law.[407] It is rather to be understood as a postponement of removal pursuant to Article 9 Return Directive. The postponement forms part of the return.[408]

Article 9(1) Return Directive provides that the removal shall be postponed for as long as a judicial or administrative body has granted a suspensory effect or if the removal would violate the principle of non-refoulement;[409] the latter provision is the most relevant to this study. Article 9(2) Return Directive regulates the cases in which removal may be postponed.[410] The Directive does not regulate the arrangements for the postponement, thereby leaving this matter to national law.[411] Nonetheless, the Member States are to observe and ensure the 'procedural safeguards' in Chapter III of the Return Directive. In this respect, *Lutz* regards the

---

403 The Commission views the expression 'other authorisation' as a catch-all provision which covers all cases that do not fall under the notion of residence permit according to Article 2 No. 16(b) SBC; Return Handbook 2017, 105 Fn 2.

404 In this sense, Return Handbook 2017, 88f; *Lutz* in *Thym/Hailbronner* Art 6 Return Directive mns 13 and 26 and *Menezes Queiroz*, Illegally Staying 155. The national law is relevant to determine the irregular status because of the fact that Art 3 No. 2 Return Directive refers to the 'conditions for entry, stay or residence in that Member State'; cf. Return Handbook 2017, 105; ECJ 7.6.2016, C-47/15, ECLI:EU:C:2016:408, *Affum*, paras 46ff; ECJ 3.6.2021, C-546/19, ECLI:EU:C:2021:432, *BZ*, paras 43–45 and ECJ *TQ*, para 71.

405 Return Handbook 2017, 98, 100. Cf. *Menezes Queiroz*, Illegally Staying 91 and *Hörich*, Abschiebungen 73, 92 with further references.

406 See Chapter 4.A.I.2.–3.

407 § 31(1a) No. 3 FPG and § 60a(3) AufenthG; cf. Fn 404.

408 See also Chapter 2.B.II.2.a.

409 See also ECJ *Gnandi*, para 47.

410 Cf. *Lutz* in *Thym/Hailbronner* Art 9 Return Directive mn 3.

411 *Lutz* in *Thym/Hailbronner* Art 9 Return Directive mn 5. See Chapter 4.A.I.

decision to postpone as falling under the notion of 'return decision'.[412] Member States have tried in part to circumvent these safeguards by not issuing a return decision, which *de facto* constitutes a postponement.[413] Alongside their rights, irregularly staying migrants are also subject to perform certain obligations if the removal is postponed during the period for voluntary departure.[414]

Consequently, legal 'toleration' of migrants accords in principle with the Return Directive as a return procedure has been initiated and a return decision issued, but not yet enforcement. Problems arise if a Member State tolerates an individual over a long period of time without granting a right to stay (long-term non-returnability).[415] Such so-called '*Kettenduldungen*' (literally: chain tolerations) or the current '*Ausbildungsduldung*' (temporary suspension of deportation for the purpose of training) in Germany are thus especially concerning from the perspective of EU law.[416]

Each Member State may grant a residence permit to an irregularly staying migrant after the return process has commenced or has concluded with legal effect.[417] In such case the third sentence of Article 6(4) Return Directive provides that the Member States are free to decide whether to withdraw the return decision or suspend it for the duration of validity of the residence permit.[418]

In short, Member States have to decide between the return procedure or regularisation according to my understanding of the Return Directive. As already indicated above, this is why the two options for the Member States are equal in nature: both have the effect of ending the irregular stay. Following the ECJ decision in *El Dridi*, the Member States must in principle issue a return decision and implement a return process,[419] yet in *Zaizoune* the ECJ emphasised that this ground rule applies without prejudice to the exceptions under Article 6(2)–(5) Return Directive.[420] The

412 *Lutz* in *Thym/Hailbronner* Art 9 Return Directive mn 5. The Commission states that postponing the removal 'should normally be adopted together with the return decision in one administrative act'; Return Handbook 2017, 132.

413 *Lutz* in *Thym/Hailbronner* Art 9 Return Directive mn 5.

414 Art 7(3) and Art 9(3) Return Directive; also *Menezes Queiroz*, Illegally Staying 101.

415 See Chapter 2.B.II.2.b.

416 See Chapter 4.A.I.2.d. and Chapter 4.E.IV.1.

417 Cf. *Augustin*, Rückführungsrichtlinie 227.

418 Cf. *Lutz* in *Thym/Hailbronner* Art 9 Return Directive mn 3.

419 See Fn 390.

420 ECJ *Zaizoune*, para 32.

Member States are free to decide at every stage of the process – even after issuing the return decision – to grant a residence permit. Consequently, the Return Directive leaves Member States the possibility to regularise irregularly staying migrants.[421]

It cannot be overlooked that in September 2018 the Commission proposed a reform the Return Directive.[422] At the time of writing (31.7.2022), these proposals have not yet been accepted,[423] and therefore closer analysis is not required. The proposals for reform would also have no effect on the general approach of the Return Directive. The Commission believes that a 'stronger and more effective'[424] return policy would be achieved by, for example, relaxing the requirements for detention. The criticism here was that an increase in the return rate is to be achieved, yet no facts or figures were presented as to why changing individual provisions should actually have such effect.[425]

II. An obligation to regularise under the Return Directive?

It is disputed whether an obligation to regularise exists under the Return Directive or, in turn, whether irregularly staying migrants have a claim to regularisation. Such obligation to grant a right to stay cannot be derived generally from Articles 3 and 8 ECHR, as discussed above.[426] However, the

421 In this sense ECJ *TQ*, paras 71f.

422 COM(2018) 634 final.

423 Cf. *NN*, Asylum seekers appealing returns must get own travel documents, euobserver.com (6.11.2018), https://euobserver.com/justice/143290 (31.7.2022).

424 *European Commission*, A stronger and more effective European return policy (12.9.2018), https://ec.europa.eu/info/sites/default/files/soteu2018-factsheet-returns-policy_en.pdf (31.7.2022). See above Introduction A. and Chapter 2.A.

425 Cf. *Machjer/Strik*, Legislating without Evidence: The Recast of the EU Return Directive, EJML 2021, 103; *Eisele*, The proposed Return Directive (recast). Substitute Impact Assessment (February 2019), http://www.europarl.europa.eu/RegData/etudes/STUD/2019/631727/EPRS_STU(2019)631727_EN.pdf (31.7.2022); *ECRE*, ECRE Comments on the Commission Proposal for a Recast Return Directive COM(2018) 634 (November 2018), https://www.ecre.org/wp-content/uploads/2018/11/ECRE-Comments-Commission-Proposal-Return-Directive.pdf (31.7.2022) and *Peers*, Lock 'em up: the proposal to amend the EU's Returns Directive, EU Law Analysis Blog (12.9.2018), http://eulawanalysis.blogspot.com/2018/09/lock-em-up-proposal-to-amend-eus.html (31.7.2022).

426 See Chapter 1.B.III., especially Chapter 1.B.III.1.b. and Chapter 1.B.III.2.–3.

future ECtHR case law needs to be observed as this could have an effect on the application and interpretation of the Return Directive.[427]

1. Opponents of an obligation to regularise

The opponents of an obligation to regularise (such as the European Commission or *Lutz*) base their argument on the ECJ decision in *Mahdi*,[428] whereby the 'purpose of the [Return Directive] is not to regulate the conditions of residence on the territory of a Member State of third-country nationals who are staying illegally and in respect of whom it is not, or has not been, possible to implement a return decision'.[429] The Return Directive 'must be interpreted as meaning that a Member State cannot be obliged to issue an autonomous residence permit, or other authorisation conferring a right to stay, to a third-country national who has no identity documents and has not obtained such documentation from his country of origin, after a national court has released the person concerned on the ground that there is no longer a reasonable prospect of removal within the meaning of Article 15(4) of that directive. However, that Member State must, in such a case, provide the third-country national with written confirmation of his situation'.[430] In this direction also goes the *M and A* as well as the *X* decision that are discussed below in Chapter 2.B.II.2.a.

One may therefore deduce that, according to the ECJ, where removal is factually[431] impossible, there is in principle no claim to the grant of a right to stay in the form of a residence permit or other authorisation to stay (and thus to regularisation) if a return decision cannot be enforced against an individual.[432] This is rather to be understood as a postponement

---

427 Also *Menezes Queiroz*, Illegally Staying 87.

428 Return Handbook 2017, 138 and *Lutz* in *Thym/Hailbronner* Art 14 Return Directive mns 13f; *Menezes Queiroz*, Illegally Staying 103, 176; *Desmond* in *Wiesbrock/Acosta Arcarazo* 76; *Farcy* in *de Bruycker/Cornelisse/Moraru* 447f.

429 ECJ *Mahdi*, para 87.

430 ECJ *Mahdi*, para 89.

431 The ECJ decisions regarding references for a preliminary ruling always concern just those legal issues in order 'to provide the national court with an answer which will be of use to it'; ECJ 4.9.2014, C-119/13 and C-120/13, ECLI:EU:C:2014:2144, *eco cosmetics* and *Raiffeisenbank*, para 32. In *Mahdi*, the migrant did not have any identity documents, therefore the response from the ECJ can only be applied to those cases in which there are factual obstacles to return.

432 ECJ *Mahdi*, paras 87f and see also Fn 428.

of removal under Article 9 of the Return Directive.[433] According to Article 14(2) of the Directive, Member States are only obliged to issue written confirmation;[434] this allows for quick verification of the residency status in case of police controls, for example.[435] The postponement of removal or the written confirmation do not in any case establish a lawful stay.

The opponents of an obligation to regularise refer not only to the decision in *Mahdi* but also to *Abdida*, the first case in which the court dealt with obstacles to return resulting from health issues. According to this decision: 'In the very exceptional cases in which the removal of a third country national suffering a serious illness to a country where appropriate treatment is not available would infringe the principle of non-refoulement, Member States cannot therefore, as provided for in Article 5 of Directive 2008/115, taken in conjunction with Article 19(2) of the Charter, proceed with such removal'.[436] The ECJ also provides that, from a procedural perspective, it is also necessary that the affected individual has a remedy with suspensive effect in order to ensure that the return decision will not be enforced before the domestic authorities and courts have decided on the potential violation of Article 3 ECHR.[437] However, the ECJ does not approach the question whether the possibility or the obligation to regularise results from an obstacle to return, but merely notes that this is at the discretion of the Member States.[438] According to the Court, the persons concerned must be granted such a legal position so that their status rights accord with the obligations resulting from the Return Directive.[439] As the ECJ qualifies such cases as the postponement of removal,[440] the persons concerned thus have the minimum rights under

433 See Chapter 2.B.I.

434 Recital 12 and Art 14(2) Return Directive. The Member States may determine the form and format of the confirmation; cf. *Lutz* in *Thym/Hailbronner* Art 9 Return Directive mn 11.

435 Return Handbook 2017, 138.

436 ECJ *Abdida*, para 48. For detail *Hinterberger/Klammer* in *Filzwieser/Taucher* 120f.

437 ECJ *Abdida*, para 53. Confirmed by ECJ *Gnandi*, paras 54 and 56ff.

438 ECJ *Abdida*, para 54 with reference to Recital 12 Return Directive.

439 For detail *Diekmann*, Menschenrechtliche Grenzen; *Hinterberger/Klammer*, Der Rechtsstatus von Geduldeten: Eine Analyse unter besonderer Berücksichtigung auf das Grundrecht der Menschenwürde in *Salomon* (ed), Der Status im europäischen Asylrecht (2020) 315 (315ff) and in English *Hinterberger/Klammer*, The Legal Status of Tolerated Aliens in Austria through the Lens of the Fundamental Right to Human Dignity, University of Vienna Law Review 2020, 46 (46ff).

440 ECJ *Abdida*, paras 57 and 59.

Article 14 Return Directive.[441] More favourable national provisions are permissible according to Article 4(3) Return Directive, provided that they are compatible with the Directive.[442] The minimum rights are, in particular, the satisfaction of basic needs as well as the provision of emergency health care and the essential treatment of illnesses during the stay in the Member State.[443] Such interpretation by the ECJ opens the floodgates to many practical problems because the discretion granted to the Member States is too broad and thus accompanied by considerable legal uncertainty. This is demonstrated especially in cases of long-term non-returnability and the resulting state of limbo for the person concerned. To sum up the argumentation in *Abdida* that is used by the opponents of an obligation to regularise: postponement under the Return Directive suffices and a regularisation is not needed.

2. Proponents of an obligation to regularise

Before I turn to the proponents of an obligation to regularise, as already stated above in the introduction, I (with the ECJ) consider a person as non-returnable when 'it is not, or has not been, possible to implement a return decision'.[444] *Menezes Queiroz* offers a further definition: 'Non-removable migrants are third-country nationals who, despite their status as irregular migrants, cannot (yet) be removed from EU territory as a result of legal, humanitarian, technical or even policy-related reasons'.[445] The author states that the non-removable persons are in a 'transitory and atypical legal situation'.[446]

The Return Directive requires Member States to choose between return or regularisation.[447] This is not readily apparent from the wording of Article 6(1) Return Directive, whereby the 'Member States shall issue a return decision to any third-country national staying illegally on their territory, without prejudice to the exceptions referred to in paragraphs 2 to 5'. The first sentence of Article 6(4) Return Directive provides, however,

---

441 Cf. *Hörich*, Abschiebungen 127f.

442 Cf. *Hörich*, Abschiebungen 28 with reference to ECJ *El Dridi*.

443 ECJ *Abdida*, paras 59f.

444 ECJ *Mahdi*, para 87.

445 *Menezes Queiroz*, Illegally Staying 182. See also below Fn 491.

446 *Menezes Queiroz*, Illegally Staying 97ff. See also the comments in Introduction C.

447 See Chapter 2.B.I.

that 'Member States may at any moment decide to grant an autonomous residence permit or other authorisation offering a right to stay for compassionate, humanitarian or other reasons to a third-country national staying illegally on their territory'. At first it appears that this provision is not an obligation to regularise as the Member States may decide at their own discretion whether to grant a residence permit to an irregularly staying migrant.[448] Conversely, Article 6(1) Return Directive obliges Member States to issue a return decision. An obligation to regularise could thus only exist in as far as the broad discretion for the Member States is removed entirely.

In my reading, the first sentence of Article 6(4) Return Directive provides an obligation to regularise in two circumstances. I agree with *Hörich* that such obligation exists in all cases in which the return would violate the principle of non-refoulement,[449] yet at the same time I believe that such obligation exists in all cases in which there are permanent obstacles to returning the migrant concerned. As *Acosta Arcarazo*, the arguments for an obligation to regularise in both of these cases are derived from the Return Directive itself:[450] the Member States must terminate the irregular stay either by enforcing the return decision or by granting a right to stay.[451] Issuing the return decision requires enforceability, indeed initiating the return procedure presupposes the possibility that it is successfully implemented to terminate the stay.[452] Member States are therefore faced with an obligation to regularise in all cases in which the decision to return cannot be enforced. The Return Directive gives no scope for long-term irregularity,[453] and it is for this reason that the discretion under the first sentence

448 See Chapter 2.B.I.

449 Cf. *Hörich*, Abschiebungen 125f. See also *Acosta Arcarazo*, The Charter, detention and possible regularization of migrants in an irregular situation under the Returns Directive: Mahdi, CMLRev 2015, 1361 (1377).

450 *Acosta Arcarazo*, CMLRev 2015, 1377f. In the same vein *Desmond*, The Return Directive: clarifying the scope and substance of the rights of migrants facing expulsion from the EU in *King/Kuschminder* (eds), Handbook of Return Migration (2022) 137 (146f).

451 See Chapter 2.B.I.

452 *Hörich*, Abschiebungen 92.

453 As the Commission does not derive an obligation to regularise from the Return Directive and assumes that the Member States will in principle issue a return decision, it also assumes that this practice will increase 'the absolute number of cases in which Member States issue return decisions which cannot be enforced due to practical or legal obstacles for removal'; Return Handbook 2017, 137. Consequent, the Commission accepts situations of long-term irregularity which often arise, as is shown in practice; see Chapter 4.A.I.

of Article 6(4) is in fact dissolved. Such view is best expressed in the European Commission's Return Handbook 2017: 'Member States are obliged to issue a return decision to any third-country national staying illegally on their territory, unless an express derogation is foreseen by Union law [...]. Member States are not allowed to tolerate in practice the presence of illegally staying third-country nationals on their territory without either launching a return procedure or granting a right to stay. This obligation on Member States to either initiate return procedures or to grant a right to stay aims at reducing "grey areas", to prevent exploitation of illegally staying persons and to improve legal certainty for all involved'.[454] This approach – to reduce and prevent 'grey areas' – has been recently also confirmed by the ECJ.[455] The 'postponement of removal'[456] in Article 9 Return Directive also accords with this approach, but by its nature the term 'postponement'[457] incorporates a distinct temporal element that excludes 'permanent' postponement. Consequently, such wording cannot cover cases of permanent non-return.

Such interpretation is supported by the *effet utile* principle ('principle of effectiveness'), whereby provisions of EU law are afforded the most effectiveness as possible.[458] The ECJ attaches considerable weight to the *effet utile* principle in the removal process,[459] with 'an effective removal and repatriation policy [...] with full respect for [...] fundamental rights'[460] at its core. The Court in *Affum* stated, for instance, that imposing a sentence of imprisonment before the transfer to another Member State would 'would delay the triggering of that procedure and thus his actual removal, thereby undermining the directive's effectiveness'.[461] Furthermore, the ECJ has also dealt with the 'effectiveness' of the removal process in relation to rejected applications for international protection in *Gnandi* and with the

454 Return Handbook 2017, 100.

455 ECJ *BZ*, para 57; see, however, also Chapter 2.B.II.2.a.

456 See Chapter 2.B.I.

457 The German and Spanish versions use the term *Aufschub* and *aplazamiento*, respectively.

458 Cf. *Öhlinger/Potacs*, EU-Recht und staatliches Recht: Die Anwendung des Europarechts im innerstaatlichen Bereich[6] (2017) 15.

459 See also ECJ 14.9.2017, C-184/16, ECLI:EU:C:2017:684, *Petrea*, paras 57, 62 and 65; ECJ *X* and *Y*, paras 34–36 and 43f.

460 ECJ *Mahdi*, para 38 with reference to Recitals 2 and 11.

461 ECJ *Affum*, para 88. The German version of the decision refers to *praktische Wirksamkeit* ('practical effectiveness'), see *Hörich*, Abschiebungen 283 with further references.

rights of the defence under the Return Directive in *MG* and *NR*.[462] In addition, 'Article 8(1) of Directive 2008/115 requires Member States, in order to ensure the effectiveness of return procedures, to take all measures necessary to carry out the removal of the person concerned, namely, pursuant to Article 3, point 5, of that directive, the physical transportation of the person concerned out of that Member State'.[463] Each of these findings by the Court is based on the premise of 'an effective removal and repatriation policy […] with full respect for […] fundamental rights'.[464] Accordingly, the discretion afforded to the Member States under Article 6(4) is removed should it affect the 'effectiveness' of the Return Directive and thus be contrary to an effective removal policy. Long-term irregularity contradicts the aforementioned EU requirements and are thus not to be considered as 'effective'.[465]

The ECJ decision in *UN* also needs to be mentioned here. Even though it deals with voluntary return, the ECJ elaborates that the voluntary compliance with the obligation to return has priority over the forced removal.[466] However, the Court then continues that if a person wants to regularise his or her stay within the period of voluntary return, the Return Directive does not preclude this possibility.[467] Said period can be extended by the Member State 'until the completion of a procedure to regularise his or her stay'.[468] According to *UN*, the only limit to such an extension are the grounds laid down in Article 7(4) Return Directive, with no discernible absolute time limit. The ECJ only refers to the fact that any extension must be 'appropriate' and 'necessary because of the specific circumstances of each case'.[469]

The *UN* decision is ground-breaking in so far as the ECJ states for the first that Member States may wait for a person to fulfil the requirements of a specific regularisation before proceeding with deportation. More specifically, the ECJ held that an extension of the period for voluntary departure

---

462 ECJ *Gnandi*, para 50 and ECJ 10.9.2013, C-383/13 PPU, ECLI:EU:C:2013:533, *MG* and *NR*, paras 36 and 41f.

463 ECJ *Zaizoune*, para 33 and also ECJ *TQ*, para 79.

464 ECJ *Mahdi*, para 38 with reference to Recitals 2 and 11.

465 In this sense ECJ *TQ*, para 80; see further ECJ *BZ*, para 57. On the question of effectiveness see also Introduction B., Chapter 2.C.I. and Chapter 4.A.

466 ECJ *UN*, para 50 with further references.

467 ECJ *UN*, para 51.

468 ECJ *UN*, para 58 and see also paras 54 and 56 and see in general Article 7(2) Return Directive.

469 ECJ *UN*, para 62.

'may be extended for a reasonable period in the light of the circumstances of the case, such as the length of stay, the existence of dependent children attending school or the existence of other family and social links'.[470] This development in the case law that specifically refers to Article 6(4) Return Directive is not (yet) laying down an obligation to regularise,[471] but it does explicitly mention regularisations as an effective measure to end irregular stay and confirms the approach taken in this study. The position taken by the ECJ seems convincing due to the necessary and foreseeable steps that Member States and the concerned migrants may take during the extension of the period of voluntary return. In these cases, the end of the irregular stay seems foreseeable in contrast to permanently non-returnable migrants.

Hence and in my reading, the first sentence of Article 6(4) Return Directive establishes an obligation to regularise in the two cases outlined below: the option to return is not enforceable and the effectiveness of the Return Directive cannot be guaranteed otherwise.[472] The right to respect for private and family life under Article 8 ECHR and Article 7 CFR is not analysed in detail here as it would extend far beyond the scope of this study.[473] This also applies to an examination of whether an obligation to regularise can be derived from the inviolability of human dignity under Article 1 CFR[474] or if such a right exists regarding unaccompanied minors.[475]

a) Principle of non-refoulement under the ECHR and CFR

The first group of cases concerns the principle of non-refoulement as understood in human rights law under the ECHR and the CFR. The principle anchored in Article 19(2) CFR will thus also be examined, but not

470 ECJ *UN*, para 63.

471 ECJ *UN*, para 64.

472 Similar with regard to *effet utile*, *Menezes Queiroz*, Illegally Staying 176; similar in relation to permanently non-returnable, *Klarmann*, Illegalisierte Migration 292–294.

473 On ECtHR case law see Fn 343 and 501 and ECJ *X*, paras 83ff.

474 On the relationship between Art 1 CFR, the Return Directive and the State obligation to satisfy the basic needs of non-returnable persons, see *Hinterberger/Klammer* in *Salomon* and *Hinterberger/Klammer*, University of Vienna Law Review 2020.

475 Cf. *Bast/von Harbou/Wessels*, REMAP 202 with reference to ECJ *TQ*.

Article 33 Refugee Convention.[476] If a return and consequently the return decision violate this principle, Member States are obliged to grant a right to stay. As *Hörich* correctly asserts, viewed from a procedural standpoint the grant of a right to stay is the only option if issuing a return decision constitutes a breach of the non-refoulement principle.[477] The discretion under Article 6(4) Return Directive is removed. Interpreting this provision in line with fundamental rights therefore turns the 'may [...] decide' into a 'must [...] decide'.[478] Such interpretation of the Return Directive does not stem from the ECHR, but from Article 51(1) in conjunction with Article 19(2) CFR.[479] In such instances the possibility for the Member State to decide to terminate the irregular stay either by return or regularisation in effect becomes an obligation to regularise. This is to be assessed independently of the fact that Article 9(1)(a) Return Directive also allows for the postponement of removal in such cases. Following the structure of the Directive, postponement is subordinate to the return decision or its implementation. Hence, the postponement may only become relevant if a return decision is issued – in my interpretation this is prohibited due to the non-refoulement principle. The interpretation advocated here is supported by ECJ case law which places the protection of fundamental rights at the core of the interpretation of directives: 'In the final analysis, while the Directive leaves the Member States a margin of appreciation, it is sufficiently wide to enable them to apply the Directive's rules in a manner consistent with the requirements flowing from the protection of fundamental rights'.[480] Furthermore, as has been noted, the Return Directive aims to create an 'an effective removal and repatriation policy [...] with full respect for [...] fundamental rights'.[481]

In March 2021, the ECJ stated in *M and A* that a return decision cannot be issued since this would violate the principle of non-refoulement.[482] This approach was confirmed in November 2022 in the *X* decision.[483] Somehow

---

476 See Chapter 1.B.III.1.

477 *Hörich*, Abschiebungen 125f and see also *Berger/Tanzer* in *Salomon* 247 and *Frik/Fux*, Subsidiärer Schutz und die Akteursproblematik – Vorgaben für eine unions- und gleichheitsrechtskonforme Novellierung, migraLex 2019, 43 (49).

478 In this sense *Acosta Arcarazo*, CMLRev 2015, 1375ff.

479 ECJ *Gnandi*, para 51 and ECJ *X and Y*, paras 27 and 31.

480 ECJ 27.6.2006, C-540/03, ECLI:EU:C:2006:429, *Parliament/Council*, para 104; see also ECJ 4.3.2010, C-578/08, ECLI:EU:C:2010:117, *Chakroun*, paras 44 and 63.

481 ECJ *Mahdi*, para 38 with reference to Recitals 2 and 11.

482 ECJ 24.3.2021, C-673/19, ECLI:EU:C:2021:127, *M and A*, paras 40, 42, 45f.

483 ECJ 22.11.2022, C-69/21, ECLI:EU:C:2022:913, *X*, paras 58f and 76.

puzzling is the decision in *BZ*. In sharp contrast to the position taken in this study, and only three months after the *M and A* decision, the ECJ held that a return decision has to be issued, even though it cannot be enforced because of the principle of non-refoulement.[484] The *M and A* as well as the *X* case thus seem to be an argument against the proposed obligation to regularise as the ECJ does not establish such an obligation.[485]

The analysis of Austrian, German and Spanish law will show that the approach in these legal systems accords in principle with the view expressed here.[486] However, although in my opinion Member States are subject to an obligation to regularise as issuing the return decision would violate the principle of non-refoulement, there are circumstances in which the Member States still issue a return decision but postpone it according to Article 9(1)(a) Return Directive.

b) Permanently non-returnable

The second group concerns cases in which migrants are permanently non-returnable for factual reasons.[487] For example, the return is impossible due to the lack of travel documents,[488] whereby the country of origin refuses to readmit the person concerned. A Member State is obliged to grant a right to stay if the return decision – and consequently the return – is permanently unenforceable, despite taking all necessary measures to implement it.[489] My interpretation accords with the aim of the Return Directive to eliminate all forms of irregularity and uncertainty concerning residency, be this via a return decision and (forced) deportation or by granting a right to stay.[490]

However, questions surround the point in time from which the non-removal of an irregularly staying migrant is deemed permanent. Following the definition advocated by *Lutz*, a person is permanently 'non-returnable' in the sense of a predictive decision if there is no longer a reasonable prospect of removal within the meaning of Article 15(4) Return Directive

---

484 ECJ *BZ*, paras 58f.
485 ECJ *M and A*, para 43 and ECJ *X*, paras 84–87, in particular para 86; cf. *Lutz* in *Thym/Hailbronner* Art 6 Return Directive mn 32a.
486 See Chapter 4.A.
487 See Chapter 1.B.III.1.b.
488 See the Travel Document Regulation.
489 See Fn 463.
490 See above, Chapter 2.B.II.2.

and thus the person concerned has to be released immediately.[491] An indication for determining permanent non-removal could lie in the maximum period for detention, namely 18 months. In principle the detention is limited to 6 months, but this may be extended by a further 12 months if, despite all reasonable efforts by the Member State, the removal is likely to last longer, e.g. due to the aforementioned factual reasons.[492] *Lutz* takes the 18-month *de facto* residency as the basis for his proposed EU regularisation measure aimed at 'non-returnable returnees' who cooperate with the national authorities.[493] One could therefore argue that the Return Directive imposes an obligation upon the Member States to regularise if they cannot remove a person within 18 months.[494]

The starting point for this 18-month period could be the date on which the return decision is legally effective. An alternative would be, for example, the date of the decision. This would be far easier to determine, but the decision is of course only enforceable by the Member State once it has gained legal effect. Ultimately it will be for the ECJ (or the EU legislator)[495] to determine the relevant point at which the migrant becomes permanently non-returnable thus triggering the aforementioned obligation to grant a right to stay.

Where the practice in the Members States is concerned, it should be noted that this currently does not accord with the remarks above. I only need to refer here to Germany, where the competent authorities have the possibility to 'tolerate' persons on a yearly basis, which often results in so-called '*Kettenduldungen*' (literally: chain tolerations).[496] According to the ECtHR, the protection under Article 8 ECHR typically only extends to 'settled migrants',[497] which is why in a similar case the court decided that such 'chain tolerations' are in principle compatible with Article 8 ECHR. However, the protection can also extend to irregularly staying migrants: in *Jeunesse/Netherlands* the ECtHR held that a factual, 'tolerated'

491 *Lutz*, EJML 2018, 30f and 39f. See also ECJ *Mahdi*, para 89.

492 Art 15(5) and (6) Return Directive.

493 *Lutz*, EJML 2018, 48.

494 In the same sense *Bast/von Harbou/Wessels*, REMAP 206.

495 See Chapter 5.

496 In the same sense *Bast/von Harbou/Wessels*, REMAP 201 and see Chapter 4.A.I.2.c.

497 ECtHR *Butt/Norway*, para 78; for criticism *Da Lomba*, Vulnerability and the Right to Respect for Private Life as an Autonomous Source of Protection against Expulsion under Article 8 ECHR, Laws 2017/6/32, 3ff and especially 10ff and *Dembour*, Migrants 442–481.

and irregular stay exceeding 16 years triggered the obligation for the State to grant residency under Article 8 ECHR.[498] In contrast to German law, the term 'tolerated' used by the ECtHR does not refer to formal toleration. The situation is better compared with Spain, where there is a (non-statutory) tolerated and irregular stay.[499] Furthermore, the ECtHR took further factors into consideration, for example the fact that all members of the applicant's family are Dutch nationals and the fact that the applicant did not have a criminal record. The ECtHR was faced with a further unusual case of a 'stateless migrant' in *Hoti/Croatia*[500] in which the applicant had lived for almost 40 years in Croatia, in part legally and in part tolerated by the State, thus having a claim to regularisation.[501] It is to be noted for German law that § 25(5) AufenthG provides that 'a foreigner who is enforceably required to leave the federal territory may be granted a temporary residence permit if departure is impossible in fact or in law' if the person has been tolerated for 18 months and the other requirements are satisfied.[502] There is no legal claim, but the provision can be viewed as a starting point to transpose the aforementioned obligation to grant a right to stay in cases where the situation as non-returnable is permanent. The current '*Ausbildungsduldung*' is another German provision that appears to contradict the Return Directive:[503] it suspends the deportation for the purpose of training for three years.[504]

III. Interim conclusion

In simple terms, Member States must choose between the return procedure or regularisation. They remain free to grant a residence permit at any stage of the process or even after issuing the return decision and thus the

---

498 ECtHR *Jeunesse/Netherlands*, para 116.

499 See Chapter 4.A.I.1.

500 See further also ECtHR 26.6.2012, *Kurić/Slovenia*, 26828/06, paras 339–362.

501 ECtHR *Hoti/Croatia*, paras 118–124; cf. *Swider*, Hoti v. Croatia – a landmark decision by the European Court of Human Rights on residence rights of a stateless person, European Network on Statelessness Blog (3.5.2018), https://www.statelessness.eu/blog/hoti-v-croatia-landmark-decision-european-court-human-rights-residence-rights-stateless-person (31.7.2022).

502 See Chapter 4.C.II.2.

503 ECJ *TQ*, paras 69ff and cf. *Roß*, EuGH, 14.01.2021 - C-441/19: Anforderungen an eine Rückkehrentscheidung gegenüber einem Minderjährigen, NVwZ 2021, 550 (552).

504 See in detail Chapter 4.E.IV.1.

Return Directive does not exclude the possibility for the Member States to regularise irregularly staying migrants. However, ECJ case law and scholarly opinions have fuelled the debate whether there is an obligation to regularise under the Return Directive. I argue that Article 6(4) Return Directive obliges the Member States to grant a right to stay to irregularly staying migrants in two sets of circumstances: the return would violate the principle of non-refoulement as per the ECHR and CFR or where the obstacles preventing the removal of the migrant concerned are permanent. Here the Member States no longer have the discretion awarded by the first sentence of Article 6(4) Return Directive as the alternative, namely return, is not enforceable.

C. EU competences under Article 79(1) TFEU

Following the insights into EU immigration policy concerning irregular migration in general and the Return Directive, the focus now shifts to the mandates and competences anchored in Article 79(1) TFEU: 'The Union shall develop a common immigration policy aimed at ensuring, at all stages, the efficient management of migration flows, fair treatment of third-country nationals residing legally in Member States, and the prevention of, and enhanced measures to combat, illegal immigration and trafficking in human beings'. This raises the question of the objectives, possibilities and barriers that underpin these concepts and how these are to be assessed. The reference to 'immigration' includes both regular and irregular migration as well and the entry and subsequent stay.[505] I will analyse the three relevant fields, placing emphasis on the prevention of, and enhanced measures to combat irregular migration (I.) before addressing the development of a common immigration policy at all stages (II.) and the fair treatment of third-country nationals (III.).

I. Prevention and enhanced measures to combat irregular migration

The Treaty of Maastricht first contained a provision in which 'combatting unauthorized immigration, residence and work' was stipulated as a matter

505 Cf. *Thym* in *Hofmann/Löhr* 195f with further references and *Bast*, Illegaler Aufenthalt und europarechtliche Gesetzgebung, ZAR 2012, 1 (1).

of 'common interest' for the then European Community.[506] However, neither the Treaty of Amsterdam nor the Treaty of Nice contained a similarly worded provision of this kind.[507] It was first in 2009, with the entry into force of the Treaty of Lisbon, that the objectives of EU primary law were redefined and established.[508] Although the proposed Treaty establishing a Constitution for Europe never entered into force, its Article III-267 is identical to the current Article 79(1) TFEU.[509]

Preventing and taking enhanced measures to combat irregular migration reflects the direction of EU immigration policy.[510] As human trafficking is excluded from the following analysis, I will not discuss Article 79(2)(d) TFEU, namely the measures to combat trafficking in persons. The objective and the content of the term 'prevention' are especially clear. The classic risk-avoidance approach shall nip irregular migration in the bud.[511] Particular groups, especially poorly qualified or economic migrants,[512] should be deterred from entering the EU.[513] The EU shall achieve this objective above all through preventative measures.[514]

The second element concerns the proverbial 'fight' against irregular migration. The EU Treaties contain more than 20 uses of the terms 'combat' or 'combatting', for example in relation to crime, terrorism, fraud, discrimination, racism and xenophobia, immigration, or climate change.[515] Literally, 'combat' means 'a fight between two people or things'; 'to try to stop something unpleasant or harmful from happening or increasing'.[516] Reducing the number of irregularly staying migrants has meant that the

506 Art K1(3)(c) TEC.

507 See Art 63(3) and (4) TEC in the version OJ 1997 C 340/1 as well as OJ 2001 C 80/1.

508 Cf. *Peers*, EU Justice 448ff.

509 Also *Weiß* in *Streinz* (ed), EUV/AEUV Kommentar[3] (2018) Art 79 AEUV mn 6. For a comparison see *Hellmann*, Der Vertrag von Lissabon (2009) 239f.

510 *Rossi* in *Calliess/Ruffert* (eds), EUV/AEUV Kommentar[5] (2016) Art 79 AEUV mns 6 and 9 refer to the provision as '*kompetenzleitend*' (literally 'guiding the competence'). *Weiß* in *Streinz* Art 79 AEUV mn 2 refers to '*recht klar definierten Zielen*' ('clearly defined objectives').

511 Cf. *Bast*, Aufenthaltsrecht 75ff.

512 Cf. *Tewocht*, Drittstaatsangehörige 286ff, especially 449.

513 Also *Thym* in *Kluth/Heusch* (eds), BeckOK Ausländerrecht (30th edn, 1.7.2020) Art 79 AEUV mn 15 with regard to the competence in Art 79(2)(c) TFEU.

514 See for instance COM(2001) 672 final, 9.

515 TEU: Arts 3(2), 43; TFEU: Arts 10, 19(1), 67(3), 75, 79(1), 79(2)(d), 86(1) and (4), 88(1), 151, 153(1)(j), 168(1) and (5), 191(1), 208(1), 325(2) and (4).

516 *Cambridge Dictionary*, 'combat', https://dictionary.cambridge.org/dictionary/english/combat (31.7.2022).

'fight' against irregular migration has become a paradigm of EU immigration policy. One reason for this is the control Member States seek to have over the composition of its resident population.[517] *Ter Steeg* has stated that the political direction of immigration policy in the field of 'illegal' immigration clearly relates to warding off irregular migrants,[518] since irregular migration is viewed exclusively as a negative form of migration.[519] *Cholewinski* even refers to a 'war on irregular migration',[520] whereas *Engbersen* is accurate in describing the restrictive policy towards irregularly entering and staying migrants with the expression 'Panopticon Europe'.[521] The risk-aversion approach considers certain categories of migrants a particular problem, specifically those without entry or residence permits.[522] In this respect the control approach under administrative law refers foremost to the prevention and monitoring of dangerous individuals.[523] *Costello* even goes so far as to claim that 'combatting' irregular migration within the EU has developed a life of its own: 'This EU policy discourse on illegal migration sets up an institutional practice around "illegal" migration that is detached from the subtleties of the law'.[524] *Boswell* opines that irregular migration is a necessary structural feature of restrictive immigration policies and of liberal democratic states.[525] Despite these political developments, the constitutional purposes and the competences do not specify the content of 'combat'. It would thus be useful to interpret this term as being fulfilled if the number of irregularly staying migrants is reduced by whatever means.[526] Such interpretation could also apply to the German (*Bekämpfung*), Spanish (*lucha*), Portuguese (*combate*), French

517 *Hampshire*, Immigration.

518 *Ter Steeg*, Einwanderungskonzept 423 with further refences; cf. also *Cholewinski*, European Policy on Irregular Migration: Human Rights Lost? in *Bogusz/Cholewinski/Cygan/Szyszczak* (eds), Irregular Migration and Human Rights: Theoretical, European and International Perspectives (2004) 159 (159f).

519 See also *Niessen*, International Migration on the EU Foreign Policy Agenda, EJML 1999, 483 (489, 493).

520 Cf. *Cholewinski* in *Baldaccini/Guild/Toner* 305.

521 *Engbersen* in *Guiraudon/Joppke* 223. Cf. on the term panopticism *Foucault*, Discipline and Punish: The Birth of the Prison[2] (1995) 195ff.

522 Cf. *Bast*, Aufenthaltsrecht 75ff.

523 Cf. *Bast*, Aufenthaltsrecht 79ff.

524 *Costello*, Human Rights 66 refers in this context to *Samers*, An Emerging Geopolitics of 'Illegal' Immigration in the European Union, EJML 2004, 25.

525 *Boswell* in *Azoulai/De Vries* 42ff.

526 See COM(2015) 453 final, 2 or COM(2017) 200 final.

(*lutte*), Slovenian (*boj*), Italian (*contrasto*), Polish (*zwlaczenie*) and Danish (*bekæmpelse*) versions.

This also arises in view of the link between the purposes in Article 79(1) TFEU and the competences listed in Article 79(2) TFEU – the 'central provision'[527] for all matters of immigration law.[528] Measures under Article 79(2) TFEU may only be adopted in order to fulfil the mandates under Article 79(1) TFEU.[529] This means specifically that every EU legislative act in the areas of immigration must fulfil one of the aforementioned purposes – it must therefore be possible for the measure in question to achieve the purpose, at least in the abstract. *Rossi* accurately describes this as a 'functional limitation'.[530] However, the TFEU is neutral with regard to the question of how the specified purpose is achieved, just as long as it can be achieved.

Each EU legislative act must therefore fulfil a particular purpose. The fact that a measure must at least be able to achieve a particular objective on the basis of primary law requirements indicates that primary law requires such acts to have a particular degree of effectiveness. This allows one to define what constitutes the effectiveness of legislation or a legislative provision, which is especially important for the theory developed in this study: 'combatting' irregularly staying migrants at Union level will be more effective with EU regularisations that supplement the EU's current return policy. Furthermore, these comments also play a key role in examining the second (and third) research question.[531]

Based on the above, the question whether the EU can pass a regularisation legislation to 'combat' irregular migration as per Article 79(1) TFEU or whether such legislation must serve to prevent irregular migration, or concerns return,[532] can be answered as follows: a regularisation act must accord with the purpose of 'combatting' irregular migration. In this respect the Council of the European Union views regularisations as an instrument in the fight against 'illegal immigration'. Accordingly, the 2008 European Pact on Immigration and Asylum leaves the Member States the

527 *Bast* in *Fischer-Lescano/Kocher/Nassibi* 76.

528 For detail, Chapter 2.D.

529 ECJ 18.12.2014, C-81/13, ECLI:EU:C:2014:2449, *United Kingdom/Council*, paras 41f; ECJ 26.12.2013, C-431/11, ECLI:EU:C:2013:589, *United Kingdom/Council*, para 63.

530 *Rossi* in *Calliess/Ruffert* Art 79 AEUV mn 9 (*'funktionale Begrenzung'*).

531 See Introduction B.

532 In this sense, *Thym* in *Kluth/Heusch* Art 79 AEUV mn 2.

option to use case-by-case regularisations.[533] The Member States should, however, refrain from so-called regularisation programmes.[534] The discretion not to issue a return decision but to instead award a residence permit to an irregularly staying migrant was subsequently codified in the Return Directive.[535]

However, under the *Realpolitik* standpoint, an EU regularisation measure is not on the horizon as the EU institutions are hardly favourable towards regularisations, fuelling remarks such as an 'anti-regularization ethos'.[536] Furthermore, *Lutz* has noted that, even where non-returnable migrants are concerned, a harmonised approach at EU level was not in the common interests of the Member States in 2018 as they consider that the existing EU *acquis* would suffice.[537]

II. Development of a common immigration policy aimed at ensuring, at all stages, the effective management of migration flows

The TFEU stipulates that the substantive requirements in Article 79(1) TFEU are to be ensured in the course of developing a common immigration policy at all stages and for the effective management of migration flows. In referring to the progressive harmonisation of this policy area, *Muzak* defines 'at all stages' as meaning that the immigration policy has to develop on a step-by-step basis and successively.[538]

Thym considers that the Treaty obligation to ensure effective migration management is based on a comprehensive regulatory approach 'in all stages'.[539] This means that EU migration law is to be understood as a 'pro-

533 *Council of the European Union*, European Pact on Immigration and Asylum (24.9.2008), 13440/08, 7.

534 On this term see Chapter 1.B.I. and Chapter 3.C.I.

535 In this sense, *Costello*, Human Rights 99 and see in detail Chapter 2.B.I.

536 *Costello*, Human Rights 98ff. In a similar direction, *Desmond* in *Wiesbrock/Acosta Arcarazo* 72–74; cf. also *Machjer/Strik*, EJML 2021, 122ff and *Bast/von Harbou/Wessels*, REMAP 205ff as well as in detail Chapter 5.A.

537 *Lutz*, EJML 2018, 49f.

538 *Muzak* in *Mayer/Stöger* (eds), Kommentar zu EUV und AEUV (1.12.2012, rdb.at) Art 79 AEUV mn 2. Similarly *Kortländer* in *Schwarze/Becker/Hatje/Schoo* (eds), EU-Kommentar[4] (2019) Art 79 AEUV mn 4.

539 *Thym* in *Kluth/Heusch* Art 79 AEUV mn 1. See also *Kortländer* in *Schwarze/Becker/Hatje/Schoo* Art 79 AEUV mn 5.

cess of a change in legal status'[540] and thus at the end of each process there is either a 'long-term visa or residence permit' pursuant to Article 79(2)(a) TFEU or a 'removal and repatriation' pursuant to Article 79(2)(c).[541] Expanding on *Thym's* view, the EU legislator is urged to include in its policy all stages and circumstances of third-country nationals. The latter is also arguable upon closer analysis of the meaning of the term 'immigration policy' as this includes both regular and irregular migration as well as the entry and subsequent stay.[542] This is supported by the Article 63(3)(a) TEC in the version of the Treaty of Nice (now Article 79(2)(a) TFEU), which allowed for the adoption of 'measures on immigration policy' and thus to establish residence rights for third-country nationals.[543]

A combination of these two approaches is the most convincing to interpret this requirement under EU law. *Muzak* states that the term 'stage'[544] implies a temporal aspect which has to be viewed with respect to the constant political developments and allows for full harmonisation within the limitations of Article 79(4) and (5) TFEU.[545] In turn, *Thym* considers that EU immigration policy has to cover all third-country nationals on a personal and substantive level, regardless of their residency status.

III. Fair treatment of third-country nationals

Under Article 79(1) TFEU the EU common immigration policy shall aim at ensuring the fair treatment of third-country nationals residing legally in Member States – this aim accords with the competence provided in Article 79(2)(b) TFEU.[546] Furthermore, Article 67(2) TFEU stipulates that EU common policy on asylum, immigration and external border control shall be fair towards third-country nationals. By not limiting the personal scope of application to third-country nationals residing legally, the EU

540 '*Prozess rechtlichen Statuswandels*': *Thym* in *Kluth/Heusch* Art 79 AEUV mn 2 with reference to *Thym*, Migrationsverwaltungsrecht (2010) 18–24.
541 See Chapter 2.D.I.–II.
542 *Bast*, ZAR 2012, 1; cf. also *Thym* in *Hofmann/Löhr* 195f with further references.
543 See Chapter 2.D.I.
544 Note that *Muzak* refers to the German version of the TFEU, i.e. '*Phase*'.
545 On Art 79(4) and (5) TFEU see Chapter 2.D.II.1.–2.
546 See above all *Bast*, Aufenthaltsrecht 143; for detail see below Chapter 2.D.II.

immigration policy thus has to be fair towards all third-country nationals, even those without a right to stay.[547]

Nonetheless, the notion of fair treatment is not sufficiently precise to allow for conclusions on its meaning or significance. For instance, *Bast* views the notion as an equitable principle that calls for a political search to balance the interests concerned, but without determining the content of the result.[548] *Rossi* goes furthest in his interpretation, noting that the most striking aspect is the vagueness of fair treatment under Article 79(1) TFEU, which certainly means more than granting those rights that are guaranteed by the fundamental rights in national law and under the ECHR and CFR.[549] As the fundamental rights under the CFR in principle form the yardstick for irregularly staying migrants,[550] it is questionable how in *Rossi's* opinion further rights can be derived if Article 79(1) TFEU is itself 'vague'. *Peyrl* takes a different standpoint by interpreting 'fair treatment' as a quasi-objective requirement subsuming thereunder the access to the labour market.[551] For *Peyrl,* fair treatment also encompasses access to the labour market, since denying third-country nationals access to the labour market without objective justification would contradict EU primary law as this would not constitute fair treatment.

Each of these different possible interpretations allow for the assertion that the EU legislator has to take into account all third-country nationals, i.e. also irregularly staying migrants.[552] In line with developing a common immigration policy at all stages, a balance must be found between the conflicting interests of the Member States or the EU and the groups of persons concerned. As the example of non-returnable persons clearly demonstrates, the EU ignores the residency situation of particular categories of migrants.[553] Moreover, as is readily apparent from the above, this does not accord with either of the stated purposes under EU primary law. Whether such a broad interpretation as proposed by *Rossi* or *Peyrl* can be derived from Article 79(1) TFEU cannot be conclusively clarified at this point as

547 Cf. *Peers*, EU Justice 449; coming to the same result *Kortländer* in *Schwarze/Becker/Hatje/Schoo* Art 79 AEUV mn 5.

548 *Bast*, Aufenthaltsrecht 143. See also *Thym*, CMLRev 2013, 722 Fn 66 with further references.

549 *Rossi* in *Calliess/Ruffert* Art 79 AEUV mn 6.

550 See *Hörich*, Abschiebungen 30–33.

551 *Peyrl*, Zuwanderung und Zugang zum Arbeitsmarkt von Drittstaatsangehörigen in Österreich (2018) 22.

552 Similarly *Peyrl*, Arbeitsmarkt 22.

553 See Chapter 2.B.II.2.b.

it requires a more in-depth discussion. Nonetheless, it hardly allows for a subjective right, but there are good reasons supporting the proposal for a principle of 'quasi-objectivity'.[554]

D. Primary law competences under Article 79(2) TFEU

Following the analysis of the purposes derived from the TFEU the spotlight now shifts to the question whether and, if so,[555] what competences the EU has in the field of irregular migration and regularisations.[556] The question of how the specified purpose is achieved has been discussed above.[557] The relevant competence is anchored in Article 79(2) TFEU. The EU and the Member States share competence in the principal area of freedom, security and justice.[558] This means that the Member States may exercise their competences as long as and to the extent that the EU has not legislated in that particular area:[559] EU legislation can prevent Member States from passing 'parallel rules'.[560] However, here the limitations under Article 79(4) and (5) TFEU as well as the principles of proportionality and subsidiarity are to be observed.[561]

The competences correspond in essence to Article 63(3) and (4) TEC introduced via the Treaty of Maastricht and amended via the Treaty of Amsterdam and the Treaty of Nice. Article III-267 of the proposed Treaty establishing a Constitution for Europe not only made linguistic changes but also expanded the content.[562] The Constitution never entered into force, but its Article III-267 is identical to Article 79(1) TFEU. The competences allow the EU to cover all immigration matters,[563] though neither

554 *Peyrl*, Arbeitsmarkt 22 referring to a *Quasi-Sachlichkeitsgebot*.

555 *Thym* in *Grabitz/Hilf/Nettesheim* Art 79 AEUV mn 29 refers here to the 'whether' in relation to the conferral of the residence permit and to the 'how' in relation to the scope of the status.

556 Cf. the question already posed by *Bast*, ZAR 2012, 1. See further also *Bast* in *Fischer-Lescano/Kocher/Nassibi*.

557 See above, Chapter 2.C.I.

558 Art 4(2)(j) TFEU.

559 *Bast*, Aufenthaltsrecht 144.

560 Cf. *Öhlinger/Potacs*, EU-Recht 16f.

561 See especially Chapter 2.D.II.1.–2. and Chapter 2.D.IV.

562 Cf. *Kortländer* in *Schwarze/Becker/Hatje/Schoo* Art 79 AEUV mn 1.

563 As expressed in the Final Report of the Working Group X Freedom, Security and Justice with regard to the former competences stipulated in Art 63(3) and (4) TEC in the version OJ 2001 C 80/1; *European Convention*, CONV 426/02

the competences nor the constitutional purposes provide details on how these are to be performed.[564]

As a final remark, the correct competence is decisive for the legality of EU legislative acts, otherwise the act may be annulled following judicial review under Article 263 TFEU. According to ECJ case law, this arises from the main aim of a measure.[565] It is also possible to culminate a number of competences, depending on the legislation.[566] The competences in Article 79(2) TFEU do not entail different legal consequences,[567] thus the EU legislator can avoid the annulment of a measure by merely selecting the relevant competences.

The following sections will first analyse the possible competences (I.–III.) before addressing the principles of proportionality and subsidiarity (IV.).

I. Conditions of entry and residence

Article 79(2)(a) TFEU states that the EU may adopt measures concerning 'the conditions of entry and residence, and standards on the issue by Member States of long-term visas and residence permits'. The provision concerns the core of EU immigration law,[568] though the competence is executed in a decentral manner by the national authorities.[569]

The provision does not distinguish whether the addressees of the rule reside in or outside of the EU or whether or not they have a residence

---

(2.12.2002) 5. Also in this sense *Thym* in *Grabitz/Hilf/Nettesheim* Art 79 AEUV mn 23 and *Kortländer* in *Schwarze/Becker/Hatje/Schoo* Art 79 AEUV mn 1.

564 Cf. *Bast*, Aufenthaltsrecht 145.

565 On identifying the 'correct' legal basis ECJ 6.11.2008, C-155/07, ECLI:EU:C:2008:605, *Parliament/Council*, para 35; ECJ 19.7.2012, C-130/10, ECLI:EU:C:2012:472, *Parliament/Council*, para 43; ECJ 6.5.2014, C-43/12, ECLI:EU:C:2014:298, *Commission/Parliament* and *Council*, para 30; in this sense also ECJ 17.3.1993, C-155/91, ECLI:EU:C:1993:98, *Commission/Council*, paras 19 and 21. See also the opinion of Advocate General Kokott 17.7.2014, C-81/13, ECLI:EU:C:2014:2114, *United Kingdom/Council*, para 49.

566 See also *Rossi* in *Calliess/Ruffert* Art 79 AEUV mn 10 and *Thym* in *Grabitz/Hilf/Nettesheim* Art 79 AEUV mn 29.

567 Cf. *Bast*, Aufenthaltsrecht 147.

568 *Thym* in *Grabitz/Hilf/Nettesheim* Art 79 AEUV mn 23.

569 Cf. *Bast*, Aufenthaltsrecht 146; similarly *Thym* in *Grabitz/Hilf/Nettesheim* Art 79 AEUV mn 34.

permit.[570] Consequently, this provides the basis for the EU to determine regularisations.[571] An EU measure could establish the lawful residence of irregularly staying migrants. It would be possible on the one hand to stipulate specific requirements for awarding residence permits but also, on the other hand, the substantive as well as formal requirements for the loss or revocation of the residence permit.[572]

The term 'residence permit' stipulated in primary law is of considerable significance for the group of persons analysed here, namely third-country nationals residing in a Member State.[573] It has been defined in EU secondary legislation, namely in Article 1(2)(a) Residence Permit Regulation,[574] which excludes visas from its scope. The period for which the permit is valid arises from a systematic interpretation of the terms 'short-stay' and 'long-term' used in EU primary law.[575] Article 79(2)(a) TFEU concerns the long-term visa, whereas Article 77(2)(a) TFEU refers to short-stay residence permits (for instance, visas under the Visa Regulation).[576] Prior to the Treaty of Lisbon, EU primary law drew a distinction based upon a three-month stay,[577] but this was repealed with the new Treaty. Nonetheless, the majority of scholars continue to use such 'benchmark'.[578]

---

570 *Bast* in *Fischer-Lescano/Kocher/Nassibi* 88; cf. the wording of Art 79(2)(a) AEUV.

571 Expressly agreeing *Bast*, Aufenthaltsrecht 147; *Thym* in *Kluth/Heusch* Art 79 AEUV mn 10; *Schieber*, Komplementärer Schutz 311f. Affirming in principle, but not exploring the question, *Rossi* in *Calliess/Ruffert* Art 79 AEUV mn 11; *Kotzur* in *Geiger/Khan/Kotzur* (eds), EUV/AEUV Kommentar[6] (2017) Art 79 AEUV mn 6; *Weiß* in *Streinz* Art 79 AEUV mns 12f; *Hoppe* in *Lenz/Borchardt* (eds), EU-Verträge Kommentar[6] (2012) Art 79 AEUV mns 3f; *Muzak* in *Mayer/Stöger* Art 79 AEUV mn 6; *Progin-Theuerkauf* in *Van der Groeben/Schwarze/Hatje* (eds), Europäisches Unionsrecht: Band 2[7] (2015) Art 79 AEUV mn 15; *Peers*, EU Justice 326ff. Contrary view, *Menezes Queiroz*, Illegally Staying 170. The author comes to the conclusion – albeit without clear reasoning – that the EU does not have any competence to pass regularisations at EU level.

572 Cf. *Bast*, Aufenthaltsrecht 145 and *Thym* in *Kluth/Heusch* Art 79 AEUV mns 9–11. For instance, the procedural requirements in the Return Directive may serve as an illustration; cf. *Hörich*, Abschiebungen 71ff and Chapter 2.B.

573 See the wording of Art 79(2)(a) TFEU; cf. also *Muzak* in *Mayer/Stöger* Art 79 AEUV mn 6; for a differing opinion *Bast*, Aufenthaltsrecht 146.

574 See also Art 2(2)(c) Single Permit Directive.

575 Cf. *Thym* in *Grabitz/Hilf/Nettesheim* Art 79 AEUV mn 24.

576 In detail *Muzak* in *Mayer/Stöger* Art 77 AEUV mns 21ff and *Peyrl*, Arbeitsmarkt 19–21.

577 See Art 62(2)(b) TEC in the version OJ 2001 C 80/1.

578 *Muzak* in *Mayer/Stöger* Art 77 AEUV mns 14, 21 and Art 79 AEUV mn 1; *Hoppe* in *Lenz/Borchardt* Art 77 AEUV mn 9 assumes a strict 3-month limit; also *Weiß* in *Streinz* Art 79 AEUV mn 12, who views the 3-month limit as 'conveyed'; see

Accordingly, long-term stays under Article 79 TFEU are understood as those longer than three months whereas short-term applies to stays up to three months.

II. Status and free movement rights of legally resident third-country nationals

According to Article 79(2)(b) TFEU, the EU can regulate 'the definition of the rights of third-country nationals residing legally in a Member State, including the conditions governing freedom of movement and of residence in other Member States'. The competence thereby encompasses the authority to define the status and rights of free movement of legally resident third-country nationals.[579] This aspect is linked to the purpose of ensuring fair treatment of third-country nationals.[580]

The competence does not appear at first to be decisive for a regularisation act. Closer analysis tells a different story, however: the nature of the status rights accompanying the residence permit is a key issue. On the one hand, third-country nationals granted such a right to stay under a regularisation framework could gain access to employment or social security benefits.[581] On the other hand, the EU legislator is afforded the possibility to design the right in such a way that – alongside the issuing Member State – it also has an effect across the entire EU and thus in all Member States.[582] In consequence, residence rights granted within a legislative framework on regularisation could not only include certain status rights but could also acquire an effect similar to the right to free movement throughout the EU which Article 21(1) TFEU grants to Union citizens.

---

also *Kortländer* in *Schwarze/Becker/Hatje/Schoo* Art 79 AEUV mn 10 and *Rossi* in *Calliess/Ruffert* Art 79 AEUV mn 11. More cautiously, *Thym* in *Grabitz/Hilf/Nettesheim* Art 79 AEUV mn 24, who refers to a few months. *Bast*, Aufenthaltsrecht 146 also does not see a strict limit and affords the EU legislator flexibility.

579 Cf. *Muzak* in *Mayer/Stöger* Art 79 AEUV mns 13ff.

580 Cf. *Bast*, Aufenthaltsrecht 143 and see Chapter 2.C.III.

581 Cf. *Weiß* in *Streinz* Art 79 AEUV mn 15; *Muzak* in *Mayer/Stöger* Art 79 AEUV mn 13; *Kortländer* in *Schwarze/Becker/Hatje/Schoo* Art 79 AEUV mn 18; in depth *Bast*, Aufenthaltsrecht 147–152.

582 See *Bast*, Aufenthaltsrecht 146; *Muzak* in *Mayer/Stöger* Art 79 AEUV mns 14f; *Thym* in *Grabitz/Hilf/Nettesheim* Art 79 AEUV mn 31. For detail see Chapter 2.D.I.

1. Integration

Article 79(4) permits the EU to provide 'support and coordination'[583] and to promote the integration of third-country nationals: 'The European Parliament and the Council, acting in accordance with the ordinary legislative procedure, may establish measures to provide incentives and support for the action of Member States with a view to promoting the integration of third-country nationals residing legally in their territories, excluding any harmonisation of the laws and regulations of the Member States'. Measures on this basis may not comprehensively regulate the field of integration. According to *Kotzur*, Article 79(4) TFEU should secure a degree of variety of national measures in the field of integration, with the author emphasising the role of State sovereignty.[584] Nonetheless, *Thym* notes that certain aspects may be harmonised at EU level to the extent in so far as they do not concern integration on the whole.[585]

Kortländer understands the notion integration as the social security benefits, language and other development programmes aimed specifically at immigrants.[586] In his view a harmonisation of these aspects would contradict Article 79(4) TFEU. However, this interpretation pushes the boundaries of the possible meanings as clarification is lacking on the core content on integration.[587] The weightier argument is that harmonisation of individual aspects of integration must indeed be possible under the respective competences as these would otherwise be limited too greatly. Such an open concept therefore cannot allow for the conclusion whereby the competences are curtailed.

In my opinion, one may conclude that the EU legislator could equip residence rights with social security benefits (or free movement rights) in future EU regularisation legislation. Such rights would concern and regulate aspects surrounding integration without being affected by the limitations under Article 79(4) TFEU.

---

583 Art 2(5) TFEU; cf. *Thym* in *Kluth/Heusch* Art 79 AEUV mn 22 and in *Schwarze/Becker/Hatje/Schoo* Art 79 AEUV mn 24.

584 Cf. *Kotzur* in *Geiger/Khan/Kotzur* Art 79 AEUV mn 11.

585 *Thym* in *Kluth/Heusch* Art 79 AEUV mn 24.

586 *Kortländer* in *Schwarze/Becker/Hatje/Schoo* Art 79 AEUV mn 19.

587 See just *Hailbronner/Arévalo* in *Hailbronner/Thym* (eds), EU Immigration and Asylum Law. A Commentary[2] (2016) Art 4 Family Reunification Directive mn 20.

2. Access to the labour market

Article 79(5) TFEU allows the Member States to retain the right to 'determine volumes of admission of third-country nationals coming from third countries to their territory in order to seek work, whether employed or self-employed'. Member States may therefore introduce quantitative restrictions on access to the labour market, such as quotas.[588] The wording 'in order to seek work' is, however, not ideal as the quotas on residence permits should apply to those in employment and not those seeking employment, which is to be understood as 'taking up employment for the first time'.[589] Article 79(5) TFEU is therefore aimed at economic migration.

The wording 'coming from third countries to their territory' is especially relevant for this study. It is clear that the competence retained by the Member States only applies to third-country nationals travelling (for the first time) from outside of the EU to a Member State, thereby entering the EU.[590] '[C]oming from third countries' therefore excludes the application to third-country nationals who travel from one Member State to another.

In this study, the persons concerned are already staying irregularly in a Member State.[591] There can be no objection on the basis of Article 79(5) TFEU if a regularisation at EU level does not grant access to the labour market – this is readily apparent from the wording 'to seek work, whether employed or self-employed'. However, it is unclear if the Member States could object under Article 79(5) TFEU should the EU introduce regularisations that grant third-country nationals access to the labour market alongside a right to stay.

On the one hand, one could argue that the Member States may also regulate the access to the labour market with regard to those persons who have already entered irregularly. Such national quotas that apply to third-country nationals entering lawfully could thus be circumvented by irregular entry. According to Article 79(5) TFEU, the Member States could

588 Cf. *Peyrl*, Arbeitsmarkt 16–18 and *Rossi* in *Calliess/Ruffert* Art 79 AEUV mn 34.

589 *Bast*, Aufenthaltsrecht 151 with reference to *Ter Steeg*, Einwanderungskonzept 458f.

590 See also *European Convention*, CONV 426/02, 2.12.2002, 5; further *Peyrl*, Arbeitsmarkt 17f; *Muzak* in *Mayer/Stöger* Art 79 AEUV mn 29; *Kortländer* in *Schwarze/Becker/Hatje/Schoo* Art 79 AEUV mn 6; *Peers*, Legislative Update: EU Immigration and Asylum Competence and Decision-Making in the Treaty of Lisbon, EJML 2008, 219 (244).

591 See Chapter 1.A.II.1.

thus apply quotas to third-country nationals entering irregularly who have not since resided lawfully and had access to the labour market.

On the other hand, there is the legitimate opinion that the wording 'from third countries [...] in order to seek work, whether employed or self-employed' covers those persons who actually enter from a third country[592] for the purpose of entering into employment and not those who are already resident.[593] It is therefore irrelevant if the third-country national has entered regularly or irregularly since the TFEU does not make such specific reference.

This study proposes the following interpretation: Article 79(5) TFEU would not apply and could not be invoked by the Member States if EU legislation were to grant access to the labour market together with a right to stay. The main purpose underlying Article 79(5) TFEU is to allow for quotas of economic migrants in the sense of those taking up employment for the first time.[594] A possible Regularisation Directive would not aim foremost at economic migration, but rather at 'combatting' irregular stays.[595] In this respect, the Student and Researchers Directive is comparable secondary legislation as it aims at education, not economic migration.[596] The residence permit[597] for students also includes access to the labour market;[598] national quotas on admission are excluded.[599] The Student and Researchers Directive may therefore be compared with a future Regularisation Directive as neither are primarily concerned with economic migration.

---

592 See *Peyrl*, Arbeitsmarkt 17f.

593 Also *Peers*, EJML 2008, 244. *Bast*, Aufenthaltsrecht 150 refers to *'ansässigen'* (resident) third-country nationals, which does not offer clarity as to whether lawful residency is required.

594 *Bast*, Aufenthaltsrecht 151 with reference to *Ter Steeg*, Einwanderungskonzept 458f.

595 See Chapter 5 on the further objectives.

596 Recitals 37 and 39 Students and Researchers Directive.

597 See Arts 11 and 17f Students and Researchers Directive.

598 Art 24 Students and Researchers Directive. According to Art 24(3) Students and Researchers Directive, the Member State shall determine the maximum number of hours per week, which shall not be less than 15 hours per week. As such, one could object that students do not qualify as workers under Art 45(1) TFEU. However, this is contrary to ECJ case law which provides that a person qualifies as a worker for the purposes of the TFEU even if they work less than ten hours per week; ECJ 4.2.2010, C-14/09, ECLI:EU:C:2010:57, *Hava Genc/Land Berlin*, paras 25f.

599 Recital 39 and Art 6 Students and Researchers Directive.

Each of these aspects leads to the assertion that a Regularisation Directive would prevent the Member States from imposing national quotas on third-country nationals regularised on the basis of an EU Regularisation Directive and limiting their (first) access to the labour market. The reservation according to Article 79(5) TFEU does not apply as the Regularisation Directive does not concern economic migration. The quantitative restrictions on access to the labour market via national quotas would thus violate EU primary law.

III. Illegal immigration and unauthorised residence

Article 79(2)(c) TFEU provides that the EU 'shall' adopt measures concerning 'illegal immigration and unauthorised residence, including removal and repatriation of persons residing without authorisation'. It therefore allows not only for preventative measures but also those to carry out return obligations.[600] This competence formed the basis for the Return Directive, for instance.[601]

The competence under Article 79(2)(c) TFEU falls within the broader policy objective to prevent and combat 'illegal immigration'.[602] 'Unauthorised residence' is understood as complementing 'residing legally in a Member State',[603] a distinction in primary law which is manifested in secondary law in the Return Directive. Article 79(2)(c) TFEU thus allows to enact rules regarding the residence of 'illegally staying third-country nationals'.[604] This competence may therefore not serve as a basis for a lawful stay and thus does not come into question for enacting regularisations.[605]

However, the EU legislator could certainly harmonise the issue of legal toleration,[606] for example as far as several successive tolerations reach a minimum duration.[607] For secondary law, the aforementioned postpone-

600 *Bast*, Aufenthaltsrecht 147; see also *Thym* in *Kluth/Heusch* Art 79 AEUV mn 15.

601 More precisely, the Return Directive was based on Art 63(3)(b) TEC in the version OJ 2001 C 80/1.

602 Cf. *Bast* in *Fischer-Lescano/Kocher/Nassibi* 77–79.

603 Art 79(2(b) and (c) TFEU; cf. *Bast*, Aufenthaltsrecht 147.

604 Art 3 No. 2 Return Directive.

605 Cf. *Thym* in *Kluth/Heusch* Art 79 AEUV mn 15 and *Bast*, Aufenthaltsrecht 146f.

606 *Schieber*, Komplementärer Schutz 312 refers to an '*Aussetzung der Abschiebung*' ('suspension of removal') in EU law.

607 Cf. *Bast*, Es gibt kein solidarisches Asylsystem in Europa, Verfassungsblog (21.10.2013), http://verfassungsblog.de/es-gibt-kein-solidarisches-asylsystem-in-e

ment of removal under Article 9 Return Directive could offer a possible link.[608] Toleration at Member State level could therefore serve as a model, which exists in different forms in both Austria and Germany and, under the respective national law, does not constitute lawful residence.[609] Article 79(2)(c) TFEU would exclude the grant of status rights to tolerated persons and to irregularly staying migrants on the basis of EU law.[610] The grant of free movement rights within the EU is already ruled out as the persons concerned do not even have a right to stay in a Member State.

IV. Proportionality and subsidiarity

Measures passed in accordance with Article 79(2) TFEU must adhere to the principles of proportionality and subsidiarity – general principles which apply to all EU legislative acts.[611] The principle of proportionality provides that EU legislative acts 'shall not exceed what is necessary to achieve the objects of the Treaties'.[612] In accordance with the principle of subsidiarity the EU shall only act in areas that do not fall within its exclusive competence if the objective of the proposed action 'can rather, by reason of the scale or effects of the proposed action, better be better achieved at Union level'.[613] The European Commission examines both principles in relation to its proposals for legislation.[614]

Problems do not arise with regard to the principle of proportionality, but the question remains whether a Regularisation Directive could breach the principle of subsidiarity. The ECJ examines whether in passing legislation 'the EU legislator was entitled to consider, on the basis of a detailed statement, that the objective of the proposed action could be better

---

uropa/ (31.7.2022) as well as *Bast/Thym*, Streitgespräch zum rechtlichen Zustand des europäischen und deutschen Asylsystems, vorgänge 208 Issue 4/2014, 4 (8f).

608 See Chapter 2.B.I.

609 § 31(1a) No. 3 FPG and § 60a(3) AufenthG and in detail Chapter 4.A.I.3.b. and Chapter 4.A.I.2.b.

610 Cf. *Bast* in *Fischer-Lescano/Kocher/Nassibi* 78.

611 Art 5(3) and (4) TEU as well as Art 69 TFEU; cf. *Thym* in *Kluth/Heusch* Art 69 AEUV mns 1f and *Thym* in *Kluth/Heusch* Art 79 AEUV mn 9 with regard to competence referred to here.

612 Art 5(4) TEU.

613 Art 5(3) TEU.

614 Cf. Protocol (No 2) on the application of the principles of subsidiarity and proportionality, OJ 2008 C 115/206.

achieved at EU level'.[615] The principle of subsidiarity could potentially be breached if one were to argue that it is not necessary for the EU to act as sufficient regularisation measures have already been created at national level, as shown in Part II.[616] However, there are several objections to this argument.

Firstly, the return deficit reveals that the mandate to 'combat' irregular migration cannot be achieved to a sufficient degree by the Member States alone.

Secondly, the Member States indeed regulate regularisations in various different forms,[617] yet each regularisation is accompanied by the grant of a right to stay. In this way, the issuing Member State establishes through regularisations the lawful residence of formerly irregularly staying migrants.[618]

Thirdly, each of such residence permits issued by a Member State entitle third-country nationals subject to a visa[619] to move freely within the Schengen Area.[620]

It follows from the above that the regularisations under national law already have legal and factual effects on the other Member States. Determining the exact extent of the effects and consequences of such regularisations requires in-depth empirical research,[621] which cannot be undertaken within the scope of this study.

The 'pull factor' concerning future irregular migration is a further argument not only for the breach of the principle of subsidiarity but also, in principle, against any type of regularisation.[622] As the comparison in Part II will show, different regularisation systems already exist in the Member States. It is therefore initially unclear as to why the introduction of

615 ECJ 4.5.2016, C-547/14, ECLI:EU:C:2016:325, *Philip Morris*, para 218.

616 Some regularisations are even regulated at regional or local level; see Chapter 4.D.II.1.

617 See Chapter 4.

618 See just Art 1(2)(a) Residence Permit Regulation or Art 2(2)(c) Single Permit Directive. The procedure under Art 6(2) Return Directive applies if a residence permit issued by a Member State does not allow for a stay in the other Schengen States; cf. Fn 396.

619 See Annex I Visa Regulation.

620 According to Art 21 Schengen Agreement and Art 6(1)(b) SBC and in so far as the remaining requirements under Art 6(1) SBC are fulfilled.

621 In this sense, *Triandafyllidou/Vogel* in *Triandafyllidou* 298f and for a highly-convincing paper see *Kraler*, Journal of Immigrant and Refugee Studies 2019.

622 *Schieber*, Komplementärer Schutz 321f covers this under the heading '*Vermeidung irregulärer Migrationsbewegungen*' ('avoidance of irregular migration flows').

an EU legal framework for regularisation should lead to quantitatively 'more' irregular migration. In any case, the lack of reliable research does not clarify whether or not an EU Regularisation Directive would have such a 'pull-effect'.[623]

The 'pull-effect' argument has been invoked by States and politicians, yet without offering any evidence thereof.[624] Several authors are correct in highlighting that the situation is far more complex and requires consideration of many different factors which are difficult to control politically.[625]

It is therefore necessary to refer to a 2014 empirical study that used the Eurostat arrest statistics relating to irregularly staying migrants. *Wehinger* indeed comes to the conclusion that regularisation programmes have a limited effect on future irregular migration, yet he notes in the same breath that one must nonetheless be cautious in interpreting his result, in particular because of the low reliability of the data.[626] *Wehinger* states further that '[h]owever, the alternative, a large illegal population residing in the country, can be more costly than an amnesty: social costs from increased criminality, missing out on tax revenues, signalling the impotence of the state [...] and worse job matching because of reduced mobility of

623 *Mimentza Martin*, Die sozialrechtliche Stellung von Ausländern mit fehlendem Aufenthaltsrecht: Deutschland und Spanien im Rechtsvergleich (2012) 149–252 for instance presents that not even social security benefits, which were the highest in the Basque region, have led to a 'pull-factor' regarding those irregularly staying migrants who lived in a different part of Spain.

624 Cf. *Parliamentary Assembly of the Council of Europe*, Regularisation programmes for irregular migrants. Report 11350 (6.7.2007), https://www.unhcr.org/4b9fac519.pdf (31.7.2022) A.7, A.13, A.16, B.4, B.28, B.29 and B.92; COM(2004) 412 final, 17; *Baldwin-Edwards/Kraler*, REGINE (January 2009) 43, 57, 83, 131; *Bausager/Møller/Ardittis*, Study on the situation of third-country nationals pending return/removal in the EU Member States and the Schengen Associated (11.3.2013), https://home-affairs.ec.europa.eu/system/files/2020-09/11032013_sudy_report_on_immigration_return-removal_en.pdf (31.7.2022) 82f.

625 *Baldwin-Edwards/Kraler*, REGINE (January 2009) 131 and 109; see also *Helbling/Leblang*, Controlling immigration? How regulations affect migration flows, European Journal of Political Research 2018, 1.

626 'Besides the quality of the data, one should be concerned by the possibility of influential omitted variables. It was not possible in the framework of this study to take into consideration exogenous shocks such as a deterioration of general circumstances in the sending countries. Besides that, clear data on enforcement measures are not available, and so enforcement could be controlled for only in a rough manner. Finally, apprehensions of illegal immigrants are not equal to illegal immigration'; *Wehinger*, International Journal of Migration and Border Studies 2014, 240f.

the illegal workforce'.[627] These negative effects of the EU return policy and the aforementioned deficit in the return of irregularly staying migrants could be lessened or lowered by an EU Regularisation Directive.[628]

As indicated above, further empirical research is necessary to take serious stock of the actual extent and effects of an EU legal framework for regularisation.[629] Subsequent policy decisions can thus be made on the basis of a correct factual basis ('evidence-based policymaking').[630] Just how many migrants each year may acquire a right to stay on the basis of a Regularisation Directive proposed in Chapter 5 will depend greatly on the requirements or on how many migrants are actually staying irregularly in the EU.[631]

In conclusion, an EU legal framework for regularisation would not violate the principle of subsidiarity. It can counteract the fragmentation of regularisations at national level illustrated in Chapter 4 and ensure a harmonised approach by the Member States.[632] EU rules could 'combat' irregular migration more effectively and reduce the number of migrants without a right to stay. The introduction of binding rules would indeed limit the Member States' broad discretion in this field, but in return the EU and the Member States could regain the credibility in EU return policy that actually functions.

627 *Wehinger*, International Journal of Migration and Border Studies 2014, 241. See also *Rosenberger/Ataç/Schütze*, Nicht-Abschiebbarkeit: Soziale Rechte im Deportation Gap, Österreichische Gesellschaft für Europapolitik Policy Brief (12.6.2018).

628 See Introduction A.

629 Accurately, *Mitsilegas*, Measuring Irregular Migration: Implications for Law, Policy and Human Rights in *Bogusz/Cholewinski/Cygan/Szyszczak* (eds), Irregular Migration and Human Rights: Theoretical, European and International Perspectives (2004) 29 (30f, 38f); *Kovacheva/Vogel*, WP 4/2009, 2; *Triandafyllidou/Vogel* in *Triandafyllidou* 292 and more recently *González Beilfuss/Koopmans*, Legal pathways to regularisation of illegally staying migrants in EU Member States (2021), https://admigov.eu/upload/Deliverable_27_Legal_pathways_Gonzales.pdf (31.7.2022) 29f.

630 Cf. *Triandafyllidou/Vogel* in *Triandafyllidou* 298f. Furthermore, the high costs of such studies have not been overlooked; cf. *Vogel/Jandl*, Introduction to the Methodological Problem in *Kraler/Vogel* (eds), Report on Methodological Issues. Clandestino Project (November 2008) 5 (5).

631 Cf. *Triandafyllidou/Vogel* in *Triandafyllidou* 298 with further references; see also Introduction A.

632 In this sense see also *Schieber*, Komplementärer Schutz 333f.

E. Summary

This chapter has focused on the question whether EU primary law covers a regularisation policy. I first outlined the EU immigration policy with regard to irregular migration in general, whereby I understand immigration policy to comprise each EU policy rooted in primary law, specifically Article 79 TFEU. This covers both the entry as well as the residence of third-country nationals. Overall, the EU continues with the (restrictive) policy outlined in the introduction to this study.[633] The Commission states that it has strived since the 2015 Agenda on Migration to achieve a balanced migration policy that is fair, robust and realistic. However, this requires critical examination whether these objectives can also actually be achieved (or are even achievable) through the legal instruments in place.

The spotlight then panned to the Return Directive. In short, this Directive places the Member States in a position to choose between the return procedure or regularisation. Member States retain the discretion to grant a right to stay at each stage of the process or even after issuing the return decision. The Return Directive therefore leaves the Member States the possibility to regularise irregularly staying migrants. Nonetheless, in light of the ECJ case law and diverse scholarly opinions it is disputed whether there is an obligation to regularise under the Return Directive. I argue that Article 6(4) Return Directive provides two sets of circumstances in which the Member States are obliged to grant irregularly staying migrants a right to stay: where the return would violate the principle of non-refoulement under the ECHR and CFR, and where the non-returnability of the migrant concerned is permanent. In both sets of circumstances the discretion afforded to the Member States under the first sentence of Article 6(4) Return Directive is removed entirely as the alternative option to return is not enforceable.

Furthermore, I have also focused on the three relevant EU mandates in Article 79(1) TFEU, directing the most attention to the prevention of and enhanced measures regarding 'illegal immigration'. The following may thus be stated with regard to the question whether the EU may, based on the task to 'combat' irregular immigration, pass legislation regarding regularisation or whether such legislation must concern the prevention of irregular migration or return of irregularly staying migrants: passing such legislation must accord with the purpose to 'combat illegal immigration'. This interpretation is also favoured by the Council of the European Union,

633 See Introduction A.

which views regularisations as an instrument in the 'fight against illegal immigration'. Accordingly, in the 2008 European Pact on Immigration and Asylum the Council left the possibility open for the Member States to use case-by-case regularisations. The Member States should, however, refrain from so-called regularisation programmes. The discretion not to issue a return decision but to instead award a residence permit to an irregularly staying migrant was subsequently codified in the Return Directive.

The final step was an examination of the competences in primary law in which I conclude that Article 79(2)(a) and (b) TFEU grant the EU legislator extensive competence to enact regularisations. The substantive provisions, the procedure as well as the accompanying status and free movement rights could be regulated in EU legislation. Rights to stay granted under national law could be equipped with such rights. With Article 79(2)(c) TFEU as a foundation, EU law could create a type of tolerated status. An EU legal framework for regularisation would also be in line with the principle of subsidiarity. It can therefore be affirmed that EU primary law would cover an EU regularisation policy.

Part II – A comparison of Austrian, German and Spanish law

Following the conceptional insights into irregular migration and regularisations as well as the discussion of the EU regulatory competences in Part I, Part II turns to a comparative analysis of regularisations in Austrian, German and Spanish law, thereby demonstrating that regularisations are widespread at national level.[634] I apply the critical-contextual approach to compare the relevant laws in these jurisdictions.[635]

The comparison of different national laws bears the risk of a 'homeward trend', in this case to Austrian law and is addressed by comparing reflexively.[636] This approach broadens the view and helps to start a discussion between the 'home' and the 'other' legal systems. However, the risk of a homeward trend is avoided as best as possible through the use of independent legal terms and by drawing upon the knowledge acquired during the research periods in each jurisdiction like described in the preface. Furthermore, with regard to the translation into English, official translations are used, in so far as they are available. This allows me to look in the best possible way 'from the outside in' and examine the chosen legal systems from a sufficient distance.[637]

It is important to emphasise a particular feature of Spanish law. Whereas Austrian and German law affix letters to provisions that have been added at a later stage to the legislation (e.g. §§ 46, 46a and 46b FPG), Spanish law uses 'bis' and 'ter', respectively (e.g. Article 2bis and 2ter LODYLE). Furthermore, as the term Asylum Act (*Asylgesetz*) applies to the corresponding legislation in both Austria and Germany, (A) and (G) are used to indicate whether the term Asylum Act refers to the Austrian or German legislation.

Chapter 3 – Context for the integrated comparison

An integrated comparison does not merely describe national law via separate national reports. It rather focuses on assessing the comparison of the

634 On the choice of these three EU Member States see Introduction D.II.1.
635 See Introduction D.I.–II.
636 See Introduction D.I.1.
637 See Introduction D.II.1.

underlying purposes, which requires details on the context. Accordingly, this chapter analyses and prepares the context in the chosen jurisdictions: Austria (A.), Germany (B.) and Spain (C.).[638]

The framework arising from the analysis serves as a reference point for the comparisons in Chapter 4, thus avoiding unnecessary repetitions. The following will focus on particular topics that serve to create an introductory overview of the three jurisdictions: each analysis begins with an account of the historical development of the respective national laws regarding residency of foreigners (*Ausländer*), or aliens (*Fremde*) in cases where the original German terminology differs. However, the emphasis is placed on the main developments since 1945 as the developments prior to 1945 play hardly any role in modern law. In the interests of this study, the spotlight is cast on the treatment of irregularly staying foreigners, and of course on regularisations.

The description of the legal status of foreigners refers, inter alia, to access to the labour market.[639] In principle this includes every type of employed activity, including self-employment. This study does not focus on self-employment because the employment of persons without a right to stay is far more relevant. After all, one of the central demands of irregularly staying migrants is that they be given access to the labour market with a right to stay.[640] Unless stated otherwise, the term 'employment' used in the following therefore refers to an employer-employee relationship, not self-employed activities. Rather than 'illegal employment', the term 'undocumented employment' is used to describe the employment of a person who does not have the required work permit. This is to be assessed irrespective of the question whether the person in question is registered for social security.[641] Furthermore, the legal status of foreigners will also be viewed in relation to access to healthcare as well as to social security bene-

638 The order in the original German version was Germany, Austria and Spain (i.e. alphabetically in relation to the German translations *Deutschland*, *Österreich* and *Spanien*).

639 Cf. *Camas Roda*, Trabajo decente e inmigrantes en España: Un estudio sobre los derechos laborales de los trabajadores migrantes y del objetivo internacional del trabajo decente (2016) 13ff on the close relationship between migration and employment.

640 Cf. *Varela Huerta*, Soziologie der Migrationskämpfe: Die Transformation der Bewegung der „Papierlosen“ in Barcelona in eine MigrantInnenbewegung in *Fischer-Lescano/Kocher/Nassibi* (eds), Arbeit in der Illegalität: Die Rechte von Menschen ohne Aufenthaltspapiere (2012) 159 (160f, 165); see also Introduction D.II.1.

641 Cf. *Triguero Martínez*, Migraciones 2014, 452.

fits.[642] Healthcare refers to the coverage by (statutory) health insurance. Social security benefits are all 'benefits', as understood in the colloquial sense. The study will not focus on any particular financial compensation or support for certain groups (such as child support) or each type of benefit to support integration, but rather primarily on those benefits that safeguard one's survival. The current law in relation to the relevant regularisations will also be outlined; Chapter 4 provides the necessary details.

Finally, the competences and the domestic authorities responsible for foreigners as well as the judicial protection are presented. It is important to indicate the features of the protection available as they concern fundamental rights, though the scope is limited here to those instruments that allow a person to appeal against decisions in which the authorities do not grant a right to stay or tolerated status. Through this presentation, I continue the adopted perspective of irregularly staying migrants.[643]

A. Austria

Austria is a democratic republic with nine *Bundesländer* (Federal States).[644] The basic principles underpinning the constitution[645] include the so-called democratic principle, the republican principle, the federal principle and the rule of law.[646] Austria may be described as a social state, despite the lack of such express description in the constitution.[647]

Austria is a 'country of immigration'.[648] This is clear from the population growth between 1961 and 2015 in which the population increased

642 Cf. *Camas Roda*, Trabajo decente 130ff on the particular need to protect migrants.

643 See Introduction D.II.3.

644 Arts 1 and 2(2) B-VG; cf. *Öhlinger/Eberhard*, Verfassungsrecht[13] (2022) mns 330ff and *Berka*, Verfassungsrecht[8] (2021) mns 1ff.

645 For an introduction to the history of the Austrian constitution see *Stelzer*, The Constitution of the Republic of Austria (2011) 1ff.

646 *Berka*, Verfassungsrecht mns 114ff; *Öhlinger/Eberhard*, Verfassungsrecht mns 62–88a and *Stelzer*, Constitution 32ff.

647 *Kaspar*, Sozialhilferechtliche Differenzierung aufgrund des Aufenthaltsstatus von subsidiär Schutzberechtigten: Ausschluss nach dem NÖ MSG – VfGH 28. Juni 2017, E 3297/2016, juridikum 2017, 476 (480); for detail *Wiederin*, Sozialstaatlichkeit im Spannungsfeld von Eigenverantwortung und Fürsorge, VVDStRL 2005/64, 53 (69–72).

648 See only *Fassmann/Reeger*, Austria: From guest worker migration to a country of immigration. IDEA WP No. 1 (December 2008).

by 1.2 million through migrants alone.[649] Approximately 17.1% of the population does not have Austrian citizenship (1 January 2021).[650]

Refugees, asylum seekers and migrants have long be seen the subject of intense debate in Austrian media and politics,[651] especially as a result of the 'long summer of migration 2015'.[652] Such topics were often dealt with in the context of 'securitisation',[653] with considerable focus directed towards the 'fear' of 'foreign infiltration' or that foreigners will abuse the social security system.[654] In general, the debate surrounding refugees

649 Cf. *Musil*, Migration und Asyl in Österreich – Ein statistischer Überblick, 1961–2016 in *Eppel/Reyhani* (eds), Handbuch Asyl- und Fremdenrecht (2016) Register 1 Chapter 2; *EMN*, Die Gestaltung der Asyl- und Migrationspolitik in Österreich (December 2015), https://www.emn.at/wp-content/uploads/2017/01/Organisationsstudie_AT-EMN-NCP_2016.pdf (31.7.2022) 27–40 and for detail *Fassmann/Münz*, Einwanderungsland Österreich? Historische Migrationsmuster, aktuelle Trends und politische Maßnahmen (1995).

650 See *Statistik Austria*, Bevölkerung nach Staatsangehörigkeit und Geburtsland, https://www.statistik.at/statistiken/bevoelkerung-und-soziales/bevoelkerung/bevoelkerungsstand/bevoelkerung-nach-staatsangehoerigkeit/-geburtsland (31.7.2022).

651 Cf. *Langthaler/Muhič/Dizdarevič/Sohler/Trauner*, Zivilgesellschaftliche und politische Partizipation und Repräsentanz von Flüchtlingen und AsylwerberInnen in der EU (February 2009), http://archiv.asyl.at/projekte/node/synthese_case studies.pdf (31.7.2022) 14–31; *Ataç*, Die diskursive Konstruktion von Flüchtlingen und Asylpolitik in Österreich seit 2000 in *Hunger/Pioch/Rother* (eds), Migrations- und Integrationspolitik im europäischen Vergleich – Jahrbuch Migration 2012/2013 (2014) 113; *Drüeke/Fritsche*, Geflüchtete in den Medien – Medien für Geflüchtete, Medien Journal 2015/4, 12; *Sponholz*, Als der Sommer zu Ende ging: Die Flüchtlingsdebatte im Wiener Wahlkampf auf Facebook, SWS-Rundschau 2016/3, 371; *Huber-Mumelter/Waitz*, Regelungen des dauerhaften Verbleibs von Fremden in Österreich und in der Schweiz – ein rechtsvergleichender Überblick zum aktuellen Stand im Asyl- und Aufenthaltsrecht, FABL 1/2009-I, 12 (14). On the debate in Germany, see Chapter 3.B.I. below.

652 For an overview of the resulting legislation see *Hinterberger*, Das österreichische Asylgesetzänderungsgesetz 2016 in *Bungenberg/Giegerich/Stein* (eds), ZEuS-Sonderband: Asyl und Migration in Europa – rechtliche Herausforderungen und Perspektiven (2016) 185 (188 with further references) and Introduction A.

653 For detail on the EU see *Huysmans*, The European Union and the Securitization of Migration, Journal of Common Market Studies 2000/38, 751.

654 See *Langthaler/Muhič/Dizdarevič/Sohler/Trauner*, Zivilgesellschaftliche und politische Partizipation und Repräsentanz von Flüchtlingen und AsylwerberInnen in der EU (February 2009) 30f and also Chapter 2.C.I.

and the (relatively high) number of asylum applications has always had considerable influence on the legislative process.[655]

I. Historical development of the law on aliens

The term *Fremdenrecht* (law on aliens) is typically used to describe the field of law that regulates the position of non-Austrian citizens in Austria. The official English translations of Austrian legislation (in particular the AsylG) translate '*Fremde*' as 'alien', which will be used in the following for reasons of consistency and to draw a distinction to the term '*Ausländer*' (foreigner) used in German legislation. Together with asylum law these are some of the most complicated fields of law in the Austrian legal system, as is shown by the near annual reforms since 2005.[656] The *Fremdenrecht* concerns in principle everyone who is not an Austrian citizen.[657]

The German National Socialist Police Order on Foreigners (*NS-Ausländerpolizeiverordnung*)[658] formed the basis for the Austrian Aliens' Police Act of 1954.[659] It is already clear from the title of this legislation that migration was discussed in the context of police law.[660] When it was enacted, the Aliens' Police Act of 1954 was merely purged of the most prominent racist terminology and provided Austria with a wealth of legal instruments to remove aliens from the country using measures to termi-

655 Especially with regard to the law on aliens and on asylum. See just *Bauer*, Zuwanderung nach Österreich (January 2008), http://www.politikberatung.or.at/fileadmin/_migrated/media/Zuwanderung-nach-Oesterreich.pdf (31.7.2022) 4ff und *Reyhani*, Einleitende Bemerkungen – Asyl- und Fremdenrecht im Kontext in *Eppel/Reyhani* (eds), Handbuch Asyl- und Fremdenrecht (2016) Register 1 Chapter 1 5ff.

656 Cf. *Muzak*, Die Kasuistik, Komplexität und Kurzfristigkeit des österreichischen Fremdenrechts in *ÖJT* (ed), 19. ÖJT Band I/2: Migration und Mobilität (2016) 23; *Hinterberger* in *Bungenberg/Giegerich/Stein* 188 with further references; *Peyrl*, Arbeitsmarkt 313; *Reyhani* in *Eppel/Reyhani* Register 1 Chapter 1 2f. In this respect also *Wiederin*, Aufenthaltsbeendende Maßnahmen im Fremdenpolizeirecht (1993) 1–7.

657 § 2(4) No. 1 FPG.

658 See below, Chapter 3.B.I.

659 See BGBl 75/1954 and §§ 15 and 17 Aliens' Police Act of 1954; cf. *Grösel*, Fremde von Staats wegen. 50 Jahre »Fremdenpolitik« in Österreich (2016) 47.

660 Cf. *Pöschl*, Zusammenfassung des Gutachtens in *ÖJT* (ed), 19. ÖJT Band I/2: Migration und Mobilität (2016) 14 (14).

nate their residence.[661] The Aliens' Police Act of 1954 was in force for over 30 years.[662] Its rules, however, need to be viewed in the context of the foreign recruitment from 1960 onwards.[663] High economic growth and low unemployment rates pushed the social partners[664] to negotiate opening the labour market to foreign guest workers (*Gastarbeiter*), which at the time was subject to strict regulations.[665] From 1961 onwards a certain number of 'foreign' guest workers were allowed to work temporarily in Austria in order to provide the 'cheap' labour that was lacking at the time,[666] partly due to the fact that Austrian workers emigrated to Germany.[667] The majority of the guest workers were from Turkey and the Former Republic of Yugoslavia. Although in principle the Austrian policy was to only allow the guest workers to stay for one year, most stayed in Austria permanently.[668] The aforementioned regulations on aliens law expressed the economic interests of Austria and the labour market.[669]

The need for foreign guest workers dropped considerably following the oil crisis in the mid-1970s and the resulting recession. Austria therefore attempted to stem and restrict migration of workers as much as possible due to the negative public perception of guest workers.[670] The 1969 Passport Act (*Paßgesetz 1969*[671]) already offered a legal instrument that was used

661 See §§ 3ff Aliens' Police Act of 1954 and the impressive explanations in *Grösel*, Fremde 47 and 56 as well on the development of measures terminating residency from 1954 *Wiederin*, Aufenthaltsbeendende Maßnahmen 1–7.

662 *Wiederin*, Aufenthaltsbeendende Maßnahmen 1 with further references.

663 Cf. *Grösel*, Fremde 46ff and 52ff with further references.

664 Typically comprising employer and employee associations; at establishment, the social partners were the *Bundeswirtschaftskammer* (Federal Chamber of Commerce), the *Österreichischer Arbeiterkammertag (Bundesarbeitskammer;* Federal Chamber of Labour), the *Österreichischer Gewerkschaftsbund* (Austrian Trade Union Federation) and the *Präsidentenkonferenz der Landwirtschaftskammer* (Presidents of the Chambers of Agriculture); cf. *Kietaibl*, Arbeitsrecht I[11] (2021) 82f.

665 Cf. *Grösel*, Fremde 52ff.

666 See the 'Raab-Olah-Agreement' signed in 1961 by the Federal Chancellor *Julius Raab* and the President of Austrian Trade Union Federation, *Franz Olah*. Cf. *Fassmann/Reeger*, IDEA WP No. 1 (December 2008) 22f.

667 Cf. *Bauer*, Zuwanderung (January 2008) 5.

668 Cf. *Fassmann/Reeger*, IDEA WP No. 1 (December 2008) 22 and 24; *Bauer*, Zuwanderung (January 2008) 6; *Pöschl* in *ÖJT* 16.

669 *Fassmann/Reeger*, IDEA WP No. 1 (December 2008) 23 and *EMN*, Die Gestaltung der Asyl- und Migrationspolitik in Österreich (December 2015) 29.

670 Cf. *Fassmann/Reeger*, IDEA WP No. 1 (December 2008) 22.

671 BGBl 422/1969.

ever increasingly.[672] Furthermore, additional restrictions were imposed in 1975 with the Employment of Foreign Nationals Act (*Ausländerbeschäftigungsgesetz*; AuslBG), which is still in force today (albeit following several reforms).[673] Whereas few foreign workers came to Austria, the number of immigrants remained at a constant high due to the influx of guest workers' families.[674] Austrian politics did not take this factor of immigration into consideration.

Following the collapse of the iron curtain and the resulting war in Yugoslavia,[675] the higher number of asylum applications at the start of the 1990s brought further legislative restrictions and a 'tougher' stance towards refugees and aliens in general. Both events saw hundreds of thousands of people flee to Austria, with the foreign population rising from approx. 400,000 to approx. 690,000. This forms the background for the notable Asylum Act of 1991 (*Asylgesetz 1991*[676]) as well as the 1993 Aliens Act (*Fremdengesetz 1993*[677]) and the Residence Act (*Aufenthaltsgesetz 1993*[678]).[679] The 1993 Aliens Act introduced for the first time many rules then unknown, such as inspection powers for the police, deportation offences and new provisions of criminal law.[680] The 1993 Residence Act contained, inter alia, a rule on applications from abroad, the distinction according to the purpose of the stay and a quota system.[681] Overall, the Austrian legislator had made targeted attempts to manage immigration.[682]

The 1993 Aliens and Residence Acts were amalgamated in the 1997 Aliens Act (*Fremdengesetz 1997*; FrG), which was labelled a 'recodification':[683] according to *Muzak*, it raised the standards under the rule of law and basic rights and the guarantee of a degree of security during the residence. § 10(4) FrG lays the foundation for the 'residence permits for exceptional circumstances' (*Aufenthaltstitel aus berücksichtigungswürdigen*

672 Cf. *Muzak* in *ÖJT* 24f, who refers to § 25 Paßgesetz 1969.
673 Cf. *EMN*, Die Gestaltung der Asyl- und Migrationspolitik in Österreich (December 2015) 29f.
674 Cf. *Fassmann/Reeger*, IDEA WP No. 1 (December 2008) 22f.
675 Cf. *Huber-Mumelter/Waitz*, FABL 1/2009-I, 14 and *Bauer*, Zuwanderung (January 2008) 7f.
676 BGBl 8/1992; cf. Entwicklung *Wiederin*, Aufenthaltsbeendende Maßnahmen 5.
677 BGBl 838/1992.
678 BGBl 466/1992.
679 On the development *Wiederin*, Aufenthaltsbeendende Maßnahmen 4–7.
680 *Muzak* in *ÖJT* 25.
681 *Muzak* in *ÖJT* 25.
682 *Fassmann/Reeger*, IDEA WP No. 1 (December 2008) 25f.
683 *Muzak* in *ÖJT* 26f.

Gründen), or in other words, the Austrian regularisations.[684] According to this provision, a residence permit was to be issued *ex officio* in exceptional circumstances for humanitarian reasons.[685] In comparison to rights of residence, the grant of a permit in such cases was 'privileged'[686] because it was possible despite certain grounds that would otherwise give cause to refuse a visa.[687] 'Exceptional circumstances' existed if the alien has been exposed to a danger within the meaning of § 57(1) and (2) FrG,[688] such as refugees from war-torn countries, victims of human trafficking or where there is the threat of torture in the sense of the non-refoulement principle.[689] An application was not possible at the time, only the grant *ex officio*. An application only first became possible from 1 January 2003 through the 2002 reform[690] of the Aliens Act and Asylum Act (A), however only until 31 December 2005.[691] At the same time, the grant of such a humanitarian residence permit required the consent of the Minister of the Interior (*Bundesminister für Inneres*).[692] An approach that was declared to be in conformity with the constitution.[693]

The so-called Aliens Law Package of 2005 (*Fremdenrechtspaket 2005*) was not only significant but also marked a major turning point.[694] This bundle of legislation repealed the FrG and replaced it with the Aliens' Police Act (*Fremdenpolizeigesetz*; FPG), the Asylum Act (*Asylgesetz*; AsylG (A)), and the Settlement and Residence Act (*Niederlassungs- und Aufenthaltsgesetz*;

---

684 See Chapter 3.A.III.

685 Cf. *Wiederin*, Die Einreise- und Aufenthaltstitel nach dem Fremdengesetz 1997, ecolex 1997, 719.

686 Cf. *Wiederin*, ecolex 1997.

687 Note that in the Austrian legal terminology, the technical term *Sichtvermerk* was used instead of *Visum*; cf. *Muzak*, Die Aufenthaltsberechtigung im österreichischen Fremdenrecht (1995) 27.

688 § 10(4) 2nd Sent. FrG.

689 Cf. *Wiederin*, ecolex 1997.

690 BGBl I 126/2002.

691 § 14(2) 3rd Sent. FrG in the version BGBl I 126/2002; ErläutRV 1172 BlgNR 21. GP, 29 and cf. *Peyrl*, Neuregelung des Aufenthaltsrechts aus humanitären Gründen („Bleiberecht"), DRdA 2009, 283 (283 Fn 1).

692 § 90(1) FrG in the version BGBl I 126/2002; cf. ErläutRV 1172 BlgNR 21. GP, 28 and 36.

693 VfGH 13.12.1999, G 2/99.

694 Cf. *Muzak* in *ÖJT* 27f and *EMN*, Die Gestaltung der Asyl- und Migrationspolitik in Österreich (December 2015) 27ff.

NAG),[695] and transposed numerous EU directives into Austrian law.[696] The Aliens' Police Act regulates matters such as the order of removal measures where asylum or subsidiary protection is not granted or withdrawn, and the grant of visas – in short, all matters concerning the policing of aliens. In Austria, the Asylum Act contains the legislative provisions on the asylum procedure and the grant of 'residence permits for exceptional circumstances'. The Settlement and Residence Act concerns the rights to settle and reside, thereby contributing to migration management. The new legislation continues to pursue the predominant 'restrictive immigration policy'.[697]

For the first time, the then called 'residence permits for humanitarian reasons' (*Aufenthaltstitel aus humanitären Gründen*) were anchored in the Settlement and Residence Act.[698] However, the person could (again) not apply for such permits, they could only be awarded *ex officio*.[699] It was only in the year 2008 in which the Austrian Constitutional Court (*Verfassungsgerichtshof*; VfGH) removed the *ex officio* requirement on the grounds of the rule of law.[700] The Court's decision was transposed into legislation via the so-called 'reform of the right to remain' of 2009 (*'Bleiberechtsnovelle' 2009*), which led to a reform of the 'residence permits for humanitarian reasons'[701] and provided an express right to apply for such permits.[702]

The most significant residence permit was and remains the so-called *Bleiberecht*: the 'right to remain'.[703] Such permit is awarded when the competent authority determines that the removal was permanently inadmissible due to the right to respect for private and/or family life.[704] Depending

695 See BGBl I 75/1997 and BGBl I 100/2005. For a short overview of the content of the legislation see *Huber-Mumelter/Waitz*, FABL 1/2009-I, 14–20.

696 Cf. ErläutRV 952 BlgNR 22. GP, 2.

697 *Huber-Mumelter/Waitz*, FABL 1/2009-I, 35.

698 §§ 72–75 NAG in the version BGBl I 2005/100; see also ErläutRV 952 BlgNR 22. GP, 147f.

699 For criticism, *Mayer*, Das humanitäre Bleiberecht – ein schrankenloses Ermessen, migraLex 2008, 36; *Bachmann*, Das Bleiberecht – eine vorläufige Bilanz, migraLex 2010, 95 (95f with further references) and *Peyrl*, Autoritäre Tendenzen im Aufenthaltsrecht seit 2006, juridikum 2018, 103 (112f).

700 VfGH 27.6.2008, G 246/07; cf. *Bachmann*, migraLex 2010, 95.

701 Cf. *Bachmann*, migraLex 2010, 95; *Peyrl*, DRdA 2009, 283; *Huber-Mumelter/Waitz*, FABL 1/2009-I, 16f and ErläutRV 88 BlgNR 24. GP, 1f.

702 §§ 43(2), 44(3) and (4) as well as 69a(1) NAG in the version BGBl I 29/2009.

703 §§ 43(2) and 44(3) NAG in the version BGBl I 29/2009 and see Chapter 4.B.III.

704 For detail *Gruber*, „Bleiberecht" und Art 8 EMRK in FS Rudolf Machacek and Franz Matscher (2008) 159; *Peyrl*, DRdA 2009, 284f and *Bachmann*, migraLex 2010, 97ff. On the balance of interests see also *Heißl*, Die Ausweisung

on which requirements were satisfied, a limited or unlimited 'settlement permit' could be granted, which differed in the grant of access to the labour market.[705] In addition, a rule regarding 'old cases' was created for 'exceptional circumstances'[706] which were narrowly unable to reach the threshold of Article 8 ECHR.[707] One requirement was for the person concerned to have been continuously resident in Austria since 1 May 2004, whereby the residence must have been lawful for at least half of the that time. In practice, a limited 'settlement permit' was granted under the 'old case' rule mainly to those rejected asylum seekers whose asylum proceedings had lasted for far too long.[708] The award of a limited 'settlement permit' required the consent of the Minister of the Interior,[709] which was deemed constitutional, though the Minister in exercising the right to grant consent is bound by the same legislative criteria as the competent authority making its decision.[710] Furthermore, the general requirements such as health insurance and accommodation also had to be satisfied, although according to *Peyrl* these requirements could only be fulfilled by engaging a sponsor.[711] The 2009 'reform of the right to remain' also introduced the 'special protection residence permit' ('*Aufenthaltsbewilligung – Besonderer Schutz*').[712] Such permit required, for instance, that a delay in enforcement was issued more than once for at least one year[713] or that the person was a victim of human trafficking. To a broad extent, the delay in enforcement was a precursor to the instrument of toleration known today.[714]

---

in der Judikatur der Höchstgerichte, ZfV 2008, 1145. For detail on the examination and award in the asylum process see *Marth*, Das Bleiberecht im Asylverfahren, migraLex 2009, 45.

705 § 8(2) Nos. 3 and 4 NAG in the version BGBl I 29/2009.

706 § 44(4) NAG in the version BGBl I 29/2009.

707 VwGH 29.4.2010, 2009/21/0255 on § 44(4) NAG in the version BGBl I 29/2009; cf. *Peyrl*, DRdA 2009, 286.

708 See also *Peyrl*, DRdA 2009, 286 Fn 26 and *Bachmann*, migraLex 2010, 99.

709 § 74 FPG in the version BGBl I 29/2009.

710 VfGH 27.6.2008, G 246/07. The Minister was advised by a board that gave recommendations in cases regarding exceptional circumstances; § 75 FPG in the version BGBl I 29/2009.

711 *Peyrl*, DRdA 2009, 286.

712 § 69a NAG in the version BGBl I 29/2009.

713 § 46(3) in conjunction with § 46(1) FPG in the version BGBl I 29/2009.

714 In this sense *Hinterberger/Klammer*, Das Rechtsinstitut der fremdenpolizeilichen Duldung, migraLex 2015, 73 (77f) and see for detail, Chapter 4.A.I.3.

Further significant reforms include the 2009 and 2011 Acts amending the Law on Aliens (*Fremdenrechtsänderungsgesetz 2009*[715] and *Fremdenrechtsänderungsgesetz 2011*[716]) as well as the Aliens' Authorities Restructuring Act of 2012 (*Fremdenbehördenneustrukturierungsgesetz 2012*[717]) and the Aliens' Authorities Restructuring Act – Amendment Act of 2013 (*Fremdenbehördenneustrukturierungsgesetz-Anpassungsgesetz 2013*).[718] The latter two Acts marked a further turning point in the Austrian law concerning asylum and aliens: they implemented the reform of the administrative courts with regard to asylum and aliens law[719] and enacted the Act establishing the Federal Office for Immigration and Asylum (*Bundesamt für Fremdenwesen und Asyl-Einrichtungsgesetz*[720]; BFA-G) and the Act on the Proceedings of the Federal Office for Immigration and Asylum (*Bundesamt für Fremdenwesen und Asyl-Verfahrensgesetz*; BFA-VG), whereby the Federal Office for Immigration and Asylum was created as a new authority in asylum and alien police proceedings. At the same time, the 'residence permits for exceptional circumstances' were reformed,[721] which will be analysed in detail below.[722] In 2015, the Act amending the Law on Aliens (*Fremdenrechtsänderungsgesetz 2015*[723]) reformed, for example, toleration according to § 46a FPG.[724] This was followed by further reforms in 2017,[725] which made changes regarding qualified workers with the 'Red-White-Red – Card' (*Rot-Weiß-Rot – Karte*) or the duty for asylum seekers, whose appli-

715 BGBl I 122/2009; cf. *Szymanski*, Das Fremdenrechtsänderungsgesetz 2009 oder der Boulevard freut sich, doch das Recht ist für Rechtsanwender und Rechtsunterworfene schwer durchschaubar, migraLex 2009, 99.

716 BGBl I 38/2011; cf. *Schmied*, Die aufenthaltsbeendenden Maßnahmen im Fremdenpolizeigesetz nach dem Fremdenrechtsänderungsgesetz 2011 – eine Bankrotterklärung der Fremdenrechtslegistik, Zeitschrift der Unabhängigen Verwaltungssenate 2011, 149.

717 BGBl I 87/2012.

718 BGBl I 68/2013.

719 Cf. *Muzak* in *ÖJT* 29f.

720 For details see https://www.bfa.gv.at/ (31.7.2022).

721 Cf. *Fouchs/Schweda*, Die Neuregelung der humanitären Aufenthaltstitel im Asylrecht, migraLex 2014, 58.

722 See Chapter 3.A.III.1.

723 BGBl I 70/2015.

724 For an overview, *Szymanski*, Und das Hamsterrad dreht sich … (Teil I). Zum Fremdenrechtsänderungsgesetz 2015, migraLex 2015, 54 and *Szymanski*, Und das Hamsterrad dreht sich … (Teil II). Zum Fremdenrechtsänderungsgesetz 2015, migraLex 2016, 18.

725 BGBl I 145/2017.

cation was dismissed, to accept accommodation in a designated district.[726] Additional reforms followed in 2018,[727] which brought provisions linked to an order for custody to secure deportation of asylum seekers or accelerated withdrawal of asylum status.[728]

Legislation passed in June 2019 established a Federal Agency for Reception and Support Services company with limited liability (*Bundesagentur für Betreuungs- und Unterstützungsleistungen Gesellschaft mit beschränkter Haftung*; BBU).[729] This measure received considerable criticism as provision of legal advice and return counselling was placed solely in the hands of a government-owned agency.[730] The corresponding legislation entered into force on 1 August 2018, with the Federal Agency for Reception and Support Services operating from 1 July 2020.[731]

The long political tug-of-war concerning the reform of the Aliens' Police Act ended in December 2019 with further amending legislation.[732] This legislation created a provisional legal solution for those asylum seekers whose application has been rejected by final decision, but who had already started an apprenticeship.[733]

II. Legal status

Before turning to the 'residence permits for exceptional circumstances', I shall first describe the legal status of aliens under current law, directing the attention to the general aspects of residence law, employment, access to social benefits and to healthcare.

---

726 For an overview, *Peyrl*, Das Fremdenrechtsänderungsgesetz 2017 und die Novelle des AuslBG 2017 oder die jährlichen Grüße des Murmeltiers, DRdA-infas 2017, 387 and *Völker/Krumphuber*, Fremdenrechtsänderungsgesetz 2017 und Fremdenrechtsänderungsgesetz 2017 Teil II in *Filzwieser/Taucher* (eds), Asyl- und Fremdenrecht. Jahrbuch 2017 (2017) 63.

727 BGBl I 56/2018.

728 For an overview, *Krisper/Krumphuber*, Fremdenrechtsänderungsgesetz 2018 in *Filzwieser/Taucher* (eds), Asyl- und Fremdenrecht. Jahrbuch 2018 (2018) 79.

729 BBU-Errichtungsgesetz in the version BGBl I 53/2019 (BBU-G).

730 See *Frik*, Verstaatlichte Rechtsberatung im Asylverfahren, juridikum 2021, 214 (214ff with further references); VfGH 13.12.2022, E 3608/2021-28. On the BBU's tasks see § 2(1) BBU-G.

731 § 2 (2) BBU-G.

732 BGBl I 110/2019.

733 See Chapter 4.E.IV.1.

1. (Un)lawful residence

§ 31 FPG stipulates the situations in which an alien resides lawfully or unlawfully in Austria. The provision contains an exhaustive list of each situation that determines lawful residence.[734] The residence in cases that do not fall under the list is thus deemed unlawful;[735] this also applies to toleration.[736]

A procedure to impose a removal measure is to be initiated against aliens who are residing unlawfully and have been apprehended.[737] For third-country nationals, this concerns a return decision.[738] Once this decision becomes enforceable, the third-country national is required to leave without delay once the deadline for voluntary departure has lapsed.[739]

For Austrian law, the situation in which the alien's application for international protection under the Asylum Act (A) is rejected or dismissal is especially important.[740] There will be a return decision if the applicants receive neither asylum status, subsidiary protection status, a 'special protection residence permit' nor a 'residence permit for reasons of Article 8 ECHR'.[741] The same also applies in cases in which the asylum status is withdrawn and no subsidiary protection is granted, or the subsidiary protection status is withdrawn.[742] The Federal Office for Immigration and Asylum has to proceed in the same way if an application is made for a 'residence permit for exceptional circumstances'. In principle the Federal Office for Immigration and Asylum has to issue a return decision if the application is rejected or dismissed,[743] though there is an exception where a final and (still) valid return decision has already been issued and the circumstances of the case have not changed in the meanwhile.[744]

734 § 31(1) FPG.
735 § 31(1a) FPG.
736 § 31(1a) No. 3 FPG; see Chapter 4.A.I.3.
737 See §§ 52ff FPG.
738 § 52 FPG.
739 § 52(8) FPG.
740 § 10 AsylG (A).
741 For detail *Hinterberger*, Asyl- und Fremdenpolizeirecht (2017) 4f, 27f, 37, 71.
742 §§ 7 and 9 AsylG (A); see Chapter 4.A.I.3.a.
743 § 52(3) FPG and § 10(3) AsylG (A). See also Fn 832 below.
744 VwGH 16.12.2015, Ro 2015/21/0037.

2. Employment

The Employment of Foreign Nationals Act (*Ausländerbeschäftigungsgesetz*) provides the relevant legislative framework to determine whether aliens (foreigners[745]) may undertake 'non-self-employed activities' in Austria:[746] in principle this requires approval. Accordingly, aliens who are residing unlawfully are denied access to the labour market, which (with one exception) also includes tolerated persons.[747]

The approval to take up employment is expressed via the term *Beschäftigungsbewilligung* ('employment permit'). The grant of such permit is linked to lawful residence.[748] The employment permit is usually granted to the employer and the workplace stated in the application.[749] Accordingly, the employees themselves cannot apply for an employment permit.[750] The permit terminates with the end of employment.[751] *Peyrl* is thus convincing when stating that the permit is a considerable disadvantage for a migrant as it is linked to a specific employer and ceases *ipso iure* upon termination of the employment relationship.[752]

An employment permit is issued subject to particular requirements,[753] whereby the labour-market test is particularly significant: the Labour Market Service (*Arbeitsmarktservice*) examines whether the conditions and development of the labour market allow the employment of the alien.[754] This is the case if there is neither an Austrian national nor a foreigner[755] available on the labour market who is ready and able to perform the

---

745 The *Ausländerbeschäftigungsgesetz* uses the term 'foreigner' (*Ausländer*) to describe those who do not possess Austrian nationality; § 2(1) AuslBG.

746 See for those foreigners who according to § 1(2) AuslBG are excluded from the scope of the AuslBG *Deutsch/Nowotny/Seitz*, Ausländerbeschäftigungsrecht Kommentar[3] (2021) § 1 AuslBG mns 2ff and *Marhold/Başar*, Erwerbstätigkeit von AusländerInnen in Österreich: Die Hürden und Fallen der AusländerInnenbeschäftigung, juridikum 2016, 93 (95ff).

747 Cf. *Hinterberger*, DRdA 2018, 107–109.

748 §§ 3ff AuslBG; *Deutsch/Nowotny/Seitz*, Ausländerbeschäftigungsrecht §§ 3ff AuslBG.

749 See just §§ 4(1) and 19(1) AuslBG.

750 Cf. *Marhold/Başar*, juridikum 2016, 98.

751 §§ 6 and 7(6) AuslBG.

752 *Peyrl*, Arbeitsmarkt 261.

753 § 4(1) and (3) AuslBG.

754 § 4(1) AuslBG; for detail *Deutsch/Nowotny/Seitz*, Ausländerbeschäftigungsrecht § 4 AuslBG mns 4ff.

755 Such as EEA-citizens; § 2(6) AuslBG.

position advertised.[756] The employer is legally entitled to be granted an employment permit if all the necessary requirements are met.[757]

The implementation of the Single Permit Directive into Austrian law[758] greatly limited the scope of the employment permit as since then only selected groups, such as tolerated persons who were previously entitled to asylum or subsidiary protection, or holder of a 'standard residence permit' or 'special protection residence permit' are covered.[759] All other aliens receive a residence title that typically includes access to employment.

3. Social benefits

Both basic welfare benefits[760] as well as a needs-based minimum benefit system are generally available in Austria to aliens in need of assistance.[761] A so-called Basic Welfare Agreement (*Grundversorgungsvereinbarung*; GVV) concerning aliens in need of assistance and protection was reached between the federal government and the *Länder*.[762] Asylum seekers are generally entitled to receive basic welfare benefits.[763] Furthermore, unlawfully residing aliens in need of protection are entitled to basic welfare benefits if they cannot be deported for legal or factual reasons.[764] However, such persons are not entitled to receive basic welfare benefits prior to being tolerated.[765]

---

756 § 4b(1) AuslBG; for more detail on this provision see *Deutsch/Nowotny/Seitz*, Ausländerbeschäftigungsrecht § 4b AuslBG.

757 Cf. *Deutsch/Nowotny/Seitz*, Ausländerbeschäftigungsrecht § 4 AuslBG mn 2.

758 BGBl I 72/2013.

759 Cf. *Deutsch/Nowotny/Seitz*, Ausländerbeschäftigungsrecht § 4 AuslBG mn 2.

760 See Grundversorgungsgesetz – Bund 2005 in the version BGBl I 53/2019; for detail *Frahm*, Zugang zu adäquater Grundversorgung für Asylsuchende aus menschenrechtlicher Perspektive, juridikum 2013, 464.

761 However, see in detail *Haas/Matti*, Verfassungsrechtliche Aspekte der Gewährung von materieller Grundsicherung an Personen mit humanitärem Aufenthaltsrecht, migraLex 2021, 58.

762 Art 15a B-VG-Vereinbarung (*Bund-Länder-Vertrag* – an agreement between the federal government and the *Länder*). Cf. *Öhlinger/Eberhard*, Verfassungsrecht mns 318–321 with further references.

763 Art 2(1) No. 1 GVV.

764 Art 2(1) No. 4 GVV; for more detail on this provision *Frahm*, juridikum 2013, 469f.

765 See Chapter 4.A.I.3.b.

Until 2019, the needs-based minimum benefit system represented the 'third or last social safety net'[766] in Austria and should protect against poverty and social exclusion. It has applied in cases in which the preceding systems of social security, employment or other social transfers did not guarantee a set minimum income. The laws of the *Länder* originally applied to determine the entitlement to needs-based minimum benefits,[767] with the federal government first passing nationwide legislation in 2019.[768] Such step was subject to intense public discussion since 2017, with the federal government presenting a federal draft for a minimum income in November 2018 (*Sozialhilfe-Grundsatzgesetz* – Fundamental Act on Social Assistance).[769] This draft proposed a lump-sum payment of 863 euro/month,[770] though with a general five-year waiting period for third-country nationals. The Fundamental Act on Social Assistance was adopted in spring 2019 and entered into force on 1 June 2019.[771] Together with the implementing legislation[772] of the *Länder*, it replaces the need-based minimum benefit system.[773] On 12 December 2019, the Austrian Constitutional Court repealed the provisions on the employment qualification bonus (also referred to as the 'skill bonus') and the maximum rate for children for being incompatible with the constitution.[774]

---

766 Cf. *Kammer für Arbeiter und Angestellte*, Sozialleistungen im Überblick 2020[22] (2020) 391f.

767 On the constitutional concerns regarding the development see *Hiesel*, Mindestsicherung neu. Erste Gedankenskizzen, juridikum 2017, 80; *Sußner*, Warten auf … ? Verfassungs- und unionsrechtliche Perspektiven auf den Mindestsicherungszugang nach einem positiv abgeschlossenen Asylverfahren (NÖ MSG), juridikum 2017, 207; *Kaspar*, juridikum 2017, 476.

768 *Pfeil*, (Vorläufiges) Aus für die einheitliche Mindestsicherung, ÖZPR 2017/14, 24.

769 Ministerialentwurf Sozialhilfe-Grundsatzgesetz 2018, 104/ME 26. GP.

770 *Fritzl*, Mindestsicherung: Die Reform im Detail, diepresse.com (28.11.2018), https://diepresse.com/home/innenpolitik/5537388/Mindestsicherung_Die-Reform-im-Detail (31.7.2022).

771 BGBl I 41/2019; for detail *Pfeil*, „Sozialhilfe neu" – viele Verschärfungen, aber wenig Vereinheitlichung, ÖZPR 2019/18, 26; *Leitner*, Das neue Sozialhilfe-Grundsatzgesetz, Arbeits- und SozialrechtsKartei 2019, 304.

772 These are to be passed and to enter into force within seven months after the entry into force of the Fundamental Act on Social Assistance.

773 Cf. *Leitner*, Arbeits- und SozialrechtsKartei 2019, 304.

774 VfGH 12.12.2019, G 164/2019-25, G 171/2019-24; cf. *Kaspar*, Aktuelles zum Sozialhilfe-Grundsatzgesetz. VfGH 12.12.2019, G 164/2019 ua: Höchstsätze für Kinder sowie „Arbeitsqualifizierungsbonus" verfassungswidrig, juridikum 2020, 141.

4. Healthcare

Healthcare coverage in Austria is linked to employment, the receipt of a pension or qualification as a family member.[775] Coverage also extends to recipients of basic welfare benefits and of needs-based minimum benefits.[776]

III. General remarks on 'residence permits for exceptional circumstances'

It is to be noted from the outset that one particular type of regularisation in Austria does not fall into the category of *Aufenthaltstitel aus berücksichtigungswürdigen Gründen* – the 'residence permit for exceptional circumstances' – namely the 'Red-White-Red – Card plus' for unaccompanied minors in the care of foster parents or the child and youth service.[777] Said permit will be discussed in Chapter 4.C.IV.

1. Overview

The Aliens' Authorities Restructuring Act (*Fremdenbehördenneustrukturierungsgesetzes*[778]) entered into force on 1 January 2014, transferring the 'residence permits for exceptional circumstances' from the Settlement and Residence Act to Chapter 7 of the Asylum Act (A), where they were newly regulated.[779] The responsibility for such permits rests with the Federal Office for Immigration and Asylum, which was also created in 2014.[780] Within the Austrian Asylum Act itself, the current provisions on the residence permits are unfamiliar to the system as, unlike the notion of

---

775 See §§ 4–12 ASVG; cf. *Homberger/Güntner*, Responses to Migrants with Precarious Status in Vienna: Frames, Strategies and Evolving Practices (October 2022), https://www.compas.ox.ac.uk/wp-content/uploads/LoReMi-Responses-to-Migrants-with-Precarious-Status-in-Vienna-Frames-Strategies-and-Evolving-Practices.pdf (20.12.2022) 15ff.

776 For criticism *Lukits*, Die gesetzliche Krankenversicherung von Asylwerbern und Asylberechtigten, migraLex 2017, 14 (15ff with further references).

777 § 41a NAG.

778 BGBl I 87/2012.

779 §§ 54ff AsylG (A); cf. ErläutRV 1803 BlgNR 24. GP, 44.

780 § 3(2) No. 2 BFA-VG.

refugee and the subsidiary protection, they are not directly related to the procedure for international protection as prescribed by EU law.[781]

The Federal Office for Immigration and Asylum decision is issued as a *Bescheid*:[782] an administrative decision addressed to those subject to the law.[783] Austrian law features 25 residence permits, though the different forms of residence titles in asylum procedures and short-term permits (visas) are not included.[784] The category of 'residence permit for exceptional circumstances' may be distinguished on the basis of the reasons for which they are granted: 'residence permit for reasons of Article 8 ECHR' (*Aufenthaltstitel aus Gründen des Art 8 EMRK*), 'residence permit in particularly exceptional cases' (*Aufenthaltstitel in besonders berücksichtigungswürdigen Fällen*), and 'special protection residence permit' (*Aufenthaltsberechtigung besonderer Schutz*). They may further be distinguished regarding the scope of entitlements according to § 54 AsylG (A), which will be discussed in detail below: 'standard residence permit' (*Aufenthaltsberechtigung*), 'residence permit plus' (*Aufenthaltsberechtigung plus*) and 'special protection residence permit' (*Aufenthaltsberechtigung besonderer Schutz*).

Although the statistics on asylum now contain data on the 'residence permit for exceptional circumstances', it is nonetheless unclear which specific permits are included. Until 2019, the statistical category 'humanitarian residence permits' merely covered the 'residence permits for reasons of Article 8 ECHR' or 'special protection residence permits',[785] thus there has been no official data on 'residence permits in particularly exceptional cases'. However, such data was provided for the first time in a study published in 2019: 169 'residence permits in particularly exceptional cases' were granted between 2014 and 2018.[786]

---

781 Cf. *Muzak* in *ÖJT* 47.

782 § 12 BFA-VG.

783 Cf. *Raschauer*, Verwaltungsrecht mns 812ff.

784 *Peyrl*, Arbeitsmarkt 3 Fn 8.

785 'If an application for asylum is to be dismissed, the authority is to examine ex officio or upon application, whether a "residence permit for exceptional circumstances" for the purposes of the Asylgesetz 2005 may be granted as a "humanitarian residence permit"'; *Bundesministerium für Inneres*, Asylstatistik 2017 (2017), https://www.bmi.gv.at/301/Statistiken/files/Jahresstatistiken/Asyl-Jahresstatistik_2017.pdf (31.7.2022) 54.

786 *Bassermann*, Überblick über nationale Schutzstatus in Österreich (May 2019), https://www.emn.at/wp-content/uploads/2019/09/emn-natioanler-bericht-2019_nationale-schutzstatus.pdf (31.7.2022) 24–26.

According to the statistics, 2621 'residence permits for exceptional circumstances were granted in 2020, with 12,569 negative decisions.[787] The statistics distinguished for the first time between whether these permits were awarded in relation to an application for asylum (2185) or – as is relevant for this study – on the basis of an irregular stay (436).[788] In 2021, 1355 'residence permits for exceptional circumstances' were issued.[789] Detailed statistics were published for the first time in 2022.[790]

The data is nonetheless to be viewed on the whole with a critical eye as, for example, there is no information on the year in which the application procedures were initiated, the exact type of permit that was granted as well as the meaning of a 'final negative decision' (*'rechtskräftig negative Entscheidung'*).[791] However, the low number of permits granted highlights the subordinate role played by residence permits for exceptional circumstances in Austrian law at present, especially when put into comparison with the number of final decisions in asylum procedures. In 2020, there were 8069 positive decisions, 9567 negative decisions and 3221 other decisions.[792]

2. Administrative procedure

The 'residence permit for exceptional circumstances' may be applied for or be considered *ex officio* in the asylum procedure. It is particularly relevant for this study that the application may be made in circumstances of an irregular stay, thereby allowing 'residence permits for exceptional circumstances' to qualify as regularisations. Although the *ex officio* procedure is not relevant for this study, it will nonetheless be examined, though from a contextual perspective. Furthermore, I shall also present the general requirements for the grant of residence permits, the grounds for refusal as well as the end of the procedure.

---

787 *Bundesministerium für Inneres*, Asylstatistik 2020 (2020), https://www.bmi.gv.at/301/Statistiken/files/Jahresstatistiken/Asyl_Jahresstatistik_2020.pdf (31.7.2022) 44–49.

788 *Bundesministerium für Inneres*, Asylstatistik 2020 (2020) 28.

789 9728/AB 27. GP, 15.

790 *Bundesministerium für Inneres*, Detail-STATISTIK – Kennzahlen BFA – 2022 – 1.-2. Quartal (July 2022), https://www.bmi.gv.at/301/Statistiken/files/2022/Detailstatistik_BFA_Kennzahlen_1-2_Quartal_2022.pdf (31.7.2022) 6f.

791 See in this regard also 146/E 27. GP (24.3.2021).

792 *Bundesministerium für Inneres*, Asylstatistik 2020 (2020) 6.

a) Application

The application for a 'residence permit for exceptional circumstances' is to be filed in person with the Federal Office for Immigration and Asylum,[793] even if the alien does not have a right of residence at the time of application. The type of permit sought is to be described in detail,[794] otherwise the Federal Office for Immigration and Asylum has to issue an application for cure.[795] According to the principles of Austrian administrative law, the requirements must be fulfilled not only at the time of the application but – in short – at the time of the decision by the competent authority[796] or competent court[797].

Where an alien is residing unlawfully, it is especially relevant that a right to stay[798] does not result from an application for a 'residence permit for exceptional circumstances' nor is a decision and execution of a removal measure prevented.[799] However, the Austrian Asylum Act provides an exception whereby the Federal Office for Immigration and Asylum shall defer the execution of deportation implementing a return decision until such application has been finally decided on (*de facto* protection against deportation) if:[800] the procedure for the rendering of a return decision was initiated only after the filing of an application and the general require-

---

793 § 58(5) AsylG (A).

794 § 58(6) AsylG (A).

795 § 13(3) AVG.

796 Cf. *Hengstschläger/Leeb*, AVG (1.4.2021, rdb.at) § 39 AVG mns 41–42/1. See regarding the Settlement and Residence Act VwGH 22.2.2018, Ra 2018/22/0018 or on the grant of asylum under the Asylum Act (A) VwGH 3.5.2016, Ra 2015/18/0212.

797 VwGH 21.10.2014, Ro 2014/03/0076.

798 § 58(13) 1st Sent. AsylG (A) and § 16(5) BFA-VG. Alternative view in *Filzwieser/Frank/Kloibmüller/Raschhofer* (eds), Kommentar Asyl- und Fremdenrecht (2016) § 55 AsylG mn 7, § 56 AsylG mn 6 and § 57 AsylG mn 5 with reference to VwGH 22.10.2009, 2009/21/0293. *Filzwieser/Frank/Kloibmüller/Raschhofer* refer to the decisions of the VwGH concerning the previous law according to which a general right can be derived to await the decision on an application in accordance with §§ 55–57 AsylG (A) in the national territory.

799 For detail on the previous provision § 44b(3) NAG in the version BGBl I 122/2009 *Völker*, Verschafft die bloße Antragstellung auf einen „humanitären" Aufenthaltstitel ein Bleiberecht? VfGH versus VwGH, migraLex 2010, 60.

800 § 58(13) 4th Sent. AsylG (A).

ments for a 'residence permit in particularly exceptional cases' are met, thus increasing the likelihood that the residence permit will be granted.[801]

b) Grant *ex officio*

The 'special protection residence permit' and the 'residence permit for reasons of Article 8 ECHR' are also considered by the Federal Office for Immigration and Asylum in the application procedure when there are neither grounds for asylum nor the award of subsidiary protection. From a procedural perspective, the grant of a special protection residence permit is considered first,[802] followed by the 'residence permits for reasons of Article 8 ECHR' as part of the imposition *ex officio* of a removal decision.[803] Put simply, such *ex officio* consideration is always necessary when an application for asylum is rejected – the first two points of the decision (asylum and subsidiary protection) – or asylum is withdrawn in a withdrawal procedure and no subsidiary protection is issued, or subsidiary protection is withdrawn.[804]

If the 'special protection residence permit' and the 'residence permits for reasons of Article 8 ECHR' are considered in the asylum procedure, they do not qualify as regularisations in these cases as the alien has a right to stay during the asylum procedure, thereby not satisfying the definition of regularisation.[805] However, consideration *ex officio* does indeed show how each of these 'residence permits for exceptional circumstances' are intertwined with the asylum procedure and are thus of contextual importance.

---

801 See Chapter 4.D.II.2.a.

802 § 10(2) and § 58(1) AsylG (A); cf. *Filzwieser/Frank/Kloibmüller/Raschhofer*, Asyl- und Fremdenrecht § 55 AsylG mn 3.

803 In this sense *Filzwieser/Frank/Kloibmüller/Raschhofer*, Asyl- und Fremdenrecht § 55 AsylG mn 3.

804 §§ 7 and 9 AsylG (A); see Chapter 4.A.I.2.a.

805 See Chapter 1.A.II.1.

c) General requirements for the grant of residence permits and grounds for refusal

§ 60 AsylG (A) contains the general requirements for the grant of 'residence permits for exceptional circumstances'.[806] However, it is more appropriate to use the term 'grounds for refusal' as the criteria stated in the provision are in effect reasons not to grant the residence permit.[807] The conflict with public interest is one such example,[808] with the 2017 amendments to the Law on Aliens providing two explicit circumstances in which this is the case, such as where the alien's behaviour cannot exclude a close relationship to extremist or terrorist groups.[809]

A valid return decision in conjunction with a ban on entry is a further ground for refusal.[810] This applies only to the 'residence permit in particularly exceptional cases' and the 'special protection residence permit'.[811] Conversely, it follows that one may apply for any of the 'residence permits for exceptional circumstances' in so far as 'merely' a return decision has been issued against an alien who has been residing unlawfully.

Moreover, aliens are subject to a general duty of cooperation in the procedure to grant a 'residence permit for exceptional circumstances'. If this duty is not performed, the procedure for the issuance of a residence permit to be granted *ex officio* shall be discontinued or the application shall be rejected.[812] This may apply where identity documents (e.g. valid travel documents) are not presented, though the possibility for an application for cure remains.[813] If, despite instructions by the Federal Office for Immigration and Asylum, such application is not made, the application for the residence permit is to be rejected and the procedure ends.[814]

From a procedural law standpoint, all applications for a 'residence permit for exceptional circumstances' are to be rejected if there are no altered

806 VwGH 14.4.2016, Ra 2016/21/0077.

807 § 60(2) AsylG (A) is excluded. This refers only to the residence permit in particularly exceptional cases and therefore does not represent a general requirement for granting a 'residence permit for exceptional circumstances'; see Chapter 4.D.II.2.

808 § 60(3) AsylG (A).

809 Cf. ErläutRV 1523 BlgNR 25. GP, 44f.

810 § 60(1) No. 1 AsylG (A) refers to § 52 in conjunction with § 53(2) or (3) FPG.

811 VwGH 16.12.2015, Ro 2015/21/0037.

812 § 58(11) AsylG (A); cf. VwGH 30.6.2015, Ra 2015/21/0039.

813 § 4(1) No. 3 in conjunction with § 8(1) No. 1 Asylgesetz-Durchführungsverordnung in the version BGBl II 93/2022.

814 See just VwGH 15.9.2016, Ra 2016/21/0206.

circumstances vis-à-vis a previous application.[815] Particular features arise in the instances of *res iudicata* regarding 'residence permits for reasons of Article 8 ECHR'.[816]

d) End of the procedure

The decision (not) to grant a residence permit is made in an administrative decision concluding the procedure.[817] If the residence permit is granted *ex officio* or upon application, the Federal Office for Immigration and Asylum shall issue the residence entitlement card if the part of the administrative decision concluding the procedure has become final.[818] Furthermore, distinctions are to be drawn regarding the scope of the entitlements: the 'standard residence permit' may only be granted to those persons who satisfy the necessary requirements for the 'residence permit for reasons of Article 8 ECHR' or the 'residence permit in particularly exceptional cases', which will be discussed in more detail in Chapter 4.[819] Alongside these, further requirements apply to the 'residence permit plus', which include basic knowledge of German (A2)[820] or, at the time of decision, the pursuit of a permitted occupation from which the earnings exceed the marginal earnings threshold (2022: 485.85 euro/month[821]).[822] The 'residence permit for exceptional circumstances' combines[823] that they are temporary and permit residence for a 12-month period.[824] Where a residence permit is issued, a prior return decision shall be no longer relevant.[825]

815 § 58(10) AsylG (A).
816 VwGH 16.12.2015, Ro 2015/21/0037.
817 § 58(3), (4), (7) and (8) AsylG (A).
818 § 58(4) 1st Sent. and (7) AsylG (A).
819 See Chapter 4.B.III.1., Chapter 4.C.III.1. and Chapter 4.D.II.2.a.
820 The AsylG (A) refers to § 9 IntG in the version BGBl I 76/2022, which concerns module 1 of the integration agreement.
821 § 5(2) ASVG.
822 § 55(1) No. 2 AsylG (A) and § 56(1) No. 3 in conjunction with § 56(2) AsylG (A).
823 See for instance VwGH 14.4.2016, Ra 2016/21/0077 and 16.9.2015, Ro 2015/22/0026. For detail, *Hinterberger*, DRdA 2018, 111.
824 § 54(2) 1st Sent. AsylG (A); cf. VwGH 14.4.2016, Ro 2016/21/0077.
825 § 60(3) No. 2 FPG. On lifting the return decision including a ban on entry VwGH 16.12.2015, Ro 2015/21/0037.

The 'residence permit plus' affords the holder unrestricted access to the labour market.[826] The 'standard residence permit' and the 'special protection residence permit' allow the pursuit of a (self) employed occupation, though an employment permit is required for employment in accordance with the Employment of Foreign Nationals Act.[827] Unlike the 'standard residence permit', no labour-market test is conducted for a 'special protection residence permit'.[828] In this respect, *Peyrl* correctly states that in principle the employment permit in such cases conforms with EU law.[829] His analysis focuses primarily on the Single Permit Directive, according to which the Member States issue a single permit for employment and residency.[830] I have already discussed elsewhere that the access to the labour market that differs between the 'special protection residence permit' and 'standard residence permit' is unconstitutional as there is no objective justification for the different requirements.[831]

The Federal Office for Immigration and Asylum typically has to issue a return decision when rejecting or dismissing the application.[832] The same also applies in the asylum procedure when it is determined during an *ex officio* consideration of the 'residence permit for reasons of Article 8 ECHR' or the 'special protection residence permit' that the requirements have not been met.[833]

3. Consolidation of residence

The possibility to change to a right to settle and reside is available to aliens who have held a 'residence permit for exceptional circumstances' for 12 months. Those holding a 'special protection residence permit' can

826 § 54(1) No. 1 AsylG (A) and § 17 AuslBG.

827 §§ 4ff AuslBG; cf. VwGH 14.4.2016, Ra 2016/21/0077.

828 § 4(7) No. 5 AuslBG; cf. *Deutsch/Nowotny/Seitz*, Ausländerbeschäftigungsrecht § 4 AufenthG mns 41 and 54. See also § 4(3) No. 9 AuslBG.

829 *Peyrl*, Arbeitsmarkt 320f.

830 Art 6 Single Permit Directive.

831 *Hinterberger*, DRdA 2018, 111.

832 § 52(3) FPG and § 10(3) AsylG (A). Cf. VwGH 21.9.2017, Ra 2017/22/0128 para15 and 14.4.2016, Ra 2016/21/0077 para 25 regarding the exception under § 10(3) 2nd Sent. in conjunction with § 58(9) AsylG (A).

833 § 10(1) AsylG (A) and § 52(2) FPG. See VwGH 12.11.2015, Ra 2015/21/0023 regarding the special protection residence permit.

therefore either renew[834] this permit or acquire a 'Red-White-Red – Card plus'. A timely[835] application means that the applicant shall continue to be lawfully resident until the application is finally decided upon.[836] In this respect, the effects of such application resemble the 'fictitious effects' under the German Residence Act, whereby a right to a fictitious permitted or tolerated stay arises *ipso iure* upon application for a residence permit (or an extension thereof).[837] The application for renewal application has not only the legal effect that a 'special protection residence permit' will be granted if the requirements are satisfied but rather a 'Red-White-Red – Card plus' will be issued if the following additional requirements are met:[838] German language competence at A2 level, a legal entitlement to suitable accommodation, adequate health insurance and that the residence does not impose a financial burden on the State.[839] The examination of the additional requirements is conducted *ex officio*, though the Federal Office for Immigration and Asylum has to inform without delay the authority competent pursuant to the Settlement and Residence Act.[840] If the Federal Office for Immigration and Asylum informs that the additional requirements have been met, the 'Red-White-Red – Card plus' is to be issued without any further examination.[841] The Red-White-Red – Card plus' affords unrestricted access to the labour market[842] and is valid for two years.[843] However, if the additional requirements are not met, a 'special protection residence permit' is to be granted once more.[844]

According to § 41a(9) Nos. 1 and 2 NAG, aliens with a 'standard residence permit' or a 'residence permit plus' may only apply for a 'Red-

834 Pursuant to § 59(4) AsylG (A), the BFA is to make the decision to renew the 'special protection residence permit' within a four-month period; cf. *Ecker*, Schnittstellen zwischen AsylG 2005 und NAG unter besonderer Berücksichtigung von „Bleiberecht" und Familienzusammenführung in *Filzwieser/Taucher* (eds), Asyl- und Fremdenrecht. Jahrbuch 2016 (2016) 83 (99).

835 Though at the earliest three months before the period of validity expires.

836 § 59(1) AsylG (A).

837 See Chapter 3.B.V.1.

838 § 59(4) AsylG (A).

839 § 59(4) No. 3 in conjunction with § 60(2) AsylG (A).

840 § 59(5) AsylG (A).

841 ErläutRV 1803 BlgNR 24. GP, 51.

842 § 3(1) AuslBG and § 8(1) No. 2 NAG; for details *Peyrl*, Die Neuordnung der Arbeitskräftemigration nach Österreich („Rot-Weiß-Rot-Karte"), DRdA 2011, 476 and *Kreuzhuber*, Arbeitsmigration nach Österreich – Eckpunkte und erste Erfahrungen zur Rot-Weiß-Rot-Karte, ZAR 2014, 13.

843 § 41(5) 1st Sent. NAG.

844 § 59(4) AsylG (A).

White-Red – Card plus'; there is no grant *ex officio*.[845] The Federal Office for Immigration and Asylum is to grant a 'Red-White-Red – Card plus' to aliens holding a 'residence permit plus' or a 'standard residence permit' for 12 months and with German language competence at A2 level or who, at the time of the decision, are pursuing an occupation and thereby exceeding the minimum earnings threshold.[846] There is a legal entitlement to receive the 'Red-White-Red – Card plus' if the requirements are met.[847] The application for a 'Red-White-Red – Card plus' is to be deemed an initial application pursuant to the Settlement and Residence Act.[848] As it is not an application for renewal, the question of the legal nature surrounding the residency arises above all in connection with obtaining permanent settlement, in so far as the 'Red-White-Red – Card plus' is only issued after the 'standard residence permit' or 'residence permit plus' expires. The Supreme Administrative Court (*Verwaltungsgerichtshof*; VwGH) has held in this respect that the stay is to be considered unlawful upon expiration of the 'standard residence permit' or 'residence permit plus' due to the initial application for the 'Red-White-Red – Card plus'.[849]

If the requirements for a 'Red-White-Red – Card plus' are not met, the legislation provides neither for a new 'standard residence permit' or 'residence permit plus' nor for the renewal (as is also the case for the 'special protection residence permit').[850] A 'settlement permit' will be granted in such cases.[851] However, it appears questionable from the perspective of equal treatment that the 'settlement permit' excludes the pursuit of a non-self-employed occupation[852] and thereby worsens the legal position of the person concerned.[853] Aliens holding a 'standard residence permit' even continue to meet the same requirements. If they held a 'residence permit plus', they met the additional requirements on at least one occasion.

845 ErläutRV 1803 BlgNR 24. GP, 77.

846 See Chapter 3.A.III.2.d.

847 *Peyrl* in *Abermann/Czech/Kind/Peyrl* (eds), NAG Kommentar^2 (2019) § 41a NAG mn 16.

848 ErläutRV 1803 BlgNR 24. GP, 73f and VwGH 23.6.2015, Ra 2014/22/0199.

849 ErläutRV 1803 BlgNR 24. GP, 45. For a differing view see *Ecker* in *Filzwieser/Taucher* 99f.

850 ErläutRV 1803 BlgNR 24. GP, 45.

851 § 43(3) NAG; for detail see *Kind* in *Abermann/Czech/Kind/Peyrl* (eds), NAG Kommentar^2 (2019) § 43 NAG mns 9–18.

852 § 8(1) No. 4 NAG. In contrast, a self-employed occupation may be pursued.

853 *Peyrl*, Arbeitsmarkt 316, who refers in this context to a '*Bestrafung*' (punishment).

Although they no longer meet these requirements, there is seemingly no objective justification for this worsened legal position.

4. Drawing distinctions

It is appropriate at this juncture to explore § 62 of the Austrian Asylum Act concerning the 'right of residence for displaced persons'.[854] In the 1990s, refugees from Bosnia and Herzegovina or Croatia were taken in due to the war in Yugoslavia.[855] The provision represents the transposition of the Temporary Protection Directive into Austrian law, which is why since 1999 it – as well as the previous provisions – has had no relevance in practice.[856] Only the activation of the Temporary Protection Directive in March 2022 because of Russia's invasion of the Ukraine effected a change in this regard.[857] A notable feature is that the temporary right is not granted by an administrative decision (*Bescheid*), but rather by an order (*Verordnung*[858]) of the Austrian federal government.[859] This provision acquires a special status,[860] whereby the grant of the right is possible without a separate decision and examination of the requirements. § 62 AsylG (A) does not meet the definition of a regularisation and is excluded from the scope of this study.[861]

---

854 § 62 AsylG used to be in § 76 NAG prior to the legislation in BGBl I 87/2012; cf. ErläutRV 1803 BlgNR 24. GP, 41. § 29 FrG was the relevant provision before the Settlement and Residence Act entered into force; see ErläutRV 952 BlgNR 22. GP, 148. As the provision has more or less remained the same, the comments in *Muzak*, Die Aufenthaltsberechtigung für „De-facto-Flüchtlinge" durch Verordnung der Bundesregierung, ÖJZ 1999, 13, still remain relevant.

855 Cf. *Asylkoordination/Diakonie/Volkshilfe/Integrationshaus/SOS Mitmensch* (eds), Ein Jahr „Bleiberecht": Eine Analyse mit Fallbeispielen (April 2010), http://s3web0314.peakserver.net/wp-content/uploads/2015/02/bleiberechtsbericht_03_10.pdf (31.7.2022) 4.

856 See the order of the federal government which concerns the right to reside granted to refugees fleeing the war in Kosovo and which amends the *Niederlassungsverordnung* 1999 (Settlement Order), BGBl II 133/1999; cf. *Muzak*, ÖJZ 1999.

857 *Vertriebenen-Verordnung* (Order on Displaced Persons), BGBl II 92/2022.

858 On the meaning of *Verordnung* in Austrian administrative law *Raschauer*, Verwaltungsrecht mns 724ff.

859 Cf. *Muzak*, ÖJZ 1999.

860 See also *Muzak*, ÖJZ 1999.

861 See Chapter 1.A.II.3.a.

It is to be noted that the residence permits under the Settlement and Residence Act in which an application is possible under § 21(2) of this legislation are generally not examined here as they are also typically not regularisations as understood in this study.[862] §§ 30a and 41a(10) NAG will be discussed in Chapter 4.D.I.1.a. and Chapter 4.C.V., respectively.

IV. Competences and authorities regarding aliens' law

In line with the federal principle underpinning the constitution,[863] the Federal Constitutional Law (*Bundesverfassungsgesetz*; B-VG) generally divides the legislative and enforcement competences between the Austrian federal government and the *Länder*.[864] In this respect, the competence concerning the legislation and enforcement regarding aliens and asylum lies mainly with the federal government.[865] The Federal Office for Immigration and Asylum was established on 1 January 2014,[866] which in the course of indirect federal administration, i.e. through the *Länder*,[867] is responsible for areas such as the grant and withdrawal of asylum and subsidiary protection in relation to applications for international protection, the grant of 'residence permits for exceptional circumstances', the removal order, declaring 'toleration' as well as imposing removal measures.[868] The competences that are central to this study thus fall within the scope of the responsibilities assigned to the Federal Office for Immigration and Asylum. The relevant provisions are to be found in the Act on the Proceedings of the Federal Office for Immigration and Asylum, the Asylum Act (A) and the Aliens' Police Act. Matters concerning the Aliens' Police Act are a part of special administrative law.[869] The procedures contained therein are therefore subject to provisions in statutes such as the General Admin-

862 See Chapter 1.A.II., for detail see *Kind* in *Abermann/Czech/Kind/Peyrl* § 21 NAG mns 19–23.

863 Art 2(1) B-VG. Cf. *Berka*, Verfassungsrecht mns 155ff.

864 Arts 10–15 B-VG; *Öhlinger/Eberhard*, Verfassungsrecht mns 235–289.

865 Art 10(1) No. 3 and 7 B-VG; cf. *Muzak* in *Kolonovits/Muzak/Piska/Perthold/Strejcek* 189 and in general on the competence under Art 10 B-VG *Öhlinger/Eberhard*, Verfassungsrecht mns 241–243.

866 See BGBl I 87/2012 and § 1 BFA-VG.

867 This arises *e contrario* from § 102(1) and (2) B-VG; cf. *Muzak* in *Kolonovits/Muzak/Piska/Perthold/Strejcek* 189 and in general on direct federal administration *Raschauer*, Verwaltungsrecht mn 261.

868 § 3(2) BFA-VG.

869 Cf. *Muzak* in *Kolonovits/Muzak/Piska/Perthold/Strejcek*.

istrative Procedure Act (*Allgemeines Verwaltungsverfahrensgesetz*; AVG), to the extent that they are not covered by the *lex specialis* provisions in the Aliens' Police Act, the Asylum Act (A) or the Act on the Proceedings of the Federal Office for Immigration and Asylum.

The field of 'immigration and emigration' is also relevant.[870] It is to be enforced via indirect federal administration.[871] According to the Settlement and Residence Act, the competent *Land* authorities are responsible for issuing, rejecting and withdrawing residence titles from aliens who reside or seek to reside in Austria, as well as the documentation of any existing rights of residence under EU law.[872]

V. Judicial protection

The Austrian judiciary can be divided into the ordinary courts responsible for civil and criminal matters, and the courts with jurisdiction in public law. The latter covers the administrative courts and the constitutional court,[873] which offer aliens particular judicial protection against acts by administrative authorities. In this respect, the rule of law, whose main element is anchored in the legality principle in Article 18 of the Federal Constitutional Law, is especially relevant as it provides that the entire public administration is bound by the law.[874] This is to be examined and ensured by the institutions such as the administrative courts and the constitutional court which provide judicial protection.[875]

1. Administrative jurisdiction

The administrative jurisdiction was subject to considerable reforms in 2012 which took effect on 1 January 2014 and which now comprises two

870 Art 10(1) No. 3 B-VG.
871 § 3(1) NAG.
872 § 1(1) NAG.
873 Cf. *Berka*, Verfassungsrecht mns 895ff.
874 Cf. *Berka*, Verfassungsrecht mns 190ff, 492ff as well as *Öhlinger/Eberhard*, Verfassungsrecht mns 597ff.
875 VfGH 11.12.1986, G 119/86 with further references.

instances.[876] The administrative courts are the courts of first instance.[877] Austria follows the '9 + 2' approach: each *Land* has its own administrative court with a Federal Administrative Court (*Bundesverwaltungsgericht*; BVwG) and a Federal Financial Court (*Bundesfinanzgericht*; BFG) at federal level.

The Federal Administrative Court is the first instance court for complaints against decisions from the Federal Office for Immigration and Asylum and thus competent for the areas relevant to this study.[878] The Federal Administrative Court can and in part must rule on the merits.[879] Following a ruling of the Federal Administrative Court,[880] the period for filing a complaint against a decision by the Federal Office for Immigration and Asylum is in principle four weeks, as applies in general to administrative proceedings.[881] However, reforms in 2018[882] introduced a shorter, two-week period with regard to rejections that were linked to a removal measure.[883] This therefore affects the dismissal decisions concerning the 'residence permits for exceptional circumstances'. Exceptions apply with regard to unaccompanied minors or where the removal measure is linked to the statement that the deportation is inadmissible.[884]

The Supreme Administrative Court (*Verwaltungsgerichtshof*; VwGH) is competent in the second instance. This Court pronounces, inter alia, on the decisions of the Federal Administrative Court.[885] The appeal against rulings of the Federal Administrative Court concerns points of law (*Revision*[886]), for which a six-week period applies.[887] The complainant may apply

---

876 BGBl I 51/2012; cf. *Wessely*, Grundrechtliche Aspekte der Verwaltungsgerichte in *Larcher* (ed), Handbuch Verwaltungsgerichte: Die Grundlagen der Verwaltungsgerichtsbarkeit I. Instanz (2013) 204 (205).

877 Art 129 B-VG; cf. *Öhlinger/Eberhard*, Verfassungsrecht mns 650ff.

878 § 7(1) No. 1 BFA-VG; see in general Art 130(1) No. 1 B-VG.

879 §§ 7ff and 28 VwGVG; cf. *Kolonovits/Muzak/Stöger*, Verwaltungsverfahrensrecht mns 820ff.

880 VfGH 26.9.2017, G 134/2017-12, in which the Constitutional Court held that the two-week period for complaints is unconstitutional.

881 § 7(4) VwGVG and § 16(1) BFA-VG.

882 BGBl I 56/2018.

883 § 16(1) BFA-VG.

884 See Chapter 4.A.I.3.

885 Cf. *Öhlinger/Eberhard*, Verfassungsrecht mns 663ff and *Holoubek/Lang* (eds), Das Verfahren vor dem Verwaltungsgerichtshof (2015).

886 Art 133(1) No. 1 B-VG. A distinction is to be drawn between ordinary and extraordinary appeal on points of law (*Revision*).

887 § 26(1) VwGG.

for legal aid if he or she does not have sufficient funds.[888] The complainant must be represented by legal counsel.

2. Constitutional jurisdiction

The Federal Constitutional Law is the most relevant source of Austrian constitutional law. However, there are also numerous other federal constitutional laws as well as individual provisions and key guarantees of basic rights, which are each on the same level as the constitution.[889] One may refer here to the Basic Law on the General Rights of Nationals (*Staatsgrundgesetz*[890]) or the ECHR as examples. The latter has direct effect in Austria due to its constitutional rank,[891] which is why its provisions may be examined by the Constitutional Court as 'constitutionally guaranteed rights'.[892]

The Constitutional Court (*Verfassungsgerichtshof*; VfGH) is the central ruling body in relation to constitutional jurisdiction.[893] In principle the complainant may bring a complaint against a ruling by the Federal Administrative Court before the Constitutional Court,[894] for which a six-week period applies.[895] The complainant may apply for legal aid if he or she does not have sufficient funds.[896] The complainant must be represented by legal counsel.

---

888 § 61 VwGG refers to the provisions of the Austrian Code of Civil Procedure (ZPO), in particular §§ 63ff ZPO are applicable.

889 Cf. *Öhlinger/Eberhard*, Verfassungsrecht mns 6ff.

890 Staatsgrundgesetz in the version BGBl 684/1988.

891 BGBl 210/1958 in the version BGBl III 68/2021.

892 Art 144 B-VG; cf. *Öhlinger/Eberhard*, Verfassungsrecht mn 131 and *Berka/Binder/Kneihs*, Die Grundrechte[2] (2019) 34ff with further references.

893 Cf. *Berka*, Verfassungsrecht mns 987ff and *Öhlinger/Eberhard*, Verfassungsrecht mns 984ff as well as a historical outline in *Holzinger/Frank*, Die Verfassungsgerichtsbarkeit – Essenz und Wandlung in FS 150 Jahre Wiener Juristische Gesellschaft (2017) 169 (171ff).

894 Art 144 B-VG.

895 § 82(1) VfGG.

896 § 82(3) VfGG refers to § 64 ZPO.

B. Germany

The 'Federal Republic of Germany is a democratic and social federal state' (Article 20(1) GG) comprising 16 *Länder* (Federal States). Germany may also be referred to as an immigration country.[897] According to the statistics from the Federal Statistical Office (*Statistisches Bundesamt*), on 31 December 2019 approx. 12.7% of the population were foreigners (10.6 from 83.2 million).[898]

I. Historical development of residency law

The German term *Ausländerrecht* (law on foreigners) is typically used to describe German immigration law,[899] though there is the increasing trend to use the term *Aufenthaltsrecht* (residency law), as is also true for this study.[900] This field of law has developed under the considerable influences on the continuous, heated discussion on the topics of refugees, migrants, and all associated issues.[901] However, it is important to draw a distinction

897 Cf. only *Unabhängige Kommission „Zuwanderung"*, Zuwanderung gestalten – Integration fördern (2001), http://www.jugendsozialarbeit.de/media/raw/Zuwanderungsbericht_pdf.pdf (31.7.2022) 1; *Bast*, DÖV 2013, 221; *Kießling*, Fremdenpolizeirecht im Rechtsstaat (?) – Zu Herkunft und Zukunft des Ausweisungsrechts, ZAR 2016, 45 (52); *Farahat* in *Baer/Lepsius/Schönberger/Waldhoff/Walter* 337 refers to a 'superdiverse immigration society' (*'superdiversen Einwanderungsgesellschaft'*).

898 Cf. *Statistisches Bundesamt*, Bevölkerung und Erwerbstätigkeit 2020: Ausländische Bevölkerung – Ergebnisse des Ausländerzentralregisters (29.3.2021), https://www.destatis.de/DE/Themen/Gesellschaft-Umwelt/Bevoelkerung/Migration-Integration/Publikationen/Downloads-Migration/auslaend-bevoelkerung-2010200207004.pdf (31.7.2022) 18.

899 See only *Bergmann/Dienelt* (eds), Kommentar Ausländerrecht[12] (2018). The term *Fremdenrecht* (law on aliens) was previously used as is similar today in Austria (see Chapter 3.A.I.); see *Doehring*, Neuregelungen des deutschen Fremdenrechts durch das „Ausländergesetz" von 1965, ZaöRV 1965, 478.

900 See *Bast*, Aufenthaltsrecht and *Huber/Eichenhofer/Endres de Oliveira*, Aufenthaltsrecht (2017) mn 1.

901 See, in general, *Herbert*, Ausländerpolitik 9ff or 299ff and on the refugee debate, *Becker*, Die Flüchtlingsdebatte in den Medien Deutschlands – Eine korpus- und diskurslinguistische Untersuchung der Konzeptualisierung von Angst, Sprachreport 2016/2, 1; *Hemmelmann/Wegner*, Flüchtlingsdebatte im Spiegel von Medien und Parteien, Communicatio Socialis 2016/1, 21.

to asylum law, which is regulated in the German Asylum Act (*Asylgesetz*; AsylG (G)).

In Germany, residency law forms a specific part of police law,[902] but is treated ever increasingly as a separate and specific part of administrative law.[903] The term '*Ausländer*' is legally defined in the most important source of German residency law,[904] the Residence Act (*Aufenthaltsgesetz*; AufenthG), and applies to anyone who is not German as defined in Article 116(1) GG.[905] The English translation of the Residence Act translates '*Ausländer*' as 'foreigner', which is the term used in the following.

The National Socialist Police Order on Foreigners is of particular historical significance, as – comparable with Austria[906] – it formed the basis for the 1965 Foreigners Act (*Ausländergesetz 1965*), which in turn repealed the aforementioned National Socialist Police Order on Foreigners.[907] According to the National Socialist Police Order on Foreigners, foreigners had no claim to residency – the rules adopted the standpoint of voluntary hospitality, for which the foreigner had to prove him- or herself worthy.[908] The authorities gave permission to stay at their own discretion.[909] Interestingly, special permission was required at that time in order to pursue employment.[910] Furthermore, the authorities were not only empowered to use force but also had to use force when removing the foreigner from the country.[911]

As a result of the events during and following the Second World War, the majority of immigrants in Germany in the 1950s were displaced persons and refugees.[912] Prior to 1959/1960, only very few foreigners living in Germany were employed. The economic boom during these years shifted political considerations towards the recruitment of migrant workers (so-

---

902 Cf. *Hailbronner*, Asyl- und Ausländerrecht[5] (2021) mn 8.
903 Cf. *Huber/Eichenhofer/Endres de Oliveira*, Aufenthaltsrecht mn 1 with further references.
904 Cf. only *Huber/Eichenhofer/Endres de Oliveira*, Aufenthaltsrecht mn 1.
905 § 2(1) AufenthG; see *Huber/Eichenhofer/Endres de Oliveira*, Aufenthaltsrecht mns 9ff for further terms used in the AufenthG.
906 See above Chapter 3.A.I.
907 § 55(2) Act of 28.4.1965 (BGBl I 353). See *Doehring*, ZaöRV 1965.
908 § 1 NS-Ausländerpolizeiverordnung.
909 § 2(1) NS-Ausländerpolizeiverordnung.
910 § 2(2) NS-Ausländerpolizeiverordnung.
911 § 7(5) NS-Ausländerpolizeiverordnung.
912 Cf. *Herbert*, Ausländerpolitik 192–197.

called *Gastarbeiter*),[913] who should alleviate the shortages on the German labour market. The 1955 recruitment agreement between Germany and Italy (*deutsch-italienisches Anwerbeabkommen*) marked the introduction of a programme to recruit migrant workers. Shortly before, the National Socialist Police Order on Foreigners and the Reich Order on Foreign Workers of 23 January 1933 (*reichsdeutsche Verordnung über ausländische Arbeitnehmer*[914]) were reintroduced and therefore the continuation of National Socialist legislation regarding foreigners.[915]

The numbers of migrant workers increased considerably following further recruitment agreements concluded until 1967 (Greece, Spain, Turkey, Portugal and Yugoslavia). The notion that migrant employees were 'reservists' played a significant role in passing the 1965 Foreigners Act,[916] in which migrant workers were generally only granted a temporary one year right to stay, which was linked to the respective employer. The relevant authorities were again equipped with considerable discretion in each decision relating to the residency.

Despite the short recession in 1967, the number of migrant workers increased and peaked in 1973; Turkish nationals formed the largest group from 1972 onwards.[917] The first negative effects of this migrant programme were already emerging at this time as it became increasingly clear that the migrant workers in Germany – as in Austria – would not only want to remain in Germany but also to bring over their families. The end of recruitment in 1973 was one response, with the 1973 oil crisis given as the cause. The political and public debate turned then to the long-term consequences of migration that was only intended to be temporary, for instance the costs for social inclusion, unemployment or social security. Ending the recruitment should fully cut off the influx of migrant workers from countries that were not part of the European Community.

The years 1973–1990 saw intense public and political debate. On the one hand, migrant inflow should be avoided, yet on the other hand, foreigners already residing in Germany should be 'integrated' as best as possible. The

---

913 See only *Oltmer/Kreienbrink/Sanz Díaz* (eds), Das „Gastarbeiter"-System. Arbeitsmigration und ihre Folgen in der Bundesrepublik Deutschland und Westeuropa (2012).

914 Imperial Law Gazette I 26/1933.

915 Cf. *Kießling*, ZAR 2016, 46.

916 Cf. *Herbert*, Ausländerpolitik 211f.

917 Cf. *Luft*, Die Anwerbung türkischer Arbeitnehmer und ihre Folgen (5.8.2014), https://www.bpb.de/internationales/europa/tuerkei/184981/gastarbeit (31.7.2022).

'non-perception of a *de facto* immigration situation'[918] was subsequently politically anchored in various reports and guidelines. Although 'integration' was at least always mentioned, the focus of the political measures was limited to restricting migrant inflow and promoting the return of foreigners already living in Germany.

The Foreigners Act of 1965 was replaced by the 1990 Foreigners Act, which after numerous failed drafts was ultimately accepted. This new legislation was not as restrictive as the preceding drafts, but continued to negate the fact that Germany had become an immigration country.

Just as its predecessor, the later Foreigners Act did not contain any comprehensive provision or prospect for foreigners to regularise their residency in the event they did not have a right to stay.[919] The policy towards foreigners always pursued the maxim that irregularly staying foreigners should never be 'rewarded' with a right to stay. As *Hailbronner* correctly states, a possibility for regularisation did exist – broadly speaking – in the form of a 'two-stage process'.[920] First, the irregularly staying foreigner had to be formally tolerated.[921] Regularisation was therefore possible by granting, in a second step, the foreigner a right to stay. This shows the tight link between tolerated status and regularisation, which still exists today. The main path out of irregularity was therefore by granting an individual residence title (*Aufenthaltsbefugnis*) pursuant to § 30 AuslG 1990,[922] over which the foreigners authority (*Ausländerbehörde*) had considerable discretion.[923]

Following the 1990 Foreigners Act, asylum policy became the beating heart of the (political and public) heated debate. The increased numbers of asylum applications, first from eastern Europe and then from former Yugoslavia, led from the mid-1980s to tighter controls in asylum procedural law. Furthermore, the amendment of the fundamental right to asylum was a hotly debated issue, which ultimately resulted in a compromise in 1993 – the so-called *Asylkompromiss*.[924] Above all, the right to asylum was

918 *Herbert*, Ausländerpolitik 245: '*Nichtwahrnehmung einer faktischen Einwanderungssituation*'.
919 Cf. *Hailbronner* in *de Bruycker* 252.
920 In this sense, *Hailbronner* in *de Bruycker* 253f. See also *Kraler*, Journal of Immigrant and Refugee Studies 2019, 102.
921 §§ 55f AuslG 1990; cf. *Hailbronner* in *de Bruycker* 264.
922 Cf. *Hailbronner* in *de Bruycker* 252.
923 Cf. *Hailbronner* in *de Bruycker* 264f.
924 See the contributions in *Luft/Schimany* (eds), 20 Jahre Asylkompromiss. Bilanz und Perspektiven (2014).

considerably restricted by the introduction of the notions safe country of origin (*sicherer Herkunftsstaat*) and safe third country (*sicherer Drittstaat*). The number of applications could be drastically lowered with one fell swoop, but at the same time the key question whether Germany would need immigration legislation was merely put on ice.[925]

An ever recurring question concerned the treatment of rejected asylum applications from persons who could not be deported.[926] Regularisations thus now became part of the political debate. In 1995, for example, a legislative proposal included a rule governing old cases in which asylum seekers had been living in Germany for a lengthy period.[927] As other proposals, this also failed and consequently no uniform legislative possibility was created to regularise the stay of those denied asylum.[928] The reason was the supposed 'pull factor'[929] of regularisations and the alleged unfavourable public opinion.[930] Nonetheless, an alternative political solution was found. Alongside the aforementioned 'residency title' pursuant to § 30 AuslG 1990, regularisation could also be achieved in part by a 'residency title' under § 32 AuslG 1990: the highest *Land* authority (*oberste Landesbehörde*) issues in agreement with the Federal Ministry of the Interior (*Bundesinnenministerium*) an 'order' (*Anordnung*) on the basis of this provision,[931] which allows a precisely defined group of persons to acquire a 'residency title'. These 'orders' have a quasi-legislative status, ranking below statutory instruments (*Rechtsverordnungen*).[932] For instance, in 1996 a hardship rule for foreign families who had been staying in Germany for many years was passed via an 'order' according to § 32 AuslG 1990.[933] Several such 'orders' were passed between 1995 and 2007, each with different requirements and

925 Cf. *Herbert*, Ausländerpolitik 320ff.
926 Cf. *Hailbronner* in *de Bruycker* 254.
927 BT-Drs 13/3877.
928 Cf. *Hailbronner* in *de Bruycker* 254f.
929 See e.g. BT-Drs 13/1189, 6.
930 Cf. *Hailbronner* in *de Bruycker* 254 and also 252.
931 This decision is often discussed in relation to the Standing Conference of the Minister of the Interior and *Land* senators of the interior; cf. *Hailbronner* in *de Bruycker* 269f.
932 Cf. *Huber/Eichenhofer/de Oliveira*, Aufenthaltsrecht mn 456 with further references.
933 On the transposition, see BT-Drs 13/9936.

applying to different groups.[934] According to *Hailbronner*, they are to be qualified as 'regularisation programmes'.[935]

All of these discussions culminated in the 'immigration compromise' and the 2005 Immigration Act (*Zuwanderungsgesetz 2005*),[936] described by *Bast* as a total revision of the migration law in force.[937] This Act contains 15 articles including the Residence Act (*Aufenthaltsgesetz*; AufenthG) and the Freedom of Movement Act/EU (*Freizügigkeitsgesetz/EU*[938]), as well as amendments to individual pieces of legislation, such as the Act on Benefits for Asylum Seekers (*Asylbewerberleistungsgesetz*; AsylbLG). The heart and most important source of the current residency law is, however, the Residence Act.[939] This legislation introduced a paradigm shift, which is expressed in the dichotomy of migration opportunity and an expectation of integration.[940] The Residence Act serves in principle to manage and limit the influx of foreigners into Germany.[941] It regulates the entry, residence, economic activity and integration of foreigners.

The perhaps most significant 'order' was issued following the enactment of the Residence Act, with § 23(1) AufenthG (the successor to § 32 AuslG 1990) as the basis.[942] By means of the so-called decision on the right to remain (*Bleiberechtsbeschluss*) from 17 November 2006, nationwide (i.e. harmonised) minimum requirements for a rule on a right to remain were

---

934 For a comprehensive and detailed overview see *Bundesministerium für Inneres*, Verwaltungsvorschriften des Innenministeriums zum Ausländerrecht (VwV-AuslR-IM) ABSCHNITT B II Eingeschränkt gültige Bleiberechtsregelungen (nur Verlängerungen) (2.11.2010) and *Hailbronner* in *de Bruycker* 256ff.

935 *Hailbronner* in *de Bruycker* 263f: 'Regularisation decisions based upon Sec. 32 of the Aliens Law are not meant to provide for a general pattern of regularisation for clandestine immigrants but rather as an instrument to accommodate the special needs and interests of particular groups after a long residence in Germany'.

936 Act of 30.7.2004 (BGBl I 1950); cf. *Unabhängige Kommission „Zuwanderung"*, Zuwanderung (2001) 16 as well as *Huber*, Das Zuwanderungsgesetz, NVwZ 2005, 1.

937 *Bast*, DÖV 2013, 214.

938 Freizügigkeitsgesetz/EU in the version of 9.7.2021 (BGBl I 2467).

939 Cf. *Huber/Eichenhofer/de Oliveira*, Aufenthaltsrecht mn 1.

940 Cf. *Bast*, Aufenthaltsrecht 218ff; for an alternative view *Hailbronner*, Asyl- und Ausländerrecht mn 8, who speaks of a '*Dreiklang Steuerung, Begrenzung und Integration*' ('triad of management, limitation and integration').

941 § 1(1) AufenthG; cf. *Hailbronner*, Asyl- und Ausländerrecht mn 14.

942 Cf. *Huber/Eichenhofer/de Oliveira*, Aufenthaltsrecht mn 455.

set in law.[943] It is contextually significant that comprehensive rules governing old cases were created for the first time for persons who had been living in Germany for several years under a 'tolerated' status.[944] These rules, which are now found in §§ 104a and 104b AufenthG,[945] served in turn as a template for §§ 25a and 25b AufenthG.[946]

The Residence Act has since undergone numerous amendments,[947] with the most important arising from the transposition of EU directives regarding residence and asylum law (2007[948] and 2011[949]) and the 2008 Act on the Management of Labour Migration (*Arbeitsmigrationssteuerungsgesetz 2008*[950]). Further legislation was passed as a consequence of the 'long summer of migration 2015', for instance the 2015 Act to Expediate the Asylum Process (*Asylverfahrensbeschleunigungsgesetz 2015*[951]), the Act to Amend the Right to Remain (*Bleiberechtsänderungsgesetz*[952]) and the 2017 Act to Improve the Enforcement of the Obligation to Leave (*Gesetz zur besseren Durchsetzung der Ausreisepflicht 2017*[953]). The Labour Migration Act of 2017 (*Arbeitsmigrationsgesetz 2017*[954]) is also to be included in this list.

In 2019, the German Parliament (*Bundestag*) passed a number of legislative measures referred to as the *Migrationspaket*[955] – the 'migration pack-

943 Available under http://www.fluechtlingsinfo-berlin.de/fr/pdf/Bleiberecht_IMK_2006.pdf (31.7.2022).

944 Cf. BT-Drs 16/4503 and *Zentrum für Politik, Kultur und Forschung Berlin*, Expertise zur Umsetzung des IMK-Bleiberechtsbeschlusses vom 17. November 2006 (January 2008), http://www.fluchtort-hamburg.de/fileadmin/pdf/EQUAL/080114_Expertise_IMK-Bleiberechtsbeschluss.pdf (31.7.2022).

945 See also Chapter 3.B.III.4.

946 See below, Chapter 4.B.I.–II.

947 Cf. *Bast*, DÖV 2013, 215; *Hailbronner*, Asyl- und Ausländerrecht mns 8–14.

948 Act of 19.8.2007 (BGBl I 1970).

949 Act of 22.11.2011 (BGBl I 2258).

950 Act of 20.12.2008 (BGBl I 2846).

951 Act of 20.10.2015 (BGBl I 1722). Cf. *Neundorf*, Neuerungen im Aufenthalts- und Asylrecht durch das Asylverfahrensbeschleunigungsgesetz, NJW 2016, 5 and *Kluth*, Das Asylverfahrensbeschleunigungsgesetz, ZAR 2015, 337.

952 Act of 27.7.2015 (BGBl I 1386). Cf. *Beichel-Benedetti*, Die Neuregelung der Abschiebungshaft im Gesetz zur Neubestimmung des Bleiberechts und der Aufenthaltsbeendigung, NJW 2015, 2541 or *Huber*, Das Gesetz zur Neubestimmung des Bleiberechts und der Aufenthaltsbeendigung, NVwZ 2015, 1178.

953 Act of 20.7.2017 (BGBl I 2780); cf. *Hörich/Tewocht*, Zum Gesetz zur besseren Durchsetzung der Ausreisepflicht, NVwZ 2017, 1153.

954 Act of 27.5.2017 (BGBl I 1106).

955 Cf. *Kluth*, Next Steps: Die Gesetze des Migrationspakets 2019 folgen jeweils eigenen Pfaden, NVwZ 2019, 1305; *Hoffmann*, Das „Migrationspaket" im Überblick, InfAuslR 2019, 409 and the contributions in the supplement

age'.[956] The measures relevant to this study are the Skilled Immigration Act (*Fachkräfteeinwanderungsgesetz*[957]), the Orderly Return Act (*Geordnete-Rückkehr-Gesetz*[958]), the Toleration Act (*Duldungsgesetz*[959]) and the Third Act to amend the Act on Benefits for Asylum Seekers (*Drittes Gesetz zur Änderung des AsylbLG*[960]). This legislation had enormous effects on the legal framework.

The Orderly Return Act entered into force on 21 August 2019, the Third Act to amend the Act on Benefits for Asylum Seekers on 1 September 2019 and the Toleration Act on 1 January 2020. The bulk of the Skilled Immigration Act entered into force on 1 March 2020. According to *Kluth*, the Skilled Immigration Act and the Toleration Act support the interests of the labour market in acquiring additional skilled workers, whereas the Orderly Return Act prioritises the State's interests in managing the return of migrants.[961] The Third Act to amend the Act on Benefits for Asylum Seekers makes the necessary changes to the social benefits received.

As in Austria, Germany has also made numerous reforms since the Residence Act, which has resulted in an ever more complex legal framework that has received justified criticism.[962]

---

to Asylmagazin 8–9/2019, such as *Informationsverbund Asyl und Migration*, Neuregelungen durch das Migrationspaket, Das Migrationspaket – Beilage zum Asylmagazin 8-9/2019, 2.

956 See *Roßbach*, Bundestag beschließt Gesetzespaket zu Abschiebung und Migration, Süddeutsche Zeitung (7.6.2019), https://www.sueddeutsche.de/politik/migration-bundestag-geordnete-rueckkehr-gesetz-1.4478900 (31.7.2022) and *Lau*, Ein kleines Ja und ein großes Nein, Zeit Online (7.6.2019), https://www.zeit.de/politik/deutschland/2019-06/migrationspaket-grosse-koalition-abschiebung-zuwanderung (31.7.2022).

957 Act of 15.8.2019 (BGBl I 1307); cf. BT-Drs 19/8285.

958 Act of 15.8.2019 (BGBl I 1294); cf. BT-Drs 19/10047. The official title is *Zweites Gesetzes zur besseren Durchsetzung der Ausreisepflicht*.

959 Act of 8.7.2019 (BGBl I 1021); cf. BT-Drs 19/8286. The official title is *Gesetz über Duldung bei Ausbildung und Beschäftigung*.

960 Act of 13.8.2019 (BGBl I 1290); cf. BT-Drs 19/10052.

961 *Kluth*, NVwZ 2019, 1306 and see further *Thym*, Geordnete Rückkehr und Bleiberechte im Dschungel des Migrationsrechts, ZAR 2019, 353 (353ff). For criticism, *Hruschka*, Ad-Hoc-Reparaturbetrieb statt kohärenter Rechtsrahmen: das „Geordnete-Rückkehr-Gesetz", Verfassungsblog (21.5.2019), https://verfassungsblog.de/ad-hoc-reparaturbetrieb-statt-kohaerenter-rechtsrahmen-das-geordnete-rueckkehr-gesetz/ (31.7.2022).

962 See especially the preface in *Marx*, Aufenthalts-, Asyl- und Flüchtlingsrecht[7] (2020) as well as *Thym*, ZAR 2019, 362.

II. Legal status of foreigners

Before addressing the 'residence permits for humanitarian reasons', this section describes the legal status of foreigners in residence law, beginning with legal status of the residence, followed by the access to employment, social benefits and healthcare.

1. (Un)lawful residence

The first sentence of § 4(1) AufenthG requires foreigners to have a residence title to enter and stay in Germany.[963] The Residence Act distinguishes between different types of residence titles,[964] though the 'temporary residence permit' (*befristete Aufenthaltserlaubnis*) is central to this study. In principle the residence is subject to a 'reservation of permission'.[965] Accordingly, a person without a residence title and with no other right to stay is staying unlawfully on German territory.

As the system under the Residence Act does not, in principle, have any scope for an unregulated stay,[966] a tolerated stay also falls under the notion of an unlawful stay.[967] This assertion also applies to the block on issuing a residence title,[968] which will be discussed in more detail below.[969]

Furthermore, foreigners must also be in possession of a recognised and valid passport or passport substitute in accordance with the 'passport obligation' (*Passpflicht*).[970] This also includes substitute identification papers according to § 48(2) AufenthG, which can be issued to a person who is neither in possession of a passport nor can be reasonably expected to obtain one.[971]

---

963 Cf. *Huber/Eichenhofer/Endres de Oliveira*, Aufenthaltsrecht mns 37f. Exceptions exist for EU citizens or nationals of associated third countries.

964 § 4(1) AufenthG and see below, Chapter 3.B.III.1.

965 No. 4.1.0.1 AVV-AufenthG.

966 *Gordzielik/Huber* in *Huber/Mantel* (eds), Kommentar Aufenthaltsgesetz/Asylgesetz[3] (2021) § 60a AufenthG mn 7 with further references.

967 See Chapter 4.A.I.2.

968 § 10(3) 2nd Sent. AufenthG.

969 See Chapter 3.B.III.2.c.

970 § 3 AufenthG and § 2ff Aufenthaltsverordnung in the version of 20.8.2021 (BGBl I 3682); cf. *Huber/Eichenhofer/Endres de Oliveira*, Aufenthaltsrecht mns 28ff.

971 Cf. *Stoppa/Lehnert* in *Huber/Mantel* (eds), Kommentar Aufenthaltsgesetz/Asylgesetz[3] (2021) § 48 AufenthG mns 4–6.

In contrast to Austrian law,[972] an obligation to leave the country is imposed *ipso iure* upon a foreigner who is staying unlawfully,[973] though the law determines the cases in which a person does not have or no longer has a residence title: termination[974] or revocation[975] of the title or the foreigner is expelled.[976] This requires a distinction to whether the obligation to leave can be enforced.[977]

A particularly important case concerns the application for issuing or extending a (humanitarian) residence permit, which is denied by the relevant authority, whereupon the authority also issues a deportation order.[978] In comparison to the terminology used in Austrian law, such unfavourable decision for the applicant is referred to as a denial (*Ablehnung*) and not as a rejection (*Abweisung*).[979] Furthermore, as discussed below,[980] it is also to be considered that the appeal against the denial or the deportation order typically does not have a suspensive effect. The obligation to leave the country is therefore enforceable as soon as the statutory period has expired and where the court has not granted provisional relief.[981] In principle, the Residence Act requires the foreigner to leave Germany without delay, unless a particular period for departure is in place.[982] In the latter case, the period is between 7 and 30 days.[983]

Expulsion under § 53 AufenthG imposes an obligation to leave the country on foreigners,[984] who, for example, present a danger to Germany. In such instances, the public interest in expulsion is weighed against the

972 In Austrian law, foreigners can be staying unlawfully, but imposing an obligation to leave the country upon aliens in general requires a procedure in which the corresponding measure issue is issued, see Chapter 3.A.II.1.

973 § 50(1) AufenthG; cf. *Huber/Eichenhofer/Endres de Oliveira*, Aufenthaltsrecht mns 1045–1049.

974 § 51 AufenthG. cf. *Hörich*, Abschiebungen 78–80.

975 § 52 AufenthG.

976 §§ 53–56 AufenthG; cf. *Hörich*, Abschiebungen 80ff.

977 See § 58(2) AufenthG; cf. *Marx*, Aufenthalts-, Asyl- und Flüchtlingsrecht § 7 mn 330.

978 Cf. *Marx*, Aufenthalts-, Asyl- und Flüchtlingsrecht § 2 mn 240.

979 See above Chapter 3.A.II.1.

980 See Chapter 3.B.V.1.

981 § 58(2) AufenthG; cf. *Marx*, Aufenthalts-, Asyl- und Flüchtlingsrecht § 7 mn 330.

982 § 50(2) AufenthG; cf. *Marx*, Aufenthalts-, Asyl- und Flüchtlingsrecht § 7 mn 331.

983 § 59(1) 1st Sent. AufenthG.

984 On the current discussions and for a convincing opinion that expulsion is to be viewed as a return decision as under the Return Directive, *Hörich*, Abschiebungen 86f and 90.

foreigner's interests in remaining.[985] A residence title expires when the foreigner is expelled and may be enforced, i.e. deportation, when the obligation to leave is executable.[986]

Furthermore, a person who is staying unlawfully and is not tolerated is criminally liable pursuant to § 95(1) No. 2 AufenthG when he or she is enforceably required to leave the country.[987] This criminal offence falls under the criminal law relating to foreigners (*Ausländerstrafrecht*);[988] it is punishable by imprisonment for up to one year or a fine. A breach of the obligation to possess a recognised and valid passport is also a punishable offence under the Residence Act.[989] The offences under German law therefore differ from their classification as administrative offences under Austrian and Spanish law.[990]

2. Employment

Prior to the Skilled Immigration Act, foreigners were only entitled to pursue a so-called *Erwerbstätigkeit* – an 'economic activity' as per the English translation of the Residence Act – if they were in possession of the relevant residence permit.[991] The introduction of the legislation brought about a 'paradigm shift'[992] whereby from 1 March 2020 every residence title is linked with the right to engage in 'economic activity', unless expressly prohibited by law.[993]

---

985 Cf. *Huber/Eichenhofer/Endres de Oliveira*, Aufenthaltsrecht mns 1087ff.

986 § 58(2) AufenthG.

987 Cf. *Hörich/Bergmann* in *Huber/Mantel* (eds), Kommentar Aufenthaltsgesetz/Asylgesetz[3] (2021) § 95 AufenthG mns 29ff.

988 Cf. on German criminal law for foreigners, *Hörich/Bergmann* in *Huber/Mantel* Vorbemerkung zu § 95 AufenthG mns 1ff.

989 § 95(1) No. 1 AufenthG.

990 For criticism see *Hörich/Bergmann* in *Huber/Mantel* Vorbemerkung zu § 95 AufenthG mn 11, who propose the classification as administrative offences (*Ordnungswidrigkeiten*). On Austrian law, see Chapter 3.A.II.1. and for Spanish law, Chapter 3.C.II.1.

991 § 4(2) and (3) AufenthG in the version of 12.7.2018 (BGBl I 1147); cf. *Huber/Eichenhofer/Endres de Oliveira*, Aufenthaltsrecht mns 44f.

992 *Klaus/Hammer*, Fachkräfteeinwanderungsgesetz (FEG): Signal mit Fragezeichen oder echter Quantensprung?, ZAR 2019, 137 (137); also *Dippe*, „Zuckerbrot und Peitsche" in den gesetzlichen Neuerungen ab März 2020, Asylmagazin 2020, 55 (58). *Kluth*, NVwZ 2019, 1306 refers to a 'structural realignment'.

993 § 4a(1) AufenthG.

This shift from a general prohibition subject to permission to general permission subject to prohibition will, however, have hardly any effect in practice:[994] each residence title still has to indicate whether or not there are any restrictions on the pursuit of employment.[995]

According to § 2(2) AufenthG, economic activity covers both employment and self-employment. It is therefore first necessary to examine whether the residence permit also entitles the foreigner to engage in an economic activity.[996] Where there is no such entitlement, the competent foreigner's authority may issue permission, which is usually subject to the approval of the Federal Employment Agency (*Bundesagentur für Arbeit*).[997] Such approval is not required if the foreigner possesses a 'residence permit for humanitarian reasons'.[998] The labour-market test (*Vorrangprüfung*[999]) no longer applies.[1000]

In turn this implies that an unlawfully staying foreigner is in principle not entitled to pursue employment. Accordingly, the same also applies to tolerated persons,[1001] though this will be discussed in more detail below.[1002]

3. Social benefits

A distinction is to be drawn between the Unemployment Benefits II (*Arbeitslosengeld II*, commonly referred to as *Hartz IV*), general social assistance and 'special' social assistance.[1003] In general, the claims to social assistance are directly linked to type of residence permit issued.

Foreigners are equally entitled to claim the Unemployment Benefits II under the Social Insurance Code II (SGB II), which provide a basic income to job-seekers. Unlike the name suggests, the benefits are not paid

994 In this sense, *Klaus/Hammer*, ZAR 2019, 137 and *Kluth*, NVwZ 2019, 1306.
995 § 4a(2) and (3) AufenthG; cf. BT-Drs 19/8285, 86f.
996 For a list of all permits see *Frings/Janda/Keßler/Steffen*, Sozialrecht für Zuwanderer² (2018) mn 56.
997 Cf. *Frings/Janda/Keßler/Steffen*, Sozialrecht mns 57–65.
998 § 31 BeschV.
999 The term *Arbeitsmarktprüfung* is used in Austria, see Chapter 3.A.II.2.
1000 Cf. just *Frings/Janda/Keßler/Steffen*, Sozialrecht mn 834 with regard to the residence permit according to § 25(5) AufenthG.
1001 § 32(1) 1st Sent. BeschV.
1002 See Chapter 4.A.I.2.b.
1003 Cf. *Mimentza Martin*, Die sozialrechtliche Stellung 128 and 133.

from unemployment insurance. A person is eligible when he or she is employable, in need of assistance and is aged 16 and above.[1004]

This does not apply, inter alia, to persons who are entitled under the Act on Benefits for Asylum Seekers or do not have a residence title.[1005] Foreigners who are in possession of a 'residence permit for humanitarian reasons' are therefore eligible to receive benefits;[1006] a claim for social assistance according to the Social Insurance Code XII may also be considered.[1007] Which of these claims to social benefits exists is determined on the basis of the complicated rules regarding the residence permit issued.[1008]

A person in possession of a 'residence permit for humanitarian reasons' merely receives the lower benefits[1009] in accordance with the Act on Benefits for Asylum Seekers.[1010] Such an exception applies to foreigners with a residence permit according to § 25(5) AufenthG.[1011] The Third Act to amend the Act on Benefits for Asylum Seekers, which entered into force on 1 September 2019, restructured the basic benefits under § 3 of the Act on Benefits for Asylum Seekers and codified the rates in a new provision, namely § 3a.[1012]

The Social Insurance Codes do not apply to foreigners who are enforceably required to leave the country and are therefore excluded from the claims to social assistance under these Codes. However, a claim to 'special' social assistance under the Act on Benefits for Asylum Seekers may arise where there is no claim under the Social Insurance Code II or XII.[1013] According to the Act on Benefits for Asylum Seekers, where benefits have

---

1004 § 7(1) 1st Sent. SGB II.

1005 § 7(1) 2nd Sent. Nos. 2, 3 SGB II. On the general provisions and general exclusions for foreigners, *Frings/Janda/Keßler/Steffen*, Sozialrecht mns 87ff.

1006 § 7(1) 3rd Sent. SGB II. Cf. *Frings/Janda/Keßler/Steffen*, Sozialrecht mn 106.

1007 § 23 SGB XII. Cf. *Frings/Janda/Keßler/Steffen*, Sozialrecht mns 130–144 and *Groth* in *Rolfs/Giesen/Keikebohm/Udsching* (eds), BeckOK Sozialrecht (62nd edn, 1.9.2021) § 23 SGB XII mns 1ff.

1008 Cf. *Frings/Janda/Keßler/Steffen*, Sozialrecht mns 690ff.

1009 The amounts paid are lower than under the SGB II and SGB XII. See §§ 1a and 3 AsylbLG for the extent of the benefits. Cf. *Schneider*, NZS-Jahresrevue 2017 – Asylbewerberleistungsgesetz, NZS 2018, 559 (560–563) and *Frings/Janda/Keßler/Steffen*, Sozialrecht mns 146 and 150–159.

1010 § 1 AsylbLG defines the groups who are eligible; cf. *Frings/Janda/Keßler/Steffen*, Sozialrecht mn 147.

1011 For detail, Chapter 4.C.II.

1012 Cf. *Genge*, Das geänderte Asylbewerberleistungsgesetz, Das Migrationspaket – Beilage zum Asylmagazin 8–9/2019, 14 (15–18).

1013 Cf. *Frings/Janda/Keßler/Steffen*, Sozialrecht mns 145ff.

been paid over a period of at least 18 months, foreigners have a claim to analogous benefits under the Social Code XII if they themselves have not influenced the duration of their stay by an abuse of rights and have remained in Germany without a significant interruption.[1014] 'Analogous benefits' (*Analogieleistungen*) means that the benefits follow the rates under the Social Code II.[1015] The Third Act to amend the Act on Benefits for Asylum Seekers extended the required minimum period of prior residence from 15[1016] to 18 months.[1017]

4. Healthcare

The Social Code V applies in Germany to claims from statutory health insurance; its § 5 determines who is subject to the obligation to have health insurance. Foreigners receiving the Unemployment Benefits II have to be insured.[1018] As noted above,[1019] the receipt of social assistance does not give rise to compulsory insurance. A person without a residence title may trigger a claim to insurance under statutory health insurance by being employed and receiving an income.[1020] If they do not have the required permit, they are undocumented workers.[1021] In short, a foreigner staying unlawfully in Germany generally does not have a claim to be insured under the statutory health insurance scheme.

Foreigners who receive benefits under the Act on Benefits for Asylum Seekers are only insured via this legislation and are not covered under the statutory health insurance regime. In comparison to the latter, the healthcare provided pursuant to the Act on Benefits for Asylum Seekers only concerns the treatment of acute illnesses and pain;[1022] this includes

---

1014 § 2(1) AsylbLG; cf. *Frings/Janda/Keßler/Steffen*, Sozialrecht mns 179ff and *Korff* in *Rolfs/Giesen/Keikebohm/Udsching* (eds), BeckOK Sozialrecht (62nd edn, 1.9.2021) § 2 AsylbLG mns 1–16.

1015 *Schneider*, NZS 2018, 563.

1016 This is the time frame required in Germany for a typical asylum process; cf. BT-Drs 18/2592, 19 with further references.

1017 § 2(1) AsylbLG; for criticism *Genge*, Das Migrationspaket – Beilage zum Asylmagazin 8–9/2019, 18f.

1018 § 5(1) No. 2a SGB V; cf. *Frings/Janda/Keßler/Steffen*, Sozialrecht mn 102.

1019 See Chapter 3.B.II.3.

1020 § 5(1) No. 1 SGB V. See also § 7(4) Sozialgesetzbuch Viertes Buch in the version of 28.6.2022 (BGBl I 969) and §§ 98a-98c AufenthG.

1021 See Chapter 3.B.II.2.

1022 § 4(1) AsylbLG. In depth, *Frings/Janda/Keßler/Steffen*, Sozialrecht mns 160f.

pregnancy and birth.[1023] The recipients of analogous benefits under § 2 AsylbLG also receive benefits included under health insurance.[1024]

III. General remarks on residence permits for humanitarian reasons

§§ 22–26 AufenthG contain the provisions on residence granted for reasons of international law or on humanitarian or political grounds. These provisions are especially relevant for the present study and will be referred to collectively as 'residence permits for humanitarian reasons' (*Aufenthaltserlaubnisse aus humanitären Gründen*).[1025] They were introduced via the 2005 Immigration Act, though were modelled on the corresponding provisions in the Foreigners Act of 1990, and have since been reformed on several occasions.[1026] The 'residence permit for the purpose of employment for qualified foreigners whose deportation has been suspended' under § 19d AufenthG is the only regularisation in Germany that does not fall under the category 'humanitarian reasons' and is thus discussed elsewhere.[1027]

1. Overview

Each residence permit under the Residence Act is linked to a particular purpose underlying the residency.[1028] In principle there are five broad purposes in the Residence Act, though these are divided into over 50 separate categories of permits.[1029] It is thus not surprising that *Groß* describes the level of detail concerning the purposes as unusually high in comparison to other legal systems.[1030] However, it is surprising that the Residence Act

---

1023 In this sense *Schneider*, NZS 2018, 564.

1024 § 264(2) SGB V; cf. *Frings/Janda/Keßler/Steffen*, Sozialrecht mn 190.

1025 *Marx*, Aufenthalts-, Asyl- und Flüchtlingsrecht § 5; cf. *Huber/Eichenhofer/Endres de Oliveira*, Aufenthaltsrecht mn 438.

1026 Cf. *Huber/Eichenhofer/Endres de Oliveira*, Aufenthaltsrecht mn 404 with reference to §§ 30–35 AuslG 1990.

1027 See Chapter 4.E.IV.

1028 Cf. *Groß*, AöR 2014, 423.

1029 In addition to those discussed here, these are education purposes, economic activity, family reasons and special rights of residence.

1030 *Groß*, AöR 2014, 426; similarly critical *Bast*, DÖV 2013, 216 with further references and *Bergmann/Eichenhofer/Hörich/Janda/Nestler/Stamm/Tewocht/Vogt*, Einwanderungsgesetz: Hallescher Entwurf zur Neuordnung der Dogmatik des Aufenthaltsrechts (2019) 68–71.

now only recognises three 'basic types'[1031] of residence titles: 'temporary', 'permanent' and the 'EU long-term residence'.[1032] The 'EU Blue Card', the 'ICT Card' and the 'Mobile ICT Card' have not been included in this list.[1033] In comparison, Austrian law features 25 different types of residence permits.[1034]

Residence titles are a beneficial administrative act, i.e. an administrative measure which establishes or confirms a right or legal advantage – a *begünstigender Verwaltungsakt*, to use the German terminology.[1035] Since the Residence Act, a residence title combines in one administrative decision the different decisions made by the foreigners authority concerning the entry, residence and access to the labour market.[1036]

According to the statistics, at the end of 2020 approx. 71,000 individuals held a residence permit as a result of a right to remain or an admission from abroad,[1037] approx. 54,000 due to long term residence and unreasonable departure[1038] and approx. 19,000 for humanitarian or personal reasons.[1039] Approximately 9,000 individuals held a residence permit due to individual hardship pursuant to § 23a AufenthG.[1040]

2. Administrative procedure

The general provisions of administrative law, specifically the Administrative Procedure Act (*Verwaltungsverfahrensgesetz*; VwVfG), apply to the administrative procedure concerning the grant of a residence permit.[1041]

1031 *Bast*, DÖV 2013, 216, who prior to entry into force of the Act of 29.8.2013 (BGBl I 3484) and the introduction of the 'EU long-term residence permit' spoke of two 'basic types'.

1032 §§ 4(1), 7, 9 and 9a AufenthG.

1033 §§ 18b(2), 19 and 19b AufenthG.

1034 See above Chapter 3.A.III.1.

1035 See *Groß*, AöR 2014, 423f.

1036 *Bast*, DÖV 2013, 216 with reference to § 4(2) and (3) AufenthG. The provision has since been rephrased by the Skilled Immigration Act; see Chapter 3.B.II.2.

1037 §§ 18a, 22, 23(1), 25a, 25b and 104a AufenthG.

1038 § 25(5) AufenthG.

1039 § 25(4) AufenthG.

1040 BT-Drs 19/32579, 2; see for 2018 BT-Drs 19/17236, 2 and for 2017 BT-Drs 19/633, 2.

1041 Cf. *Marx*, Aufenthalts-, Asyl- und Flüchtlingsrecht § 2 mn 220.

a) Application

In principle the Residence Act stipulates the requirement to apply for and the extension of a residence permit.[1042] Where an application is made for a 'residence permit for humanitarian reasons', the competent foreigners authority as well as the administrative court upon appeal have to examine a claim to issue a residence permit in accordance with every provision of the Residence Act that comes into consideration.[1043] For example, if a foreigner applies for a residence permit where deportation to a specific state is banned (§ 25(3) AufenthG),[1044] the competent foreigners authority is to examine all of the other (humanitarian) grounds that come into consideration to issue a residence permit.

The time limits for 'residence permits for humanitarian reasons' vary according to the reason for the permit, though it may be issued for a maximum of three years.[1045] This aspect will be discussed in more detail in Chapter 4 in relation to the different regularisations.

According to § 12(2) AufenthG, each residence permit may be issued and extended subject to conditions, such as a geographic restriction. § 12a(1) AufenthG requires particular attention as it is a *lex specialis* rule concerning a place of residence for foreigners to whom a 'residence permit for humanitarian reasons' has been granted for the first time pursuant to §§ 22, 23 or 25(3) AufenthG.[1046]

It is also necessary in this context to draw attention to the second sentence of § 11(4) AufenthG, which concerns the application for a 'residence permit for humanitarian reasons' despite a ban on entry and residence.[1047] According to this provision, the ban is to be revoked in order to allow the grant of a (humanitarian) residence permit.[1048] The draft legislation makes specific reference to §§ 25(4a)–(5) as well as 25a and 25b AufenthG.[1049]

1042 § 81(1) AufenthG; cf. *Marx*, Aufenthalts-, Asyl- und Flüchtlingsrecht § 2 mns 233–235 and *Huber/Eichenhofer/Endres de Oliveira*, Aufenthaltsrecht mn 1384.

1043 *Marx*, Aufenthalts-, Asyl- und Flüchtlingsrecht § 5 mn 1 with further references and cf. *Huber/Eichenhofer/Endres de Oliveira*, Aufenthaltsrecht mn 420.

1044 See Chapter 4.A.II.2.

1045 § 26 AufenthG; cf. *Huber/Eichenhofer/Endres de Oliveira*, Aufenthaltsrecht mn 639.

1046 Cf. *Huber/Eichenhofer/Endres de Oliveira*, Aufenthaltsrecht mns 662–682; see Chapter 4.A.II.2.

1047 Cf. *Huber/Eichenhofer/Endres de Oliveira*, Aufenthaltsrecht mns 441f.

1048 Cf. BT-Drs 18/4097, 37.

1049 See below Chapter 4.B.I.–II., Chapter 4.C.II. as well as Chapter 4.D.I.2.

b) General requirements for granting residence titles and grounds for denial

Diverse general requirements need to be met in order to grant a residence title.[1050] As is usual under German administrative law, these must be met at the time of the decision by the authority or administrative court.[1051] The Residence Act distinguishes between the requirements that are to be met 'as a rule' and those that 'must' be met.[1052] The latter requirements include the possession of the visa required for entry and that, in the visa application, the key information required for granting the title has already been given. These requirements may be waived[1053] when granting a 'residence permit for humanitarian reasons' as it may have been impossible or unreasonable to leave the country for the visa process.[1054]

§ 5(3) AufenthG contains a special rule for 'residence permits for humanitarian reasons' as usually not all of the requirements under § 5 AufenthG have to be met in order for such permits to be granted.[1055] Accordingly, foreigners meeting such requirements should have 'the possibility of a legal residence status for the duration of the humanitarian crisis'[1056] because, in the majority of these cases, the stay cannot be ended anyway.

§ 5(1) AufenthG lists the criteria that, as a rule, are to be met in order to grant a residence title. The criteria can be divided into two categories: positive and negative. Whereas secure subsistence,[1057] established identity,[1058] and the obligation to acquire a passport[1059] constitute the positive require-

---

1050 § 5(1) and (2) AufenthG.

1051 § 113 VwGO; cf. *Marx*, Aufenthalts-, Asyl- und Flüchtlingsrecht § 2 mn 244 with further references and *Decker* in *Posser/Wolff* (eds), BeckOK VwGO (53rd edn, 1.4.2020) § 113 VwGO mns 21f. On the relevant exceptions in the procedure see mns 22.3–22.5.

1052 Cf. *Huber/Eichenhofer/Endres de Oliveira*, Aufenthaltsrecht mn 422.

1053 § 5(3) 2nd Sent. AufenthG.

1054 *Huber/Eichenhofer/Endres de Oliveira*, Aufenthaltsrecht mn 435.

1055 No. 5.3.0.1 AVV-AufenthG and BTS-Drs 15/420, 70. Cf. also *Huber/Eichenhofer/Endres de Oliveira*, Aufenthaltsrecht mns 86–92 and 423.

1056 No. 5.3.0.1 AVV-AufenthG.

1057 In detail *Huber/Eichenhofer/Endres de Oliveira*, Aufenthaltsrecht mns 12ff and 65, for the exception under § 5(3) AufenthG, mns 427–429.

1058 For detail see *Huber/Eichenhofer/Endres de Oliveira*, Aufenthaltsrecht mns 28ff and mn 430 for the exception under § 5(3) AufenthG.

1059 See above, Chapter 3.B.II.1. and for detail *Huber/Eichenhofer/Endres de Oliveira*, Aufenthaltsrecht mn 75 and mn 435 for the exception under § 5(3) AufenthG.

ments, the lack of public interest in the expulsion[1060] and of a threat or endangerment to national interests form the negative requirements.[1061] These may also be waived in accordance with the special rule applicable to 'residence permits for humanitarian reasons'.

The Residence Act also contains further reasons for denying the grant of a residence permit, such as in the case of an especially serious interest in expulsion under § 54(1) No. 2 or No. 4 AufenthG.[1062] This also applies to 'residence permits for humanitarian reasons'.[1063]

c) Restriction after an asylum process

Particular rules apply to the grant of a residence title upon completion of an asylum process, thereby showing the close links to the 'residence permits for humanitarian reasons'.[1064] According to the first sentence of § 10(3) AufenthG, a foreigner whose asylum application has been incontestably rejected or who has withdrawn the asylum application may be granted a 'residence permit for humanitarian reasons' before leaving the federal territory.[1065] This provision excludes the grant of a residence permit for a different purpose. Special rules apply if the application for asylum has been rejected for being manifestly unfounded on the basis of specific reasons, such as fraud.[1066] In general, such individuals may not be granted any residence permit whatsoever, though two exceptions apply: where the requirements for a residence permit are met in the event deportation to a specific state is banned (§ 25(3) AufenthG)[1067] or where there is a claim to grant a residence title.[1068] Furthermore, a 'residence permit for

1060 In detail, *Huber/Eichenhofer/Endres de Oliveira*, Aufenthaltsrecht mns 67–70 and mn 431 for the exception under § 5(3) AufenthG.

1061 For further information see *Huber/Eichenhofer/Endres de Oliveira*, Aufenthaltsrecht mns 71–74 and mn 431 for the exception under § 5(3) AufenthG.

1062 § 5(4) AufenthG.

1063 *Huber/Eichenhofer/Endres de Oliveira*, Aufenthaltsrecht mns 436f and No. 5.4.2 AVV-AufenthG.

1064 Similar to Austria, the *ex officio* examination of two 'residence permits for exceptional circumstances', see Chapter 3.A.III.2.b.

1065 § 10(3) 1st Sent. AufenthG.

1066 § 10(3) 2nd Sent. AufenthG; cf. *Huber/Eichenhofer/Endres de Oliveira*, Aufenthaltsrecht mn 138.

1067 See Chapter 4.A.II.2.

1068 For detail see *Huber/Eichenhofer/Endres de Oliveira*, Aufenthaltsrecht mns 139–141 and 439f with further references.

the purpose of employment for qualified foreigners whose deportation has been suspended' under § 19d(3) AufenthG may also be issued despite the restriction on granting a residence title.[1069] Such restriction has been the subject of long-standing criticism as it leads to a cycle of tolerations despite efforts towards integration and obstacles to departure or deportation through no fault of the foreigner in question.[1070] Moreover, it also raises concerns about the compatibility with requirements under international and EU law.[1071]

3. Consolidation of residence

§ 8(1) AufenthG provides that an extension of a residence permit is subject to the same regulations as granting such permit. For 'residence permits for humanitarian reasons', however, § 26(2) AufenthG excludes an extension 'if the obstacle to departure or other grounds precluding a termination of residence have ceased to apply'. This provision serves to clarify and emphasise that the 'residence permits for humanitarian reasons' embody the principle of temporary protection.[1072] As a result, the requirements for granting an extension must continue to be met and observed as at the time the permit was first issued.[1073] The exclusion of an extension does not apply to those 'residence permits for humanitarian reasons' which open the possibility for long-term residence,[1074] i.e. most of those analysed in Chapter 4.[1075]

As noted above, a residence permit is always granted in relation to a particular purpose and therefore a change of purpose is generally excluded when the permit is extended. § 25(4) 2nd Sent. AufenthG thus allows a derogation from § 8(1) and (2) AufenthG to extend a residence permit

1069 Cf. *Huber/Eichenhofer/Endres de Oliveira*, Aufenthaltsrecht mn 142.

1070 *Deutscher Anwaltverein*, Stellungnahme zur Abschaffung des § 10 Absatz 3 Satz 2 Aufenthaltsgesetz (AufenthG) (April 2013), https://dav-migrationsrecht.de/files/page/0_47513700_1402160616s.pdf (31.7.2022) 3.

1071 The *Deutsche Anwaltverein* gives Art 8 ECHR and the provisions from the Return Directive and the Family Reunification Directive as examples; cf. *Deutscher Anwaltverein*, Stellungnahme (April 2013).

1072 No. 26.2 AVV-AufenthG.

1073 No. 26.2 AVV-AufenthG.

1074 In this sense. *Huber/Eichenhofer/Endres de Oliveira*, Aufenthaltsrecht mn 644.

1075 §§ 25(4) 2nd Sent., 25(4a) 3rd Sent., 25a and 25b AufenthG. §§ 104a and 104b AufenthG are not included in the analysis; see Chapter 3.B.III.4.

in cases of exceptional hardship.[1076] The application of this provision is subject to the requirements that the extension is not possible under the general provisions and that the foreigner is in possession of a residence permit.[1077]

According to § 25(3) AufenthG, a permanent settlement permit (*Niederlassungserlaubnis*) may also be granted to a foreigner with a 'residence permit for humanitarian reasons'. Such permanent settlement permit has been described as 'the highest level of consolidated residence'[1078] in German residence law as it is not subject to any time or employment limitations. Such permit requires the foreigner to have been in possession of a residence permit for five years.[1079] The duration of residence during the asylum procedure counts towards this qualifying period.[1080] A permanent residence permit may be granted accordingly to children who entered Germany before reaching the age of 18.[1081]

4. Drawing distinctions

To narrow the scope of the study, the following only refers to those provisions which, although they concern 'residence permits for humanitarian reasons', are not to be analysed. § 22 AufenthG concerns the permit for the purpose of 'admission from abroad'. As the name already indicates, the foreigner must be abroad for the provision to apply. The same applies to the resettlement of persons seeking protection according to § 23(4) AufenthG.[1082] Accordingly, these residence permits do not constitute regularisations for the purposes of this study and are therefore not included in the analysis.

The 'residence permit […] for reasons of international law, on humanitarian grounds or in order to uphold the political interests' under § 23(1)

1076 Cf. *Maaßen/Kluth* in *Kluth/Heusch* (eds), BeckOK Ausländerrecht (30th edn, 1.7.2021) § 25 AufenthG mns 78f.

1077 On the requirements, see *Maaßen/Kluth* in *Kluth/Heusch* § 25 AufenthG mns 80ff.

1078 *Huber/Eichenhofer/Endres de Oliveira*, Aufenthaltsrecht mn 929: '*die höchste Stufe der aufenthaltsrechtlichen Verfestigung*'.

1079 § 26(4) 1st Sent. § 9(2) AufenthG.

1080 § 26(4) 3rd Sent. AufenthG and cf. *Huber/Eichenhofer/Endres de Oliveira*, Aufenthaltsrecht mn 655.

1081 § 26(4) 4th Sent. in conjunction with § 35 AufenthG.

1082 Cf. *Huber/Eichenhofer/Endres de Oliveira*, Aufenthaltsrecht mns 479ff.

AufenthG is also not analysed as part of the comparison in Chapter 4. A detailed analysis is not included as there are presently no 'orders' pursuant to § 23(1) AufenthG that are in force, thus preventing an in-depth analysis.[1083] § 32 AuslG 1990, which is of historical significance and precedes § 23(1) AufenthG, has already been described in detail.[1084]

The provisions governing old cases (§§ 104a and 104b AufenthG) have also been discussed.[1085] These served as a model for the current §§ 25a and 25b AufenthG, which will be examined more closely in Chapter 4.B.I.–II. Although §§ 104a and 104b AufenthG are still in force, they are of little relevance as they are linked to a particular date (1 July 2007).[1086] As the analysis concerns §§ 25a and 25b AufenthG, an additional examination of §§ 104a and 104b AufenthG is not necessary.

Furthermore, § 24 AufenthG concerns the 'granting of residence for temporary protection'. This provision is rooted in the Temporary Protection Directive, which is why it will not be examined in detail.[1087] The same applies to residence permits for persons entitled to asylum,[1088] with refugee status[1089] or entitled to subsidiary protection[1090] as such persons do not fall within the scope of this study.[1091] This same reason applies to the approval for admission ordered to safeguard special political interests pursuant to § 23(2) AufenthG.[1092]

The residence permit for 'urgent humanitarian or personal grounds or due to substantial public interests' under § 25(4) 1st Sent. AufenthG will not be analysed as such permit is only issued for a maximum of six months [1093] It is therefore excluded from the analysis in Chapter 4 because it does not satisfy the minimum duration for granting a right to stay.[1094]

1083 Toleration under § 60a(1) AufenthG, which refers in its 2nd Sent. to § 23(1) AufenthG, will also not be analysed; see Chapter 4.A.I.2.a.

1084 See Chapter 3.B.I.

1085 See Chapter 3.B.I.

1086 In this sense, *Huber/Eichenhofer/Endres de Oliveira*, Aufenthaltsrecht mn 688.

1087 See above Chapter 1.B.IV.1.

1088 § 25(1) AufenthG.

1089 § 25(2) 1st Sent. AufenthG.

1090 § 25(2) 1st Sent. AufenthG.

1091 See above Introduction D.II.1.

1092 Cf. *Huber/Eichenhofer/Endres de Oliveira*, Aufenthaltsrecht mns 470ff.

1093 § 26(4) 1st Sent. AufenthG.

1094 See the introductory remarks in Chapter 4.

IV. Competences and authorities in residence law

Article 30 GG stipulates that the 'exercise of state powers and the discharge of state functions' – i.e. the direct state administration – is in principle 'a matter for the *Länder*'[1095] and thus executed by the *Länder*. The individual provisions regarding the competences then distinguish between legislation and administration.[1096]

Beginning with the provisions concerning legislation: Article 74(1) No. 4 GG ('law relating to residence and establishment of foreign nationals') is presently the most relevant provision on the competence in residency law, though one must also bear in mind Article 73(1) No. 3 GG ('immigration and emigration') and Article 74(1) No. 6 GG ('matters concerning refugees and expellees').[1097] *Bast* describes Article 74(1) No. 4 GG as a well secured special regulatory law for the federal government whereby the *Länder* have no legislative scope.[1098]

The *Länder* undertake the administration and are in principle bound by legislation and act in a sovereign manner (i.e. under public law).[1099] Accordingly, Article 83 GG stipulates that the *Länder* shall execute federal laws (such as the Residence Act) 'in their own right'.[1100] The domestic execution of residency law lies with the foreigners authorities of the *Länder*,[1101] though the Federal Office for Migration and Refugees (*Bundesamt für Migration und Flüchtlinge*; BAMF) is responsible for the execution of matters pertaining to asylum and certain decisions regarding residency under the German Asylum Act.[1102] The BAMF is an 'autonomous federal higher authority' within the meaning of Article 87(3) 1st Sent. GG.

1095 *Maurer/Waldhoff*, Verwaltungsrecht § 22 mn 1 and see Arts 83ff GG.
1096 Arts 72ff and 83ff GG.
1097 On the relationship between the different provisions, see *Bast*, Aufenthaltsrecht 118–139.
1098 Cf. *Bast*, Aufenthaltsrecht 119 with further references.
1099 See Fn 1095. Cf. *Maurer/Waldhoff*, Verwaltungsrecht § 1 mns 25f and § 9 mns 12–14.
1100 Cf. *Maurer/Waldhoff*, Verwaltungsrecht § 22 mn 3.
1101 § 71(1) 1st Sent. AufenthG; cf. *Bast*, DÖV 2013, 216 and *Marx*, Aufenthalts-, Asyl- und Flüchtlingsrecht § 2 mn 221.
1102 § 5(1) AsylG (G); cf. *Huber/Eichenhofer/Endres de Oliveira*, Aufenthaltsrecht mns 1729–1732.

V. Judicial protection

Judicial protection in Germany can be distinguished between the jurisdictions of the administrative courts and the constitutional court, which will be described below. Beforehand, however, it is necessary to explain the significance of a subjective right under public law. According to Article 19(4) GG, every person whose rights are violated by public authority may have recourse to the courts.[1103] Where the claimant has a subjective right, the decision by the administrative authority will be examined in full by the courts.[1104] It is important to note with regard to the German administrative courts that the administrative authority and the person concerned are in principle on equal footing as parties to the proceedings.[1105]

1. Administrative jurisdiction

Three types of actions may be brought before the Administrative Court (*Verwaltungsgericht*; VG) with respect to acts by administrative authorities: an action for recission (*Anfechtungsklage*), an action for a declaratory judgment (*Feststellungsklage*) and an action for enforcement (*Verpflichtungsklage*).[1106] In the event the application for a residence permit is rejected, the applicant may bring an action for enforcement; an action for recission is brought in relation to a deportation warning, however.[1107] *Marx* is correct in noting in this regard that, for reasons of procedural law, both actions are always to be filed together.[1108] The aforementioned actions do not have any suspensive effect in these cases.[1109] The action for enforcement targets the 'issuance of an administrative act'.[1110] With regard to actions for recission, the administrative court is to examine the lawful-

---

1103 *Maurer/Waldhoff*, Verwaltungsrecht § 8 mn 5.

1104 See with regard to a subjective right § 42(2) VwGO; *Maurer/Waldhoff*, Verwaltungsrecht § 8 mn 5 with further references and § 8 mns 6ff on the requirements.

1105 *Maurer/Waldhoff*, Verwaltungsrecht § 8 mn 5.

1106 §§ 1ff VwGO.

1107 §§ 42ff VwGO; cf. *Maurer/Waldhoff*, Verwaltungsrecht § 10 mns 80–83.

1108 *Marx*, Aufenthalts-, Asyl- und Flüchtlingsrecht § 2 mn 244 with further references.

1109 § 84(1) No. 1 AufenthG. See generally § 80 VwGO.

1110 *Maurer/Waldhoff*, Verwaltungsrecht § 10 mn 82.

ness of the administrative act; the act is to be revoked if it is unlawful and in so far as the rights of the person concerned have been violated.[1111]

Provisional relief pursuant to § 80(5) VwGO must be sought to prevent the threat of deportation (and unpermitted residency). An application for provisional relief may be made if the application for a residence permit (or an extension) has triggered effects under § 81(3) and (4) AufenthG.[1112] These are so-called 'fictitious effects',[1113] meaning that a right to a fictitious permitted or tolerated stay arises *ipso iure* upon application for a residence permit (or an extension). If such application does not have any fictitious effect because of the obligation to leave the country is enforceable (irrespective of the application), the person concerned is to request an interim order (*einstweilige Anordnung*) under § 123 VwGO.[1114] In comparison to § 80(5) VwGO, considerably stricter requirements apply to the interim order.[1115] For the enforcement of the obligation to leave it means that the obligation generally becomes enforceable once the time limit has lapsed. Where there has been an application for provisional relief, the obligation to leave first becomes enforceable after the proceedings are concluded with legal effect.[1116]

The administrative courts examine the legality of the administrative acts.[1117] The decision is binding and conclusive.[1118] However, an exception applies if the administrative authority is afforded a margin of discretion.[1119] The discretion of interest to this study always aims at the legal consequences of a statutory provision.[1120] In such cases the administrative authority has the right to a 'final decision'.[1121] The administrative courts only examine the legality of the decision and whether the discretion was exercised within the legislative boundaries – the '*Ermessens(rechts)bindung*'

1111 § 113(1) VwGO.
1112 Cf. *Marx*, Aufenthalts-, Asyl- und Flüchtlingsrecht § 2 mns 245f.
1113 Cf. *Marx*, Aufenthalts-, Asyl- und Flüchtlingsrecht § 2 mns 248–264.
1114 Cf. *Huber/Eichenhofer/Endres de Oliveira*, Aufenthaltsrecht mn 1398.
1115 Cf. *Marx*, Aufenthalts-, Asyl- und Flüchtlingsrecht § 2 mns 247 and 281ff.
1116 § 58(2) AufenthG; cf. *Marx*, Aufenthalts-, Asyl- und Flüchtlingsrecht § 2 mn 240.
1117 *Maurer/Waldhoff*, Verwaltungsrecht § 7 mn 4.
1118 Cf. *Maurer/Waldhoff*, Verwaltungsrecht § 7 mn 5.
1119 On the scope of discretion and on the open legal term see *Maurer/Waldhoff*, Verwaltungsrecht § 7 mns 26ff.
1120 Cf. *Maurer/Waldhoff*, Verwaltungsrecht § 7 mn 7.
1121 *Maurer/Waldhoff*, Verwaltungsrecht § 7 mn 6 with further references.

in German legal terminology.[1122] A person has a claim to a correct decision made by the competent authority within the scope of its discretion.[1123]

An appeal on points of fact and law (*Berufung*) may be made within one month to the competent Higher Administrative Court (*Oberverwaltungsgericht*; OVG).[1124] From this point, those concerned must be represented by an authorised legal representative.[1125] Applications for legal aid may be made throughout all proceedings before the administrative courts.[1126] An appeal on a point of law (*Revision*) may be made within one month to the Federal Administrative Court (*Bundeverwaltungsgericht*; BVerwG).[1127] Furthermore, there is the possibility under certain circumstances to proceed directly from the Administrative Court to the Federal Administrative Court, thus 'leapfrogging' the Higher Administrative Court.[1128]

2. Constitutional jurisdiction

The Federal Constitutional Court (*Bundesverfassungsgericht*; BVerfG) may examine the constitutionality of State acts. The constitutional complaint is especially important for natural persons: it is an extraordinary legal remedy[1129] that may be brought by any natural person whose basic rights (Articles 1 to 19 GG) or certain comparable rights[1130] have been violated by a public authority (mostly by the courts or an administrative authority). § 93(1) BVerfGG stipulates that in principle the constitutional complaint shall be lodged within one month commencing from the decision.[1131]

1122 § 40 VwVfG; cf. *Maurer/Waldhoff*, Verwaltungsrecht § 7 mn 17.
1123 Cf. *Maurer/Waldhoff*, Verwaltungsrecht § 8 mn 15.
1124 §§ 124ff VwGO.
1125 § 67(4) VwGO.
1126 § 166 VwGO refers to the provisions of the *Zivilprozessordnung* (Code of Civil Procedure) in the version of 24.6.2022 (BGBl I 959).
1127 §§ 132ff VwGO.
1128 § 134 VwGO.
1129 Art 93(1) No. 4a GG and §§ 90ff BVerfGG.
1130 Arts 20(4), 33, 38, 101, 103 and 104 GG.
1131 § 93(1) BVerfGG.

C. Spain

Spain is a social and democratic State; its political form is that of a parliamentary monarchy.[1132] Spain comprises 17 *Comunidades Autónomas* ('autonomous communities').[1133] As Austria and Germany, the term 'country of immigration' also applies to Spain, at the latest from the end of the 1980s.[1134] Spain is still recovering from the 2008 'economic crisis', which hit the country especially hard, bursting the property bubble.[1135] This has also changed the influx of migrants. Generally, a significantly lower number of foreigners are migrating to Spain, with many foreigners and Spanish citizens leaving the country.[1136] One of the main reasons for this exodus was (and is) the high level of unemployment and the losses in the casual labour sector due to the 'economic crisis'.[1137] Between 2012 and 2017 alone, approx. 812,000 fewer foreigners were residing in Spain,[1138] though this distracts from the fact that between 2008 and 2014 the number of Spanish citizens with a foreign background rose from 1,037,663 to 1,729,335.[1139] 150,000 foreigners became Spanish citizens in

---

1132 Art 1 CE; for detail *López Guerra/Espín/García Morillo/Pérez Tremps/Satrústegui*, Derecho Constitucional: Vol I[11] (2018).

1133 Arts 143–158 CE.

1134 Cf. *Delgado Godoy*, Política de inmigración y cambio de gobierno in *Palomar Olmeda* (ed), Tratado de Extranjería[5] (2012) 113 (115–117); *Gómez Díaz*, Seguridad Social de los extranjeros. Inmigración y Seguridad Social, una gestión integrada in *Balado Ruiz-Gallegos* (ed), Inmigración, Estado y Derecho: Perspectivas desde el siglo XXI (2008) 883 (883) or *Cerdán/Maas*, Ein Überblick über die Neuerungen im spanischen Ausländerrecht, ZAR 2010, 105 (105). See also *Delgado Godoy*, Inmigración, política y acción pública en España: 1985-2019 in *Palomar Olmeda* (ed), Tratado de Extranjería[6] (2020) 91 (91ff).

1135 See only *Iglesias Martínez*, La inmigración que surgió del frío. Población de origen inmigrante y nuevos retos de las políticas de integración tras la crisis, Estudios Empresariales 2015/2 No. 148, 1 (1).

1136 Cf. *Camas Roda*, Trabajo decente 98.

1137 Cf. *Carbajal García*, El arraigo como circunstancia excepcional para poder residir y trabajar legalmente en España, Revista de Derecho Migratorio y Extranjería 2012/29, 55 (57) and *Sabater/Domingo*, A New Immigration Regularization Policy: The Settlement Program in Spain, International Migration Review 2012/46, 191 (214f).

1138 Cf. *Instituto Nacional de Estadística*, Cifras de Población a 1 de enero de 2017, Estadística de Migraciones 2016, Datos Provisionales (29.6.2017), https://www.ine.es/prensa/cp_2017_p.pdf (31.7.2022) 1.

1139 Cf. *Iglesias Martínez*, Estudios Empresariales 2015/2 No. 148, 5f.

2016 alone,[1140] with most enjoying the relaxed citizenship requirements for persons with Latin American roots.[1141] In this respect, there is overall no 'decrease' in the foreign population.[1142] On 1 January 2021, 5.4 million foreigners were living in Spain, i.e. approx. 11.4% of the registered population (47.3 million).[1143] A rise in the foreign population following the 'economic crisis' can first be seen in 2018.[1144]

In contrast to Austria and Germany, issues concerning foreigners do not play an especially dominant role in the public debate.[1145] It is also to be emphasised that the asylum law does not rank especially high in relation to the other aspects of the law on foreigners.[1146] This is underlined by the fact that only a fraction of foreigners holding a 'temporary residence permit for exceptional circumstances' (*residencia temporal por circunstancias excepcionales*) have received such permit on the grounds of international protection (*protección internacional*). One reason is the rejection of two-thirds of asylum applications.[1147] On the whole, the number of applications for asylum have increased slightly in past years,[1148] but the humanitarian and political crisis in Venezuela led in 2019 to an enormous increase in the

---

1140 *NN*, España concedió la nacionalidad a 150.000 extranjeros en 2016, un 32% más, eleconomista.es (9.4.2018), https://www.eleconomista.es/economia/noticias/9057786/04/18/Espana-fue-el-segundo-pais-de-la-UE-que-mas-extranjeros-nacionalizo-en-2016-segun-Eurostat.html (31.7.2022).

1141 Cf. *Sabater/Domingo*, International Migration Review 2012/46, 215.

1142 In that sense *Iglesias Martínez*, Estudios Empresariales 2015/2 No. 148, 5f.

1143 Cf. *Instituto Nacional de Estadística*, Avance de la Estadística del Padrón Continuo a 1 de enero de 2021 – Datos provisionales (20.4.2021), https://www.ine.es/prensa/pad_2021_p.pdf (31.7.2022) 1.

1144 Cf. *Poncini*, La población extranjera en España aumenta por primera vez desde la crisis, elpais.com (24.8.2018), https://elpais.com/politica/2018/04/24/actualidad/1524564519_812661.html (31.7.2022).

1145 Cf. *Iglesias Martínez*, Estudios Empresariales 2015/2 No. 148, 9.

1146 See the numbers in *Fernández Bessa/Brandariz García*, 'Perfiles' de deportabilidad: el sesgo del sistema de control migratorio desde la perspectiva de nacionalidad, Estudios penales y criminológicos 2017/27, 307 (338f) and further *Defensor del Pueblo*, Estudio sobre el asilo en España (June 2016), https://www.defensordelpueblo.es/wp-content/uploads/2016/07/Asilo_en_Espa%C3%B1a_2016.pdf (31.7.2022).

1147 *Sanmartín*, España rechaza dos de cada tres solicitudes de asilo, elmundo.es (18.6.2018), https://www.elmundo.es/espana/2018/06/18/5b276a2ee2704ecd3f8b45d4.html (31.7.2022).

1148 See just *NN*, España ya lleva 17.000 peticiones de asilo en 2018 y podría superar su récord, aunque rechaza la mayoría, europapress.es (18.6.2018), https://www.europapress.es/sociedad/noticia-espana-ya-lleva-17000-peticiones-asilo-2018-podria-superar-record-rechaza-mayoria-20180618143346.html (31.7.2022).

number of temporary residence permits granted to Venezuelans on the grounds of international protection (*residencia temporales por protección internacional*).[1149]

I. Historical development of the law on foreigners

The 'history' of the Spanish law on foreigners (*derecho de extranjería*) is shorter than in other Member States.[1150] The situation regarding foreigners was subject to considerable discretion held by the authorities, especially under the Franco dictatorship from 1939–1975. In contrast, the adoption of the Spanish Constitution in 1978 brought a positive development in the form of Article 13(1) CE, which states that foreigners shall enjoy the fundamental rights guaranteed by the constitution.[1151] The Spanish Constitutional Court (*Tribunal Constitucional*) has interpreted this provision on the basis of human dignity,[1152] with the effect that several of the fundamental rights also apply to irregularly staying foreigners.[1153] Foreigners

1149 Cf. *Ministerio de Trabajo, Migraciones y Seguridad Social*, Flujo de autorizaciones de residencia concedidos a extranjeros 2019: Principales resultados (November 2020), https://extranjeros.inclusion.gob.es/ficheros/estadisticas/operaciones/flujos/2019/Residentes_PRFlujo2019.pdf (31.7.2022) 11 and 16.

1150 Cf. *Pico Lorenzo*, Nuestra errática normativa sobre extranjería. Especial referencia a las regularizaciones y al arraigo, Jueces para la democracia 2002, 62 (62f) and *Solanes Corella*, Un balance tras 25 años de leyes de extranjería en España: 1985-2010, Revista del Ministerio de Trabajo e Inmigración 2010, 77 (97f).

1151 In general on foreigners' fundamental rights in Spain, *Fernández Pérez*, Los derechos fundamentales y libertades públicas de los extranjeros en España: Una visión desde la doctrina del tribunal constitucional (2016); *Aja* (ed), Los derechos de los inmigrantes en España (2009) and *García Ruiz*, La condición de extranjero y el Derecho Constitucional español in *Revenga Sánchez* (ed), Problemas constitucionales de la inmigración: una visión desde Italia y España (2005) 489.

1152 STC 107/1984, ECLI:ES:TC:1984:107; cf. *Pico Lorenzo*, Jueces para la democracia 2002, 63 and *Rodríguez/Rubio-Marín*, The constitutional status of irregular migrants: testing the boundaries of human rights protection in Spain and the United States in *Dembour/Kelly* (eds), Are Human Rights for Migrants? Critical Reflection on the Status of Irregular Migrants in Europe and the United States (2011) 73.

1153 STC 236/2007, ECLI:ES:TC:2007:236; STC 257/2007, ECLI:ES:TC:2007:257; cf. *Flores*, Los derechos fundamentales de los extranjeros irregulares in *Revenga Sánchez* (ed), Problemas constitucionales de la inmigración: una visión desde Italia y España (2005) 153; *Camas Roda*, Trabajo decente 80f and *Cerdán/Maas*, ZAR 2010, 107.

(*extranjeros*) are legally defined as those who do not have Spanish nationality.[1154]

In 1985, Spain passed for the first time an organic law (*Ley Orgánica*[1155]),[1156] which regulated the rights and freedoms of foreigners in Spain: Organic Law 7/1985 (LOE).[1157] This single piece of legislation contained all provisions regarding foreigners,[1158] with emphasis on entry and deportation. When viewed in context, this law is explained by Spain's accession to the European Community in 1986, with Spain showing to the other Member States that foreigners may not travel to Spanish territory without further requirements.[1159] Accordingly, the entry criteria were so restrictive that they were practically impossible to fulfil.[1160] For instance, entry not only required a visa but also a signed employment contract with a Spanish company.[1161] This thus had the effect that most foreigners entered irregularly;[1162] regular entry was possible under some circumstances via a tourist visa, though such persons were staying irregularly at the latest once the permitted time period lapsed. In addition, the requirements for deportation were so broadly worded that with their wide discretion the competent authorities were able to impose deportation at any time.[1163]

The LOE was restrictive for foreigners, but it did not prevent an increase in immigration. On the contrary, various other factors impacted on immigration, causing an enormous rise from the end of the 1980s and reaching its peak in 2005.[1164] In addition to the increase in absolute terms, the num-

1154 Art 1 LODYLE; cf. *Monereo Pérez/Gallego Morales*, Art 1 LODYLE in *Monereo Pérez/Fernández Avilés/Triguero Martínez* (eds), Comentario a la ley y al reglamento de Extranjería, Inmigración e Integración Social[2] (2013) 43.

1155 Cf. On the legal nature of organic laws *Parejo Alfonso*, Lecciones de Derecho Administrativo[11] (2021) 209ff.

1156 Cf. *Aja*, La evolución de la normativa sobre inmigración in *Aja/Arango* (eds), Veinte Años de Inmigración en España: Perspectiva jurídica y sociológica (1985-2004) (2006) 17 (17–20). No higher-ranking law was in force before.

1157 Cf. *Aja* in *Aja/Arango* 20ff and *Fernández Pérez*, Derechos fundamentales 125.

1158 *Solanes Corella*, Revista del Ministerio de Trabajo e Inmigración 2010, 78.

1159 Cf. *Fernández Pérez*, Derechos fundamentales 125.

1160 Cf. *Aja* in *Aja/Arango* 21; correctly *Fernández Pérez*, Derechos fundamentales 125ff.

1161 Cf. *Solanes Corella*, Revista del Ministerio de Trabajo e Inmigración 2010, 79.

1162 Cf. *Solanes Corella*, Revista del Ministerio de Trabajo e Inmigración 2010, 82.

1163 Cf. *Aja* in *Aja/Arango* 21f; *Fernández Pérez*, Derechos fundamentales 126 and *Solanes Corella*, Revista del Ministerio de Trabajo e Inmigración 2010, 79.

1164 Cf. *Moya Malapeira*, La evolución de control migratorio de entrada en España in *Aja/Arango* (eds), Veinte Años de Inmigración en España: Perspectiva jurídica y sociológica (1985-2004) (2006) 47 (47).

ber of irregularly staying foreigners also increased. The economic boom at the end of the 1990s brought a greater need for cheap labour, for instance in construction and agriculture, with the foreign population taking on the lion's share.[1165] Many of these jobs were (and still are) performed by irregularly staying foreigners working without documentation. *Sabater/Domingo* are correct in noting that this was not viewed as a problem, but rather a necessity to maintain the blooming economy.[1166] In short, Spain was (and is) especially attractive as a 'country of immigration'. As *González-Enríquez* states: 'First, there is the existence of this strong and rather vibrant informal economy where irregular migrants can find employment. Second, the relatively positive social attitudes towards migrants, in comparison with other European countries, third, the traditional tolerance towards illegality embedded in South European political culture, and, fourth, the treatment of social rights for irregular migrants in Spanish laws. Since the year 2000 irregular migrants enjoy free access to the public health system and to education (from 3 to 16 years) in the same conditions as Spaniards or regular migrants with the only condition of register themselves in the municipal register (the *Padrón*)'.[1167] As will be seen in the following, these statements still hold water.

A political debate therefore flared up in 1991,[1168] which led to the use of extraordinary 'regularisation programmes'[1169] (*procesos de normalización*).[1170] These type of regularisation programmes were introduced as instruments to lower the number of irregularly staying foreigners.[1171] The regularisation programmes are extraordinary procedures in the Spanish law on foreigners which aim to convert an irregular into a regular stay.[1172] As a rule, the programmes were announced in advance to reach a larger group of applicants. Irregularly staying foreigners therefore had a particular period of time to apply for a residence permit, and often also an

1165 Cf. *Iglesias Martínez*, Estudios Empresariales 2015/2 No. 148, 2ff.

1166 *Sabater/Domingo*, International Migration Review 2012/46, 215.

1167 *González-Enríquez*, Undocumented Migration: Country Report Spain. Clandestino Project (January 2009) 7.

1168 Cf. *Pico Lorenzo*, Jueces para la democracia 2002, 65f.

1169 See Chapter 1.B.I.

1170 Cf. *Solanes Corella*, Revista del Ministerio de Trabajo e Inmigración 2010, 82.

1171 Cf. *González-Enríquez*, Spain, the Cheap Model. Irregularity and Regularisation as Immigration Management Policies, EJML 2009, 139. Cf. *Aja* in *Aja/Arango* 24.

1172 *Sánchez Alonso*, La Política Migratoria en España: Un análisis de largo plazo, Revista Internacional de Sociología 2011, 243 (249, 259, 262).

employment permit.[1173] The measures targeted undocumented workers who could demonstrate a certain degree of 'integration' or that they were firmly rooted.[1174]

This type of policy towards foreigners became manifest in the years thereafter,[1175] rooting Spain's long tradition to regularise irregular stays.[1176] Regularisation programmes were undertaken in 1985 and 1991, with approx. 108,000 residence permits granted in 1991.[1177] A contingent[1178] of foreigners was regularised each year between 1993 and 1999 – the procedures can be seen as precursors to the regularisation mechanisms.[1179] Although these were hidden regularisation procedures, the legislation did not refer to these as such or in similar terms.[1180] A much larger regularisation programme was carried out in the year 2000.[1181] Here it is interesting to note that until 2004, the majority of foreigners were in fact staying irregularly despite the programmes.[1182]

The policy towards foreigners during the 1990s has been criticised by *Aja* for exhibiting two extremes: on the one hand, no appropriate entry conditions were established – the regularisations were 'just' of undocu-

1173 Cf. *Gortázar* in *de Bruycker* 334f.

1174 Cf. *Pico Lorenzo*, Jueces para la democracia 2002, 65f and *Gortázar* in *de Bruycker* 293. The latter does however note that some regularisations were also aimed at unsuccessful applicants for asylum.

1175 Cf. *Solanes Corella*, Revista del Ministerio de Trabajo e Inmigración 2010, 80f.

1176 Cf. for an overview until 2001 *Puerta Vílchez* in *Moya Escudero* 391; furthermore *Gortázar* in *de Bruycker* 301ff; *González-Enríquez*, EJML 2009; *Arango/Finotelli*, Country Report Spain in *Baldwin-Edwards/Kraler* (eds), REGINE Regularisations in Europe: Appendix A Country Studies (January 2009), https://home-affairs.ec.europa.eu/system/files/2020-09/regine_appendix_a_january_2009_en.pdf (31.7.2022) 83 and *Pico Lorenzo*, Jueces para la democracia 2002, 65ff.

1177 Cf. the detailed collection of newspaper articles and papers in *Comisión Española de Ayuda al Refugiado*, Dossier: Proceso de regularización de trabajadores extranjeros ilegales (1991); *Pico Lorenzo*, Jueces para la democracia 2002, 65f and on the requirements *Gortázar* in *de Bruycker* 301–304 and 319–322.

1178 Annually, covering between 20,000 and 30,000 individuals; cf. *Aja* in *Aja/Arango* 24 and on the requirements *Gortázar* in *de Bruycker* 305f and 326–329.

1179 Cf. *Pico Lorenzo*, Jueces para la democracia 2002, 66. On the regularisation programme in 1999 see *Trinidad García*, Revista de Derecho Migratorio y Extranjería 2002/1, 99–104.

1180 Cf. *Gortázar* in *de Bruycker* 294.

1181 Cf. in detail *Gortázar* in *de Bruycker* 305.

1182 Cf. *Cabellos Espiérrez/Roig Molés*, El tratamiento jurídico del extranjero en situación regular in *Aja/Arango Joaquín* (eds), Veinte Años de Inmigración en España: Perspectiva jurídica y sociológica (1985-2004) (2006) 113 (114).

mented foreign workers who had been staying in Spain for years without a residence permit. The argument put forward by *Aja* at this point is probably aimed at the extreme of 'rewarding' irregularly staying foreigners for breaking the law.[1183] On the other hand, *Aja* counters the creation of a 'serious' policy by stating that the annual regularisation programmes have been a 'pull effect' for further irregular migration. The assumed 'pull factor' has been reflected in the media coverage[1184] of the regularisation programmes.[1185] This can presumably be explained by their specific features, such as the intention to draw in a large number of applications or that this is a government's answer to a particular political situation. As already noted,[1186] there is no scientific evidence to maintain the assumption that regularisation programmes (and regularisations) attract foreigners without a right to enter or reside. Furthermore, several authors view the recourse to such 'extraordinary' legal instruments as a failure of the former Spanish policy towards foreigners.[1187] This opinion cannot, however, be fully supported as the programmes also corrected errors or hardships that the law at the time did not take into account, thus allowing the 'integration' of those concerned.

Several important changes were heralded by the Organic Law 4/2000 (LODYLE),[1188] which is still in force today, albeit following numerous reforms; the implementation regulations (REDYLE) accompanying the LODYLE are also significant. In addition, guidelines (*instrucciónes*) are also to be observed – these do not have the status as law, but are of decisive importance for the administrative authorities in relation to the provisions

---

1183 Cf. for similar arguments *Serrano Villamanta* in *Balado Ruiz-Gallegos* 554 and for criticism Chapter 2.D.IV.

1184 Cf. on the 2005 regularisation programme *Schweizerisches Bundesamt für Migration*, Spanien: Die Regularisierungsaktion 2005 (7.7.2005), 4 and *Möller-Holtkamp*, Legalisierungspolitik in Spanien in der Kritik, dw.com (12.5.2005), https://www.dw.com/de/legalisierungspolitik-in-spanien-in-der-kritik/a-1581274 (31.7.2022).

1185 Cf. *Pérez/Leraul*, El arraigo en España. De figura excepcional a instrumento de gobernanza de las migraciones, Comunicación aceptada para el VII Congreso de las Migraciones Internacionales en España (11–13.4.2012) 5f.

1186 See Chapter 2.D.IV.

1187 *Fernández Pérez*, Derechos fundamentales 126f; in this sense also *Serrano Villamanta* in *Balado Ruiz-Gallegos* 554; *Trinidad García*, Revista de Derecho Migratorio y Extranjería 2002/1, 100 as well as *Solanes Corella*, Revista del Ministerio de Trabajo e Inmigración 2010, 80.

1188 On the political development, *Aja* in *Aja/Arango* 27.

of the law on foreigners.[1189] For the first time, the legal status of foreigners was clearly and conclusively regulated by the LODYLE with reference to the previous case law of the Spanish Constitutional Court.[1190] Overall, the LODYLE is designed around the residence permit.[1191] This Organic Law recognised foreigners as a structural part of Spanish society, as is apparent from the use of the term 'integration' (*integración*) in the title.[1192] *Pico Lorenzo* is, however, more critical in her assessment that the law on foreigners does not have any clear objectives, even describing it as 'muddled'.[1193] Where irregularly staying foreigners are concerned, the LODYLE states several basic rights, such as the access to healthcare and education. Unlike the regularisation programmes, regularisation mechanisms were also introduced that could be accessed at any time.[1194] The regularisations based on a foreigner's roots (*arraigo*) are still in force today.[1195]

The law on foreigners was reformed a short time after the LODYLE was passed, with the victory of the conservative *Partido Popular* in the 2000 parliamentary elections considered one of the main reasons.[1196] Closer analysis of the reform shows that the basic structure of the Organic Law 8/2000 was maintained and only some aspects were fully reformed.[1197] Most of the provisions were tightened to provide adequate legal instruments to 'combat' irregular migration, which was increasing at the time.[1198]

1189 See just *Moreno Rebato*, Circulares, instrucciones y órdenes de servicio: naturaleza y régimen jurídico, Revista de Administración Pública 1998/147, 159.

1190 *Aja* in *Aja/Arango* 27 and *Solanes Corella*, Revista del Ministerio de Trabajo e Inmigración 2010, 82–85.

1191 Cf. *Triguero Martínez*, Migraciones 2014, 438f.

1192 On the development of the notion of integration in the Organic Law 2/2009 see Art 2ter LODYLE; cf. *Solanes Corella*, Revista del Ministerio de Trabajo e Inmigración 2010, 93f and *Cerdán/Maas*, ZAR 2010, 106.

1193 *Pico Lorenzo*, Jueces para la democracia 2002, 63f.

1194 Cf. *Triguero Martínez*, Migraciones 2014, 438f.

1195 Cf. *Triguero Martínez*, Migraciones 2014, 439 as well as *Pérez/Leraul*, El arraigo en España (11–13.4.2012) 3f and *Pico Lorenzo*, Jueces para la democracia 2002, 68f.

1196 Cf. *Solanes Corella*, Revista del Ministerio de Trabajo e Inmigración 2010, 84 and *Aja* in *Aja/Arango* 29f.

1197 Cf. *Aja* in *Aja/Arango* 30f.

1198 Cf. *Ruiz Paredes*, La regulación de la extranjería. Enfoque mercantil. Aproximación al empresariado inmigrante en España in *Balado Ruiz-Gallegos* (ed), Inmigración, Estado y Derecho: Perspectivas desde el siglo XXI (2008) 631 (633–635).

The last extraordinary regularisation programme[1199] was undertaken in 2005 and was also the most extensive.[1200] Irregularly staying foreigners could apply for a residence permit from February to March 2005, with the main requirements being continuous residence and registration in a Spanish municipality since August 2004.[1201] An employment contract was also required as a means to suppress the employment of undocumented foreign workers.[1202] A person could acquire not only a residence permit but also an employment permit if there was a future employment relationship of at least six months. The validity of both permits was linked to the registration for social security;[1203] this is still required for a regularisation based on 'roots'.[1204] This approach avoided the submission of pseudo employment contracts for the sole purpose of acquiring a residence permit. Altogether there were approx. 700,000 applications during this time, of which approx. 578,000 (83%) were successful.[1205]

One notable aspect is the fact that the application was to be made by the future employer, not the foreigner.[1206] As with the registration for social security, this requirement was to also ensure the existence of an actual employment relationship. The 2005 regularisation programme was considered a success in tackling the employment of undocumented workers.[1207]

1199 Cf. the heading of the transitional provision 3 REDYLE in the version of the Royal Decree 2393/2004.

1200 REDYLE in the version of the Royal Decree 2393/2004; cf. *Arango/Finotelli* in *Baldwin-Edwards/Kraler* 85ff.

1201 Cf. for an overview *Aguilera Izquierdo*, El acceso de los inmigrantes irregulares al mercado de trabajo: Los procesos de regularización extraordinaria y el arraigo social y laboral, Revista del Ministerio de Trabajo y Asuntos Sociales 2006, 175 or *Gómez Díaz* in *Balado Ruiz-Gallegos* 887ff.

1202 *Gómez Díaz* in *Balado Ruiz-Gallegos* 888, even claims in this context that it is still the largest measure undertaken against the employment of undocumented workers in Spain.

1203 Cf. *Gómez Díaz* in *Balado Ruiz-Gallegos* 895ff.

1204 See Chapter 4.E.I.

1205 Cf. on the statistics *Gómez Díaz* in *Balado Ruiz-Gallegos* 891ff and *Cerezo Mariscal*, La gestión de los procesos de la irregularidad estructural y sobrevenida en España. Análisis maquetado del arraigo, Revista de Derecho 2015, 657 (672).

1206 Cf. *Gómez Díaz* in *Balado Ruiz-Gallegos* 887.

1207 Cf. *Gómez Díaz* in *Balado Ruiz-Gallegos* 887f; more generally *González Calvet*, El arraigo como instrumento de regularización individual y permanente del trabajador inmigrante indocumentado en el reglamento de extranjería aprobado por el RD 2393/2004, de 30 de diciembre, Revista de Derecho Social 2007/37, 105 (107).

Regularised foreigners would now pay social security contributions from their regular and documented employment. Furthermore, the return to irregularity and undocumented employment should also be prevented by the possibility to extend the residence permit.[1208] However, the political rejection of these regularisation programmes by other EU Member States ultimately resulted in the statement in the European Pact on Immigration and Asylum that Member States should now only use 'case-by-case regularisation'.[1209] The Pact is not legally binding, but Spain has since followed this 'case-by-case' approach and not undertaken any further regularisation programmes.[1210]

The aforementioned importance of foreign workers for the Spanish economy is worth highlighting.[1211] According to *Gómez Díaz*, the extraordinary regularisation programmes are closely linked to efforts to regulate the labour market and find solutions to its realities and needs.[1212] *Camas Roda* and *Triguero Martínez* go further in stating that the immigration policy not only depends on but is also guided by the labour market.[1213] This is shown, for instance, by the fact that under Prime Minister *Zapatero* the main responsibility for the development of migration policy was transferred from the Ministry of the Interior to the (then) Ministry of Labour (*Ministerio de Trabajo*).[1214] The responsibility currently lies with the Secretary of State for Migration (*Secretaría de Estado de Migraciones*) in the Ministry of Inclusion, Social Security and Migration (*Ministerio de Inclusión, Seguridad Social y Migraciones*).

The Organic Law 10/2011 introduced improvements to the 'temporary residence permit and employment permit for extraordinary circumstances for foreign victims of human trafficking' and the 'temporary residence

1208 See on this development, which originated in the 1991 regularisation programme, *Gortázar* in *de Bruycker* 335.

1209 *Council of the European Union*, European Pact on Immigration and Asylum (24.9.2008), 13440/08, 7.

1210 Also in this sense *Sabater/Domingo*, International Migration Review 2012/46, 214f.

1211 Cf. *Fernández Bessa/Brandariz García*, Transformaciones de la penalidad migratoria en el contexto de la crisis económica: El giro gerencial del dispositivo de deportación, Revista para el Análisis del Derecho 2016/4, 1 (4 with further references).

1212 Cf. *Gómez Díaz* in *Balado Ruiz-Gallegos* 887.

1213 Cf. *Camas Roda*, Trabajo decente 82 with further references; for the development see *Triguero Martínez*, Migraciones 2014, 441–447.

1214 Cf. *Donaire Villa/Moya Malapeira* in *Boza Martínez/Donaire Villa/Moya Malapeira* 545f.

permit and employment permit for extraordinary circumstances for foreign women who are victims of gender based violence'.[1215] In comparison to Austrian and German laws, it is notable that since 2009 there have been hardly any reforms to the Spanish law on foreigners.[1216] One exception was in July 2022, when the Spanish government passed the Royal Decree (*Real Decreto*) 629/2022 and reformed the 'roots' (*arraigo*) regularisations.[1217] Like in past reforms, the situation of the Spanish labour market was the decisive reason for this reform, in particular to be able to respond swiftly to the growing imbalances of the labour market.[1218] These have been partly caused by the COVID-19 pandemic. One major novelty is the introduction of a new type of 'roots' regularisation, the so-called training roots (*arraigo para la formación*) that is inspired by the German 'toleration for the purpose of training'.[1219] In this way, the Spanish government wants to incorporate into the labour market foreigners who are living in Spain and work precariously and/or undocumented. Hence, the Spanish government explicitly addresses and tries to tackle this situation.

Currently (31 July 2022) there is a popular legislative initiative for an extraordinary regularisation of foreigners (*Iniciativa Legislativa Popular para una Regularización Extraordinaria de Personas Extranjeras*) running to regularise between 390,000 and 470,000 irregularly staying foreigners in Spain.[1220] This initiative is called *esenciales* (essentials) and is led by migrant organisations and supported by numerous actors of civil society. 500,000 signatures are necessary to ensure that the proposed legislation is addressed.[1221]

II. Legal status of foreigners

Before detailing the current law on 'temporary residence permits for exceptional circumstances', I will first describe the legal status of foreigners, focusing on the general aspects regarding residency law, employment, social benefits, and healthcare.

1215 BOE 180 of 28.7.2011. See Chapter 4.D.I.4.–5.
1216 See Chapter 3.A.I. and Chapter 3.B.I.
1217 See Chapter 3.C.III.1.
1218 Royal Decree 629/2022, BOE 179 of 27.7.2022, 107697.
1219 Royal Decree 629/2022, BOE 179 of 27.7.2022, 107698 and see Chapter 4.E.III. and Chapter 4.E.IV.1.
1220 For more information see https://esenciales.info/ (31.7.2022).
1221 Art 87(3) CE.

1. (Un)lawful residence

The Spanish law on foreigners distinguishes in principle between minor, serious, and very serious offences (*infracciones leves, graves y muy graves*).[1222] Under Spanish law, an irregular stay is – with one exception[1223] – a serious offence.[1224] Foreigners who do not meet the requirements for entry and/or residence are required to leave the country.[1225] As a rule, a separate deportation procedure is initiated against a foreigner who has been caught without a valid right to stay.[1226] This can result in deportation or a fine.[1227] The decision regarding deportation takes legal effect and is enforceable at the moment it is rendered.[1228]

In comparison to Austrian and German law, a negative decision regarding residency does not automatically result in a removal measure.[1229] There is merely the aforementioned obligation to leave the country,[1230] with the

---

1222 Arts 52, 53 and 54 LODYLE; cf. *Solanes Corella*, Revista del Ministerio de Trabajo e Inmigración 2010, 81 and *Palomar Olmeda*, La potestad sancionadora pública en materia de extranjería in *Palomar Olmeda* (ed), Tratado de Extranjería[6] (2020) 455 (459ff).

1223 According to Arts 52(b) and 55(1)(a) LODYLE, failing to renew the residence permit within the first three months after it has expired is only a minor offence punishable with a fine; cf. *Arrese Iriondo*, La problemática jurídica de las situaciones irregulares: la expulsión como sanción a la situación irregular, Revista de Derecho Migratorio y Extranjería 2010/25, 73 (74 and 83–86).

1224 Art 53(1)(a) LODYLE; cf. *Boza Martínez*, El procedimiento sancionador en general y, particularmente, los procedimientos de expulsión in *Boza Martínez/Donaire Villa/Moya Malapeira* (ed), Comentario a la reforma de la ley de extranjería (LO 2/2009) (2011) 261 (263ff); *Castanedo García*, Examen de la jurisprudencia existente relativa a los artículos 57 y 58 de la ley orgánica 4/2000, de 11 de enero y su desarrollo reglamentario, y las sentencias de distintos tribunales superiores de justicia sobre la materia, Revista de Derecho Migratorio y Extranjería 2014/36, 261 (262); *Lorenzo Jiménez*, La expulsión de extranjeros que se encuentran en trámite de regularización, Revista de Derecho Migratorio y Extranjería 2015/38, 13 (24f).

1225 Art 28(3)(c) LODYLE and Art 24 REDYLE.

1226 On the distinction between ordinary (*ordinario*) and preferential (*preferente*) procedure see Arts 226–233 and 234–237 REDYLE; for detail *Arrese Iriondo*, Revista de Derecho Migratorio y Extranjería 2010/25, 80–82.

1227 See Chapter 4.A.I.1.

1228 Arts 21(2) and 63(7) LODYLE; cf. *Lorenzo Jiménez*, Revista de Derecho Migratorio y Extranjería 2015/38, 32.

1229 For Austria, see Chapter 3.A.II.1. and for Germany Chapter 3.B.II.1.

1230 Art 24 REDYLE.

decision on deportation subject to the outcome of a separate deportation process.

2. Employment

According to the heading to Article 10 LODYLE, foreigners have a right to work and to social security.[1231] However, it is not an unrestricted right as the wording suggests:[1232] the right to work depends on a work permit.[1233] The requirements set in the LODYLE therefore need to be met in order to receive a work permit that allows the holder to engage in remunerated activities, be this through self-employment or otherwise.[1234] According to Article 36(1) LODYLE, this requires a work permit as well as a residence permit,[1235] which are usually issued together.[1236] The holder must register with the social security authorities in order for the permits to be valid.[1237] As mentioned above, this serves to tackle fraud and abuse in relation to employment contracts, and to ensure the legality of the employment relationships.[1238] Undocumented employment is therefore to be prevented and 'fought' as best as possible.

The 'temporary residence permit for exceptional circumstances' system requires the application for a work permit to be made simultaneously with the application for a residence permit or during the period in which the application is valid.[1239] This does not apply to residence permits granted

---

1231 Cf. *Camas Roda*, Trabajo decente 79–82.

1232 Art 35 CE; cf. *Monereo Pérez/Triguero Martínez*, Art 10 LODYLE in *Monereo Pérez/Fernández Avilés/Triguero Martínez*, Comentario a la ley y al reglamento de Extranjería, Inmigración e Integración Social[2] (2013) 203.

1233 Cf. *Barcelón Cobedo*, Autorización de Residencia por motivos laborales. Régimen general in *Boza Martínez/Donaire Villa/Moya Malapeira* (eds), La nueva regulación de la inmigración y la extranjería en España (2012) 364 (365ff).

1234 Cf. *Monereo Pérez/Triguero Martínez* in *Monereo Pérez/Fernández Avilés/Triguero Martínez* 203 and *Nieves Moreno Vida*, Art 36 LODYLE in *Monereo Pérez/Fernández Avilés/Triguero Martínez* (eds), Comentario a la ley y al reglamento de Extranjería, Inmigración e Integración Social[2] (2013) 614 (614).

1235 Cf. *Nieves Moreno Vida* in *Monereo Pérez/Fernández Avilés/Triguero Martínez* 614, 618ff.

1236 Apart from exceptional cases such as foreigners convicted of criminal offences; cf. *Nieves Moreno Vida* in *Monereo Pérez/Fernández Avilés/Triguero Martínez* 619.

1237 Arts 36(2) and 67(7) REDYLE, as well as Art 128(6) REDYLE.

1238 Cf. *Nieves Moreno Vida* in *Monereo Pérez/Fernández Avilés/Triguero Martínez* 620.

1239 Art 129(2) REDYLE: cf. *Serrano Villamanta* in *Balado Ruiz-Gallegos* 575 and *Esteban de la Rosa*, Art 31 LODYLE in *Monereo Pérez/Fernández Avilés/Triguero*

on the basis of 'roots', as in such instances the residence permit and work permit are granted together.[1240] Consequently, the general requirements for issuing a work permit must also be met,[1241] such as an employment contract with the future employer.[1242] If an application is made for a work permit concerning employment as an employee (*por cuenta ajena*), there is no test of the Spanish labour market.[1243] This differs greatly from the ordinary residency system.[1244] As in Austria and Germany, the national labour-market test is a measure used to manage migration inflow on the basis of economic criteria and by favouring the national (and equivalent) population.[1245]

As the work permit is tied to a right to stay, persons residing irregularly in Spain cannot lawfully engage in employed activities;[1246] any employment is therefore undocumented.[1247] However, at the same time this does not mean that they do not have the same rights as lawfully employed foreigners.[1248]

3. Social benefits

Irregularly staying foreigners are entitled to basic social services and benefits.[1249] The extent of the services and benefits provided varies consider-

Martínez (eds), Comentario a la ley y al reglamento de Extranjería, Inmigración e Integración Social[2] (2013) 491 (508f).

1240 Art 129(1) REDYLE and see Chapter 3.C.III.2.

1241 Art 129(2) REDYLE, which refers to Arts 64(3) and 105(3) REDYLE; cf. *García Vitoria*, Residencia por Circunstancias Excepcionales. El Arraigo in *Boza Martínez/Donaire Villa/Moya Malapeira* (eds), La nueva regulación de la inmigración y la extranjería en España (2012) 287 (304).

1242 Art 64(3)(b) REDYLE; see Chapter 4.E.1. on social roots.

1243 Cf. *Serrano Villamanta* in *Balado Ruiz-Gallegos* 556 and *Carbajal García*, Revista de Derecho Migratorio y Extranjería 2012/29, 57.

1244 In detail, *Camas Roda*, Trabajo decente 86ff.

1245 See Chapter 3.A.II.2. and Chapter 3.B.II.2.

1246 Cf. *Pérez Milla*, De un status laboral mínima para situaciones de migración irregular, Revista de Derecho Migratorio y Extranjería 2004/5, 9 (20ff).

1247 On the effects of undocumented employment on the employment relationship itself see Art 36(3) LODYLE and *Nieves Moreno Vida* in *Monereo Pérez/ Fernández Avilés/Triguero Martínez* 625, and *González Calvet*, Revista de Derecho Social 2007/37, 108–112.

1248 Cf. *Camas Roda*, Trabajo decente 143ff.

1249 Art 14(3) LODYLE; cf. *Mimentza Martin*, Die sozialrechtliche Stellung 245 with further references and *Vázquez Garranzo*, Los servicios sociales y

ably across Spain as the responsibility lies with the autonomous communities.[1250] Basic benefits include, for example, the minimum income for integration (*renta mínima de inserción*),[1251] which serves to ease the pressing needs of particular groups.[1252] Furthermore, a top-up housing allowance (*prestación complementaria de vivienda*) and assistance to overcome particular social challenges or integration assistance (*ayudas a la inserción*) are further benefits.[1253]

Foreigners who are residing regularly in Spain will be included[1254] in the contribution-based social security system and are entitled to social services and benefits under the same conditions as Spaniards.[1255] This includes a basic pension, a basic income in the event of reduced income, benefits for disabled children as well as medical treatment for persons in need.[1256]

4. Healthcare

Prior to the Royal Decree 16/2012[1257], all foreigners registered in the municipal register were guaranteed access to healthcare, irrespective of their residence status.[1258] For *González-Enríquez*, this was a reason why migrants

la dependencia in *Palomar Olmeda* (ed), Tratado de Extranjería[6] (2020) 1145 (1163ff).

1250 Cf. *Vázquez Garranzo* in *Palomar Olmeda* 1158–1163, 1171f and *Mimentza Martin*, Die sozialrechtliche Stellung 243ff with further references.

1251 Cf. *Vázquez Garranzo* in *Palomar Olmeda* 1181ff.

1252 STC 239/2002, ECLI:ES:TC:2002:239.

1253 Cf. *Mimentza Martin*, Die sozialrechtliche Stellung 243–257 with a detailed description of the situation in the Basque Country.

1254 Art 7(1) Real Decreto Legislativo 8/2015, de 30 de octubre, por el que se aprueba el texto refundido de la Ley General de la Seguridad Social, BOE 261 of 31.10.2015 in the version of 27.7.2022; cf. *Pajuelo*, La protección social de los extranjeros en España in *Palomar Olmeda* (ed), Tratado de Extranjería[6] (2020) 991 and *Mimentza Martin*, Die sozialrechtliche Stellung 214 and 257ff.

1255 Art 14(1) LODYLE; cf. *Camas Roda*, Trabajo decente 140f and *Mimentza Martin*, Die sozialrechtliche Stellung 242f and 245ff.

1256 *Mimentza Martin*, Die sozialrechtliche Stellung 242f.

1257 Real Decreto-ley 16/2012, de 20 de abril, de medidas urgentes para garantizar la sostenibilidad del Sistema Nacional de Salud y mejorar la calidad y seguridad de sus prestaciones, BOE 98 of 24.4.2012 in the version of 1.7.2017.

1258 Cf. *Sangüesa Ruiz*, El derecho a la salud de los extranjeros residentes en situación irregular: sobre la legitimidad constitucional del RD-Ley 16/2012, Revista Electrónica del Departamento de Derecho de la Universidad de la

found Spain to be particularly 'attractive'.[1259] However, since the Royal Decree 16/2012, distinctions are to be drawn between third-country nationals:[1260] minors continue to have the same access as Spanish nationals. In addition, irregularly staying foreigners of full age only have access to healthcare services in cases of pregnancy and emergencies due to serious illness or accidents. A residence permit is otherwise required for access to healthcare services.[1261] Despite the limitations by the central government, the autonomous communities have almost entirely reintroduced the access to healthcare services for irregularly staying foreigners.[1262]

The Royal Decree 27/2018[1263] was passed in July 2018, reversing considerable parts of the reforms via Royal Decree 16/2012,[1264] including the reintroduction at the level of the central government of unrestricted healthcare for irregularly staying foreigners.[1265] Now (as before), proof of registration in the municipal register must be furnished. In addition, proof of identity such as a passport or similar document must be presented, though the person concerned still has access to healthcare services even if such document does not exist.[1266]

Rioja 2015, 233 (234f) and *Mimentza Martin*, Die sozialrechtliche Stellung 306f.

1259 *González-Enríquez*, Clandestino Project (January 2009) 7.

1260 Cf. *Fernández Pérez*, Derechos fundamentales 101f.

1261 Cf. *Sangüesa Ruiz*, Revista Electrónica del Departamento de Derecho de la Universidad de la Rioja 2015, 234f; for criticism *Fernández Pérez*, Derechos fundamentales 243ff and *Red Acoge*, Los efectos de la exclusión sanitaria en las personas inmigrantes más vulnerables (July 2015).

1262 Cf. *Sangüesa Ruiz*, Revista Electrónica del Departamento de Derecho de la Universidad de la Rioja 2015, 237f; *Ramírez de Castro*, Los «sin papeles» deberán estar 6 meses empadronados para tener asistencia sanitaria, abc.es (2.9.2015), https://www.abc.es/sociedad/20150902/abci-interior-sanidad-irregulares-201509012119.html (31.7.2022); *Mouzo Quintans*, El Parlamento blinda hoy la sanidad universal, elpais.com (15.7.2017), https://elpais.com/ccaa/2017/06/14/catalunya/1497459112_092105.html (31.7.2022).

1263 Real Decreto-ley 7/2018, de 27 de julio, sobre el acceso universal al Sistema Nacional de Salud, BOE 183 of 30.7.2018.

1264 *Gómez Zamora*, Comentario al Real Decreto-ley 7/2018, de 27 de julio, sobre el acceso universal al Sistema Nacional de Salud, Gabilex 2018, 281 (281ff).

1265 *NN*, Sanidad establece tres requisitos para atender gratuitamente a los «sin papeles», abc.es (10.7.2019), https://www.abc.es/sociedad/abci-sanidad-establece-tres-requisitos-para-atender-gratuitamente-sin-papeles-201907101948_noticia.html (31.7.2022).

1266 *De Benito*, Los migrantes tendrán sanidad desde el primer día sin necesidad de padrón, elpais.com (17.7.2018), https://elpais.com/politica/2018/07/16/actualidad/1531764444_944908.html (31.7.2022).

III. General remarks on 'temporary residence permits for exceptional circumstances'

The Spanish regularisations to be compared belong to the category *residencias temporales por circunstancias excepcionales*[1267] – 'temporary residence permits for exceptional circumstances'.[1268] One exception concerns the residence permit for children not born in Spain, which will be analysed in more detail in Chapter 4.C.I.

The 'temporary residence permits for exceptional circumstances' are extraordinary because certain requirements, which would otherwise need to be met in the course of an ordinary residence permit, do not apply.[1269] In this respect, the most important exemption is by far the exclusion of the visa requirement at the time of application,[1270] though it is also significant that the applicant does not need to have sufficient financial means.[1271] The decisions on residence permits relevant to this study are usually issued in the form of a decision (*resolución* or *decisión*),[1272] which exhausts the administrative procedure.[1273]

1. Overview

At the latest since the last regularisation programme in 2005, regularisation mechanisms have become an established approach in Spanish law to

1267 On exceptional circumstances see *Peña Pérez*, Arraigo, circunstancias excepcionales y razones humanitarias: Evolución histórica dentro del derecho de extranjería, Revista de Derecho Migratorio y Extranjería 2012/30, 35 (43f).

1268 Art 31(3) LODYLE and Arts 123ff REDYLE; cf. *Esteban de la Rosa*, Art 31 LODYLE in *Monereo Pérez/Fernández Avilés/Triguero Martínez* 503–509.

1269 *Serrano Villamanta* in *Balado Ruiz-Gallegos* 553; cf. also *Triguero Martínez*, Migraciones 2014, 439f.

1270 Art 31(3) LODYLE; cf. *Serrano Villamanta* in *Balado Ruiz-Gallegos* 553f and *García Vitoria* in *Boza Martínez/Donaire Villa/Moya Malapeira* 287.

1271 Cf. *Serrano Villamanta* in *Balado Ruiz-Gallegos* 572.

1272 Cf. *Boza Martínez/Donaire Villa/Moya Malapeira* in *Boza Martínez/Donaire Villa/Moya Malapeira* 19.

1273 Disposición adicional 14 REDYLE; cf. *Conde Antequera*, Art 21 LODYLE in *Monereo Pérez/Fernández Avilés/Triguero Martínez* (eds), Comentario a la ley y al reglamento de Extranjería, Inmigración e Integración Social[2] (2013) 337 (339).

offering a permanent path out of irregularity.[1274] These were introduced, inter alia, due to changes surrounding migration,[1275] especially the rising numbers of foreigners residing in Spain.[1276] Strictly speaking, there have already been 'hidden' regularisation possibilities since the first Organic Law of 1985, which were extended[1277] foremost by the LODYLE and ultimately defined and reconceptualised as 'roots' (*arraigo*) by the Organic Law 8/2000.[1278] *Heredia Fernández* welcomes this codification as there is no longer the need to use regularisation programmes to lower the number of irregularly staying foreigners.[1279] The Organic Law 14/2003 introduced Article 31(3) LODYLE in the form that is mostly still in force today.[1280] In terms of the numbers issued, the 'temporary residence permits for exceptional circumstances' have first gained in relevance since the end of the last regularisation programme in 2005.[1281]

Current Spanish law affords foreigners the possibility to apply at any time (i.e. without needing to wait for an extraordinary regularisation programme) to apply for a 'temporary residence permit for exceptional circumstances'. In some circumstances they may even be legally entitled to such a residence permit as the competent authorities have very limited discretion.[1282] *Cerezo Mariscal* even goes so far to state that, broadly speaking, these types of residence permits have since become 'ordinary' in na-

---

1274 Cf. *Cerezo Mariscal*, Revista de Derecho 2015, 659, 668; *Serrano Villamanta* in *Balado Ruiz-Gallegos* 554 and *Pérez/Leraul*, El arraigo en España (11–13.4.2012) 5.

1275 Cf. *González Calvet*, Revista de Derecho Social 2007/37, 105f.

1276 See above Chapter 3.C.I.

1277 Art 29(3) LODYLE; cf. *Trinidad García*, Revista de Derecho Migratorio y Extranjería 2002/1, 105ff and *Peña Pérez*, Revista de Derecho Migratorio y Extranjería 2012/30, 46ff.

1278 Art 31 LODYLE and Art 45 REDYLE in the version of the Royal Decree 2393/2004 and see Chapter 3.C.I.

1279 *Heredia Fernández*, Las situaciones de los extranjeros en España in *Moya Escudero* (ed), Comentario sistemático a la ley de extranjería (2001) 53 (67); see however also Chapter 3.C.I.

1280 Cf. *Fernández Collados*, Régimen de entrada, permanencia y salida de los extranjeros en España in *Palomar Olmeda* (ed), Tratado de Extranjería[6] (2020) 373 (423f) and *González Calvet*, Revista de Derecho Social 2007/37, 119ff.

1281 See also *González Calvet*, Revista de Derecho Social 2007/37, 119 and see the statistics in *Pérez/Leraul*, El arraigo en España (11–13.4.2012) 7.

1282 Cf. *Esteban de la Rosa*, Art 31 LODYLE in *Monereo Pérez/Fernández Avilés/Triguero Martínez* 503 and *Triguero Martínez*, Migraciones 2014, 448f.

ture.[1283] For instance, on 31 December 2019 approx. 83,800 foreigners held a 'temporary residence permit for exceptional circumstances'[1284] – a total of 29.3% of all temporary residence permits (*autorizaciónes de residencia temporal*). However, it is to be noted that (as in Austria[1285]) there is no precise data to determine how many permits were issued and under which circumstances.[1286]

2. Roots

The vast majority of foreigners who hold a 'temporary residence permit for exceptional circumstances' acquired such permit on the basis of 'roots'. For instance, in 2019 there were 40,005 foreigners with a residence permit issued on the grounds of 'roots', with 43,861 issued for other reasons. In 2018, approx. 88.2% of all foreigners were in possession of a 'temporary residence permit for exceptional circumstances' issued on the grounds of 'roots'.[1287] The increase in permits for other grounds arises primarily from

---

1283 Cf. *Cerezo Mariscal*, Revista de Derecho 2015, 682. See also *Triguero Martínez*, Migraciones 2014, 440, 450.

1284 Cf. *Ministerio de Trabajo, Migraciones y Seguridad Social*, Flujo de autorizaciones de residencia concedidos a extranjeros 2019: Principales resultados (November 2020) 14 and 16. This is more than double compared to the previous year (31.12.2018 – 41,653); cf. *Ministerio de Trabajo, Migraciones y Seguridad Social*, Flujo de autorizaciones de residencia concedidos a extranjeros 2018: Principales resultados (26.11.2019), https://extranjeros.inclusion.gob.es/ficheros/estadisticas/operaciones/flujos/2018/Residentes_PRFlujo2018.pdf (31.7.2022) 14. The increase results in particular from the '*residencia temporales por protección internacional*' granted to Venezuelans.

1285 See Chapter 3.A.III.1.

1286 The statistics distinguish between the requirements for 'roots' and those for humanitarian and other reasons (*razones humanitarias y otras*). The latter are defined as: 'La categoría "Razones humanitarias y otras" incluye las autorizaciones que se conceden por circunstancias excepcionales por: Razones de Protección internacional, Razones humanitarias, Colaboración con autoridades, Seguridad nacional o interés público, Mujeres víctimas de violencia de género, Colaboración contra redes organizadas y Víctimas de trata de seres humanos'; *Ministerio de Trabajo, Migraciones y Seguridad Social*, Flujo de autorizaciones de residencia concedidos a extranjeros 2019: Principales resultados (November 2020) 20.

1287 Cf. *Ministerio de Trabajo, Migraciones y Seguridad Social*, Flujo de autorizaciones de residencia concedidos a extranjeros 2018: Resultados detallados (15.11.2019), https://extranjeros.inclusion.gob.es/ficheros/estadisticas/operaciones/flujos/2018/Detallados_flujonacional2018.xlsx (31.7.2022) Table 6.

the 'residence permit for international protection' (*residencia temporal por protección internacional*) issued to Venezuelans.[1288] The official statistics may no longer distinguish between the different types of roots, yet it is clear from the literature that 'social roots' play – quantitively speaking – the most important role, followed by 'family roots', with 'employment roots' being of least importance. For instance, of the 747,685 applications for a 'temporary residence permit for exceptional circumstances' between 2006 and 2014, only 6.44% and 1.65% were granted on the basis of family roots and employment roots, respectively.[1289] In this regard, 'roots' is the most important path away from an irregular status, both in practice and in terms of scale.[1290] This is clear not only from the aforementioned statistics but also from the list in the legislation. Since the REDYLE, the 'roots' requirements belong to the 'temporary residence permit for exceptional circumstances'[1291] and are even listed within this category before the 'temporary residence permit for international protection'.[1292]

With the reform in 2022, apart from the social, employment and family roots, a new type of roots was introduced, the so-called training roots (*arraigo para la formación*). However, as the law has only recently come into force, there are no statistics available as yet.

The term 'roots' used in the Spanish law on foreigners described three different types of 'residence permits',[1293] for which the LODYLE,[1294] the Organic Law 8/2000,[1295] the Organic Law 14/2003 as well as the Royal

See also the statistics on the regularisations issued between 2002 and 2012 in *Pérez/Leraul*, El arraigo en España (11–13.4.2012) 6–9, and more generally in *Carbajal García*, Revista de Derecho Migratorio y Extranjería 2012/29, 56f.

1288 Cf. *Ministerio de Trabajo, Migraciones y Seguridad Social*, Flujo de autorizaciones de residencia concedidos a extranjeros 2019: Principales resultados (November 2020) 11 and 16.

1289 Cf. *Cerezo Mariscal*, Revista de Derecho 2015, 673, 676f and 680.

1290 Cf. *Serrano Villamanta* in *Balado Ruiz-Gallegos* 561 and *García Vitoria* in *Boza Martínez/Donaire Villa/Moya Malapeira* 287. Cf. on the development *Triguero Martínez*, Migraciones 2014, 440 and 450.

1291 Art 123(1) REDYLE and cf. *Triguero Martínez*, Migraciones 2014, 449.

1292 Cf. *Goizueta Vértiz*, La entrada a España, los visados y las situaciones de los extranjeros en España: estancia y residencia e irregularidad y arraigo in *Boza Martínez/Donaire Villa/Moya Malapeira* (eds), Comentario a la reforma de la ley de extranjería (LO 2/2009) (2011) 157 (160).

1293 Art 124 REDYLE.

1294 Art 29(3) LODYLE; cf. *González Calvet*, Revista de Derecho Social 2007/37, 116–118.

1295 Art 31(3) LODYLE; cf. *González Calvet*, Revista de Derecho Social 2007/37, 118f.

Decree 2393/2004[1296] played an important role.[1297] Before this legislative development, however, the term was already used by the courts from the mid-1990s and influenced the legislative development.[1298] For instance, deportation decisions based on the 'rootedness' of foreigners in Spain were described as disproportionate if they violated Article 8 ECHR.[1299] In this respect, the Spanish Constitutional Court determined several criteria that are to be observed.[1300] This may be compared with the development of the 'right to remain' in Austria, which is now anchored in law as the 'residence permit for reasons of Article 8 ECHR'.[1301]

The term 'roots' is therefore an undefined legal term,[1302] influenced by the courts[1303] and now forming a part of the legislation itself.[1304] The three – since 2022 four – types are all based on the foreigner's roots and settlement in Spain,[1305] which is why it may be referred to as an instrument to consolidate the integration into Spanish society.[1306] Nonetheless, *García Vitoria* uses the example of the right to respect one's private life to criticise that there are gaps between the judicial interpretation and the

---

1296 Art 45 REDYLE in the version Real Decreto 2393/2004.

1297 On the legislative development of the term 'rootedness' in Spanish law see *Triguero Martínez*, Migraciones 2014, 437–440; *Massó Garrote*, El nuevo reglamento de extranjería (2002) 40f; *Carbajal García*, Revista de Derecho Migratorio y Extranjería 2012/29, 62–65. Cf. also *Serrano Villamanta* in *Balado Ruiz-Gallegos* 561ff with further references. The author shows that continuous residence is the most important criterion (563).

1298 Cf. *González Calvet*, Revista de Derecho Social 2007/37, 116–119 and *Ques Mena*, El arraigo, social, económico y familiar en el Derecho de extranjería. Tratamiento legal y jurisprudencial, Diario la Ley 2008/7067, 1 (2 with further references).

1299 Cf. *García Vitoria*, El impacto de la jurisprudencia del Tribunal Europeo de Derechos Humanos en la expulsión de inmigrantes, Revista General de Derecho Constitucional 2015/20, 1 (14–16) and *González Calvet*, Revista de Derecho Social 2007/37, 116–118.

1300 *Cerezo Mariscal*, Revista de Derecho 2015, 670f.

1301 See Chapter 4.B.III. and Chapter 4.C.III.

1302 Cf. more detail *Peña Pérez*, Revista de Derecho Migratorio y Extranjería 2012/30, 37–43 and on the origin of the term *Carbajal García*, Revista de Derecho Migratorio y Extranjería 2012/29, 58ff.

1303 *Triguero Martínez*, Migraciones 2014, 436f with further references.

1304 Art 124 REDYLE; on the development of the term in the law on foreigners see Chapter 3.C.I.

1305 Cf. *Cerezo Mariscal*, Revista de Derecho 2015, 670f and *Ques Mena*, Diario la Ley 2008/7067, 1–5. For instance ATC 54/2010, ECLI:ES:TC:2010:90A, FJ 4f.

1306 Cf. *Triguero Martínez*, Migraciones 2014, 449.

types covered by the legislation, which are not compatible with Article 8 ECHR.[1307]

Viewed overall, I consider the regularisations based on 'roots' to have contributed to solving and removing systematic and structural weaknesses in the Spanish law on foreigners.[1308] They have become an established solution to reduce the ever-increasing number of irregularly staying foreigners. *Sabater/Domingo* are therefore entirely correct in referring to a 'New Immigration Regularisation Policy'.[1309] In contrast to the regularisation programmes, they have not resulted in a media and political uproar,[1310] and – from the rule of law perspective – offer an appropriate solution.

3. Administrative procedure

a) Application

Foreigners are free to apply for a 'temporary residence permit for exceptional circumstances' or apply for several different types of residence permits at the same time.[1311] This is notable in so far as it opens the possibility to apply for two residence permits (e.g. on the basis of social roots and on the basis of humanitarian reasons), with the chance that one of the two applications may be successful. In principle Article 128 REDYLE regulates the procedure, though there are some exceptions for particular permits.[1312]

The foreigner is to apply in person for a 'temporary residence permit for exceptional circumstances'.[1313] This does not reflect the general approach in Spanish administrative law,[1314] thus attracting criticism as being unconstitutional.[1315] Depending on the type of permit, different documents are

---

1307 Cf. *García Vitoria*, Revista General de Derecho Constitucional 2015/20, 15ff and see Chapter 4.C.V.1. on family roots.

1308 Cf. *Cerezo Mariscal*, Revista de Derecho 2015, 669f and 673ff; see also *Sabater/Domingo*, International Migration Review 2012/46, 213 and also *González Calvet*, Revista de Derecho Social 2007/37, 126f.

1309 Cf. *Sabater/Domingo*, International Migration Review 2012/46, 191.

1310 Cf. *González-Enríquez*, EJML 2009, 149.

1311 STSJ Castilla-La Mancha 225/2016, ECLI:ES:TSJCLM:2016:225.

1312 Cf. *Fernández Collados* in *Palomar Olmeda* 430f. See especially Arts 132–134 REDYLE, Arts 136–137 REDYLE and Art 144 REDYLE as well as Art 186 REDYLE.

1313 Art 128(5) REDYLE; cf. *Fernández Collados* in *Palomar Olmeda* 431.

1314 Cf. *García Vitoria* in *Boza Martínez/Donaire Villa/Moya Malapeira* 300f.

1315 Cf. *Fernández Pérez*, Derechos fundamentales 258–264.

to be presented at the time of the application, though a passport is generally required.[1316] It therefore follows that the requirements for issuing the permit must be met both at the time of the application and also at the time of the decision.[1317]

Unlike Austrian law, Spanish law generally does not provide for the *ex officio* grant of residence permits.[1318] However, certain authorities may encourage the grant of a temporary residence permit for exceptional circumstances due to the 'collaboration with public authorities, or for reasons of national security or public interest'.[1319]

If the requirements for a 'temporary residence permit for exceptional circumstances' are met, the permit is valid for one year.[1320]

b) Grounds for refusal and rejection

The grant of a residence permit is subject to the (negative) requirement that the foreigner must not have a criminal record (*antecedentes penales*) in Spain or in any of the countries in which the foreigner has previously resided over the past five years.[1321] The Spanish Constitutional Court has determined that this requirement conforms to the constitution as it serves to protect public order.[1322] A further reason for refusal is that the foreigner is not listed in SIS for refusal of entry.[1323]

An ongoing deportation procedure or the existence of a valid deportation generally constitute reasons to reject an application for a 'temporary residence permit for exceptional circumstances' made after the procedure

---

1316 Art 128(1)(a) REDYLE; cf. *García Vitoria* in *Boza Martínez/Donaire Villa/Moya Malapeira* 301 and *Fernández Collados* in *Palomar Olmeda* 431f.

1317 Art 128(1) REDYLE.

1318 See Chapter 3.A.III.2.a.

1319 See Chapter 4.F.I.

1320 Art 130(1) REDYLE.

1321 Art 31(5) LODYLE; cf. Instrucción DGI/SGJR/06/2008, 2f; *Esteban de la Rosa*, Art 31 LODYLE in *Monereo Pérez/Fernández Avilés/Triguero Martínez* 494f and *Triguero Martínez*, Migraciones 2014, 451, and *Ques Mena*, Diario la Ley 2008/7067, 7f with further references regarding 'roots'.

1322 ATC 54/2010, ECLI:ES:TC:2010:90A, FJ 4; for criticism see *Fernández Pérez*, Derechos fundamentales 287.

1323 Art 31(5) LODYE; cf. *Esteban de la Rosa*, Art 31 LODYLE in *Monereo Pérez/Fernández Avilés/Triguero Martínez* 495.

is initiated or the deportation decision is given.[1324] Article 214(2) and (3) REDYLE provide an exception, whereby the application is admissible and, at the same time, the legally binding deportation is to be revoked *ex officio*.[1325] The exception applies if the deportation has not been enforced and the deportation is not merely for reasons of irregularity and/or undocumented employment.[1326] Furthermore, the authority must come to the initial conclusion that the requirements for the permit applied for are met.[1327] This means that every foreigner who has not yet been deported may apply for a 'temporary residence permit for exceptional circumstances' and can thus undergo a process of regularisation.[1328] Moreover, the grant of the residence permit also revokes the removal measure.

If the foreigner has applied for a 'temporary residence permit for exceptional circumstances' before the deportation proceedings are initiated, and if such proceedings are pending after the application, the latter are to be suspended until a decision on the residence permit has been taken.[1329] This transposes Article 6(5) Return Directive.[1330] The deportation proceedings end if the residence permit is granted,[1331] but the proceedings will continue if the requirements for the residence permit are not met.

1324 Disposición adicional 4(1) LODYLE; see also Art 241 REDYLE; cf. *García Vitoria* in *Boza Martínez/Donaire Villa/Moya Malapeira* 301f and *Lorenzo Jiménez*, Revista de Derecho Migratorio y Extranjería 2015/38, 24, 27–29.

1325 Cf. *García Vitoria* in *Boza Martínez/Donaire Villa/Moya Malapeira* 302 and *Boza Martínez* in *Boza Martínez/Donaire Villa/Moya Malapeira* 274. For court decisions, see e.g. STSJ Andalucía 3694/2016, ECLI:ES:TSJAND:2016:3694.

1326 Art 53(a) and (b) LODYLE.

1327 Cf. *Defensor del Pueblo*, Sugerencia (20.5.2016), Queja 15004478.

1328 Here one may merely note the social roots; *Defensor del Pueblo*, Sugerencia (20.5.2016), Queja 15004478 and see Chapter 4.E.I.

1329 Art 63(6) LODYLE and Art 241(1) REDYLE; cf. *Lorenzo Jiménez*, Revista de Derecho Migratorio y Extranjería 2015/38, 25–30 and *Boza Martínez* in *Boza Martínez/Donaire Villa/Moya Malapeira* 273f.

1330 In this sense *Lorenzo Jiménez*, Revista de Derecho Migratorio y Extranjería 2015/38, 26 and 28.

1331 Cf. *Luján Alcaraz*, Art 63 LODYLE in *Monereo Pérez/Fernández Avilés/Triguero Martínez* (eds), Comentario a la ley y al reglamento de Extranjería, Inmigración e Integración Social[2] (2013) 1019 (1024).

4. Consolidation of residence

Articles 130 and 202 REDYLE regulate the transition from a 'temporary residence permit for exceptional circumstances' to a different type of residence permit.[1332] The basic notion underpinning the Spanish legislation is that the 'exceptional circumstances' regarding the residence status should not be extended. The foreigners concerned should rather (be able to) change to the ordinary residency system.[1333] Accordingly, foreigners entitled to stay for at least one year due to the 'temporary residence permit for exceptional circumstances' may acquire a residence permit under the 'ordinary' system, though the visa requirement does not apply.[1334] For instance, it is possible to acquire a 'residence permit and work permit (employed or self-employed)', which is limited to two years.[1335] Whether the foreigner meets the requirements of this type of residence permit varies depending on whether the foreigner had a work permit.[1336] If this is the case, the foreigner may apply for the 'residence permit and work permit' subject to the requirements in Article 71 REDYLE. In comparison, if the foreigner has not had a work permit, the employer may apply for the 'residence permit and work permit', though in this case Article 202(3) REDYLE provides that the requirements under Article 64 REDYLE are to be met.

The application for such 'residence permit and work permit' may be made up to 60 days prior to the expiry of the period of validity.[1337] This therefore extends the residence permit to the conclusion of the procedure. The same applies in the cases in which the application is submitted within 90 days after the date on which the period of validity expires. However, the delayed application initiates the proceedings for an administrative penalty.[1338]

1332 Cf. *Fernández Collados* in *Palomar Olmeda* 452f and *Abarca Junco/Alonso-Olea García/Lacruz López/Martín Dégano/Vargas Gómez-Urrutia*, Inmigración y Extranjería: Régimen jurídico básico[5] (2011) 219f.

1333 Cf. *Serrano Villamanta* in *Balado Ruiz-Gallegos* 556.

1334 Art 201(1) REDYLE.

1335 Art 202(2)–(4) REDYLE and *García Vitoria* in *Boza Martínez/Donaire Villa/Moya Malapeira* 306.

1336 Cf. *García Vitoria* in *Boza Martínez/Donaire Villa/Moya Malapeira* 306 and *Fernández Collados* in *Palomar Olmeda* 452f.

1337 Art 130(5) REDYLE.

1338 See the last sentence of Art 130(5) REDYLE and Art 52(b) LODYLE, which concerns such offence to be minor; cf. *García Vitoria* in *Boza Martínez/Donaire Villa/Moya Malapeira* 305f.

A renewal (*renovación*) or extension (*prórroga*) of a 'temporary residence permit for exceptional circumstances' is only possible in certain situations.[1339] This creates problems in cases in which a person does not meet the requirements for an ordinary residence permit, as such person would fall back into irregularity.[1340] In this respect, the REDYLE does not provide an answer to the question whether, in such cases, it is possible to apply once again for the same 'temporary residence permit for exceptional circumstances'. Regarding the Regularisation Programme 2005 and the post-2006 'roots' requirements, *Sabater/Domingo* have analysed how many individuals continued to be legally resident after one year or fell back into an irregular status.[1341] For employment roots and social roots, after one year approx. 24% and 29.2% of the regularised foreigners were once again staying irregularly as they could not acquire any other type of residence permit. Both authors therefore favour a modification of the 'roots' requirements to accord with the new economic conditions, especially those stemming from the 'economic crisis'.[1342]

5. Drawing distinctions

The LODYLE provides a temporary residence permit and/or work permit in non-regulated cases of special relevance (*autorización temporal y/o trabajo en supuestos no reguladas de especial relevancia*),[1343] whereby there is a distinction between two circumstances.

On the one hand, the Secretary of State for Migration (*Secretaría de Estado de Migraciones*) may grant a temporary residence permit in exceptional circumstances that are not covered by the REDYLE. The decision is based on a report by the Secretary of State for Security (*Secretaría de Estado de Seguridad*). As there are no further details about the minimum

1339 Art 130(2) REDYLE and see Chapter 4.F.I.

1340 For criticism *García Vitoria* in *Boza Martínez/Donaire Villa/Moya Malapeira* 305 and *Defensor del Pueblo*, Recomendación (20.1.2014), Queja 12276555.

1341 *Sabater/Domingo*, International Migration Review 2012/46, 206f and 213. See also *Baldwin-Edwards*, Regularisations and Employment in Spain. REGANE Assessment Report (February 2014), https://mpra.ub.uni-muenchen.de/59812/1/MPRA_paper_59812.pdf (31.7.2022) 15f.

1342 *Sabater/Domingo*, International Migration Review 2012/46, 215.

1343 Art 123(2) 2nd Sent. REDYLE; Disposición adicional 1(4) REDYLE. Cf. *García Vitoria* in *Boza Martínez/Donaire Villa/Moya Malapeira* 299f and *Ques Mena*, Diario la Ley 2008/7067, 10f.

requirements that are to be met, an analysis here would not be appropriate and is therefore not undertaken.

On the other hand, such residence permits may be granted based on an order from the Council of Ministers (*Consejo de Ministros*), which details the precise requirements.[1344] As above, this process will also not be analysed as it is not clear whether such orders have already been made or exist, their content, and accordingly the minimum requirements.

Finally, it should be pointed out that the courts can expand upon the 'temporary residence permits for exceptional circumstances' regulated by the LODYLE and REDYLE.[1345] Furthermore, two other residence permits are discussed in connection with the 'residence permit for a child not born in Spain', though these will not be analysed in this study for reasons to be explained below.[1346]

IV. Competences and authorities regarding the law on foreigners

In principle the competence concerning immigration and the status of foreigners lies exclusively with the federal state.[1347] However, this prevailing doctrine has changed over the past decades, with limited competences now held by the autonomous communities[1348] as a result of the reform of various statutes of autonomy (*Estatuto de Autonomía*), the Organic Law 2/2009 and the (conciliatory) decisions of the Spanish Constitutional Court.[1349] In this respect, the reports (*Informe*) to be compiled by the autonomous com-

1344 Cf. for detail Disposición adicional 1(4) REDYLE.

1345 Cf. *Giménez Bachmann*, La situación jurídica de los inmigrantes irregulares en España, Dissertation 2014, Universitat Abab Oliba CEU, https://www.tdx.cat/handle/10803/295836#page=1 (31.7.2022) 175.

1346 See Chapter 4.C.I.

1347 Art 149(1) No. 2 CE; cf. *Roig*, Autonomía e inmigración: competencias y participación de las Comunidades Autónomas y los Entes locales en materia de inmigración in *Revenga Sánchez* (ed), Problemas constitucionales de la inmigración: una visión desde Italia y España (2005) 359.

1348 Cf. on the development *Donaire Villa/Moya Malapeira*, Marco competencial y organización administrativa de la inmigración in *Boza Martínez/Donaire Villa/Moya Malapeira* (eds), La nueva regulación de la inmigración y la extranjería en España (2012) 521 (521ff).

1349 STC 31/2010, ECLI:ES:TC:2010:31.

munities in relation to the 'temporary residence permit' on the grounds of 'social roots' are an example of their limited competences.[1350]

The foreigners' offices (*Oficina de Extranjería*) are typically responsible for matters concerning foreigners,[1351] such as granting residence permits or conducting the proceedings concerning administrative penalties.[1352] These offices are subordinate to the government delegations or sub-delegations (*Delegaciones y Subdelegaciones del Gobierno*), which in turn are subordinate to the Ministry for Territorial Policy and Public Function (*Ministerio de la Política Territorial y Función Pública*).

The municipal register (*Padrón*) also plays a key role, as the entry serves as evidence of the time spent in Spain,[1353] which is significant to demonstrate 'social roots', for example.[1354] As noted above, registration in the municipal register is also necessary in order to access healthcare services.[1355] Entry in the register requires only an official document, such as a passport, as proof of one's identity; irregularly staying foreigners may in principle therefore also be registered.[1356] Registration is even encouraged by the state.[1357] Even the possibility for the foreigner's offices or the Civil Guard (*Guardia Civil*) to access the register (e.g. to determine a foreigner's place of residence) has not reduced the number of registrations.[1358]

1350 Cf. *Donaire Villa/Moya Malapeira* in *Boza Martínez/Donaire Villa/Moya Malapeira* 536f and see Chapter 4.E.I.

1351 Arts 259–263 REDYLE and cf. *Donaire Villa/Moya Malapeira* in *Boza Martínez/ Donaire Villa/Moya Malapeira* 549ff.

1352 Art 261 REDYLE and Disposición adicional 1 REDYLE; cf. *García Vitoria* in *Boza Martínez/Donaire Villa/Moya Malapeira* 300 and *Donaire Villa/ Moya Malapeira* in *Boza Martínez/Donaire Villa/Moya Malapeira* 549f.

1353 Cf. *Cerdán/Maas*, ZAR 2010, 109.

1354 See Chapter 4.E.I.

1355 See Chapter 3.C.II.4.

1356 Cf. *González-Enríquez* in *Triandafyllidou* 250.

1357 Along these lines, *González-Enríquez*, Clandestino Project (January 2009) 20ff.

1358 Disposición adicional 5(2) LODYLE; for criticism *Fernández Pérez*, Derechos fundamentales 265–270 with further references.

V. Judicial protection

The constitutional right to effective judicial protection (*Tutela Judicial Efectiva*[1359]) applies to regularly and irregularly staying foreigners.[1360] They may access the administrative courts as well as the constitutional court to safeguard their rights.

1. Administrative jurisdiction

The jurisdiction of the administrative courts (*Jurisdicción Contencioso-Administrativa*) is well established in Spain and allows the full control of any administrative act, particularly those of the executive.[1361] The administrative courts (*Juzgados de lo Contencioso-Administrativo*) are part of the ordinary jurisdiction.[1362]

Before addressing this topic in more detail, it is first necessary to briefly discuss the administrative remedies available.[1363] It is possible to lodge an appeal for reversal (*Recurso de Reposición*)[1364] against a decision on residence that usually exhausts the administrative channels.[1365] The appeal for reversal is directed against the foreigners' office issuing the order[1366] – an ordinary appeal (*Recurso Ordinario de Alzada*) addressed to a higher-ranking administrative body would not be admissible.[1367] The appeal does not have a suspensive effect.[1368] This remedy is optional, i.e. it may, but

---

1359 Art 24 CE and Art 20(1) LODYLE; cf. *González García*, Algunas cuestiones sobre el derecho a la tutela judicial efectiva de los extranjeros a la luz de la jurisprudencia constitucional y de la Ley Orgánica 2/2009, Teoría y Realidad Constitucional 2010, 515 (518ff).

1360 Cf. *González García*, Teoría y Realidad Constitucional 2010, 521.

1361 LJCA and cf. *Parejo Alfonso*, Derecho Administrativo 1185ff.

1362 Arts 3 and 24 Ley Orgánica 6/1985, de 1 de julio, del Poder Judicial, BOE 157 of 2.7.1985 in the version of 27.7.2022; cf. *Parejo Alfonso*, Derecho Administrativo 1190f.

1363 Cf. on the previous law *Conde Antequera* in *Monereo Pérez/Fernández Avilés/Triguero* 337–339.

1364 Arts 123f LPAC.

1365 Disposición adicional 14 REDYLE and see Fn 1273.

1366 On the responsibilities of the foreigners' office, see Chapter 3.C.IV.

1367 Arts 121f LPAC; cf. On the 'Recurso Ordinario de Alzada' *Parejo Alfonso*, Derecho Administrativo 1152f.

1368 See just Art 117 LPAC; cf. *Parejo Alfonso*, Derecho Administrativo 1151 and 1157ff as well as *García Vitoria*, Revista General de Derecho Constitucional 2015/20, 9f with regard to deportation decisions.

does not have to be pursued in order to subsequently proceed down the route of the administrative courts. A one-month period applies for lodging the appeal.[1369]

If the foreigner resorts to an appeal for reversal, the foreigners' office examines whether or not the arguments raised are valid. An appeal to the administrative courts is not possible until a decision on the appeal for reversal,[1370] which – unlike in the administrative courts – is to be made within one month.[1371] If there is no decision in this period, the 'silence' is viewed as a rejection.[1372]

A 'contentious administrative appeal' (*Recurso Contencioso-Administrativo*) may be lodged following the optional appeal for reversal or directly after receiving the rejection of the application.[1373] In principle this has no suspensive effect. However, according to Articles 129ff LJCA it is possible at any stage of the proceeding before the administrative courts to apply for a temporary injunction, which has suspensive effect.[1374] The administrative courts then decide by means of a judgment (*Sentencia*) and can revoke the administrative act if it is unlawful and/or on the merits of the case.[1375] A two-month period applies for lodging the appeal in relation to ordinary procedures,[1376] though a ten-day period applies in special procedures concerning the protection of fundamental rights.[1377] In contrast to administrative proceedings, the complainant must be represented by legal counsel in proceedings before the administrative court.[1378] The complainant may

---

1369 Art 124(1) LPAC.

1370 Art 123(2) LPAC; cf. *Parejo Alfonso*, Derecho Administrativo 1153f.

1371 Cf. *Parejo Alfonso*, Derecho Administrativo 1154 with reference to STC 40/2007, ECLI:ES:TC:2007:40.

1372 Cf. on the previous law *Conde Antequera* in *Monereo Pérez/Fernández Avilés/Triguero Martínez* 339.

1373 Art 25 LJCA; cf. on the procedure before the administrative courts *Parejo Alfonso*, Derecho Administrativo 1229ff and *Conde Antequera* in *Monereo Pérez/Fernández Avilés/Triguero Martínez* 340 regarding the law on foreigners.

1374 For detail *Parejo Alfonso*, Derecho Administrativo 1240ff; *Conde Antequera* in *Monereo Pérez/Fernández Avilés/Triguero Martínez* 346–350 on the ordinary procedure and *Mercader Uguina/Tolosa Tibiño*, Art 24 LODYLE in *Monereo Pérez/Fernández Avilés/Triguero Martínez* (eds), Comentario a la ley y al reglamento de Extranjería, Inmigración e Integración Social^2 (2013) 371 (376) on the special procedure.

1375 Arts 67 and 71(1) LJCA.

1376 Art 46(1) LJCA.

1377 Art 115(1) LJCA.

1378 Art 23 LJCA.

apply for free legal representation if he or she does not have sufficient funds.[1379]

At first, a single judge decides upon the appeal brought before the administrative court.[1380] If the decision by the administrative court is again insufficient, an appeal (*Recurso de Apelación*) may be brought before the High Court (*Tribunal Superior de Justicia*) of an autonomous community.[1381] An extraordinary appeal (*Recurso de Casación*) may be brought thereafter before the Supreme Court (*Tribunal Supremo*).[1382]

The jurisdiction of the administrative courts features ordinary and special procedures, though in each case it is possible to bring the aforementioned legal remedies or to lodge an appeal against the decision. The foreigner may have recourse to both procedures simultaneously or to only one of the two.[1383] The ordinary procedure is conducted for foreigners as a so-called fast-track procedure (*Procedimiento Abreviado*).[1384] The special procedure may be conducted on the grounds of protection of fundamental rights (*Procedimiento para la Protección de los Derechos Fundamentales*).[1385] This requires the allegation that a fundamental right has been violated through a discriminatory act.[1386] As will be explained below, a constitutional complaint may only be lodged on grounds of the violation of

1379 Ley 1/1996, de 10 de enero, de asistencia jurídica gratuita, BOE 11 of 12.1.1996 in the version of 5.6.2021, and Art 22(3) LODYLE; cf. *Colomer Hernández*, Los extranjeros y los tribunales españoles in *Palomar Olmeda* (ed), Tratado de Extranjería[6] (2020) 653 (664ff) and with regard to deportation decisions *Arrese Iriondo*, Revista de Derecho Migratorio y Extranjería 2010/25, 90f.

1380 Art 8(4) LJCA; cf. *Conde Antequera* in *Monereo Pérez/Fernández Avilés/Triguero Martínez* 341f.

1381 Arts 81ff LJCA.

1382 Art 88 LJCA; cf. *Huelin Martínez de Velasco*, La nueva casación contencioso-administrativa (primeros pasos), Revista General de Derecho Constitucional 2017/24, 1.

1383 Cf. *Mercader Uguina/Tolosa Tibiño* in *Monereo Pérez/Fernández Avilés/Triguero Martínez* 375 with further references.

1384 Art 78(1) LJCA; cf. *Parejo Alfonso*, Derecho Administrativo 1259ff and *Conde Antequera* in *Monereo Pérez/Fernández Avilés/Triguero Martínez* 343.

1385 Art 53(2) CE in conjunction with Art 24 LODYLE and Arts 114–122 LJCA; cf. *Conde Antequera* in *Monereo Pérez/Fernández Avilés/Triguero Martínez* 343–345 and *Mercader Uguina/Tolosa Tibiño* in *Monereo Pérez/Fernández Avilés/Triguero Martínez* 371.

1386 Cf. *Conde Antequera* in *Monereo Pérez/Fernández Avilés/Triguero Martínez* 344.

particular fundamental rights.[1387] The special procedure has preferential status.[1388] A ten-day period applies to claims lodged under the special procedure.[1389]

2. Constitutional jurisdiction

The Spanish Constitutional Court (*Tribunal Constitucional*) also plays a key role in the judicial protection of foreigners.[1390] This court does not belong to the jurisdiction of ordinary courts, but is described as an independent, special jurisdiction.[1391]

According to the Spanish Constitution, any citizen may submit an appeal for constitutional protection (*Recurso de Amparo Constitucional*) against the violation of his or her fundamental rights and liberties protected by the constitution.[1392] A 20 or 30-day period applies, depending on whether the appeal is against an administrative act or court decision.[1393] The appeal may be made against every act by a public body which violates a fundamental right or freedom.[1394] The appeal for constitutional protection is both quantitively and qualitatively the most important and most frequently invoked instrument of the Constitutional Court.[1395] Legal representation is necessary, though some exceptions apply.[1396] Any natural or legal person with a legitimate interest may lodge an appeal for constitutional protection,[1397] including foreigners.[1398] From the perspective of

1387 Cf. *Mercader Uguina/Tolosa Tibiño* in *Monereo Pérez/Fernández Avilés/Triguero Martínez* 372 and *Conde Antequera* in *Monereo Pérez/Fernández Avilés/Triguero Martínez* 343.

1388 Art 114(3) LJCA.

1389 Art 115(1) LJCA.

1390 Art 53(2) in conjunction with Art 21(1) LODYLE and *Fernández Pérez* Art 57 LODYLE in *Monereo Pérez/Fernández Avilés/Triguero Martínez*, Comentario a la ley y al reglamento de Extranjería, Inmigración e Integración Social[2] (2013) 900 (921).

1391 *Carrillo*, La jurisdicción constitucional española y el caso chileno, Revista de Derecho 2001, 75 (75).

1392 Arts 53(2) and 161(1)(b) CE; cf. *Pérez Tremps*, Sistema de Justicia Constitucional[3] (2019) 121ff and 21ff on the court in general.

1393 Arts 43(2) and 44(2) LOTC; cf. *Pérez Tremps*, Justicia Constitucional 143.

1394 Art 41(2) LOTC.

1395 Cf. *Pérez Tremps*, Justicia Constitucional 123.

1396 Art 81(1) LOTC.

1397 Art 162(b) CE.

1398 Cf. *Pérez Tremps*, Justicia Constitucional 133f.

those affected, the constitutional complaint is the last legal remedy that serves to protect fundamental rights due to its subsidiary nature.[1399] In other words, the claim concerning the violation of the fundamental rights has been unsuccessful in the ordinary legal process and no further appeals are possible thereunder.[1400] For foreigners, the administrative court procedure discussed above is available as an ordinary legal process.[1401]

The extraordinary nature of the constitutional appeal is to be emphasised as it may only be lodged with regard to the fundamental rights and freedoms anchored in the Spanish Constitution,[1402] e.g. the traditional rights and freedoms such as the right to life (Article 15 CE) or the freedom of expression (Article 20 CE). Nonetheless, the distinction between the protection of the family (Article 39 CE) and the right to family privacy (Article 18 CE) has been criticised as the appeal for constitutional protection only applies to the latter.[1403]

VI. Summary – The special status of regularisations in the laws concerning residency and foreigners

The above description shows the particular status held by regularisations in the laws on residency, and foreigners in the Member States. The similarities and distinctions in the historical development have allowed a special category of decisions granting the right to stay to emerge in all three Member States. Where the comparison is concerned, it is especially worthwhile to present the (structural) differences and similarities once more in greater depth and to consolidate these to gain a more complete impression of the topic.

Generally, the regularisations in all three Member States have a privileged status in comparison to the decisions which grant the right to stay under the 'ordinary' system. It means therefore that the requirements do not necessarily need to be met or that certain legislative grounds for

---

1399 Cf. *Pérez Tremps*, Justicia Constitucional 125.

1400 STC 186/1997, ECLI:ES:TC:1997:186, FJ 2; cf. *Pérez Tremps*, Justicia Constitucional 135ff.

1401 See Chapter 3.C.V.1.

1402 Arts 14–29 and 30(2) CE and cf. *Pérez Tremps*, Justicia Constitucional 126f with further references.

1403 Cf. *Díaz Crego/García Vitoria*, Los derechos de los migrantes in *García Roca* (ed), ¿Hacia una globalización de los derechos? El impacto de las sentencias del Tribunal Europeo y de la Corte Interamericana (2017) 363 (394–398).

denying the right do not apply. One such example is the visa requirement, which does not apply to the analysed regularisations in any of the three Member States.

Although there are some exceptions, set terminology applies at national level to summarise the regularisations: *Aufenthaltstitel aus berücksichtigungswürdigen Gründen* (residence permits for exceptional circumstances) in Austria, *Aufenthaltserlaubnisse aus humanitären Gründen* (residence permits for humanitarian reasons) in Germany and *residencias temporales por circunstancias excepcionales* (temporary residence permits for exceptional circumstances) in Spain.

One may cautiously state that the 'temporary residence permits for exceptional circumstances' in Spain are no longer 'exceptional' as they constitute 30% of all temporary residence permits, with the regularisation based on 'roots' (especially 'social roots') being particularly relevant. The statistics for Austria show that regularisations do not play an important role, though one must bear in mind that the statistics lack detail in some areas and thus their actual relevance is debatable. For Germany, it is clear from the figures that a notable number of foreigners hold a 'residence permit for humanitarian grounds'.

It must be possible in all three Member States for an irregularly staying migrant to apply for the decisions granting a right to stay, as otherwise they would not satisfy the definition of a regularisation. The *ex officio* consideration of the 'special protection residence permit' and of the 'residence permits for reasons of Article 8 ECHR' in the asylum process in Austria also plays an important role and shows the close links between these two 'residence permits for exceptional circumstances' and asylum law. This is shown for Germany with the restrictions on granting a residence title after the asylum process has been completed, but also that (similar to Austria) the national bans on deportation are to be examined. To satisfy the regularisation definition,[1404] these will only constitute regularisations in those cases in which the application may be made whilst residing irregularly and not when examined in the asylum process.[1405] Asylum law is not analysed in this study, but remarks concerning asylum law give context since the development of regularisations in Austria and Germany is closely related to the (in part) high number of asylum applications and the related political debates.[1406] This is one of the reasons why reforms of residence and asylum

1404 See Chapter 1.A.
1405 See Chapter 4.A.I.2.a.
1406 For Germany see *Kraler*, Journal of Immigrant and Refugee Studies 2019, 102.

laws have been made on a near annual basis over the past two decades. The picture in Spain is different, however, as the regularisations have developed on a broader scale and are especially one of the consequences of the rapid increase in foreigners until 2005. This development is not closely related to the number of asylum applications and as such there was not a constant stream of reforms.

Regularisation programmes were implemented in Spain in the early 1990s to offer foreigners a path out of irregularity. This instrument was used almost annually, with regularisation mechanisms first established in 2005. Unlike Austria and Germany, regularisations in Spain have always been very closely dependent on the economy and the labour market or are linked more closely to economic considerations. Regularisation programmes were never used in Austria due to the regularisation mechanisms introduced at the end of the 1990s. Germany, however, adopted a hybrid approach, with the use of regularisation mechanisms from the start of the 1990s and regularisation programmes from the mid-1990s. Nowadays, the same type of regularisations (i.e. regularisation mechanisms) features in all three Member States, which will subject to the comparative analysis in Chapter 4.

The legal status of foreigners also plays an important role in the development of regularisations, whereby considerable differences between the legislative provisions may be observed. One notable feature of the Spanish system is the access to social benefits and healthcare that is afforded to irregularly staying foreigners. This is a marked difference to the situation in Austria and Germany, as the irregular status is therefore less precarious.[1407] Access to employment, however, is similar in the three Member States as a specific permit is required, which is linked to the lawful residence or the decision granting a right to stay. In Germany, the Skilled Immigration Act (*Fachkräfteeinwanderungsgesetz*) also brought a change in approach as the right to engage in an economic activity was granted with each residence title unless prohibited by law. However, this shift from 'reserving permis-

---

1407 This has become an even greater problem during the COVID-19 pandemic: the effect of not affording such groups access to healthcare can 'harm' the general population; cf. *Kohlenberger*, Fehlender Gesundheitszugang von Migranten schadet allen, Falter.at (13.5.2020), https://cms.falter.at/blogs/thinktank/2020/05/13/warum-gefluechtete-besonders-corona-gefaehrdert-sind/ (31.7.2022); for detail *Raposo/Violante*, Human Rights Review 2021 and *Desmond*, The European Approach to Irregular Migration in Pandemic Times: The More Things Change, the More They Stay the Same? in *Czech/Heschl/Lukas/Nowak/Oberleitner* (eds), European Yearbook on Human Rights (2021) 285 (302ff).

sion' to 'reserving prohibition' will have hardly any effect in practice as it still must be ascertainable from each residence title whether economic activity is permitted and whether it is subject to any limitations. Several authors note that in this respect the employment of undocumented workers is or has become 'tolerated' in Spain.

The analysis of the national laws shows further that administrative or judicial penalties may apply to (un)lawful residence. In Austria, the negative outcome in a procedure to grant a 'residence permit for exceptional circumstances' automatically results in a removal measure, which may be subsequently enforced. In Germany, the rejection of an application for a 'residence permits for humanitarian reasons' leads to a deportation order, which may be subsequently enforced. Spanish law, however, takes an entirely different approach: the rejection of an application for a residence permit does not automatically result in a removal measure. There is indeed an obligation to leave the country, but is only enforceable following a separate decision on deportation.

All three Member States provide that an existing removal measure may – to varying degrees – constitute a ground for refusal to grant a residence permit. In Austria, a valid return decision including a ban on entry constitutes a reason to refuse a 'residence permit for exceptional circumstances'. An application for a 'residence permit for humanitarian reasons' is denied in Germany if there is a particularly serious interest in expulsion within the meaning of § 51(1) Nos. 2 or 4 AufenthG. An ongoing deportation procedure or a pending deportation constitutes a ground for rejection under Spanish law, provided that the application for a 'temporary residence permit for exceptional circumstances' is only made after the deportation procedure has been initiated or the deportation order has been issued. However, the application is admissible (and the deportation is to be revoked) if the deportation order was issued merely because of the irregular stay or undocumented employment as the competent authority draws the initial conclusion that the requirements for the permit are met.

The respective authorities responsible for matters concerning residency and foreigners do not exhibit any distinctive characteristics. Furthermore, different legal instruments are available in each case to foreigners in proceedings before the administrative as well as before the constitutional courts. Differences exist, however, with regard to whether the legal instrument has suspensive effect. This is especially relevant for rejections/dismissals in Austria and Germany because these types of decisions give rise to a removal measure.

Chapter 4 – The purpose-based integrated comparison of regularisations

The context provided in Chapter 3 now allows for the focus to shift to the comparative analysis of regularisations. The critical-contextual method is used,[1408] whereby instead of a 'traditional' comparison via national reports, the regularisations are categorised, compared and assessed in an integrated approach based on their purpose.[1409] They will be reviewed in light of their compatibility with the relevant provisions of international and EU law, though for the former only the ECHR will be examined in detail.[1410]

The regularisations are not categorised from a formal perspective. For example, the Austrian 'special protection residence permit' in § 57 AsylG (A) unites three sets of circumstances, whereby each is valid as a separate regularisation as the grounds for granting the permit vary in each case.[1411] In principle separate sets of circumstances fall under separate regularisation purposes or sub-categories if they specify different grounds for granting the regularisation.

Regularisations may also serve more than one purpose and thus fall under more than one sub-category. The most relevant purpose will be determined by balancing the interests surrounding the regularisation, thereby allowing for a clean methodological approach. The State's main interest in approving the right to stay serves as the main argument as, unlike the migrant's own interest, the State's interest is at the forefront on the understanding of a contractualistic understanding of the decisions granting the right to stay.[1412]

Within each purpose the regularisations are structured by the extent of their scope, for which I refer to the minimum duration. The order is alphabetical (Austria, Germany, Spain) where two or more regularisations have the exact same minimum duration.

The definition of a regularisation given in Chapter 1 is used for the comparative analysis, but narrowed down even further.[1413] Only those rights to stay are examined where lawful residence is granted for at least 12 months – this minimum duration is used as the distinguishing criterion. However, with regard to some regularisations under German law, the

1408 See Introduction D.I.
1409 See Introduction D.II.2. and Chapter 1.B.II.
1410 See Introduction D.II.1.
1411 See Chapter 4.A.II.1. and Chapter 4.D.I.1.
1412 See above, Chapter 1.B.II.
1413 See Chapter 1.A.II.

stay can be limited from six months to two or three years.[1414] These are nevertheless included in the analysis as the statutory minimum period may be exceeded.

I adopt an uniform approach to the comparison and begin with a discussion of the conditions for granting the right to stay and then the nature of the right to stay itself, in so far as this has not already been presented in Chapter 3.[1415] Acquiring a full picture of each regularisation therefore requires the corresponding explanations in Chapter 3 for context. The general requirements for the grant or refusal are thus not repeated. Access to the labour market, access to social benefits, and judicial protection are only presented in more detail if these differ from the general comments in Chapter 3. Again, the terms appropriate to the respective legal system are used: foreigners (Germany and Spain) and aliens (Austria).[1416]

A. Non-returnability

I. Toleration

Toleration[1417] comprises a legislative mechanism and non-statutory toleration, whereby in the following toleration as a legislative mechanism describes the statutory rules in Austria and Germany that qualify as a postponement of removal according to Article 9 Return Directive.[1418] 'Non-statutory toleration' refers to the (legal) situation in Spain.

The order of the regularisations is based on the extent of the entitlements. As there is no minimum duration without a right to stay, the order is as follows: the statutory and non-statutory situation is first analysed for Spain, where there is no legal instrument comparable to toleration, just situations of *de facto* toleration. This non-statutory toleration is thus another means to express an irregular stay. In contrast, both Austrian and German law feature a legal instrument known as toleration (*Duldung*), which may under the circumstances be described as a qualified irregular

1414 See Chapter 4.B.I.2., Chapter 4.C.II.2. and Chapter 4.D.I.2.
1415 See for example the 'residence permits for exceptional circumstances' in Chapter 3.A.III.2.d.
1416 See the introductory remarks in Part II.
1417 See Chapter 1.B.III.1.a.
1418 See Chapter 2.B.I.

stay or as a step towards a right to stay.[1419] As the minimum duration determines the order, Germany is analysed before Austria.

1. Spain: non-statutory toleration and irregularity

Unlike in Austria and Germany, Spanish law does not feature a legal instrument comparable with toleration. There is, however, a type of 'factual' toleration, i.e. situations in which an irregular stay is tolerated (*situación tolerada de la estancia irregular*).[1420] *Sagarra Trias* has expressed this as situations in which the foreigners may live irregularly on a legal basis: '*el extranjero "legalmente" podrá vivir irregularmente*'.[1421] Despite criticisms, the Spanish legislator (knowingly) still does not regulate this situation,[1422] but this issue was addressed implicitly through the introduction of the 'residence permit for reasons of training roots' in 2022.[1423]

As noted above in Chapter 3, an irregular stay constitutes a serious offence under Spanish law[1424] and usually initiates a separate deportation process, in which the principle of proportionality must be respected.[1425] In comparison to Austria and Germany, the rejection of an application for a residence permit does not automatically lead to a removal measure.[1426] Spanish law instead provides for two different procedural options for an irregularly staying foreigner: a fine or deportation.[1427]

1419 See Chapter 1.B.III.1.a.

1420 Cf. *García Vitoria* in *Boza Martínez/Donaire Villa/Moya Malapeira* 289; *Sainz de la Maza Quintanal*, Ultima ratio. El proceso de expulsión de inmigrantes en situación irregular en España, Dissertation 2015, Universidad Complutense de Madrid, https://eprints.ucm.es/34472/ (31.7.2022) 41.

1421 *Sagarra Trias*, Un nuevo 'status' de extranjero en España (El inmigrante, irregular, empadronado, residente trabajando y con orden de expulsión), Revista de Derecho Migratorio y Extranjería 2002/1, 89 (96).

1422 *Arrese Iriondo*, Revista de Derecho Migratorio y Extranjería 2010/25, 94f.

1423 See Chapter 4.E.III.

1424 Art 53(1)(a) LODYLE and see Chapter 3.C.II.1.

1425 Arts 55(3) and 57(1) LODYLE as well as Arts 222(3) and 242(1) 1st Sent. REDYLE; cf. *Arrese Iriondo*, Revista de Derecho Migratorio y Extranjería 2010/25, 77f.

1426 See Chapter 3.C.II.1.

1427 *Arrese Iriondo*, Revista de Derecho Migratorio y Extranjería 2010/25, 75–82.

Prior to the ECJ's decision in *Zaizoune* in 2015, foreigners subject to a deportation process because of an irregular stay were usually fined.[1428] This was justified on the basis of Article 57(1) LODYLE, which stipulates that a specific reason is required for deportation.[1429] By imposing a fine, foreigners were 'factually' tolerated and staying irregularly as the obligation to leave the country was not enforced.[1430] The Spanish law on foreigners does not allow a fine and deportation to be imposed simultaneously.[1431]

However, in *Zaizoune* the ECJ criticised the Spanish law, deeming it incompatible with the Return Directive:[1432] imposing a fine would not constitute an efficient removal of irregularly staying foreigners due to the lack of enforcement. The Spanish government sought to argue that an obligation to leave the country would always follow even where only a fine is imposed,[1433] but this was rejected by the ECJ. This decision was followed by the Spanish courts, which determined that deportation is to be ordered for an irregularly staying foreigner, not a fine.[1434]

The ECJ case law seemed quite robust in this regard, yet the *UN* decision made clear that it is still in progress and sometimes an unexpected U-turn is necessary. The ECJ held – in contrast to *Zaizoune* – that imposing a fine is actually compatible with the Return Directive as it entails an obligation

---

1428 On the tense relationship with the Return Directive prior to *Zaizoune* see *Boza Martínez* in *Boza Martínez/Donaire Villa/Moya Malapeira* 270 and *González Saquero*, La Directiva 'retorno' y el alcance de la armonización del procedimiento de expulsión de extranjeros. WP on European Law and Regional Integration No. 6 (2011), https://ucm.es/data/cont/docs/595-2013-11-07-la%20directiva%20retorno.pdf (31.7.2022) 12–15.

1429 Cf. *Castanedo García*, Revista de Derecho Migratorio y Extranjería 2014/36, 263f. See however Art 242(1) REDYLE.

1430 *Arrese Iriondo*, Revista de Derecho Migratorio y Extranjería 2010/25, 94f with further references.

1431 Art 57(3) LODYLE:

1432 ECJ *Zaizoune*, paras 32ff; cf. *Gortázar Rotaeche*, Return Decisions and Domestic Judicial Practices: Is Spain Different? in *de Bruycker/Cornelisse/Moraru* (eds), Law and Judicial Dialogue on the Return of Irregular Migrants from the European Union (2020) 63 (70ff). *Acosta Arcarazo/Romano*, The Returns Directive and the Expulsion of Migrants in an Irregular Situation in Spain, EU Law Analysis Blog (2.5.2015), www.eulawanalysis.blogspot.co.uk/2015/05/the-returns-directive-and-expulsion-of.html (31.7.2022); *Fernández Rojo*, La detención de extranjeros en situación irregular: impacto de la directiva 2008/115/CE y la jurisprudencia del TJUE en la legislación española, Revista de Derecho Comunitario Europeo 2016, 233 (242ff).

1433 Art 28(3)(c) LODYLE and Art 24 REDYLE.

1434 STSJ Galicia 6738/2016, ECLI:ES:TSJGAL:2016:6738, FJ 4; STSJ Aragón 1005/2016, ECLI:ES:TSJAR:2016:1005.

to leave within a prescribed period of time, 'unless, before that period expires, that third-country national's stay is regularised by a national authority. It is only where, on expiry of that period, that [the third-country] national has neither regularised his/her situation nor departed voluntarily, that the competent authority must adopt a removal decision'.[1435] This has been elaborated above in Chapter 2.B.II.2.

The Spanish legislation and practice, which still allows a fine to be imposed for irregularity, is therefore now (finally) in line with EU law. There is a factual toleration in these circumstances as the obligation to leave the country cannot be enforced.

This status may arise in two additional circumstances. *Boza Martínez* refers here to the distinction between the impossibility to order deportation and to enforce it.[1436] The impossibility to order deportation concerns each of the criteria listed in Article 57(5) LODYLE. According to Article 57(5)(d) LODYLE, this applies in cases in which a person was lawfully resident and employed, but cannot be deported due to the unemployment benefits (*prestación de desempleo*) received after the residence permit expires.[1437] Where applicable, the criteria in Article 57(5) LODYLE are to be considered, thus rendering a deportation order unlawful and thus impossible. However, it is not clear how the authorities are to proceed in such situations (e.g. whether a fine may be imposed) due to the lack of corresponding provisions in procedural law.[1438]

The impossibility to enforce the deportation extends to all cases in which deportation has become impossible since it was ordered, for instance due to pregnancy or because it would violate the non-refoulement principle.[1439] Again, procedural law does not provide the authorities with rules on how to proceed in such circumstances. In principle Article 57(4) LODYLE allows for the revocation of a decision on deportation, though

---

1435 ECJ *UN*, para 46 and see also para 49.

1436 See Art 57(5) and (6) LODYLE and *Boza Martínez* in *Boza Martínez/Donaire Villa/Moya Malapeira* 271.

1437 STS 1864/2008 – ECLI:ES:TS:2008:1864, FJ 7; cf. *Nieves Moreno Vida* in *Monereo Pérez/Fernández Avilés/Triguero Martínez* 627f. The Supreme Court further states that this can in no way concern cases of undocumented employment, as otherwise it would be a kind of hidden regularisation, because the persons could not be deported due to receiving unemployment benefits (despite undocumented employment).

1438 Cf. *Boza Martínez* in *Boza Martínez/Donaire Villa/Moya Malapeira* 270f.

1439 Art 57(6) LODYLE and Art 246(7) REDYLE; cf. *Consejo de Estado*, Dictamen 320/2016 (12.5.2016). The deportation may not present a risk to the health or the pregnancy of the woman and unborn child.

there is no specific provision which allows for revocation under these particular circumstances.[1440] Likewise, there are no rules where the impossibility of deportation has been ascertained.[1441] From a procedural perspective, it is only possible to tackle the deportation in the administrative courts, whereby the competent court could decide to suspend the deportation,[1442] though this is only possible where a complaint against the deportation has been filed.[1443]

It can therefore be maintained that the non-statutory toleration of an irregularly staying foreigner can arise in three different cases.[1444] Such foreigners languish in this state of limbo until they meet the requirements for a 'temporary residence permit for exceptional circumstances'. The decision to deport will be revoked in such cases.[1445] In a broader sense, it is thus possible to claim factual toleration of irregularly staying foreigners in Spain.[1446] This also means that the Spanish state accepts all the resulting effects, such as the precarious living situations. However, there is a balance in this respect due to the access to social benefits, even during the irregular stay and the less onerous (at least in comparison to Austria and Germany) requirements to acquire a residence permit, as the example of 'social rootedness' shows.[1447] Overall, irregularly staying foreigners have many possibilities for regularisation at their disposal, irrespective whether they are tolerated 'outside of the law'.

2. Germany: statutory toleration

Foreigners are generally to be deported where they are obliged under § 50(1) AufenthG to leave the country and this obligation is enforce-

---

1440 Cf. *Boza Martínez* in *Boza Martínez/Donaire Villa/Moya Malapeira* 270f.

1441 *Boza Martínez* in *Boza Martínez/Donaire Villa/Moya Malapeira* 271f makes this suggestion.

1442 Art 129 LJCA.

1443 See Chapter 3.C.V.1.

1444 Cf. *Fernández Bessa/Brandariz García*, Revista para el Análisis del Derecho 2016/4, 8f.

1445 For detail see Chapter 3.C.III.3.b.

1446 Cf. *Sagarra Trias*, Revista de Derecho Migratorio y Extranjería 2002/1, 96; *González-Enríquez*, Clandestino Project (January 2009) 7, 17f; *Arrese Iriondo*, Revista de Derecho Migratorio y Extranjería 2010/25, 94f; *Sabater/Domingo*, International Migration Review 2012/46, 215f.

1447 Chapter 4.E.I.

able.[1448] However, toleration (*Duldung*) was introduced as an instrument in Germany via § 60a AufenthG as it is often not possible to enforce deportation directly. Toleration therefore concerns the temporary suspension of deportation; it does not remove the obligation to leave the country or the enforceability thereof.[1449] In Germany, as in Austria, toleration does not result in lawful residence.[1450] According to the statistics, approx. 243,656 foreigners were tolerated in mid-2021,[1451] a considerable number in comparison to Austria and a reflection of the important role this instrument plays in German residence law.[1452]

a) Requirements

The number of requirements for toleration under § 60a AufenthG is so extensive that a thorough explanation would simply breach the boundaries of this study.[1453] For instance, the 2017 Act to Improve the Enforcement of the Obligation to Leave (*Gesetz zur besseren Durchsetzung der Ausreisepflicht*) introduced toleration to examine an acknowledgement of paternity, which is now anchored in § 60(2) 4th Sent. AufenthG.[1454] Toleration 'for the purpose of training' is found in § 60c AufenthG and is discussed in relation to the 'temporary residence permit for the purpose of employment for qualified foreigners whose deportation has been suspended'.[1455] The same applies for 'toleration for the purpose of employment', which will be discussed in relation to the 'residence in the case of permanent integration' and the 'residence permit for the purpose of employment for qualified foreigners'.[1456] Furthermore, the Orderly Return Act (*Geordnete-Rückkehr-Gesetz*), which entered into force on 21 August 2019, introduced toleration 'for persons whose identity is not yet verified' in § 60b AufenthG – also

1448 § 58(2) AufenthG and see Chapter 4.A.I.2.
1449 *Gordzielik/Huber* in *Huber/Mantel* § 60a AufenthG mn 63.
1450 § 60a(3) AufenthG and see Chapter 4.A.I.3.
1451 BT-Drs 19/32579, 31ff.
1452 See Chapter 4.A.I.3.
1453 For a historical overview, *Wittmann*, Vom migrationspolitischen Mindeststandard zum „Bleiberecht im Duldungsgewand" – Entwicklungslinien der deutschen Migrations- und Integrationsgesetzgebung im Bereich der Duldung, ZAR 2020, 183.
1454 Cf. *Hörich/Tewocht*, NVwZ 2017, 1156.
1455 See Chapter 4.E.IV.1.
1456 See Chapter 4.B.I. and Chapter 4.E.IV.1.

known as *'Duldung light'* or *'Duldung minus'*.[1457] This basis for toleration will be covered below as part of the discussion on the factual obstacles to deportation.

Toleration is characterised by the legal and factual impossibility surrounding deportation, and thus why only the 'basic' elements are presented. For this study, the separate grounds for toleration pursuant to § 60a(2) 1st Sent. AufenthG (the obstacles to deportation) are relevant.[1458] They will be divided into legal and factual obstacles.[1459] § 60a(2) AufenthG states that deportation is to be suspended for as long as deportation is impossible in fact or in law and no residence permit is granted.[1460] Impossibility in this context refers to the question whether deportation can be effected in a timely manner or whether it is excluded due to legal or factual obstacles.[1461] According to the Federal Administrative Court, this is to be judged irrespective of whether the foreigner could leave the country voluntarily.[1462] § 60a(2) 1st Sent. AufenthG provides a legal entitlement to temporary suspension of deportation, i.e. to toleration, in such cases.[1463]

Deportation may be legally impossible due to reasons stemming from statute, constitutional law, EU law or customary international law,[1464] though the relationship between the individual concerned and the State is decisive.[1465] The 'national deportation bans' pursuant to § 60(5) or (7) AufenthG are especially relevant to this study as both extend beyond the international protection under the Qualification Directive and – procedurally speaking – are subordinate to it.[1466] These are therefore viewed as

---

1457 Cf. *Eichler*, Das Sanktionsregime der „Duldung light". Die neue „Duldung für Personen mit ungeklärter Identität" nach § 60b AufenthG, Das Migrationspaket – Beilage zum Asylmagazin 8–9/2019, 64; *Thym*, ZAR 2019, 354f and *Hruschka*, Verfassungsblog (21.5.2019).

1458 Cf. *Hoffmann*, Asylmagazin 2010, 369f.

1459 See just *Marx*, Aufenthalts-, Asyl- und Flüchtlingsrecht § 7 mns 342–347.

1460 Cf. *Hörich*, Abschiebungen 122.

1461 *Gordzielik/Huber* in *Huber/Mantel* § 60a AufenthG mn 15.

1462 *Huber/Eichenhofer/Endres de Oliveira*, Aufenthaltsrecht mn 1202 with further references. This is only relevant once a permit has been granted according to § 25(5) AufenthG; see Chapter 4.C.II.

1463 Cf. *Gordzielik/Huber* in *Huber/Mantel* § 60a AufenthG mn 14 with further references.

1464 Cf. *Funke-Kaiser* in *Berlit* (ed), Gemeinschaftskommentar zum Aufenthaltsgesetz (110th edn, March 2021) § 60a AufenthG mn 168.

1465 Cf. *Gordzielik/Huber* in *Huber/Mantel* § 60a AufenthG mn 21.

1466 Cf. *Hruschka* in *Huber/Mantel* (eds), Kommentar Aufenthaltsgesetz/Asylgesetz³ (2021) Vorbemerkung vor Abschnitt 2. Schutzgewährung mn 21 and *Hruschka/Mantel* in *Huber/Mantel* (eds), Kommentar Aufenthaltsgesetz/Asylgesetz³

a 'third category of protection'[1467] after the protection of refugees and subsidiary protection. The 'national deportation bans' are relevant to this study both as grounds for toleration as well as requirements for granting residence permits under § 25(3) and (5) AufenthG,[1468] thus exhibiting a dual character. Decisions on toleration generally rest with the foreigners authority, though the Federal Office for Migration and Refugees is to be included in decisions on both 'national deportation bans' and determines if these requirements are met.[1469] Furthermore, one must also bear in mind that the 'national deportation bans' are also examined in the asylum process. The 'national deportation bans' are now distinguished by 'internal' (i.e. domestic) and 'external' (i.e. in the state of destination) bans on deportation.[1470]

A deportation ban is characterised as 'internal' where the deportation would violate a right that is legally protected in Germany. The 'national deportation bans' are examined under § 60(5) and (7) AufenthG.[1471] A 'residence permit for persons who are enforceably required to leave the country, but whose departure is legally or factually impossible', may be granted where the deportation is permanently impossible.[1472] Such an 'internal obstacle' for health reasons may also be derived from Article 2(2) 1st Sent. GG – the right to life and physical integrity.[1473] Distinctions may also be drawn between an inability to travel in a narrow and a broader sense. The narrow meaning describes cases in which a serious deterioration in health or a risk to life or health arises in connection with the deportation procedure. In a broad sense, the inability to travel also refers to the deportation itself, but here the associated serious risk of a substantial or even life-threatening deterioration in health is decisive. This may be shown by, for example, terminating vital medical treatment, a high-risk pregnancy, an acute and serious risk of suicide, or an impending birth.[1474]

(2021) § 60 AufenthG mn 17 as well as *Koch* in *Kluth/Heusch* (eds), BeckOK Ausländerrecht (30th edn, 1.7.2020) § 60 AufenthG mn 2.

1467 *Marx*, Aufenthalts-, Asyl- und Flüchtlingsrecht § 5 mn 36.

1468 See Chapter 4.A.II.2. and Chapter 4.C.II.

1469 § 72(2) AufenthG; cf. *Marx*, Aufenthalts-, Asyl- und Flüchtlingsrecht § 5 mns 36f.

1470 Cf. *Marx*, Aufenthalts-, Asyl- und Flüchtlingsrecht § 7 mn 342.

1471 *Hoffmann*, Asylmagazin 2010, 369f.

1472 See Chapter 4.C.II.

1473 Cf. *Gordzielik/Huber* in *Huber/Mantel* § 60a AufenthG mn 24.

1474 Cf. *Gordzielik/Huber* in *Huber/Mantel* § 60a AufenthG mns 25f.

The ban on deportation is 'external' in nature where there are risks related to the state of destination which may arise through the deportation.[1475] This means that the deportation may not violate the obstacles anchored in the ECHR,[1476] which are again examined according to § 60(5) and (7) AufenthG. A residence permit may be granted in instances in which the deportation to the state of destination is banned and subsidiarily for persons who are enforceably required to leave the country, but whose departure is legally or factually impossible – in other words where the deportation is permanently impossible.[1477] The grounds for exclusion are also to be considered since, in some circumstances, only toleration is possible despite the impossibility surrounding the deportation.[1478] Additionally, numerous legal grounds for toleration also exist (such as the protection against deportation under Article 6 GG and Article 8 ECHR), though only a brief reference will be made here.[1479]

Factual obstacles to deportation concern the type and manner in which the statutory obligation to leave the country is enforced.[1480] For instance, the deportation may not be factually enforceable or is only possible with disproportionate effort or considerable delays because,[1481] for example, travel documents are missing or because the state of destination refuses to take the person concerned.[1482] Statelessness may also be a factual obstacle.[1483] An illness may also prevent deportation as travel or transport are not possible.[1484] In contrast to the factual reasons in Austria, there is no examination of whether the impossibility has been caused by the foreigner him- or herself.[1485] Whether the deportation could not be enforced because of the foreigner's own fault is in principle 'only' relevant with regard to social benefits and access to the labour market, as this allows

1475 Cf. *Hoffmann*, Asylmagazin 2010, 369f.

1476 Cf. *Hruschka/Mantel* in *Huber/Mantel* § 60 AufenthG mns 26–28.

1477 See Chapter 4.A.II.2. and Chapter 4.C.II.

1478 See Chapter 4.A.II.2.b.

1479 Cf. *Huber/Eichenhofer/Endres de Oliveira*, Aufenthaltsrecht mns 1204–1206 with further references and see also Chapter 4.C.II.1.

1480 *Gordzielik/Huber* in *Huber/Mantel* § 60a AufenthG mn 16.

1481 BT-Drs 11/6321, 76 on the previous version of § 55 AuslG 1990.

1482 *Huber/Eichenhofer/Endres de Oliveira*, Aufenthaltsrecht mn 1203 with further references.

1483 Cf. *Marx*, Aufenthalts-, Asyl- und Flüchtlingsrecht § 7 mns 348–351.

1484 See VGH Kassel, Judgment of 11.5.1992, 13 UE 1608/91, Entscheidungssammlung zum Ausländer- und Asylrecht 045 No. 2, on the case of a life-threatening illness (specifically a confirmed suicide risk).

1485 See Chapter 4.A.I.3.a.

to refuse to grant an employment permit.[1486] The examination on this second level appears more expedient as it determines the suspension of deportation (which in fact cannot be enforced anyway) even if it is the fault of the foreigner and he or she is only subsequently 'punished' for his or her behaviour in accessing employment or social benefits. Furthermore, fault on the part of the foreigner plays a role in subsequently obtaining a residence permit.[1487]

A reference to § 60b AufenthG, introduced via the Orderly Return Act, is also necessary when discussing the factual obstacles to deportation.[1488] Tolerated status according to § 60a(4) AufenthG is granted to foreigners who are enforceably required to leave the country where there is reason to suspect that they cannot be deported for reasons for which they themselves are responsible.[1489] The corresponding certificate confirming the suspension of deportation in such cases features the additional wording 'for persons whose identity is not verified'. This therefore constitutes a 'subcategory'[1490] under toleration. According to § 60b(1) 1st Sent. AufenthG, the authorities have no discretion with regard to the question whether the foreigner is responsible for the obstacle to deportation.[1491] 'Specific' obligations to acquire a passport also exist in § 60(3) AufenthG alongside the already existing obligation to acquire a passport.[1492] The toleration of 'persons whose identity is not verified' applies not only to every foreigner who first acquired such status after the law entered into force on 21 August 2019 but also to all who were tolerated beforehand and whose tolerated status was extended or granted for another reason.[1493] § 60b AufenthG does not apply to foreigners who are tolerated for the purpose of training or employment.[1494]

Extensive sanctions accompany the toleration of 'persons whose identity is not verified', which impact primarily on the status (prohibition of em-

1486 § 60a(6) No. 2 AufenthG and see Chapter 4.A.I.2.b.

1487 See Chapter 4.C.II.1.

1488 Cf. *Wittmann/Röder*, Aktuelle Rechtsfragen der Duldung für Personen mit ungeklärter Identität gem. § 60b AufenthG, ZAR 2019, 362.

1489 § 60b(1) 2nd Sent. AufenthG.

1490 *Eichler*, Das Migrationspaket – Beilage zum Asylmagazin 8–9/2019, 64.

1491 This is apparent from the wording 'is granted'. In this sense, see *Eichler*, Das Migrationspaket – Beilage zum Asylmagazin 8–9/2019, 65.

1492 For criticism see *Eichler*, Das Migrationspaket – Beilage zum Asylmagazin 8–9/2019, 65–68.

1493 § 105(1) AufenthG.

1494 § 105(3) AufenthG and see Chapter 4.E.IV.1.

ployment and reduction of social benefits).[1495] Furthermore, the length of time of such toleration does not count towards the future toleration of persons in vocational training or employment (the so-called *Vorduldungszeiten*).[1496] This will have notable effects on acquiring a residence permit according to §§ 25a and 25b AufenthG and a toleration for vocational training and employment, which is why it greatly worsens the prospects under residence law.[1497] According to *Eichler*, it implements a long intended stigmatism and disenfranchisement of an entire group.[1498] However, it should be noted that it is possible at a later time to undertake the reasonable efforts to acquire a passport and thus 'cure' the failure to perform this obligation.[1499] In this case the obligation to cooperate will be regarded as performed and the foreigner will be issued with a certificate confirming the tolerated status under § 60a(4) AufenthG without the additional wording for 'persons whose identity is not verified'.[1500] The cure therefore allows the duration of toleration prior to the issuance of toleration for 'persons whose identity is not verified' to again have effect under residence law and can be subsequently credited to the previous periods of residence for §§ 25a and 25b AufenthG.[1501] Overall, the toleration of 'persons whose identity is not verified' is to be regarded as a qualified irregular stay for the purposes of this study.[1502]

By introducing the toleration of 'persons whose identity is not verified', the law in Germany begins to resemble the existing law in Austria.[1503] For instance, it is examined whether the foreigner is responsible for rendering deportation impossible and accordingly receives tolerated status only as a 'person whose identity is not verified'. It is for these reasons that the legal situation prior to the Orderly Return Act is preferable. According to the

---

1495 See Chapter 4.A.I.2.b.

1496 § 60b(5) 1st Sent. AufenthG; cf. BT-Drs 19/10047, 39.

1497 Cf. *Eichler*, Das Migrationspaket – Beilage zum Asylmagazin 8–9/2019, 71 and see Chapter 4.B.I.1.–2. and Chapter 4.E.IV.1.

1498 *Eichler*, Das Migrationspaket – Beilage zum Asylmagazin 8–9/2019, 64: '*die seit langem beabsichtigte Stigmatisierung und Entrechtung einer ganzen Personengruppe*'.

1499 § 60b(4) AufenthG and see Chapter 4.E.IV.1.

1500 § 60b(4) 4th Sent. AufenthG.

1501 *Eichler*, Das Migrationspaket – Beilage zum Asylmagazin 8–9/2019, 71 with reference to BT-Drs 19/10047, 39.

1502 See Chapter 1.B.I.a.

1503 See Chapter 4.A.I.3.a.

statistics, by mid-2021 8.9% of all tolerated persons were tolerated on be basis of an 'unverified identity'.[1504]

b) Status

Tolerated status is to be issued in writing in the form of a certificate.[1505] It is a beneficial administrative act (*begünstigender Verwaltungsakt*) under German administrative law.[1506] Such type of act gives rise to or confirms a right or legal advantage.[1507] According to *Gordzielik/Huber*, toleration qualifies as an 'other authorisation offering a right to stay' under the Return Directive,[1508] though this opinion is not watertight as toleration under the Residence Act does not establish a lawful stay.[1509] It is rather to be understood as a 'postponement of removal' pursuant to Article 9 Return Directive, as is also expressed by the use of 'temporary suspension' in the English translation of the Residence Act.[1510]

The toleration period varies roughly between three months and one year,[1511] though in principle the duration is determined by 'how long an obstacle to deportation is likely to prevent the enforcement of the obligation to leave the country'.[1512] Nonetheless, it is disputed whether the requirements to cooperate during the deportation procedure may lead to a shorter period.[1513] According to § 95(1) No. 2(c) AufenthG, it is not punishable to reside in Germany without a necessary residence title if the deportation has been suspended (i.e. the person is tolerated);[1514] this also applies even if the certificate was not issued, but the statutory require-

1504 BT-Drs 19/32579, 31.

1505 § 60a(4) AufenthG. See § 78(7) AufenthG with regard to the content of such a certificate.

1506 Cf. *Gordzielik/Huber* in *Huber/Mantel* § 60a AufenthG mn 72.

1507 § 48(1) 2nd Sent. VwVfG.

1508 *Gordzielik/Huber* in *Huber/Mantel* § 60a AufenthG mn 64 with further references. See also *Huber/Eichenhofer/Endres de Oliveira*, Aufenthaltsrecht mn 1194.

1509 § 60a(3) AufenthG.

1510 See Chapter 2.B.I.

1511 For details see § 60a(1) and (2) AufenthG.

1512 *Marx*, Aufenthalts-, Asyl- und Flüchtlingsrecht § 7 mn 410.

1513 In this sense, *Marx*, Aufenthalts-, Asyl- und Flüchtlingsrecht § 7 mn 410; for criticism see *Gordzielik/Huber* in *Huber/Mantel* § 60a AufenthG mn 66.

1514 Cf. *Hörich/Bergmann* in *Huber/Mantel* § 95 AufenthG mns 44–49 and see also Chapter 3.B.II.1.

ments are met.[1515] § 60a(5) 4th Sent. AufenthG provides that there is to be notification of deportation if a persons was tolerated for more than one year and this has been revoked.[1516] This obligation to notify was repealed by the Act to Improve the Enforcement of the Obligation to Leave in so far as the person concerned did not cooperate in the procedure.[1517]

Pursuant to § 61(1) 1st Sent. AufenthG, the stay of a foreigner who is enforceably required to leave the country is restricted in geographic terms to the territory of the *Land* concerned.[1518] This geographic restriction expires automatically after three months of uninterrupted residence in the respective *Land*.[1519]

The tolerated person may not be employed during the first three months, though the foreigners authority may grant the approval to engage in employment after three months.[1520] This therefore constitutes a general prohibition unless permission is granted.[1521] This was not changed by the Skilled Immigration Act in 2020. According to *Schuster/Voigt*, the foreigners authority should exercise its discretion under § 4(4) AufenthG regarding the grant of an employment permit positively provided that the requirements for prohibiting employment are not met.[1522] However, tolerated persons may be generally prohibited from engaging in employed activities if they have entered Germany to obtain benefits under the Act on Benefits for Asylum Seekers, if measures to terminate their stay cannot be carried out for reasons for which they are responsible, or they are nationals of a safe country of origin[1523] under § 29a Asylum Act (G) and

---

1515 *Hörich/Bergmann* in *Huber/Mantel* § 95 AufenthG mn 45 with further references.

1516 § 60a(5) 4th Sent. AufenthG.

1517 For criticism, *Hörich/Tewocht*, NVwZ 2017, 1156.

1518 Cf. *Gordzielik* in *Huber/Mantel* (eds), Kommentar Aufenthaltsgesetz/Asylgesetz[3] (2021) § 61 AufenthG mn 7.

1519 § 61(1)b AufenthG. Critical, *Hörich/Tewocht*, NVwZ 2017, 1156 on the extended possibility to order a geographic restriction introduced in 2017 by the Act to Improve the Enforcement of the Obligation to Leave.

1520 § 32 BeschV.

1521 Cf. *Mimentza Martin*, Die sozialrechtliche Stellung 170ff.

1522 *Schuster/Voigt*, Neuerungen beim Arbeitsmarktzugang – Die Schere geht auseinander, Asylmagazin 2020, 64 (69).

1523 For criticism on the use of the notion of a safe country of origin, *Werdermann*, Die Vereinbarkeit von Sonderrecht für Asylsuchende und Geduldete aus sicheren Herkunftsstaaten mit Art. 3 GG, ZAR 2018, 11.

the application for asylum was filed after 31 August 2015 and has been denied.[1524]

Kluth/Breidenbach consider the mandatory requirements to be especially relevant in practice if the tolerated person has brought about the obstacle to deportation with his or her own deceit concerning his or her identity or nationality or by furnishing false information.[1525] In contrast to Austrian law, this 'only' leads to a general ban on employment, whereas in Austria this is a reason for refusing to issue the card for tolerated persons (*Karte für Geduldete*) and, hence, not acquiring a tolerated status.[1526] Self-employment was prohibited until the Skilled Immigration Act entered into force on 1 March 2020, since then it may be approved.[1527]

Tolerated persons are entitled to claim benefits under the Act on Benefits for Asylum Seekers during the first 18 months.[1528] However, various reasons can apply to limit these benefits to a six-month period,[1529] for example if the person has entered the country for the purpose of claiming benefits or is responsible for rendering the deportation impossible.[1530] The Third Act to amend the AsylbLG, which entered into force on 1 September 2019, restructured and extended the restrictions under § 1a AsylbLG.[1531] Following the first 18 months, tolerated persons are entitled to analogous benefits under the Social Insurance Code XII if they have not abused their rights to influence the length of their stay.[1532] This legislation extended the duration of the previous stay from 15 to 18 months.[1533]

1524 § 60a(6) AufenthG; cf. *Kluth/Breidenbach* in *Kluth/Heusch* § 60a AufenthG mns 49–59 and *Gordzielik/Huber* in *Huber/Mantel* § 60a AufenthG mns 70f; *Schuster/Voigt*, Asylmagazin 2020, 70ff.

1525 *Kluth/Breidenbach* in *Kluth/Heusch* § 60a AufenthG mn 53. For detail, *Hörich/Putzar-Sattler*, Mitwirkungspflichten im Ausländerrecht: Rechtsgutachten zu den Voraussetzungen von Sanktionen bei Nichtmitwirkung (November 2017), https://www.fluechtlingsrat-lsa.de/wp-content/uploads/2017/11/fluera_lsa_gutachten_2017_Mitwirkungspflichten_im_Auslaenderrecht.pdf (31.7.2022) 11f.

1526 See Chapter 4.A.I.3.a.

1527 Cf. *Schuster/Voigt*, Asylmagazin 2020, 72 with reference to § 4a(4) AufenthG.

1528 § 1(1) No. 4 AsylbLG; cf. *Korff* in *Rolfs/Giesen/Keikebohm/Udsching* § 1 AsylbLG mns 15–17.

1529 See §§ 1a(1)–(3) and 14(1) AsylbLG; cf. *Schneider*, NZS 2018, 561f.

1530 Cf. *Korff* in *Rolfs/Giesen/Keikebohm/Udsching* § 1a AsylbLG mns 10–15 and 16–22.

1531 Cf. *Genge*, Das Migrationspaket – Beilage zum Asylmagazin 8–9/2019, 20f.

1532 § 2 AsylbLG; see Fn 1014.

1533 § 2(1) AsylbLG. For criticism see *Genge*, Das Migrationspaket – Beilage zum Asylmagazin 8–9/2019, 18f.

Tolerated persons are excluded from receiving benefits under the Social Insurance Code II and standard welfare benefits.[1534]

Finally, it should be pointed out that the toleration of 'persons whose identity is not verified' has brought about more severe legal consequences.[1535] Such tolerated foreigners are subject to an employment ban and benefit reductions according to § 1a(3) AsylbLG.[1536] Furthermore, they are subject to the residence requirement pursuant to § 61(1d) AufenthG, i.e. the geographic restriction.[1537]

c) Legal protection

The refusal to suspend deportation (i.e. closing the door to toleration) is not contestable,[1538] though an action for enforcement (*Verpflichtungsklage*) may be brought.[1539] Such action does not have a suspensive effect as toleration is merely a measure of administrative enforcement.[1540] An application for provisional relief under § 123(1) 1st Sent. VwGO may be submitted to temporarily suspend the enforcement of the deportation.[1541]

d) Regularisation prospects

'Chain tolerations' (*Kettenduldungen*) are a considerable problem in practice.[1542] The term is used to describe the situation in which a foreigner is tolerated over several years, though the essence of the toleration is only to temporarily suspend deportation.[1543] In my opinion, such long-term toler-

---

1534 § 7(1) 2nd Sent. No. 3 SGB II and § 23(2) SGB XII; cf. *Groth* in *Rolfs/Giesen/Keikebohm/Udsching* § 23 SGB XII mn 15.

1535 See Chapter 4.A.I.2.a.

1536 § 60b(5) 2nd Sent. AufenthG. Cf. *Eichler*, Das Migrationspaket – Beilage zum Asylmagazin 8–9/2019, 70f.

1537 § 60b(5) 3rd Sent. AufenthG.

1538 § 83(2) AufenthG. In general on the procedure, see §§ 68ff VwGO and *Maurer/Waldhoff*, Verwaltungsrecht § 10 mn 77.

1539 § 42(1) VwGO; cf. *Marx*, Aufenthalts-, Asyl- und Flüchtlingsrecht § 7 mn 423.

1540 § 80(2) VwGO; cf. *Kluth/Breidenbach* in *Kluth/Heusch* § 60a AufenthG mn 63.

1541 Cf. *Hailbronner*, Asyl- und Ausländerrecht mn 1158.

1542 See Chapter 2.B.I., Chapter 2.B.II.2.b. and Chapter 3.B.III.2.c.

1543 See specifically the tables in *Wendel*, Kettenduldung. Bleiberechtsregelungen und parlamentarische Initiativen 2000 – 2014 (August 2014), http://www.flue

ation is not compatible with the Return Directive as there is an obligation to award a residence permit in cases of permanent non-returnability.[1544]

Overall, the 'chain tolerations' show that many tolerated persons remain as such, with a number of high hurdles to jump to acquire residence permit. In the meanwhile, German law features some statutory possibilities for tolerated persons to become regularised.[1545] Some even offer a possible solution to the problem of 'chain tolerations'. Nonetheless, *Marx* remains correct in his assessment that the phenomenon still remains in practice.[1546] In this respect, toleration in Germany is generally to be understood as a preliminary step towards acquiring a right to stay as many of the residence permits for humanitarian reasons may be acquired for different reasons.[1547]

3. Austria: statutory toleration

Aliens residing unlawfully in Austrian territory do not face the prospect of automatic deportation: an enforceable legislative basis is necessary, which is provided by a return decision.[1548] Deportation must be legally admissible and factually possible. However, it is often rendered impossible by a legal or factual obstacle. The Austrian legislator therefore created 'toleration' as a legal instrument to apply in such cases.[1549] The low issue rate[1550] of the card for tolerated persons (*Karte für Geduldete*) underlines that 'toleration' merely has a shadowy existence in Austria, especially when compared with the statistics for Germany.[1551] One reason for this trend appears to be the considerable discretion held by the Federal Office for

chtlingsrat-brandenburg.de/wp-content/uploads/2014/08/Kettenduldung.pdf (31.7.2022) 5–7.

1544 See Chapter 2.B.II.2.b.

1545 On § 25(5) AufenthG see Chapter 4.C.II. On § 25a AufenthG see Chapter 4.B.II. On § 25b AufenthG see Chapter 4.B.I. On § 19d AufenthG see Chapter 4.E.IV. On § 23a AufenthG see Chapter 4.D.II.1.

1546 *Marx*, Aufenthalts-, Asyl- und Flüchtlingsrecht § 7 mn 341.

1547 See Chapter 1.B.III.1.a.

1548 §§ 46 and 52 FPG.

1549 On the historical development of toleration in Austria see *Hinterberger/Klammer*, migraLex 2015, 77f.

1550 According to the statistics provided by the Austrian Federal Ministry for the Interior, only 215 cards were issued in the year 2020, see 4901/AB 27. GP, 29.

1551 See Chapter 4.A.I.2.

Immigration and Asylum (as well its rather restrictive interpretation) with regard to the grounds for toleration.[1552]

Temporary inadmissibility is to be distinguished from the inadmissibility of a return decisions due to Article 8 ECHR, which results in a 'residence permit for reasons of Article 8 ECHR'.[1553]

a) Requirements

In contrast to German law, Austrian law distinguishes merely between legal and factual grounds for toleration, which will be analysed in detail below. Legal obstacles to deportation arise in cases in which the deportation would violate a constitutionally-protected right under the ECHR, specifically Articles 2, 3 or 8.[1554] The principle of non-refoulement plays a particularly important role:[1555] if there are non-refoulement reasons that exclude a return to a third-country, a return decision must (since 2017) be issued in accordance with § 52(9) FPG, and at the same time the inadmissibility of the deportation must be declared and the person must be tolerated.[1556]

The FPG provides three groups of legal obstacles to deportation. The first group (§ 46(1) No. 1 FPG) concerns the non-refoulement principle. This can only concern countries other than the country of origin as the FPG explicitly states that an application related to the country of origin constitutes an application for international protection.[1557]

The second group (§ 46a(1) No. 2 FPG) concerns those cases in which the asylum status or the subsidiary protection is withdrawn due to a criminal offence,[1558] yet the non-refoulement principle excludes the return to the country of origin.[1559] The Federal Office for Immigration and Asylum

1552 Cf. *Frahm*, juridikum 2013, 469f; *Hinterberger/Klammer*, migraLex 2015, 79f; *Peyrl*, Arbeitsmarkt 323 and *Geiger*, migraLex 2019, 5–7.

1553 See Chapter 4.B.III. and Chapter 4.C.III.

1554 § 46a(1) Nos. 1, 2 and 4 FPG. See Fn 891 and 892.

1555 See Chapter 1.B.III.1.b. and Chapter 2.B.II.2.a.

1556 See also VwGH 21.12.2017, Ra 2017/21/0125.

1557 § 51(2) FPG, cf. VwGH 28.8.2014, 2013/21/0218 and 20.12.2016, Ra 2016/21/0109.

1558 For refugees, the offence must be particularly serious (§ 6(1) No. 4 AsylG (A)). Subsidiary protection will be withdrawn for crimes under § 17 StGB (A) (§ 9(2) No. 3 AsylG (A)).

1559 A further scenario also comes into consideration: a person commits a crime during the asylum process and meets the necessary requirements to be entitled

has to pronounce this in the order at the same time as the withdrawal and has to tolerate the person concerned.[1560] Following the reforms in 2017 the Federal Office for Immigration and Asylum also has to issue a return decision.[1561] The legislator's intention was that delinquency goes hand in hand with the loss of status rights and that the legal position of these persons is therefore massively restricted.[1562]

The third group (§ 46a(1) No. 4 FPG) comprises the cases in which the deportation would constitute a violation of the right to respect one's private and family life, i.e. Article 8 ECHR. § 9(1)–(3) BFA-VG contain the interests to be balanced.[1563] The return decision is temporarily inadmissible in such instances, as is shown by the example of an advanced (high risk) pregnancy.[1564] In contrast to the temporary inadmissibility, the Federal Office for Immigration and Asylum or Federal Administrative Court may also determine that the return decision is permanently inadmissible due to the private and family life of the person concerned.[1565] Specifically, this concerns cases in which the threatened Article 8 ECHR violation is based on circumstances that are not merely temporary in nature; a 'residence permit for reasons of Article 8 ECHR' is to be granted in such cases.[1566]

Toleration, however, also acknowledges the circumstances in which deportation is factually impossible for reasons for which the person concerned is not responsible. The Federal Office for Immigration and Asylum requires the authorisation from the country of origin (a so-called certificate of return or travel document) in order to perform the deportation. If such authorisation is not issued by the respective representative authority abroad (*Vertretungsbehörde*), the alien cannot be deported and there is a factual obstacle to deportation.

---

to asylum or subsidiary protection. Such person will be granted the relevant status, which will then be immediately withdrawn due to the criminal offence.

1560 There is thus an exception from the constitutive effect of issuing the card; see Fn 1576.

1561 § 52(9) FPG.

1562 ErläutRV 330 BlgNR 24. GP, 9.

1563 See Chapter 4.B.III.1.

1564 VwGH 28.4.2015, Ra 2014/18/0146. The fact that medical treatment is carried out in Austria is also relevant as in the case in question it may significantly increase the person's interest in remaining in Austria. The rules on maternity protection are also applicable, for example §§ 3ff Mutterschutzgesetz in the version BGBl I 87/2022 (Maternity Protection Act), according to which women in the pre- and postpartum period require rest.

1565 § 9(3) BFA-VG.

1566 See Chapter 4.B.III. and Chapter 4.C.III.

The decisive aspect is whether the deportation is impossible due to acts by the alien concerned. § 46a(3) FPG therefore provides that reasons attributable to the alien shall in all cases exist if: the alien conceals his or her identity, fails to comply with a summons for the purpose of clarifying his or her identity or procuring a replacement travel document, or the alien does not cooperate in the steps necessary to obtain a replacement travel document or frustrates the taking of such steps. Furthermore, there must be a causal link between the acts or omissions listed in § 46a(3) FPG and the reasons for the impossibility of deportation.[1567] The authorities have broad discretion in this respect,[1568] though this has been limited by the courts on several occasions. For instance, the notification by the Austrian representative authority that the identity and/or nationality cannot be determined does not allow for the conclusion that the person concerned has made an inaccurate declaration about his or her identity.[1569] Since 2017, every alien is expressly required to obtain a travel document from the competent foreign authority (embassy or consulate) and to take all necessary actions that are necessary for this.[1570] This especially concerns the application for the document by the alien him- or herself and providing accurate information on his or her identity (name, date of birth, nationality and address).[1571] The alien has to prove that he or she has performed this obligation to cooperate. Where necessary,[1572] the Federal Office for Immigration and Asylum may summon the alien to the competent foreign representative authority to acquire a travel document (or similar).[1573]

1567 VwGH 30.6.2016, Ra 2016/21/0078 para 17 with reference to ErläutRV 1078 BlgNR 24, 27.

1568 In Austrian terminology, discretion (*Ermessen*) means that the authority is not bound to a particular decision, but has a number of different options to choose from; cf. *Raschauer*, Verwaltungsrecht mn 573. In turn, the scope of the discretion may not be so broad that the rule becomes indeterminate and thus unconstitutional pursuant to Art 18(1) B-VG. On the different types of discretion, *Raschauer*, Verwaltungsrecht mns 574–580.

1569 VwGH 30.6.2015, Ra 2014/21/0040.

1570 § 46(2) FPG; for criticism see *Klammer*, Beugehaft nach dem FPG in *Filzwieser/Taucher* (eds), Asyl- und Fremdenrecht. Jahrbuch 2018 (2018) 147 (150–154) and *Geiger*, Die Beugehaft zur Durchsetzbarkeit von Mitwirkungspflichten im Rahmen des Fremdenpolizeigesetzes, migraLex 2019, 2 (4–7).

1571 § 36(2) BFA-VG.

1572 § 46(2b) FPG.

1573 § 46(2a) FPG; for criticism see *Klammer* in *Filzwieser/Taucher* 150–154.

b) Status

The Federal Office for Immigration and Asylum has to issue a card for tolerated persons (*Karte für Geduldete*; hereinafter just 'card') if the relevant requirements are met.[1574] In principle a person first acquires tolerated status once the card is issued,[1575] and thus this is why this act has constitutive effect.[1576] As the name indicates, the stay is not lawful and the obligation to leave the country still remains.[1577] In other words, the stay in Austria is merely temporary.[1578] The card may be withdrawn if the requirements are no longer met.[1579] There is no constitutive effect of issuing the card if the toleration was finally determined at an earlier point in time pursuant to § 46a(6) FPG – this primarily concerns the cases in which the Federal Office for Immigration and Asylum or Federal Administrative Court have held that the deportation is inadmissible due to a criminal conviction.

From a legal standpoint, issuing the card and the corresponding status gives rise to particular rights which allow the tolerated person to be distinguished from other irregularly staying aliens. The card is valid for one year from its date of issue.[1580] In principle the unlawful stay is punishable with a fine,[1581] but no such offence is committed where there is tolerated status.[1582] An application for a card under § 46a FPG has no procedural effects on the threat of deportation, which is enforceable despite such application.

Generally, persons staying irregularly – including those who are tolerated – are denied access to the labour market, though there is an exception for those individuals whose asylum or subsidiary protection status has been withdrawn (or not granted), but whose deportation is inadmissible due to the principle of non-refoulement.[1583] Such persons have the possibility to engage in employment after receiving the relevant employment

1574 For example, VwGH 31.8.2017, Ro 2016/21/0019, paras 29ff. See VwGH 16.5.2012, 2012/21/0053 on extending 'toleration'.

1575 § 46a(4) and (5) FPG.

1576 VfGH 29.11.2016, E 847/2016. An exception exists if the toleration was finally determined at an earlier point in time. See Fn 1560.

1577 §§ 31(1a) No. 3 and 46(1) FPG.

1578 § 46a(4) and (5) FPG.

1579 VwGH 31.8.2017, Ro 2016/21/0019, para 30.

1580 § 46a(5) 1st Sent. FPG.

1581 § 120(1)(a) FPG.

1582 § 120(5) No. 2 FPG.

1583 § 46a(1) No. 2 FPG.

permit.[1584] I have already discussed elsewhere that such unequal treatment is unconstitutional in so far as it violates the fundamental requirement of decent living conditions.[1585]

As already outlined in Chapter 3, a claim to basic welfare benefits is only available to those irregularly staying aliens who cannot be deported due to legal or factual reasons.[1586] There is thus no right to basic welfare benefits until the impossibility of deportation and thus tolerated status has been determined.[1587]

c) Legal protection

The appeals described in Chapter 3.A.V. may be lodged if an application for tolerated status is rejected or dismissed.[1588]

d) Regularisation prospects

Regularisation is possible for persons who are tolerated pursuant to § 46a(1) Nos. 1 or 3 FPG. Both of these sets of circumstances are therefore considered a preliminary step towards acquiring a right to stay.[1589] Tolerated persons may apply for a 'special protection residence permit' after one year, thereby regularising their stay.[1590] The other sets of circumstances (i.e. § 46a(1) Nos. 2 or 4 FPG) are consequently just considered a qualified irregular stay. In addition, it is also conceivable that one may apply for a 'residence permit for reasons of Article 8 ECHR'.[1591] This type of residence permit is available to irregularly staying persons irrespective of whether they have tolerated status. Where tolerated persons are concerned, this regularisation is not considered a chance for regularisation as the tolerated stay is not a requirement for this type of residence permit.

1584 § 4(1) No. 1 AuslBG; see Chapter 3.A.II.2.
1585 *Hinterberger*, DRdA 2018, 106–109.
1586 Art 2(1) No. 4 GVV.
1587 See Chapter 3.A.II.4. For criticisms with regard to Art 1 CFR *Hinterberger/Klammer* in *Salomon* 349 and *Hinterberger/Klammer*, University of Vienna Law Review 2020, 74.
1588 § 7(1) No. 1 BFA-VG.
1589 See Chapter 1.B.III.1.a.
1590 See Chapter 4.A.II.1.
1591 See Chapter 4.B.III. and Chapter 4.C.III.

II. Non-refoulement under the ECHR and CFR or factual reasons[1592]

The following describes the Austrian 'special protection residence permit' (*Aufenthaltsberechtigung besonderer Schutz*) before the German 'residence permit for banned deportation to a specific state' (*Aufenthaltserlaubnis bei zielstaatsbezogenen Abschiebungsverboten*) and the Spanish 'temporary residence permit for humanitarian reasons' (*autorización de residencia temporal por razones humanitarias*) as each are granted for (at least) one year. As there is no difference in duration, the national jurisdictions are therefore presented in alphabetical order.

1. Austria: 'special protection residence permit'

A special protection residence permit may be granted based upon the circumstances listed in § 57(1) AsylG (A).[1593] § 57(1) No. 1 AsylG (A) will be analysed here, with Nos. 2 and 3 discussed in the context of vulnerability, specifically victim protection.[1594]

§ 57(1) No. 1 AsylG (A) applies to tolerated persons. Its legal grounds are derived from Article 3 ECHR, with the Return Directive providing the basis for its factual grounds. The last official statistics were published in 2013, according to which only 27 'special protection residence permits' were granted.[1595] Despite the lack of recent statistics, it can be assumed from the low number of cards issued to tolerated persons that a low number of 'special protection residence permits' have been issued.[1596] Such permits therefore have almost no relevance in practice.

a) Requirements

The main requirement according to § 57(1) No. 1 AsylG (A) is for the tolerated person to have been tolerated pursuant to § 46a(1) Nos. 1 or 3 FPG

1592 See Chapter 1.B.III.1.b.

1593 § 57(1) AsylG (A) and ErläutRV 1803 BlgNR 24. GP, 47.

1594 See Chapter 4.D.I.1.

1595 *Bundesministerium für Inneres*, Niederlassungs- und Aufenthaltsstatistik 2013 (2013), https://www.bmi.gv.at/302/Statistik/files/Niederlassungs_und_Aufenthaltsstatistik_Jahresstatistik_2013.pdf (31.7.2022) 37. There were only 15 extensions.

1596 See Chapter 4.A.I.3.

since at least one year and the requirements 'continue to be met'. It is for the Federal Office for Immigration and Asylum to examine whether the requirements 'continue to be met', though the Supreme Administrative Court has ruled that the Federal Office for Immigration and Asylum is bound by the fact that the alien possesses a card for tolerated persons.[1597] Furthermore, the alien may not constitute a danger to the Republic of Austria or have been convicted of a crime[1598]. An alien may not receive a 'special protection residence permit' if international protection (asylum or subsidiary protection) has been withdrawn.[1599]

b) Right to stay

See the discussion in Chapter 3.A.III.2.d.

2. Germany: 'residence permit for banned deportation to a specific state'

The residence permit because of the banned deportation to a specific state under § 25(3) AufenthG may be issued if the departure from the country is impossible for legal reasons and it is not expected that the obstacles to departure will cease in the foreseeable future.[1600] The 'national deportation bans' according to § 60(5) and (7) AufenthG[1601] are to be understood as derivatives of Article 3 ECHR and the Return Directive, despite being a purely national means to protection against deportation, which fall within the regulatory competences at national level.[1602]

The 'national deportation bans' are also relevant in relation to the 'residence permits for persons who are enforceably required to leave the country, but whose departure is legally or factually impossible'. By

---

1597 VwGH 31.8.2017, Ro 2016/21/0019, para 32.

1598 See § 17 StGB (A). In some circumstances the final judgment of a foreign court may be considered equivalent to a judgment of an Austrian court; § 73 StGB (A).

1599 §§ 7 and 9 AsylG (A). § 57(1) No. 1 AsylG (A) makes no express reference to § 46(1) No. 2 FPG. See Chapter 4.A.I.3.a.

1600 See Chapter 4.C.II.

1601 See Chapter 4.A.I.2.a.

1602 *Hruschka/Mantel* in *Huber/Mantel* § 60 AufenthG mn 18; agreeing *Koch* in *Kluth/Heusch* § 60 AufenthG mns 39f.

mid-2021, 127,261 foreigners held a residence permit pursuant to § 25(3) AufenthG.[1603]

a) Requirements

§ 60(5) and (7) AufenthG refer to the ban of deportation to a specific state, though § 60(5) AufenthG is derived primarily from the ECHR.[1604] Article 3 ECHR may be mentioned here, but there are other 'deportation bans' under the ECHR that are to be guaranteed – such as the exclusion from subsidiary protection.[1605] § 60(7) AufenthG can be derived above all from the German Basic Law – the *Grundgesetz*.[1606] If there is a ban on deportation to a specific state, the grant of the residence permit under § 25(3) takes priority over the residence permit under § 25(5) AufenthG due to the more extensive rights it affords.[1607]

A further case may be given in the event an illness cannot be treated in the specific state of destination.[1608] There is only a 'concrete threat' if the foreigner's health would significantly worsen if he or she is deported.[1609] Determining a threat requires consideration of all the circumstances related to the state of destination, especially those that can worsen the foreigner's conditions.[1610] § 60(2) 2nd Sent. AufenthG stipulates that it must be a life-threatening or serious illness which would significantly worsen if the foreigner is deported.[1611] It is not necessary for medical care in the state of destination to be equivalent to medical care in Germany.[1612] Furthermore, sufficient medical care generally also exists where it is guaranteed only in part of the state of destination.[1613] The person concerned can therefore be

1603 BT-Drs 19/32579, 6.
1604 *Hruschka/Mantel* in *Huber/Mantel* § 60 AufenthG mns 26ff.
1605 Cf. *Hruschka/Mantel* in *Huber/Mantel* § 60 AufenthG mn 32.
1606 Cf. *Hruschka/Mantel* in *Huber/Mantel* § 60 AufenthG mn 18.
1607 See Chapter 4.C.II.1.
1608 See also *Koch* in *Kluth/Heusch* § 60 AufenthG mn 28.
1609 NVwZ-RR 2012, 529 mn 34 with further references.
1610 Cf. *Hager*, Abschiebung trotz schwerer Krankheit? Die gesetzlichen Neuregelungen zu Abschiebungshindernissen aus gesundheitlichen Gründen, Asylmagazin 2016, 160 (161).
1611 *Hager*, Asylmagazin 2016, 162. Cf. NVwZ-RR 2012, 529 mn 34 with further references. For criticism see *Hager*, Asylmagazin 2016, 161.
1612 § 60(7) 3rd Sent. AufenthG; cf. *Thym*, Die Auswirkungen des Asylpakets II, NVwZ 2016, 409 (412).
1613 § 60(7) 4th Sent. AufenthG.

expected to go to a certain part of the country in order to make use of the sufficient healthcare available there.[1614] The German legislator introduced this rule to reduce the obstacles to deportation on alleged health grounds, as the authorities are faced with major challenges in both quantative and qualitative terms.[1615] The residence permit has been viewed as being compatible in principle with ECtHR case law.[1616]

b) Right to stay

As has been noted above, the 'national deportation bans' under § 60(5) and (7) AufenthG serve as a third category of protection after the protection of asylum seekers and refugees, and subsidiary protection.[1617] This study has already considered that these bans serve as a basis for toleration, though here they serve as requirements for granting a residence permit. The foreigners authority is responsible for deciding upon an application under § 25(3) AufenthG, though only after consulting the Federal Office for Migration and Refugees.[1618]

As in relation to § 25(5) AufenthG, it is relevant that the Federal Office for Migration and Refugees carries out the examination of the 'national deportation bans' during the deportation procedure.[1619] In these cases, which can be described as national subsidiary protection, the residence permit discussed here is again not to be qualified as regularisation. It is more important for this study that the application for the residence permit can be made during the status as a tolerated person,[1620] as this fulfils the notion of a regularisation.

A residence permit is to be granted for at least one year where the ban on deportation to a specific state is formally acknowledged.[1621] An exception exists, however, if the grounds for exclusion apply.[1622] On the one hand, this concerns cases in which it is apparent from the foreigner's

1614 For criticism, see *Hager*, Asylmagazin 2016, 162.
1615 Cf. BT-Drs 18/7538, 11.
1616 For detail on two points contrary to international and EU law, see *Hinterberger/Klammer* in *Filzwieser/Taucher* 139.
1617 See Chapter 4.A.I.2.a.
1618 § 72(2) AufenthG.
1619 See just § 42 1st Sent. AsylG (G).
1620 See Chapter 4.A.I.2.a.
1621 § 25(3) AufenthG; cf. *Maaßen/Kluth* in *Kluth/Heusch* § 25 AufenthG mns 55–57.
1622 § 25(3) 1st and 2nd Sent. AufenthG.

file or statements that deportation to another state is possible and reasonable.[1623] On the other hand, this exception concerns cases in which the foreigner has repeatedly or grossly breached the obligation to cooperate, thereby making the deportation to another state impossible or unreasonable,[1624] for instance by furnishing falsified documents.[1625] Furthermore, there is a list of mandatory grounds for denying the application, with the commission of a serious criminal offence playing an especially significant role.[1626] If such a ground for exclusion applies, the person concerned is only tolerated and not to be granted a residence permit.[1627]

Prior to the Skilled Immigration Act in 2020, the residence permit under § 25(3) AufenthG did not directly allow the foreigner to work, but instead required permission from the foreigners authority.[1628] § 4a(1) 1st Sent. AufenthG has since greatly improved the situation by providing that foreigners holding a residence title may pursue an 'economic activity' (i.e. employment and self-employment).[1629] Where a residence permit is issued due to the ban on deportation to a specific state, the foreigner is also entitled to benefits under the Social Insurance Code II or social assistance under the Social Insurance Code XII.[1630]

1623 For detail see *Göbel-Zimmermann/Hupke* in *Huber/Mantel* (eds), Kommentar Aufenthaltsgesetz/Asylgesetz³ (2021) § 25 AufenthG mns 15–20.

1624 See BVerwG, Judgment of 22.11.2005, 1 C 18/04, NVwZ 2006, 711.

1625 VGH München Beck Rechtssache 2005, 16071. However, the stated grounds for exclusion may not be applied when interpreting the law in accordance with the Directive if a 'deportation ban' is established according to § 60(7) AufenthG when implementing the Qualification Directive; see *Maaßen/Kluth* in *Kluth/Heusch* § 25 AufenthG mn 32.

1626 See § 25(3) 3rd Sent. AufenthG; for detail see *Göbel-Zimmermann/Hupke* in *Huber/Mantel* § 25 AufenthG mns 23–28. These were introduced when transposing Art 17 Qualification Directive.

1627 Cf. *Marx*, Aufenthalts-, Asyl- und Flüchtlingsrecht § 5 mn 41 and see Chapter 4.A.I.2.a.

1628 § 31 BeschV and on the previous law cf. *Maor* in *Kluth/Heusch* (eds), BeckOK Ausländerrecht (18th edn, 1.5.2018) § 4 AufenthG mn 30.

1629 Cf. *Schuster/Voigt*, Asylmagazin 2020, 65f.

1630 Cf. *Frings/Janda/Keßler/Steffen*, Sozialrecht mn 756 and *Huber/Eichenhofer/Endres de Oliveira*, Aufenthaltsrecht mn 546.

3. Spain: 'temporary residence permit for humanitarian reasons' where the visa application in the state of origin is impossible

Article 126(3) REDYLE allows the grant of a 'temporary residence permit for exceptional circumstances' to foreigners who meet the requirements for a temporary residence permit or a residence permit and employment permit, but who cannot go to the country of origin to apply for a visa due to the threat to their own safety or of their family (*autorización temporal por razones humanitarias – imposibilidad de trasladarse al país de origen para solicitar el visado*).[1631] This type of residence permit falls under 'humanitarian reasons' within the category 'temporary residence permit for exceptional circumstances', which also includes two other grounds.[1632]

According to *García Vitoria*, this is the final part of the 'international protection' (*protección internacional*) under Spanish law as it concerns every person who does not receive either asylum or subsidiary protection.[1633] This type of residence permit is relevant to this study as it may be understood as an expression of the non-refoulement principle in the sense of Article 3 ECHR, which attempts to close the gap in protection between international protection per the Qualification Directive and the non-refoulement principle.[1634] However, it is to be noted here that the application is subject to the irregular status, thus satisfying the definition of regularisation. There is no provision for *ex officio* consideration in the asylum process.

a) Requirements

It must be impossible for the foreigner to go to the country of origin to apply for a visa. Unlike the requirements for international protection, this could cover all cases in which the journey would constitute a violation of the non-refoulement principle. This is apparent from the wording '*imposibilidad de trasladarse*',[1635] though the risk must be specified in a report. Article 35(7) LODYLE and Article 196(1) REDYLE each contain a similar

1631 Cf. *Peña Pérez*, Revista de Derecho Migratorio y Extranjería 2012/30, 44–46.
1632 Art 126 REDYLE and see Chapter 4.D.I.3. and Chapter 4.D.II.1.
1633 Cf. *García Vitoria* in *Boza Martínez/Donaire Villa/Moya Malapeira* 298.
1634 See Chapter 1.B.III.1.b.
1635 In this sense see *Trinidad García*, Residencia temporal por circunstancias excepcionales: el arraigo laboral y social, Revista de Derecho Migratorio y Extranjería 2005/9, 133 (153).

expression with regard to unaccompanied minors who cannot be returned (*imposibilidad de retorno* and *repatriación*).[1636] However, the precise meaning is not clear,[1637] thus giving rise to considerable uncertainty.[1638]

The High Court of Justice of Castilla-La Mancha (*Tribunal Superior de Justicia* de *Castilla-La Mancha*) held that this requirement was met in the following circumstances: a Colombian national had contributed as a protected witness to uncovering a drug network.[1639] However, this network subsequently became aware of the witness' statements, which thus would have placed him and his family in great danger if they were to return to Colombia. A statement by the local *Guardia Civil* confirmed the witness' contribution as well as the risks of returning to Colombia. The Court therefore affirmed the requirement as returning to Colombia to apply for a visa would have endangered the safety of the witness and of his family.

b) Right to stay

The residence permit is usually granted for one year, though an application for an employment permit may be made together with this residence permit.[1640]

III. Interim conclusion

The non-refoulement principle and the Return Directive form the standard against which the purpose 'non-returnability' underpinning the regularisation is measured. The latter obliges the Member States to end the irregular stay either by return or by granting a right to stay. The view advocated here maintains that two regularisation obligations result from the

---

1636 Cf. *Ruiz Legazpi*, Los problemas jurídicos de la inmigración infantil in *Balado Ruiz-Gallegos* (ed), Inmigración, Estado y Derecho: Perspectivas desde el siglo XXI (2008) 507 (527f) and *Cobas Cobiella*, Menores y Extranjería: Situaciones de regularización, Revista Boliviana de Derecho 2015/20, 100 (113f).

1637 See *Heredia Fernández* in *Moya Escudero* 60 on the previous law.

1638 *Lázaro González/Benlloch Sanz*, Ciudadanía e integración: menores no acompañados, trata de seres humanos y víctimas de violencia de género in *Palomar Olmeda* (ed), Tratado de Extranjería[6] (2020) 881 (899f) referring to the wording in Art 196(1) REDYLE.

1639 STSJ Castilla-La Mancha 225/2016, ECLI:ES:TSJCLM:2016:225.

1640 Arts 129(2) and 130(1) REDYLE; see Chapter 3.C.II.2.

Return Directive. On the one hand, an obligation applies when the return would violate the non-refoulement principle. If one does not follow this view, there is merely special protection against deportation for migrants on the basis of the non-refoulement principle, but no obligation to grant a right to stay. On the other hand, according to the view advocated here, there is a regularisation obligation under the Return Directive in cases of permanent non-returnability, i.e. if a person cannot be deported by the respective Member State within 18 months.

Where the comparative analysis of the 'non-returnability' purpose is concerned, it can be stated at the outset that Austria and Germany, on the one hand, and Spain, on the other, have found different ways of dealing with irregularly staying foreigners (aliens) who are non-returnable. This already became clear in Chapter 3 during the discussion of the different ways of accessing social benefits and healthcare.[1641]

Spanish law does not regulate the situation of irregularly staying migrants who cannot be deported.[1642] One can speak of a factual or non-statutory toleration of irregularly staying foreigners in the circumstances identified as either no regulations exist or it is unclear how the authorities are to proceed in these situations. Contrastingly, the system of toleration was created in Austria and Germany, which represents a temporary solution for legal and factual obstacles to deportation and is intended to increase the level of legal certainty. In view of the assessment criterion, this solution is to be assessed as the most effective solution as it does not leave the persons in an even greater state of limbo and the Member States have such more control. The removal measure can thereby be enforced if the obstacle to deportation ceases, or if this is not the case, the migrant can be granted a residence permit. It should be emphasised that irregularly staying foreigners are only entitled to social benefits, access to healthcare and, under certain circumstances, access to employment once they have tolerated status. Many cases of toleration can be qualified as a preliminary step to a right to stay. Furthermore, a distinction must be made between factual and legal obstacles to deportation.

Two problems exist in Austria with regard to the *de facto* obstacles to deportation. On the one hand, the alien must not have caused the obstacles to deportation him- or herself, otherwise no card for tolerated persons and consequently no 'special protection residence permit' may be granted. On the other hand, the Federal Office for Immigration and

1641 See Chapter 3.D.
1642 With the exception of those residence permits still to be discussed.

Asylum has too much discretion in assessing whether the obstacles to deportation are attributable to the alien. This has the effect that the aliens are *de facto* not deportable, but (for the reasons explained) are also not tolerated. They thus find themselves in a similar situation as in Spain, although under Spanish law there is at least access to social benefits and healthcare for irregularly staying foreigners. Whether the departure is self-inflicted has so far been examined in Germany 'only' with regard to the entitlement to social benefits and access to employment, but not with regard to the decision whether the person is tolerated. This seems to be the most appropriate solution for the factual obstacles to deportation. Since the Orderly Return Act, however, the legal situation in Germany has come closer to that of Austria through the introduction of a special ground for toleration: 'persons whose identity is not verified'. The grant of such a toleration entails far-reaching sanctions compared to other grounds for toleration. Those periods in which one is a 'person whose identity is not verified' do not count as periods preceding the toleration. Since 21 August 2019, the legal situation for such tolerated persons thus leads to a serious deterioration of their prospects under residence law, especially with regard to obtaining the residence permits pursuant to §§ 25a and 25b AufenthG.[1643] Furthermore, a closer look reveals that the 'residence permit for persons who are enforceably required to leave the country, but whose departure is legally or factually impossible',[1644] cannot be issued if the departure could not be enforced due to the actions of the foreigner. The problem of 'self-infliction' is therefore only shifted to another level. The German solution still seems to be the more expedient in comparison to the Austrian, even if the Orderly Return Act has worsened the situation. Those affected at least have a legally secured status and, depending on the reason for toleration, access to social benefits and access to the labour market, albeit limited. The German solution, however, involves a different problem. Since it is not possible to obtain a right to stay in these cases, many foreigners remain 'stuck' in toleration for several years. The term 'chain toleration' describes this phenomenon.

With regard to the legal obstacles to deportation, specifically Article 3 ECHR, it is evident that foreigners can be granted tolerated status in Austria as well as in Germany. When measured against the opinion expressed here that in such cases there is an obligation to regularise, these persons should immediately receive a right to stay. Neither the Austrian nor the

---

1643 See Chapter 4.B.I.–II.
1644 See Chapter 4.C.II.

German 'toleration' meets this requirement. If one takes the opposite view, that in the case of a threatened violation of the non-refoulement principle there is special protection against deportation, but no obligation to regularise, toleration is then an effective mechanism in so far as a right to stay can actually be obtained afterwards.

In Spain, the foreigners concerned are either *de facto* tolerated or they can obtain a 'temporary residence permit for humanitarian reasons' due to the impossibility of going to the country of origin to apply for a visa. However, due to the very open wording, this type of residence permit does not seem to cover very many cases in practice and contributes to great legal uncertainty. The legal situation in Spain is thus hardly compatible with the requirements of Article 3 ECHR in the circumstances in which the persons are only *de facto* tolerated, as the status is so precarious and uncertain. If one includes the obtaining of the temporary residence permit, one could possibly come to the conclusion that the protection against deportation required by Article 3 ECHR is fulfilled. In addition, the view expressed in this study that there is an obligation to regularise in these cases is also followed.

As a first step it should be noted that the creation of a separate legal institution is an effective solution to prevent irregularly staying migrants who cannot be deported due to legal and factual obstacles to deportation from remaining in a state of limbo. For reasons of legal certainty, granting tolerated status for one year (as in Austrian law) is an appropriate approach. Austria and Germany provide different prospects for regularisation based on the tolerated status, which accord in essence with the obligation to regularise in the case of permanent non-returnability or the imminent violation of the non-refoulement principle.

In addition to toleration, a total of three regularisations were analysed in the three Member States, which enable the acquisition of a right to stay because of legal or factual obstacles to deportation. German law provides for a 'residence permit for banned deportation to a specific state' which, for example, covers circumstances in which subsidiary protection has been withdrawn or the person is excluded from subsidiary protection altogether. The 'banned deportation to a specific state' offers foreigners the possibility of obtaining a residence permit if they suffer from an illness that cannot be treated in the state of destination. The residence permit is granted for one year if such 'deportation ban' has been formally established and there are no grounds for exclusion. This is relevant in practice because the foreigners are only tolerated should grounds for exclusion exist. A residence permit for banned deportation to a specific state can be derived, inter alia, from Article 3 ECHR and offers protection against deportation by granting a right to stay. However, if there is a ground for exclusion, the person is only to be tolerated. An obligation to regularise is thus not followed in these cases.

The 'special protection residence permit' in Austrian law stipulates that aliens can obtain a one-year residence title if they have been tolerated for one year. Nonetheless, it is a problem that not all persons tolerated due to the imminent violation of the non-refoulement principle may obtain this residence permit. This applies foremost to the situations in which the person was entitled to asylum or subsidiary protection, but this was withdrawn because the person concerned committed a crime. The exclusion of this group of persons may be one of the reasons for the limited practical significance of this particular residence permit. Persons who were entitled to asylum or subsidiary protection thus remain in a tolerated status unless another residence permit can be obtained, with the 'residence permit for reasons of Article 8 ECHR' being the most prominent. For the remaining tolerated persons, however, this residence permit represents the decisive prospect for regularisation. In accordance with the standard of assessment, it can thus be stated that it is indeed possible to obtain a residence permit in accordance with the obligation to regularise set out here, but impossible for a significant group of persons. All of the discussed circumstances under Austrian law fulfil the special protection against deportation. If one assumes that an obligation to regularise exists, however, it must be pointed out that this obligation is contradicted by those cases that are excluded from the prospect of regularisation.

As already indicated, Spanish law contains a residence permit for those situations that go beyond international protection within the meaning of the Qualification Directive. As the provisions are broadly worded, there is great legal uncertainty as to whether and in which cases the requirements are met.

Thus, in a second step, it should be noted that three different regularisations exist in the three Member States analysed here. This already shows the distinctions present in this field of law. All three Member States have created regulations that prevent imminent non-refoulement violations pursuant to Article 3 ECHR. Nonetheless, they differ in their requirements for granting the permit and the grounds for exclusion, with considerable differences in whether deportation is temporarily suspended or whether a right to stay can be obtained immediately.

B. Social ties

The German 'residence permit in the case of permanent integration' (*Aufenthaltserlaubnis bei nachhaltiger Integration*) will be analysed first as it can be granted from six months to a maximum of two years. This is followed by a description of the 'residence permit for well-integrated juveniles and young adults' (*Aufenthaltserlaubnis für gut integrierte Jugendliche und Heranwachsende*), which allows a stay from six months to a maximum of three years. The Austrian 'residence permit for reasons of Article 8 ECHR' (*Aufenthaltstitel aus Gründen des Artikel 8 EMRK*) is then presented in relation to the right to respect one's private life as it may be granted for a minimum period of one year.

I. Germany: 'residence permit in the case of permanent integration'

The 'residence permit in the case of permanent integration' under § 25b AufenthG was introduced in 2011 together with the 'residence permit for well-integrated juveniles and young adults' in § 25a AufenthG. Both entered into force on 1 August 2015 and are derived from Article 8 ECHR.[1645] Where tolerated persons are concerned, § 25b AufenthG created for the first time the prospect of residence independent of age and a specific date.[1646] According to recent statistics, since mid-2021 there are 7,841 foreigners with a residence permit pursuant to § 25b AufenthG.[1647]

Furthermore, it is to be noted that the so-called Toleration Act (*Duldungsgesetz*), which entered into force on 1 January 2020, created a 'toleration for the purpose of employment' (*Beschäftigungsduldung*).[1648] This is relevant as foreigners (and their immediate family) who have had such tolerated status for 30 months, may acquire a residence permit in the case

1645 *Marx*, Aufenthalts-, Asyl- und Flüchtlingsrecht § 5 mn 138.

1646 Act of 23.6.2011 (BGBl I 1266). See *Röder*, §§ 25a und b AufenthG – Hiergeblieben!? Die neuen Bleiberechte bei gelungener Integration, Asylmagazin 2016, 108.

1647 BT-Drs 19/32579, 23.

1648 Cf. *Röder/Wittmann*, Spurwechsel leicht gemacht? Überlegungen zur neuen Ausbildungs- und Beschäftigungsduldung, Das Migrationspaket – Beilage zum Asylmagazin 8–9/2019, 23 (31ff); *Rosenstein/Koehler*, Beschäftigungsduldung – eine Bewertung der Neuregelung aus Sicht der Praxis, ZAR 2019, 223.

of permanent integration provided other criteria are met.[1649] This will be discussed in more detail in Chapter 4.E.IV.1.

1. Requirements

The main requirement for granting a 'residence permit in the case of permanent integration' is that the person concerned has a tolerated status pursuant to § 60(2) AufenthG, or a 'permission to remain' pursuant to § 55 AsylG (G), or holds a temporary residence or permanent settlement permit. For the purposes of this study and the definition of a regularisation, it is imperative that the applicant has tolerated status when applying for the residence permit.[1650] This requires particular consideration of the new rules introduced by the Orderly Return Act, especially those concerning the toleration of 'persons whose identity is not verified'.[1651] § 105(3) AufenthG stipulates that the duration of such tolerated status does not count towards the future 'toleration for the purpose of employment'.[1652] This drastically worsens the prospects under residence law for tolerated 'persons whose identity is not verified'. However, one must not forget that it is possible at a later time to undertake the reasonable efforts to acquire a passport and thus 'cure' the failure to perform this obligation.[1653] In this case the obligation be regarded as met and the certificate issued to the tolerated person will not contain the additional wording for 'persons whose identity is not verified'.[1654] The cure therefore allows the duration of toleration prior to the issuance of toleration for 'persons whose identity is not verified' to again have effect under residence law and can be subsequently credited to the previous periods of residence for §§ 25a and 25b AufenthG.[1655]

'Permanent integration' is also required. § 25b(1) 2nd Sent. AufenthG lists a series of requirements that are to be met, though the explanations accompanying the legislation state that comparable efforts at integration

1649 § 25b(6) AufenthG; cf. BT-Drs 19/8286, 13f.
1650 See Chapter 1.A.II.1.
1651 § 60b AufenthG.
1652 See Chapter 4.A.I.2.a.
1653 § 60b(4) AufenthG and see Chapter 4.E.IV.1.
1654 § 60b(4) 4th Sent. AufenthG.
1655 *Eichler*, Das Migrationspaket – Beilage zum Asylmagazin 8–9/2019, 71 with reference to BT-Drs 19/10047, 39.

may allow the grant of residence permit under § 25b AufenthG even if not all of the requirements under § 25b(1) 2nd Sent. AufenthG are met.[1656]

Another requirement is eight years uninterrupted residence in Germany because the deportation was suspended (i.e. the stay was tolerated), on the basis of permission to remain pending the asylum decision or by holding a temporary residence or permanent settlement permit. Here *Röder* is correct in arguing that six years residence will also suffice if there are further efforts at integration.[1657] A minimum six-year period applies if the foreigner is living with a minor, unmarried child[1658] as a family unit, for at least six years.[1659] The residence must be 'without interruption', though short interruptions up to three months are harmless.[1660]

Further requirements include the condition that the foreigner is committed to the free democratic basic order[1661] and possesses a basic knowledge of the legal and social system and the prevailing way of life in Germany.[1662]

The foreigner must also be integrated economically.[1663] On the one hand, this may be achieved by having a secure subsistence.[1664] In this respect it suffices if the foreigner can cover from his or her own resources more than half of the amount required,[1665] though the temporary receipt of benefits is not detrimental to his or her application.[1666] On the other hand, the explanations accompanying the legislation correctly highlight the difficulty in finding employment due to the uncertain residence status.[1667] It therefore suffices to consider the foreigner's previous education, training, income and family situation to determine whether 'it is to be ex-

1656 BT-Drs 18/4097, 42.

1657 *Röder*, Asylmagazin 2016, 109f with reference to BT-Drs 18/4097, 23.

1658 The legislation refers to a 'child', though it does not have to be the applicant's child; see *Röder*, Asylmagazin 2016, 109.

1659 Depending on the circumstances, a shorter period may also suffice.

1660 Cf. BT-Drs 18/4097, 43 and *Röder*, Asylmagazin 2016, 110.

1661 § 25b(1) No. 2 AufenthG. For criticism see *Röder*, Asylmagazin 2016, 111. This is more extensive than as required under § 25a(1) No. 5 AufenthG; see Chapter 4.B.II.1.

1662 As for the permanent settlement permit, these may be proven through participation in an orientation course; cf. No. 9.2.1.8 AVV-AufenthG. According to *Röder*, Asylmagazin 2016, 111 it is not clear why the exception under § 25b(3) AufenthG does not apply.

1663 § 25(1) No. 3 AufenthG.

1664 § 2(3) 1st Sent. AufenthG.

1665 *Röder*, Asylmagazin 2016, 111.

1666 § 25b(1) 3rd Sent. AufenthG; for detail see *Röder*, Asylmagazin 2016, 112.

1667 Cf. BT-Drs 18/4097, 43.

pected' that the foreigner will be able to ensure his or her subsistence. An elementary oral command of the German language equivalent to A2 level is also required and may be met in a pragmatic manner by being able to communicate with the foreigners authority without an interpreter.[1668] Pursuant to § 25b(3) AufenthG, these two requirements (economic integration and oral command of German) are waived if they cannot be fulfilled due to a physical or mental illness or disability or old age.

Finally, school-age children must be able to furnish proof that they are 'actually' attending school.[1669] Unlike for the residence permit under § 25a AufenthG, the attendance need not be 'successful'.[1670]

§ 25b(2) AufenthG contains two express grounds for exclusion: firstly, where deportation has been prevented or delayed due to intentionally providing false information or deceit with regard to identity or nationality. *Hörich/Putzar-Sattler* draw attention to the fact that the wording is much narrower than under § 25(5) 3rd Sent. AufenthG, thus the foreigner must have acted knowingly and intentionally.[1671] Secondly, a residence permit may not be granted if there is an especially serious or serious public interest in expelling the foreigner within the meaning of § 54(1) or (2) Nos. 1 and 2 AufenthG.[1672] Such interest arises if, for example, the foreigner has links to an extremist or terrorist organisation or has intentionally committed a criminal offence.[1673] Furthermore, § 25b(5) 2nd Sent. AufenthG provides that residence permit may be granted in derogation from the aforementioned block on issuing a residence title in certain cases in which an application for asylum has been rejected.[1674]

1668 § 25b(1) No. 4 AufenthG; cf. BT-Drs 18/4097, 44.

1669 § 25b(1) No. 5 AufenthG.

1670 See Chapter 4.B.II.1.

1671 *Hörich/Putzar-Sattler*, Mitwirkungspflichten im Ausländerrecht: Rechtsgutachten zu den Voraussetzungen von Sanktionen bei Nichtmitwirkung (November 2017), 9 refer to the identical wording under § 25a(2) 1st Sent. No. 1 AufenthG; see Chapter 4.B.II.1. The wording is almost identical besides that in § 25b(2) 1st Sent. No. 1 AufenthG the word 'intentionally' is used in comparison to § 25a(2) 1st Sent. No. 1 AufenthG.

1672 For detail see *Bergmann/Putzar-Sattler* in *Huber/Mantel* (eds), Kommentar Aufenthaltsgesetz/Asylgesetz[3] (2021) § 54 AufenthG.

1673 BT-Drs 18/4097, 44.

1674 See Chapter 3.B.III.2.c.

2. Right to stay

The residence permit is to be granted and extended for no more than two years,[1675] though as for § 25a AufenthG there is a degree of discretion.[1676] The residence permit allows the holder to pursue an economic activity according to § 4a(1) 1st St AufenthG.[1677] In principle a residence permit under § 25b AufenthG allows the holder to claim the Unemployment Benefits II (*Arbeitslosengeld II*) under the Social Security Code II or social assistance under the Social Security Code XII.[1678]

An extension is possible pursuant to § 8(1) AufenthG. The requirement of tolerated status does not need to be met again, the economic integration does, however.[1679] In addition to an application for a residence permit pursuant to § 25b AufenthG, a secondary application for a residence permit pursuant to § 25(5) AufenthG may also be submitted.[1680]

3. Family members: derivate right to stay

§ 25b(4) AufenthG states that a residence permit is to be granted to the spouse, civil partner and minor, unmarried children living with the foreigner who has become permanently integrated into the way of life in Germany. In other words, the family members have a derivative right to a residence permit under § 25b AufenthG. With the exception of the period of uninterrupted residence, the family member must satisfy the other requirements as described above.[1681] The legal status is comparable to that of the respective beneficiary of a residence permit under § 25b(1) AufenthG.[1682]

1675 §§ 25b(5) 1st Sent. and 26(1) 1st Sent. AufenthG.

1676 *Röcker* in *Bergmann/Dienelt* (eds), Kommentar Ausländerrecht[13] (2020) § 25b AufenthG mns 4f and *Röder*, Asylmagazin 2016, 114 and 116.

1677 This is no longer expressly regulated in § 25b(5) 2nd Sent. AufenthG following the Skilled Immigration Act; cf. BT-Drs 19/8285, 32.

1678 *Frings/Janda/Keßler/Steffen*, Sozialrecht mn 869.

1679 *Röder*, Asylmagazin 2016, 108 and 114.

1680 Along this line, see *Röcker* in *Bergmann/Dienelt* § 25b AufenthG mn 8 and see Chapter 4.C.II.

1681 See Chapter 4.B.I.1.

1682 *Röder*, Asylmagazin 2016, 114f.

II. Germany: 'residence permit for well-integrated juveniles and young adults'

The 'residence permit for well-integrated juveniles and young adults' refers to the integration in Germany and – just as for the 'residence permit in the case of permanent integration' – may be derived from Article 8 ECHR.[1683] According to the explanatory documents, it shall offer well-integrated, tolerated juveniles and young adults their own opportunity to acquire a right to stay,[1684] especially because it is independent of the cut-off date, unlike the earlier regulations in §§ 104a and 104b AufenthG governing old cases.[1685] In mid-2021, 12,819 foreigners had a residence permit pursuant to § 25a AufenthG.[1686]

1. Requirements

According to § 25a(1) AufenthG, a juvenile or young adult is to be granted a residence permit if he or she has successfully attended school in Germany for at least four years without interruption. The terms 'juvenile' (*Jugendliche*) and 'young adult' (*Heranwachsende*) are defined in accordance with the Youth Court Act (*Jugendgerichtsgesetz*; JGG):[1687] a 'juvenile' means anyone who has reached the age of 14 but not yet 18 years; 'young adult' means anyone who has reached the age of 18 but not yet 21 years (§ 1 JGG). An application is admissible if it is filed before the foreigner reaches the age of 14 or 21.[1688] These age limits are now less restrictive following the Act to Amend the Right to Remain (*Bleiberechtsänderungsgesetz*).[1689] This legislation also lowered the period of prior residence from six to four years, giving the provision a much broader scope of application. As for the 'residence permit in the case of permanent integration',[1690] this period must also be 'without interruption', though short trips abroad do

1683 *Marx*, Aufenthalts-, Asyl- und Flüchtlingsrecht § 5 mn 138.
1684 BR-Drs 704/1/10, 4.
1685 See Chapter 3.B.III.4.
1686 BT-Drs 19/32579, 23.
1687 Jugendgerichtsgesetz in the version of 25.6.2021 (BGBl I 2099); cf. BT-Drs 18/4097, 42.
1688 § 25a(1) No. 3 AufenthG. For detail see *Röder*, Asylmagazin 2016, 115 and *Röcker* in *Bergmann/Dienelt* § 25a AufenthG mns 10 and 14.
1689 *Röder*, Asylmagazin 2016, 115.
1690 See Chapter 4.B.I.1.

not have a detrimental effect.[1691] The integration is shown primarily by the successful attendance at school, though the wording refers both to the actual four-year attendance as well as the acquisition of a recognised qualification.[1692]

The 'residence permit for well-integrated juveniles and young adults' also requires the foreigner to be tolerated in the sense of § 60a(2) AufenthG, or to have a permission to remain pending an asylum decision or to hold a temporary residence or permanent settlement permit. Again, the new rules introduced by the Orderly Return Act in 2019 must be taken into consideration, especially those concerning the toleration of 'persons whose identity is not verified'.[1693]

Furthermore, there may not be any concrete evidence to suggest a lack of commitment to the German free democratic basic order, i.e. this requirement is met if there is no evidence to the contrary.[1694] It also needs to be apparent in consideration of the foreigner's efforts at integration and way of life that the foreigner will be able to integrate into the German way of life.[1695]

According to § 25a(1) 3rd Sent. AufenthG, the residence permit is to be denied if deportation has been suspended on the basis of false information furnished by the foreigner or on the grounds of deception by the foreigner as to his or her identity or nationality. This corresponds basically with the exclusion for a 'residence permit in the case of permanent integration' and thus the explanations above apply.[1696]

2. Right to stay

The residence permit is to be granted, though as for § 25b AufenthG there is a degree of discretion.[1697] The permit may be issued and extended in each instance for a maximum of three years.[1698] It allows the holder to

---

1691 *Röcker* in *Bergmann/Dienelt* § 25a AufenthG mn 11.

1692 *Röcker* in *Bergmann/Dienelt* § 25a AufenthG mns 12f; contrast with *Röder*, Asylmagazin 2016, 116.

1693 § 60b AufenthG and see Chapter 4.B.I.1. for detail.

1694 § 25a(1) No. 5 AufenthG. *Röder*, Asylmagazin 2016, 116.

1695 *Röcker* in *Bergmann/Dienelt* § 25a AufenthG mn 15.

1696 See Chapter 4.B.I.1.

1697 *Röder*, Asylmagazin 2016, 116.

1698 § 26(1) 1st Sent. AufenthG.

pursue an economic activity according to § 4a(1) 1st Sent. AufenthG.[1699] An extension is possible pursuant to § 8(1) AufenthG, though the requirements concerning the maximum age and tolerated status do not need to be met again.[1700] In principle a residence permit under § 25a AufenthG allows the holder to claim the Unemployment Benefits II under the Social Insurance Code II or social assistance under the Social Insurance Code XII.[1701]

In addition to an application for a residence permit pursuant to § 25a AufenthG, a secondary application for a residence permit pursuant to § 25(5) AufenthG may also be submitted.[1702]

3. Family members: derivate right to stay

§ 25a(2) AufenthG allows the grant of a residence not only to parents or a parent having the right of care and custody of a foreign minor who holds a residence permit under § 25a AufenthG but also to minor children, a spouse or civil partner. This takes into account the protection of family life as understood by Article 6 GG and Article 8 ECHR.[1703] In principle the spouse and civil partner must live with the permit holder as a family unit and must satisfy all requirements already listed in relation to § 25a(1) AufenthG.[1704] Particular reference is to be made here to the independent means of subsistence, for which stricter requirements apply than for a 'residence permit in the case of permanent integration'.[1705] Minor, unmarried children merely have to be living with the permit holder as a family unit.[1706]

1699 This is no longer expressly regulated in § 25a(4) AufenthG since the Skilled Immigration Act; cf. BT-Drs 19/8285, 32.

1700 *Röder*, Asylmagazin 2016, 116.

1701 *Frings/Janda/Keßler/Steffen*, Sozialrecht mn 853.

1702 In this sense, *Röcker* in *Bergmann/Dienelt* § 25a AufenthG mn 6 and see Chapter 4.C.II.

1703 *Röcker* in *Bergmann/Dienelt* § 25a AufenthG mn 21.

1704 § 25a(2) 3rd Sent. AufenthG and see Chapter 4.B.II.1.

1705 See Chapter 4.B.I.3.

1706 § 25a(2) 5th Sent. AufenthG.

III. Austria: 'residence permits for reasons of Article 8 ECHR'

It is readily apparent from the name 'residence permits for reasons of Article 8 ECHR' that such permits are based on the right to respect for one's private and family life under Article 8 ECHR.[1707] It is also referred to as a *Bleiberecht* – a right to remain.[1708] This type of residence permit has two elements. The following will focus on the general requirements and the right to respect for private life; the right to respect for family life is discussed in relation to 'family unity'. As described above,[1709] there are no reliable statistics for the category of 'residence permits for exceptional circumstances' in Austria and therefore it is not clear how many of these permits are granted annually.

1. Requirements

The return decision has to be permanently inadmissible for reasons of private and family life.[1710] The Federal Office for Immigration and Asylum is to balance the alien's interests in remaining in Austria for reasons of private (and family) life against the interests of the Austrian state in removing the alien.[1711] Austrian law has codified the balance of interests required by the ECtHR in statute law.[1712] According to § 9(2) BFA-VG, consideration is due to the type, duration and legality of the stay,[1713] an actual family life,[1714] the degree to which the private life is worthy of protection,[1715] the degree of integration, the ties to the country of origin,[1716] and the lack of a

1707 See just VwGH 4.8.2016, Ra 2015/21/0249.
1708 See *Oswald*, Bleiberecht.
1709 See Chapter 3.A.III.1.
1710 § 9(2) BFA-VG.
1711 VfGH 29.9.2007, B 1150/07 and VwGH 12.11.2015, Ra 2015/21/0101; in detail *Oswald*, Bleiberecht; *Hinterberger*, Asyl- und Fremdenpolizeirecht 66–69; *Rössl*, Staatsangehörige zweiter Klasse?, FABL 2/2017-I, 37 (38).
1712 A comparable balance of interests has developed in Germany in relation to § 25(5) AufenthG; see Chapter 4.C.II.1. However, one difference is that the various criteria are not anchored in law. Several criteria that have been developed in the case law on Art 8 ECHR are, however, anchored in §§ 25a and 25b AufenthG; see Chapter 4.B.I.–II.
1713 VwGH 23.6.2015, Ra 2015/22/0026.
1714 VfGH 28.6.2003, G 78/00.
1715 VwGH 28.4.2015, Ra 2014/18/0146.
1716 VfGH 10.3.2011, B 1565/10 ua.

criminal record. A case-by-case assessment of all of the facts is necessary in order to determine whether the return decision constitutes an inadmissible violation of the areas protected by Article 8 ECHR.[1717]

With regard to private life and the degree of integration, the Federal Office for Immigration and Asylum has to take into account in particular whether the alien has undergone education or training during his or her stay in Austria, activity and memberships in associations, and whether he or she has taken steps towards integration into the labour market.[1718] All facts that have come to the attention of the Federal Office for Immigration and Asylum during its investigation must be taken into account with regard to the substantive assessment of integration and private and family life. In practice, it is therefore recommended to submit a statement informing the Federal Office for Immigration and Asylum of all relevant facts.

According to case law, where the stay in Austria is more than ten years, the personal interest in remaining prevails over Austria's interest in deportation, provided that the alien has integrated him- or herself professionally and socially and his or her behaviour does not pose a threat to public order and security.[1719] However, it must also be taken into account whether the private life was created at a time when the persons concerned were aware of their insecure residence status.[1720] Furthermore, according to case law, the length of stay can depend on the alien's actions, such as not presenting a passport.[1721] It therefore follows from the above that the Austrian 'right to remain' refers to 'roots' that have already taken hold, whereas it will be shown that in comparison the 'social roots' in Spain refer in principle to future roots.[1722] An application for a 'residence permit for reasons of Article 8 ECHR' is to be rejected if there are no altered circumstances which necessitate a further evaluation or a re-evaluation of the return decision (*res iudicata*).[1723]

1717 VwGH 6.9.2018, Ra 2018/18/0026 with further references.
1718 See only for past employment VwGH 15.3.2018, Ra 2017/21/0203.
1719 VwGH 10.9.2018, Ra 2018/19/0169 with further references.
1720 § 9(2) No. 8 BFA-VG; VwGH 15.3.2018, Ra 2018/21/0034.
1721 VwGH 29.8.2018, Ra 2018/22/0180 with further references.
1722 See Chapter 4.E.I.
1723 § 58(10) AsylG (A) and VwGH 16.12.2015, Ro 2015/21/0037 for detail.

2. Right to stay

The general explanations in Chapter 3.A.III.2.d. apply here. The Federal Office for Immigration and Asylum has to grant a 'standard residence permit' if it comes to the conclusion that the return decision is permanently inadmissible due to the need to protect private and family life. A 'residence permit plus' is to be granted if the alien also meets the additional requirements. It should be emphasised that the alien – in comparison to the other 'residence permits for exceptional circumstances' – is legally entitled to a residence permit if he or she satisfies the requirements.[1724] The authorities have no discretionary powers in this regard.[1725]

Furthermore, it is to be noted that in the case of a rejection of an application for a 'residence permit for reasons of Article 8 ECHR', the law does not provide for an examination of the requirements of § 57 AsylG (A), i.e. the 'special protection residence permit'.[1726]

IV. Interim conclusion

The analysis has shown that the three Member States recognise humanitarian considerations as a legitimate reason for granting a right to stay due to 'social ties'. Here, the right to respect one's private life anchored in Article 8 ECHR serves as the legal standard. According to ECtHR case law, there is no general obligation to grant a right to stay, though such right may be granted in exceptional circumstances. It instead suffices that States protect the migrants concerned from possible expulsion.

The German 'residence permit in the case of permanent integration' and the German 'residence permit for well-integrated juveniles and young adults' overlap in several respects. 'Integration' is at the heart of both, despite the differences regarding the respective personal scope of application: the 'residence permit for well-integrated juveniles and young adults' aims at persons between the ages of 14 and 21, a much narrower scope of application than the 'residence permit in the case of permanent integration',

1724 In this sense, *Filzwieser/Frank/Kloibmüller/Raschhofer*, Asyl- und Fremdenrecht § 55 AsylG mn 2.

1725 Since 2015, the Federal Administrative Court may also decide on the grant of a 'residence permit for reasons of Article 8 ECHR'; see *Filzwieser/Frank/Kloibmüller/Raschhofer*, Asyl- und Fremdenrecht § 55 AsylG mn 5.

1726 VwGH 12.11.2015, Ra 2015/21/0101 and 16.12.2016, Ra 2015/21/0166.

which applies in principle to all tolerated foreigners.[1727] Furthermore, the 'residence permit for well-integrated juveniles and young adults' also requires four years of successful school attendance in Germany, which serves to demonstrate that integration has been 'achieved'. In contrast, the 'residence permit in the case of permanent integration' requires the person to have been residing in Germany for eight years on the basis of tolerated status or through permission to remain. Economic integration is also a requirement for the 'residence permit in the case of permanent integration', whereby the foreigner shows that he or she is able to sustain him- or herself. However, it is possible to determine that this ability is 'to be expected' on the basis of certain criteria. This is particularly relevant for tolerated persons due to their insecure residence status and the resulting difficulty in finding employment. In addition, oral German language skills at A2 level are required and can be demonstrated when appearing before the authorities. A reason for refusal that applies to both residence permits is that deportation may not be suspended on the basis of false information provided by the person concerned. Both are to be granted for two ('residence permit in the case of permanent integration') or three ('residence permit for well-integrated juveniles and young adults') years if the requirements are met and grant entitlement to social benefits and access to employment. The statistics show that the 'residence permit for well-integrated juveniles and young adults' is granted to about twice as many foreigners as the 'residence permit in the case of permanent integration'. This can probably be explained by the – relatively – simpler requirements.

Both residence permits have the special feature of a derivative residence permit for family members. The custodial parent or the minor siblings of a well-integrated juvenile or young adult can thus acquire a right to stay, provided that they live in a family unit with him or her. Although this takes into account the protection of the family within the meaning of Article 6 GG and Article 8 ECHR, it would be more appropriate for the family members to be granted an independent right to stay and, put simply, not be 'dependent' on the original beneficiary.

The Austrian 'residence permit for reasons of Article 8 ECHR' is the third and final right to stay falling under the regularisation purpose 'social ties'. In contrast to the two German residence permits, this particular Austrian residence permit has an entirely different structure and is strongly

1727 However, one must also consider the provisions introduced by the Orderly Return Act in 2019, specifically those concerning 'persons whose identity is not verified'; see Chapter 4.A.I.2.a. and Chapter 4.B.I.1.–2.

oriented towards the ECtHR case law on Article 8 ECHR. Despite a lack of statistics, it may be assumed that this is the most important regularisation in Austrian law because the requirements are easier to meet when compared to the requirements for the other regularisations. A list of criteria is thus anchored in statute law, according to which a balancing of interests is to be carried out between the private (or family) interests of the foreigner in remaining in Austria and the Austrian interests in removal. Overall, the Austrian 'right to remain' therefore refers to a person who is firmly rooted. Compared to the German residence permits, the Austrian variant appears to be more 'flexible', but it is also more difficult to 'know' in which cases a right to stay will be granted. From the perspective of legal certainty, therefore, clearly defined conditions for granting residence permits seem to be preferable, though they have the disadvantage that they generally do not take into account all the reasons that speak for or against the alien's remaining in the country.

In short, both Austria and Germany comply in principle with the protection against expulsion according to Article 8 ECHR (private life). Spanish law does not provide a residence permit on grounds of 'social ties' and thus one may be forgiven for thinking that Spain is not meeting its obligations under international law. A closer look shows the protection against expulsion under Article 8 ECHR is provided by other residence permits, especially the temporary residence permit on grounds of 'social roots'.[1728] This type of permit is primarily granted on the basis of an employment contract and therefore falls under 'employment and training' discussed below.

C. Family unity

The first regularisation discussed in relation to the purpose of 'family unity'[1729] is the Spanish 'residence permit for a child not born in Spain' (*residencia del hijo no nacido en España de residente*) as the duration of the residence permit is usually derived from a parent or guardian and is generally not granted for a minimum period. This is followed by the residence permit granted in Germany to persons who are enforceably required to leave the country, but whose departure is legally or factually impossible (*Aufenthaltserlaubnis für vollziehbar Ausreisepflichtige, wenn die Ausreise aus*

1728 See Chapter 4.E.I.
1729 See already Chapter 1.B.III.3.

rechtlichen oder tatsächlichen Gründen unmöglich ist), as such permit can be granted for a period of six months up to a maximum of three years. The Austrian 'residence permits for reasons of Article 8 ECHR' (*Aufenthaltstitel aus Gründen des Artikel 8 EMRK*) is then presented, which is limited to one year. The analysis turns to the Austrian 'Red-White-Red – Card plus' for unaccompanied minor aliens in the care of foster parents or the child and youth service (*'Rot-Weiß-Rot – Karte plus' für unbegleitete minderjährige Fremde in Obhut von Pflegeeltern oder des Kinder- und Jugendhilfeträgers*), which is granted for two years and, finally, to the Spanish 'temporary residence permit on grounds of family roots' (*autorización de residencia temporal por razones de arraigo familiar*), which in certain cases is granted for five years.

I. Spain: 'residence permit for a child not born in Spain'

Article 186 REDYLE stipulates that minors,[1730] who are not born in Spain, may be granted a residence permit. According to *Fernández Collados*, the features of this type of permit allow for its classification as 'residence for reasons of roots' even though it is not listed in Article 124 REDYLE.[1731] It is also commonly referred in Spain to as 'rooted minors' (*arraigo menores*). The statistics do not contain precise information on how many residence permits were granted for this reason.[1732] There are many arguments for the assertion that the 'residence permit for a child not born in Spain' is derived in principle from Article 8 ECHR, especially with regard to the respect for the best interests of the child.[1733]

According to Article 185 REDYLE, children born in Spain to foreigners lawfully residing in Spain will automatically acquire the same residence permit to which any of their parents are entitled.[1734] This is not a regularisation as understood by this study and therefore this provision will not be discussed.[1735] Furthermore, Article 35(7) LODYLE provides that

---

1730 See on the legal status of minors in the Spanish law on foreigners *Cobas Cobiella*, Revista Boliviana de Derecho 2015/20, 105ff.

1731 Cf. *Fernández Collados* in *Palomar Olmeda* 424f.

1732 See Chapter 3.C.III.1. See however *Lázaro González/Benlloch Sanz* in *Palomar Olmeda* 902f, who assumes that very few have been granted.

1733 Art 3(1) UN Convention on the Rights of the Child.

1734 Cf. *Cobas Cobiella*, Revista Boliviana de Derecho 2015/20, 108.

1735 See Chapter 1.A.II.

an unaccompanied minor[1736] will be staying lawfully from the moment the public administration assumes guardianship.[1737] In a broad sense, the assumption of guardianship could constitute a regularisation, but will not be analysed as it is not a separate, individual decision that grants a right to stay.[1738] The guardian may subsequently apply for a residence permit,[1739] but this only has a declarative effect in this case. A considerable problem in practice is posed by the situation where minors reach the age of majority and the guardian has not applied for a residence permit, which is why the minor's stay becomes irregular.[1740] In this case, an application for a separate 'temporary residence permit for exceptional circumstances' can be made according to Article 198 REDYLE.[1741]

1. Requirements

The child must be a minor[1742] who has resided in Spain for a continuous two-year period. Where minors are of compulsory school age (6–17), they must also show that they have regularly attended school.[1743] This resem-

1736 Cf. in general on unaccompanied minors *Pérez Rey*, Art 35 LODYLE in *Monereo Pérez/Fernández Avilés/Triguero Martínez* (eds), Comentario a la ley y al reglamento de Extranjería, Inmigración e Integración Social² (2013) 584 and *Asín Cabrera*, La residencia y protección de los menores inmigrantes no acompañados in *Boza Martínez/Donaire Villa/Moya Malapeira* (eds), La nueva regulación de la inmigración y la extranjería en España (2012) 307 (308ff).

1737 Cf. *Lázaro González/Benlloch Sanz* in *Palomar Olmeda* 901–904.

1738 See Chapter 1.A.II.3.a.

1739 Art 196 REDYLE; cf. on the procedure and the requirements *Asín Cabrera* in *Boza Martínez/Donaire Villa/Moya Malapeira* 315–317 and *Pérez Rey* in *Monereo Pérez/Fernández Avilés/Triguero Martínez* 609–611.

1740 On the problems when reaching the age of majority, see *Pérez Rey* in *Monereo Pérez/Fernández Avilés/Triguero Martínez* 611; *Asín Cabrera* in *Boza Martínez/Donaire Villa/Moya Malapeira* 317ff and *Gimeno Monterde*, Menores extranjeros no acompañados. Una cuestión compleja para las políticas públicas y sociales, Revista de Derecho Migratorio y Extranjería 2010/25, 55 (58–61).

1741 Cf. *Pérez Rey* in *Monereo Pérez/Fernández Avilés/Triguero Martínez* 611f and *Asín Cabrera* in *Boza Martínez/Donaire Villa/Moya Malapeira* 319f.

1742 On the problems in proving minority *Defensor del Pueblo*, ¿Menores o Adultos? Procedimientos para la determinación de la edad (2012), https://www.defensordelpueblo.es/wp-content/uploads/2015/05/2011-09-Menores-o-Adultos-Procedimientos-para-la-determinaci%C3%B3n-de-la-edad1.pdf (31.7.2022) and *Ruiz Legazpi* in *Balado Ruiz-Gallegos* 511ff.

1743 Art 186(2) REDYLE; cf. *Fernández Collados* in *Palomar Olmeda* 424f.

bles the requirement for the German 'residence permit in the case of permanent integration'.[1744]

Furthermore, at least one parent of the child concerned must be residing lawfully. This is also provided for by law for children whose guardian is a lawfully residing foreigner or Spaniard, or if the guardian is an institution established in Spain.[1745] In any case the parent or guardian must prove that they have adequate accommodation[1746] and the necessary financial resources.[1747] In 2022, an adult with one child had to prove an income of more than 868 euro.[1748]

2. Right to stay

The application may only be made by a parent or the guardian. The 'residence permit for a child not born in Spain' constitutes one of the 'temporary residence permits for exceptional circumstances', though some procedural provisions as well as the extension procedure are based on the family reunification provisions.[1749]

The duration of the residence permit is determined by the duration of the residence permit of the parent or guardian.[1750] If the parent or guardian is an EU citizen, the residence permit is limited to five years. When the minor reaches working age (16), the residence permit also entitles him to take up any gainful employment.[1751] *Cobas Cobiella* rightly points out that this provision is of particular relevance, as it automatically enables entry into the labour market when the minor reaches working age.[1752]

1744 See Chapter 4.B.I.1.

1745 Art 186(1) REDYLE.

1746 Cf. for detail Instrucción DGI/SGRJ/2011.

1747 Art 186(1) REDYLE in conjunction with Art 18(2) LODYLE.

1748 According to Art 54 REDYLE, the necessary financial resources represent more than 150% of the monthly public revenue index (*Indicador Público de Renta de Efectos Múltiples*; IPREM). In 2022, the IPREM was set at 579,02 euro; www.iprem.com.es/ (31.7.2022).

1749 Art 186(4) REDYLE; cf. *Fernández Collados* in *Palomar Olmeda* 425 and *Cobas Cobiella*, Revista Boliviana de Derecho 2015/20, 109.

1750 Art 186(3) REDYLE.

1751 Art 186(5) REDYLE; cf. *Cobas Cobiella*, Revista Boliviana de Derecho 2015/20, 110.

1752 *Cobas Cobiella*, Revista Boliviana de Derecho 2015/20, 109.

II. Germany: 'residence permit for persons who are enforceably required to leave the country, but whose departure is legally or factually impossible'

Pursuant to § 25(5) AufenthG, a foreigner who is enforceably required to leave Germany may be granted a residence permit if departure is legally or factually impossible and the obstacle to deportation is not likely to be removed in the foreseeable future.[1753] The same also applies for the 'residence permit for banned deportation to a specific state'.[1754] It is essential that the obstacle to deportation must not be 'temporary'[1755] and that the person cannot leave the country, though the term 'departure' (*Ausreise*) covers both the compulsory return as well as the voluntary departure.[1756]

The protection against deportation in § 60(5) and (7) AufenthG is pure German law in origin and falls under the remaining national competence,[1757] though one must not forget that the provision can also be derived from international and EU law, more precisely Article 3 ECHR and the Return Directive.[1758] This type of residence permit also requires an assessment of Article 8 ECHR and therefore falls under the purpose 'family unity'. The factual obstacles to deportation indeed make it possible to grant a residence permit, which in turn suggest that the residence permit may fall under the sub-category 'non-refoulement under the ECHR and CFR or factual reasons' under 'non-returnability', though this is not the decisive reason for granting the permit and therefore it would be inappropriate to discuss this permit in that context.

The residence permit was introduced in order to solve the aforementioned problem of 'chain tolerations' (*Kettenduldungen*),[1759] though this has only been partially successful.[1760] One reason is that it is incredibly difficult to acquire a residence permit where there are factual obstacles

1753 Cf. *Göbel-Zimmermann/Hupke* in *Huber/Mantel* § 25 AufenthG mn 53 and *Maaßen/Kluth* in *Kluth/Heusch* § 25 AufenthG mn 127.

1754 See Chapter 4.A.II.2.

1755 *Göbel-Zimmermann/Hupke* in *Huber/Mantel* § 25 AufenthG mn 58.

1756 Cf. *Maaßen/Kluth* in *Kluth/Heusch* § 25 AufenthG mn 128 with further references.

1757 *Hruschka/Mantel* in *Huber/Mantel* § 60 AufenthG mn 18; in agreement *Koch* in *Kluth/Heusch* § 60 AufenthG mns 39f.

1758 See Chapter 1.B.III.1.b.

1759 Cf. *Marx*, Aufenthalts-, Asyl- und Flüchtlingsrecht § 5 mn 73 with further references.

1760 Cf. *Maaßen/Kluth* in *Kluth/Heusch* § 25 AufenthG mns 123f and see Chapter 4.A.I.2.d.

to deportation as certain acts by the foreigner, which prevent the departure, are grounds for denying the application.[1761] By mid-2021 over 51,000 foreigners held a residence permit under § 25(5) AufenthG,[1762] thereby making it the most important regularisation in German law.

1. Requirements

According to case law from the Federal Administrative Court, 'internal obstacles to deportation' according to § 60(5) and (7) AufenthG are primarily taken into consideration in relation to § 25(5) AufenthG,[1763] though the right to respect for family life under Article 8 ECHR is afforded a special status.[1764] However, the 'residence permit for well-integrated juveniles and young adults' (§ 25a AufenthG) and the 'residence permit in the case of permanent integration' (§ 25b AufenthG) have greatly narrowed the scope of § 25(5) AufenthG.[1765] The examination of whether there is a right to respect for private or family life under Article 8 ECHR follows the usual rules, whereby there is first an examination of whether there is an infringement of the protected right and whether this is proportional.[1766] Unlike Austrian law, German law does not codify the required balance of interests.[1767] However, the protection of one's private life applies especially to foreigners who have resided in Germany for several years and are accordingly 'rooted'.[1768] The tolerated stay is also to be taken into account.[1769] The protection of one's family life applies between spouses or

1761 See Chapter 4.C.II.1.
1762 BT-Drs 19/32579, 22.
1763 See Chapter 4.A.I.2.a.
1764 Cf. *Göbel-Zimmermann/Hupke* in *Huber/Mantel* § 25 AufenthG mns 67ff; *Marx*, Aufenthalts-, Asyl- und Flüchtlingsrecht § 5 mn 75 with further references.
1765 See Chapter 4.B.I. –II.
1766 Cf. *Welte*, Die Wahrung des Grundsatzes der Verhältnismäßigkeit im Ausweisungsrecht, InfAuslR 2019, 176.
1767 See Chapter 4.B.III.1.
1768 Cf. *Marx*, Aufenthalts-, Asyl- und Flüchtlingsrecht § 5 mns 79f and 83–85; *Eckertz-Höfer*, Neuere Entwicklungen in Gesetzgebung und Rechtsprechung zum Schutze des Privatlebens, ZAR 2008, 41; *Eckertz-Höfer*, Neuere Entwicklungen in Gesetzgebung und Rechtsprechung zum Schutze des Privatlebens: Fortsetzung des Beitrags aus Heft 2/2008, ZAR 2008, 93.
1769 Cf. *Marx*, Aufenthalts-, Asyl- und Flüchtlingsrecht § 5 mns 90f.

in the parent-child relationship, which requires consideration of the actual family life.[1770]

Furthermore, the "national deportation bans' under § 60(5) and (7) AufenthG may also lead to the grant of the residence permit discussed here. This requires, however, consideration of the relationship to the 'residence permit for banned deportation to a specific state' under § 25(3) AufenthG.[1771] Where such a ban exists, the permit pursuant to § 25(3) AufenthG takes 'priority'[1772] as it affords better access to the labour market and social benefits. However, if there are grounds for exclusion under § 25(3) 2nd Sent. AufenthG, the grant of a residence permit according to § 25(5) AufenthG can be considered subsidiarily.

A residence permit may only be issued if the foreigner is prevented from leaving the country through no fault of his or her own.[1773] According to § 25(5) 4th Sent. AufenthG, fault is deemed to exist in particular if the foreigner furnishes false information, deceives the authorities with regard to his or her identity or nationality or fails to meet reasonable demands to eliminate the obstacles to departure. *Hörich/Putzar-Sattler* aptly state that a residence permit cannot be issued if departure has been prevented or substantially delayed due to an act or omission attributable to the foreigner – there must be a causal link between the foreigner's behaviour and the existence of an obstacle to departure.[1774] At the same time, however, the two authors emphasise that the foreigners authority has a 'duty to inform and instigate' the possible removal of these obstacles. The overall conclusion is that the behaviour of the person concerned plays a central role in the issuance of this residence permit and that it is difficult in practice to issue it due to factual obstacles since voluntary entry into the country of origin will often be possible.[1775] This is probably one of the reasons why the prevention of the 'chain toleration' phenomenon intended by the legislator has not been fully successful. [1776] The law may provide a prospect of regularisation, but this is illusionary as it often cannot be achieved.

1770 Cf. *Marx*, Aufenthalts-, Asyl- und Flüchtlingsrecht § 5 mns 79, 81–85.

1771 See Chapter 4.A.II.2.

1772 *Huber/Eichenhofer/Endres de Oliveira*, Aufenthaltsrecht mn 590: '*vorrangig*'.

1773 § 25(5) 3rd Sent. AufenthG.

1774 *Hörich/Putzar-Sattler*, Mitwirkungspflichten im Ausländerrecht: Rechtsgutachten zu den Voraussetzungen von Sanktionen bei Nichtmitwirkung (November 2017), 8.

1775 In this sense, *Marx*, Aufenthalts-, Asyl- und Flüchtlingsrecht § 5 mn 78.

1776 See Chapter 4.I.2.d and Chapter 4.C.II.

2. Right to stay

The statements made on the residence permit pursuant to § 25(3) AufenthG are also relevant for the residence permit under § 25(5) AufenthG.[1777] As already explained, the foreigners authority (after consulting the Federal Office for Migration and Refugees[1778]) decides whether there is a 'national deportation ban' at its own discretion.[1779] However, if a person has already been tolerated for 18 months, the discretionary rule becomes a mandatory rule.[1780] The residence permit can be issued for a maximum of three years, but under certain circumstances for a maximum of six months, as long as 'the foreigner has not been legally resident in the federal territory for at least 18 months'.[1781]

As a side note, the 'national deportation bans' are also examined in the asylum process and determined by the Federal Office for Migration and Refugees if the requirements are met.[1782] The residence permit can be applied for subsequently, whereby the foreigners authority is bound by the decision of the Federal Office for Migration and Refugees.[1783] However, this case does not qualify as a regularisation and is therefore not dealt with in more detail.

Until the Skilled Immigration Act, the residence permit under § 25(5) AufenthG did not directly entitle the holder to engage in employed activities; rather, a permit from the foreigners authority was required. Now, access to employment, which also includes self-employment, results directly from § 4a(1) 1st Sent. AufenthG.[1784] This represents a significant improvement.

The residence permit is accompanied by a claim to social benefits according to the Act on Benefits for Asylum Seekers if the decision on the suspension of deportation (i.e. toleration) was made less than 18

1777 See Chapter 4.A.II.2.b.

1778 § 72(2) AufenthG.

1779 Cf. *Maaßen/Kluth* in *Kluth/Heusch* § 25 AufenthG mn 151.

1780 § 25(5) 2nd Sent. AufenthG; cf. *Maaßen/Kluth* in *Kluth/Heusch* § 25 AufenthG mns 152–154.

1781 § 26(1) 1st Sent. AufenthG.

1782 § 31(1) 4th Sent. AsylG (G) and see Chapter 4.A.I.2.a.

1783 § 42 1st Sent. AsylG (G); cf. however *Marx*, Aufenthalts-, Asyl- und Flüchtlingsrecht § 5 mns 36f.

1784 Cf. *Schuster/Voigt*, Asylmagazin 2020, 65f.

months beforehand.[1785] Holders of a residence permit pursuant to § 25(5) AufenthG receive benefits pursuant to § 1(1) No. 3(c) AsylbLG until this point in time (18-month suspension of deportation).[1786] After receiving benefits for a period of at least 18 months under the Act on Benefits for Asylum Seekers, they are entitled to analogous benefits under the Social Insurance Code XII if they have not abusively influenced the duration of their stay themselves and have resided in Germany without significant interruption.[1787] The required period of prior residence was extended from 15 to 18 months following the Third Act to amend the Act on Benefits for Asylum Seekers.[1788]

III. Austria: 'residence permits for reasons of Article 8 ECHR'

As is clear from the name, the 'residence permits for reasons of Article 8 ECHR' are based on the right to respect for one's private and family life under Article 8 ECHR.[1789] It is also referred to as a *Bleiberecht* – a right to remain.[1790] This type of residence permit has two elements. The following will focus on the right to family life.[1791] As already noted,[1792] there are no reliable statistics for the category of 'residence permits for exceptional circumstances' in Austria, and therefore it is not clear how many of these permits are granted annually.

1. Requirements

As already described in Chapter 4.B.III., the granting of a 'residence permit for reasons of Article 8 ECHR' requires a balancing of the (private and) family interests of the alien to remain in Austria and the public interest of the Austrian state in the removal. According to case law, the separation of

---

1785 Cf. *Voigt*, Die wundersame Welt des § 25(5) AufenthG, Asylmagazin 2015, 152 and *Frings/Janda/Keßler/Steffen*, Sozialrecht mn 836.

1786 Cf. *Korff* in *Rolfs/Giesen/Keikebohm/Udsching* § 1 AsylbLG mns 11–14.

1787 § 2(1) AsylbLG; see Fn 1014.

1788 For criticism see *Genge*, Das Migrationspaket – Beilage zum Asylmagazin 8–9/2019, 18f.

1789 See just VwGH 4.8.2016, Ra 2015/21/0249.

1790 See *Oswald*, Bleiberecht.

1791 See Chapter 4.B.III.

1792 See Chapter 3.A.III.1.

spouses, for example, is only admissible if great weight is to be attached to the public interest in the removal, e.g. if the alien commits a criminal offence or has always intended to circumvent the regulations in the law regarding aliens.[1793] The commitment of the alien to his or her spouse is of particular importance in the relation to the balance of interests. According to the Supreme Administrative Court, in such a case more detailed findings must be made on the living conditions of the alien and his or her spouse, in particular on the living conditions, the nature of their occupations and the income earned, but also, for example, on the question of the command of the German language as well as on the ties to the country of origin and the possibility and reasonableness of leading a family life outside Austria.[1794] For a family life to exist within the meaning of Article 8 ECHR, however, it is not a matter of a formal marriage, but rather of close personal and factual family ties expressed in a number of circumstances, such as living together, the length of the relationship or having children together.[1795]

The best interests of the child are at the centre of the consideration of interests concerning children and minors.[1796] The Supreme Administrative Court attaches particular importance to the ties to the home country, especially where the children were born, in which country and in which cultural and linguistic environment they lived, where they completed their schooling, whether they speak the language of the home country, and especially whether they are of an adaptable age.[1797]

1793 VwGH 6.9.2018, Ra 2018/18/0026 with further references.

1794 VwGH 2.5.2018, Ra 2018/18/0159.

1795 VwGH 29.11.2017, Ra 2017/18/0425 with reference to ECtHR case law.

1796 See just VwGH 30.8.2017, Ra 2017/18/0070–0072 with further references and Art 3(1) UN Convention on the Rights of the Child; cf. see also Bericht der unabhängigen Kommission für den Schutz der Kinderrechte und des Kindeswohls im Asyl- und Fremdenrecht (13.7.2021), https://www.bmj.gv.at/dam/jcr:0a8466e4-c24a-4fd2-bfbc-c8b11facba2f/Bericht%20der%20Kindeswohlkommission_13.%20Juli%202021%20(Langfassung).pdf (31.7.2022) and Leitfaden „Kindeswohl im Asyl- und Fremdenrecht", https://www.bvwg.gv.at/Kindeswohl_-_Leitfaden_Fassung_02_2022.pdf?8mk1yf (31.7.2022).

1797 VwGH 21.3.2018, Ra 2017/18/0333 and see § 9(2) No. 5 BFA-VG.

2. Right to stay

Reference is made to the explanations in Chapter 3.A.III.2.d. and Chapter 4.B.III.2.

IV. Austria: 'Red-White-Red – Card plus' for unaccompanied minor aliens in the care of foster parents or the child and youth service'

§ 41a(10) NAG contains a regularisation according to which a 'Red-White-Red – Card plus' (*Rot-Weiß-Rot – Karte plus*) is to be issued to unaccompanied minor aliens in the care of foster parents or the child and youth service. It is the only regularisation in Austrian law that does not fall under the category of 'residence permits for exceptional circumstances'.[1798]

This residence permit was previously regulated by § 69(1) No. 4 NAG until the amendments via BGBl I 87/2012. Although it was the only one of the four sets of circumstances covered by that provision which fell under the category 'special protection', it was not subsequently included as a 'special protection residence permit'.[1799] According to statistics, only 68 minors held a 'Red-White-Red – Card plus' in January 2021, which indicates that the residence title is not very significant in practice.[1800] The 'Red-White-Red – Card plus' is in principle derived from Article 8 ECHR, as it primarily serves to protect the best interests of the child.[1801] Without being able to go into detail, however, it likely exceeds the obligation under human rights law.

1798 However, § 30a NAG is also to be taken into consideration; see Chapter 4.D.I.1.a. and Fn 1847 especially.

1799 ErläutRV 1803 BlgNR 24. GP, 46. On § 69a(1) No. 4 NAG see *Kutscher/Völker/Witt*, Niederlassungs- und Aufenthaltsrecht² (2010) 182.

1800 *Bundesministerium für Inneres*, Niederlassungs- und Aufenthaltsstatistik (January 2021), https://www.bmi.gv.at/312/statistiken/files/NAG_2021/Niederlassungs_und_Aufenthaltsstatistik_Jaenner_2021.pdf (31.7.2022) 47.

1801 See also Art 3(1) UN Convention on the Rights of the Child and in this sense *Peyrl* in *Abermann/Czech/Kind/Peyrl* § 41a NAG mn 18.

1. Requirements

The only requirement to obtain such a residence permit stipulates that the person has to be an unaccompanied minor alien.[1802] This term is legally defined as an alien under the age of 18 who is not accompanied by an adult[1803] responsible for him or her by law.[1804]

Furthermore, the minors must be in the care of foster parents or the child and youth service on a more than temporary basis on the basis of a court order, by virtue of the law or an agreement between the natural parents and the child and youth service. The foster parents are deemed to be 'legal representatives' within the meaning of § 19 NAG.[1805]

It appears from the wording of the legislation that only § 11(1) Nos. 1–3 NAG may constitute obstacles to issuing the card as § 11(1) Nos. 4–6 NAG and § 11(2) NAG do not apply. Accordingly, an existing ban on entry or residence may be an obstacle. It is nonetheless unclear whether § 11(1) No. 3 NAG actually applies: an enforceable return decision is a reason for refusal if 18 months have not passed since the person left the country.[1806] § 11(3) NAG provides that the residence permits covered thereunder may also be granted despite an obstacle to issuance if this is necessary to respect the right to respect for private and family life within the meaning of Article 8 ECHR.[1807] The criteria listed in § 11(3) NAG correspond to the criteria in § 9(2) BFA-VG, which applies to 'residence permits for reasons of Article 8 ECHR'.[1808]

1802 However, a second requirement existed prior to the 2017 Act amending the Law on Aliens. This was repealed as it was no longer appropriate; ErläutRV 1523 BlgNR 25. GP, 9.

1803 § 2(1) No. 17 NAG.

1804 § 2(4) No. 1 NAG in conjunction with § 21(2) Allgemeines Bürgerliches Gesetzbuch in the version BGBl I 145/2022 (Austrian Civil Code).

1805 According to VwGH 21.3.2017, Ra 2015/22/0160 the relevant provisions of the Austrian Civil Code (§§ 184–185) are used to interpret the term 'foster parents'.

1806 *Peyrl* in *Abermann/Czech/Kind/Peyrl* § 41a NAG mn 18 assumes that the gap was not intended and therefore argues that the existence of a valid return decision is not detrimental to the claim.

1807 Cf. *Peyrl/Czech* in *Abermann/Czech/Kind/Peyrl* (eds), NAG Kommentar^2 (2019) § 11 NAG mns 30ff.

1808 See Chapter 4.B.III. and Chapter 4.C.III.

2. Right to stay

The 'Red-White-Red – Card plus' may be granted *ex officio* or upon a well-founded application.[1809] § 3(1) NAG stipulates that the Governor (*Landeshauptmann*) is the competent authority. With the exception of Vienna, the district administration authorities have been empowered via an order (*Verordnung*).[1810]

Pursuant to § 41(5) 1st Sent. NAG, the 'Red-White-Red – Card plus' is valid for two years and allows unrestricted access to the labour market.[1811] The explanations in Chapter 3.A.II.3. apply vis-à-vis social benefits.

V. Spain: 'temporary residence permit for reasons of family roots'

Article 124(3) REDYLE concerns the 'temporary residence permit for reasons of family roots' (*autorización de residencia temporal por razones de arraigo familiar*).[1812] As discussed above, the 'roots' are one of the main paths out of irregularity in the Spanish law on foreigners.[1813] Be that as it may, family roots are, quantitively speaking, not as important as social roots. This type of regularisation is derived in principle from Article 8 ECHR.[1814]

1. Requirements

The REDYLE draw a distinction between two sets of circumstances,[1815] however the Royal Decree 629/2022 reformed Article 124(3) REDYLE and now three sets of circumstances are stated. In this respect, *Carbajal García's*

1809 Cf. *Peyrl* in *Abermann/Czech/Kind/Peyrl* § 41a NAG mn 18 concerning the cases in which one is entitled to receive the card.

1810 Cf. *Czech* in *Abermann/Czech/Kind/Peyrl* (eds), NAG Kommentar² (2019) § 3 NAG mns 6f.

1811 § 3(1) AuslBG and § 8(1) No. 2 NAG and see the references in Fn 842.

1812 On the development of 'family roots' *Cerezo Mariscal*, Revista de Derecho 2015, 680 and on the previous law *Iglesias Sánchez*, La regularización de la situación administrativa de los padres de menores españoles en situación irregular, Revista de Derecho Migratorio y Extranjería 2010/3, 35.

1813 See Chapter 3.C.III.2.

1814 See Chapter 3.C.III.2.

1815 Cf. *Cerezo Mariscal*, Revista de Derecho 2015, 680f.

observation with regard to the previous law is still valid. The author considers the regularisation to be easily achievable in privileged cases as 'only' one set of circumstances has to be met alongside the general requirements.[1816]

Article 124(3)(a) REDYLE, introduced in 2011 and reformed in 2022, concerns the minor's parents or guardian. The minor has to be a Spanish citizen. According to Article 17(1)(a) Código Civil[1817], those born of a Spanish mother or father are Spaniards by birth.[1818] Article 124(3)(a) REDYLE further requires the parent or guardian to be responsible for the minor and living with him or her or must comply with the parental obligations in respect of the minor;[1819] this provision also includes family members of EU citizens.[1820] The Royal Decree 629/2022 supplemented the wording of this provision. It further stipulates that a foreigner might obtain this residence permit if he or she provides support to a Spaniard with a disability for the exercise of their legal capacity, provided that the foreigner who provides this support is in charge of the person with a disability and lives with him or her. Hence, this reform contributed to the fact that Article 124(3)(a) REDYLE now falls within the scope of this study.[1821]

The Royal Decree 629/2022 also reformulated and (newly) introduced Article 124(3)(b) REDYLE which is now available to the spouse or registered partner of a Spanish citizen (*cónyuge o pareja de hecho acreditada de ciudadano o ciudadana de nacionalidad española*). Furthermore, ascendants over 65 years of age, or dependents under 65 years of age, descendants under 21 years of age, or dependents over 21 years of age, of a Spanish citizen, or of their spouse or registered partner, fall within the ambit of said permit.

1816 *Carbajal García*, Revista de Derecho Migratorio y Extranjería 2012/29, 68.

1817 Real Decreto de 24 de julio de 1889 por el que se publica el Código Civil, BOE 206 of 25.7.1889 in the version of 16.12.2021.

1818 Cf. *Boza Martínez*, La regularización de los progenitores de menores de nacionalidad española y la necesidad de una solución reglamentaria a la cuestión. WP 1/2011 (9.2.2011), http://idpbarcelona.net/docs/public/wp/workingpaper5.pdf (31.7.2022) 4 and *Álvarez Rodríguez/Marrero González*, Attribution of Spanish Nationality to Children Born in Spain with the Purpose of Avoiding Situations of Statelessness at Birth in *Carrera Nuñez/de Groot* (eds), European Citizenship at the Crossroads: The Role of the European Union on Loss and Acquisition of Nationality (2015) 267.

1819 Cf. *Cerezo Mariscal*, Revista de Derecho 2015, 681.

1820 See TSJ País Vasco 170/2017, ECLI:ES:TSJPV:2017:1252, FJ 4.

1821 See Chapter 1.B.IV.2.

The requirement in Article 124(3)(c) REDYLE, which actually existed prior to the Royal Decree 629/2022, applies to those children whose mother or father was originally a Spanish citizen.[1822] This can be proven by referring to the entry of the birth in the civil register, which contains information on the parents' nationality.[1823]

The term 'family' – within the whole *arraigo* system – is limited to the immediate family, i.e. the spouse, registered partner and lineal relatives in the first degree.[1824] *García Vitoria* criticises this narrow definition as being incompatible with Article 8 ECHR as it excludes siblings who live together[1825] or couples who are neither married nor registered partners.[1826]

2. Right to stay

The residence permit according to Article 124(3)(c) REDYLE is valid for one year.[1827] The permits issued for reasons of 'rootedness' share the common feature that they also encompass a work permit.[1828] This privileges 'rootedness' within the 'temporary residence permits for exceptional circumstances'. It does not apply to minors who have not yet reached working age (16 years).[1829]

The residence permits according to Article 124(3)(a) and (b) REDYLE are granted for five years and entitle the holder to work as an employee or self-employed person.

1822 Before the Royal Decree 629/2022, this was set out in Article 124(3)(b) REDYLE.

1823 Cf. Instrucción DGI/SGJR/10/2008, 3f. For criticism, see *Cerezo Mariscal*, Revista de Derecho 2015, 680f, who notes that there are considerable problems in recognising former citizens of the Spanish Sahara – a Spanish colony until 1975.

1824 Cf. *Triguero Martínez*, Migraciones 2014, 453f.

1825 See however the case law cited in *Esteban de la Rosa*, Art 31 LODYLE in *Monereo Pérez/Fernández Avilés/Triguero Martínez* 505.

1826 Cf. *García Vitoria*, Revista General de Derecho Constitucional 2015/20, 14ff.

1827 Art 130(1) REDYLE. However, see Art 124(3)(a) REDYLE.

1828 Art 129(1) REDYLE; cf. *Serrano Villamanta* in *Balado Ruiz-Gallegos* 564 and see Chapter 3.C.II.2.

1829 Art 129(1) REDYLE; cf. *Fernández Collados* in *Palomar Olmeda* 434.

VI. Interim conclusion

The right to respect for family life under Article 8 ECHR serves as the legal standard with regard to the purpose of the regularisation 'family unity'. It is generally not necessary to grant a right to stay in order to comply with the protection against expulsion pursuant to Article 8 ECHR.

The Spanish 'residence permit for a child not born in Spain' covers minors who have been residing in Spain for at least two years and, where applicable, attending school. This is complicated by the requirements that one parent or guardian must be residing lawfully and have sufficient financial resources. As a result, the length of the right to stay is derived from the duration of the residence permit of the parent or guardian.

At the same time, the Austrian 'Red-White-Red – Card plus' for unaccompanied minor aliens in the care of foster parents or child and youth service is to be understood as an expression of Article 8 ECHR, especially with regard to the best interests of the child, which is also stipulated in the UN Convention on the Rights of the Child. Similar to the Spanish residence permit, the person concerned must be a minor, but the main difference is that only 'unaccompanied' minors are eligible under Austrian law. There is a parallel in that minors who are in the care of the child and youth service fall within the personal scope of application. The Spanish law on foreigners stipulates that an institution established in Spain must be the guardian. The Austrian 'Red-White-Red – Card plus' is valid for two years and thus one year longer than the Spanish residence permit.

The Austrian 'residence permits for reasons of Article 8 ECHR' requires an examination of the proportionality of a removal measure with regard to the impact on one's (private) and family life, which is to be undertaken during the asylum procedure or upon application. Despite a lack of statistics, it may be assumed that this is the most important regularisation in Austrian law because the requirements are easier to meet when compared to the requirements for the other regularisations. In principle, Austrian law accords with the protection against expulsion under Article 8 ECHR as it has codified the required balance of interests in statute law.

The German 'residence permit for persons who are enforceably required to leave the country, but whose departure is legally or factually impossible' targets internal obstacles to deportation, though gives special consideration to Article 8 ECHR and the associated balance between interests of private/family life and the public interest in expulsion. German law therefore meets the obligation under Article 8 ECHR to guarantee foreigners special protection against expulsion where there is an existing private/family life.

At the same time, Article 3 ECHR has left its mark as the German law also covers cases falling under this provision.[1830] Furthermore, as already explained in Chapter 4.A.III., it is extremely difficult in practice to obtain this residence permit if there are factual obstacles to deportation ('chain toleration' being the key phrase here), as it is a ground for refusal if the foreigner is at fault for the obstacle. The residence permit is granted on the basis of an application. It is contextually significant that it is also examined *ex officio* in the asylum procedure, subsequently after the asylum, refugee and subsidiary protection status. It is a particular feature of German law that the wording is open regarding the grant of the permit 'for a maximum of three years', but under certain circumstances 'for no longer than six months', as long as the foreigner 'has not been legally resident in the federal territory for at least 18 months'. Quantitively speaking, the 'residence permit for persons who are enforceably required to leave the country, but whose departure is legally or factually impossible' is the most important regularisation in German law.

The Spanish 'temporary residence permit for reasons of family roots' may be understood as implementing Article 8 ECHR. In contrast to the Austrian 'residence permits for reasons of Article 8 ECHR' or the German 'residence permit for persons who are enforceably required to leave the country, but whose departure is legally or factually impossible', the Spanish law on this residence permit does not mandate a balance of interests. It instead stipulates three specific sets of circumstances which were reformed by the Royal Decree 629/2022. Interestingly, Article 124(3)(a) REDYLE now stipulates that a foreigner might obtain this residence permit if he or she provides support to a Spaniard with a disability for the exercise of their legal capacity, provided that the foreigner who provides this support is in charge of the person with a disability and lives with him or her. Additionally, the residence permit is granted for an exceptionally long period, five years, and entitles the holder to work both employed and self-employed. The scope of family members is however very narrow and thus not all cases protected by Article 8 ECHR are covered. Several of these cases are covered by other regularisations in Spanish law, though 'social roots' merit particular attention.

1830 However, the relationship to the 'residence permit for banned deportation to a specific state' under § 25(3) AufenthG is also to be considered. If such a ban exists, the residence permit under § 25(3) AufenthG takes priority as it offers better access to the labour market and social benefits.

Overall, the balance of interests established in ECtHR case law on Article 8 ECHR has had an effect on the regularisations. This is especially clear in Austria and Germany. Austria has even created a regularisation particular to unaccompanied minors. For Germany, regularisations that fall under other regularisation purposes should not be disregarded, as these are partly granted for family reasons – for instance the 'residence permit in the case of permanent integration' and the 'residence permit for well-integrated juveniles and young adults' both feature a derivative right to stay for family members. Spain has taken the opposite path by anchoring three specific sets of circumstances in law. This solution appears to be too rigid and does not appear to fully reconcile with all aspects of Article 8 ECHR, even though the reform via the Royal Decree 629/2022 has expanded the scope of application of this regularisation. Be that as it may, one must bear in mind that several types of cases are covered by other regularisations, such as 'social roots'.

D. Vulnerability[1831]

I. Victim protection[1832]

This section begins with a description of the Austrian 'special protection residence permit' for victims of crimes (*Aufenthaltsberechtigung besonderer Schutz für Opfer von Straftaten*) and the German 'residence permit for prosecution of criminal offences' (*Aufenthaltserlaubnis zur Strafverfolgung*) as both are granted for one year, though in some circumstances the latter may be granted for two years. The three Spanish residence permits are then analysed in order to present the particularly victim-friendly Spanish protection regime in the best possible way. The Spanish 'temporary residence permit for humanitarian reasons' for victims of a crime (*autorización temporal por razones humanitarias – víctimas de delitos*) is valid for one year; the Spanish 'temporary residence permit and work permit for exceptional circumstances for foreign victims of human trafficking' (*autorización de residencia y trabajo por circunstancias excepcionales de extranjeros víctimas de trata de seres humanos*) and the 'temporary residence permit and work permit for exceptional circumstances for foreign women who are victims

1831 See Chapter 1.B.III.4.
1832 See Chapter 1.B.III.4.a.

of gender-based violence' (*autorización de residencia temporal y trabajo de mujeres extranjeras víctimas de violencia de género*) are granted for five years.

1. Austria: 'special protection residence permit' for victims of a crime

In addition to tolerated persons,[1833] the 'special protection residence permit' may also be granted to witnesses and victims of human trafficking or cross-border trade in prostitution, and victims of violence. The provision therefore serves to protect witnesses and victims.[1834] Accordingly, it is more appropriate to subsume this residence permit under the purpose of the regularisation 'victim protection' and not under 'other national interests'.[1835]

The protection relating to victims of human trafficking is based on obligations under international and EU law, in particular Article 8 Human Trafficking Directive.[1836] It is an autonomous mechanism under national law to protect victims of violence from further violence.[1837] The most recent official statistics date from 2013, when 'special protection residence permits' were granted to six victims of human trafficking and three victims of violence.[1838] As noted above, there are no current statistics, but it is reasonable to assume from the 2013 statistics that this part of Austrian law is of no particular relevance in practice.

a) Requirements

According to § 57(1) No. 2 AsylG (A), granting a 'special protection residence permit' requires the purpose of guaranteeing the prosecution of acts punishable by the courts or of asserting and enforcing civil-law claims in connection with such punishable acts, in particular to witnesses or

1833 See Chapter 4.A.II.1.

1834 *Peyrl/Neugschwendtner/Schmaus*, Fremdenrecht 194 and see also ErläutRV 1803 BlgNR 24. GP, 47f.

1835 See Chapter 4.F.

1836 ErläutRV 1803 BlgNR 24. GP, 47.

1837 ErläutRV 1803 BlgNR 24. GP, 47. See also VwGH 30.8.2017, Ra 2017/18/0119 and 12.11.2015, Ra 2015/21/0023.

1838 *Bundesministerium für Inneres*, Niederlassungs- und Aufenthaltsstatistik 2013 (2013) 37. There were only 6 (victims of human trafficking) and 16 (victims of violence) extensions.

victims of human trafficking or cross-border trade in prostitution. The explanations accompanying the legislation state that victim cooperation is not an objective requirement.[1839] Such objective requirement instead exists if criminal proceedings have already been initiated or civil claims have been asserted.[1840] The corresponding application shall be rejected as inadmissible if no criminal proceedings have been initiated or no civil-law claims have been asserted.[1841] The Federal Office for Immigration and Asylum has to decide on an application under § 57(1) No. 2 AsylG (A) within six weeks. The explanations accompanying the legislation justify this accelerated procedure for reasons of victim protection, according to which a quick reaction by the authority is facilitated to a considerable extent by legal certainty.[1842] The 'low threshold' takes account of the protection afforded to the victim.

§ 57(1) No. 3 AsylG (A) stipulates that victims of violence may receive a residence permit if it is necessary to protect them against further violence.[1843] It will suffice if criminal proceedings have been initiated or an interim injunction[1844] has or could have been issued. The application shall be rejected if this requirement is not met.[1845] According to the explanations to the Aliens Law Package of 2005, the provision is addressed foremost to victims of domestic violence.[1846] In addition, victims of forced marriages or partnerships may under certain circumstances receive a 'special protection residence permit' under § 57(1) No. 3 AsylG (A).[1847]

1839 However, see in this regard *Stiller*, Trafficked Third-Country Nationals: Detection, Identification and Protection in Austria (October 2021), https://www.emn.at/wp-content/uploads/2022/06/emn-study-2022-trafficked-third-country-nationals-detection-identification-and-protection-in-at.pdf (31.7.2022) 28 referring to *Schlintl/Sorrentino*, Residence permits, international protection and victims of human trafficking: Durable Solutions Grounded in International Law. Final Report (February 2021), https://lefoe.at/wp-content/uploads/2021/05/REST-Final-Report-2.pdf (31.7.2022) 25.

1840 Cf. ErläutRV 1803 BlgNR 24. GP, 47.

1841 § 59(3) 1st Sent. (A) and cf. ErläutRV 1803 BlgNR 24. GP, 47.

1842 ErläutRV 1803 BlgNR 24. GP, 48.

1843 § 57(1) No. 3 AsylG (A) and VwGH 5.5.2015, Ra 2014/22/0162.

1844 §§ 382b or 382c Exekutionsordnung in the version BGBl I 86/2021 (Enforcement Code).

1845 § 57(4) AsylG (A); ErläutRV 1803 BlgNR 24. GP, 48. But see also VwGH 5.5.2015, Ra 2014/22/0162.

1846 ErläutRV 1803 BlgNR 24. GP, 47. Along these lines ErläutRV 1077 BlgNR 24. GP, 10.

1847 § 30a NAG; ErläutRV 1803 BlgNR 24. GP, 76. It is somewhat unusual that the provision is stipulated in the NAG. This also applies to the 'Red-White-Red –

Before issuing the special residence permit according to § 57(1) Nos. 2 and 3 AsylG (A), the Federal Office for Immigration and Asylum shall obtain a substantiated opinion from the competent *Land* police directorate.[1848] This allows the police directorate to become aware of the applications under § 57 AsylG (A) and to report to the Federal Office for Immigration and Asylum without being restricted in the performance of its duties.[1849]

b) Right to stay

The explanations in Chapter 3.A.III.2.d. and Chapter 4.A.II.1.b. apply accordingly.

2. Germany: 'residence permit for prosecution of criminal offences'

The German 'residence permit for humanitarian reasons' contains two sets of circumstances aimed at the prosecution of specific criminal offences. The name indeed first suggests that it falls under the purpose 'other national interests',[1850] but the main purpose of the two sets of circumstances is to protect victims.[1851] This is also supported by the fact that the stay may be extended beyond the conclusion of criminal proceedings.[1852] Here the importance of the cooperation with the competent prosecution and court authorities is not overlooked.[1853]

According to § 25(4a) AufenthG, there is a 'residence permit for the victims of human trafficking', which was introduced when transposing Article 8 Human Trafficking Directive.[1854] The focus is on securing the

Card plus' for unaccompanied minor aliens in the care of foster parents or the child and youth service; see above Chapter 4.C.IV.

1848 § 57(2) AsylG (A).

1849 ErläutRV 1803 BlgNR 24. GP, 47.

1850 See Chapter 4.F.

1851 See Recital 9 Human Trafficking Directive and *Röcker* in *Bergmann/Dienelt* § 25 AufenthG mns 79ff. For a contrasting view see *Koch* in *Kluth/Hornung/Koch* (eds), Handbuch Zuwanderungsrecht[3] (2020) § 4 mns 965 and 982.

1852 See Chapter 4.D.I.2.b.

1853 In this sense, *Marx*, Aufenthalts-, Asyl- und Flüchtlingsrecht § 5 mn 60 with further references and 66.

1854 No. 25.4a.0.1 AVV-AufenthG and *Marx*, Aufenthalts-, Asyl- und Flüchtlingsrecht § 5 mn 60.

safety of the victims of human trafficking as well as providing suitable support in order to successfully prosecute the offenders.[1855] § 25(4b) AufenthG contains a 'residence permit for victims of undocumented employment', which was introduced when transposing Article 13(4) Employers Sanctions Directive.[1856] The 'residence permit for victims of undocumented employment' was modelled on the 'residence permit for the victims of human trafficking',[1857] thus it is appropriate to analyse the provisions together. Only 77 foreigners held a residence permit under § 25(4a) or (4b) AufenthG in mid-2021,[1858] therefore highlighting that this type of permit is almost irrelevant in practice.

a) Requirements

The foreigner has to have been a victim of a criminal offence under §§ 232–233a German Criminal Code (*Strafgesetzbuch*):[1859] human trafficking, forced prostitution, forced labour, exploitation of labour, and exploitation involving deprivation of liberty. It suffices that the public prosecutor's office is investigating on the basis of concrete facts.[1860] The presence of the victim must be necessary for the criminal proceedings and be considered appropriate, whereby his or her expected statements are of particular relevance.[1861] The consideration by the public prosecutor's office or the criminal court that the foreigner's presence in Germany is appropriate is binding on the foreigners authority.[1862]

It follows that the person concerned must have agreed to testify as a witness in order to fall within the scope of the residence permit.[1863] The Human Trafficking Directive grants the person concerned a 'reflection period' to take an informed decision as to whether to cooperate with the

1855 No. 25.4a.0.1 AVV-AufenthG.

1856 Cf. *Maaßen/Kluth* in *Kluth/Heusch* § 25 AufenthG mn 116.

1857 Cf. *Maaßen/Kluth* in *Kluth/Heusch* § 25 AufenthG mn 116.

1858 BT-Drs 19/32579, 21.

1859 Strafgesetzbuch in the version of 11.7.2022 (BGBl I 1082); *Herker*, Bleiberecht für Opfer von Hasskriminalität (2022) 318ff, advocates for a legal change and inclusion of victims of hate crimes.

1860 No. 25.4a.1.1 AVV-AufenthG.

1861 *Maaßen/Kluth* in *Kluth/Heusch* § 25 AufenthG mns 102f.

1862 *Maaßen/Kluth* in *Kluth/Heusch* § 25 AufenthG mn 107.

1863 See Art 5 Human Trafficking Directive and *Maaßen/Kluth* in *Kluth/Heusch* § 25 AufenthG mn 105.

authorities.[1864] If the foreigners authority has concrete indications that a person who is obliged to leave the country is a victim of human trafficking or undocumented employment,[1865] it must set a deadline for leaving the country that allows the victim to make a decision, again by granting a suitable reflection period.[1866] The foreigners authority or the criminal prosecution authority must inform the victim of the reflection period.[1867] The Human Trafficking Directive does not require lawful residence during the reflection period,[1868] which is why German law only grants tolerated status in such cases.[1869]

It is also important that the victim no longer has any ties to the defendant.[1870] Finally, it should be pointed out that an existing entry and residence ban does not prevent the issuance of a 'residence permit for victims of human trafficking'.[1871]

The 'residence permit for victims of undocumented employment' is aimed at foreigners who were engaged in undocumented employment under particularly exploitative conditions or as minors. The only difference to the 'residence permit for the victims of human trafficking' is that they must be victims of a criminal offence under the Act to Combat Undocumented Employment (*Schwarzarbeitsbekämpfungsgesetz*) or the Act on Temporary Employment Businesses (*Arbeitsnehmerüberlassungsgesetz*).[1872]

Other provisions of the Residence Act may apply to the victims of other offences, i.e. neither human trafficking nor undocumented employment,[1873] such as § 25(4) 1st Sent. AufenthG ('residence permit for urgent humanitarian or personal reasons or substantial public interests').[1874] Furthermore, a toleration pursuant to § 60a(2) 2nd Sent. AufenthG may be

1864 Art 6 Human Trafficking Directive .
1865 See the introductory remarks in Chapter 3.
1866 See Art 6(2) Human Trafficking Directive .
1867 See Art 5 Human Trafficking Directive and in this sense *Maaßen/Kluth* in *Kluth/Heusch* § 25 AufenthG mn 109.
1868 Art 6(3) Human Trafficking Directive .
1869 § 60a(5) AufenthG; cf. *Marx*, Aufenthalts-, Asyl- und Flüchtlingsrecht § 5 mn 61.
1870 Cf. No. 25.4a.2.2 AVV-AufenthG.
1871 Cf. *Maaßen/Kluth* in *Kluth/Heusch* § 25 AufenthG mn 106.
1872 §§ 10(1) and 11(1) No. 3 Schwarzarbeitsbekämpfungsgesetz in the version of 25.6.2021 (BGBl I 2099) and § 15a Arbeitsnehmerüberlassungsgesetz in the version of 18.3.2022 (BGBl I 466).
1873 *Maaßen/Kluth* in *Kluth/Heusch* § 25 AufenthG mn 100.
1874 Cf. *Marx*, Aufenthalts-, Asyl- und Flüchtlingsrecht § 5 mns 49–54.

granted if the foreigner is needed as a witness in criminal proceedings.[1875] However, the examination of the so-called *Prozessduldung*, i.e. toleration due to criminal proceedings, is subordinate to the residence permit discussed here.[1876]

b) Right to stay

The residence permits pursuant to § 25(4a) and (4b) are in principle issued and extended for one year.[1877] The foreigners authority is to consult the competent authority, namely the public prosecutor's office or the criminal court.[1878] The residence permits generally only ensure a temporary stay and therefore the foreigners authority has to decide whether the person concerned will have to leave the country following the proceedings.[1879] Only toleration pursuant to § 60a(2) 2nd Sent. AufenthG comes into consideration if this is not the case.[1880]

The one-year period does not apply if humanitarian or personal reasons or public interests require the foreigner's further presence in Germany, as the residence permit is granted for two years in these cases.[1881]

The residence permit can also be issued for longer than one or two years where there are justified reasons. According to the General Administrative Provisions on the Residence Act (AVV-AufenthG), such a case exists if it is needed for the foreigner to remain due to the investigations by the public prosecutor's office and/or the trial exists for longer than the one or two-year period. § 25(4a) 3rd Sent. and (4b) 3rd Sent. AufenthG provide the circumstances in which the period may be extended.

Holders of a residence permit pursuant to § 25(4a) or (4b) AufenthG are generally entitled to Unemployment Benefit II under the Social Insurance Code II or social assistance under Social Insurance Code XII.[1882] The Skilled Immigration Act did not make any changes with regard to employment. Although employment is not allowed by law, it can be ap-

---

1875 Cf. BT-Drs 16/5065, 187.
1876 *Kluth/Breidenbach* in *Kluth/Heusch* § 60a AufenthG mn 22.
1877 § 26(1) 5th Sent. AufenthG; cf. *Maaßen/Kluth* in *Kluth/Heusch* § 25 AufenthG mn 110.
1878 § 72(6) AufenthG; cf. *Maaßen/Kluth* in *Kluth/Heusch* § 25 AufenthG mn 112.
1879 *Maaßen/Kluth* in *Kluth/Heusch* § 25 AufenthG mn 101.
1880 See Chapter 4.A.I.2.a.
1881 § 26(1) 5th Sent. AufenthG.
1882 *Frings/Janda/Keßler/Steffen*, Sozialrecht mns 806 and 824.

proved by the foreigners authority,[1883] whereby the approval of the Federal Employment Agency (*Bundesagentur für Arbeit*) is not required according to § 31 BeschV.

3. Spain: 'temporary residence permit for humanitarian reasons' for victims of crimes

The 'temporary residence permit for humanitarian reasons' for victims of crimes (*autorización temporal por razones humanitarias – víctimas de delitos*) is one of the 'temporary residence permits for exceptional circumstances', more specifically it is one of three types of humanitarian reasons.[1884] The residence permit is rooted in national law as there are no indications for inspirations from international or EU law. The statistics do not shed light on just how many of these residence permits have been granted.[1885]

a) Requirements

The permit may only be granted to foreigners who are victims of certain offences.[1886] The Law 4/2015 (LEVD) grants further rights to the victims.[1887] The offences are characterised by their links to situations of particular vulnerability:[1888]

- Crimes against employee rights;[1889]
- Crimes motivated by racist, anti-Semitic or other discriminatory reasons; and
- Violent crimes carried out in the family environment, i.e. domestic violence (*en el entorno familiar*).[1890]

1883 § 25(4a) 3rd Sent. and § 25(4b) 4th Sent. AufenthG.
1884 Art 126(1) REDYLE and see Chapter 4.A.II.3. and Chapter 4.D.II.1.
1885 See Chapter 3.C.III.1.
1886 Art 126(1) REDYLE.
1887 Cf. *Gutiérrez Sanz*, El anteproyecto de ley orgánica del estatuto de la víctima del delito y la víctima adulta del delito de trata de seres humanos con fines de explotación sexual, Revista de Derecho Migratorio y Extranjería 2014/37, 13.
1888 Cf. *García Vitoria* in *Boza Martínez/Donaire Villa/Moya Malapeira* 296f.
1889 Arts 311–315 CP.
1890 Cf. Ley 27/2003, de 31 de julio, reguladora de la Orden de protección de las víctimas de la violencia doméstica, BOE 183 of 1.8.2003, and in general on domestic violence against women *Defensor del Pueblo*, La violencia domestica contra las mujeres (1998), https://www.defensordelpueblo.es/wp-content/upl

This latter group will probably apply in circumstances that are not covered by the 'temporary residence permit and work permit for exceptional circumstances for foreign women who are victims of gender-based violence' discussed below.[1891]

In order to prove that one has been the victim of such a crime, Article 126 (1) REDYLE requires a final court decision (*resolución judicial finalizadora*). The Spanish Supreme Court has interpreted this requirement as constitutional, though in a different context.[1892] However, *Serrano Villamanta* criticises this requirement as severely restricting the scope of the application because of the lengthy wait for a court decision.[1893] A regularisation on the basis of social roots will therefore often come into question before a 'temporary residence permit for humanitarian reasons' for victims of crimes.[1894]

According to *Esteban de la Rosa* and other authors, the application for the 'residence permit for humanitarian reasons' for victims of crimes can already be made where there is a court order for the protection of the victim of domestic violence.[1895] However, the residence permit can only be granted after the conclusion of the court proceedings. This is why it would be more appropriate to extend the protection regime for foreign women who have been victims of gender-related violence to the residence permit discussed here.[1896] This would mean better protection as the application for the residence permit may be made at the moment of the court order, thus allowing the victim to receive a provisional 'temporary residence permit and work permit' at an earlier stage.[1897]

---

oads/2015/05/1998-01-La-violencia-dom%C3%A9stica-contra-las-mujeres.pdf (31.7.2022).

1891 Cf. *García Vitoria* in *Boza Martínez/Donaire Villa/Moya Malapeira* 296 and see Chapter 4.D.I.5.

1892 STS 782/2007, ECLI:ES:TS:2007:782, FJ 11.

1893 *Serrano Villamanta* in *Balado Ruiz-Gallegos* 559; agreeing *García Vitoria* in *Boza Martínez/Donaire Villa/Moya Malapeira* 297.

1894 See Chapter 4.E.I.

1895 In this sense, *Esteban de la Rosa*, Art 31 LODYLE in *Monereo Pérez/Fernández Avilés/Triguero Martínez* 506 and *Lázaro González/Benlloch Sanz* in *Palomar Olmeda* 941f as well as *Trinidad García*, Revista de Derecho Migratorio y Extranjería 2005/9, 151.

1896 Cf. *Lázaro González/Benlloch Sanz* in *Palomar Olmeda* 941f.

1897 See Chapter 4.D.I.5.b.

b) Right to stay

The residence permit is usually granted for one year.[1898] An application for a work permit is to be submitted separately.[1899]

4. Spain: 'temporary residence permit and work permit for exceptional circumstances for foreign victims of human trafficking'

Article 59bis LODYLE and Articles 140–146 REDYLE contain the main provisions on the 'temporary residence permit and work permit for exceptional circumstances for foreign victims of human trafficking' (*autorización de residencia y trabajo por circunstancias excepcionales de extranjeros víctimas de trata de seres humanos*),[1900] with Article 177bis CP containing the corresponding provision in criminal law.[1901]

Article 59bis LODYLE was introduced by the Organic Law 2/2009,[1902] which transposed the provisions of the 2004 Human Trafficking Directive.[1903] On the national level, the Framework protocol for the protection of victims of human trafficking (*Protocolo Marco de Protección de las Víctimas de Trata de Seres Humanos*) was passed on 28 October 2010, with additional rights for victims of crime provided via the Law 4/2015 (LEVD).[1904] Furthermore, the aforementioned provisions are significantly influenced by international documents such as the Council of Europe Convention on Action against Trafficking in Human Beings of 16 May 2005[1905] or

1898 Art 130(1) REDYLE.

1899 Art 129(2) REDYLE; see Chapter 3.C.II.2.

1900 Minors are subject to special rules, which are not analysed here; cf. *Vicente Palacio*, Art 59bis LODYLE in *Monereo Pérez/Fernández Avilés/ Triguero Martínez* (eds), Comentario a la ley y al reglamento de Extranjería, Inmigración e Integración Social[2] (2013) 957 (969f).

1901 STS 4668/2016, ECLI:ES:TS:2016:4668 and cf. *Vicente Palacio*, Art 59bis LODYLE in *Monereo Pérez/Fernández Avilés/Triguero Martínez* 958–961.

1902 Cf. *Vicente Palacio*, Art 59bis LODYLE in *Monereo Pérez/Fernández Avilés/ Triguero Martínez* 957f and *Díaz Morgado*, La residencia de víctimas de trata de personas y la residencia por colaboración contra redes organizadas in *Boza Martínez/Donaire Villa/Moya Malapeira* (eds), La nueva regulación de la inmigración y la extranjería en España (2012) 340f and 351f.

1903 Cf. *Vicente Palacio*, Art 59bis LODYLE in *Monereo Pérez/Fernández Avilés/ Triguero Martínez* 957f.

1904 Cf. *Gutiérrez Sanz*, Revista de Derecho Migratorio y Extranjería 2014/37, 13ff.

1905 Art 59bis(1) LODYLE refers to Art 10 of said Convention.

the Protocol to Prevent, Suppress and Punish Trafficking in Persons, Especially Women and Children, supplementing the UN Convention against Transnational Organized Crime of 2000.

The protection of victims of human trafficking is at the core[1906] of this regularisation and thus it is not discussed in the context of 'other national interests'.[1907] Due to the lack of precise detail in the statistics, it is unclear how many residence permits of this kind have been issued.[1908]

a) Identification of potential victims

The identification of the potential victims is the first key step in granting this type of residence permit.[1909] Any person or authority who is aware of the existence of a potential victim of human trafficking is to immediately inform the competent police authority for the investigation of the offence or the delegate or subdelegate of government.[1910] This may occur, for example, in relation to a control by the Labour and Social Security Inspectorate (*Inspección de Trabajo y Seguridad Social*), in the course of a deportation process or at any other time.[1911]

The competent authorities are subject to a duty to inform once there are reasonable indications (*indicios razonables*) that there is a potential victim of human trafficking.[1912] They must inform these foreigners in writing and

---

1906 Along this line, *Vicente Palacio*, Art 59bis LODYLE in *Monereo Pérez/Fernández Avilés/Triguero Martínez* 960f; *Díaz Morgado*, La residencia de víctimas de trata de personas y la residencia por colaboración contra redes organizadas in *Boza Martínez/Donaire Villa/Moya Malapeira* 342f. According to *Lázaro González/Benlloch Sanz* in *Palomar Olmeda* 927 the main focus is to ease the prosecution of offences.

1907 See Chapter 4.F.

1908 See Chapter 3.C.III.1.

1909 Cf. *Díaz Morgado*, La residencia de víctimas de trata de personas y la residencia por colaboración contra redes organizadas in *Boza Martínez/Donaire Villa/Moya Malapeira* 353.

1910 Art 141(1) REDYLE and Instrucción DGI/SGRJ/6/2011, 3; cf. *Lázaro González/Benlloch Sanz* in *Palomar Olmeda* 928f.

1911 Instrucción DGI/SGRJ/6/2011, 3; cf. also *Díaz Morgado*, La residencia de víctimas de trata de personas y la residencia por colaboración contra redes organizadas in *Boza Martínez/Donaire Villa/Moya Malapeira* 354 and *Vicente Palacio*, Art 59bis LODYLE in *Monereo Pérez/Fernández Avilés/Triguero Martínez* 962.

1912 Cf. *Díaz Morgado*, La residencia de víctimas de trata de personas y la residencia por colaboración contra redes organizadas in *Boza Martínez/Donaire Villa/Moya Malapeira* 354f.

in a language that they understand of the protections available to them, and in particular about the residence permit.[1913] Furthermore, they must also provide information on the social and health benefits to which the foreigner is entitled.[1914]

The competent police units, i.e. those trained in human trafficking investigation,[1915] examine and, if necessary, establish whether the person concerned is a victim of human trafficking.[1916] Victim identification is a particularly delicate and important phase.[1917] The great vulnerability of the victims must be observed.[1918]

During the identification phase and the recovery and reflection period, no deportation proceedings may be initiated because the victim is staying irregularly.[1919] A deportation procedure that has already been initiated or a pending deportation must be suspended. The new rule introduced by the Organic Law 10/2011 is very welcome from the victim's perspective, as the victims now do not have to fear that deportation proceedings will be initiated when they approach the authorities with their concerns.[1920]

b) Recovery and reflection period

Following the identification of potential victims, the competent police unit will send within 48 hours an opinion on the granting of a recovery and reflection period to the competent delegate or subdelegate of govern-

---

1913 Art 59bis(2) LODYLE and Art 141(1) REDYLE; cf. Instrucción DGI/SGRJ/6/2011, 2.

1914 Cf. *Lázaro González/Benlloch Sanz* in *Palomar Olmeda* 929.

1915 Cf. *Díaz Morgado*, La residencia de víctimas de trata de personas y la residencia por colaboración contra redes organizadas in *Boza Martínez/Donaire Villa/Moya Malapeira* 353 and *Defensor del Pueblo*, Recomendación (23.5.2016), Queja 16002509.

1916 Arts 141(2) and 142 REDYLE; cf. Instrucción DGI/SGRJ/6/2011, 2.

1917 Cf. *Díaz Morgado*, La residencia de víctimas de trata de personas y la residencia por colaboración contra redes organizadas in *Boza Martínez/Donaire Villa/Moya Malapeira* 353–355.

1918 Cf. Instrucción DGI/SGRJ/6/2011, 1.

1919 Art 59bis(2) LODYLE and Art 141(2) REDYLE and Instrucción DGI/SGRJ/6/2011, 3.

1920 In this sense, *Díaz Morgado*, La residencia de víctimas de trata de personas y la residencia por colaboración contra redes organizadas in *Boza Martínez/Donaire Villa/Moya Malapeira* 355.

ment,[1921] which makes a final decision within five days.[1922] If the five-day period expires without a response, the silence is considered as approval.[1923] If there are reasonable indications that the person is a trafficking victim, a recovery and reflection period is granted. This phase is granted for at least 90 days and must continue until the victim is ready to decide on a possible cooperation with the prosecution authorities with regard to the offences.[1924]

In addition to the aforementioned suspension of a possible deportation or deportation proceedings, the victim's stay is regularised during the recovery and reflection period.[1925] According to Article 59bis(2) LODYLE, this also applies to the victim's children if they are in Spain at the time the parent is deemed a victim of human trafficking.[1926] This includes both underage and disabled adult children.[1927] Theoretically, other persons are also eligible if they have a special relationship with the victim and the grant of the right to stay is necessary for the victim's cooperation with the authorities.[1928] The extension of protection to all these persons serves to remove all possible obstacles that could prevent the victim from cooperating with the authorities.[1929]

1921 Cf. *Lázaro González/Benlloch Sanz* in *Palomar Olmeda* 930 and *Díaz Morgado*, La residencia de víctimas de trata de personas y la residencia por colaboración contra redes organizadas in *Boza Martínez/Donaire Villa/Moya Malapeira* 356.

1922 Art 142(3) REDYLE; cf. *Vicente Palacio*, Art 59bis LODYLE in *Monereo Pérez/Fernández Avilés/Triguero Martínez* 963.

1923 In this cases the recovery and reflection period is granted for a minimum of 90 days; Art 59bis(2) LODYLE.

1924 Art 59bis(2) LODYLE; for detail see *Lázaro González/Benlloch Sanz* in *Palomar Olmeda* 929f.

1925 Art 59(2) LODYLE; cf. for detail Art 142(6) REDYLE; Instrucción DGI/SGRJ/6/2011, 4. *Vicente Palacio*, Art 59bis LODYLE in *Monereo Pérez/Fernández Avilés/Triguero Martínez* 964 who considers that a 'provisional residence permit and work permit' is to be granted from the recovery and reflection phase onwards. However, this does not result either from the legislation or from the cited guidelines on the law on foreigners, as such permit is granted only at a later time; see Chapter 4.D.I.4.b.

1926 Cf. *Vicente Palacio*, Art 59bis LODYLE in *Monereo Pérez/Fernández Avilés/Triguero Martínez* 966f.

1927 For detail see Instrucción DGI/SGRJ/6/2011, 3f.

1928 Cf. *Fernández Pérez*, Derechos fundamentales 237 and *Díaz Morgado*, La residencia de víctimas de trata de personas y la residencia por colaboración contra redes organizadas in *Boza Martínez/Donaire Villa/Moya Malapeira* 357f.

1929 In this sense *Díaz Morgado*, La residencia de víctimas de trata de personas y la residencia por colaboración contra redes organizadas in *Boza Martínez/Donaire*

During the recovery and reflection period, the competent police unit has to ensure the safety and protection of the victims and, if applicable, the children.[1930] The relevant guidelines on the law on foreigners states that the authorities have to provide for the subsistence of the persons concerned,[1931] which is probably understood to mean social benefits.[1932]

At the end of the recovery and reflection period, the competent authority evaluates the victim's situation to order a possible extension of this period.[1933] If the period is extended, the time limit of the 'provisional residence permit and work permit' for the victim and, if applicable, for the children is also extended.

If, after providing the necessary information by means of an opinion, the delegate or subdelegate of government comes to the conclusion that the conditions for granting the recovery and reflection period are not met, the application can be rejected or subsequently revoked.[1934] Reasons for rejection may include the protection of public order and the fact that the victim's status was wrongly invoked.[1935] The law stipulates that the dismissal must be justified and contestable.[1936]

c) Exemption from administrative penalties and 'provisional residence permit and work permit'

Article 59bis(4) LODYLE allows the delegate or subdelegate of government to exempt the victim from the administrative penalties because of

---

Villa/Moya Malapeira 358 and *Vicente Palacio*, Art 59bis LODYLE in *Monereo Pérez/Fernández Avilés/Triguero Martínez* 965.

1930 Cf. *Vicente Palacio*, Art 59bis LODYLE in *Monereo Pérez/Fernández Avilés/Triguero Martínez* 964f and *Díaz Morgado*, La residencia de víctimas de trata de personas y la residencia por colaboración contra redes organizadas in *Boza Martínez/Donaire Villa/Moya Malapeira* 357.

1931 Cf. Instrucción DGI/SGRJ/6/2011, 5.

1932 Cf. *Vicente Palacio*, Art 59bis LODYLE in *Monereo Pérez/Fernández Avilés/Triguero Martínez* 964 with further references.

1933 Art 59bis(2) LODYLE; cf. Instrucción DGI/SGRJ/6/2011, 5f.

1934 Art 59bis(3) LODYLE; cf. *Díaz Morgado*, La residencia de víctimas de trata de personas y la residencia por colaboración contra redes organizadas in *Boza Martínez/Donaire Villa/Moya Malapeira* 358f.

1935 Cf. *Lázaro González/Benlloch Sanz* in *Palomar Olmeda* 931.

1936 Cf. *Fernández Pérez*, Derechos fundamentales 237 and in general the remarks on judicial protection in Chapter 3.C.V.

the irregular stay and from the resulting deportation.[1937] Moreover, Article 59bis(4) LODYLE also suggests that the foreigner may be exempted from all other administrative penalties.[1938] On the one hand, the prosecution authorities can request the exemption from the delegate or subdelegate of government based on the victim's cooperation. On the other hand, the delegate or subdelegate of government may exempt victims in light of their 'personal situation'[1939].[1940]

The exemption has an important legal effect,[1941] as the person concerned must subsequently be informed of the possibility to apply for a 'temporary residence permit and work permit' or of assisted voluntary return.[1942] The application is submitted to the delegate or subdelegate of government,[1943] who in turn forwards it to the competent office. In principle the application must include a copy of the passport, although this may be waived if obtaining it poses a risk to the victim.[1944] Depending on whether the application is based on cooperation in criminal proceedings or on the victim's personal situation, the Secretary of State for Security (*Secretaría de Estado de Seguridad*) or the Secretary of State for Migration (*Secretaría de Estado de Migraciones*) is responsible.[1945] The competent delegate or subdelegate of government attaches two opinions to the application, one relating to the administrative and personal situation of the for-

1937 Art 143(1) REDYLE makes express reference to Art 53(1)(a) LODYLE.

1938 In this sense *Díaz Morgado*, La residencia de víctimas de trata de personas y la residencia por colaboración contra redes organizadas in *Boza Martínez/Donaire Villa/Moya Malapeira* 347 referring to the near-identical wording in Art 59(3) LODYLE; see Chapter 4.F.II.2.

1939 According to the legislative materials, there is a lack of clarity surrounding the meaning of the victim's personal situation; cf. *Díaz Morgado*, La residencia de víctimas de trata de personas y la residencia por colaboración contra redes organizadas in *Boza Martínez/Donaire Villa/Moya Malapeira* 361 Fn 473.

1940 Cf. *Vicente Palacio*, Art 59bis LODYLE in *Monereo Pérez/Fernández Avilés/Triguero Martínez*, 966 and *Díaz Morgado*, La residencia de víctimas de trata de personas y la residencia por colaboración contra redes organizadas in *Boza Martínez/Donaire Villa/Moya Malapeira* 359f.

1941 Cf. *Vicente Palacio*, Art 59bis LODYLE in *Monereo Pérez/Fernández Avilés/Triguero Martínez* 966.

1942 Art 144 REDYLE.

1943 Art 144(2) REDYLE.

1944 Art 59bis(4) LODYLE.

1945 Furthermore, it is also possible to make two applications at the same time: one regarding cooperation and the other regarding the victim's personal situation; Art 144(1) REDYLE; cf. *Lázaro González/Benlloch Sanz* in *Palomar Olmeda* 932.

eigner and the other to the substantive assessment of the proceedings.[1946] If latter opinion is favourable, the foreigner is immediately granted a 'provisional residence permit and work permit'.[1947] It should be emphasised here that the residence is therefore lawful until the procedure is concluded. Moreover, the foreigner is entitled to engage in employment.[1948] The 'provisional residence permit and work permit' can also be granted to the victim's children upon application.[1949]

If the foreigner or his or her children, as the case may be, are not exempt from the administrative criminal liability, the suspension of the administrative criminal proceedings or the enforceability of the expulsion will be lifted.[1950] In these cases it is not possible to apply for a 'temporary residence permit and work permit for exceptional circumstances for foreign victims of human trafficking'. However, it is still possible to apply for another 'temporary residence permit for exceptional circumstances' and, as a result, the deportation proceedings will remain suspended.[1951]

d) Right to stay

The 'temporary residence permit and work permit' granted is valid for five years and does not have any territorial restrictions or limitations on the work that may be undertaken.[1952] Just as with the 'provisional residence permit and work permit', a residence permit can again be applied for the victim's children and, if the victim meets the requirements, can also be granted to the children.[1953] One must also emphasise here that Article 144(5) REDYLE refers to the fact that after the five years there may be an application for a long term residence permit (*residencia de larga*

1946 Art 144(3); cf. *Díaz Morgado*, La residencia de víctimas de trata de personas y la residencia por colaboración contra redes organizadas in *Boza Martínez/Donaire Villa/Moya Malapeira* 361f.
1947 Art 144(4) REDYLE.
1948 Art 144(4) REDYLE.
1949 Cf. Instrucción DGI/SGRJ/6/2011, 4f.
1950 Art 143(2) REDYLE.
1951 Art 143(3) REDYLE and see Chapter 3.C.III.3.b.
1952 Art 144(5) REDYLE.
1953 Cf. Instrucción DGI/SGRJ/6/2011, 4f.

duración),[1954] whereby the periods under the 'provisional residence and work permit' count towards the required five years.[1955]

If the application for a 'temporary residence permit and work permit' is unsuccessful, no such permit is granted and the 'provisional residence permit and work permit' is no longer valid.[1956] The person concerned will therefore be staying irregularly, but may apply for a different 'temporary residence permit for exceptional circumstances' to become regularised once again. The application is taken into account in the (resumed) deportation procedure and in any case the deportation procedure will be discontinued if the permit is granted.[1957]

5. Spain: 'temporary residence permit and work permit for exceptional circumstances for foreign women who are victims of gender-based violence'

Article 31bis LODYLE and Articles 131–134 REDYLE stipulate the requirements for the 'temporary residence permit and work permit for exceptional circumstances for foreign women who are victims of gender-based violence' (*autorización de residencia temporal y trabajo de mujeres extranjeras víctimas de violencia de género*).[1958] On a broader level, the Organic Law 1/2004 (LOMPIVG) created general provisions concerning the protection against gender-based violence.[1959] The Organic Law 10/2011

1954 Art 32 LODYLE. See also the Long Term Residence Directive.

1955 Cf. *Vicente Palacio*, Art 59bis LODYLE in *Monereo Pérez/Fernández Avilés/Triguero Martínez* 968.

1956 Art 144(6) REDYLE.

1957 Arts 144(7) and 241(2) REDYLE; in this sense *Lázaro González/Benlloch Sanz* in *Palomar Olmeda* 931f and see Chapter 3.C.III.3.b. on Art 241(2) REDYLE.

1958 Cf. on the women who were victims of gender-based violence *Toledo Larrea*, Análisis de la situación jurídico-social de las mujeres extranjeras víctimas de violencia de género acogidas en los recursos integrales para víctimas de violencia de género de la administración autonómica andaluza, Revista de Derecho Migratorio y Extranjería 2014/37, 53 (54–56).

1959 On the notion of gender-based violence see Art 1(3) LOMPIVG; for detail see *Acale Sánchez*, La Residencia de mujeres víctimas de violencia de género in *Boza Martínez/Donaire Villa/Moya Malapeira* (eds), Comentario a la reforma de la ley de extranjería (LO 2/2009) (2011) 321 (322ff); *Lázaro González/Benlloch Sanz* in *Palomar Olmeda* 935ff as well as *Esteban de la Rosa*, Art 31bis LODYLE in *Monereo Pérez/Fernández Avilés/Triguero Martínez* (eds), Comentario a la ley y al reglamento de Extranjería, Inmigración e Integración Social^2 (2013) 519 (524–527).

amended Article 31bis LODYLE, which has not been amended since.[1960] Furthermore, since 2015 the LEVD provides specific rights to victims of gender-based violence.

Like the victims of human trafficking,[1961] the victims of gender-based violence receive particular protection due to their vulnerability.[1962] The introduction of this purely domestic residence permit is justified by the fact that in 2013 and 2014 alone, 37% of those killed by domestic violence were foreign women.[1963] If one considers that approx. 11.4% of the Spanish population are foreigners, the scale of the problem becomes clear.[1964] However, as precise statistics are lacking, it is not possible to determine how many residence permits were granted to protect victims of domestic violence.[1965]

a) Report

Article 131 REDYLE stipulates that a report implying gender-based violence will suspend any deportation proceedings, which were initiated due to the irregular stay, until the criminal proceedings have ended.[1966] However, no deportation proceedings will be opened if the authorities first learn of the irregularity through said report.[1967] It is clear from this provi-

1960 Cf. *Fernández Pérez*, Derechos fundamentales 235ff. On the previous law see *Díaz Morgado*, La residencia de mujeres víctimas de violencia de género in *Boza Martínez/Donaire Villa/Moya Malapeira* (eds), La nueva regulación de la inmigración y la extranjería en España (2012) 223 and *Acale Sánchez* in *Boza Martínez/Donaire Villa/Moya Malapeira* 329–332.

1961 See Chapter 4.D.I.4.

1962 Cf. Instrucción DGI/SGRJ/6/2011, 1; see further *Acale Sánchez* in *Boza Martínez/Donaire Villa/Moya Malapeira* 338f.

1963 *Consejo General del Poder Judicial*, Informe sobre víctimas mortales de la violencia de género y de la violencia doméstica en el ámbito de la pareja o ex pareja en el año 2015 (2015) 17. Along this line, *Acale Sánchez* in *Boza Martínez/Donaire Villa/Moya Malapeira* 321f and *Lázaro González/Benlloch Sanz* in *Palomar Olmeda* 935.

1964 See Chapter 3.C.

1965 See Chapter 3.C.III.1.

1966 See also Art 31bis LODYLE; cf. *Esteban de la Rosa*, Art 31bis LODYLE in *Monereo Pérez/Fernández Avilés/Triguero Martínez* 529ff.

1967 Cf. *Acale Sánchez* in *Boza Martínez/Donaire Villa/Moya Malapeira* 333 and *Lázaro González/Benlloch Sanz* in *Palomar Olmeda* 942f.

sion that the residence situation is subordinate to the protection against further violence.[1968]

Where a report is made, the authority is to inform the person concerned of the rights under the LOMPIVG and LODYLE.[1969] In particular, Article 27 LOMPIVG concerns the special social benefits for women who have little financial means and have difficulty to access the labour market due to their personal situation.[1970]

b) Court protection order and 'provisional residence permit and work permit'

Article 31bis(3) LODYLE and Article 132(1) REDYLE both provide that a foreign woman, who is staying irregularly,[1971] may apply for a 'temporary residence permit for exceptional circumstances' from the time a court protection order (*orden de protección*)[1972] has been issued.[1973] However, where there is no order, the possibility to apply will depend on whether there is a report by the public prosecutor on indications of gender-based violence.[1974] An application for residence may also be made vis-á-vis the victim's children. The children must be minors or, if they are of full age, have a disability and are not objectively capable of providing for their needs.[1975]

1968 Also *Esteban de la Rosa*, Art 31bis LODYLE in *Monereo Pérez/Fernández Avilés/ Triguero Martínez* 529–531.

1969 Cf. on the interplay between this legislation *Esteban de la Rosa*, Art 31bis LODYLE in *Monereo Pérez/Fernández Avilés/Triguero Martínez* 528ff.

1970 Cf. *Esteban de la Rosa*, Art 31bis LODYLE in *Monereo Pérez/Fernández Avilés/ Triguero Martínez* 525ff. On the rights under the LOMPIVG see *Toledo Larrea*, Revista de Derecho Migratorio y Extranjería 2014/37, 57ff.

1971 *Lázaro González/Benlloch Sanz* in *Palomar Olmeda* 941 favour analogous application to women staying regulary, whose stay is only temporarily lawful, e.g. due to a visa.

1972 *Dalli Almiñana*, La violencia de género y el acceso de las víctimas extranjeras en situación administrativa irregular a los servicios sanitarios: consecuencias del real decreto-ley 16/2012, Revista de Derecho Migratorio y Extranjería 2014/36, 39 (48f with further references) notes that it is often difficult in practice to obtain a court order.

1973 The application is possible until the criminal proceedings have been concluded or at the latest until six months after the proceedings; see Art 134(1)(b) REDYLE and *Lázaro González/Benlloch Sanz* in *Palomar Olmeda* 943.

1974 Cf. *Lázaro González/Benlloch Sanz* in *Palomar Olmeda* 940f, 944.

1975 Arts 133(1) and 134(1)(a) REDYLE.

The competent delegate or subdelegation of government shall submit *ex officio*[1976] a 'provisional residence permit and work permit' to the victim and, if necessary, to her children, provided there is a court protection order or report from the public prosecutor's office.[1977]

c) Right to stay

The public prosecutor's office is to inform the competent foreigners office and the competent police station[1978] of the content of the court decision.[1979] The key aspect is whether the criminal proceedings conclude with a conviction or judgment that the woman has been a victim of gender-based violence.[1980] If this is the case, the woman is to be granted a 'temporary residence permit and work permit for exceptional circumstances for foreign women who are victims of gender-based violence' within 20 days.[1981] The 'provisional residence permit and work permit' thus automatically becomes a temporary permit.[1982] Any deportation proceedings that have been suspended will be finally discontinued and no penalty will be issued on the basis of the irregular stay.[1983] Furthermore, it should be pointed out that, in contrast to other 'temporary residence permits for exceptional circumstances', a criminal record does not exclude the grant of the residence permit.[1984] The same goes for the requirement for being listed in the SIS for refusal of entry.

1976 Cf. *Acale Sánchez* in *Boza Martínez/Donaire Villa/Moya Malapeira* 336 and *Dalli Almiñana*, Revista de Derecho Migratorio y Extranjería 2014/36, 49.

1977 Art 31bis(3) LODYLE and Art 133 REDYLE.

1978 Cf. *Esteban de la Rosa*, Art 31bis LODYLE in *Monereo Pérez/Fernández Avilés/Triguero Martínez* 532f.

1979 Art 134 REDYLE.

1980 Art 31bis(4) LODYLE and Art 134 REDYLE. According to the guidelines regarding the law on foreigners, this is not an exhaustive list, which is why any (court) decision can be used if it can be used to derive the woman' status as a victim; Instrucción DGI/SGRJ/6/2011, 2

1981 Art 134(1)(a) REDYLE; cf. *Acale Sánchez* in *Boza Martínez/Donaire Villa/Moya Malapeira* 337.

1982 Cf. *Esteban de la Rosa*, Art 31bis LODYLE in *Monereo Pérez/Fernández Avilés/Triguero Martínez* 527.

1983 Art 134(1)(c) REDYLE; cf. *Esteban de la Rosa*, Art 31bis LODYLE in *Monereo Pérez/Fernández Avilés/Triguero Martínez* 530.

1984 As per *Acale Sánchez* in *Boza Martínez/Donaire Villa/Moya Malapeira* 333 and *Lázaro González/Benlloch Sanz* in *Palomar Olmeda* 943ff. For a contrasting view,

The residence permit is valid for five years[1985] and is accompanied by a work permit.[1986] If the person concerned has also applied for a residence permit for her underage children who were also residing in Spain at the time the violence was reported, these children will receive a residence permit of the same duration. Minors are only granted a work permit when they reach the age of 16.[1987] If such a residence permit has not yet been applied for, the women concerned must be informed of this possibility.[1988]

If there is no court decision that establishes the status as a victim, the 'provisional residence permit and work permit' automatically loses its validity and the application for a 'temporary residence permit and residence authorisation' is refused.[1989] The woman concerned may, however, apply for another 'temporary residence permit for exceptional circumstances'.[1990] For example, the aforementioned 'residence permit for humanitarian reasons' for victims of crimes comes into consideration if they are victims of domestic violence.[1991] After a refusal, the deportation procedure is generally resumed, whereby the application for another 'temporary residence permit for exceptional circumstances' must be taken into account.[1992] If the requirements for a residence permit are met, the deportation proceedings are discontinued.[1993]

---

see *Esteban de la Rosa*, Art 31bis LODYLE in *Monereo Pérez/Fernández Avilés/Triguero Martínez* 530f.

1985 Art 134(1)(a) REDYLE; cf. *Acale Sánchez* in *Boza Martínez/Donaire Villa/Moya Malapeira* 333.

1986 Art 134(1)(a) REDYLE. The national labour market situation is not taken into consideration; cf. *Lázaro González/Benlloch Sanz* in *Palomar Olmeda* 942.

1987 Cf. *Lázaro González/Benlloch Sanz* in *Palomar Olmeda* 944.

1988 See Fn 1973.

1989 Art 134(2)(a) REDYLE; cf. *Acale Sánchez* in *Boza Martínez/Donaire Villa/Moya Malapeira* 337.

1990 Cf. *Acale Sánchez* in *Boza Martínez/Donaire Villa/Moya Malapeira* 337f.

1991 Cf. *Acale Sánchez* in *Boza Martínez/Donaire Villa/Moya Malapeira* 334 and see Chapter 4.D.I.3.

1992 Art 134(2)(c) REDYLE; cf. *Esteban de la Rosa*, Art 31bis LODYLE in *Monereo Pérez/Fernández Avilés/Triguero Martínez* 531.

1993 Art 241(2) REDYLE. See Chapter 3.C.III.3.b.

II. Other cases of hardship

This section on other cases of hardship[1994] begins with the German 'granting residence in case of hardship', as this is not subject to a minimum period, but rather a maximum three-year period. This is followed by the Austrian 'residence permit in particularly exceptional cases' and the Spanish 'temporary residence permit for humanitarian reasons' due to sudden serious illness, as these are both limited to one year.

1. Germany: 'granting residence in cases of hardship'

The German 'granting residence in cases of hardship' is a regularisation applicable in especially difficult cases of hardship in order to find a humanitarian solution based on the foreigner's vulnerability.[1995] It is the last 'residence permit for humanitarian reasons' under the German system.[1996] The permit is rooted in domestic law and to be interpreted accordingly as it is not derived from any higher-ranking sources. By the end of 2020, 9,093 foreigners held a residence permit pursuant to § 23a AufenthG.[1997]

a) Requirements

§ 23a AufenthG applies to a foreigner who is enforceably required to leave Germany.[1998] A hardship commission (*Härtefallkommission*) established by the *Land* government by virtue of a statutory instrument may deal with particular cases of hardship.[1999] However, the foreigner is not legally entitled to this.[2000]

1994 See Chapter 1.B.III.4.b.

1995 No. 23a.0.1 AVV-AufenthG.

1996 See also *Röcker* in *Bergmann/Dienelt* § 23a AufenthG mn 5, according to whom the wording 'in derogation from' (*abweichend von*) means that § 23a AufenthG is subsidiary in its relationship to the other 'residence permits for humanitarian reasons'.

1997 BT-Drs 19/32579, 13.

1998 § 23a(1) 1st Sent. AufenthG.

1999 Cf. *Röcker* in *Bergmann/Dienelt* § 23a AufenthG mns 3f.

2000 § 23a(2) 2nd and 3rd Sent. AufenthG; cf. *Röcker* in *Bergmann/Dienelt* § 23a AufenthG mn 9.

The provision determines a specific multi-stage procedure,[2001] according to which the hardship commission can file a 'hardship petition' to the supreme *Land* authority. This is not an obstacle to deportation and does not have a suspensive effect.[2002] If the supreme *Land* authority concludes that there is in fact a case of hardship, it issues an order to the competent foreigners authority to grant a residence permit.[2003] *Maaßen/Kluth* are succinct in their description of the hardship process as one that is designed in a purely humanitarian manner, not subject to judicial review and, in comparison to all other provisions of the Residence Act, extra-judicial.[2004] The residence permit may be granted even if it deviates from the requirements for issuing and extending a residence permit under the AufenthG.[2005]

Whether the hardship petition is filed will depend on whether there are urgent humanitarian or personal grounds that have been established and justify the foreigner's continued presence in the federal territory.[2006] This includes, for example, serious health problems, extreme circumstances, permanent participation in working life or long periods of residence, though these will depend on the rules under *Land* law.[2007] *Schwantner* concludes, however, that secured subsistence is of particular significance.[2008] In any case, the grant of a residence permit must be necessary to especially urgent circumstances in the individual case.[2009] A case of hardship will generally not be considered if the foreigner has committed a 'serious

2001 *Maaßen/Kluth* in *Kluth/Heusch* § 23a AufenthG mn 2.

2002 *Maaßen/Kluth* in *Kluth/Heusch* § 23a AufenthG mn 12.

2003 The supreme *Land* authority is not bound by the hardship petition; cf. *Röcker* in *Bergmann/Dienelt* § 23a AufenthG mn 20.

2004 *Maaßen/Kluth* in *Kluth/Heusch* § 23a AufenthG mn 3. For criticism see *Schönebroicher*, Rechtsstaat auf Abwegen? – Die neue „Härtefallklausel" des Ausländerrechts, ZAR 2004, 351 (355ff) and from the perspective of constitutional law *Kluth*, Die Beurteilung der Härtefallkommission nach § 23a AufenthG aus dem Blickwinkel des Verfassungsrechts, ZAR 2022, 204.

2005 See Chapter 3.B.III.2.b.

2006 § 23a(2) 4th Sent. AufenthG.

2007 Cf. *Schwantner*, Zur Arbeit der Härtefallkommissionen, Asylmagazin 2016, 63 (63f).

2008 *Schwantner*, Asylmagazin 2016, 64.

2009 Cf. *Röcker* in *Bergmann/Dienelt* § 23a AufenthG mns 11f.

offence'[2010] or if a concrete date has already been set for the foreigner's removal.[2011]

b) Right to stay

According to the general rule in § 26(1) 1st Sent. AufenthG, the residence permit may be granted for a maximum of three years. The hardship procedure gives rise to differences vis-à-vis the means of legal protection.[2012] The residence permit entitles the foreigner to engage in employment pursuant to § 4a(1) 1st Sent. AufenthG.[2013] Holders of a residence permit pursuant to § 23a AufenthG are generally entitled to the Unemployment Benefits II pursuant to the Social Insurance Code II or social assistance pursuant to the Social Insurance Code XII.[2014]

2. Austria: 'residence permit in particularly exceptional cases'

The 'residence permit in particularly exceptional cases' is a purely national means of protection and extends beyond the international obligations under Article 8 ECHR. As noted above,[2015] there are generally no Austrian statistics for 'residence permits for exceptional circumstances', though statistics from a study published in 2019 show that 169 residence permits were issued between 2014 and 2018.[2016] It is therefore reasonable to state that the 'residence permits in particularly exceptional cases' are of little relevance in practice.

2010 Cf. *Röcker* in *Bergmann/Dienelt* § 23a AufenthG mn 13 and *Maaßen/Kluth* in *Kluth/Heusch* § 23a AufenthG mn 8.

2011 § 23a(1) 3rd Sent. AufenthG. For criticism see *Schwantner*, Asylmagazin 2016, 63, referring to the possibility in § 59(1) 3rd Sent. AufenthG to waive the warning of an intention to deport.

2012 For detail see *Röcker* in *Bergmann/Dienelt* § 23a AufenthG mns 23–26.

2013 This used to be expressly regulated in § 23a(2) 5th Sent. AufenthG; cf. BT-Drs 19/8285, 31 and *Schuster/Voigt*, Asylmagazin 2020, 65.

2014 *Frings/Janda/Keßler/Steffen*, Sozialrecht mn 935.

2015 See Chapter 3.A.III.1.

2016 *Bassermann*, Überblick über nationale Schutzstatus in Österreich (May 2019) 24–26.

a) Requirements

A 'residence permit in particularly exceptional cases' requires proof that the alien has been resident in Austria for a continuous period of five years, whereby the alien must have been lawfully resident for three years of this period. The residence permit also applies to aliens residing unlawfully, and is thus relevant to this study. According to *Fouchs/Schweda*, 'resident in the federal territory for a continuous period' (*durchgängiger Aufenthalt im Bundesgebiet*) is to be understood as according to the law until 1 January 2014.[2017] Following the Supreme Administrative Court's case law of the time, therefore, short stays in Austria and abroad, especially for visiting purposes, do not interrupt the continuous period necessary for the permit.[2018] A stay abroad would only interrupt this period if accompanied by a change in the centre of the alien's life. The corresponding Spanish law is much more specific in this respect and allows stays abroad up to a total of 120 days in relation to 'temporary residence permits for reasons of social roots'.[2019]

Pursuant to § 56(3) AsylG (A), the Federal Office for Immigration and Asylum shall also take into account the 'degree of integration, in particular the ability to earn his or her living, education, vocational training, employment and knowledge of the German language'.[2020] Unlike the 'residence permit for reasons of Article 8 ECHR', the very high threshold of private or family life does not have to be met.[2021] According to the Supreme Administrative Court, the residence permit aims to settle particularly exceptional 'old cases'.[2022]

Further key requirements include the legal entitlement to accommodation deemed in conformity with local accommodation, adequate health insurance as well as fixed and regular income.[2023] As a guideline, the income for an unmarried person in 2022 is set at approx. 1000 euro/month

2017 *Fouchs/Schweda*, migraLex 2014, 61 with further references; concurring *Kind* in *Abermann/Czech/Kind/Peyrl* § 43 NAG mns 17f.

2018 VwGH 20.8.2013, 2012/22/0122.

2019 See Chapter 4.E.I.a.

2020 See also VwGH 11.6.2014, 2013/22/0356.

2021 See just VwGH 19.12.2019, Ra 2019/21/0308. See Chapter 4.B.III. and Chapter 4.C.III.

2022 On the provision under the previous law VwGH 29.4.2010, 2009/21/0255.

2023 § 60(2) AsylG (A). Cf. on the provision under the previous law VwGH 25.3.2010, 2010/21/0088.

and approx. 1600 euro/month for a married couple,[2024] though the Federal Office for Immigration and Asylum does have to make a prediction in this respect.[2025] In principle this means that the alien must be self-sufficient. According to the Supreme Administrative Court, however, it suffices if there are sufficiently concrete prospects, such as an employment contract.[2026] Prior to a decision of the Austrian Constitutional Court in 2021, asylum seekers could access the labour market only in theory and not in practice, which is why rejected asylum seekers could not satisfy the self-sufficiency requirement.[2027] However, since June 2021 the access to the labour market is legally and factually open to asylum seekers.[2028] Irregularly staying aliens have (still) no access to the labour market.[2029] In this respect, it is to be noted that these requirements may be met by a sponsorship declaration.[2030] As a final requirement, the residence permit may only be granted if it does not significantly harm Austrian relations with another state or another subject of international law.

In practice this residence permit should probably be aimed at cases of lengthy asylum procedures (rejected asylum seekers), since the stay is lawful during the ongoing procedure.[2031] If an asylum procedure neither leads to the grant of asylum nor the status as a beneficiary of subsidiary protection and if it has lasted longer than three years, it is therefore possible to apply for this type of residence permit. The very high hurdles and the requirement of self-sufficiency seem to make it impossible to obtain this type of permit.[2032] However, the regained access to the labour market for asylum seekers, which exists again in fact since June 2021, could lead to a higher number of residence permits in the future.

2024 § 11(5) NAG in conjunction with § 293 ASVG.

2025 VwGH 18.3.2010, 2008/22/0637; 21.6.2011, 2009/22/0060 and 23.11.2017, Ra 2017/22/0144.

2026 VwGH 15.12.2011, 2008/21/0002.

2027 On the access to the labour market for asylum seekers prior to the VfGH ruling see *Peyrl*, Arbeitsmarkt 302ff.

2028 VfGH 23.6.2021, V 95-96/2021-12. See also the decree 14.7.2021, 2021-0.502.591 and *Deutsch/Nowotny/Seitz*, Ausländerbeschäftigungsrecht Vorwort.

2029 See Chapter 3.A.II.2.

2030 § 2(1) No. 26 AsylG (A); VwGH 11.6.2014, 2013/22/0356 and in this sense *Filzwieser/Frank/Kloibmüller/Raschhofer*, Asyl- und Fremdenrecht § 56 AsylG mn 2.

2031 § 13(1) AsylG (A).

2032 See *Bassermann*, Überblick über nationale Schutzstatus in Österreich (May 2019) 49, who takes a similar direction.

b) Right to stay

Reference is made here to the explanations in Chapter 3.A.III.2.d. Furthermore, it is to be noted that there is no provision allowing an *ex officio* grant and therefore the 'residence permit in particularly exceptional cases' is only granted upon application.[2033] An ongoing procedure to impose a removal measure does not prevent a well-founded application.[2034] If the requirements are met, there is protection against deportation until there is a final decision, if the procedure for rendering a return decision was initiated only after the application was filed.[2035]

3. Spain: 'temporary residence permit for humanitarian reasons' – sudden serious illness

The Spanish law on foreigners provides a 'temporary residence permit for humanitarian reasons' in cases in which the foreigner suddenly suffers a serious illness (*autorización temporal por razones humanitarias – enfermedad sobrevenida grave*). The other two residence permits issued for humanitarian reasons have been discussed above.[2036] Although here the term 'humanitarian reasons' suggests that the analysis would be better placed under 'social ties',[2037] the argument for a discussion in the context of 'vulnerability' carries greater weight: the most significant reason for granting the permit is the link to a vulnerable situation, namely a sudden, serious illness. In principle this regularisation qualifies as purely domestic, but may be derived from Article 3 ECHR as recent ECtHR case law suggests.[2038] One could therefore consider an analysis under 'non-returnability' (under 'non-refoulement under the ECHR and CFR or factual reasons'), but this would not give sufficient heed to the domestic nature of this particular right to stay. The number of residence permits granted on the basis of a sudden, serious illness cannot be ascertained from the statistics.[2039]

In addition, a separate residence permit exists for minors who have travelled to Spain under a temporary programme for the purposes of medical

2033 VwGH 15.3.2018, Ra 2018/21/0034.
2034 § 56(1) AsylG (A).
2035 § 58(13) 4th Sent. AsylG (A); see Chapter 3.A.III.2.a.
2036 See Chapter 4.A.II.3. and Chapter 4.D.I.3.
2037 See Chapter 4.B.
2038 For detail see *Hinterberger/Klammer* in *Filzwieser/Taucher*.
2039 See Chapter 3.C.III.1.

treatment.[2040] In contrast to the 'temporary residence permit for humanitarian reasons', the minors do not have to prove a sudden illness – they are travelling lawfully to Spain to receive medical treatment, for which a clinical report must be presented.[2041] This is therefore not a regularisation for the purposes of this study and is not subject to analysis.[2042]

a) Requirements

A 'temporary residence permit for humanitarian reasons' may be granted to foreigners who can prove that they are suffering from a sudden, serious illness.[2043] 'Sudden' means that the illness was first diagnosed after entry into Spain,[2044] thereby avoiding the situation in which a serious illness was diagnosed just for the purposes of travelling to Spain for treatment.[2045] The proof of a 'sudden' illness does not appear to be compatible with the recent ECtHR case law concerning Article 3 ECHR,[2046] as the person concerned cannot acquire the 'temporary residence permit for humanitarian reasons', is therefore staying irregularly and in effect merely tolerated.[2047]

The proof of a serious illness and sudden onset is to be furnished via a clinical report – this is central to the decision on granting the type of residence permit discussed here.[2048] Furthermore, it is to be proven that treatment in Spain is adequate and not available in the country of origin.[2049] There must also be evidence that an interruption to or non-receipt of the medical treatment would seriously endanger the person's health or life.[2050] From a procedural perspective, Article 246(7) REDYLE is relevant

2040 Arts 126(2) and 187 REDYLE.

2041 Cf. *Giménez Bachmann*, Dissertation 2014, 299.

2042 See Chapter 1.A.II.1.

2043 Art 126(2) REDYLE.

2044 STS 782/2007, ECLI:ES:TS:2009:782, FJ 9; *Defensor del Pueblo*, Sugerencia (14.7.2017), Queja 17012408; *Defensor del Pueblo*, Sugerencia (24.2.2015), Queja 12009749; for criticism see *Giménez Bachmann*, Dissertation 2014, 295f with further references.

2045 STSJ Madrid 6102/2009, ECLI:ES:TSJM:2009:6102 and see *Giménez Bachmann*, Dissertation 2014, 295.

2046 ECtHR 13.12.2016, *Paposhvili/Belgium*, 41738/10 and *Hinterberger/Klammer* in *Filzwieser/Taucher* for detail.

2047 See Chapter 4.A.I.1.

2048 STSJ Madrid 628/2015, ECLI:ES:TSJM:2015:628.

2049 Cf. STSJ Madrid 11645/2009, ECLI:ES:TSJM:2009:11645.

2050 Cf. *García Vitoria* in *Boza Martínez/Donaire Villa/Moya Malapeira* 297.

here, whereby an expulsion (i.e. the deportation) is to be suspended if the measure poses a risk to the health of a sick person.

b) Right to stay

The residence permit is usually valid for one year[2051] and is in principle not accompanied by an employment permit.[2052] However, an application for an employment permit may be submitted in parallel.[2053]

III. Interim conclusion

The fourth category of the purpose of the regularisation is characterised by targeting vulnerable persons or situations and is divided into two subcategories. Whereas 'victim protection' is measured against the standards in EU law (above all the Human Trafficking Directive and the Employers Sanctions Directive), 'other hardships' are not derived from international or EU law and are thus purely domestic in nature.

According to the Human Trafficking Directive and the Employers Sanctions Directive, the Member States must grant the victims of certain criminal offences the possibility of obtaining a residence permit, though the Member States have the discretion regarding the definition of the conditions and the decision to grant the residence permit.

Spanish law contains separate provisions concerning the regularisation of victims of human trafficking and for women who are victims of gender-based violence. The former represents an exemplary implementation of the Human Trafficking Directive. The latter creates an effective protection regime for the problem of violence against foreign women. The very similar temporary residence permits and work permits are characterised by particularly detailed regulations that are very much guided by the needs of the victims. The procedure is divided into several 'phases'. First of all, the focus is on the identification of the victims and a recovery and reflection phase, each of which is prescribed by law. Subsequently, the foreigner may

2051 Cf. *García Vitoria* in *Boza Martínez/Donaire Villa/Moya Malapeira* 304.

2052 Art 129(1) REDYLE.

2053 Art 129(2) REDYLE; cf. *García Vitoria* in *Boza Martínez/Donaire Villa/Moya Malapeira* 304. On the requirements see Arts 63(4) and 105(3) REDYLE. Cf. also *Giménez Bachmann*, Dissertation 2014, 297.

be exempted from any administrative penalties, for example in relation to an irregular stay. The exemption triggers an important legal consequence, as the person concerned must then be informed of the possibility to apply for a 'temporary residence permit and work permit'. A 'provisional residence permit and work permit' may be granted after the application, which underlines the extraordinarily victim-friendly approach, as the residence is therefore lawful until the conclusion of the proceedings. It should also be emphasised that the two Spanish residence permits are issued for a period of five years, which is by far the longest time limit in comparison to the Austrian and German law and thus enables the acquisition of a long-term residence permit. Furthermore, the residence permit granted is accompanied by a work permit.

At the risk of jumping the gun, 'other national interests' concerns a further regularisation that is structurally similar to the Spanish residence permits falling under 'vulnerability': the 'temporary residence permit for exceptional circumstances due to collaboration in the fight against organised networks'. However, this additional regularisation, which transposes the Employers Sanctions Directive, requires cooperation with the authorities and is thus discussed in the context of 'other national interests'.[2054]

Spanish law also features a third type of regularisation, namely the 'temporary residence permit for humanitarian reasons' for victims of crime, which is linked to situations of particular vulnerability, such as crimes against employee rights or crimes whose motive is based on racist, anti-Semitic or other discriminatory grounds. This residence permit is problematic in so far as it requires the submission of a final court decision, which could take several years. Nevertheless, it might be often the case that a 'temporary residence permit for reasons of social roots' can be applied for and granted beforehand.

The Austrian 'special protection residence permit' for victims of crime follows a similar direction. It merely determines that victims of violence shall be protected against further violence by receiving a residence permit and covers the victims of human trafficking or cross-border trade in prostitution, or victims of domestic violence or of forced marriage/partnership. In contrast to its Spanish counterparts, there is no sophisticated procedure that protects the victim's interests. Furthermore, granting the residence permit requires the purpose of guaranteeing the prosecution of acts punishable by the courts or of asserting and enforcing civil-law claims in connection with such punishable acts. This requirement greatly narrows

2054 See Chapter 4.F.II.

the scope of application. The 'special protection residence permit' is valid for one year and, depending on the circumstances, offers restricted or unrestricted access to the labour market.

The spotlight was then directed towards the German 'residence permit for prosecution of criminal offences'. This may be granted to the victims of human trafficking or undocumented employment, which requires an assessment of the relevant provisions of criminal law. As under Austrian law, German law requires the victim's presence in Germany to be necessary and considered appropriate with regard to the criminal proceedings. In comparison to the Spanish provisions concerning victims of human trafficking or gender-based violence, the German residence permit is worse or just as poor as the Austrian 'special protection residence permit'. This is also shown in practice, where the German 'residence permit for prosecution of criminal offences' plays practically no role due to the extensive requirements.

One may therefore observe that all three Member States comply with the requirements under EU law and provide regularisations for victims of human trafficking or exploitative working conditions. Be that as it may, there are notable differences in how the protection is designed. In contrast to the victim-friendly system in Spain, Austrian and German law appear to be very minimalist and, in addition to the interests of the victim, focus primarily on the purpose of criminal justice.

The category 'vulnerability' also features the sub-category 'other cases of hardship'. This sub-category is purely domestic in nature. As it is derived just from the national legal systems, there are no obligations under international or EU law that are to be met or observed.

'Granting residence in cases of hardship' under German law is the last possibility for irregularly staying foreigners, and was introduced for precisely this reason. The foreigner cannot apply for this type of regularisation, instead there is an extra-judicial process designed on a purely humanitarian basis. It covers all types of particularly urgent circumstances in an individual case and is a 'catch-all' solution for cases that do not fall into other categories of residence permits. Nonetheless, it is to be criticised from the perspective of an individual's rights as it is not issued upon application by the person concerned and is subject to a distinct procedure in which the principles under the Residence Act do not apply.

The 'residence permits in particularly exceptional cases' are a peculiar feature of Austrian law. It was introduced to allow for the prospect of regularisation in instances of lengthy asylum procedures in which no residence status was granted. In principle it targets those (ir)regularly staying aliens who do not reach the high threshold of private and family life in the sense of Article 8 ECHR. The statistics highlight that the permit has a near-irrelevant role in practice due to the extensive hurdles that have to be overcome. In addition to five years' continuous residence, the alien must have the ability to be self-sufficient – a criterion that is nearly impossible to fulfil where there is a lack of access to the labour market. Nonetheless, the regained access to the labour market for asylum seekers since June 2021 could lead to a higher number of residence permits in the future.

The Spanish 'temporary residence permit for humanitarian reasons' due to sudden serious illness is a purely domestic instrument, but in light of recent ECtHR case law could be understood as an expression of Article 3 ECHR. The requirement that adults must prove the sudden onset of the illness does not seem to be compatible with international law; this requirement does not apply to minors. Overall, however, it is positive that Spanish law features an independent right to stay for seriously ill persons.

The sub-category 'other cases of hardship' shows that each of the three Member States has developed a regularisation that is to be viewed as a distinctly national instrument aimed at the protection of vulnerable individuals or situations where there is no other possibility to acquire a right to stay.

E. Employment and training

The purpose 'employment and training'[2055] comprises four regularisations identified from the comparison of the national laws. I will first present the Spanish 'temporary residence permit for reasons of social roots', the 'temporary residence permit for reasons of employment roots' and the 'temporary residence permit for reasons of training roots' as these are each valid for one year/twelve months. The attention is then directed to the German 'residence permit for the purpose of qualified foreigners whose deportation has been suspended', as this is issued for a period of two years.

I. Spain: 'temporary residence permit for reasons of social roots'

The 'temporary residence permit for reasons of social roots' (*autorización de residencia temporal por razones de arraigo social*) is the most common in

2055 See Chapter 1.B.III.5.

practice and the most important regularisation in Spain.[2056] Even though it already worked quite well in practice, it was reformed by the Royal Decree 629/2022 – with the words of the Spanish legislator – to even better address the needs of the Spanish labour market.[2057]

This type of residence permit could fall under 'social ties' as well as 'employment and training'. For the former, the name alone offers justification as well as the fact that in certain circumstances any form of integration has to be proven.[2058] Nonetheless, the focus lies on the submission of an employment contract and thus the discussion under the purpose 'employment and training'. The previous law also referred expressly to the 'foreign employee'.[2059]

Similar to the Austrian 'right to remain',[2060] the social roots have developed from the case law on disproportionate expulsion decisions according to Article 8 ECHR.[2061] Initially, the case law took a similar path, but ultimately both regularisations were anchored in a different manner in law. In principle the social roots under Spanish law refer to future roots,[2062] whereas the Austrian 'right to remain' refers to established roots.[2063] 'Social roots' under Spanish law is now perhaps most comparable with the Austrian 'residence permit in particularly exceptional cases' under § 56 AsylG (A), especially with respect to the proof of continuous residency.[2064] It can thus be stated that the regularisation may in principle be derived from Article 8 ECHR, but due to its codification in national law, it takes a step beyond this human rights obligation and is to be understood as a provision of purely national law.

2056 See Chapter 3.C.III.2.

2057 Royal Decree 629/2022, BOE 179 of 27.7.2022, 107698.

2058 Cf. *Triguero Martínez*, Migraciones 2014, 455 and *Cerezo Mariscal*, Revista de Derecho 2015, 676.

2059 Art 45(2)(b) REDYLE in the version Royal Decree 2393/2004 and the accompanying Instrucción del 22 de junio de 2005 de la Dirección General de Inmigración, http://fmrmurcia.info/UPLOAD/DOCUMENTO/instruccion%20arraigo%20_definitiva_%20_1_.pdf (31.7.2022) 1.

2060 See Chapter 4.B.III.1. and Chapter 4.C.III.1.

2061 See Chapter 3.C.III.2.

2062 *Carbajal García*, Revista de Derecho Migratorio y Extranjería 2012/29, 82. *González Calvet*, Revista de Derecho Social 2007/37, 108 who is correct in noting that a minimum residence period is required as otherwise the 'social roots' do not come into consideration.

2063 See Chapter 4.B.III. and Chapter 4.C.III.

2064 See Chapter 4.F.I.

1. Requirements

The 'temporary residence permit for reasons of social roots' requires continuous residence in Spain for three years.[2065] According to the accompanying guidelines, the entry in the municipal register (*Padrón*) serves as the most important evidence for continuous residence,[2066] though in principle any evidence accepted by law will suffice,[2067] such as health insurance statements, bank statements, the transfer of funds to a bank account abroad, or certificates from language or integration courses. A period of continuous residence is necessary, though stays abroad do not have any detrimental effect if the total duration is less than 120 days.[2068]

As for employment roots,[2069] evidence of employment relationships is also to be furnished.[2070] Prior to the Royal Decree 629/2022 this required a signed employment contract for at least one year. In principle the applicant only needed to present one employment contract of the required duration, even though it was possible in certain sectors to fulfil the one-year period by furnishing multiple employment contracts.[2071] The agricultural sector, which is a key source of income for foreigners in Spain, was one such example.[2072]

According to the newly formulated Article 124(2)(b) REDYLE, the foreigner must present an employment contract signed by the worker and employer, which guarantees at least the minimum interprofessional wage (*salario mínimo interprofesional*), or that established by the applicable collective bargaining agreement. The contract must stipulate a minimum of 30 working hours per week.[2073] In the agricultural sector, two or more contracts with different employers may still be presented, each of them

---

2065 Cf. *Triguero Martínez*, Migraciones 2014, 453; *Ques Mena*, Diario la Ley 2008/7067, 6.

2066 Cf. Instrucción del 22 de junio de 2005 de la Dirección General de Inmigración, 2.

2067 Cf. Instrucción DGI/SGRJ/3/2011, 3.

2068 Cf. Instrucción del 22 de junio de 2005 de la Dirección General de Inmigración, 2.

2069 See Chapter 4.E.II.

2070 *Camas Roda*, Trabajo decente 96.

2071 Cf. *Carbajal García*, Revista de Derecho Migratorio y Extranjería 2012/29, 67, who welcomed its introduction as it offered greater flexibility to the applicant.

2072 Cf. *Iglesias Martínez*, Estudios Empresariales 2015/2 No. 148, 3ff.

2073 The contract may have a duration of at least 20 hours in cases where it is accredited that the worker is in charge of minors or persons who require support measures for the exercise of their legal capacity.

linked together. The presentation of several contracts in the same or different occupations, working partially and simultaneously for more than one employer, is also permitted.

The competent foreigners office may acquire an opinion on the employment contract from the Labour and Social Security Inspectorate (*Inspección de Trabajo y Seguridad Social*).[2074] It must be possible for the employment relationship to begin upon receiving the residence permit,[2075] which highlights how Spanish immigration policies fall under the policy objectives concerning the labour market.[2076]

An exception of the requisite to provide an employment contract applies in cases in which the foreigner has sufficient financial resources (currently 491.63 euro/month).[2077] This is a significant reduction in comparison to the applicable rules before the Royal Decree 629/2022. The competent autonomous community may propose an exception to this requirement in its report to the foreigners office if there is such evidence.[2078]

Furthermore, either social integration into Spanish society or a family relationship must be proven.[2079] Evidence of social integration is made in the form of a report submitted by the foreigner.[2080] This is issued by the competent autonomous community or the town hall,[2081] for which the authority has 30 days commencing from the submission of the application. [2082] The report should address, inter alia, the previous duration

2074 Cf. Carbajal García, Revista de Derecho Migratorio y Extranjería 2012/29, 71ff.

2075 Cf. Carbajal García, Revista de Derecho Migratorio y Extranjería 2012/29, 71ff. The employment relationship is conditional on receiving the residence permit. On the control of the actual start of employment see Chapter 4.E.I.2.

2076 Cf. *Nieves Moreno Vida* in *Monereo Pérez/Fernández Avilés/Triguero Martínez* 624; along these lines regarding the Royal Decree 2393/2004 *Gómez Díaz* in *Balado Ruiz-Gallegos* 887. For a different view see *Triguero Martínez*, Migraciones 2014, 455, who notes that there is no need to present an employment contract if the foreigner proves that he or she has sufficient financial resources.

2077 Art 124(2)(c) REDYLE refers to the Minimum Vital Income (*Ingreso Mínimo Vital*); see https://www.seg-social.es/wps/portal/wss/internet/Trabajadores/Prestaciones PensionesTrabajadores/65850d68-8d06-4645-bde7-05374ee42ac7 (31.7.2022).

2078 Cf. *Belgrano Ledesma*, Solicitar una autorización de residencia temporal por arraigo social, Iuris 2010/151, 59 (61f).

2079 Art 124(2)(c) REDYLE and Instrucción DGI/SGRJ/3/2011.

2080 Art 128(2)(b) REDYLE; cf. for detail Instrucción del 22 de junio de 2005 de la Dirección General de Inmigración, 4 and 8–10, which specifies the submission of a report.

2081 Art 68(3) LODYLE; cf. *Cerezo Mariscal*, Revista de Derecho 2015, 679 and *Camas Roda*, Trabajo decente 96f.

2082 Art 124(2)(c) REDYLE.

of stay at the address of registration, the foreigner's financial resources, the relations with legally resident family members and the integration efforts on the basis of the professional-social and cultural integration programmes.[2083]

If the report is not issued within the 30-day period, the integration can also be proven otherwise.[2084] The foreigner can independently present any certificates of professional-social or cultural integration programmes.[2085] In addition, proof can be furnished that the foreigner has adequate housing and sufficient financial resources.[2086] The report of the autonomous community or the respective town hall is not binding on the foreigners authority.[2087] However, the competent foreigners authority must give reasons for deviating from a positive report by the competent autonomous community or town hall.[2088]

Family relationships with regularly residing foreigners must be presented as an alternative to providing evidence of social integration.[2089] Only spouses or registered partners and first-degree relatives (children and parents) fall under the narrow definition of family.[2090] The family relationship must be proven by means of a document recognised in Spain.[2091]

Finally, it is to be pointed out that social roots could be linked to another condition for granting a residence permit by issuing an instruction under the law on foreigners: the examination of the national labour market situation.[2092] The introduction of this condition would severely limit the scope of application of social roots and its effectiveness in practice.[2093]

2083 Art 124(2) REDYLE as well as Art 68(3) LODYLE. Cf. Instrucción DGI/SGRJ/3/2011 and the example of Madrid given in *Pérez/Leraul*, El arraigo en España (11–13.4.2012) 12f.

2084 Art 124(2) REDYLE; cf. *Triguero Martínez*, Migraciones 2014, 454.

2085 Cf. *Camas Roda*, Trabajo decente 97.

2086 Cf. *Camas Roda*, Trabajo decente 97f and *Triguero Martínez*, Migraciones 2014, 455. In so far as the resources are from self-employed activities, this will be viewed positively, see STSJ Castilla y León 2957/2015, ECLI:ES:TSJCL:2015:2957.

2087 Cf. *Belgrano Ledesma*, Iuris 2010/151, 61.

2088 Cf. Instrucción DGI/SGRJ/3/2011, 6.

2089 Art 124(2) REDYLE.

2090 Cf. *Triguero Martínez*, Migraciones 2014, 453f.

2091 Art 128(2)(b) REDYLE and cf. Instrucción del 22 de junio de 2005 de la Dirección General de Inmigración, 3.

2092 Art 124(5) REDYLE and see further Art 65 REDYLE.

2093 Cf. *Triguero Martínez*, Migraciones 2014, 445f with further references.

However, this requirement has not been introduced in any corresponding instruction yet.

2. Right to stay

In general, the permit is issued for one year.[2094] Further details are provided in Chapter 4.C.V.2. To determine the actual start of employment, the person concerned must be registered for social security within one month of the procedure;[2095] the validity of the residence permit is suspended until registration. [2096] This prevents recourse to false employment contracts.[2097] Said requirement does not have to be met in cases where the foreigner has been exempted from presenting an employment contract.[2098]

If the person takes up employment without being registered for social security by the employer, registration can be requested directly from the Social Security Treasury General (*Tesorería General de la Seguridad Social*) so that the residence permit comes into effect.[2099]

II. Spain: 'temporary residence permit for reasons of employment roots'

Article 124(1) REDYLE offers a further regularisation: the 'temporary residence permit for reasons of employment roots' (*arraigo laboral*).[2100] This type of residence permit is subsumed under 'employment and training' as employment relationships are the main requirement.[2101] The 'roots' have indeed sprouted from the case law concerning Article 8 ECHR, but this

---

2094 Art 130(1) REDYLE.

2095 Art 128(6) REDYLE; cf. *García Vitoria* in *Boza Martínez/Donaire Villa/Moya Malapeira* 303.

2096 Art 67(7) REDYLE.

2097 For detail on this problem see *Carbajal García*, Revista de Derecho Migratorio y Extranjería 2012/29, 57 and 78–80 and *Nieves Moreno Vida* in *Monereo Pérez/Fernández Avilés/Triguero Martínez* 624f.

2098 Art 128(6) REDYLE; cf. *Fernández Collados* in *Palomar Olmeda* 433.

2099 Cf. Instrucciones Provisionales sobre Arraigo Laboral del Ministerio de Trabajo y Asuntos Sociales (3.8.2005), http://www.intermigra.info/archivos/legislacion/ARRAIGOLABORAL.pdf (31.7.2022).

2100 Art 124(1) REDYLE.

2101 Cf. *Triguero Martínez*, Migraciones 2014, 451f.

residence permit is to be understood as purely national in nature as it extends beyond the obligations under the ECHR.[2102]

1. Requirements

A continuous stay in Spain for a period of two years is required.[2103] An absence for up to 90 days will not have a detrimental effect on the application.[2104] The Royal Decree 629/2022 has supplemented the provision with the wording that the foreigner has to be irregularly staying at the time of application. The Spanish legislator attempted to further clarify that the residence permit is not only open to undocumented working foreigners – like before – but also to foreigners who work in a documented manner.[2105]

In addition, the applicant must demonstrate the existence of employment relationships of no less than six months in duration. The term 'employment relationship' is interpreted broadly.[2106] It covers all types of employee-employer relationships with one or more employers.[2107] The provision is therefore directed specifically at undocumented foreign workers.[2108] *Triguero Martínez* welcomes the fact that the period to be proven is now only six months – half the time as was required under the previous law (before the Royal Decree 557/2011).[2109]

One key problem in practice is, however, the documentation concerning the employment relationship. Usually, the employee is to notify the Labour and Social Security Inspectorate.[2110] However, this strikes fear into many foreigners:[2111] their undocumented employment and irregular resi-

2102 See Chapter 3.C.III.2. and Chapter 4.E.I.
2103 Art 124(1) REDYLE.
2104 Cf. Instrucciones Provisionales sobre Arraigo Laboral del Ministerio de Trabajo y Asuntos Sociales (3.8.2005).
2105 Royal Decree 629/2022, BOE 179 of 27.7.2022, 107698.
2106 Cf. Instrucciones Provisionales sobre Arraigo Laboral del Ministerio de Trabajo y Asuntos Sociales (3.8.2005).
2107 Cf. *González Calvet*, Revista de Derecho Social 2007/37, 124f and *García Vitoria* in *Boza Martínez/Donaire Villa/Moya Malapeira* 290.
2108 See only Royal Decree 629/2022, BOE 179 of 27.7.2022, 107698.
2109 *Triguero Martínez*, Migraciones 2014, 453; cf. *Carbajal García*, Revista de Derecho Migratorio y Extranjería 2012/29, 65.
2110 Cf. *Fernández Collados* in *Palomar Olmeda* 432f; *Camas Roda*, Trabajo decente 96 and *García Vitoria* in *Boza Martínez/Donaire Villa/Moya Malapeira* 290.
2111 Cf. *Cerezo Mariscal*, Revista de Derecho 2015, 675.

dence status are unlawful[2112] and thus there is the risk of deportation.[2113] Furthermore, the employer receives a fine[2114] in cases of undocumented employment and must also pay the outstanding social security contributions.[2115]

Before the Royal Decree 629/2022, the employment relationship may have been also demonstrated via a court decision (*resolución judicial*)[2116] or by any other means.[2117] The burden of proving the employment relationship therefore rested with the undocumented employee,[2118] if the Labour and Social Security Inspectorate did not coincidentally 'uncover' the undocumented employment in the course of a routine inspection.[2119] The reform in 2022 brought changes in this regard. The employment relationship and its duration may still be proven by any means. However, Article 124(1) REDYLE now specifies that proof shall be provided of the performance, in the last two years, of an employment activity involving, in the case of employed work, at least 30 hours per week over a period of 6 months or 15 hours per week over a period of 12 months, and in the case of self-employment, a continuous activity of at least 6 months.

Despite the intention to 'combat' irregular stays as well as undocumented employment, the aforementioned problem of proving employment relations meant – before the Royal Decree 629/2022 – that the numbers of this type of residence permit were low. Only 1.65% of all applications made (12,406) on the basis of 'roots' between 2006 and 2014 (747,685) and 1.54% of all 'temporary residence permits for reasons of roots' granted during this period, concerned employment roots.[2120] *Fernández Collados* even goes so far as to claim that, due to the difficulty of meeting the

2112 Art 53(1)(a) and (b) LODYLE; cf. *Camas Roda*, Trabajo decente 96.

2113 See Chapter 3.C.II.1.

2114 Art 54(1)(d) in conjunction with Art 55(1)(c) LODYLE; the minimum fine for undocumented employment is 10,000 euro.

2115 Cf. *González Calvet*, Revista de Derecho Social 2007/37, 124f.

2116 Cf. Instrucciones Provisionales sobre Arraigo Laboral del Ministerio de Trabajo y Asuntos Sociales (3.8.2005).

2117 Instrucción DGI/SGRJ/3/2011. For a contrasting view see *Carbajal García*, Revista de Derecho Migratorio y Extranjería 2012/29, 66 and *González Calvet*, Revista de Derecho Social 2007/37, 120. On the problems in practice see *Defensor del Pueblo*, Sugerencia (12.7.2017), Queja 16004439.

2118 Cf. *Solanes Corella*, Combatiendo la inmigración irregular: la insuficiencia de las regularizaciones y las sanciones in *Alberdi Bidaguren/Goizueta Vértiz* (eds), Algunos retos de la inmigración en el siglo XXI (2008) 201 (215f).

2119 Cf. *Triguero Martínez*, Migraciones 2014, 452.

2120 Cf. *Cerezo Mariscal*, Revista de Derecho 2015, 675.

requirements, the 'temporary residence permits for reasons of employment roots' deter employers from undocumented employment of foreigners rather than serving as an effective regularisation for foreigners staying irregularly and engaging in undocumented employment.[2121] However, it remains to be seen if the Royal Decree 629/2022 solves this problem with the reform of Article 124(1) REDYLE and the establishment of a new residence permit in Article 127(2) REDYLE.[2122]

2. Right to stay

The residence permit is granted for one year.[2123] Further information may be found in Chapter 4.C.V.2.

III. Spain: 'temporary residence permit for reasons of training roots'

The Royal Decree 629/2022 introduced a new type of *arraigo*, the so-called 'temporary residence permit for reasons of training roots' (*arraigo para la formación*) which is set out in Article 124(4) REDYLE. The role model is the German 'toleration for the purpose of training'.[2124] However, in contrast to the German toleration, the Spanish model is more generous as it grants irregularly staying foreigners an immediate right to stay. Nevertheless, the main idea was borrowed from the German approach: foreigners might 'earn' their right to residency.[2125]

1. Requirements

The foreigner has to prove that he or she has been in Spain for a continuous period of at least two years.[2126] The stay might be regular or irregular

---

2121 *Fernández Collados* in *Palomar Olmeda* 432f.

2122 See Chapter 4.F.I.

2123 Art 130(1) REDYLE.

2124 Royal Decree 629/2022, BOE 179 of 27.7.2022, 107698 and see Chapter 4.E.IV.1.

2125 See Chapter 4.E.IV.1.

2126 See already the remarks on how to prove the continuous residency in Chapter 4.E.I.1. on social roots.

during this time.[2127] The main requirement to obtain this residence permit is, however, that the foreigner is willing

- to undertake training for employment that is regulated (*formación reglada para el empleo*);
- to obtain a certificate of professionalism (*certificado de profesionalidad*), i.e. an official accreditation of a professional qualification;
- to undertake a training leading to the award of a certificate of technical competence (*una formación conducente a la obtención de la certificación de aptitud técnica*); or
- to complete a professional qualification required to practice a specific occupation (*habilitación profesional necesaria para el ejercicio de una ocupación específica*).[2128]

Hence, the foreigner obtains the residence permit before even starting the training as the foreigner must provide proof of enrolment within three months of notification of the decision granting the residence permit.[2129] If the proof of enrolment is not submitted within this period, the foreigners office may terminate the residence permit. This seems a suitable solution to check if the foreigner is actually willing to undertake training.

Even though this is a general requirement for all 'temporary residence permits for exceptional circumstances',[2130] Article 124(4)(a) REDYLE explicitly mentions that the grant of said residence permit is subject to the (negative) requirement that the foreigner must not have a criminal record (*antecedentes penales*) in Spain or in any of the countries in which the foreigner has previously resided over the past five years.

2. Right to stay

The residence permit is granted for 12 months. This residence permit may be extended only once for another 12-month period in cases where the training lasts longer than 12 months or its duration exceeds the duration of the first permit granted.[2131]

Once the training has been completed, and for the duration of the residence permit, the foreigner may submit an application for a 'residence and

---

2127 Royal Decree 629/2022, BOE 179 of 27.7.2022, 107698.
2128 Art 124(4)(b) REDYLE.
2129 Art 124(4)(b) REDYLE.
2130 Art 31(5) LODYLE.
2131 Art 124(4)(b) REDYLE.

work permit as an employed person' (*autorización de residencia temporal y trabajo por cuenta ajena*).[2132] This is an explicit way to consolidate his or her residence. The application must include an employment contract signed by the worker and the employer that guarantees at least the minimum interprofessional wage, or that established by the applicable collective bargaining agreement, at the time of the application, and proof of having completed the training provided for in the residence application. The 'residence and work permit as an employed person' will be valid for two years.

IV. Germany: 'residence permit for the purpose of employment for qualified tolerated foreigners'

The Skilled Immigration Act reformed all of Chapter 2, Part 4 AufenthG, i.e. the provisions on 'residence for the purpose of economic activity' (*Aufenthalt zum Zweck der Erwerbstätigkeit*).[2133] Following the reform the 'residence permit for the purpose of employment for qualified tolerated foreigners' (*Aufenthaltserlaubnis für qualifizierte Geduldete zum Zweck der Beschäftigung*) was moved as of the 1 March 2020 from § 18a AufenthG to § 19d AufenthG, though the content generally remained the same.[2134] In addition, the Toleration Act changed the rules surrounding the 'toleration for the purpose of training' (*Ausbildungsduldung*) and created a 'toleration for the purpose of employment' (*Beschäftigungsduldung*).[2135]

The 'residence permit for the purpose of employment for qualified tolerated foreigners' under § 19d AufenthG is the only regularisation in this study which does not fall under the 'residence permits for humanitarian reasons'.[2136] It was introduced as a response to the shortage of skilled workers[2137] and is closely linked to the residence granted in cases of 'hardship'.[2138] In the words of *Groß/Tryjanowski*, one may refer to 'utilitarian'

2132 Art 38 LODYLE and Arts 62ff REDYLE.

2133 Cf. *Kluth*, NVwZ 2019, 1306–1308 and *Klaus/Hammer*, ZAR 2019, 137ff.

2134 BT-Drs 19/8285, 102.

2135 See Chapter 4.B.I. and Chapter 4.E.IV.1.

2136 § 19d AufenthG falls under Chapter 2, Part 4 AufenthG: residence for the purpose of economic activity; cf. also No. 18a.0 AVV-AufenthG.

2137 In general on this term from an economic perspective, *Rahner*, Fachkräftemangel und falscher Fatalismus (2018).

2138 Cf. *Dienelt/Dollinger* in *Bergmann/Dienelt* (eds), Kommentar Ausländerrecht[13] (2020) § 19d AufenthG mn 1 and see Chapter 4.D.II.1.

motivations for granting a permit of this type.[2139] The 'residence permit for the purpose of employment for qualified tolerated foreigners' is to be understood as a purely national regularisation.

At the end of 2018 there were only 410 foreigners in possession of such a residence permit,[2140] which is probably due to the difficulty of meeting the requirements for issue.[2141] The numbers have risen sharply in recent years, showing an increase in importance. One reason might be the three-year 'toleration for the purpose of training' and the fact that this can be followed by the two-year residence permit described below (the '3 + 2 regulation').[2142] Hence, by mid-2021 already 4,220 migrants held a 'residence permit for the purpose of employment for qualified tolerated foreigners'.[2143]

1. Requirements

The residence permit is only available to tolerated persons.[2144] According to the General Administrative Provisions on the Residence Act , the permit is granted on the basis of the vocational qualification and the integration into the labour market.[2145] As such, the most important requirement is the completion of formal vocational training, which includes training of at least two years.[2146] In the same vein, a course of study at a higher education institution or vocational training to become a skilled worker in Germany can be completed.[2147] If the foreigner has acquired a foreign qualification, proof that skilled work was performed continuously for three years in

2139 *Groß/Tryjanowski*, Der Status von Drittstaatsangehörigen im Migrationsrecht der EU – eine kritische Analyse, Der Staat 2009, 259 (261, 272).

2140 BT-Drs 19/17236, 12–14.

2141 Cf. *Dienelt/Dollinger* in *Bergmann/Dienelt* § 19d AufenthG mn 4; *Stiegeler*, Geduldete Fachkräfte – Wem hilft § 18a AufenthG?, Asylmagazin 2009, 11.

2142 See Chapter 4.E.IV.1.

2143 BT-Drs 19/32579, 10.

2144 In this sense *Dienelt/Dollinger* in *Bergmann/Dienelt* § 19d AufenthG mn 3 and see Chapter 4.A.I.2.

2145 No. 18a.0 AVV-AufenthG.

2146 § 19d(1) No. 1(a) AufenthG and § 6(1) 2nd Sent. BeschV; cf. No. 18a.1.1.1 AVV-AufenthG.

2147 § 19d(1) No. 1(a) and (b) AufenthG; cf. No. 18a.1.1.1 and 18a.1.1.2 AVV-AufenthG and for detail *Dienelt/Dollinger* in *Bergmann/Dienelt* § 19d AufenthG mns 6–8.

Germany will suffice,[2148] though the foreigner and his or her family members must not have relied on benefits during this period.[2149] The residence permit requires the approval from the Federal Employment Agency, which assesses the foreigner's qualifications,[2150] though no labour-market test is undertaken.

The tolerated person must also have a concrete offer of employment that corresponds to the professional qualification.[2151] This is comparable to the 'social roots' requirement in Spain.[2152] The residence permit intends to enable the persons concerned to actually exercise the acquired professional qualification by acquiring lawful residence and a work permit.[2153] Such link between employment and exercise has been described as giving German 'refugee policy' a new structural framework: rejected asylum seekers may now earn their 'right to remain' by demonstrating their success on the labour market.[2154] The 'paradigm shift' already indicated by the introduction of the residence permit is continued also by the Skilled Immigration Act and the Toleration Act.[2155]

Furthermore, the foreigner must also satisfy the following additional requirements. The foreigner

- has sufficient living space and sufficient command of the German language (B1);
- has not intentionally deceived the foreigners authority as to the circumstances of relevance and has not intentionally delayed or obstructed official measures to the end the residence;
- has no links to extremist or terrorist organisations and has not been convicted of an offence intentionally committed.[2156]

2148 § 19d(1) No. 1(c) AufenthG; cf. No. 18a.1.1.3 AVV-AufenthG.

2149 Cf. No. 18a.1.1.3 AVV-AufenthG.

2150 § 19d(2) 1st Sent. AufenthG; cf. No. 18a.1.0 and 18a.2.1 AVV-AufenthG.

2151 Cf. BT-Drs 16/10288, 9 and *Dienelt/Dollinger* in *Bergmann/Dienelt* § 19d AufenthG mns 3 and 32.

2152 See Chapter 4.E.I.

2153 Cf. BT-Drs 16/10288, 9 and No. 18a.0 AVV-AufenthG.

2154 *Schammann*, Eine meritokratische Wende? Arbeit und Leistung als neue Strukturprinzipien der deutschen Flüchtlingspolitik, Sozialer Fortschritt 2017/66, 741 (750).

2155 *Schuler*, Ein Paradigmenwechsel, trotz allem, zeit.de (19.12.2018), https://www.zeit.de/politik/deutschland/2018-12/fachkraefteeinwanderungsgesetz-bundeskabinett-arbeitsmigration (31.7.2022) and in this sense *Wittmann*, ZAR 2020, 187.

2156 § 19d(1) Nos. 2–7 AufenthG; for detail see *Dienelt/Dollinger* in *Bergmann/Dienelt* § 19d AufenthG mns 17–31.

The block on issuing a residence title following the asylum procedure does not apply to the 'residence permit for the purpose of employment for qualified tolerated foreigners'.[2157]

Reference should also be made here to the 'toleration for the purpose of training'.[2158] The 2015 Act to Amend the Right to Remain introduced training as grounds for tolerating foreigners under the age of 21 who do not come from safe countries of origin. This was reformed in 2016 by the Integration Act (*Integrationsgesetz*[2159]). The 'toleration for the purpose of training' serves to provide tolerated persons and companies with greater legal certainty during the training period and for a limited period thereafter as well as simplifying the procedural aspects.[2160] Although problems exist with regard to the different implementations and interpretations of the *Länder*, which leads to very restrictive outcomes,[2161] there are the prospects for permanent residence and thus the description as a 'right to stay dressed as toleration'.[2162] The 'toleration for the purpose of training' is therefore to be considered an initial step in acquiring a right to stay,[2163] which is also expressed by the description as a '3 + 2 regulation' (three years toleration + two years right to stay). In mid-2021, 6,393 foreigners held a 'toleration for the purpose of training' and 3,251 were in possession of a 'toleration for the purpose of employment'.[2164]

The Toleration Act entered into force on 1 January 2020, thereby repealing § 60a(2) 4th–12th Sent. AufenthG, providing new rules on the 'toleration for the purpose of training'[2165] in § 60c AufenthG and introducing the

---

2157 § 19d(3) AufenthG and see Chapter 3.B.III.2.c.

2158 For information on the requirements see *Dollinger* in *Bergmann/Dienelt* (eds), Kommentar Ausländerrecht[13] (2020) § 60c AufenthG mns 10ff.

2159 Act of 31.7.2016 (BGBl I 1939).

2160 BT-Drs 18/8615, 48.

2161 Cf. *Eichler*, Die „neue" Ausbildungsduldung: Möglichkeiten und Hindernisse in der Umsetzung des § 60a Abs. 2 S. 4 ff., Asylmagazin 2017, 177.

2162 *Röder/Wittmann*, Aktuelle Rechtsfragen der Ausbildungsduldung, ZAR 2017, 345 (352); *Wittmann*, ZAR 2020, 187.

2163 See Chapter 1.B.III.1.a.

2164 BT-Drs 19/32579, 31.

2165 For detail see *Rosenstein/Koehler*, Die neue Ausbildungsduldung – eine notwendige Überarbeitung, InfAuslR 2019, 266; *Wittmann/Röder*, Aktuelle Rechtsfragen der Ausbildungsduldung gem. § 60c AufenthG, ZAR 2019, 412.

'toleration for the purpose of employment'[2166] in § 60d AufenthG.[2167] This sought to provide an initial response to the shortage of skilled workers in Germany by drawing on domestic workers.[2168] The 'toleration for the purpose of training' is aimed primarily at qualified vocational training,[2169] whereas the 'toleration for the purpose of employment' targets lesser qualifications.[2170] The aforementioned 'paradigm shift' is highlighted by the fact that both tolerations serve as a 'bridge' to a fully-fledged right to stay.[2171] As before, the newly regulated 'toleration for the purpose of training' makes it possible to obtain the 'residence permit for the purpose of employment for qualified tolerated foreigners' discussed here, whereby § 19d(1a) AufenthG stipulates that the foreigner is entitled to a residence permit after successfully concluding the vocational training.[2172] This perhaps explains why there has been a continuous increase in the number of such permits.[2173] The foreigner is entitled to a 'toleration for

---

2166 For detail see *Röder/Wittmann*, Das Migrationspaket – Beilage zum Asylmagazin 8–9/2019, 23; *Rosenstein/Koehler*, ZAR 2019, 223; *Funke-Kaiser*, § 60d AufenthG als abschließende Regelung für die Ermöglichung einer Beschäftigung von geduldeten Ausländern und Ausländerinnen, ZAR 2020, 90.

2167 See also BT-Drs 19/8286, 14ff and Anwendungshinweise des Bundesministeriums des Innern, für Bau und Heimat zum Gesetz über Duldung bei Ausbildung und Beschäftigung (20.12.2019), https://www.bmi.bund.de/SharedDocs/downloads/DE/veroeffentlichungen/themen/migration/anwendungshinweise-zum-gesetz-ueber-duldung-bei-ausbildung.pdf?__blob=publicationFile&v=2 (31.7.2022).

2168 Along this line, *Kluth*, NVwZ 2019, 1308f and *Rosenstein/Koehler*, InfAuslR 2019, 266.

2169 According to § 2(12a) AufenthG, vocational training is only qualified if it lasts for at least two years; cf. also Anwendungshinweise des Bundesministeriums des Innern, für Bau und Heimat zum Gesetz über Duldung bei Ausbildung und Beschäftigung (20.12.2019) mn 60c.1.0.2.

2170 *Kluth*, NVwZ 2019, 1309.

2171 *Röder/Wittmann*, Das Migrationspaket – Beilage zum Asylmagazin 8–9/2019, 24. Cf. on 'toleration for the purpose of employment' *Welte*, Beschäftigungsmöglichkeiten für geduldete Ausländer, infAuslR 2020, 225 (228).

2172 Cf. Anwendungshinweise des Bundesministeriums des Innern, für Bau und Heimat zum Fachkräfteeinwanderungsgesetz (6.8.2021), https://www.bmi.bund.de/SharedDocs/downloads/DE/veroeffentlichungen/themen/migration/anwendungshinweise-fachkraefteeinwanderungsgesetz.pdf?__blob=publicationFile&v=5 (31.7.2022) mn 19d.1a.1.

2173 See Chapter 4.E.IV.

the purpose of training', if the requirements are met.[2174] Asylum seekers are 'privileged' where the 'toleration for the purpose of training' is concerned.[2175] There is also an entitlement to receive 'toleration for the purpose of employment'.[2176] The newly created 'toleration for the purpose of employment' may be used to obtain a 'residence in the case of permanent integration'.[2177]

Finally, the question remains whether the 'toleration for the purpose of employment' is compatible with the Return Directive. According to *Roß*,[2178] an incompatibility arises due to the case law in *TQ* in which the ECJ – drawing on the requirement of effectiveness[2179] – again emphasised that Member States must either deport irregularly staying migrants or grant a right to stay in order to satisfy their obligations under EU secondary law.[2180] The decision in *TQ* concerns an unaccompanied minor, whose application for asylum was unsuccessful. Following the decision, his or her stay was therefore irregular but 'tolerated' until he or she reached the age of majority.[2181] However, the Dutch authorities did not carry out an adequate investigation to ensure that adequate reception facilities exist in the country of return. The facts of the case in *TQ* are somewhat different, yet it provides valid arguments for the view that the three-year 'toleration for the purpose of employment' violates EU law.

The decision in *TQ* is the first time the ECJ has commented upon a lengthy 'toleration' period in a Member State, whereby the period in *TQ* was a maximum of three years.[2182] From a dogmatic standpoint, there are two possible consequences for German residency law:

It could be argued that Germany would have to deport persons 'tolerated for the purpose of employment' as the toleration cannot be applied due

2174 Cf. Anwendungshinweise des Bundesministeriums des Innern, für Bau und Heimat zum Gesetz über Duldung bei Ausbildung und Beschäftigung (20.12.2019) mn 60c.1.0.

2175 Cf. *Röder/Wittmann*, Aktuelle Rechtsfragen der Ausbildungsduldung gem. § 60c AufenthG, ZAR 2019, 412 (414).

2176 Cf. *Rosenstein/Koehler*, ZAR 2019, 228; concurring *Welte*, Die Wahrung des Prinzips der abschließenden Normierung im Aufenthaltsgesetz am Beispiel der Beschäftigungsduldung, ZAR 2020, 87 (87).

2177 See § 25b(6) AufenthG and Chapter 4.B.I.

2178 *Roß*, NVwZ 2021, 552.

2179 ECJ *TQ*, paras 79f.

2180 For detail see Chapter 2.B.II.2.b.

2181 ECJ *TQ*, para 31.

2182 ECJ *TQ*, para 63.

to the primacy of EU law. However, this is contradicted by the fact that Germany 'deliberately' suspends the deportation for three years.

In my opinion, there are better reasons why a claim to regularisation under EU law arises at the time when a 'toleration for the purpose of training' is granted or when the requirements are met: the discretion of the Member State in Article 6(4) Return Directive is reduced to zero. I would thus classify this regularisation obligation under the category 'permanently non-returnable'.[2183]

Spain took a similar path to Germany and introduced a new regularisation that explicitly mentions this kind of toleration as its role model.[2184] In contrast, Austria has followed the opposite path and will, where the decision is final, deport asylum seekers without making an exception for those undergoing an apprenticeship.[2185] Until the 2019 reform, an apprenticeship ended automatically as soon as an asylum process was completed and final.[2186] Such approach was criticised, inter alia, due to the supposed shortage of skilled workers in Austria.[2187] However, a decision by the Supreme Administrative Court precludes the consideration of apprenticeship in a shortage occupation as a public interest in favour of the alien,[2188] and thus the interests of the domestic labour market are not covered by Article 8 ECHR.[2189] There have also been further developments and heated political debates surrounding the question of how Austria should deal with rejected asylum seekers who have started an apprenticeship. In September 2019, a resolution was adopted in the National Council, according to which a pragmatic solution for asylum and apprenticeship

---

2183 For detail see Chapter 2.B.II.2.b.

2184 See Chapter 4.E.III.

2185 See *NN*, Abgelehnte Asyl-Lehrlinge werden nun doch abgeschoben, diepresse.com (12.9.2018), https://diepresse.com/home/innenpolitik/5494875/Abgelehnte-AsylLehrlinge-werden-nun-doch-abgeschoben (31.7.2022).

2186 § 14(2)(f) Berufsausbildungsgesetz in the version BGBl I 86/2022 (Act on Vocational Education), and *Peyrl*, Arbeitsmarkt 306.

2187 See *NN*, WKÖ-Studie: In Österreich fehlen 162.000 Fachkräfte, sn.at (31.8.2018), https://www.sn.at/wirtschaft/oesterreich/wkoe-studie-in-oesterreich-fehlen-162-000-fachkraefte-39460492 (31.7.2022); *Fink/Titelbach/Vogtenhuber/Hofer*, Gibt es in Österreich einen Fachkräftemangel? Analyse anhand von ökonomischen Knappheitsindikatoren (December 2015), https://irihs.ihs.ac.at/id/eprint/3891/1/IHS_Fachkräftemangel_Endbericht_09122015_final.pdf (31.7.2022).

2188 VwGH 28.2.2019, Ro 2019/01/0003-3 and 15.7.2019, Ra 2019/18/0108. For criticism see *Reyhani/Nowak*, Beschäftigung von Asylsuchenden (4.7.2018).

2189 VwGH 28.2.2019, Ro 2019/01/0003-3, para 47 with further references.

should be found.[2190] Specifically, the Federal Minister of the Interior was asked to ensure that the approx. 900 asylum seekers complete their apprenticeship and cannot be deported during this time.

The National Council finally passed an amendment to the Alien Act (the *Fremdenrechtsänderungsgesetz* 2019) at the beginning of December 2019. § 55a FPG now stipulates that the time limit for voluntary departure is suspended for the purpose of completing an apprenticeship programme that has already commenced.[2191] The obligation to leave the country thus does not arise until the apprenticeship has been completed. In effect, the provision 'discretely postpones'[2192] forced deportation, but which is designed differently than the previously existing toleration.[2193] From the perspective of EU law, § 55a FPG is to be considered as compatible following the recent ECJ decision in *UN*.[2194]

The provision only applies to those asylum seekers who started their apprenticeship before the law came into force and whose proceedings have not yet been finally concluded.[2195] It is significant from a contextual perspective that – similar to Germany – economic interests were decisive for this amendment.[2196] However, this is only a temporary solution and it is unclear what the permanent solution will be.[2197] Since a ruling of the

2190 109/E 26. GP (19.9.2019).

2191 Cf. *Peyrl*, Neuregelung der Möglichkeit zur Beendigung einer Lehre von AsylwerberInnen nach negativem Abschluss des Asylverfahrens, DRdA-infas 2020, 121 and *Hinterberger*, Die Beendigung der Lehre von abgewiesenen AsylwerberInnen gem § 55a FPG, ÖJZ 2020, 640. See also VwGH 8.3.2021, Ra 2020/14/0291.

2192 *NN*, Keine Abschiebung: Asylwerber können Lehre abschließen, diepresse.com (11.12.2019), https://www.diepresse.com/5736996/keine-abschiebung-asylwerber-konnen-lehre-abschliessen (31.7.2022), using the expression *ein schlichter Aufschub*. See also § 125(31)–(34) FPG.

2193 See Chapter 4.A.I.3.

2194 See Chapter 2.B.II.2.

2195 10267/BR 27. GP and *NN*, AsylwerberInnen in Lehre: Vier-Fraktionen-Einigung im Nationalrat, Parlamentskorrespondenz No. 1183 (11.12.2019), https://www.parlament.gv.at/PAKT/PR/JAHR_2019/PK1183/#XXVII_A_00087 (31.7.2022). Those who have committed a criminal offence or have attempted to deceive the authorities about their identity during the asylum procedure are also excluded; § 55a(2) FPG.

2196 *NN*, Asylwerbende in Lehre: Einigung im Budgetausschuss, Parlamentskorrespondenz No. 1156 (3.12.2019), https://www.parlament.gv.at/PAKT/PR/JAHR_2019/PK1156/index.shtml (31.7.2022).

2197 According to § 126(23) FPG the rule is only effective for four years since its entry into force on 28.12.2019. See also *Konrad*, Modernes Bleiberecht: Wir brauchen sehr schnell eine Lösung, diepresse.com (7.12.2019), https://www.die

Austrian Constitutional Court in 2021, asylum seekers have at least (again) generally access to the labour market.[2198]

2. Right to stay

The residence permit is valid for two years.[2199] As is clear from its nature, it entitles the holder to engage in employment during this period. Unrestricted access to the labour market is allowed only after the two-year period of residence, provided that the foreigner has been employed in a position commensurate with the vocational qualification throughout this time.[2200] During the period of employment, foreigners are entitled to benefits under the basic security scheme for job-seekers and, after termination of the employment relationship, to social benefits under the Social Insurance Code II.[2201]

V. Interim conclusion

The purpose 'employment and training' is not influenced by international and EU law, but is purely national in nature. In principle there are no specific provisions of international and EU law that are to be observed.

This purpose engages first with 'social roots', which have the most significance in Spanish law. These have developed from the court decisions concerning disproportionate expulsion, but have been codified quite differently from the regularisations in Austria or Germany. Social roots basically refers to future roots, whereas the Austrian 'right to remain' refers to roots that have already taken hold. Spanish law sets specific requirements for granting the right to stay, which the foreigners can actually meet, as the statistics show. Even though it already worked quite well in practice, it was reformed with the Royal Decree 629/2022 to even better address the needs of the Spanish labour market. For instance, the relevant Spanish law requires three years' residence and since the Royal Decree 629/2022

---

presse.com/5734477/modernes-bleiberecht-wir-brauchen-sehr-schnell-eine-losung (31.7.2022).

2198 See Chapter 4.D.II.2.

2199 § 19d(1a) AufenthG.

2200 § 19d(2) 3rd Sent. AufenthG and § 9 BeschV; cf. *Dienelt/Dollinger* in *Bergmann/Dienelt* § 19d AufenthG mn 34 with further references.

2201 Cf. *Frings/Janda/Keßler/Steffen*, Sozialrecht mns 635f.

an employment contract for 30 hours per week signed by the worker and employer, which guarantees at least the minimum interprofessional wage or that established by the applicable collective bargaining agreement. An exception of this requisite applies in cases in which the foreigner has sufficient financial resources. Contextually speaking, this regularisation may be explained by the relationship between the Spanish migration policy and the interests of labour market policy. Here one can speak of utilitarian motivations. The examination of the beginning of the employment relationship is an especially effective rule, since this is made dependent on registration for social security. Until that time, the validity of the residence permit remains suspended. In addition to the employment contract and the duration of residence, social integration or a family relationship must be proven. In this respect, social integration has elements of both the purposes 'social ties' and 'family unity' and therefore, as already indicated, also covers factual circumstances falling under Article 8 ECHR.

From a quantitative perspective, 'employment roots' are not relevant in Spanish law, especially when compared to 'social roots'. Nonetheless, the basic idea behind offering undocumented foreign workers the prospect of regularisation appears praiseworthy. The two-year residence period is usually not the problem in obtaining this residence permit, but rather the fact that past employment relationships have to be proven. The required notification to the Labour and Social Security Inspectorate deters too many foreigners due to the consequences. Interestingly, one author considers that the regularisation misses its actual purpose and instead serves as a deterrent for employers. It will be seen if the reform via the Royal Decree 629/2022 solves this problem and gives greater relevance to this residence permit.

Additionally, the Royal Decree 629/2022 introduced a new type of roots, the so-called 'temporary residence permit for reasons of training' whereby the German 'toleration for the purpose of training' was the role model. However, in contrast to the German toleration, the Spanish model is more generous as it grants irregularly staying foreigners right away a right to stay. In this case, the foreigner has to prove that he or she has been in Spain for a continuous period of at least two years and is willing to enter into a training. Practically relevant and an appropriate solution seems the approach that the foreigner obtains the residence permit before even starting the training as the foreigner must provide proof of enrolment within three months of notification of the decision granting the residence permit.

The 'residence permit for the purpose of employment for qualified tolerated foreigners' is a peculiar feature of German residency law which was enacted due to the shortage of skilled workers. Interestingly, its role in practice has been limited because – just like employment roots in Spain – it is hardly possible to meet the very high requirements, however, showing an increase in importance. This is probably due to the introduction of the three-year 'toleration for the purpose of training' and the fact that this can be followed by the two-year residence permit (the '3 + 2 regulation'). The residence permit shall offer the prospect of regularisation to tolerated persons who have completed qualified vocational training. In addition, a concrete job offer must be available – this requirement is similar to the relevant requirement of social roots. Furthermore, the foreigner must also have a command of the German language at B1 level and sufficient living space at his or her disposal. The statement that foreigners residing unlawfully can earn their 'right to remain' holds water. The 'paradigm shift' already indicated by the introduction of the residence permit is also continued by the Skilled Immigration Act and the Toleration Act.

It is also to be noted that German law has created a basis for toleration for young foreigners who complete vocational training in Germany. Despite the practical problems, the basic idea underpinning the 'toleration for the purpose of training' under § 60c AufenthG seems to be an approach that is capable of meeting the presupposed requirements of the German economy. The Toleration Act continued this approach by creating a 'toleration for the purpose of employment' in § 60d AufenthG. Austria has taken the opposite direction, since an apprenticeship undertaken by an asylum seeker will automatically end when the asylum application is unsuccessful and he or she can consequently be deported. However, following further intense political debates, an amendment to the Aliens' Police Act was passed in the National Council in December 2019. This amendment provides that the time limit for voluntary departure is suspended for the purpose of completing vocational training. Accordingly, the obligation to leave the country does arise until the apprenticeship has been completed. It is significant that – similar to Germany – economic interests were decisive for this amendment. However, the solution is only temporary and it is not clear what the permanent solution will be.

Before concluding this section it is necessary to refer to another finding: there is no Austrian regularisation falling within the category 'employment and training', which is why the question of a functional equivalent arises.[2202] Austrian legislation seems to have deliberately refrained from creating regularisations for those cases that are linked to employment or training in the broader sense. This was already indicated above, as rejected asylum seekers can only continue their apprenticeship under certain conditions. This underlines another result of the analysis, which I will discuss further in the summary. Compared to Germany and Spain, Austrian law is the most restrictive with regard to regularisations.[2203]

F. Other national interests

'Other national interests'[2204] concerns two residence permits under Spanish law: the 'temporary residence permit for exceptional circumstances due to the collaboration with public authorities, or for reasons of national security or public interest' (*autorización de residencia temporal por circunstancias excepcionales de colaboración con autoridades públicas, razones de seguridad nacional o interés público*), which is granted for one year, and the 'temporary residence permit for exceptional circumstances due to collaboration in the fight against organised networks' (*autorización de residencia temporal por circunstancias excepcionales por colaboración contra redes organizadas*), which is granted for five years.

I. Spain: 'temporary residence permit for exceptional circumstances due to the collaboration with public authorities, or for reasons of national security or public interest'

Article 127 REDYLE provides that a temporary residence permit may be granted 'for exceptional circumstances due to the collaboration with public authorities, or for reasons of national security or public interest'. This provision was reformed via the Royal Decree 629/2022, which introduced Article 127(2) REDYLE as a new provision. The former content of Article 127 REDYLE simply became Article 127(1) REDYLE. This type of permit extends beyond the obligations under international and EU law. The lack

2202 Cf. *Piek*, ZEuP 2013, 66, 70 and 73f; in general on the functional method see Introduction D.I.1.
2203 See Chapter 4.G.
2204 See Chapter 1.B.III.6.

of precise information in the statistics means that it is not possible to state how many permits of this kind have been issued.[2205]

1. Requirements

Pursuant to Article 127(1) REDYLE, a residence permit may be granted to persons who collaborate with the administrative, police, tax or judicial authorities on matters outside the fight against organised networks. The two residence permits in relation to the fight against organised networks will be discussed separately.[2206]

It is possible to obtain a residence permit on the grounds of 'collaboration' or 'national security' or 'public interest', if justified by one of these grounds. 'National security' and 'public interest' are undefined terms whose meaning can neither be determined from the relevant literature[2207] nor from the case law[2208]. Here it is important to note the decision of the High Court of Justice of Castilla-La Mancha in a case discussed under the 'temporary residence permit for humanitarian reasons' for victims of crimes:[2209] the person concerned was a protected witness who contributed to uncovering a drug network, resulting in the arrest of several individuals and confiscation of various laboratories, which would have satisfied the requirement of 'collaboration' with the public authorities.[2210] However, it is not clear why the circumstances of this case did not fall under the 'temporary residence permit for exceptional circumstances due to collaboration in the fight against organised networks'.[2211]

It is therefore apparent from the above that it is not clear in all three cases which factual circumstances will actually lead to a right to stay, which is why a corresponding legal clarification would be desirable.[2212]

2205 See Chapter 3.C.III.1.

2206 Cf. *García Vitoria* in *Boza Martínez/Donaire Villa/Moya Malapeira* 298 and see Chapter 4.F.II.

2207 Cf. for instance *García Vitoria* in *Boza Martínez/Donaire Villa/Moya Malapeira* 298f or *Fernández Collados* in *Palomar Olmeda* 426f.

2208 Cf. for instance STS 5515/2016, ECLI:ES:TS:2016:5515 and STSJ Castilla-La Mancha 225/2016, ECLI:ES:TSJCLM:2016:225.

2209 STSJ Castilla-La Mancha 225/2016, ECLI:ES:TSJCLM:2016:225, FJ 3 and see Chapter 4.D.I.4.a.

2210 On the term collaboration see also Chapter 4.F.II.

2211 See Chapter 4.F.II.

2212 For a similar analysis see Chapter 4.F.II.1.

A step into this direction seems to be the Royal Decree 629/2022 which lays down in the new Article 127(2) REDYLE that a residence permit may be granted to persons who collaborate with the relevant labour authority. Collaboration in this case is specified as demonstrating the existence of the person working in an undocumented situation of no less than six months in duration in the last year. Said employment relationship has to be proven to the Labour and Social Security Inspectorate by any means. Furthermore, if the Labour and Social Security Inspectorate or subsequently a court has established a violation of the committed offence (undocumented work), the person must also submit the respective administrative or court decision. Article 127(2) REDYLE appears to resemble the 'temporary residence permit for reasons of employment roots' and, hence, it is probable that some of the same problems arise, such as foreigners being too afraid of the consequences – like deportation – to actually contact the Labour and Social Security Inspectorate.[2213]

2. Right to stay

The residence permit pursuant to Article 127(1) REDYLE is issued for one year.[2214] Article 128(5) REDYLE determines which authority is responsible for issuing the permit.[2215] The Secretary of State for Security has jurisdiction in matters concerning collaboration with the police, tax or judicial authorities or in cases of national security. The applications are to be accompanied by a report from the appropriate headquarters of the law enforcement authorities (*Jefatura de las Fuerzas y Cuerpos de Seguridad*) or the tax or judicial authority that has conducted the respective procedure with regard to cooperation, giving the reasons for granting the permit.[2216] In these cases, the residence permit may – in contrast to the other 'temporary residence permits for exceptional circumstances'[2217] – be extended if the Secretary of State for Security concludes that the reasons for granting the permit still remain.[2218]

2213 See Chapter 4.E.II.1.
2214 Art 130(1) REDYLE.
2215 Cf. *García Vitoria* in *Boza Martínez/Donaire Villa/Moya Malapeira* 300.
2216 Art 128(5) REDYLE and cf. *García Vitoria* in *Boza Martínez/Donaire Villa/Moya Malapeira* 299.
2217 See Chapter 3.C.III.4.
2218 Cf. *García Vitoria* in *Boza Martínez/Donaire Villa/Moya Malapeira* 305.

The Secretary of State for Migration is responsible in cases concerning the collaboration with other administrative authorities and for reasons of public interest.[2219] Alongside the application to the competent authority, Article 127(1) 2nd Sent. REDYLE also indicates that the responsible authorities may urge (*instar*) the grant of a residence permit. For instance, the competent tax administration authority can urge the issuance of a residence permit at the Office of the Secretary of State for Security, provided there is sufficient collaboration from the person concerned.

The responsible authority for the newly established residence permit according to Article 127(2) REDYLE is the Directorate-General for Migration (*Dirección General de Migraciones*). The residence permit is valid for one year and enables the persons concerned to work (employed or self-employed). The residence may be applied by the foreigner or may be granted *ex officio* by the competent labour authority.

II. Spain: 'temporary residence permit for exceptional circumstances due to collaboration in the fight against organised networks'

Article 59 LODYLE and Articles 135–139 REDYLE feature two 'temporary residence permit for exceptional circumstances which may be granted to foreigners due to collaboration in the fight against organised networks'. The two residence permits differ only in terms of the authority with which the foreigner collaborates. In terms of the necessary collaboration in the fight against organised networks, they also differ from the residence permit according to Article 127 REDYLE.[2220] It is not clear from the statistics how many residence permits were granted on the basis of this provision.[2221]

Introducing this residence permit created a legal incentive for victims, witnesses or other injured parties in contributing to the prosecution of

2219 Art 128(5)(b) REDYLE

2220 Cf. *Esteban de la Rosa,* Art 31 LODYLE in *Monereo Pérez/Fernández Avilés/Triguero Martínez* 506 and see Chapter 4.F.I.1.

2221 See Chapter 3.C.III.1.

the perpetrators[2222] of certain (administrative) offences.[2223] This not only strengthens the collaboration between irregularly staying foreigners and the authorities but also improves the prosecution and conviction of criminals.[2224] At first blush it appears that these two residence permits go beyond the provisions of international and EU law and offer better protection for those foreigners who collaborate with the authorities. However, closer analysis reveals that victims of exploitative employment may also obtain the residence permit discussed here. Since this can be derived from Article 13(4) Employers Sanctions Directive, as has already been explained in relation to 'vulnerability' and 'victim protection',[2225] this also represents an implementation of EU law.

1. Requirements

Article 59(1) LODYLE stipulates that the foreigner must be residing irregularly.[2226] Furthermore, the foreigner must be a victim, witness or have been injured in relation to one of the following (administrative) offences:[2227] smuggling of human beings, irregular immigration,[2228] labour

2222 Or participants; cf. *Vicente Palacio*, Art 59 LODYLE in *Monereo Pérez/Fernández Avilés/Triguero Martínez* (eds), Comentario a la ley y al reglamento de Extranjería, Inmigración e Integración Social² (2013) 942 (942).

2223 Cf. *Díaz Morgado*, La residencia de víctimas de trata de personas y la residencia por colaboración contra redes organizadas in *Boza Martínez/Donaire Villa/Moya Malapeira* 343f.

2224 See also *Vicente Palacio*, Art 59 LODYLE in *Monereo Pérez/Fernández Avilés/Triguero Martínez* 943.

2225 See Chapter 1.B.III.4.a. and Chapter 4.D.I.

2226 Cf. *Díaz Morgado*, La residencia de víctimas de trata de personas y la residencia por colaboración contra redes organizadas in *Boza Martínez/Donaire Villa/Moya Malapeira* 344f and *Vicente Palacio*, Art 59 LODYLE in *Monereo Pérez/Fernández Avilés/Triguero Martínez* 946.

2227 Cf. *Díaz Morgado*, La residencia de víctimas de trata de personas y la residencia por colaboración contra redes organizadas in *Boza Martínez/Donaire Villa/Moya Malapeira* 345f; *Vicente Palacio*, Art 59 LODYLE in *Monereo Pérez/Fernández Avilés/Triguero Martínez* 943f and 946, and especially Instrucción DGI/SGRJ/06/2006, 2.

2228 Art 318bis CP and Art 54(1)(b) LODYLE; cf. *Vicente Palacio*, Art 59 LODYLE in *Monereo Pérez/Fernández Avilés/Triguero Martínez* 946–948.

exploitation,[2229] smuggling of workers (*tráfico ilícito de mano de obra*),[2230] or exploitation in relation to prostitution.[2231] The smuggling of human beings differs from human trafficking in so far as the person concerns consents to the unlawful transportation,[2232] whereas force or intimidation is used in relation to human trafficking.[2233] Furthermore, with regard to each act committed, the emergency situation of the persons concerned must have been exploited[2234] and the act must have been carried out by organised groups or gangs.[2235]

'Collaboration' is understood to mean both the reporting of one of the aforementioned (administrative) offences, providing essential information or materials for the proceedings and making relevant statements.[2236] According to the Spanish Supreme Court, an act does not meet the definition of collaboration if it results – so to speak – only by abiding the law.[2237] Conversely, it is not necessary that the collaboration endangers the life, freedom or property of the person concerned. [2238] According to case law, however, collaboration can be assumed if a foreigner files a complaint and makes relevant statements that lead to the identification and conviction of the offenders.[2239] Nonetheless, it remains unclear whether, for example,

---

2229 Arts 311 and 312(2) CP; cf. *Vicente Palacio*, Art 59 LODYLE in *Monereo Pérez/Fernández Avilés/Triguero Martínez* 946 and 948.

2230 Art 312(1) CP.

2231 Art 188(1) CP.

2232 Ar.t 318bis CP and cf. STS 4668/2016, ECLI:ES:TS:2016:4668

2233 Cf. *Vicente Palacio*, Art 59 LODYLE in *Monereo Pérez/Fernández Avilés/Triguero Martínez* 947.

2234 As is the wording of Art 59(1) LODYLE; cf. *Vicente Palacio*, Art 59 LODYLE in *Monereo Pérez/Fernández Avilés/Triguero Martínez* 944.

2235 For detail see *Vicente Palacio*, Art 59 LODYLE in *Monereo Pérez/Fernández Avilés/Triguero Martínez* 944f.

2236 Cf. *Vicente Palacio*, Art 59 LODYLE in *Monereo Pérez/Fernández Avilés/Triguero Martínez* 946 and *Vicente Palacio*, Art 59bis LODYLE in *Monereo Pérez/Fernández Avilés/Triguero Martínez* 966; for detail see STSJ Castilla-La Mancha 225/2016, ECLI:ES:TSJCLM:2016:225.

2237 STS 3389/2016, ECLI:ES:TS:2016:3389 and STS 3800/2016, ECLI:ES:TS:2016:3800; in these cases the person concerned merely complied with a court order.

2238 STSJ Castilla-La Mancha 225/2016.

2239 In this sense STSJ Castilla-La Mancha 225/2016, ECLI:ES:TSJCLM:2016:225; cf. *Vicente Palacio*, Art 59 LODYLE in *Monereo Pérez/Fernández Avilés/Triguero Martínez* 948f with further references.

filing a complaint would suffice in order for a permit to be granted. [2240] The authorities' (broad) discretion leads to great legal uncertainty and increases the vulnerability of victims, witnesses, etc., who collaborate with them.[2241] It would therefore be appropriate to legally define the acts that satisfy the notion of collaboration.

In contrast to the 'temporary residence permit and work permit for exceptional circumstances for foreign victims of human trafficking', collaboration is a necessary requirement. This is also why the 'temporary residence permit for exceptional circumstances due to collaboration in the fight against organised networks' was analysed under 'other national interests'. The scope of application is therefore much narrower because the victim's personal circumstances are not taken into consideration.[2242]

2. Exemption from administrative penalties

The focus now turns to the question of the authorities with which collaboration is possible. On the one hand, Article 136 REDYLE stipulates the collaboration with non-police administrative authorities (*autoridades administrativas no policiales*), whereby a guideline concerning the law on foreigners states that the Labour and Social Security Inspectorate is one such authority.[2243] On the other hand, Article 137 REDYLE concerns the collaboration with the law enforcement, tax or judicial authorities (*autoridades administrativas policiales, fiscales o judiciales*).

The authority with which a foreigner is collaborating must submit a statement to the authority responsible for the administrative penal procedure, which indicates the collaboration provided.[2244] A central point here is that the collaborating foreigners can benefit from an exemption

---

2240 Along this line *Díaz Morgado*, La residencia de víctimas de trata de personas y la residencia por colaboración contra redes organizadas in *Boza Martínez/Donaire Villa/Moya Malapeira* 346f with further references.

2241 In this sense *Díaz Morgado*, La residencia de víctimas de trata de personas y la residencia por colaboración contra redes organizadas in *Boza Martínez/Donaire Villa/Moya Malapeira* 346f and *Defensor del Pueblo*, Recomendación (23.5.2016), Queja 16002509.

2242 Cf. *Vicente Palacio*, Art 59bis LODYLE in *Monereo Pérez/Fernández Avilés/Triguero Martínez* 960f and see Chapter 4.D.I.4.c.

2243 Instrucción DGI/SGRJ/06/2006, 1.

2244 Art 135(1) REDYLE; cf. *Díaz Morgado*, La residencia de víctimas de trata de personas y la residencia por colaboración contra redes organizadas in *Boza Martínez/Donaire Villa/Moya Malapeira* 347f.

from administrative penalties, as this should serve as a further incentive for collaboration.[2245] They can be exempted from criminal liability due to irregular residency in an expulsion procedure[2246] already initiated or also in relation to any other administrative criminal procedure.[2247] The authority responsible for the administrative criminal proceedings has a duty to provide information on the exemption from administrative penalties.[2248] Conversely, if the public prosecutor's office obtains knowledge of foreigners who meet the conditions for exemption and are vital for criminal proceedings, the public prosecutor's office can request the competent authority not to enforce the expulsion order.[2249]

Based on the report outlining the collaboration, the authority responsible for the administrative penal procedure then sends a proposal to the competent delegate or subdelegate of government[2250] suggesting the exemption from criminal liability. The competent delegate or subdelegate shall then decide on the exemption and at the same time on the temporary suspension of the administrative penalty proceedings or the expulsion.[2251] The design of the exemption from administrative penalties bears resemblance to the 'temporary residence permit and work permit for exceptional circumstances for foreign victims of human trafficking'.[2252]

If liability is exempted, the foreigner is to be informed of the possibility to apply for a 'temporary residence permit for exceptional circumstances due to collaboration in the fight against organised networks'.[2253] The authority is to support the person concerned in making the application. In-

---

2245 Cf. *Vicente Palacio*, Art 59 LODYLE in *Monereo Pérez/Fernández Avilés/Triguero Martínez* 943.

2246 Art 135(1) REDYLE in conjunction with Art 53(1)(a) LODYLE; cf. *Vicente Palacio*, Art 59 LODYLE in *Monereo Pérez/Fernández Avilés/Triguero Martínez* 942f.

2247 See *Díaz Morgado*, La residencia de víctimas de trata de personas y la residencia por colaboración contra redes organizadas in *Boza Martínez/Donaire Villa/Moya Malapeira* 346f with further references.

2248 Art 59(2) LODYLE; cf. *Díaz Morgado*, La residencia de víctimas de trata de personas y la residencia por colaboración contra redes organizadas in *Boza Martínez/Donaire Villa/Moya Malapeira* 347.

2249 Art 59(4) LODYLE.

2250 See Art 135(2) REDYLE.

2251 Art 135(3) REDYLE; cf. Instrucción DGI/SGRJ/06/2006, 4.

2252 Arts 59(3) and 59bis(4) LODYLE, as well as Arts 135 and 143 REDYLE. Cf. *Vicente Palacio*, Art 59bis LODYLE in *Monereo Pérez/Fernández Avilés/Triguero Martínez* 965 and see Chapter 4.D.I.4.

2253 Arts 136(1) and 137(1) REDYLE.

stead of such an application, the person concerned also has the possibility of assisted return to the country of origin.[2254]

3. 'Provisional residence permit and work permit'

It is necessary in this context to draw a distinction between the different authorities. If the person concerned has collaborated with non-police administrative authorities, the application for a 'residence permit and work permit' is to be made to the delegate or subdelegate of government who issued the exemption. However, the Office of the Secretary of State for Migration is responsible for the decision.[2255] If there has been collaboration with the police, tax or judicial authorities, the Office of the Secretary of State for Security is responsible for issuing the permit, but the application must be submitted to the competent police unit of the foreigners office.[2256] The application is then forwarded with the aforementioned report on collaboration and a further report assessing the content of the procedure.

If the report is favourable, the person concerned is automatically granted a 'provisional residence permit and work permit', of which he or she must be informed immediately.[2257] No new application is required, which is why the report is of such great importance.[2258] The 'provisional residence permit and work permit' allows the holder to take up any employment.[2259] The 'provisional residence permit and work permit' is characterised by the fact that it is valid from the time of notification until the decision on the final 'residence permit and work permit'.[2260] However, if the report is not favourable, no 'provisional residence permit and work permit' is granted.

2254 Cf. for detail Art 138 REDYLE.
2255 Art 136 REDYLE.
2256 Art 137 REDYLE.
2257 Arts 136(3) and (4) as well as 137(3) and (4) REDYLE.
2258 Cf. *Vicente Palacio*, Art 59 LODYLE in *Monereo Pérez/Fernández Avilés/Triguero Martínez* 951.
2259 Arts 136(6) and 137(6) REDYLE.
2260 Cf. *Díaz Morgado*, La residencia de víctimas de trata de personas y la residencia por colaboración contra redes organizadas in *Boza Martínez/Donaire Villa/Moya Malapeira* 349f.

4. Right to stay

If the outcome of the final decision on the 'residence permit and work permit' is positive, the permit is issued and is valid for five years; again it entitles the holder to engage in any employment.[2261] In any case, the extension of the duration from one to five years through the REDYLE is to be emphasised[2262] as it allows for a subsequent application for a permanent residence permit.[2263] The required five years also include the period during which the person concerned held a 'provisional residence permit and work permit'.[2264]

By comparison, in the event of an unfavourable outcome, the 'provisional residence permit and work permit' is automatically invalid. The deportation process will resume, whereby a deportation will usually be ordered unless there are reasons for just imposing a fine.[2265] Where the deportation process is resumed, there must be consideration of the fact that the person concerned could apply for another 'temporary residence permit for exceptional circumstances' or may be eligible for such permit under certain circumstances.[2266] If the requirements for one of the residence permits are met, the deportation proceedings are to be discontinued.[2267]

III. Interim conclusion

'Other national interests' is a distinctly national category of regularisations as it is derived almost entirely from provisions of domestic law. As these types of regularisations have not been influenced by international or EU law (with the exception of Article 13(4) Employers Sanctions Directive),

2261 Arts 136(7) and 137(7) REDYLE.

2262 In this sense *Díaz Morgado*, La residencia de víctimas de trata de personas y la residencia por colaboración contra redes organizadas in *Boza Martínez/Donaire Villa/Moya Malapeira* 350.

2263 Art 32 LODYLE.

2264 Arts 136(7) and 137(7) REDYLE.

2265 Instrucción DGI/SGRJ/06/2006, 4; cf. *Vicente Palacio*, Art 59 LODYLE in *Monereo Pérez/Fernández Avilés/Triguero Martínez* 953.

2266 Arts 136(9) and 137(9) REDYLE; see also *Lázaro González/Benlloch Sanz* in *Palomar Olmeda* 931f concerning the 'temporary residence permit and work permit for exceptional circumstances for foreign victims of human trafficking' and the parallel provision under Art 144(7) REDYLE; see Chapter 4.D.I.4.

2267 Art 241(2) REDYLE. See Chapter 3.C.III.3.b.

the residence permit extends beyond such higher-ranking laws, which in principle do not need to be observed in this context.

The comparison has shown that only two Spanish residence permits may fall under the purpose 'other national interests'. Both regularisations grant certain public authorities the possibility to issue a residence permit to foreigners who collaborate with the authorities. Although not explicitly defined by law, 'collaboration' may be understood as reporting certain criminal offences, providing essential information or making relevant statements. Furthermore, it is also possible that the residence permit is granted on the grounds of national security or public interest, though it is not possible to determine from the literature or the case law what these notions actually mean. A clarifying step seems to be the reform via the Royal Decree 629/2022 that lays down that a residence permit may be granted to persons who collaborate with the relevant labour authority, whereby collaboration is specified as demonstrating the existence of him or her working in an undocumented situation of no less than six months in duration in the last year. However, it will be seen how this residence permit will prove itself in practice and if the same problems will arise as regarding the 'temporary residence permit for reasons of employment roots'.

The procedural aspects of these permits feature key differences. The 'temporary residence permit for exceptional circumstances for exceptional circumstances due to the collaboration with public authorities, or for reasons of national security or public interest' is only granted for one year and corresponds in essence to the procedure laid down for 'temporary residence permits for exceptional circumstances'.

In contrast, the 'temporary residence permit for exceptional circumstances due to collaboration in the fight against organised networks' is entirely different both with regard to the procedural aspects and the protection offered. For the most part, it corresponds to the residence permits granted to victims of human trafficking or foreign women who are victims of gender-based violence.[2268] Such overlaps exist because the 'temporary residence permit for exceptional circumstances due to collaboration in the fight against organised networks' serves, inter alia, to transpose Article 13(4) Employers Sanctions Directive, thus allowing victims or other parties injured by 'labour exploitation' to apply for this type of permit. Unlike the residence permit that may be granted to victims of human trafficking, the 'collaboration' with the authorities is essential. As discussed

2268 See Chapter 4.D.I.4.–5.

above, the meaning of 'collaboration' is shrouded in uncertainty. The exemption from administrative sanctions, the possibility to receive a five-year 'provisional residence permit and work permit' and the fact that the residence and work permit is issued for five years show that the rule is capable of providing legal incentives to victims, witnesses or other injured parties in the prosecution of perpetrators of the stated offences.

As in the interim conclusion regarding 'employment and training', it is necessary to highlight another result from the comparison: neither Austria nor Germany has a regularisation that falls under the purpose 'other national interests'. With regard to Austrian law, this can be explained by the generally restrictive and cautious attitude towards regularisations.[2269] For Germany, however, it can be assumed that from a contextual perspective there is no need for regularisations that serve to protect other national interests.

G. Summary – The differentiated regularisation systems

Each of the three Member States features a differentiated system of regularisations. On the one hand, the Member States grant irregularly staying migrants a right to stay based on higher-ranking laws.[2270] However, it is necessary to distinguish between the rights to stay that are mandatory to meet these obligations and those rights that go beyond the international and EU obligations. Put somewhat bluntly: the national rights to stay have been soaked in international and EU law. On the other hand, certain regularisations refer to different domestic contexts and the rights to stay are then granted on such basis. The categorisation forms a stable foundation for a future Regularisation Directive, since both the international and EU influences and the reference to contextual circumstances in the Member States have been shown.[2271]

The breakdown of all regularisations in Austria, Germany and Spain has further shown just how differentiated each individual regularisation system is. Austria is certainly at the lower end of the spectrum, since in contrast to German and Spanish law there are quantitatively fewer regularisations and these are therefore not as effective in practice, at least according to the assumptions made here. From the perspective of irregu-

2269 See Chapter 4.G.
2270 See Table 1 in Chapter 1.B.III.
2271 See the hypothesis in Chapter 1.B.V.

larly staying migrants, the situation is aggravated by the fact that due to their status they do not have access to social benefits or health and that it is very difficult to meet most of the requirements set by the legislation. The most important regularisation is probably the 'residence permit for reasons of Article 8 ECHR', whereby respect for private and family life is relevant. The 'residence permit in particularly exceptional cases' targets those (ir)regularly staying aliens who do not reach the high threshold of private and family life in the sense of Article 8 ECHR, in particular rejected asylum seekers. The statistics highlight that the permit has a near-irrelevant role in practice due to the extensive hurdles that have to be overcome. In addition to five years' continuous residence, the alien must have the ability to be self-sufficient – a criterion that is nearly impossible to fulfil where there is a lack of access to the labour market. Nonetheless, the regained access to the labour market for asylum seekers since June 2021 could lead to a higher number of residence permits in the future.

Spanish law features a wealth of regularisations. Three points are particularly noteworthy here. First, social roots, which – quantitatively speaking – is by far the most important regularisation. From the perspective of the individual, the requirements for granting a residence permit offer a pragmatic and effective way out of irregularity. Even though it already worked quite well in practice, it was reformed with the Royal Decree 629/2022 to even better address the needs of the Spanish labour market. Second, said Royal Decree additionally introduced a new type of roots, the so-called 'temporary residence permit for reasons of training' that used the German 'toleration for the purpose of training' as a role model. However, in contrast to the German toleration, the Spanish model is more generous as it grants irregularly staying foreigners an immediate right to stay. In this case, the foreigner has to prove that he or she has been in Spain for a continuous period of at least two years and is willing to take up a training. Third, Spanish law provides for regularisation for victims of human trafficking and for women who have been victims of gender-based violence. The first implements the Human Trafficking Directive in an exemplary manner and the second offers an effective system of protection for the problem of violence against foreign women. The temporary residence permits and work permits, which are very similarly structured, have a particularly sophisticated procedure that is very much framed around the needs of the victims. This procedure is divided into several 'phases', which enable the identification of the victims and to grant a 'provisional residence permit and work permit', as well as providing for an exemption from administrative penalties under certain circumstances.

German law is just as differentiated as Spanish law and features numerous regularisations. Special mention is due here to the 'residence permit in the case of permanent integration' and the 'residence permit for well-integrated juveniles and young adults', both of which can be derived from Article 8 ECHR and can be granted to tolerated persons. In this way, the German legislator has for the first time introduced a prospect of residency for this group, irrespective of age and a cut-off date, which is an expedient approach in light of the ongoing problem of 'chain tolerations'. The 'residence permit for persons who are enforceably required to leave the country, but whose departure is legally or factually impossible' is quantitatively the most important regularisation in German law. The main case of application here is again the implementation of Article 8 ECHR. Last but not least, the 'residence permit for the purpose of employment for qualified tolerated foreigners' is a peculiar feature of German residency law, enacted due to the shortage of skilled workers. Interestingly, its role in practice has been limited, however, showing an increase in importance. This is probably due to the three-year 'toleration for the purpose of training' and the fact that this can be followed by the two-year residence permit (the '3 + 2 regulation'). The statement that foreigners residing unlawfully can earn their 'right to remain' holds water.

Part III – Outlook

I examined in Part I the concepts of irregular migration and regularisations and outlined the framework under EU law. The regularisations in Austria, Germany and Spain were examined from a comparative perspective in Part II. The analyses in Parts I and II thus serve as a foundation for provoking the discussion concerning the legal instruments regarding irregularly staying migrants. Part III builds on this foundation with a proposal for a future EU Regularisation Directive. In particular, it can take stock of the advantages and disadvantages of the common and different approaches in Austria, Germany and Spain and refer to the respective national requirements and conditions to plant the seed for future EU legislation.

Chapter 5 – An EU Regularisation Directive[2272]

The following proposes an EU Regularisation Directive, though such EU legislation is presently unrealistic under the current *Realpolitik*.[2273] My proposal has already been acknowledged by *Bast/von Harbou/Wessels*, who use the title 'Directive of the European Parliament and the Council on common standards and procedures in Member States for regularizing illegally staying third-country nationals'.[2274] A regulation is not considered as the legislative form: imposing mandatory rules on the Member States without allowing any discretion in transposing the rules into national law is even less politically viable.[2275] Despite such political reality, I remain

2272 Individual sections and ideas have been published in *Hinterberger*, Maastricht Journal of European and Comparative Law 2019 and, in German, in *Hinterberger* in *Lanser/Potocnik-Manzouri/Safron/Tillian/Wieser*. See Introduction D.III.

2273 See the detail given in Chapter 2.C.I. and especially *Lutz*, EJML 2018, 49f. Also *Desmond* in *Czech/Heschl/Lukas/Nowak/Oberleitner* 312 referring to the COVID-19 pandemic.

2274 *Bast/von Harbou/Wessels*, REMAP 205ff, in particular 206.

2275 See how the negotiations concerning reforms of the Common European Asylum System and Resettlement have stalled: *Council of the European Union*, Note from the Presidency to the Council Concerning the Reform of the Common European Asylum System and Resettlement (30.5.2018), 9520/18, 4.

convinced that there are benefits to providing more detail on legislation that would supplement the EU's current immigration policy: 'There are no easy answers, but their absence does not render the quest for appropriate solutions obsolete'.[2276] In this respect, examples of scholars who have also undertaken such quest include *Menezes Queiroz*, who provides an overview of the potential balancing role of regularisations at supranational level.[2277]

It is therefore prudent to present the core content of a Regularisation Directive, but to respect the political reality by not drafting specific legislative provisions. The remarks below build on Part I, with particular emphasis on the explanations in Chapter 2 concerning with the EU's immigration policy, its objectives and competences. The comparison in Part II (Chapter 3 and Chapter 4) is, however, the central element.

This Chapter first presents the complementary notion of 'immigration from within' (A.) in which I present the reasons why current EU immigration policy concerning irregularly staying migrants needs a new direction that can be best supplemented by an EU Regularisation Directive. I then present the basic concept underpinning such a Directive (B.) and discuss the most important areas of its content (C.). Finally, I present a plea for developing the general part of EU migration law with a horizontal Regularisation Directive (D.).

A. 'Immigration from within'

The remarks at the beginning of this Chapter give rise to the question whether the EU's mandates and competences under primary law do not even (implicitly) call the EU to realign its immigration policy also with regard to irregular migration, whereby I refer specifically to the irregular stay. In this respect, the EU's push towards more effective returns accords with the TFEU, yet in the same breath it must also be recognised that the measures thus far have not been able to significantly reduce the number of irregularly staying migrants or have had only a limited effect. The poor enforcement of returns shows the need for action from the EU in the 'fight' against irregular migration.[2278] Just like returns, regularisations end

2276 *Thym*, CMLRev 2013, 734.

2277 *Menezes Queiroz*, Illegally Staying 167ff. See further *Schieber*, Komplementärer Schutz 334ff.

2278 See Introduction A., Chapter 2.A. and Chapter 2.C.I.

the irregular stay.[2279] The EU mandate to 'combat' irregular migration would be fulfilled through the use of this measure.[2280]

The analysis in Chapter 2 allowed me to conclude that Article 79(2)(a) and (b) TFEU afford the EU legislator broad competences to pass legislation on regularisations. The substantive provisions and the procedure as well as the rights attributable to the status and freedom of movement could be regulated in EU legislation.[2281] Residence permits issued on the basis of pure national law could be equipped with status and freedom of movement rights. Based on Article 79(2)(c) TFEU, EU law could also create a form of tolerated status.[2282] Two – expressed somewhat exaggeratedly – approaches thus seem conceivable for the EU's future immigration policy:

Firstly, to focus just on effective returns.[2283] Regularisations will continue not to be viewed as part of the solution. This would mean a continuation of the present policy, which aims at a more consequent enforcement of the current provisions.[2284]

Secondly, the alternative favoured here is linked to the rules under the Return Directive, supplementing these with the harmonisation of the Member States' regularisation policies.[2285] This complementary approach could be entwined with the current efforts towards more consequent enforcement and actually lower the number of irregularly staying migrants.[2286]

An EU regularisation policy would fall within the ambit of EU primary law, as shown in Chapter 2. This reform proposal would, however, not strike the core of the return policy, as the return of irregularly staying migrants would continue, as was also emphasised by the ECJ in *El Dridi*. However, the Court did stress in *Zaizoune* that the Member States may at any moment grant a residence permit instead of enforcing the return

---

2279 See Chapter 2.B.I.

2280 See Chapter 2.C.I.

2281 See Chapter 2.D.I. and Chapter 2.D.II.

2282 See Chapter 2.D.II.3.

2283 In this sense COM(2017) 200 final and see the comments in *Lutz*, EJML 2018, 49 and *Kraler*, Journal of Immigrant and Refugee Studies 2019, 94ff.

2284 See COM(2015) 668 final, 2. Cf. in this context *Bommes*, Illegale Migration in der modernen Gesellschaft – Resultat und Problem der Migrationspolitik europäischer Nationalstaaten in *Alt/Bommes* (eds), Illegalität: Grenzen und Möglichkeiten der Migrationspolitik (2006) 95 (108).

2285 Cf. *Uriarte Torrealday*, Revista de Derecho Político 2009, 315.

2286 Also *Bommes* in *Alt/Bommes*, 108. Cf. *Böhning*, International Migration 1983, 161.

procedure. My proposal is thus for regularisations to be used as a means to supplement current EU policy.

The EU has so far refrained from employing regularisations as a tool to manage immigration and thus it seems to me that the introduction of a regularisation legal framework in the form of a directive would fill a gap in the common immigration policy. Consequently, the 'fight' against irregular immigration is understood in accordance with primary law and, to quote *Bast*, as '*Einwanderung von innen*'[2287] – immigration from within. I see this as an opportunity for the EU to 'fight' irregular migration more effectively, with regularisations as the key tool in the toolbox.[2288] As has been the case so far in this study,[2289] an individual-rights perspective is adopted.

Regularisations are often criticised for 'rewarding' foreigners who have ignored the legal requirements to leave the country.[2290] Such criticism is indeed justified, but examples from construction or tax law show that the 'legalisation' of illegal structures or 'tax amnesties' are widespread.[2291] Accordingly, the criticism of this behaviour by irregularly staying migrants needs to be considered in the discussion of a Regularisation Directive, but should not be an obstacle.

This is supported by the fact that regularisations are already part of the 'toolbox' of the differentiated, contemporary migration management at national level,[2292] as was clearly shown in the comparison in Part II, in particular in Chapter 4. As under the Return Directive, they also represent – in addition to return[2293] – the main way out of irregularity.[2294] By using regularisations, the requirements under EU primary law would also be (more effectively) fulfilled; for instance, immigration policy would be further developed in all phases, i.e. continuously and with regard to all stages of residence.[2295] This would prevent the state of limbo in the administra-

2287 *Bast*, ZAR 2012, 6.

2288 In this sense *Costello*, Human Rights 101. Though see to a much lesser degree and in part with a different opinion *Menezes Queiroz*, Illegally Staying 167ff.

2289 See Introduction D.II.3.

2290 In this sense *Pico Lorenzo*, Jueces para la democracia 2002, 68f.

2291 See Chapter 1.A.

2292 Cf. *Kraler*, IMISCOE WP No. 24 (February 2009) 21 and *Desmond* in *Acosta Arcarazo/Wiesbrock* 70.

2293 See Chapter 2.B.I.

2294 Cf. *Triandafyllidou/Vogel* in *Triandafyllidou* 297.

2295 See Chapter 2.C.II.

tive practice of the Member States with regard to non-returnable persons, as recognised in ECJ case law.[2296]

A harmonised approach at EU level would counteract[2297] the fragmentation of regularisations at national level identified in the comparison in Part II and could contribute to reducing the number of persons with an irregular stay. It has already been indicated that a Regularisation Directive would bring advantages for the respective domestic budgets and the rule of law.[2298] The consistency with the principle of subsidiarity has also been discussed above, in so far as the EU makes use of regularisation as a legal instrument.[2299] Harmonisation would also lead to administrative simplifications.

Furthermore, a Regularisation Directive could contribute to the efficient management of migration flows. According to the TFEU's design, this is reflected in a convergence of the EU *acquis* and legal reality.[2300] Through regularisations the EU could reduce the enforcement deficit of returns and pursue an active migration policy that exerts influence on the legal reality.[2301] In this way, both the fundamental rights of irregularly staying migrants[2302] and the management interests of the Member States would be strengthened and satisfied by striking the appropriate balance.[2303]

B. Underlying concept – holistic approach

My concept underlying a Regularisation Directive is based on a holistic approach that addresses all irregularly staying migrants and combines the matters identified in the comparison in a single instrument. This is the best possible way to supplement the Return Directive and to harmonise the fragmentary approach pursued to date by the EU and the Member States. On a substantive level, all regularisations that fall under one of the

---

2296 See Chapter 2.B.II.2.b.

2297 In this sense also *Schieber*, Komplementärer Schutz 333f.

2298 Cf. e.g. *Bast* in *Fischer-Lescano/Kocher/Nassibi* 71 referring to *Dauvergne*, Illegal 9ff.

2299 See Chapter 2.D.IV.

2300 See also *Thym* in *Grabitz/Hilf/Nettesheim* Art 79 AEUV mn 15.

2301 *Thym* in *Grabitz/Hilf/Nettesheim* Art 79 AEUV mn 15.

2302 Cf. *Bast*, ZAR 2012, 6 and *Thym*, CMLRev 2013, 715 referring to the area of freedom, security and justice.

2303 See *Bast*, Aufenthaltsrecht 143.

six purposes of the regularisation should be covered.[2304] In other words, all those measures that are to be understood as regularisation in the sense of the present study are taken into account.[2305]

An independent Regularisation Directive could contain different conditions for issuing permits, as reflects the current practice in Austria, Germany and Spain. The Directive conceived to supplement the Return Directive should be clearly distinguished from the Return Directive, the content is indeed the same in so far as the task of 'combatting' irregular migration is concerned, but the substantive content differs entirely. I therefore propose a two-tier model to adequately address the fragmented legal landscape in the world of regularisations.

Before presenting this model, however, another option should be discussed. The Return Directive could be reformed and – in addition to Article 6(4) Return Directive – further provisions concerning regularisations could be introduced.[2306] These could define both the return procedure and minimum standards for granting residence permits, covering for instance those cases in which return is impossible for legal or factual reasons and thus making regularisation necessary.[2307] Legal reasons would result from the non-refoulement principle and the right to respect for private and family life, as discussed in Chapter 4.[2308] It would also be especially important to set procedural guarantees and strict minimum conditions for granting protection as otherwise there would be a risk that the recast Return Directive could be undermined in practice by the Member States or that the standards of international and EU law could be watered down ('race-to-the-bottom').[2309] As already indicated, however, a Regularisation Directive should be given preference over a recast Return Directive to maintain the distinction between return and regularisation in future EU legislation.

Finally, it should be noted that the Qualification Directive could also be supplemented. However, this approach will not be pursued further, as the distinction between beneficiaries of international protection and irregularly staying migrants should be maintained, especially in order not to lessen the protection afforded to the former.

2304 See Table 1 in Chapter 1.B.III.

2305 See Chapter 1.A.II.

2306 See COM(2018) 634 final on the European Commission's current proposal.

2307 See Chapter 2.B.II.2.

2308 See Chapter 4.A.II. and Chapter 4.B.–C.

2309 Cf. *Bausager/Møller/Ardittis*, Study (11.3.2013) 84.

I. First harmonisation phase

The first phase of harmonisation should comprise and define the minimum standards under international and EU law on the basis of the comparison undertaken in Part II. More precisely, this concerns Articles 3 and 8 ECHR in international law, and in EU law the Return Directive, the Human Trafficking Directive, the Qualification Directive as well as the Charter of Fundamental Rights. The corresponding ECtHR and ECJ case law must also be considered.

With regard to the first phase, this means determining all the minimum requirements for each of the regularisations that are derived from international or EU law and thus fall under the purposes of the regularisation 1 to 4.[2310] A legal entitlement to regularisation should also be determined for all of the cases in which – in line with this study – there is a regularisation obligation,[2311] such as may be derived, inter alia, from Articles 3 and 8 ECHR and the Return Directive. Such step could allow the EU to be more effective in its 'fight' against irregular migration and reduce the number of irregularly staying migrants. The provisions of higher-ranking laws should themselves serve as a basis for the minimum requirements to be set in order not to weaken the current practice in Member States, which often exceeds the level set by the higher-ranking norms.[2312]

This approach would place human rights or the corresponding EU legislation at the centre of the Regularisation Directive. With a foundation in universal human rights the Directive would have a 'cosmopolitan basis'.[2313] *Schmid-Drüner* takes a similar direction by calling in 2007 for a Directive 'for the protection of elementary fundamental rights of illegally staying migrants'.[2314] Her proposal should ensure, inter alia, the respect for the human dignity, private and family life, right to healthcare and to education of 'illegally staying migrants'.[2315] Although some of her demands in this respect do proceed in a different direction, human rights are nonetheless at the core.

2310 See Chapter 1.B.III.1.–3.

2311 See Chapter 2.B.II.2. as well as Chapter 1.B.III.2.

2312 Cf. *Bausager/Møller/Ardittis*, Study (11.3.2013) 84.

2313 As stated by *Bast*, Vom subsidiären Schutz zum europäischen Flüchtlingsbegriff, ZAR 2018, 41 (46) regarding subsidiary protection; cf. also *Bast/von Harbou/Wessels*, REMAP 205ff.

2314 *Schmid-Drüner*, Einwanderungsrecht 477: '*eine Richtlinie zum Schutz elementarer Grundrechte illegal aufhältiger Drittstaatsangehöriger*'.

2315 *Schmid-Drüner*, Einwanderungsrecht 477.

The harmonisation of regularisations based on international and EU law should not, however, lead to the fact that regularisations issued on the basis of context-specific circumstances would become incompatible with EU law.[2316] Accordingly, a provision with the same wording as Article 6(4) Return Directive should be included in the Regularisation Directive, with its first sentence being of particular relevance: 'Member States may at any moment decide to grant an autonomous residence permit or other authorisation offering a right to stay for compassionate, humanitarian or other reasons to a third-country national staying illegally on their territory'.

II. Second harmonisation phase

In a second phase, minimum standards could then be introduced regarding the purely national regularisations categorised in the purposes of the regularisation 5 and 6. The Member States would have to be given sufficient scope to be able to take into account – as is currently the case – the respective geographical, economic and political factors that have already played a role in the determining national regularisations. In light of this, no special minimum requirements should be set in order to allow the Member States to respond to domestic circumstances by means of regularisations, as they have done so far in accordance with Article 6(4) Return Directive. The regulation of aspects of procedural law would also be meaningful with regard to this type of regularisation. However, priority should be given to the first harmonisation phase, with the second phase only beginning when an agreement is reached regarding the first phase – a staggered approach, so to speak.

C. Content

Following on from the underlying concept, this section now turns to the regulatory content considered necessary for the Directive and which should be taken into account in a possible legislative process at EU level. In doing so, I will refer back to comments already made in the course of this study.

With regard to content, the 2017 Return Handbook prepared by the European Commission can serve as a starting point for the more detailed

2316 See Chapter 4.G.

design of such a directive.[2317] Amongst other things, the Handbook addresses the wide discretion of the Member States in issuing residence permits and recommends that the Member States take into account both individual and horizontal (policy-related) criteria, such as:

- 'the cooperative/non-cooperative attitude of the returnee;
- the length of factual stay of the returnee in the Member State;
- integration efforts made by the returnee;
- personal conduct of the returnee;
- family links;
- humanitarian considerations;
- the likelihood of return in the foreseeable future;
- need to avoid rewarding irregularity;
- impact of regularisation measures on migration pattern of prospective (irregular) migrants; (and)
- (the) likelihood of secondary movements within Schengen area'.[2318]

These criteria represent the most important points taken into consideration by the European Commission in the development of a regularisation legal framework already in 2017. Comparing these with the results of the comparison of Austrian, German and Spanish law, soon shows the number of overlaps. This underlines to an even greater extent the central role a comparison of national laws can play in a future Regularisation Directive.

I. Personal scope of application

The personal scope of application is an essential element of a Regularisation Directive. It should align with the Return Directive to cover all irregularly staying migrants[2319] in order to fit coherently into existing EU law and, in the sense of an 'immigration from within', contribute to the reduction of irregularly staying migrants.

II. Requirements for granting regularisations

The substantive and formal requirements must be clearly formulated and must not give the competent authorities too much discretion, otherwise

2317 Along this line *Lutz* in *Thym/Hailbronner* Art 14 Return Directive mn 14.

2318 Return Handbook 2017, 139.

2319 See also Chapter 5.D. and Chapter 1.A.II.1.

there is no legal certainty.[2320] This was clear in relation to some regularisations examined in Chapter 4.[2321] For example, in the case of the Spanish 'temporary residence permit for exceptional circumstances due to collaboration in the fight against organised networks', it is not clear how the term 'collaboration' is to be interpreted.[2322]

The comparison of the national laws has revealed several requirements that play a central role in connection with many regularisations and have thus been mentioned. The period of residence spent in the Member State is an essential requirement, whereby the quality of the residence status is assessed differently. Accordingly, periods of lawful residence are generally valued more highly than those during which the person concerned was tolerated or staying irregularly. If a measure terminating the residence of the irregular migrant exists, this can constitute a reason for refusal. As a rule, the absence of criminal convictions is a necessary requirement for granting a residence permit or, conversely, a criminal conviction may constitute a ground for refusal. Another aspect usually taken into consideration is whether the migrant was at fault for the impossibility of departure. In this context, it is assessed differently whether the cause for the impossibility of leaving the country is already taken into account when the residence permit is granted (Austria) or only when access to social benefits or the labour market is granted (Germany).[2323] The latter is to be preferred.

Furthermore, whether, and if so, under which conditions, there is a legal entitlement to regularisation. Such an entitlement should be defined for those cases in which a regularisation obligation is argued in this study.[2324] Consequently, non-returnable migrants should be granted a right to stay after a certain period of residence. This was already discussed by the Danish delegation in 1997 during the negotiations on the introduction of subsidiary protection.[2325] In line with the view expressed here that there is

---

2320 In this sense *Trinidad García*, Revista de Derecho Migratorio y Extranjería 2002/1, 101f, 110f, on the problems arising from the Spanish regularisation programme in 1999.

2321 See also Chapter 4.A.I.3.a. on the problems acquiring toleration on factual grounds in Austria.

2322 See Chapter 4.F.II.1.

2323 However, one must consider the toleration of 'persons whose identity is not verified' and its effects on German law; see in particular Chapter 4.A.I.2.a.

2324 See Chapter 2.B.II.2. and Chapter 1.B.III.2.

2325 *Council of the European Union*, Aufzeichnung der dänischen Delegation für die Gruppen „Migration“ und „Asyl“ betreffend subsidiären Schutz (17.3.1997), 6764/97, 9.

an obligation to regularise in cases of permanent non-returnability, I therefore propose a period of 18 months, which is derived from the maximum period of detention.[2326]

III. Right to stay

Further central aspects to be determined include not only the duration of the right to stay but also the possible extensions or change to a different basis for the right. It is also conceivable that EU law introduces a kind of tolerated status that proceeds the grant of a right to stay. This could provide even greater legal certainty as a 'transitional solution' under residence law, i.e. in the phase before granting a right to stay or until voluntary return. However, two points need to be considered should toleration be introduced as a precursor to a right to stay: acquiring tolerated status must not be made impossible by affording the authorities extensive discretion[2327] and long-term irregularity is to be avoided. In this latter respect, it would be counter-productive to create problems such as the 'chain tolerations' in Germany and for irregularly staying migrants to become stuck in a situation of permanent non-returnability.[2328]

A right to stay that is acquired in relation to a Regularisation Directive must in any event constitute lawful residence.[2329] Here, it is key that irregularly staying migrants are able to extend their right to stay or to switch to the 'ordinary' residence regime. In practice, many irregularly staying migrants often 'fall back' into a state of irregularity after regularisation, which is certainly a problem[2330] – the situation in Spain in the 1990s was particularly striking in connection with the regularisation programmes that were implemented.[2331] Similar problems can also be seen in current Spanish law with the different requirements for 'roots', as shown by *Sabater/Domingo*.[2332] In order to avoid a return to an irregular status, the conditions for an extension or the change to a different permit should therefore be formulated in such a way that they can be met by the mi-

2326 See Chapter 2.B.II.2.b.
2327 See Chapter 4.A.I.3.a.
2328 See Chapter 4.A.I.2.d.
2329 See Chapter 1.A.II.2.
2330 *Triandafyllidou/Vogel* in *Triandafyllidou* 295f.
2331 See *Cabellos Espiérrez/Roig Molés* in *Aja/Arango Joaquín* 114 and Chapter 3.C.I.
2332 See *Sabater/Domingo*, International Migration Review 2012/46, 203ff and Fn 1341 and 1342.

grants concerned. The explanations in Chapter 3 can be used as a starting point for this. Furthermore, it should be regulated whether permanent residence can be obtained after an extension or a change, and under which conditions this would be possible.

The right to stay should be accompanied by certain rights linked to the migrants lawful residency, in particular access to the labour market,[2333] social benefits and healthcare. In this respect, the REGANE I study from 2014 should be taken into account: the 'Feasibility Study on the Labour Market Trajectories of Regularised Immigrants within the European Union', which shows the complex relationship between regularisations and employment.[2334]

IV. Procedural aspects

A Regularisation Directive must also regulate the procedural aspects. The Return Directive and the Single Permit Directive could serve as models, particularly as the latter established a single procedure for a single residence and work permit. In addition to the procedure, the Single Permit Directive also contains procedural guarantees and certain rights, such as the right to equal treatment. Furthermore, there should also be provisions concerning the possibility of appeal, which corresponds to the right to an effective remedy according to Article 6 ECHR and Article 47 CFR.

D. Expanding general EU migration law

My proposal for harmonisation has to be designed to allow it to fit coherently into the EU and domestic immigration and residency systems. It is for this reason that I consider an independent Regularisation Directive to be the best approach. Such Directive could not only find a balance between the interests of the EU (and the Member States) and irregularly staying migrants but could also create clear basic requirements.

2333 The Member States may not invoke Art 79(5) TFEU in order to introduce national quotas for access to the labour market. See Chapter 2.D.II.2.

2334 *Kraler/Reichel/König/Baldwin-Edwards/Şimşek*, Feasibility Study on the Labour Market Trajectories of Regularised Immigrants within the European Union (REGANE I). Final Report (February 2009), https://ec.europa.eu/social/BlobServlet?docId=12612&langId=en (31.7.2022) 81. For detail see the analysis of the study in *Kraler*, Journal of Immigrant and Refugee Studies 2019.

It is prudent in this respect to refer to *Tewocht*, who has shown that only four current EU Directives (including the Return Directive) pursue a horizontal regulatory approach.[2335] *Tewocht* uses the term 'horizontal' to describe the fact that the personal and material scopes of application are comprehensive, i.e. addressed to all third-country nationals and covering all residence permits. Transferring this notion to a Regularisation Directive, it would be desirable if the Directive were to take account of all irregularly staying migrants and all types of regularisations. Adopting a sectoral approach, i.e. rules specific for individually definable groups such as non-returnable persons, would only lead to further (deliberate) differentiation.[2336]

Accordingly, the EU should make use of its competences in the sense of a horizontal regulatory approach so that a future Regularisation Directive becomes an element of the 'general part' of EU migration law.[2337] The criticism of the lack of a migration concept or the slow development of the harmonisation of the area of freedom, security and justice could thus be avoided, at least for this area.[2338]

Referring back to the complementary concept of 'immigration from within', introducing a Regularisation Directive would thus fill a gap in the common immigration policy.[2339] If one understands 'combatting' irregular immigration in accordance with EU primary law and in the sense of *Bast's* 'immigration from within',[2340] the EU has the opportunity to 'combat' irregular migration more effectively. The EU could use regularisations to reduce the enforcement deficit of returns and pursue an active migration policy that exerts influence on the legal reality.[2341] In this way, both the fundamental rights of irregularly staying migrants and the management interests of the Member States would be strengthened and satisfied through striking the necessary balance.

2335 *Tewocht*, Auf dem Weg zur Gleichstellung von Drittstaatsangehörigen und Unionsbürgern? – Zu Inhalt und Reichweite der sogenannten ‚Rahmenrichtlinie', ZAR 2012, 217 (219) and *Tewocht*, Drittstaatsangehörige 411f, 449.

2336 Cf. *Tewocht*, Drittstaatsangehörige 417ff, 449, 451.

2337 *Tewocht*, Drittstaatsangehörige 411 refers to this as a general part of European immigration law (*'allgemeiner Teil des europäischen Einwanderungsrechts'*).

2338 Cf. for criticism *Tewocht*, ZAR 2012, 219 Fn 29 with further references.

2339 See Chapter 4.A.

2340 *Bast*, ZAR 2012, 6.

2341 *Thym* in *Grabitz/Hilf/Nettesheim* Art 79 AEUV mn 15.

Bibliography

Abarca Junco/Alonso-Olea García/Lacruz López/Martín Dégano/Vargas Gómez-Urrutia, Inmigración y Extranjería: Régimen jurídico básico[5] (2011).

Acale Sánchez, La Residencia de mujeres víctimas de violencia de género in *Boza Martínez/Donaire Villa/Moya Malapeira* (eds), Comentario a la reforma de la ley de extranjería (LO 2/2009) (2011) 321.

Acosta Arcarazo, The Charter, detention and possible regularization of migrants in an irregular situation under the Returns Directive: Mahdi, CMLRev 2015, 1361.

Acosta Arcarazo/Guild, The Returns Directive in *Peers/Guild/Acosta Arcarazo/Groenendijk/Moreno-Lax* (eds), EU Immigration and Asylum Law. Vol 2: EU Immigration Law[2] (2012) 455.

Acosta Arcarazo/Romano, The Returns Directive and the Expulsion of Migrants in an Irregular Situation in Spain, EU Law Analysis Blog (2. 5. 2015), www.eulaw analysis.blogspot.co.uk/2015/05/the-returns-directive-and-expulsion-of.html (31.7.2022).

Aguilera Izquierdo, El acceso de los inmigrantes irregulares al mercado de trabajo: Los procesos de regularización extraordinaria y el arraigo social y laboral, Revista del Ministerio de Trabajo y Asuntos Sociales 2006, 175.

Aja (ed), Los derechos de los inmigrantes en España (2009).

Aja, La evolución de la normativa sobre inmigración in *Aja/Arango* (eds), Veinte Años de Inmigración en España: Perspectiva jurídica y sociológica (1985-2004) (2006) 17.

Álvarez Rodríguez/Marrero González, Attribution of Spanish Nationality to Children Born in Spain with the Purpose of Avoiding Situations of Statelessness at Birth in *Carrera Nuñez/de Groot* (eds), European Citizenship at the Crossroads: The Role of the European Union on Loss and Acquisition of Nationality (2015) 267.

Angenedt, Irreguläre Migration als internationales Problem. SWP Study (December 2007), https://www.swp-berlin.org/fileadmin/contents/products/studien/2007_S33_adt_ks.pdf (31.7.2022).

Apap/de Bruycker/Schmitter, Regularisation of Illegal Aliens in the European Union. Summary Report of a Comparative Study, EJML 2000, 263.

Apap/de Bruycker/Schmitter, Rapport de synthèse sur la comparaison des régularisations d'étrangers illégaux dans l'Union européenne in *de Bruycker* (ed), Les regularisations des étrangers illégaux dans l'union européenne. Regularisations of illegal immigrants in the European Union (2000) 24.

Arango/Finotelli, Country Report Spain in *Baldwin-Edwards/Kraler* (eds), REGINE Regularisations in Europe: Appendix A Country Studies (January 2009), https://home-affairs.ec.europa.eu/system/files/2020-09/regine_appendix_a_january_2009_en.pdf (31.7.2022) 83.

Arrese Iriondo, La problemática jurídica de las situaciones irregulares: la expulsión como sanción a la situación irregular, Revista de Derecho Migratorio y Extranjería 2010/25, 73.

Asín Cabrera, La residencia y protección de los menores inmigrantes no acompañados in *Boza Martínez/Donaire Villa/Moya Malapeira* (eds), La nueva regulación de la inmigración y la extranjería en España (2012) 307.

Asylkoordination/Diakonie/Volkshilfe/Integrationshaus/SOS Mitmensch (eds), Ein Jahr „Bleiberecht": Eine Analyse mit Fallbeispielen (April 2010), http://s3web0314.peakserver.net/wp-content/uploads/2015/02/bleiberechtsbericht_03_10.pdf (31.7.2022).

Ataç, Die diskursive Konstruktion von Flüchtlingen und Asylpolitik in Österreich seit 2000 in *Hunger/Pioch/Rother* (eds), Migrations- und Integrationspolitik im europäischen Vergleich – Jahrbuch Migration 2012/2013 (2014) 113.

Augustin, Die Rückführungsrichtlinie der Europäischen Union. Richtliniendogmatik, Durchführungspflichten, Reformbedarf (2016).

Bachmann, Das Bleiberecht – eine vorläufige Bilanz, migraLex 2010, 95.

Baer, Verfassungsvergleichung und reflexive Methode: Interkulturelle und intersubjektive Kompetenz, ZaöRV 2004, 735.

Baldaccini/Guild/Toner (eds), Whose Freedom, Security and Justice? EU Immigration and Asylum Law and Policy (2007).

Baldwin-Edwards, Regularisations and Employment in Spain. REGANE Assessment Report (February 2014), https://mpra.ub.uni-muenchen.de/59812/1/MPRA_paper_59812.pdf (31.7.2022).

Baldwin-Edwards/Kraler, REGINE Regularisations in Europe: Study on the practices in the area of regularization of illegally staying third-country nationals in the Member States of the EU. Final Report (January 2009), https://ec.europa.eu/migrant-integration/sites/default/files/2009-04/docl_8193_345982803.pdf (31.7.2022).

Barcelón Cobedo, Autorización de Residencia por motivos laborales. Régimen general in *Boza Martínez/Donaire Villa/Moya Malapeira* (eds), La nueva regulación de la inmigración y la extranjería en España (2012) 364.

Bartels, Methode und Gegenstand intersystemarer Rechtsvergleichung (1982).

Bassermann, Überblick über nationale Schutzstatus in Österreich (May 2019), https://www.emn.at/wp-content/uploads/2019/09/emn-natioanler-bericht-2019_nationale-schutzstatus.pdf (31.7.2022).

Bast, Aufenthaltsrecht und Migrationssteuerung (2011).

Bast, Es gibt kein solidarisches Asylsystem in Europa, Verfassungsblog (21.10.2013), http://verfassungsblog.de/es-gibt-kein-solidarisches-asylsystem-in-europa/ (31.7.2022).

Bast, Illegale Migration und die Rechte von illegalen Migrantinnen und Migranten als Regelungsgegenstände des Europarechts in *Fischer-Lescano/Kocher/Nassibi* (eds), Arbeit in der Illegalität: Die Rechte von Menschen ohne Aufenthaltspapiere (2012) 71.

Bast, Illegaler Aufenthalt und europarechtliche Gesetzgebung, ZAR 2012, 1.

Bast, Ursprünge der Europäisierung des Migrationsrechts in FS Kay Hailbronner (2013) 3.

Bast, Völker- und unionsrechtliche Anstöße zur Entterritorialisierung des Rechts, VVDStRL 2016/76, 278.

Bast, Vom subsidiären Schutz zum europäischen Flüchtlingsbegriff, ZAR 2018, 41.

Bast, Zehn Jahre Aufenthaltsgesetz, DÖV 2013, 214.

Bast/Thym, Streitgespräch zum rechtlichen Zustand des europäischen und deutschen Asylsystems, vorgänge 208 issue 4/2014, 4.

Bast/von Harbou/Wessels, Human Rights Challenges to European Migration Policy. The REMAP Study (2022).

Bauder, Why We Should Use the Term 'Illegalized' Refugee or Immigrant: A Commentary, IJRL 2014, 327.

Bauer, Zuwanderung nach Österreich (January 2008), http://www.politikberatung.or.at/fileadmin/_migrated/media/Zuwanderung-nach-Oesterreich.pdf (31.7.2022).

Bausager/Møller/Ardittis, Study on the situation of third-country nationals pending return/removal in the EU Member States and the Schengen Associated (11.3.2013), https://home-affairs.ec.europa.eu/system/files/2020-09/11032013_sudy_report_on_immigration_return-removal_en.pdf (31.7.2022).

Becker, Die Flüchtlingsdebatte in den Medien Deutschlands – Eine korpus- und diskurslinguistische Untersuchung der Konzeptualisierung von Angst, Sprachreport 2016/1, 1.

Beichel-Benedetti, Die Neuregelung der Abschiebungshaft im Gesetz zur Neubestimmung des Bleiberechts und der Aufenthaltsbeendigung, NJW 2015, 2541.

Belgrano Ledesma, Solicitar una autorización de residencia temporal por arraigo social, Iuris 2010/151, 59.

Bell, Comparing Public Law in *Harding/Örücü* (eds), Comparative Law in the 21st Century (2002) 235.

Berger/Tanzer, Die Rückführungsrichtlinie im Spannungsfeld von effektiver Rückführungspolitik und Grundrechtsschutz – eine Analyse unter Berücksichtigung der österreichischen Gesetzeslage in *Salomon* (ed), Der Status im europäischen Asylrecht (2020) 265.

Bergmann/Dienelt (eds), Kommentar Ausländerrecht[13] (2020).

Bergmann/Eichenhofer/Hörich/Janda/Nestler/Stamm/Tewocht/Vogt, Einwanderungsgesetz: Hallescher Entwurf zur Neuordnung der Dogmatik des Aufenthaltsrechts (2019).

Bergmann/Putzar-Sattler in *Huber/Mantel* (eds), Kommentar Aufenthaltsgesetz/Asylgesetz[3] (2021) § 54 AufenthG.

Berka, Verfassungsrecht[8] (2021).

Berka/Binder/Kneihs, Die Grundrechte[2] (2019)

Berlit, Migration und ihre Folgen – Wie kann das Recht Zuwanderung und Integration in Gesellschaft, Arbeitsmarkt und Sozialordnung steuern? (Teil 1), ZAR 2018, 229.

Berlit, Migration und ihre Folgen – Wie kann das Recht Zuwanderung und Integration in Gesellschaft, Arbeitsmarkt und Sozialordnung steuern? (Teil 2), ZAR 2018, 287.

Bernhardt, Eigenheiten und Ziele der Rechtsvergleichung im öffentlichen Recht, ZaöRV 1964, 431.

Bigo, Border Regimes Police Cooperation and Security in an Enlarged European Union in *Zielonka* (ed), Europe Unbound: Enlarging and Reshaping the Boundaries of the European Union (2003) 213.

Błuś, Beyond the Walls of Paper. Undocumented Migrants, the Border and Human Rights, EJML 2013, 413.

Boeles/den Heijer/Lodder/Wouters, European Migration Law[2] (2014).

Böhning, Regularising the Irregular, International Migration 1983, 159.

Bommes, Illegale Migration in der modernen Gesellschaft – Resultat und Problem der Migrationspolitik europäischer Nationalstaaten in *Alt/Bommes* (eds), Illegalität: Grenzen und Möglichkeiten der Migrationspolitik (2006) 95.

Bosniak, Human Rights, State Sovereignty and the Protection of Undocumented Migrants under the International Migrant Workers Convention, International Migration Review 1991, 737.

Boswell, The Politics of Irregular Migration in *Azoulai/De Vries* (eds), EU Migration Law: Legal Complexities and Political Rationales (2014) 41.

Boza Martínez, El procedimiento sancionador en general y, particularmente, los procedimientos de expulsión in *Boza Martínez/Donaire Villa/Moya Malapeira* (eds), Comentario a la reforma de la ley de extranjería (LO 2/2009) (2011) 261.

Boza Martínez, El régimen sancionador en la normativa de extranjería in *Boza Martínez/Donaire Villa/Moya Malapeira* (eds), La nueva regulación de la inmigración y la extranjería en España (2012) 471.

Boza Martínez, La regularización de los progenitores de menores de nacionalidad española y la necesidad de una solución reglamentaria a la cuestión. WP 1/2011 (9.2.2011), http://idpbarcelona.net/docs/public/wp/workingpaper5.pdf (31.7.2022).

Boza Martínez/Donaire Villa/Moya Malapeira (eds), La nueva regulación de la inmigración y la extranjería en España (2012).

Boza Martínez/Donaire Villa/Moya Malapeira (eds), Comentario a la reforma de la ley de extranjería (LO 2/2009) (2011).

Boza Martínez/Donaire Villa/Moya Malapeira, La normativa española de extranjería y asilo: evolución y características principales in *Boza Martínez/Donaire Villa/Moya Malapeira* (eds), La nueva regulación de la inmigración y la extranjería en España (2012) 15.

Bröcker, Die externen Dimensionen des EU-Asyl- und Flüchtlingsrechts im Lichte der Menschenrechte und des Völkerrechts (2010).

Bydlinski, Das bewegliche System und juristische Methodenlehre in *Bydlinski/Krejci/Schilcher/Steininger* (eds), Das Bewegliche System im geltenden und künftigen Recht (1986) 21.

Cabellos Espiérrez/Roig Molés, El tratamiento jurídico del extranjero en situación regular in *Aja/Arango* (eds), Veinte Años de Inmigración en España: Perspectiva jurídica y sociológica (1985-2004) (2006) 113.

Camas Roda, Trabajo decente e inmigrantes en España: Un estudio sobre los derechos laborales de los trabajadores migrantes y del objetivo internacional del trabajo decente (2016).

Carbajal García, El arraigo como circunstancia excepcional para poder residir y trabajar legalmente en España, Revista de Derecho Migratorio y Extranjería 2012/29, 55.

Carlin, Statement by the ICM Director James L. Cadin, International Migration 1983, 97.

Carrera/Guild, Addressing Irregular Migration, Facilitation and Human Trafficking: The EU's Approach in *Carrera/Guild* (eds), Irregular Migration, Trafficking and Smuggling of Human Beings: Policy Dilemmas in the EU (2016) 1.

Carrera/Guild/Aliverti/Allsopp/Manieri/Levoy, Fit for purpose? The Facilitation Directive and the criminalisation of humanitarian assistance to irregular migrants (2016), http://www.europarl.europa.eu/RegData/etudes/STUD/2016/536490/IPOL_STU%282016%29536490_EN.pdf (31.7.2022).

Carrera/Parkin, Protecting and Delivering Fundamental Rights of Irregular Migrants at Local and Regional Levels in the European Union (14.11.2011), https://www.ceps.eu/ceps-publications/protecting-and-delivering-fundamental-rights-irregular-migrants-local-and-regional/ (31.7.2022).

Carrillo, La jurisdicción constitucional española y el caso chileno, Revista de Derecho 2001, 75.

Castanedo García, Examen de la jurisprudencia existente relativa a los artículos 57 y 58 de la ley orgánica 4/2000, de 11 de enero y su desarrollo reglamentario, y las sentencias de distintos tribunales superiores de justicia sobre la materia, Revista de Derecho Migratorio y Extranjería 2014/36, 261.

Cerdán/Maas, Ein Überblick über die Neuerungen im spanischen Ausländerrecht, ZAR 2010, 105.

Cerezo Mariscal, La gestión de los procesos de la irregularidad estructural y sobrevenida en España. Análisis maquetado del arraigo, Revista de Derecho 2015, 657.

Cholewinski, Control of Irregular Migration and EU Law and Policy: A Human Rights Deficit in *Peers/Rogers* (eds), EU Immigration and Asylum Law: Text and Commentary (2006) 899.

Cholewinski, European Policy on Irregular Migration: Human Rights Lost? in *Bogusz/Cholewinski/Cygan/Szyszczak* (eds), Irregular Migration and Human Rights: Theoretical, European and International Perspectives (2004) 159.

Cholewinski, No Right of Entry in *Groenendijk/Guild/Minderhoud* (eds), In Search of Europe's Borders (2002) 105.

Cholewinski, The Criminalisation of Migration in EU Law and Policy in *Baldaccini/Guild/Toner* (eds), Whose Freedom, Security and Justice? EU Immigration and Asylum Law and Policy (2007) 301.

Cobas Cobiella, Menores y Extranjería: Situaciones de regularización, Revista Boliviana de Derecho 2015/20, 100.

Cole/Quintel, Data Retention under the Proposal for an EU Entry/Exit System (EES): Analysis of the impact on and limitations for the EES by Opinion 1/15 on the EU/Canada PNR Agreement of the Court of Justice of the European Union (October 2017), http://orbilu.uni.lu/bitstream/10993/35446/1/Legal%20Opinion.PDF (31.7.2022).

Colomer Hernández, Los extranjeros y los tribunales españoles in *Palomar Olmeda* (ed), Tratado de Extranjería[6] (2020) 653.

Comisión Española de Ayuda al Refugiado, Dossier: Proceso de regularización de trabajadores extranjeros ilegales (1991).

Conde Antequera, Art 21 LODYLE in *Monereo Pérez/Fernández Avilés/Triguero Martínez* (eds), Comentario a la ley y al reglamento de Extranjería, Inmigración e Integración Social[2] (2013) 337.

Consejo General del Poder Judicial, Informe sobre víctimas mortales de la violencia de género y de la violencia doméstica en el ámbito de la pareja o ex pareja en el año 2015 (2015).

Cornelisse, Immigration Detention and Human Rights: Rethinking Territorial Sovereignty (2010).

Costello, The Human Rights of Migrants and Refugees in European Law (2015).

Curran, Critiquing Günter Frankenberg's Comparative Law As Critique, German Law Journal 2020, 304.

Cyrus/Kovacheva, Undocumented Migration in Germany: Many Figures, Little Comprehension in *Triandafyllidou* (ed), Irregular Migration: Myths and Realities (2010) 125.

Czech in *Abermann/Czech/Kind/Peyrl* (eds), NAG Kommentar[2] (2019) § 3 NAG.

Da Lomba, Vulnerability and the Right to Respect for Private Life as an Autonomous Source of Protection against Expulsion under Article 8 ECHR, Laws 2017/6/32.

Dalli Almiñana, La violencia de género y el acceso de las víctimas extranjeras en situación administrativa irregular a los servicios sanitarios: consecuencias del real decreto-ley 16/2012, Revista de Derecho Migratorio y Extranjería 2014/36, 39.

Dauvergne, Making People Illegal: What Globalization Means for People and Law (2008).

De Bruycker (ed), Les regularisations des étrangers illégaux dans l'union européenne. Regularisations of illegal immigrants in the European Union (2000).

De Weck, Non-Refoulement under the European Convention on Human Rights and the UN Convention against Torture (2016).

Decker in *Posser/Wolff* (eds), BeckOK VwGO (53rd edn, 1.4.2020) § 113 VwGO.

Defensor del Pueblo, ¿Menores o Adultos? Procedimientos para la determinación de la edad (2012), https://www.defensordelpueblo.es/wp-content/uploads/2015/05/2011-09-Menores-o-Adultos-Procedimientos-para-la-determinaci%C3%B3n-de-la-edad1.pdf (31.7.2022).

Defensor del Pueblo, Estudio sobre el asilo en España (June 2016), https://www.defensordelpueblo.es/wp-content/uploads/2016/07/Asilo_en_Espa%C3%B1a_2016.pdf (31.7.2022).

Defensor del Pueblo, La violencia domestica contra las mujeres (1998), https://www.defensordelpueblo.es/wp-content/uploads/2015/05/1998-01-La-violencia-dom%C3%A9stica-contra-las-mujeres.pdf (31.7.2022).

Delgado Godoy, Inmigración, política y acción pública en España: 1985-2019 in *Palomar Olmeda* (ed), Tratado de Extranjería[6] (2020) 91.

Delgado Godoy, Política de inmigración y cambio de gobierno in Palomar Olmeda (ed), Tratado de Extranjería[5] (2012) 113.

Dembour, When Humans Become Migrants (2015).

Den Heijer/Rijpma/Spijkerboer, Coercion, Prohibition and Great Expectations: The Continuing Failure of the Common European Asylum System, CMLRev 2016, 607.

Depenheuer/Grabenwarter (eds), Der Staat in der Flüchtlingskrise: Zwischen gutem Willen und geltendem Recht (2017).

Dérens/Rico, Auf der Balkanroute, Le Monde diplomatique (Deutsche Ausgabe) April 2016, 4.

Desmond, Regularization in the European Union and the United States. The Frequent Use of an Exceptional Measure in *Wiesbrock/Acosta Arcarazo/Wiesbrock* (eds), Global Migration: Old Assumptions, New Dynamics. Vol 1 (2015) 69.

Desmond, The Development of a Common EU Migration Policy and the Rights of Irregular Migrants: A Progress Narrative?, HRLR 2016, 247.

Desmond, The European Approach to Irregular Migration in Pandemic Times: The More Things Change, the More They Stay the Same? in *Czech/Heschl/Lukas/Nowak/Oberleitner* (eds), European Yearbook on Human Rights (2021) 285.

Desmond, The Return Directive: clarifying the scope and substance of the rights of migrants facing expulsion from the EU in *King/Kuschminder* (eds), Handbook of Return Migration (2022) 137.

Deutsch/Nowotny/Seitz, Ausländerbeschäftigungsrecht Kommentar[3] (2021).

Deutscher Anwaltverein, Stellungnahme zur Abschaffung des § 10 Absatz 3 Satz 2 Aufenthaltsgesetz (AufenthG) (April 2013), https://dav-migrationsrecht.de/files/page/0_47513700_1402160616s.pdf (31.7.2022).

Díaz Crego/García Vitoria, Los derechos de los migrantes in *García Roca* (ed), ¿Hacia una globalización de los derechos? El impacto de las sentencias del Tribunal Europeo y de la Corte Interamericana (2017) 363.

Díaz Morgado, La residencia de mujeres víctimas de violencia de género in *Boza Martínez/Donaire Villa/Moya Malapeira* (eds), La nueva regulación de la inmigración y la extranjería en España (2012) 223.

Díaz Morgado, La residencia de víctimas de trata de personas y la residencia por colaboración contra redes organizadas in *Boza Martínez/Donaire Villa/Moya Malapeira* (eds), La nueva regulación de la inmigración y la extranjería en España (2012) 340.

Diekmann, Menschenrechtliche Grenzen des Rückführungsverfahrens in Europa (2016).

Dienelt/Dollinger in *Bergmann/Dienelt* (eds), Kommentar Ausländerrecht[13] (2020) § 19d AufenthG.

Dippe, „Zuckerbrot und Peitsche" in den gesetzlichen Neuerungen ab März 2020, Asylmagazin 2020, 55.

Doehring, Neuregelungen des deutschen Fremdenrechts durch das „Ausländergesetz" von 1965, ZaöRV 1965, 478.

Dollinger in *Bergmann/Dienelt* (eds), Kommentar Ausländerrecht[13] (2020) § 60c AufenthG.

Donaire Villa/Moya Malapeira, Marco competencial y organización administrativa de la inmigración in *Boza Martínez/Donaire Villa/Moya Malapeira* (eds), La nueva regulación de la inmigración y la extranjería en España (2012) 521.

Drüeke/Fritsche, Geflüchtete in den Medien – Medien für Geflüchtete, Medien Journal 2015/4, 12.

Dumon, Effects of Undocumented Migration for Individuals concerned, International Migration 1983, 218.

Düvell, Irreguläre Immigration nach Europa: Eine Einführung in *Falge/Fischer-Lescano/Sieveking* (eds), Gesundheit in der Illegalität: Rechte von Menschen ohne Aufenthaltspapiere (2009) 23.

Düvell, Paths into Irregularity: The Legal and Political Construction of Irregular Migration, EJML 2011, 275.

Düvell, The Pathways in and out of Irregular Migration in the EU: A Comparative Analysis, EJML 2011, 245.

Ebert, Rechtsvergleichung (1978).

Ecker, Schnittstellen zwischen AsylG 2005 und NAG unter besonderer Berücksichtigung von „Bleiberecht" und Familienzusammenführung in *Filzwieser/Taucher* (eds), Asyl- und Fremdenrecht. Jahrbuch 2016 (2016) 83.

Eckertz-Höfer, Neuere Entwicklungen in Gesetzgebung und Rechtsprechung zum Schutze des Privatlebens, ZAR 2008, 41.

Eckertz-Höfer, Neuere Entwicklungen in Gesetzgebung und Rechtsprechung zum Schutze des Privatlebens: Fortsetzung des Beitrags aus Heft 2/2008, ZAR 2008, 93.

ECRE, ECRE Comments on the Commission Proposal for a Recast Return Directive COM(2018) 634 (November 2018), https://www.ecre.org/wp-content/uploads/2018/11/ECRE-Comments-Commission-Proposal-Return-Directive.pdf (31.7.2022).

Ehrlich, Grundlegung der Soziologie des Rechts (1913).

Eichler, Das Sanktionsregime der „Duldung light“. Die neue „Duldung für Personen mit ungeklärter Identität“ nach § 60b AufenthG, Das Migrationspaket – Beilage zum Asylmagazin 8–9/2019, 64.

Eichler, Die „neue“ Ausbildungsduldung: Möglichkeiten und Hindernisse in der Umsetzung des § 60a Abs. 2 S. 4 ff., Asylmagazin 2017, 177.

Einwallner, Asyl- und Fremdenrecht 2010 – Bloß noch Spielball der Politik, juridikum 2010, 68.

Eisele, The External Dimension of the EU's Migration Policy (2014).

Eisele, The proposed Return Directive (recast). Substitute Impact Assessment (February 2019), http://www.europarl.europa.eu/RegData/etudes/STUD/2019/631727/EPRS_STU(2019)631727_EN.pdf (31.7.2022).

EMN, Asylum and Migration Glossary 3.0 (October 2014), https://www.emn.at/wp-content/uploads/2016/11/emn-glossary-en-version.pdf (31.7.2022).

EMN, Die Gestaltung der Asyl- und Migrationspolitik in Österreich (December 2015), https://www.emn.at/wp-content/uploads/2017/01/Organisationsstudie_AT-EMN-NCP_2016.pdf (31.7.2022).

EMN, Practical Measures to Reduce Irregular Migration. Synthesis Report (October 2012).

EMN, The different national practices concerning granting of non-EU harmonised protection statuses (December 2010).

EMN, The effectiveness of return in EU Member States 2017 (15.2.2018), http://emn.ie/files/p_201802260500242017_emn_synthesis_return_23.02.2018.pdf (31.7.2022).

Engbersen, The Unanticipated Consequences of Panopticon Europe: Residence Strategies of Illegal Immigrants in *Guiraudon/Joppke* (eds), Controlling a New Migration World (2001) 222.

Esteban de la Rosa, Art 31 LODYLE in *Monereo Pérez/Fernández Avilés/Triguero Martínez* (eds), Comentario a la ley y al reglamento de Extranjería, Inmigración e Integración Social[2] (2013) 491.

Esteban de la Rosa, Art 31bis LODYLE in *Monereo Pérez/Fernández Avilés/Triguero Martínez* (eds), Comentario a la ley y al reglamento de Extranjería, Inmigración e Integración Social[2] (2013) 519.

European Commission, Clandestino Project. Final Report (23.11.2009), http://www.statewatch.org/news/2015/mar/eu-com-clandestino-final-report-november-2009.pdf (31.7.2022).

Evan/Grisoli/Treves, Rechtssoziologie und Rechtsvergleichung in *Drobnig/Rehbinder* (eds), Rechtssoziologie und Rechtsvergleichung (1997) 35.

Farahat, Inklusion in der superdiversen Einwanderungsgesellschaft in *Baer/Lepsius/Schönberger/Waldhoff/Walter* (eds), Jahrbuch des öffentlichen Rechts der Gegenwart 66 (2018) 337.

Farahat, Progressive Inklusion: Zugehörigkeit und Teilhabe im Migrationsrecht (2014).

Farcy, Unremovability under the Return Directive: An Empty Protection? in *de Bruycker/Cornelisse/Moraru* (eds), Law and Judicial Dialogue on the Return of Irregular Migrants from the European Union (2020) 437.

Fassmann/Münz, Einwanderungsland Österreich? Historische Migrationsmuster, aktuelle Trends und politische Maßnahmen (1995).

Fassmann/Reeger, Austria: From guest worker migration to a country of immigration. IDEA WP No. 1 (December 2008).

Fernández Bessa/Brandariz García, 'Perfiles' de deportabilidad: el sesgo del sistema de control migratorio desde la perspectiva de nacionalidad, Estudios penales y criminológicos 2017/27, 307.

Fernández Bessa/Brandariz García, Transformaciones de la penalidad migratoria en el contexto de la crisis económica: El giro gerencial del dispositivo de deportación, Revista para el Análisis del Derecho 2016/4, 1.

Fernández Collados, Régimen de entrada, permanencia y salida de los extranjeros en España in *Palomar Olmeda* (ed), Tratado de Extranjería[6] (2020) 373.

Fernández Pérez, Los derechos fundamentales y libertades públicas de los extranjeros en España: Una visión desde la doctrina del tribunal constitucional (2016).

Fernández Rojo, La detención de extranjeros en situación irregular: impacto de la directiva 2008/115/CE y la jurisprudencia del TJUE en la legislación española, Revista de Derecho Comunitario Europeo 2016, 233.

Filzwieser/Frank/Kloibmüller/Raschhofer (eds), Kommentar Asyl- und Fremdenrecht (2016).

Fink/Titelbach/Vogtenhuber/Hofer, Gibt es in Österreich einen Fachkräftemangel? Analyse anhand von ökonomischen Knappheitsindikatoren (December 2015), https://irihs.ihs.ac.at/id/eprint/3891/1/IHS_Fachkräftemangel_Endbericht_0912 2015_final.pdf (31.7.2022).

Fischer-Lescano/Kocher/Nassibi, Einleitung in *Fischer-Lescano/Kocher/Nassibi* (eds), Arbeit in der Illegalität (2012) 7.

Flores, Los derechos fundamentales de los extranjeros irregulares in *Revenga Sánchez* (ed), Problemas constitucionales de la inmigración: una visión desde Italia y España (2005) 153.

Foucault, Discipline and Punish: The Birth of the Prison[2] (1995).

Fouchs/Schweda, Die Neuregelung der humanitären Aufenthaltstitel im Asylrecht, migraLex 2014, 58.

Fox-Ruhs/Ruhs, The Fundamental Rights of Irregular Migrant Workers in the EU: Understanding and reducing protection gaps (July 2022), https://www.europarl.e uropa.eu/RegData/etudes/STUD/2022/702670/IPOL_STU(2022)702670_EN.pdf (31.7.2022).

FRA, Fundamental rights of migrants in an irregular situation in the European Union. Comparative report (November 2011), https://fra.europa.eu/sites/default /files/fra_uploads/1827-FRA_2011_Migrants_in_an_irregular_situation_EN.pdf (31.7.2022).

Frahm, Zugang zu adäquater Grundversorgung für Asylsuchende aus menschenrechtlicher Perspektive, juridikum 2013, 464.

Frankenberg, Comparative Law as Critique (2019).

Frankenberg, Comparing constitutions: Ideas, ideals, and ideology—toward a layered narrative, ICON 2006, 439.

Frankenberg, Critical Comparisons: Re-thinking Comparative Law, Harvard International Law Journal 1985, 411.

Frei, Menschenhandel und Asyl: Die Umsetzung der völkerrechtlichen Verpflichtungen zum Opferschutz im schweizerischen Asylverfahren (2018).

Frei/Hinterberger/Hruschka in *Hruschka* (ed), GFK-Kommentar (2022) Art 33 GFK.

Frik, Verstaatlichte Rechtsberatung im Asylverfahren, juridikum 2021, 214.

Frik/Fux, Subsidiärer Schutz und die Akteursproblematik – Vorgaben für eine unions- und gleichheitsrechtskonforme Novellierung, migraLex 2019, 43.

Frings/Janda/Keßler/Steffen, Sozialrecht für Zuwanderer[2] (2018).

Funke-Kaiser in *Berlit* (ed), Gemeinschaftskommentar zum Aufenthaltsgesetz (110th edn, March 2021) § 60a AufenthG.

Funke-Kaiser, § 60d AufenthG als abschließende Regelung für die Ermöglichung einer Beschäftigung von geduldeten Ausländern und Ausländerinnen, ZAR 2020, 90.

Gammeltoft-Hansen, Access to Asylum: International Refugee Law and the Globalization of Migration Control (2011).

Gammeltoft-Hansen/Hathaway, *Non-Refoulement* in a World of Cooperative Deterrence, University of Michigan Law and Economics Research Paper No. 14-016 (August 2014).

García Ruiz, La condición de extranjero y el Derecho Constitucional español in *Revenga Sánchez* (ed), Problemas constitucionales de la inmigración: una visión desde Italia y España (2005) 489.

García Vitoria, El impacto de la jurisprudencia del Tribunal Europeo de Derechos Humanos en la expulsión de inmigrantes, Revista General de Derecho Constitucional 2015/20, 1.

García Vitoria, Residencia por Circunstancias Excepcionales. El Arraigo in *Boza Martínez/Donaire Villa/Moya Malapeira* (eds), La nueva regulación de la inmigración y la extranjería en España (2012) 287.

Geertz, Thick Description: Toward an Interpretive Theory of Culture in *Geertz*, The Interpretation of Cultures (1973) 3.

Geiger, Die Beugehaft zur Durchsetzbarkeit von Mitwirkungspflichten im Rahmen des Fremdenpolizeigesetzes, migraLex 2019, 2.

Genge, Das geänderte Asylbewerberleistungsgesetz, Das Migrationspaket – Beilage zum Asylmagazin 8–9/2019, 14.

Gil-Bazo, The Practice of Mediterranean States in the context of the European Union's Justice and Home Affairs External Dimension. The Safe Third Country Concept Revisited, IJRL 2006, 571.

Giménez Bachmann, La situación jurídica de los inmigrantes irregulares en España, Dissertation 2014, Universitat Abab Oliba CEU Barcelona, https://www.tdx.cat/handle/10803/295836#page=1 (31.7.2022).

Gimeno Monterde, Menores extranjeros no acompañados. Una cuestión compleja para las políticas públicas y sociales, Revista de Derecho Migratorio y Extranjería 2010/25, 55.

Glaser, Die Entwicklung des Europäischen Verwaltungsrechts aus der Perspektive der Handlungsformenlehre (2013).

Göbel-Zimmermann/Hupke in *Huber/Mantel* (eds), Kommentar Aufenthaltsgesetz/Asylgesetz[3] (2021) § 25 AufenthG.

Goizueta Vértiz, La entrada a España, los visados y las situaciones de los extranjeros en España: estancia y residencia e irregularidad y arraigo in *Boza Martínez/Donaire Villa/Moya Malapeira* (eds), Comentario a la reforma de la ley de extranjería (LO 2/2009) (2011) 157.

Gómez Díaz, Seguridad Social de los extranjeros. Inmigración y Seguridad Social, una gestión integrada in *Balado Ruiz-Gallegos* (ed), Inmigración, Estado y Derecho: Perspectivas desde el siglo XXI (2008) 883.

Gómez Zamora, Comentario al Real Decreto-ley 7/2018, de 27 de julio, sobre el acceso universal al Sistema Nacional de Salud, Gabilex 2018, 281.

González Beilfuss/Koopmans, Legal pathways to regularisation of illegally staying migrants in EU Member States (2021), https://admigov.eu/upload/Deliverable_27_Legal_pathways_Gonzales.pdf (31.7.2022).

González Calvet, El arraigo como instrumento de regularización individual y permanente del trabajador inmigrante indocumentado en el reglamento de extranjería aprobado por el RD 2393/2004, de 30 de diciembre, Revista de Derecho Social 2007/37, 105.

González García, Algunas cuestiones sobre el derecho a la tutela judicial efectiva de los extranjeros a la luz de la jurisprudencia constitucional y de la Ley Orgánica 2/2009, Teoría y Realidad Constitucional 2010, 515.

González Saquero, La Directiva „retorno“ y el alcance de la armonización del procedimiento de expulsión de extranjeros. WP on European Law and Regional Integration No. 6 (2011), https://ucm.es/data/cont/docs/595-2013-11-07-la%20directiva%20retorno.pdf (31.7.2022).

González-Enríquez, Spain: Irregularity as a Rule in *Triandafyllidou* (ed), Irregular Migration: Myths and Realities (2010) 247.

González-Enríquez, Spain, the Cheap Model. Irregularity and Regularisation as Immigration Management Policies, EJML 2009, 139.

González-Enríquez, Undocumented Migration: Country Report Spain. Clandestino Project (January 2009).

Goodwin-Gill/Lambert, The Limits of Transnational Law: Refugee Law, Policy Harmonization and Judicial Dialogue in the European Union (2010).

Gordzielik in *Huber/Mantel* (eds), Kommentar Aufenthaltsgesetz/Asylgesetz[3] (2021) § 61 AufenthG.

Gordzielik/Huber in *Huber/Mantel* (eds), Kommentar Aufenthaltsgesetz/Asylgesetz[3] (2021) § 60a AufenthG.

Gortázar Rotaeche, Return Decisions and Domestic Judicial Practices: Is Spain Different? in *de Bruycker/Cornelisse/Moraru* (eds), Law and Judicial Dialogue on the Return of Irregular Migrants from the European Union (2020) 63.

Gortázar Rotaeche, The Regularisation of Illegal Immigrants in Spain in *de Bruycker* (ed), Les regularisations des étrangers illégaux dans l'union européenne. Regularisations of illegal immigrants in the European Union (2000) 291.

Gosme, Limbo spaces between illegal and legal stay: resulting from EU management of non-removable third country nationals, Dissertation 2014, Sciences Po Paris, https://spire.sciencespo.fr/hdl:/2441/30a6ffj78696ja3eov65066e05/resources/2014iepp0037-gosme-charles-these.pdf (31.7.2022).

Grösel, Fremde von Staats wegen. 50 Jahre »Fremdenpolitik« in Österreich (2016).

Groß, Das Ausländerrecht zwischen obrigkeitsstaatlicher Tradition und menschenrechtlicher Herausforderung, AöR 2014, 421.

Groß/Tryjanowski, Der Status von Drittstaatsangehörigen im Migrationsrecht der EU – eine kritische Analyse, Der Staat 2009, 259.

Großfeld, Kernfragen der Rechtsvergleichung (1996).

Groth in *Rolfs/Giesen/Keikebohm/Udsching* (eds), BeckOK Sozialrecht (62nd edn, 1.9.2021) § 23 SGB XII.

Gruber, „Bleiberecht" und Art 8 EMRK in FS Rudolf Machacek und Franz Matscher (2008) 159.

Guild, Discretion, Competence and Migration in the European Union, EJML 1999, 61.

Guild, Who is an irregular migrant? in *Bogusz/Cholewinski/Cygan/Szyszczak* (eds), Irregular Migration and Human Rights: Theoretical, European and International Perspectives (2004) 3.

Gutiérrez Sanz, El anteproyecto de ley orgánica del estatuto de la víctima del delito y la víctima adulta del delito de trata de seres humanos con fines de explotación sexual, Revista de Derecho Migratorio y Extranjería 2014/37, 13.

Gutteridge, Comparative Law (1946).

Haas/Matti, Verfassungsrechtliche Aspekte der Gewährung von materieller Grundsicherung an Personen mit humanitärem Aufenthaltsrecht, migraLex 2021, 58.

Hager, Abschiebung trotz schwerer Krankheit? Die gesetzlichen Neuregelungen zu Abschiebungshindernissen aus gesundheitlichen Gründen, Asylmagazin 2016, 160.

Hailbronner, Asyl- und Ausländerrecht[5] (2021).

Hailbronner, The Regularisation of illegal Immigrants in Germany in *de Bruycker* (ed), Les regularisations des étrangers illégaux dans l'union européenne. Regularisations of illegal immigrants in the European Union (2000) 251.

Hailbronner/Arévalo in *Hailbronner/Thym* (eds), EU Immigration and Asylum Law. A Commentary[2] (2016) Art 4 Family Reunification Directive.

Hampshire, The Politics of Immigration (2013).

Handmaker/Mora, 'Experts': the mantra of irregular migration and the reproduction of hierarchies in *Ambrus/Arts/Hey/Raules* (eds), The Role of 'Experts' in International and European Decision-Making Processes: Advisors, Decision Makers or Irrelevant Actors? (2014) 263.

Hathaway, The Emerging Politics of Non-Entrée, Journal of Refugee Studies 1992, 40.

Heißl, Die Ausweisung in der Judikatur der Höchstgerichte, ZfV 2008, 1145.

Helbling/Leblang, Controlling immigration? How regulations affect migration flows, European Journal of Political Research 2018, 1.

Hellmann, Der Vertrag von Lissabon (2009).

Hemmelmann/Wegner, Flüchtlingsdebatte im Spiegel von Medien und Parteien, Communicatio Socialis 2016/1, 21.

Hengstschläger/Leeb, AVG (1.1.2014, rdb.at) § 7 AVG.

Hengstschläger/Leeb, AVG (1.4.2021, rdb.at) § 39 AVG.

Hengstschläger/Leeb, AVG (1.7.2005, rdb.at) § 56 AVG.

Herbert, Geschichte der Ausländerpolitik in Deutschland[2] (2017).

Heredia Fernández, Las situaciones de los extranjeros en España in *Moya Escudero* (ed), Comentario sistemático a la ley de extranjería (2001) 53.

Herker, Bleiberecht für Opfer von Hasskriminalität (2022).

Hess/Kasparek/Kron/Rodatz/Schwertl/Sontowski (eds), Der lange Sommer der Migration: Grenzregime III (2016).

Hiesel, Mindestsicherung neu. Erste Gedankenskizzen, juridikum 2017, 80.

Hinterberger, A Critical-Contextual Approach in Comparative Migration Law, International Journal of Migration and Border Studies 2023, forthcoming.

Hinterberger, A Multi-Level Governance Approach to Residence Rights of Migrants and Irregular Residence in the EU, EJML 2018, 182.

Hinterberger, An EU Regularization Directive. An effective solution to the enforcement deficit in returning irregularly staying migrants, Maastricht Journal of European and Comparative Law 2019, 736.

Hinterberger, Arbeitsmarktzugang von Fremden mit „Duldung" oder „Aufenthaltstitel aus besonders berücksichtigungswürdigenden Gründen" – Eine gleichheitsrechtliche Analyse, DRdA 2018, 104.

Hinterberger, Asyl- und Fremdenpolizeirecht (2017).

Hinterberger, Das österreichische Asylgesetzänderungsgesetz 2016 in *Bungenberg/Giegerich/Stein* (eds), ZEuS-Sonderband: Asyl und Migration in Europa – rechtliche Herausforderungen und Perspektiven (2016) 185.

Hinterberger, Die Beendigung der Lehre von abgewiesenen AsylwerberInnen gem § 55a FPG, ÖJZ 2020, 640.

Hinterberger, Die Mehrebenendimension aufenthaltsrechtlicher Irregularität. Konzeptionelle Überlegungen zum Auftreten irregulärer Migration in der EU in *Thym/Klarmann* (eds), Unionsbürgerschaft und Migration im aktuellen Europarecht (2017) 155.

Hinterberger, Eine Regularisierungsrichtlinie der EU: Eine wirksame Lösung für das Vollzugsdefizit von Rückführungen irregulär aufhältiger Migrant*innen in *Lanser/Potocnik-Manzouri/Safron/Tillian/Wieser* (eds), Social Europe? 1. Tagung junger Europarechtler*innen 2018 (2018) 45.

Hinterberger/Klammer, Abschiebungsverbote aus gesundheitlichen Gründen: Die aktuelle Rechtsprechung des EGMR und EuGH zu Non-Refoulement und deren Auswirkungen auf die österreichische, deutsche und spanische Rechtslage – eine Verbesserung der rechtlichen Situation schwer kranker Drittstaatsangehöriger? in *Filzwieser/Taucher* (eds), Asyl- und Fremdenrecht. Jahrbuch 2017 (2017) 111.

Hinterberger/Klammer, Abschiebungsverbote aus gesundheitlichen Gründen: Die aktuelle EGMR- und EuGH-Rechtsprechung zu Non-Refoulement und deren Auswirkungen auf die deutsche Rechtslage – eine Verbesserung der rechtlichen Situation schwer kranker Drittstaatsangehöriger, NVwZ 2017, 1180.

Hinterberger/Klammer, Das Rechtsinstitut der fremdenpolizeilichen Duldung, migraLex 2015, 73.

Hinterberger/Klammer, Der Rechtsstatus von Geduldeten: Eine Analyse unter besonderer Berücksichtigung auf das Grundrecht der Menschenwürde in *Salomon* (ed), Der Status im europäischen Asylrecht (2020) 315.

Hinterberger/Klammer, The Legal Status of Tolerated Aliens in Austria through the Lens of the Fundamental Right to Human Dignity, University of Vienna Law Review 2020, 46.

Hobbe, Undokumentierte Migration in Deutschland und den Vereinigten Staaten: Interne Migrationskontrollen und die Handlungsräume von Sans Papier (2004).

Hoffmann, Das „Migrationspaket" im Überblick, InfAuslR 2019, 409.

Hoffmann, Geduldet in Deutschland – Teil 1: Aufenthaltsrechtliche Auswirkungen, Asylmagazin 2010, 369.

Hoffmann, Leben in der Illegalität – Exklusion durch Aufenthaltsrecht in *Falge/Fischer-Lescano/Sieveking* (eds), Gesundheit in der Illegalität: Rechte von Menschen ohne Aufenthaltspapiere (2009) 13.

Holoubek/Lang (eds), Das Verfahren vor dem Verwaltungsgerichtshof (2015).

Holzinger/Frank, Die Verfassungsgerichtsbarkeit – Essenz und Wandlung in FS 150 Jahre Wiener Juristische Gesellschaft (2017) 169.

Homberger/Güntner, Responses to Migrants with Precarious Status in Vienna: Frames, Strategies and Evolving Practices (October 2022), https://www.compas.ox.ac.uk/wp-content/uploads/LoReMi-Responses-to-Migrants-with-Precarious-Status-in-Vienna-Frames-Strategies-and-Evolving-Practices.pdf (20.12.2022).

Hoppe in *Lenz/Borchardt* (eds), EU-Verträge Kommentar[6] (2012) Arts 77 and 79 AEUV.

Hörich, Abschiebungen nach europäischen Vorgaben (2015).

Hörich/Bergmann in *Huber/Mantel* (eds), Kommentar Aufenthaltsgesetz/Asylgesetz[3] (2021) Vorbemerkung zu § 95 AufenthG and § 95 AufenthG.

Hörich/Putzar-Sattler, Mitwirkungspflichten im Ausländerrecht: Rechtsgutachten zu den Voraussetzungen von Sanktionen bei Nichtmitwirkung (November 2017), https://www.fluechtlingsrat-lsa.de/wp-content/uploads/2017/11/fluera_lsa_gutachten_2017_Mitwirkungspflichten_im_Auslaenderrecht.pdf (31.7.2022).

Hörich/Tewocht, Zum Gesetz zur besseren Durchsetzung der Ausreisepflicht, NVwZ 2017, 1153.

Hruschka in *Huber/Mantel* (eds), Kommentar Aufenthaltsgesetz/Asylgesetz[3] (2021) Vorbemerkung vor Abschnitt 2. Schutzgewährung.

Hruschka, Ad-Hoc-Reparaturbetrieb statt kohärenter Rechtsrahmen: das „Geordnete-Rückkehr-Gesetz", Verfassungsblog (21.5.2019), https://verfassungsblog.de/ad-hoc-reparaturbetrieb-statt-kohaerenter-rechtsrahmen-das-geordnete-rueckkehr-gesetz/ (31.7.2022).

Hruschka/Mantel in *Huber/Mantel* (eds), Kommentar Aufenthaltsgesetz/Asylgesetz[3] (2021) § 60 AufenthG.

Huber, Das Gesetz zur Neubestimmung des Bleiberechts und der Aufenthaltsbeendigung, NVwZ 2015, 1178.

Huber, Das Zuwanderungsgesetz, NVwZ 2005, 1.

Huber/Eichenhofer/Endres de Oliveira, Aufenthaltsrecht (2017).

Huber-Mumelter/Waitz, Regelungen des dauerhaften Verbleibs von Fremden in Österreich und in der Schweiz – ein rechtsvergleichender Überblick zum aktuellen Stand im Asyl- und Aufenthaltsrecht, FABL 1/2009-I, 12.

Huelin Martínez de Velasco, La nueva casación contencioso-administrativa (primeros pasos), Revista General de Derecho Constitucional 2017/24, 1.

Husa, A New Introduction to Comparative Law (2015).

Huysmans, The European Union and the Securitization of Migration, Journal of Common Market Studies 2000/38, 751.

Iglesias Martínez, La inmigración que surgió del frío. Población de origen inmigrante y nuevos retos de las políticas de integración tras la crisis, Estudios Empresariales 2015/2 No. 148, 1.

Iglesias Sánchez, La regularización de la situación administrativa de los padres de menores españoles en situación irregular, Revista de Derecho Migratorio y Extranjería 2010/3, 35.

Ineli-Ciger, Temporary Protection in Law and Practice (2018).

Ineli-Ciger, Time to Activate the Temporary Protection Directive, EJML 2016, 1.

Informationsverbund Asyl und Migration, Neuregelungen durch das Migrationspaket, Das Migrationspaket – Beilage zum Asylmagazin 8–9/2019, 2.

Intergovernmental Committee for Migration, Undocumented Migrants and the Regularization of their Status, International Migration 1983, 109.

Jackson, Comparative Constitutional Law: Methodologies in *Rosenfeld/Sajó* (eds), The Oxford Handbook of Comparative Constitutional Law (2012) 54.

Jeandesboz/Rijpma/Bigo, Smart Borders Revisited: An assessment of the Commission's revised Smart Borders proposal (October 2016), http://www.europarl.europa.eu/RegData/etudes/STUD/2016/571381/IPOL_STU%282016%29571381_EN.pdf (31.7.2022).

Jellinek, Allgemeine Staatslehre[3] (1914).

Jessup, Transnational Law (1956).

Kaiser, Vergleichung im öffentlichen Recht, ZaöRV 1964, 391.

Kamba, Comparative Law: A Theoretical Framework, ICLQ 1974, 485.

Kammer für Arbeiter und Angestellte, Sozialleistungen im Überblick 2020[22] (2020).

Kaspar, Aktuelles zum Sozialhilfe-Grundsatzgesetz. VfGH 12.12.2019, G 164/2019 ua: Höchstsätze für Kinder sowie „Arbeitsqualifizierungsbonus" verfassungswidrig, juridikum 2020, 141.

Kaspar, Sozialhilferechtliche Differenzierung aufgrund des Aufenthaltsstatus von subsidiär Schutzberechtigten: Ausschluss nach dem NÖ MSG – VfGH 28. Juni 2017, E 3297/2016, juridikum 2017, 476.

Kießling, Fremdenpolizeirecht im Rechtsstaat (?) – Zu Herkunft und Zukunft des Ausweisungsrechts, ZAR 2016, 45.

Kietaibl, Arbeitsrecht I[11] (2021).

Kind in *Abermann/Czech/Kind/Peyrl* (eds), NAG Kommentar[2] (2019) §§ 21 and 43 NAG.

Kischel, Comparative Law (2019).

Kischel, Vorsicht, Rechtsvergleichung! ZVglRWiss 2005, 10.

Klammer, Beugehaft nach dem FPG in *Filzwieser/Taucher* (eds), Asyl- und Fremdenrecht. Jahrbuch 2018 (2018) 147.

Klarmann, Aspekte migrationsspezifischer Illegalisierung im Unionsrecht in *Thym/Klarmann* (eds), Unionsbürgerschaft und Migration im aktuellen Europarecht (2017) 127.

Klarmann, Illegalisierte Migration. Die (De-)Konstruktion migrationsspezifischer Illegalitäten im Unionsrecht (2021).

Klaus, Überwachung von Reisen Drittstaatsangehöriger durch das Entry/Exit System (EES): Anfang vom Ende aller Overstays?, ZAR 2018, 246.

Klaus/Hammer, Fachkräfteeinwanderungsgesetz (FEG): Signal mit Fragezeichen oder echter Quantensprung?, ZAR 2019, 137.

Kleist, Warum weit weniger Asylbewerber in Europa sind, als angenommen wird: Probleme mit Eurostats Asylzahlen, ZAR 2015, 294.

Kluth, Das Asylverfahrensbeschleunigungsgesetz, ZAR 2015, 337.

Kluth, Die Beurteilung der Härtefallkommission nach § 23a AufenthG aus dem Blickwinkel des Verfassungsrechts, ZAR 2022, 204.

Kluth, Einheitliche Europäische Zuwanderungspolitik: Vertragsrechtliche Grundlagen und Vergleich der politischen Konzeptionen. Legalisierungsmaßnahmen, ZAR 2007, 20.

Kluth, Next Steps: Die Gesetze des Migrationspakets 2019 folgen jeweils eigenen Pfaden, NVwZ 2019, 1305.

Kluth/Breidenbach in *Kluth/Heusch* (eds), BeckOK Ausländerrecht (30th edn, 1.7.2021) § 60a AufenthG.

Koch in *Kluth/Heusch* (eds), BeckOK Ausländerrecht (30th edn, 1.7.2020) § 60 AufenthG.

Koch in *Kluth/Hornung/Koch* (eds), Handbuch Zuwanderungsrecht[3] (2020) § 4.

Kohlenberger, Fehlender Gesundheitszugang von Migranten schadet allen, Falter.at (13.5.2020), https://cms.falter.at/blogs/thinktank/2020/05/13/warum-gefluechtete-besonders-corona-gefaehrdert-sind/ (16.11.2021).

Kolonovits/Muzak/Stöger, Verwaltungsverfahrensrecht[11] (2019).

Korff in *Rolfs/Giesen/Keikebohm/Udsching* (eds), BeckOK Sozialrecht (62nd edn, 1.9.2021) §§ 1, 1a and 2 AsylbLG.

Kortländer in *Schwarze/Becker/Hatje/Schoo* (eds), EU-Kommentar[4] (2019).

Koser, International Migration (2007).

Kotzur in *Geiger/Khan/Kotzur* (eds), EUV/AEUV Kommentar[6] (2017) Art 79 AEUV.

Kovacheva/Vogel, The Size of the Irregular Foreign Resident Population in the European Union in 2002, 2005 and 2008: Aggregated Estimates. WP 4/2009 (2009), https://irregular-migration.net/wp-content/uploads/2021/06/WP4_Kovacheva-Vogel_2009_EuropeEstimate_Dec09.pdf (31.7.2022).

Kraler, Fixing, Adjusting, Regulating, Protecting Human Rights – The Shifting Uses of Regularisations in the European Union, EJML 2011, 297.

Kraler, Regularisation: A misguided option or part and parcel of a comprehensive policy response to irregular migration? IMISCOE WP No. 24 (February 2009).

Kraler, Regularization of Irregular Migrants and Social Policies: Comparative Perspectives, Journal of Immigrant and Refugee Studies 2019, 94.

Kraler/Hollomey, Austria: Irregular Migration – A Phenomenon in Transition in *Triandafyllidou* (ed), Irregular Migration: Myths and Realities (2010) 41.

Kraler/Reichel/Hollomey, Undocumented Migration: Country Report Austria. Clandestino Project (November 2008/updated October 2009), https://www.eliamep.gr/wp-content/uploads/2017/12/clandestino_report_austria_final_2.pdf (31.7.2022).

Kraler/Reichel/König/Baldwin-Edwards/Şimşek, Feasibility Study on the Labour Market Trajectories of Regularised Immigrants within the European Union (REGANE I). Final Report (February 2009), https://ec.europa.eu/social/BlobServlet?docId=12612&langId=en (31.7.2022).

Kreuzhuber, Arbeitsmigration nach Österreich – Eckpunkte und erste Erfahrungen zur Rot-Weiß-Rot-Karte, ZAR 2014, 13.

Kreuzhuber/Hudsky, Arbeitsmigration (2011).

Krisper/Krumphuber, Fremdenrechtsänderungsgesetz 2018 in *Filzwieser/Taucher* (eds), Asyl- und Fremdenrecht. Jahrbuch 2018 (2018) 79.

Krüger, Eigenart, Methode und Funktion der Rechtsvergleichung im öffentlichen Recht in FS Martin Kriele (1997) 1393.

Kutscher/Völker/Witt, Niederlassungs- und Aufenthaltsrecht[2] (2010).

Lachmayer, Verfassungsvergleichung durch Verfassungsgerichte, JRP 2010, 166.

Langthaler/Muhič/Dizdarevič/Sohler/Trauner, Zivilgesellschaftliche und politische Partizipation und Repräsentanz von Flüchtlingen und AsylwerberInnen in der EU (February 2009), http://archiv.asyl.at/projekte/node/synthese_casestudies.pdf (31.7.2022).

Lazaridis, International Migration into Europe: From Subjects to Abjects (2015).

Lázaro González/Benlloch Sanz, Ciudadanía e integración: menores no acompañados, trata de seres humanos y víctimas de violencia de género in *Palomar Olmeda* (eds), Tratado de Extranjería[6] (2020) 881.

Legrand, European Legal Systems are not Converging, ICLQ 1996, 52.

Legrand, How to Compare Now, Legal Studies 1996, 232.

Leitner, Das neue Sozialhilfe-Grundsatzgesetz, Arbeits- und SozialrechtsKartei 2019, 304.

López Guerra/Espín/García Morillo/Pérez Tremps/Satrústegui, Derecho Constitucional: Vol I[11] (2018).

Lorenzo Jiménez, La expulsión de extranjeros que se encuentran en trámite de regularización, Revista de Derecho Migratorio y Extranjería 2015/38, 13.

Luft, Die Anwerbung türkischer Arbeitnehmer und ihre Folgen (5.8.2014), https://www.bpb.de/internationales/europa/tuerkei/184981/gastarbeit (31.7.2022).

Luft/Schimany (eds), 20 Jahre Asylkompromiss. Bilanz und Perspektiven (2014).

Luhmann, Politische Steuerung: Ein Diskussionsbeitrag, Politische Vierteljahresschrift 1989, 4.

Luján Alcaraz, Art 63 LODYLE in *Monereo Pérez/Fernández Avilés/Triguero Martínez* (eds), Comentario a la ley y al reglamento de Extranjería, Inmigración e Integración Social[2] (2013) 1019.

Lukan in *Holoubek/Lienbacher* (eds), GRC-Kommentar[2] (2019) Art 4 GRC.

Lüke, Humanitäre Bleiberechte außerhalb des Flüchtlingsschutzes im Rahmen des Aufenthaltsgesetzes, ZAR 2004, 397.

Lukits, Die gesetzliche Krankenversicherung von Asylwerbern und Asylberechtigten, migraLex 2017, 14.

Lutz in *Thym/Hailbronner* (eds), EU Immigration and Asylum Law. A Commentary[3] (2022) Arts 2, 6, 9 and 14 Return Directive.

Lutz, Non-removable Returnees under Union Law: Status Quo and Possible Developments, EJML 2018, 50.

Lutz, The Negotiations on the Return Directive: Comments and Material (2010).

Maaßen/Kluth in *Kluth/Heusch* (eds), BeckOK Ausländerrecht (30th edn, 1.7.2021) §§ 23a and 25 AufenthG.

Machjer/Strik, Legislating without Evidence: The Recast of the EU Return Directive, EJML 2021, 103.

Maor in *Kluth/Heusch* (eds), BeckOK Ausländerrecht (18th edn, 1.5.2018) § 4 AufenthG.

Marhold/Başar, Erwerbstätigkeit von AusländerInnen in Österreich. Die Hürden und Fallen der AusländerInnenbeschäftigung, juridikum 2016, 93.

Marth, Das Bleiberecht im Asylverfahren, migraLex 2009, 45.

Martin, The Authority and Responsibility of States in *Aleinikoff/Chetail* (eds), Migration and International Legal Norms (2003) 31.

Marx, Aufenthalts-, Asyl- und Flüchtlingsrecht[7] (2020).

Massó Garrote, El nuevo reglamento de extranjería (2002).

Mattei, Comparative Law and Critical Legal Studies in *Reimann/Zimmermann* (eds), The Oxford Handbook of Comparative Law[2] (2019) 805.

Maurer/Waldhoff, Allgemeines Verwaltungsrecht[20] (2020).

Mayer, Das humanitäre Bleiberecht – ein schrankenloses Ermessen, migraLex 2008, 36.

Menezes Queiroz, Illegally Staying in the EU: An Analysis of Illegality in EU Migration Law (2018).

Mercader Uguina/Tolosa Tibiño, Art 24 LODYLE in *Monereo Pérez/Fernández Avilés/Triguero Martínez* (eds), Comentario a la ley y al reglamento de Extranjería, Inmigración e Integración Social[2] (2013) 371.

Messinger, Schein oder Nicht Schein. Konstruktion und Kriminalisierung von „Scheinehen“ in Geschichte und Gegenwart (2012).

Michaels, The Functional Method of Comparative Law in *Reimann/Zimmermann* (eds), The Oxford Handbook of Comparative Law[2] (2019) 346.

Michaels, Was ist nichtstaatliches Recht? in *Calliess* (ed), Transnationales Recht: Stand und Perspektiven (2014) 39.

Michl, Dysfunktionale Außengrenze und binnenstaatliche Reaktion – zur unionsrechtlichen Zulässigkeit einseitiger Maßnahmen in Zeiten großer Migrationsströme in *Bungenberg/Giegerich/Stein* (eds) ZEuS-Sonderband: Asyl und Migration in Europa – rechtliche Herausforderungen und Perspektiven (2016) 161.

Migrationsrat für Österreich, Bericht des Migrationsrats (2016).

Miller/Zumbansen (eds), Comparative Law as Transnational Law (2012).

Mimentza Martin, Die sozialrechtliche Stellung von Ausländern mit fehlendem Aufenthaltsrecht: Deutschland und Spanien im Rechtsvergleich (2012).

Mitsilegas, Measuring Irregular Migration: Implications for Law, Policy and Human Rights in *Bogusz/Cholewinski/Cygan/Szyszczak* (eds), Irregular Migration and Human Rights: Theoretical, European and International Perspectives (2004) 29.

Molnár, The Interplay between the EU's Return Acquis and International Law (2021).

Monereo Pérez/Gallego Morales, Art 1 LODYLE in *Monereo Pérez/Fernández Avilés/Triguero Martínez* (eds), Comentario a la ley y al reglamento de Extranjería, Inmigración e Integración Social[2] (2013) 43.

Monereo Pérez/Triguero Martínez, Art 10 LODYLE in *Monereo Pérez/Fernández Avilés/Triguero Martínez* (eds), Comentario a la ley y al reglamento de Extranjería, Inmigración e Integración Social[2] (2013) 203.

Moraru, The Future Architecture of the EU's Return System Following the Pact on Asylum and Migration: Added Value and Shortcomings in *Thym/Odysseus Academic Network* (eds), Reforming the Common European Asylum System (2022) 187.

Moreno Rebato, Circulares, instrucciones y órdenes de servicio: naturaleza y régimen jurídico, Revista de Administración Pública 1998/147, 159.

Moreno-Lax, (Extraterritorial) Entry Controls and (Extraterritorial) Non-Refoulement in EU Law in *Maes/Foblets/de Bruycker* (eds), The External Dimensions of EU Asylum and Immigration Policy (2011) 415.

Morticelli, Human Rights of Irregular Migrants in the European Union (2021).

Motomura, Americans in Waiting (2007).

Moya Malapeira, La evolución de control migratorio de entrada en España in *Aja/Arango* (eds), Veinte Años de Inmigración en España: Perspectiva jurídica y sociológica (1985-2004) (2006) 47.

Musil, Migration und Asyl in Österreich – Ein statistischer Überblick, 1961–2016 in *Eppel/Reyhani* (eds), Handbuch Asyl- und Fremdenrecht (2016) Register 1 Chapter 2.

Muzak in *Mayer/Stöger* (eds), Kommentar zu EUV und AEUV (1.12.2012, rdb.at) Art 79 AEUV.

Muzak, Die Aufenthaltsberechtigung für „De-facto-Flüchtlinge" durch Verordnung der Bundesregierung, ÖJZ 1999, 13.

Muzak, Die Aufenthaltsberechtigung im österreichischen Fremdenrecht (1995).

Muzak, Die Kasuistik, Komplexität und Kurzfristigkeit des österreichischen Fremdenrechts in *ÖJT* (ed), 19. ÖJT Band I/2: Migration und Mobilität (2016) 23.

Muzak, Fremden- und Asylrecht in *Kolonovits/Muzak/Piska/Perthold/Strejcek* (eds), Besonderes Verwaltungsrecht[2] (2017) 187.

Nachtigall, Die Ausdifferenzierung der Duldung, ZAR 2020, 271.

Nafziger, The General Admission of Aliens under International Law, AJIL 1983, 804.

Neundorf, Neuerungen im Aufenthalts- und Asylrecht durch das Asylverfahrensbeschleunigungsgesetz, NJW 2016, 5.

Niessen, International Migration on the EU Foreign Policy Agenda, EJML 1999, 483.

Nieves Moreno Vida, Art 36 LODYLE in *Monereo Pérez/Fernández Avilés/Triguero Martínez* (eds), Comentario a la ley y al reglamento de Extranjería, Inmigración e Integración Social[2] (2013) 614.

Öhlinger/Eberhard, Verfassungsrecht[13] (2022).

Öhlinger/Potacs, EU-Recht und staatliches Recht: Die Anwendung des Europarechts im innerstaatlichen Bereich[6] (2017).

Oltmer/Kreienbrink/Sanz Díaz (eds), Das „Gastarbeiter"-System. Arbeitsmigration und ihre Folgen in der Bundesrepublik Deutschland und Westeuropa (2012).

Örücü, The Enigma of Comparative Law: Variations on a Theme for the Twenty-first Century (2004).

Oswald, Das Bleiberecht: Das Grundrecht auf Privat- und Familienleben als Schranke für Aufenthaltsbeendigungen (2012).

Pajuelo, La protección social de los extranjeros en España in *Palomar Olmeda* (ed), Tratado de Extranjería[6] (2020) 991.

Palomar Olmeda, La potestad sancionadora pública en materia de extranjería in *Palomar Olmeda* (ed), Tratado de Extranjería[6] (2020) 455.

Parejo Alfonso, Lecciones de Derecho Administrativo[11] (2021).

Parliamentary Assembly of the Council of Europe, Regularisation programmes for irregular migrants. Report 11350 (6.7.2007), https://www.unhcr.org/4b9fac519.pdf (31.7.2022).

Peers, EU Justice and Home Affairs Law. Vol 1: EU Immigration and Asylum Law[4] (2016).

Peers, Legislative Update: EU Immigration and Asylum Competence and Decision-Making in the Treaty of Lisbon, EJML 2008, 219.

Peers, Lock 'em up: the proposal to amend the EU's Returns Directive, EU Law Analysis Blog (12.9.2018), http://eulawanalysis.blogspot.com/2018/09/lock-em-up-proposal-to-amend-eus.html (31.7.2022).

Peers/Moreno-Lax, Qualification: Refugee Status and Subsidiary Protection in *Peers/Moreno-Lax/Garlick/Guild* (eds), EU Immigration and Asylum Law. Vol 3: EU Asylum Law[2] (2015) 65.

Pelzer, Regularisierung des Aufenthalts von Menschen ohne Papiere: Bausteine einer liberalen Migrationspolitik? in *Fischer-Lescano/Kocher/Nassibi* (eds), Arbeit in der Illegalität: Die Rechte von Menschen ohne Aufenthaltspapiere (2012) 143.

Peña Pérez, Arraigo, circunstancias excepcionales y razones humanitarias: Evolución histórica dentro del derecho de extranjería, Revista de Derecho Migratorio y Extranjería 2012/30, 35.

PERCO, PERCO Position Paper on the Vulnerabilities of Migrants which are caused by the Lack of a Legal Status (8.5.2015), https://drk-wohlfahrt.de/uploads/tx_ffpublication/PERCO_Position_Paper_on_Vulnerabilities_along_the_migratory_trails_to_the_EU_and_to_the_Schengen_area_03.pdf (31.7.2022).

Pérez Milla, De un status laboral mínima para situaciones de migración irregular, Revista de Derecho Migratorio y Extranjería 2004/5, 9.

Pérez Rey, Art 35 LODYLE in *Monereo Pérez/Fernández Avilés/Triguero Martínez* (eds), Comentario a la ley y al reglamento de Extranjería, Inmigración e Integración Social[2] (2013) 584.

Pérez Tremps, Sistema de Justicia Constitucional[3] (2019).

Pérez/Leraul, El arraigo en España. De figura excepcional a instrumento de gobernanza de las migraciones, Comunicación aceptada para el VII Congreso de las Migraciones Internacionales en España (11–13.4.2012).

Perruchoud/Redpath-Cross (eds), Glossary on Migration[2] (2011).

Peyrl in *Abermann/Czech/Kind/Peyrl* (eds), NAG Kommentar[2] (2019) § 41a NAG.

Peyrl, Autoritäre Tendenzen im Aufenthaltsrecht seit 2006, juridikum 2018, 103.

Peyrl, Das Fremdenrechtsänderungsgesetz 2017 und die Novelle des AuslBG 2017 oder die jährlichen Grüße des Murmeltiers, DRdA-infas 2017, 387.

Peyrl, Die Neuordnung der Arbeitskräftemigration nach Österreich („Rot-Weiß-Rot-Karte"), DRdA 2011, 476.

Peyrl, Neuregelung der Möglichkeit zur Beendigung einer Lehre von AsylwerberInnen nach negativem Abschluss des Asylverfahrens, DRdA-infas 2020, 121.

Peyrl, Neuregelung des Aufenthaltsrechts aus humanitären Gründen („Bleiberecht"), DRdA 2009, 283.

Peyrl, Zuwanderung und Zugang zum Arbeitsmarkt von Drittstaatsangehörigen in Österreich (2018).

Peyrl/Czech in *Abermann/Czech/Kind/Peyrl* (eds), NAG Kommentar[2] (2019) § 11 NAG.

Peyrl/Neugschwendtner/Schmaus, Fremdenrecht[7] (2018).

Pfeil, „Sozialhilfe neu" - viele Verschärfungen, aber wenig Vereinheitlichung, ÖZPR 2019/18, 26.

Pfeil, (Vorläufiges) Aus für die einheitliche Mindestsicherung, ÖZPR 2017/14, 24.

Pico Lorenzo, Nuestra errática normativa sobre extranjería. Especial referencia a las regularizaciones y al arraigo, Jueces para la democracia 2002, 62.

Piek, Die Kritik an der funktionalen Rechtsvergleichung, ZEuP 2013, 60.

Pollet, The Negotiations on the Return Directive: Challenges, Outcomes and Lessons learned from an NGO Perspective in *Zwaan* (ed), The Returns Directive (2011) 25.

Pöschl, Zusammenfassung des Gutachtens in *ÖJT* (ed), 19. ÖJT Band I/2: Migration und Mobilität (2016) 14.

Pound, Law in Books and Law in Action, American Law Review 1910, 12.

Progin-Theuerkauf in *Van der Groeben/Schwarze/Hatje* (eds), Europäisches Unionsrecht: Band 2[7] (2015) Art 79 AEUV.

Puerta Vílchez, La regularización de extranjeros. Art 31.3 y Disposición transitoria cuarta in *Moya Escudero* (ed), Comentario sistemático a la ley de extranjería (2001) 391.

Ques Mena, El arraigo, social, económico y familiar en el Derecho de extranjería. Tratamiento legal y jurisprudencial, Diario la Ley 2008/7067, 1.

Raffaeli, Criminalizing Irregular Immigration and the Returns Directive: An Analysis of the El Dridi Case, EJML 2011, 467.

Rahner, Fachkräftemangel und falscher Fatalismus (2018).

Raposo/Violante, Access to Health Care by Migrants with Precarious Status During a Health Crisis: Some Insights from Portugal, Human Rights Review 2021.

Raschauer, Allgemeines Verwaltungsrecht[5] (2016).

Red Acoge, Los efectos de la exclusión sanitaria en las personas inmigrantes más vulnerables (July 2015).

Rehbinder, Rechtssoziologie[8] (2014).

Renner, Ausländerrecht in Deutschland: Einreise und Aufenthalt (1998).

Reyhani, Einleitende Bemerkungen – Asyl- und Fremdenrecht im Kontext in *Eppel/Reyhani* (eds), Handbuch Asyl- und Fremdenrecht (2016) Register 1 Chapter 1.

Reyhani/Nowak, Beschäftigung von Asylsuchenden in Mangelberufen und die Zulässigkeit von Rückkehrentscheidungen (4.7.2018), https://bim.lbg.ac.at/sites/files/bim/attachments/reyhaninowak_gutachten_art_8_abs_2_emrk_04072018.pdf (31.7.2022).

Riecken, Die Duldung als Verfassungsproblem (2006).

Röcker in *Bergmann/Dienelt* (eds), Kommentar Ausländerrecht[13] (2020) §§ 23a, 25, 25a and 25b AufenthG.

Röder, §§ 25a und b AufenthG – Hiergeblieben!? Die neuen Bleiberechte bei gelungener Integration, Asylmagazin 2016, 108.

Röder/Wittmann, Aktuelle Rechtsfragen der Ausbildungsduldung gem. § 60c AufenthG, ZAR 2019, 412.

Röder/Wittmann, Aktuelle Rechtsfragen der Ausbildungsduldung, ZAR 2017, 345.

Röder/Wittmann, Spurwechsel leicht gemacht? Überlegungen zur neuen Ausbildungs- und Beschäftigungsduldung, Das Migrationspaket – Beilage zum Asylmagazin 8–9/2019, 23.

Rodríguez/Rubio-Marín, The constitutional status of irregular migrants: testing the boundaries of human rights protection in Spain and the United States in *Dembour/Kelly* (eds), Are Human Rights for Migrants? Critical Reflection on the Status of Irregular Migrants in Europe and the United States (2011) 73.

Roig, Autonomía e inmigración: competencias y participación de las Comunidades Autónomas y los Entes locales en materia de inmigración in *Revenga Sánchez* (ed), Problemas constitucionales de la inmigración: una visión desde Italia y España (2005) 359.

Rosenberger/Ataç/Schütze, Nicht-Abschiebbarkeit: Soziale Rechte im Deportation Gap, Österreichische Gesellschaft für Europapolitik Policy Brief (12.6.2018).

Rosenstein/Koehler, Beschäftigungsduldung – eine Bewertung der Neuregelung aus Sicht der Praxis, ZAR 2019, 223.

Rosenstein/Koehler, Die neue Ausbildungsduldung – eine notwendige Überarbeitung, InfAuslR 2019, 266.

Roß, EuGH, 14.01.2021 - C-441/19: Anforderungen an eine Rückkehrentscheidung gegenüber einem Minderjährigen, NVwZ 2021, 550.

Rossi in *Calliess/Ruffert* (eds), EUV/AEUV Kommentar[5] (2016) Art 79 AEUV.

Rössl, Staatsangehörige zweiter Klasse?, FABL 2/2017-I, 37.

Ruiz Legazpi, Los problemas jurídicos de la inmigración infantil in *Balado Ruiz-Gallegos* (ed), Inmigración, Estado y Derecho: Perspectivas desde el siglo XXI (2008) 507.

Ruiz Paredes, La regulación de la extranjería. Enfoque mercantil. Aproximación al empresariado inmigrante en España in *Balado Ruiz-Gallegos* (ed), Inmigración, Estado y Derecho: Perspectivas desde el siglo XXI (2008) 631.

Ryan/Mitsilegas (eds), Extraterritorial Immigration Control: Legal Challenges (2010).

Sabater/Domingo, A New Immigration Regularization Policy: The Settlement Program in Spain, International Migration Review 2012/46, 191.

Sagarra Trias, Un nuevo "status" de extranjero en España (El inmigrante, irregular, empadronado, residente trabajando y con orden de expulsión), Revista de Derecho Migratorio y Extranjería 2002/1, 89.

Sainz de la Maza Quintanal, Ultima ratio. El proceso de expulsión de inmigrantes en situación irregular en España, Dissertation 2015, Universidad Complutense de Madrid, https://eprints.ucm.es/34472/ (31.7.2022).

Samers, An Emerging Geopolitics of 'Illegal' Immigration in the European Union, EJML 2004, 25.

Sánchez Alonso, La Política Migratoria en España: Un análisis de largo plazo, Revista Internacional de Sociología 2011, 243.

Sangüesa Ruiz, El derecho a la salud de los extranjeros residentes en situación irregular: sobre la legitimidad constitucional del RD-Ley 16/2012, Revista Electrónica del Departamento de Derecho de la Universidad de la Rioja 2015, 233.

Schammann, Eine meritokratische Wende? Arbeit und Leistung als neue Strukturprinzipien der deutschen Flüchtlingspolitik, Sozialer Fortschritt 2017/66, 741.

Scharpf, Politische Steuerung und Politische Institutionen, Politische Vierteljahresschrift 1989, 10.

Schieber, Komplementärer Schutz: Die aufenthaltsrechtliche Stellung nicht rückführbarer Personen in der EU (2013).

Schlintl/Sorrentino, Residence permits, international protection and victims of human trafficking: Durable Solutions Grounded in International Law. Final Report (February 2021), https://lefoe.at/wp-content/uploads/2021/05/REST-Final-Report-2.pdf (31.7.2022).

Schmid-Drüner, Der Begriff der öffentlichen Sicherheit und Ordnung im Einwanderungsrecht ausgewählter EU-Mitgliedstaaten (2007).

Schmidt-Aßmann, Das allgemeine Verwaltungsrecht als Ordnungsidee^2 (2006).

Schmidt-Aßmann/Dagron, Deutsches und französisches Verwaltungsrecht im Vergleich ihrer Ordnungsideen, ZaöRV 2007, 395.

Schmied, Die aufenthaltsbeendenden Maßnahmen im Fremdenpolizeigesetz nach dem Fremdenrechtsänderungsgesetz 2011 - eine Bankrotterklärung der Fremdenrechtslegistik, Zeitschrift der Unabhängigen Verwaltungssenate 2011, 149.

Schneider, NZS-Jahresrevue 2017 – Asylbewerberleistungsgesetz, NZS 2018, 559.

Schönebroicher, Rechtsstaat auf Abwegen? – Die neue „Härtefallklausel" des Ausländerrechts, ZAR 2004, 351.

Schuster/Voigt, Neuerungen beim Arbeitsmarktzugang – Die Schere geht auseinander, Asylmagazin 2020, 64.

Schwantner, Zur Arbeit der Härtefallkommissionen, Asylmagazin 2016, 63.

Schwarze, Europäisches Verwaltungsrecht^2 (2005).

Serrano Villamanta, La residencia por circunstancias excepcionales. El arraigo in *Balado Ruiz-Gallegos* (ed), Inmigración, Estado y Derecho: Perspectivas desde el siglo XXI (2008) 553.

Shaw, International Law⁹ (2021).

Singleton, Migration and Asylum Data for Policy-making in the European Union: The problem with numbers. CEPS WP No. 89 (March 2016), https://www.ceps.eu/system/files/LSE%2089%20AS%20Migration%20and%20Asylum%20Data.pdf (31.7.2022).

Solanes Corella, Combatiendo la inmigración irregular: la insuficiencia de las regularizaciones y las sanciones in *Alberdi Bidaguren/Goizueta Vértiz* (eds), Algunos retos de la inmigración en el siglo XXI (2008) 201.

Solanes Corella, Un balance tras 25 años de leyes de extranjería en España: 1985-2010, Revista del Ministerio de Trabajo e Inmigración 2010, 77.

Sommermann, Bedeutung der Rechtsvergleichung für die Fortentwicklung des Staats- und Verwaltungsrechts in Europa, DÖV 1999, 1017.

Sponholz, Als der Sommer zu Ende ging: Die Flüchtlingsdebatte im Wiener Wahlkampf auf Facebook, SWS-Rundschau 2016/3, 371.

Starck, Rechtsvergleichung im öffentlichen Recht, JZ 1997, 1021.

Stelzer, The constitution of the republic of Austria (2011).

Stiegeler, Geduldete Fachkräfte – Wem hilft § 18a AufenthG?, Asylmagazin 2009, 8.

Stiller, Trafficked Third-Country Nationals: Detection, Identification and Protection in Austria (October 2021), https://www.emn.at/wp-content/uploads/2022/06/emn-study-2022-trafficked-third-country-nationals-detection-identification-and-protection-in-at.pdf (31.7.2022).

Stoppa/Lehnert in *Huber/Mantel* (eds), Kommentar Aufenthaltsgesetz/Asylgesetz[3] (2021) § 48 AufenthG.

Strban/Rataj/Šabič, Return Procedures Applicable to Rejected Asylum-Seekers in the European Union and Options for their Regularisation, Refugee Survey Quarterly 2018, 1.

Sunderhaus, Regularization Programs for Undocumented Migrants: A Global Survey on more than 60 Legalizations in all Continents (2007).

Sußner, Warten auf … ? Verfassungs- und unionsrechtliche Perspektiven auf den Mindestsicherungszugang nach einem positiv abgeschlossenen Asylverfahren (NÖ MSG), juridikum 2017, 207.

Swider, Hoti v. Croatia – a landmark decision by the European Court of Human Rights on residence rights of a stateless person, European Network on Statelessness Blog (3.5.2018), https://www.statelessness.eu/blog/hoti-v-croatia-landmark-decision-european-court-human-rights-residence-rights-stateless-person (31.7.2022).

Szymanski, Das Fremdenrechtsänderungsgesetz 2009 oder der Boulevard freut sich, doch das Recht ist für Rechtsanwender und Rechtsunterworfene schwer durchschaubar, migraLex 2009, 99.

Szymanski, Und das Hamsterrad dreht sich … (Teil I). Zum Fremdenrechtsänderungsgesetz 2015, migraLex 2015, 54.

Szymanski, Und das Hamsterrad dreht sich … (Teil II). Zum Fremdenrechtsänderungsgesetz 2015, migraLex 2016, 18.

Tapinos, Irregular Migration: Economic and Political Issues in *OECD* (ed), Combating the Illegal Employment of Foreign Workers (2003) 13.

Ter Steeg, Das Einwanderungskonzept der EU (2006).

Tewocht, Auf dem Weg zur Gleichstellung von Drittstaatsangehörigen und Unionsbürgern? – Zu Inhalt und Reichweite der sogenannten ‚Rahmenrichtlinie', ZAR 2012, 217.

Tewocht, Der Drittstaatsangehörige im Unionsrecht (2016).

Thurin, Der Schutz des Fremden vor rechtswidriger Abschiebung: Das Prinzip des Non-Refoulement nach Artikel 3 EMRK[2] (2012).

Thym in *Grabitz/Hilf/Nettesheim* (eds), Das Recht der Europäischen Union Kommentar Band I (69th edn, February 2020) Art 79 AEUV.

Thym in *Kluth/Heusch* (eds), BeckOK Ausländerrecht (30th edn, 1.7.2020) Arts 69 and 79 AEUV.

Thym, Die Auswirkungen des Asylpakets II, NVwZ 2016, 409.

Thym, EU migration policy and its constitutional rationale: A cosmopolitan outlook, CMLRev 2013, 709.

Thym, Europäische Einwanderungspolitik: Grundlagen, Gegenstand und Grenzen in *Hofmann/Löhr* (eds), Europäisches Flüchtlings- und Einwanderungsrecht (2008) 183.

Thym, Geordnete Rückkehr und Bleiberechte im Dschungel des Migrationsrechts, ZAR 2019, 353.

Thym, Migrationssteuerung im Einklang mit den Menschenrechten – Anmerkungen zu den migrationspolitischen Diskursen der Gegenwart, ZAR 2018, 193.

Thym, Migrationsverwaltungsrecht (2010).

Thym, Respect for private and family life under Article 8 ECHR in immigration cases: a human right to regularize illegal stay?, ICLQ 2008, 87.

Thym, Schutz des Aufenthalts zwischen polizeilicher Herkunft und menschenrechtlicher Neuausrichtung in *Arndt/Betz/Farahat/Goldmann/Huber/Keil/Láncos/Schaefer/Smrkolj/Sucker/Valta* (eds), 48. Assistententagung Öffentliches Recht (2008) 221.

Thym, The "refugee crisis" as a challenge of legal design and institutional legitimacy, CMLRev 2016, 1545.

Thym, When Union Citizens Turn into Illegal Migrants: The Dano Case, ELR 2015, 249.

Tohidipur, Grund- und Menschenrechte illegalisierter Migrantinnen und Migranten in *Fischer-Lescano/Kocher/Nassibi* (eds), Arbeit in der Illegalität: Die Rechte von Menschen ohne Aufenthaltspapiere (2012) 41.

Toledo Larrea, Análisis de la situación jurídico-social de las mujeres extranjeras víctimas de violencia de género acogidas en los recursos integrales para víctimas de violencia de género de la administración autonómica andaluza, Revista de Derecho Migratorio y Extranjería 2014/37, 53.

Trantas, Die Anwendung der Rechtsvergleichung bei der Untersuchung des öffentlichen Rechts (1998).

Triandafyllidou, Irregular Migration in Europe in the Early 21st Century in *Triandafyllidou* (ed), Irregular Migration: Myths and Realities (2010) 1.

Triandafyllidou/Ambrosini, Irregular Immigration Control in Italy and Greece: Strong Fencing and Weak Gate-keeping serving the Labour Market, EJML 2011, 251.

Triandafyllidou/Vogel, Irregular Migration in the European Union: Evidence, Facts and Myths in *Triandafyllidou* (ed), Irregular Migration: Myths and Realities (2010) 291.

Triguero Martínez, El arraigo y los modelos actuales jurídico-políticos de inmigración y extranjería, Migraciones 2014, 433.

Trinidad García, Los inmigrantes irregulares en la Ley 4/2000 y en su reforma: una regularización que no cesa, Revista de Derecho Migratorio y Extranjería 2002/1, 99.

Trinidad García, Residencia temporal por circunstancias excepcionales: el arraigo laboral y social, Revista de Derecho Migratorio y Extranjería 2005/9, 133.

Tushnet, Weak Courts, Strong Rights: Judicial Review and Social Welfare Rights in Comparative Constitutional Law (2009).

Unabhängige Kommission „Zuwanderung", Zuwanderung gestalten – Integration fördern (2001), http://www.jugendsozialarbeit.de/media/raw/Zuwanderungsbericht_pdf.pdf (31.7.2022).

Uriarte Torrealday, Algunas reflexiones críticas a partir de la jurisprudencia sobre inmigración irregular, Revista de Derecho Político 2009, 291.

Van Hoecke/Warrington, Legal Cultures, Legal Paradigms and Legal Doctrine: Towards a New Model for Comparative Law, ICLQ 1998, 495.

Vanderbruggen/Phelps/Sebtaoui/Kovats/Pollet, Point of No Return: The Futile Detention of Unreturnable Migrants (January 2014), https://detentionaction.org.uk/wp-content/uploads/2018/12/PONR_report.pdf (31.7.2022).

Varela Huerta, Soziologie der Migrationskämpfe: Die Transformation der Bewegung der „Papierlosen" in Barcelona in eine MigrantInnenbewegung in *Fischer-Lescano/Kocher/Nassibi* (eds), Arbeit in der Illegalität: Die Rechte von Menschen ohne Aufenthaltspapiere (2012) 159.

Vázquez Garranzo, Los servicios sociales y la dependencia in *Palomar Olmeda* (ed), Tratado de Extranjería[6] (2020) 1145.

Vicente Palacio, Art 59 LODYLE in *Monereo Pérez/Fernández Avilés/Triguero Martínez* (eds), Comentario a la ley y al reglamento de Extranjería, Inmigración e Integración Social[2] (2013) 942.

Vicente Palacio, Art 59bis LODYLE in *Monereo Pérez/Fernández Avilés/Triguero Martínez* (eds), Comentario a la ley y al reglamento de Extranjería, Inmigración e Integración Social[2] (2013) 957.

Vogel/Jandl, Introduction to the Methodological Problem in *Kraler/Vogel* (eds), Report on Methodological Issues. Clandestino Project (November 2008) 5.

Vogel/Kovacheva, Classification report: Quality assessment of estimates on stocks of irregular migrants. WP 1/2008 (2008).

Vogelrieder, Die Sanktionsrichtlinie: ein weiterer Schritt auf dem Weg zu einer umfassenden Migrationspolitik der EU, ZAR 2009, 168.

Voigt, Die wundersame Welt des § 25 Abs 5 AufenthG, Asylmagazin 2015, 152.

Völker, Verschafft die bloße Antragstellung auf einen „humanitären" Aufenthaltstitel ein Bleiberecht? VfGH versus VwGH, migraLex 2010, 60.

Völker/Krumphuber, Fremdenrechtsänderungsgesetz 2017 und Fremdenrechtsänderungsgesetz 2017 Teil II in *Filzwieser/Taucher* (eds), Asyl- und Fremdenrecht. Jahrbuch 2017 (2017) 63.

Vollmer, Policy Discourses on Irregular Migration in the EU – 'Number Games' and 'Political Games', EJML 2011, 317.

Von Busse, Die Methoden der Rechtsvergleichung im öffentlichen Recht als richterliches Instrument der Interpretation von nationalem Recht (2015).

Wehinger, Do amnesties pull in illegal immigrants? An analysis of European apprehension data, International Journal of Migration and Border Studies 2014, 231.

Weiß in *Streinz* (ed), EUV/AEUV Kommentar[3] (2018) Art 79 AEUV.

Welser/Kletečka, Grundriss des bürgerlichen Rechts: Band I[15] (2018).

Welte, Beschäftigungsmöglichkeiten für geduldete Ausländer, infAuslR 2020, 225.

Welte, Die Wahrung des Grundsatzes der Verhältnismäßigkeit im Ausweisungsrecht, InfAuslR 2019, 176.

Welte, Die Wahrung des Prinzips der abschließenden Normierung im Aufenthaltsgesetz am Beispiel der Beschäftigungsduldung, ZAR 2020, 87.

Wendel, Kettenduldung. Bleiberechtsregelungen und parlamentarische Initiativen 2000 – 2014 (August 2014), http://www.fluechtlingsrat-brandenburg.de/wp-content/uploads/2014/08/Kettenduldung.pdf (31.7.2022).

Werdermann, Die Vereinbarkeit von Sonderrecht für Asylsuchende und Geduldete aus sicheren Herkunftsstaaten mit Art. 3 GG, ZAR 2018, 11.

Wessely, Grundrechtliche Aspekte der Verwaltungsgerichte in *Larcher* (ed), Handbuch Verwaltungsgerichte: Die Grundlagen der Verwaltungsgerichtsbarkeit I. Instanz (2013) 204.

Wiederin, Aufenthaltsbeendende Maßnahmen im Fremdenpolizeirecht (1993).

Wiederin, Die Einreise- und Aufenthaltstitel nach dem Fremdengesetz 1997, ecolex 1997, 719.

Wiederin, Sozialstaatlichkeit im Spannungsfeld von Eigenverantwortung und Fürsorge, VVDStRL 2005/64, 53.

Wilderspin in *Kellerbauer/Klamert/Tomkin* (eds), The EU Treaties and the Charter of Fundamental Rights. A Commentary (2019) Art 79 TFEU.

Willen, Toward a Critical Phenomenology of "Illegality": State Power, Criminalization, and Abjectivity among Undocumented Migrant Workers in Tel Aviv, Israel, International Migration 2007, 8.

Winkelmann, 25 Jahre Schengen: Der Schengen-Acquis als integraler Bestandteil des Europarechts – Bedeutung und Auswirkung auf die Einreise- und Aufenthaltsrechte – Teil 1, ZAR 2010, 213.

Winkelmann, 25 Jahre Schengen: Der Schengen-Acquis als integraler Bestandteil des Europarechts – Bedeutung und Auswirkung auf die Einreise- und Aufenthaltsrechte, ZAR 2010, 270.

Wittmann, Vom migrationspolitischen Mindeststandard zum „Bleiberecht im Duldungsgewand" – Entwicklungslinien der deutschen Migrations- und Integrationsgesetzgebung im Bereich der Duldung, ZAR 2020, 183.

Wittmann/Röder, Aktuelle Rechtsfragen der Ausbildungsduldung gem. § 60c AufenthG, ZAR 2019, 412.

Wittmann/Röder, Aktuelle Rechtsfragen der Duldung für Personen mit ungeklärter Identität gem. § 60b AufenthG, ZAR 2019, 362.

Zentrum für Politik, Kultur und Forschung Berlin, Expertise zur Umsetzung des IMK-Bleiberechtsbeschlusses vom 17. November 2006 (January 2008), http://www.fluchtort-hamburg.de/fileadmin/pdf/EQUAL/080114_Expertise_IMK-Bleiberechtsbeschluss.pdf (31.7.2022).

Zumbansen, Carving Out Typologies and Accounting for Differences across Systems: Towards a Methodology of Transnational Constitutionalism in *Rosenfeld/Sajó* (eds), The Oxford Handbook of Comparative Constitutional Law (2012) 75.

Zweigert/Kötz, An Introduction to Comparative Law[3] (1998).

Zweigert/Puttfarken, Critical Evaluation in Comparative Law, The Adelaide Law Review 1976, 343.